THE BOURBONS OF NAPLES (1734–1825)

THE BOURBONS OF NAPLES

(1734–1825)

by

HAROLD ACTON

ff
faber and faber

This edition first published in 2009
by Faber and Faber Ltd
Bloomsbury House, 74–77 Great Russell Street, London WC1B 3DA

All rights reserved
© Harold Acton, 1957

The right of Harold Acton to be identified as author of this work
has been asserted in accordance with Section 77 of the
Copyright, Designs and Patents Act 1988

This book is sold subject to the condition that it shall not, by way of
trade or otherwise, be lent, resold, hired out or otherwise circulated
without the publisher's prior consent in any form of binding or cover other than
that in which it is published and without a similar condition including this
condition being imposed on the subsequent purchaser

A CIP record for this book is available from the British Library

ISBN 978–0–571–24901–5

TO

MY MANY EXCELLENT NEAPOLITAN FRIENDS

FEW OF WHOM WILL READ THIS BOOK

ALL OF WHOM HAVE REJOICED MY HEART

AND

STRENGTHENED MY LOVE OF HUMANITY

CONTENTS

CHAPTER I
page 13
Elisabeth Farnese's ambitions for her elder son Don Carlos—His departure for Italy, 1731—His arrival in Tuscany and Parma—Spain declares war on Austria, 1733—The Spanish invasion of Naples, 1734—Don Carlos enters his new capital, May 10—Conquest of Sicily—Coronation of King Charles in Palermo—His festive return to Naples.

CHAPTER 11
page 29
Matrimonial projects—Charles's betrothal to Maria Amalia of Saxony—The kingdom of Naples becomes independent—The King under tutelage—Santo Stefano, Montealegre and Tanucci—The first Committee of Distrust—Embellishment of the capital—The San Carlo—Opera, singers and drama—The arrival of the royal bride—Public rejoicings—The *Cuccagna*—Foundation of the Order of San Gennaro.

CHAPTER III
page 49
New palaces—Portici and Herculaneum—Royal hunting preserves and regulations—The Queen's first offspring—Montealegre succeeds Santo Stefano—The Neapolitan Fine Arts—The Sultan's ambassador—War of Austrian Succession—Commodore Martin's expedition—A new Family Compact—The King decides to march—The Battle of Velletri—A formal visit to Rome—Disgrace

of Montealegre—Fogliani succeeds him—Death of Philip V of Spain—Final emancipation of Charles.

CHAPTER IV
page 69

The birth of an Heir Apparent—A cruel disillusion—The Queen's ambitions—Squillace—Naples, France and Sardinia—The gorgeous Prince Esterhazy—The Inquisition nipped in the bud—The building of Caserta.

CHAPTER V
page 85

The *Reale Albergo dei Poveri*—Father Rocco—The *Presepe*—A ministerial reshuffle—The rise of Tanucci—The antiquities of Herculaneum—Ferdinando Galiani—Genoa and Corsica—The fatal hypochondria of Ferdinand VI of Spain.

CHAPTER VI
page 99

An architectural transformation—Reforms—Genovesi—The Prince of San Severo—Death of Ferdinand VI of Spain and succession of Charles III—Exclusion of the imbecile Heir Apparent—Ferdinand becomes Heir to the Two Sicilies—A treaty with Austria—Charles abdicates and embarks for Spain—Death of Queen Maria Amalia.

CHAPTER VII
page 111

Tanucci and the Abbé Galiani—Baiting the Pope—The famine of 1764—Ferdinand's education—The arrival of William Hamilton as British Minister—Ferdinand's coming of age, 1767—Expulsion of the Jesuits—The Tutor of the Two Sicilies—The hapless Archduchess Josepha—Eruption of Vesuvius—Ferdinand's betrothal to Archduchess Maria Carolina.

CHAPTER VIII
page 131

Maria Carolina's journey to Naples—Her reception—The Emperor Joseph's account of his visit in 1769—His description of Ferdinand; speculations about his future development—An unfavourable analysis of Tanucci's character—Joseph's summary of his impressions.

CHAPTER IX
page 155
Maria Carolina and the Freemasons—Court life rejuvenated—Large influx of foreigners—Casanova—The Prince of Francavilla—Sarah Goudar—Galiani's reluctant return—Piccinni—William Hamilton becomes a Neapolitan institution—A paternal government—English visitors—Maria Carolina's firstborn—The Queen enters the Council of State—Fall of Tanucci, 1776.

CHAPTER X
page 185
Death of the imbecile Infante Philip—Dr Gatti introduces inoculation against smallpox—The advent of John Acton—The Queen's reputed gallantries—Conflict with Spain over Acton—Sambuca's disgrace and Acton's triumph.

CHAPTER XI
page 207
Marchese Caracciolo becomes Prime Minister—The Queen's vendetta against the Spanish faction—More royal offspring—Abolition of the *Chinea*—Mrs Piozzi's impressions—Goethe on Naples—Emma Hart—Filangieri and his sprightly sister—Tischbein, Angelica Kauffmann and Hackert—Death of Charles III, 1788—Bereavements and betrothals—Death of Marchese Caracciolo—Acton becomes Minister for Foreign Affairs.

CHAPTER XII
page 229
Acton's reforms—The Colony of San Leucio—Tragic news from France—The first *émigrés*—Carnival in Naples—Death of the Emperor Joseph and succession of Leopold II—Betrothal ceremonies—The King and Queen visit Austria—Their return journey through Rome—Pleasure versus duty—Luigi de' Medici and his sister the San Marco.

CHAPTER XIII
page 245

Effects of the French Revolution on the King and Queen—Medici as chief of police—Hamilton marries Emma Hart—Death of Emperor Leopold and succession of Francis II—Relations with France—Mackau, Bassville and Sémonville—Latouche-Tréville's expedition—Bassville's murder—Execution of Louis XVI—Treaty of alliance with Great Britain—Jacobin conspiracy—Nelson arrives and Mackau departs.

CHAPTER XIV
page 269

Naples and the Siege of Toulon—Execution of Marie Antoinette—'Lomo' and 'Romo'—The *Giunta di Stato*—Jacobin excitement—The thirty-third eruption of Vesuvius—Medici and the Giordano brothers—Public execution of three conspirators—Medici's disgrace—Revolt at Palermo—Political arrests.

CHAPTER XV
page 287

Spain and France—Bonaparte and the Army of Italy—Belmonte's negotiations with Bonaparte—Armistice of June 5, 1796—Peace treaty of October 10 —Treaty of Tolentino, 1797—Leoben—The Queen's rift with Acton—Prince Augustus Frederick—Marriage of the Hereditary Prince—The Queen's opinion of Bonaparte.

CHAPTER XVI
page 307

Envoys of the French Directory—The Marquis of Gallo—General Duphot and the French occupation of Rome, 1798—Citizen Garat—Release of Medici and political prisoners—Aboukir—Nelson's enthusiastic reception at Naples—General Mack—The King's disastrous expedition to Rome—A belated appeal to the Neapolitan masses.

CHAPTER XVII
page 325

Preparations for the flight of the royal family—Complete demoralization of Mack—A rough passage with Nelson to Palermo—The Vicar General Pignatelli—Armistice with Championnet—Mack's resignation—Resistance of the Neapolitan masses—Moliterno and the 'patriots'—The brave *lazzaroni*—Betrayal: the Parthenopean Republic.

CHAPTER XVIII
page 347

The Court of Palermo—Treaties with Russia and Turkey—Sicilian pride and prejudice—Cardinal Ruffo and the Calabrian Crusade—The Queen's disgust with Mack—The cost of frenchified liberty—Eleonora Pimentel and the *Monitore Napoletano*—Republican doctrinaires—General Macdonald and the recall of Championnet.

CHAPTER XIX
page 365

The King as a family tyrant—Nelson and the Hamiltons—Progress of Cardinal Ruffo's campaign—Corsican adventurers—Civil war—Troubridge in the Bay of Naples—Austria declares war on France—A Parthenopean deputation to Paris—Republican experiments in Naples—A royalist plot—The surreptitious withdrawal of General Macdonald.

CHAPTER XX
page 385

Revolt at Castellammare di Stabia—The imposition of a miracle—Republican rejoicings—Delusions about a Franco-Spanish armada—Exploits of Admiral Caracciolo—Cardinal Ruffo in Puglia—His capture of Altamura—Russian and Turkish auxiliaries—Twilight of the Parthenopean Republic—Cardinal Ruffo at the gates of the capital—Negotiations for peace.

CHAPTER XXI
page 405

The capitulation of June 19, 1799—Nelson returns to Naples with the Hamiltons—Their disagreement with Ruffo—The Queen's indignation: 'No truce with the rebels!'—The capitulation repudiated—Caracciolo sentenced to be hanged—The King on board the *Foudroyant*—Méjean surrenders Sant' Elmo—Verdicts of the *Giunta di Stato*.

CHAPTER XXII
page 427

The King's happy return to Palermo—Rewards and celebrations—A tiff with some Turks—The Neapolitan occupation of Rome—The Queen's forebodings—Tactless behaviour of Mr Charles Lock—Bonaparte becomes First Consul.

CHAPTER XXIII
page 443

1800—The Hamiltons' recall—Arthur Paget: 'a bad beginning'—Acton's marriage—The King's 'very proper sense of danger'—The new Order of Saint Ferdinand—Luisa Sanfelice—Election of Pope Pius VII—The Queen's departure for Vienna—A chequered voyage—The capitulation of Malta—Adieu to Nelson and the Hamiltons—Hohenlinden and Marengo—The treaty of Lunéville, 1801—The Queen's dejection.

CHAPTER XXIV
page 463

The Hereditary Prince and Princess return to Naples—The Treaty of Florence—Amnesty of February 17, 1801; the *Giunta di Stato* abolished and all its records destroyed—Alquier as French ambassador—Death of the Hereditary Princess—A double marriage arranged—Treaty of Amiens—Murat visits Naples—Maria Carolina's prophecy—The King's return to Naples in June—The Queen's return in August—The Spanish nuptials of Princess Marie Antoinette—The Hereditary Prince and his child bride.

CHAPTER XXV
page 481

An exchange of courtesies: 'A single branch of olive'—Alquier's missed opportunities—Conversational indiscretions—A pen-portrait of the Queen—The new favourite Saint-Clair—The fall of Zurlo—The French occupation of Puglia—The Queen pleads with Bonaparte—The rise of Medici—Hugh Elliot—'Between Scylla and Charybdis'—The cabal against Acton—The tribulations of Gallo.

CHAPTER XXVI
page 501

The Queen's mounting exasperation—Execution of the Duke of Enghien—Alquier's rupture with Acton—Bonaparte becomes Emperor—'*Gloria in Excelsis Demonio*'—'The Emperor, your master!'—Elliot's interview with the King—The pinpricks of foreign occupation—Risk rather than self-abasement—Count Roger de Damas—'*Dunque la guerra!*'—The Queen appeals to Bonaparte.

CHAPTER XXVII
page 519

Napoleon's reply and the Queen's vindication—The Damas controversy; Damas obliged to leave—Mme de Staël visits the Queen— Napoleon King of Italy—A calculated explosion—Delayed credentials—Two Russian generals arrive in Naples—Alquier apes his master—Spanish intrigues—An earthquake—The expulsion of Prince Scherbatoff—A secret treaty with Russia—Gallo's treaty of neutrality with France—French evacuation of Puglia—Ulm—Trafalgar—The return of Damas—The departure of Alquier and landing of the Anglo-Russians.

CHAPTER XXVIII
page 539

Defensive preparations—The King's cynicism—Austerlitz: 'The dynasty of Naples has ceased to reign'—Old General Lacy's Council of War—The Queen's attempts to ward off catastrophe—A last appeal to Napoleon—Evacuation of the Anglo-Russians—The Queen's effort to organize resistance—Her last letter to Gallo—The failure of every mission—'I fear we shall never see Naples again'—A foothold in Calabria.

CHAPTER XXIX
page 557

Joseph Bonaparte enters Naples—Acton regains power in Sicily—Damas's defeat and retirement to Vienna—The Calabrian campaign continues—The Queen's party—Arrival of Sir Sidney Smith; his capture of Capri and Ponza—Rodio's execution—The Prince of Hesse-Philippsthal resists at Gaeta—Battle of Maida—Surrender of Gaeta—Courier's letters from Calabria—The young Prince of Canosa—Acton resigns and the Queen recovers power.

CHAPTER XXX
page 575

Failure of Hesse's expedition and of royalist plots at Naples—Saliceti versus Canosa—Paget on dissensions at Palermo—Tilsit—The Empress of Austria's death and the Emperor's remarriage—Canosa's difficulties—The Saliceti explosion—Napoleon's advice to his brother Joseph—Treaty between England and Sicily, March 30, 1808—Insurrection in Spain—Arrival of the Duke of Orléans—His engagement to Maria Amalia—Fruitless mission to Spain—Murat enters Naples as King, September, 1808—His capture of Capri—Stuart's lukewarm expedition—Marriage of Maria Amalia.

CHAPTER XXXI
page 595

Opposition in the Sicilian Parliament—The Peace of Schönbrunn—Napoleon's marriage to Marie Louise complicates the situation—English suspicions against the Queen—The Duke of Orléans invited to Spain—A forged letter from Napoleon—Murat's invasion of Sicily—Appeal of the Sicilian barons to Lord Amherst—The one per cent tax—Arrest of the five factious barons—Arrival of Lord William Bentinck—The Queen's stroke—Death of Acton—Compromising letters—Bentinck's duel with the Queen—The Hereditary Prince appointed Vicar General, January 16, 1812.

CHAPTER XXXII
page 613

Reinstatement of the five barons and exile of their leading opponents—Bentinck's persecution of the Queen—Moliterno's project for Italian unification—Father Caccamo's intervention—The new Sicilian Constitution—A new treaty of alliance—The Prince Vicar's illness—Disputes among the Constitutionalists—The King defiantly returns to Palermo—Bentinck bullies the King—The Duke of Orléans intervenes—The King retires from Palermo—Order for the Queen's departure—The siege of Castelvetrano—The Queen sails from Mazzara—A voyage of eight months to Vienna.

CHAPTER XXXIII
page 641

Bentinck seeks laurels in Catalonia—Murat's indecision—Political factions in Sicily—Bentinck's return and dictatorship—An election campaign—Bentinck's dream—Murat's treaty with Austria, January 11, 1814—Bentinck signs armistice between Sicily and Naples—Murat's double-dealing—Bentinck's proclamation in Leghorn, interview with Murat, and liberation of Genoa—Napoleon's abdication—King Ferdinand's restoration—Sir William A'Court succeeds Bentinck in Sicily—Louis-Philippe's advice—Maria Carolina at Hetzendorf—Her death—Ferdinand's morganatic marriage—Castlereagh's memorandum—Murat declares war on Austria, March 15, 1815—His hasty advance and retreat—The Constitution bequeathed as a parting gift—Treaty of Casalanza—Murat's flight—Miss Davies and Murat's children—Prince Leopold enters Naples—Caroline Murat passes King Ferdinand on his homeward voyage.

CHAPTER XXXIV
page 663

Regardless of the Sicilian Constitution, the King returns to Naples—His full restoration—Treaty with Austria of June 12, 1815—Bentinck forbidden to land—Murat's fatal expedition—Canosa, the Carbonari and Calderari—The Concordat of 1818—Plague at Noia and destruction of the San Carlo—Stendhal on the San Carlo's resurrection—Rossini—Betrothals of Prince Leopold and Princess Maria Carolina—The crowns of Naples and Sicily united: Ferdinand IV becomes Ferdinand I—Changes in Neapolitan society: Marchese Berio and the Archbishop of Taranto—The Villa Floridiana—The King's visit to Rome—He resolves to part with his queue.

CHAPTER XXXV
page 689

Death of Maria Luisa of Spain, followed by that of Charles IV—Visiting Russians—The Emperor and Empress of Austria and Prince Metternich—Growth of the Carbonari—The revolt at Nola—General Guglielmo Pepe leads the rebels—Carbonari gate-crashers at the royal palace—Pepe's flamboyant march into the capital—Ferdinand reluctantly swears to a Constitution—Austria's reaction—Repercussions in Sicily—Protocol of Troppau—Ferdinand invited to Laibach; his voyage and arrival on January 8, 1821—The Congress decides to interfere by force—The Constitutional Parliament declares war—Pepe's rout at Rieti on March 7—The Parliament proposes submission to the King—Flight of Carbonari leaders.

CHAPTER XXXVI
page 715

Canosa again Minister of Police—The King's return to Naples—Canosa's conflict with the Austrians and retirement—Medici and Tommasi reinstated—The King attends the Congress of Verona and proceeds to Vienna—Lady Blessington on Neapolitan society—Medici's burdens—Ferdinand's serene old age—A water-fête for the Empress Marie Louise—The King's sudden death.

NOTE AND ACKNOWLEDGEMENTS

As this history is intended for the general reader—if he still exists outside the writer's imagination—such distracting paraphernalia as footnotes have been dispensed with as much as possible.

The cult of the footnote, involving, at its apogee, a page crammed with encyclopædic detail in small type to a solitary line of text, is no doubt a proof of diligence, but it may also be a tedious form of exhibitionism. A bibliography has been provided for those interested in my chief sources: even this has had to be pruned to essentials. If all the articles perused in the *Archivio Storico per le Province Napoletane* and in *Napoli Nobilissima* had been cited in detail, the bibliography would have become a volume in itself. The hospitable *Società di Storia Patria* of Naples possesses a boundless wealth of manuscripts, books, pamphlets and journals dealing with every period of Neapolitan history, and the State Archives have recently been enriched by the acquirement of the Duke of Calabria's collection, which it would take a lifetime to study exhaustively. Fortunately the Neapolitans are addicted to their own history, so that we may expect new treasures from this yet unexplored mine.

The author desires to express his grateful acknowledgement for the generous assistance rendered him in many valuable ways by Ferdinando Acton, Prince of Leporano; Count Riccardo Filangieri, director of the *Grande Archivio*; Doctor Massimo Fittipaldi, of the *Biblioteca Nazionale*; Professor Ernesto Pontieri, the director of the *Società Napoletana di Storia Patria*, and his colleagues Professor Alfredo Parente and Signora Olga Quarta; Signora Giulia Betocchi, who loaned the author rare books from the library of her son, the late Captain Alessandro Betocchi; Doctor Gino Doria, director of the Museum of San Martino; Professor Jean Pasquier, of the Institut Français de Naples; Signora Clotilde Marghieri, in whose villa near Torre del Greco the book was begun; and above all, the late colossus and patriarch of all Neapolitan studies, the lamented Benedetto Croce.

The author also desires to express his particular gratitude to Mr Noel Blakiston, Head of the Research Department, Public Record Office, London, for his kind advice and permission to consult the documents of his province; to Miss Margaret Franklin for her sympathetic collaboration in delving through the tomes of F.O. 70 and transcribing useful excerpts; to the Hon. Sir Harold Nicolson for permission to quote from his masterly study of the Congress of Vienna; to the late Duchess of Sermoneta and Mr John Murray for permission to quote from *The Locks of Norbury*; to Sir Osbert Sitwell for his introduction to Sir Nathaniel Wraxall; and to Mr Reginald Colby for the considerate loan of books unprocurable in Italy.

Florence, September 1955

PROLOGUE

Most people, even those who have never visited Naples, are familiar with the outlines of that vast amphitheatre-city. The curve of its bay has for centuries been recognized as a masterpiece of romantic scenery. Since the infancy of engraving, the view from Mergellina, framed by the Horatian pine in the foreground, must have been reproduced by the million and reached the uttermost ends of the earth. The reality is a spectacle of voluptuous enchantment, as powerful in its masses as it is sumptuous in detail, and the cheapest tinted postcard cannot fail to convey some impression of its magnificence. Vesuvius was called 'hackneyed' by Byron, but the beauty of its slopes cannot pall like the purple passages of *Childe Harold*. Though its severed cone has lost its plume of smoke, its dormant menace never quite relaxes hold on the imagination.

The buildings, being subordinate to the grandeur of the natural panorama, are often overlooked. Their number seems greater from the distance, and their flat roofs and multi-coloured walls form an intricate mosaic which the liquid light may melt and fuse in an Oriental anonymity. But when we come to examine them separately, many speak a language of pungent individual charm, like the dialect of the people.

Naples is an architectural palimpsest prodigal of hidden surprises. While the foreground may be summarized on a travel poster, the background remains a mysterious, teeming jungle. How easy to lose oneself among all those clefts and crevices! How much there is to explore!

No other city in Europe has been ruled by so varied a succession of foreign dynasties, and each has left some trace, yet under the chaos and congestion of its growth, coiled up as in a complicated shell, many of its treasures are camouflaged. Since Palæopolis, the 'old city', and Neapolis, the 'new city', were founded by Greek colonists and merged in 328 B.C., after their inevitable conflict with Rome, sections of the original walls were embodied in later structures, and relics of their perennial tufa may be found in unexpected places. As in Rome, there was a gradual metamorphosis: the Cathedral was built over a temple of Apollo, the Church of Santi Apostoli rises on the ruins of a temple of Mercury; that of San Paolo Maggiore was once a temple of Castor and Pollux, and retains two Corinthian columns of the pristine portico. Among the pines and vines of Posillipo, derived from the old Greek words meaning a 'truce to care', other villas replaced those Greco-Roman pleasure-houses reminiscent of the epicure Pollio, so well calculated to banish melancholy and exhilarate the mind. On the whole, they are sorry substitutes. And now a crop of 'functional' apartment houses is springing up and up to spoil the landscape. The Castel dell' Ovo could not have been an improvement on the Megaris of Lucullus, but at least it is a picturesque pile, which the neighbouring hotels will never be. Life still pullulates most noisily in the twilit chasms of the Greco-Roman centre, the narrow lanes of high houses running from the Via Tribunali, where the greatest revelations reward the leisurely rover.

Naples began to assume its modern aspect under the rule of the Angevins (1266–1442), who first raised it to the dignity of a capital. The Gothic art they introduced was too frigid for the Neapolitan temperament and has left no progeny, though its petrified frost-flowers have monopolized the interest of most art historians. Romantic writers have idealized the Angevin period, with its chivalry and adventure and dramatic vicissitudes, and the halcyon days of the wise King Robert (1309–1343) left a long legacy of literary nostalgia. Yet King Robert was essentially Gallic, and he filled his court with cosmopolitans. As protector of the Guelf party he was enriched by subsidies from Florence, and he employed Florentine bankers as well as architects, sculptors and painters, many of whom, like Boccaccio, discovered a new *joie de vivre* in Naples, 'gay, peaceful and flourishing under a single sovereign', preferring it to their free but harassed republic. Boccaccio has commemorated this period most vividly, when the Castel Nuovo might have been the centre of some sophisticated court in Provence. The Angevin additions to Naples were destroyed or rebuilt by the extravagant Aragonese, whose transformation of the city was only less prodigious, considering their short rule from 1442 till 1501, than that of Charles, the first of the Neapolitan Bourbons.

One of the earliest surviving pictures of Naples viewed from the sea, the 'Tavola Strozzi' in the museum of San Martino, is a neat record of the Aragonese achievement, of which the salient features have survived. The hills were well timbered then, and must have resembled those near Florence, sprinkled with monasteries and country houses; and the town population did not exceed 50,000. The hub of local culture was the academy, which met since 1443 in King Alfonso's library in the Castel Nuovo to discuss philosophy, the elements of poetry, philology and kindred subjects; it became famous under the name of *Pontaniana*. But art and culture seem to have served an inclination for luxury and display rather than to have moderated the congenital cruelty of this dynasty. What had the elegant Latin of Pontano to do with King Ferrante's museum of mummies, the embalmed victims which he liked to keep near him, dressed as when they were alive? The nobler features of the Italian despotisms of the Renaissance, as Burckhardt wrote, are not to be found among the princes of this line.

During the next two centuries the Spanish viceroys left a profounder mark on the city's straggling development. Though its main thoroughfare is officially called Via Roma in honour of the unification of Italy, to Neapolitans it remains the Toledo, in memory of the energetic Viceroy Pedro de Toledo, who laid it out in 1536. The canals of lanes and steep staircases up the hill side, called *gradoni*, have changed little since then. Many streets and squares were widened and paved with blocks of lava; the massive castle of Sant' Elmo was rebuilt in the form of a star, with six rays which long remained impregnable. It was Pedro of Toledo's policy to concentrate the feudal barons in the metropolis so as to keep them under better control, but they created fresh problems by bringing their hordes of retainers. The population rose to 200,000 by the middle of the seventeenth century, and approached half a million by the end of the eighteenth.

At last an architectural style was imported which assumed a distinct Neapolitan character. When the baroque came to Naples, it expressed itself like a swarm of nightingales released from a golden cage. Quite apart from the patronage of the Jesuits and the Spanish viceroys, this intensely theatrical art appealed strongly to the popular fantasy. The very climate favoured it: colour clamoured for more colour; exuberance sought its complement in the most mathematical of the visual arts. It is chiefly the prodigal use of colour which distinguishes the Neapolitan from the Roman baroque. Majolica tiles glitter with the sheen of peacocks from cupolas and the cusps of bell towers among the mottled pastel shades of houses whose flat roofs resemble hanging gardens; the floors of religious and secular buildings are carpeted with tiles in lively patterns; and when we peer into churches, the polychrome of frescoes and inlaid marbles prevails over plastic effects.

'That which seemed to us most extraordinary at Naples,' wrote Misson at the end of the seventeenth century, 'was the number and magnificence of the churches. It may be justly said, that in this respect it surpasses imagination... If you would look upon rare pictures, sculptures, and the rarity of vessels of gold and silver, you need but go to the churches: the roofs, the wainscots, the walls are all covered with pieces of precious marble, most artificially laid together, or with compartments of *basso relievo*, or of joiner's work gilded, and enriched with the works of the most famous painters. There is nothing to be seen but jasper, porphyry, mosaic of all fashions, all masterpieces of art. I visited five and twenty, or thirty of these stately edifices, where one still finds oneself surprised afresh.'

This comment of a near contemporary was a measure of their success, for the Neapolitan public had a craving for surprises. A combination of virtuosity and versatility was required of the skilled artisan, and the keen competition of rival religious orders for his handiwork acted on him as a powerful stimulus. He transmuted the rhetorical flourishes of seventeenth-century poetry into marble and stucco.

An inevitable reaction set in. Under the chapter-heading 'The Triumph of the Baroque', one Ruskinian guide to Naples exclaimed:'Now we come to the *Inferno*!' But a few German critics retained a clearer sense of perspective; and in England the poetic enthusiasm of Sir Osbert and Mr Sacheverell Sitwell heralded a partial return to favour. Those obelisks called *guglie*, long damned as deplorable, 'the nadir of Baroque bad taste', were appreciated in relation to their environment; and what open-air monuments could be more flamboyantly festive? They seem to have sprung up like palm trees full-fledged from the architects' imagination.

Nearly all the baroque sculptor-architects busy in Naples during the seventeenth century were of North Italian stock, but here they 'suffered a sea-change'. In blending the grandiose with the startling, it was as if they were influenced by the volcanic atmosphere, and wished to compete with the mineral, marine and vegetable forces of nature, so that one comes to regard them as Neapolitans.

The Fanzago family hailed from Bergamo, but were to be more closely identified with their second home. Cosimo Fanzago contributed more than any other architect to the form and colour of seventeenth-century Naples, and he founded a prolific school. His masterpiece is the church and cloisters of the Certosa di San Martino, just below the castle of Sant' Elmo: both citadel and monastery dominate all views like the superimposed eyries of eagles sacred and profane. But the citadel casts no shadow on the cloisters; only passing clouds may darken this area so splendidly conceived for contemplation of the eternal. From the well-head with its three crowning obelisks to the little cemetery whose balustrade is adorned with skulls there are countless details to beguile the connoisseur. The church is a repository of the richest baroque art; the monastic halls of the Carthusians have been converted into a museum illustrating the past history of Naples. To those who can make them speak, the objects assembled here become eloquent. Old portraits, prints and drawings of scant artistic value, documents of vanished customs, the *fleur-de-lis* embroidered cloak of the knights of San Gennaro, state coaches and gilded galleys of the Bourbons, an eighteenth-century *presepe* or crib with a thousand figures to celebrate a perpetual Christmas—these conjure many a forgotten aspect of the kingdom of the Two Sicilies.

Fanzago was also responsible for the less florid *guglie* of San Gennaro and San Domenico, and for the unfinished Palazzo Donn' Anna at Posillipo, designed for Anna Carafa, wife of the Viceroy Medina, a classical honeycomb rising from the sea, haunted by siren music, such as only Claude has been able to evoke in paint. Signor Roberto Pane, to whom all lovers of Naples are indebted, has pointed out that a dishevelled grandeur 'nearly always accompanied by a mysterious atmosphere of drama not noticeable elsewhere', is characteristic of many Neapolitan buildings, since those of the seventeenth and eighteenth centuries were seldom finished, and the incomplete in architecture, especially when it has been mellowed by time, has a singular suggestive power. This applies, above all, to the Palazzo Donn' Anna.

There are copious variations on Fanzago's church façades, of which a double staircase leading to a terrace with an ample atrium is a typical feature. Among Fanzago's contemporaries, the Dominican Father Giuseppe Nuvolo distinguished himself for the originality of his roofs and cupolas, whose tiles of yellow, green and blue form airy clusters of Oriental fruit, idealized pineapples and never-bursting bubbles.

Another characteristic of Neapolitan architecture is the elaboration of the open staircase in the background of palace courtyards, with its operatic perspective of arches and vaults. The streets were usually too narrow for a boldly effective façade, but the open staircase, with its light and fanciful arcades, provides many an unexpected compensation.

So formidable was the increase of religious buildings that in the beginning of the eighteenth century a petition was sent to the Viceroy, urging him to prevent the clergy from acquiring more property. Until 1860 there were at least 400 churches, exclusive of private chapels, and about 200 houses belonging to religious orders. Most of the latter have been turned into hospitals, schools, public offices and barracks, and many have been damaged or destroyed, like Santa Chiara during the last war.

The precious few that survive are oases of tranquillity behind high walls, unknown to the passing tourist, and they cover considerable areas in the heart of the old city. The most impressive, in contrast with the din of the streets outside it, is the Convent of San Gregorio Armeno, which has managed to retain its eighteenth-century serenity. The spacious cloister garden contains a monumental fountain with marble masks and shells and prancing sea-horses—a baroque glorification of the well of Samaria. On one side of it stands Jesus, on another the Samaritan woman; from a distance these graceful figures, sculpted by Matteo Bottiglieri in 1730, seem to be walking among the orange trees. All the rooms above the arcades around this cloister open on to broad balconied terraces. Only the daughters of noble families were admitted to this convent, where everything helped to reconcile the less austere to their lot. Good food is a great consolation, and the cooking was famed for its excellence. Dr John Moore, who visited 'four of the principal nunneries' in the royal suite, wrote that 'the company were surprised, on being led into a large parlour, to find a table covered, and every appearance of a most plentiful cold repast, consisting of several joints of meat, hams, fowl, fish, and various other dishes. It seemed rather ill-judged to have prepared a feast of such a solid nature immediately after dinner; for those royal visits were made in the afternoon. The Lady Abbess, however, earnestly pressed their Majesties to sit down; with which they complied... The nuns stood behind, to serve their royal guests. The Queen chose a slice of cold turkey, which, on being cut up, turned out a large piece of lemon ice, of the shape and appearance of a roasted turkey. All the other dishes were ices of various kinds, disguised under the forms of joints of meat, fish, and fowl, as above mentioned. The gaiety and good humour of the King, the affable and engaging behaviour of the royal sisters (Queen Maria Carolina and the Princess of Saxe-Teschen), and the satisfaction which beamed from the plump countenance of the Lady Abbess, threw an air of cheerfulness on this scene; which was interrupted, however, by gleams of melancholy reflection, which failed not to dart across the mind, at sight of so many victims to the pride of family, to avarice, and superstition. Many of those victims were in the full bloom of health and youth, and some of them were remarkably handsome.'

The generally accepted tradition that the two centuries of Spanish rule were a period of utter decay is at least challenged by the continued enlargement of the city and the profusion of handsome buildings which still survive. Benedetto Croce has pointed out that the Spaniards governed Naples as they governed their own peninsula, neither better nor worse; unfortunately they were bad economists. Their character was better attuned to the Neapolitan than that of most foreigners. Their intense religiosity, their fretful sense of honour and punctilio, the importance they attached to pomps and ceremonies, their love of ostentation and contempt for manual labour, were shared by most of their subjects. At least Naples enjoyed peace for a century and a half, and the power of the aggressive barons was greatly reduced. Many were coaxed to the capital, where they soon succumbed to the pleasure of competing with each other 'in the brilliancy of their *equipages*, the number of their attendants, the richness of their dress, and the grandeur of their titles'. In the meantime they left their property to be administered by agents, and in most cases gambling and extravagance ruined their descendants.

The middle class grew wealthier, especially the bankers and

contractors of Genoese origin, and the lawyers, who invaded all government offices and climbed steadily to political power. The successful bought titles and estates; in the seventeenth century Naples had at least 119 princes, 156 dukes, 173 marquesses and several hundreds of counts. Only six or seven of the dukes and princes had estates producing from the equivalent of ten to thirteen thousand pounds sterling (old gold-standard) a year; a considerable number had fortunes of about half that value; and the annual income of many was not above one or two thousand pounds. Of the counts and marquesses, many had not above three or four hundred pounds a year of family estate, many still less, and not a few enjoyed the title without any estate whatever. Yet most foreign travellers were amazed that the richest of these could support such expensive establishments. A guest would have to pass through a dozen large rooms, usually more lofty and spacious than those in Paris and London, before reaching the dining-room, where the table was laid for between thirty to forty persons and the dishes were varied and abundant. Each guest had a footman behind his chair; other liveried servants remained in the adjacent rooms and in the entrance hall.

'No estate in England,' wrote an English traveller, 'could support such a number of servants, paid and fed as English servants are; but here the wages are very moderate indeed, and the greater number of men-servants, belonging to the first families, give their attendance through the day only and find beds and provisions for themselves. It must be remembered, also, that few of the nobles give entertainments and those who do not are said to live very sparingly; so that the whole of their revenue, whatever that may be, is exhausted on articles of show.'

In glaring contrast with these and with the army of mixed clergy, which had reached one-fortieth of the population, there was the formidable city populace, which became world-famous under the name of *lazzaroni*. Since Masaniello's rebellion in 1647, this class had given rise to fantastic legends; during the eighteenth and well on into the nineteenth century foreign travellers were quite as curious about the *lazzaroni* as they were about Vesuvius and Pompeii. The reason is not far to seek, for these were as fascinating in their way as the landscape; and their open-air life was a constant source of amusement and interest—a perpetual comic opera, for those who did not peer too close. Their voluble presence enhanced the atmosphere of seaside festivity and masquerade which the tourist expected of Naples. They were children of nature, sturdy, excitable, apparently cheerful and carefree, proliferating in primitive simplicity, sufficient unto the day, the passing minute, walking and sporting on the sea-shore naked, with no more shame than Adam in his primal innocence, and, thanks to the climate, content with little and sleeping under the stars most of the year.

Squeamish Président de Brosses called them 'the most abominable rabble, the most disgusting vermin which has ever crawled on the surface of the earth'; and under the Spanish regime the hordes of ragged beggars must have been frightening, as the name *lazzaroni* implies; probably the Abbé Galiani was correct in deriving it from the lepers, whose patron was Saint Lazarus and who were segregated in hospitals called lazarets in consequence. They became a byword for all that was thieving, treacherous, seditious, lazy and corrupt. 'There is not such another race of rogues as the common people of Naples,' Henry Swinburne concluded. But as Goethe observed with greater sympathy, the Northerner mistook for idlers those who did not toil all day. After a careful scrutiny, that universal genius exploded the common myth. The *lazzaroni* worked like anybody else, but in their own fashion, he decided, recalling those cynic philosophers who could only exist in a climate like that of Greece, for they could not have survived the winters of the North. Their way of being satisfied with so little, of living on the air of time, seemed to him a sign of inner freedom rather than of indolence. And an English contemporary of Goethe's wrote that if these poor fellows were idle, it was not their own fault; they were continually running about the streets, offering their service and begging for employment. 'Fewer riots or outrages of any kind happen', he observed, 'than might be expected in a town where the police is far from being strict, and where such multitudes of poor unemployed people meet together every day. This partly proceeds from the national character, which, in my opinion, is quiet, submissive, and averse to riot or sedition; and partly to the common people being universally sober, and never inflamed with strong and spirituous liquors, as they are in the northern countries. Iced water and lemonade are among the luxuries of the lowest vulgar; they are carried about in little barrels, and sold in halfpenny's worth. The half-naked *lazzarone* is often tempted to spend the small pittance destined for the maintenance of his family on this bewitching beverage, as the most dissolute of the low people in London spend their wages on gin and brandy; so that the same extravagance which cools the mob of the one city, tends to inflame that of the other to acts of excess and brutality.'

This maligned class had virtues ready to be drawn out by discriminating sympathy and leadership. The poorest had their own simple standards of morality and their own semi-pagan but passionate religion; they loved their families and had warm human qualities not obvious to the superficial tourist. Their heroic defence of Naples against Championnet's army in 1799 and their persistent loyalty to the Bourbons were as unpalatable as they were alarming to the Jacobin agitators and doctrinaire professors who bedevilled the later course of Neapolitan history. The *lazzaroni* were the real patriots, and they were even capable of gratitude. Instinctively they identified the Bourbons with Naples and with themselves.

In 1734, after more than two centuries as a province of Spain and Austria, Naples became the capital of an independent kingdom under Charles of Bourbon, who deserved his reputation as an enlightened monarch. A sovereign of their own had come to reside among the Neapolitans, who felt once more that they were a nation. Charles was no miracle worker: he could not suddenly transform the social system and the character of his people, or cause trade and agriculture to flourish overnight. But he transformed the capital of his new kingdom, so that the Naples we see today remains pre-eminently a city of the Bourbons. The San Carlo Theatre, the national library, the Farnese collections brought from Parma, the first treasures from Herculaneum and Pompeii, the palaces of Capodimonte, Portici and Caserta, the Albergo dei Poveri, the fine squares now called Piazza Dante and Piazza Plebiscito—wherever we turn we see some splendid relic of Charles and his successors.

No impartial historian can deny that the Two Sicilies were happier under Charles than they had been for many a long century. The benefits of independence were soon apparent, and much solid progress was made. Charles should not be blamed if this progress was not dizzily spectacular, any more than he should be blamed for the eruptions of Vesuvius or for the earthquakes of 1738 and 1750. The peasants remained in a backward condition, but as Croce exclaimed: 'After a century and a half—after the unification of Italy—were they so much better off?' Some order was restored to public finance, and a long period of peace favoured prosperity.

Ecclesiastical jurisdiction and immunities were curtailed, and at last clerical property (then about one-third of the whole kingdom) was taxed, though not beyond two per cent of its value. But Charles was more interested in the fine arts and the excavation of antiquities than in the problems of economy and legislation. The university was modernized and given a worthy home; archaeology was encouraged with notable results; there were numberless improvements in public and private life; houses were more conveniently furnished, and the use of glass windows became common; great architects, like Vanvitelli and Fuga, were commissioned to design the buildings we still admire; and Naples also became, as de Brosses wrote, 'the capital of the musical world'. Progress paved the way for more progress, until the shattering repercussions of the French Revolution.

I

Elisabeth Farnese's ambitions for her elder son Don Carlos—His departure for Italy, 1731—His arrival in Tuscany and Parma—Spain declares war on Austria, 1733—The Spanish invasion of Naples, 1734—Don Carlos enters his new capital, May 10—Conquest of Sicily—Coronation of King Charles in Palermo—His festive return to Naples.

When the Spanish Infante Don Carlos came in 1734 to plant the Bourbon dynasty in Naples, that 'piece of Heaven dropped to earth' had suffered grievously from twenty-seven years of Austrian domination after more than two centuries under Spanish viceroys good, bad and indifferent, but mostly bad. The historian Giannone lamented the exorbitant sums extorted from the Neapolitans by their Spanish overlords, not only to pay for their illnesses and funerals, but even for their wedding-and-bedding expenses. Such voted taxes, euphemistically termed donations, had become heavier and more frequent under the Austrians. Contributions for distant wars, for the christening of Hapsburg babies, for the salaries of Viennese officials, for privileges nominal and purposes mysterious, were so heaped upon the Neapolitans that with the exception of a few privileged barons they were even ready to welcome the return of the Spaniards. The Emperor Charles VI, sitting in Vienna, knew as little about the Neapolitans as they knew about him. They only knew that they were cruelly exploited by his emissaries. On the other hand, glowing accounts of Don Carlos had reached Naples before his arrival. And he was coming not as a viceroy but as a king.

Naples owed its final independence to a woman. Elisabeth Farnese, the second wife of Philip V of Spain, had never ceased to be intensely Italian. When the Farnese and Medici dynasties were on the verge of extinction, she had mounted a throne from which she tried to sway the politics of Europe. Since Philip's health was precarious, she feared an early widowhood; her sons were Philip's younger sons, and as such had no brilliant prospects. Elisabeth was determined to provide handsomely for both emergencies.

Her first aim was to secure the succession to Parma and Piacenza as a Farnese, and to Tuscany as a descendant of the Medici. It cost her twenty years of incessant intrigue to achieve this maternal ambition. Her eldest son, the Infante Charles, had been born in 1716, and the main purpose of his education had been to teach him blind obedience to his parents and to the Catholic Church. Until the age of seven he had been entrusted to a Spanish governess of the most rigid principles; after that age he had his private apartment in the Escurial, and a train of priestly tutors to cram him with all the approved subjects. A French Jesuit taught him languages, including Latin, Italian, German and French, as well as history sacred and profane. He also acquired a smattering of military tactics, naval science, geometry and fortification. Don Emanuel de Benavides y Aragon, Conde de San Esteban, a solemn statesman of immaculate pedigree, was appointed to add the final polish to an education which was never more than superficial. The Prince's predilection for hunting and shooting was encouraged, and it was to become a lifelong obsession. Open-air exercise probably contributed more than his tutors to sharpening his native wit.

Physically, Charles was short, lean and round shouldered, with a sunburnt complexion and bad teeth from which he suffered acutely. As he grew older his nose became his most prominent feature; it was a protuberance more than Roman, but his eyes were bright and clever and his expression was genial. Nobody could call him handsome, but he had 'that unruffled, Olympian air' which Sir Max Beerbohm diagnosed as so sure a sign of the Blood Royal. He was always dignified, in spite of his tendency to stoop and his simplicity of manner, though he was never quite as simple as he appeared. To impartial observers he resembled a very distinguished ram. He was taught to curb his youthful high spirits, for the Conde de San Esteban repeatedly admonished him: 'First gravity and fear of God!' His tastes were healthy and frugal: apart from hunting, which he regarded as a physical necessity, he enjoyed fishing, billiards and carpentry—he carved the pommel of his own cane—but, although he was obliged to attend the opera, and eventually built the largest of contemporary opera-houses, he disliked serious music. His piety was deep and sincere, and he was a model of filial virtue.

His great-uncle Francesco Farnese, the Duke of Parma, hoped

that Charles would restore the ebbing fortunes of his state. To ensure his succession he tried to prevent his own brother Antonio from marrying, but this mountainous bachelor was eventually persuaded by the Emperor of Austria to take a wife. When Duke Antonio died in 1731, his widow, Henrietta of Modena, fancied herself to be with child, but nobody shared her illusion. At the second Treaty of Vienna of the same year the Emperor of Austria promised to let Don Carlos take possession of Parma and Piacenza even if the problem child materialized, and to garrison Tuscany as well. The Grand Duke Gian Gastone agreed reluctantly to these stipulations. During his minority the Infante was to remain under his guardianship and that of his grandmother, the Dowager Duchess of Parma.

On October 20, 1731, Charles took leave of his parents in Seville; he knelt before them and asked for their blessing. Philip V has been portrayed by Saint-Simon and others as a grotesque figure of premature senility; his clothes were unnecessarily shabby, and he had a drawling speech and vacant expression. Not content with confessing twice a day, he required his confessors to be available at all hours, when demoniacal conflicts occurred between his conscience and his concupiscence. Yet he managed to retain a curious dignity, as well as the affection of his boisterous Queen, who seldom left his side. With tremulous deliberation he made the sign of the cross on the Infante's forehead and presented him with the jewelled sword he had formerly received from his grandfather Louis XIV. Elisabeth blessed him, too, and gave him an enormous diamond ring.

He was to travel by land as far as Antibes, stopping at Valencia and Barcelona and crossing the Pyrenees. He need never be lonely or bored, for he was well attended: from the highest dignitaries to the *mozos de retrete*, his travelling suite consisted of two hundred and fifty persons, at least some of whom could distract him from any fit of homesickness. The most important member of his household was his former tutor, the Count of San Esteban, whose name was italianized as Santo Stefano, now his chief major-domo and Philip V's plenipotentiary in Italy, who had a separate retinue. Other important members were his chief equerry Prince Corsini, the Pope's nephew; his grand chamberlain the Duke of Tursi; his secretary for despatches the Marquis of Montealegre; his first gentleman-in-waiting Don José Fernandez Miranda, a devoted courtier whose influence outlasted all others; a special protégé of his mother's, Marchese Fogliani of Piacenza; and the Neapolitan Don Lelio Carafa, brother of the opulent Duke of Maddaloni and captain of the Infante's bodyguard, a hundred strong.

Thus, at the age of fifteen, Charles left his native land, which he would not see again for nearly thirty years. At Antibes an Anglo-Spanish squadron and three Tuscan galleys awaited him; by Louis XV's orders he had been treated as a Son of France, and he was a little tired of pompous receptions. Four days later, after a stormy Christmas at sea, he landed at Leghorn on December 27. Here he was welcomed as heir presumptive by the ministers of Gian Gastone, the last Grand Duke of the Medici, who seldom left his bed in the Pitti Palace, where his debauches had become legendary. Santo Stefano proclaimed that the Infante had come in the role of a son to the Grand Duke and his sister the Electress Anna Maria, both of whom were childless. Father Ascanio, the Spanish envoy to Tuscany, brought the comforting news that the Austrians had peacefully evacuated Parma and Piacenza.

The good-natured young Prince seemed far more Italian than Spanish, and his lavishness helped to produce a favourable impression. Unfortunately he caught smallpox soon after his arrival, a disease which was often fatal in his family. This caused widespread alarm, since the Tuscans were delighted with this promising heir, if only as a safeguard against the dreaded Austrians. During his illness everything possible was done to amuse him. The British envoy, Sir Horace Mann, relates that he had recourse to the following pastime while he was confined to his bedroom: 'His pages used to fix little hooks to fine threads or wires that hung down unobserved in different parts of the room, which were all fastened to a sort of a bell-rope within his bed; which hooks, when properly baited by the sly pages, with the wigs of his courtiers, he with a sudden jerk, drew them up to the top of the room. Mr Skinner, then consul there— the most ridiculous dressing creature I ever saw—was often served so. He commonly wore his own hair, which was black; but on very great occasions he put on a white wig, with four tails and a vast deal of powder over his black locks.' The Prince's health was prayed for with particular fervour; and he recovered so quickly that he was soon chasing wild boar in the Pisan Maremma.

On March 9, 1732, he made his formal entry to Florence. Guns saluted him from the fortresses as he advanced in a splendid procession along streets hung with tapestry all the way to the cathedral, under whose echoing dome the *Te Deum* was sung by eight choirs of three hundred musicians, while the guns repeated their salvos in the distance. The Grand Duke and his sister, who were on such bad terms that they avoided each other, awaited him separately in the Pitti Palace, where a regal apartment had been prepared for him.

Gian Gastone had become cynically resigned to the adoption of a 'political son'. After signing his last will and testament, declaring the Infante Charles his successor, he remarked that he had just got a son and heir by a stroke of his pen which he had not been able to get in thirty-four years of marriage. He lay in bed as usual during his visit, which simplified etiquette considerably. The young Prince struggled to disguise his amazement at the Grand Duke's appearance, like a bloated turkey-cock under a ponderous wig. On the other hand, Gian Gastone took kindly to his guest. He treated him with fatherly tenderness, we are told, and among the presents he gave him was a small open phaeton with silver fittings and velvet lining, which he drove with two donkeys through the Boboli gardens.

For three nights Florence was illuminated, and dazzling fireworks exploded from the tower of the Palazzo Vecchio. Every day there were military parades and bands playing in the public squares, but whenever he could the Prince went off hunting. In the evening he would politely sit through one act of the opera in the Pergola Theatre, smothering his yawns until he could retire. His obsession with hunting was such that on leaving a room lined with tapestry, among the figures on which was that of a horse, he would always raise his leg, as if he were about to ride. Sir Horace Mann wrote that when the Prince was lodged in the Pitti, 'he amused himself by shooting with a bow and arrow at the birds in the fine tapestry-hangings of his rooms, and was become so very dextrous that he seldom missed the eye he aimed at. John Gaston was much displeased when he was told how sadly his precious meubles of the Gobelins were treated by the expertness of his pupil; so that, the first time the young Prince went out, orders were given to remove the tapestry and to put up damask with gold fringe and lace in the place of it. When the young sportsman returned home, both he and his Spanish court were surprised and even offended to see so great an alteration; but John Gaston sent him word that, as the weather was growing warmer, he was fearful that the Prince's health might have suffered by the heat of the winter furniture. He was forced to accept of the excuse, but lamented much the loss of his amusement.' Such notions of entertainment perplexed the cultured Florentines, but the Prince's generosity compensated for his lack of seriousness.

On June 24, the feast of Florence's patron saint, John the Baptist, Gian Gastone, without consulting the Emperor of Austria, allowed Charles to receive homage from the Tuscan Senate and provinces, which were represented at this annual function by men on horseback carrying banners and by wooden towers decorated with historical symbols and coats-of-arms. Charles, who now styled himself Grand Prince of Tuscany, sat on a raised platform before the Palazzo Vecchio while each banner was hoisted and lowered in front of him. The pageantry was unusually gay, for it was an age since the Florentines had had an opportunity to rejoice: Gian Gastone had long been a recluse invisible to most of his subjects, and his father before him had been the gloomiest of bigots. The thorny problem of the Tuscan succession appeared to be solved with the sanction of a jubilant people.

The Austrians were furious. They protested that Charles was still a minor; he should have waited for imperial investiture and a special dispensation on account of his age. His parents told him to disregard the Emperor's protests. Already the Spanish garrisons were installed: Spain had regained a firm foothold in Italy. In October Charles proceeded to Parma and Piacenza amid similar celebrations. The medal struck to commemorate the occasion had for its device a lady with a lily in her hand, and for its legend *Spes publica*. A *carrousel* of sixteen horsemen with verses by the honey-tongued Frugoni, who called it 'The Arrival of Ascanius in Italy', was given in the Teatro Farnese. The words *Parma Resurget* were blazoned across the front of the ducal palace. This annoyed the Austrians even more, but Elisabeth Farnese was past caring. The ambitions of that pugnacious Queen had begun to soar beyond Tuscany and Parma.

In the meantime Charles wrote to his parents that Colorno, the summer residence of the Farnese, was far superior to their new palace at San Ildefonso, the building of which had not yet been completed, and that the fertile plains of Parma appealed more to his taste than the hills of Tuscany. In this he was a true child of the eighteenth century. He was visited twice by Cardinal Alberoni, who had retired to Piacenza; and the septuagenarian statesman must have been gladdened at the sight of this Prince, whose birth had coincided with his first political triumphs and who now promised to realize his most cherished ambitions.

When the War of the Polish Succession broke out after the death of Augustus II in 1733, Elisabeth, who was not interested in Poland unless one of her sons could rule it, seized this chance to attack Austria in its most vulnerable spot. On November 7 France and Spain signed the Treaty of the Escurial, guaranteeing each other's possessions and securing Parma, Piacenza, the reversion to Tuscany, and all Italian conquests to the Infante Charles. The latter were subject to the terms of the Treaty of Turin, which France had signed previously with Charles Emmanuel of Savoy but which Spain had refused to ratify. According to these Charles Emmanuel was promised the State of Milan, while Don Carlos was to receive Naples, Sicily and the Tuscan seaports called the Presidi, which Philip II of Spain had kept when he granted Siena as a fief to the Grand Duke Cosimo de' Medici.

In December Spain declared war on Austria. At the same time forty thousand Frenchmen commanded by Marshal de Villars crossed the Alps, joined the forces of Charles Emmanuel, and conquered Lombardy, while thirty thousand Spaniards under the Count of Montemar landed at Leghorn. Montemar was to guard the Po against an Austrian descent from the eastern Alps, but Charles Emmanuel refused to collaborate with him unless the Treaty of Turin was signed. Elisabeth Farnese had as sound reasons for mistrusting this treaty as Charles Emmanuel had for mistrusting her. So Montemar was told to leave him alone and prepare for the conquest of Naples.

Don Carlos was enjoying the placid amenities of his new principality when he heard that a greater career was reserved for him. He was to be titular Commander-in-Chief of the Spanish army in Italy. On his eighteenth birthday, January 20, 1734, he declared himself to be of age, 'free to rule and administer our States independently', though in fact he was still subordinate to his parents. His mother wrote him an eloquent letter bidding him conquer the Two Sicilies, 'which elevated into a free kingdom, will be yours. Go forth and win: the most beautiful crown in Italy awaits you.' Montemar joined him in Parma, and after removing the richest heirlooms of the Farnese family and entrusting the regency to his grandmother, the Dowager Duchess, he left for Florence in February. Again he received an ovation, but he could only stay two weeks. Gian Gastone bade him a tearful farewell, realizing that the whole question of the Tuscan succession would have to be hammered out again over his exhausted body, while Tuscany might become a general battleground. The conquest of Naples was bound to deprive him of this becoming heir. The Florentines shared Gian Gastone's gloomy forebodings.

For the young Prince himself everything was glorious, a triumphal progress. On March 5 he reviewed his army at Perugia, and within a few days he received encouraging reports from Naples: the people were said to be preparing a rapturous welcome. Pope Clement XII, who still claimed Parma as a lapsed fief and expected some compensation, made no difficulty about allowing the Spanish to pass through his states. The Roman aristocracy came crowding to pay the Prince their respects at Monterotondo; and from here a proclamation was issued to the people of the Two Sicilies on March 14, 1734, 'in the name of Don Carlos, by the grace of God Infante of Spain, Duke of Parma, Piacenza and Castro, etc., Hereditary Grand Prince of Tuscany and Generalissimo of the armies of His Catholic Majesty in Italy'. This contained a despatch from Philip V, explaining his desire to recover his two lost kingdoms and save them from the excessive violence, oppression and tyranny of the Austrians. He declared that his sole aim was to restore Naples to happiness and prosperity. He was ready to let bygones be bygones. In the meantime he had authorized the Infante Charles to grant dispensations and free pardons both general and particular, to confer privileges and abolish every tax invented by the insatiable greed of the Austrian government. The Prince added that he confirmed these pledges. His progress was leisurely and bountiful. After crossing the Neapolitan frontier he was met by the Abbot of Montecassino, who entertained him at the famous abbey. Nowhere did he encounter the slightest resistance.

The Emperor Charles VI paid no heed to his viceroy's urgent appeals for reinforcements, and the pro-Austrian Marshal Giovanni Carafa had barely 7,000 troops at his disposal. The Viceroy Visconti was ordered to raise 600,000 ducats for defence, while the nobility were to raise recruits; in both cases they failed. Prince Pignatelli di Monteleone's efforts to conscript a regiment ended in a public riot and his few recruits ran away. Admiral Pallavicini had only three frigates and four galleys to defend Naples against the

Spanish fleet, whose vanguard had seized Procida and Ischia while Prince Charles was still on papal territory.

The Austrian Emperor had also launched a proclamation, but in spite of his 'certainty of final victory over an enemy that broke laws human and divine in attempting to usurp the kingdom which Divine Providence had entrusted to his care', the gist of this was: 'I rely upon your efforts... Rest assured that I shall ever be mindful of the troubles and sacrifices which the hostile invasion may cause you.'

The pro-Austrian party in Naples declared to deaf ears that Don Carlos would descend upon them in a spirit of wrathful revenge. The viceroy did not know where to turn for funds, since the Emperor had almost drained the treasury. In addition to copious extra taxes, a new 'donation' to Vienna was imposed, of which only one-sixth could be collected, and there was a frantic run on the banks to withdraw deposits. The nobles whose loyalty was dubious were banished, and these slipped straight over to the Spanish camp. Leaving the military control of the capital to Marshal Carafa, Count Traun entrenched himself with some 4,600 infantry and cavalry in the narrow gorges of Mignano to check the Bourbon advance. But he was by-passed by 5,000 Spanish grenadiers, who crossed the neighbouring wooded heights unobserved. Traun could only retreat hurriedly towards Capua, leaving most of his baggage behind him.

The Viceroy Visconti sent his family and treasures to Rome, where they were joined by other important refugees of the Austrian faction. He garrisoned the Nuovo, Ovo and Sant' Elmo castles, and put a committee of citizens in charge of public safety. Then, after a last futile appeal for more money—'since the foe were drawing near he had to leave and therefore required a donation', as he expressed it—he escaped to Puglia, accompanied by Marshal Carafa and General Pignatelli di Belmonte with 2,000 Austrian infantry and 400 cavalry. According to Monsignor Celestino Galiani, the viceroy's confessor, the Marshal's panic lowered everybody's morale: he wept in front of his officers and rushed orders and counter-orders in hysterical confusion. Apart from the folly of dividing his troops into small units and bottling up a thousand in the fortresses of Naples and Baia, he would have been more sensible to march to Pescara, where he could have maintained communications with his garrisons in Capua and Gaeta. But in his many blunders Monsignor

Galiani detected 'the hand of God, which is wont to transfer kingdoms from one people to another precisely when injustice and oppression have reached their limit'.

The Infante Charles advanced by short, easy stages, scattering *largesse*, giving time for the legend of his munificence to precede him. On April 9 he entered Maddaloni, which belonged to the pro-Spanish branch of the powerful Carafa family. The Duke received him under an awning at the city gate, where he was greeted with continuous cheers and the discharge of petards and muskets. The same evening eighteen Neapolitan deputies knelt before him and kissed hands; then they sat in a circle and were allowed to remain covered as grandees of Spain while one of them, the Prince of Centola, delivered a harangue, after which their master of ceremonies presented him with the gilded keys of the city and the book of privileges bound in vellum and gold. Since time immemorial these deputies (*eletti*) represented the wards (*seggi* or *sedili*) of the municipality. Five of these wards were governed by committees of nobles; the sixth belonged exclusively to the people, in this case the rich merchants and professional classes, governed by a mayor called the *Eletto del Popolo*. They met in handsome open porticoes to discuss business and local taxation, and the privileges conferred on them by former kings were 'intended as a decoy to draw the fierce vassal out of his den, and soften his independent spirit in the gentle atmosphere of courts and cities'. As most of them consisted of the feudal nobility, they were rigidly conservative. The tribunal of San Lorenzo administered the provisioning of the city, and its greatest pride was a diploma conferring on it the dignities of a Spanish grandee in perpetuity. After listening to the speeches of these deputies the Prince replied briefly in Spanish, acknowledging their submission and confirming their privileges.

While Montemar was to pursue the retreating Austrians, the Count de Charny, an illegitimate grandson of Gaston d'Orléans in the Spanish service, was to attack the garrisons. The formidable looking castle of Sant' Elmo surrendered after five days, and the others capitulated in rapid succession. The Neapolitans said that the belligerents had reached a preliminary agreement, and would not waste powder and shot except to *épater les bourgeois*. After the surrender of Sant' Elmo, Count de Charny invited his defeated opponent the Count of Lossada and his chief officers to dinner, and these returned the compliment by holding a reception in his honour the same evening. Similar courtesies were repeated after the surrender of the Castel dell' Ovo, which had been bombarded 'with the utmost humanity'.

During the siege of Castel Nuovo the Florentine agent Intieri wrote that the Neapolitans were so inquisitive that many ventured through the firing line. 'The besieged, no less considerate of the city than the besiegers, make signs with a handkerchief when they decide to fire and give warning in a loud voice so that the populace can withdraw, and when these are out of danger they proceed. Before destroying a small house, they allowed time for the furniture to be removed. As soon as a cannon is fired the lowest people run up to search for the ball, and the garrison waits before firing again. Last evening the crowd obstructed the outer gate of the castle. Towards dusk the garrison shouted to them to go away, and since nobody paid any attention it was necessary to let off an arquebus and one was killed. Curiosity is not restricted to the lower orders: the more educated and members of the nobility draw up in their carriages, although they keep at a safer distance.'

Under such circumstances any siege could be prolonged. That of Castel Nuovo cost each side three casualties, and its surrender was chiefly due to the mutiny of 400 members of the garrison bored with their confinement; half of them were quite ready to go over to the Spaniards. The Bourbon lilies were hoisted the same evening, and the castle was illuminated with torches and lamps forming the inscription: 'Long live the reigning Philip V and Elisabeth.' The strolling players, dancers and jugglers returned to throng the piazza as before.

By May 10 everything was in order for the state entry of Prince Charles. The nobility went to meet him at the Porta Capuana, through which the kings and conquerors of Naples had always passed. Very slowly the procession advanced through Via Tribunali, which differs now but slightly from what it was then: first richly caparisoned horses led by grooms, then the Prince's equerries handsomely mounted, the Prince riding between Santo Stefano and Prince Corsini, followed by horsemen scattering money among the crowd. Don Lelio Carafa wound up the procession with the royal bodyguard. Even that sacred oracle, the blood of San Gennaro, had given clear indication of favouring Don Carlos by liquefying out of season. At last the Prince dismounted before the cathedral. After being blessed by the aged Archbishop, Cardinal Pignatelli, he presented a rare collar of diamonds and rubies to the city's patron saint, and amid bugles and thundering cannon proceeded to the royal palace, where he dined in public.

'Dear Naples will be more beautiful than ever!' the people exclaimed, and for three nights in succession the city was illuminated, with an effect all the more brilliant for being unusual. We have been spoiled in some respects by electricity. As the Florentine Intieri wrote, an account of the rejoicings would be incomplete without the vivid gestures accompanying the words of these people to express their spontaneous affection for the new sovereign: 'Imagine the words of these kindly spokesmen, ragged, dirty and far from neat or fashionable. Either they wear no stockings or these are torn and loose, and their shoes are in the same condition. The women, attracted to the scene by the general jubilation, are of the same character as their husbands, and perhaps more singular. A vast horde of this species went to congratulate the royal Infante on the day he drove to visit Our Lady of the Carmine with the Count of Santo Stefano and Prince Corsini. They cried out that His Royal Highness was lovely, and that his face was like that of San Gennaro as it appears in his statue, made of an unknown metal; that he had been depicted as ugly but now they found him as beautiful as the sun. They exhorted him to bring his lady viceroy to live happily in Naples and beget at least twelve boys... And for a long time they continued with their compliments which, if none too delicate, betoken a great affection.'

Remembering the warm welcome extended to the Austrians in 1707, the reactionaries were bitter. Most of the die-hards had fled; others, still hoping for an Austrian victory, stayed on to conspire against the Bourbon dynasty. They were disarmed by the geniality of the Spaniards, who were altogether friendlier than their arrogant forebears. What if Prince Charles was young and inexperienced? The portents were all in his favour. On April 20 the Venetian resident Vignola wrote that everybody in Naples was certain that, when the Two Sicilies were conquered, the Prince would assume 'the title of King of Italy, the very idea of which delights the nobility here to the highest degree'. At the same time the Florentine agent reflected the trend of topical speculation. 'What renders this people happy,' he wrote on April 16, 'springs from the belief that His Royal Highness will be their king. Certainly his chief ministers have encouraged this hope, which has been increased by the words of his oath, swearing to respect their privileges *himself* and by the order given to the chief chaplain Galiani to pronounce, in prayers for the King, "*pro serenissimo principe nostro Carolo*", without any mention of King Philip. There is also another project being discussed to bring Italy on a par with Germany, with the Pope corresponding to the Emperor and Bologna to Ratisbon. The members of the Italic body would be the Pope, the King of Naples and Sicily, Tuscany (to which the architect has united Parma and Piacenza with Massa di Carrara and what are now called the Presidi), Venice (to which Mantua should be allotted), the Duke of Savoy (fortified by the State of Milan), the Duke of Modena, and the Republics of Lucca and Genoa. This project, which at present may sound fabulous and platonic, was mentioned by a prominent personage... and it is certain that the Spanish ministers serving His Royal Highness publicly declare that they recognize the truth of Boccalini's maxim, that the kingdoms of Italy, united to Spain, enfeebled the latter.'

The dream of an Italian confederation, as Nicola Nicolini remarked, based on a supposition that it would be as easy to expel the Austrians from Lombardy as from the South of Italy, did not survive a brief midsummer's night. But the prominent personage referred to was probably Santo Stefano, and his project reflects the change in the Spanish outlook. This was due to the influence of their Italian Queen, who owed her political education to Alberoni. The Cardinal had hoped to unite all the Italian states into a league, expel the Austrians and re-Italianize the peninsula; but he was far in advance of his age.

The happiest of Neapolitan rumours was soon confirmed. On May 15 it was published that Philip V of Spain had ceded all his rights to the kingdoms of Naples and Sicily to his son Charles. Once more Naples had become the capital of an independent state. But the whole kingdom was not conquered yet. On May 25 the Austrians were crushingly defeated at Bitonto, but the strategic forts of Pescara, Gaeta and Capua continued to resist. The former was the first to capitulate after a siege of thirty-eight days. 'The Old Pretender', James III Stuart, sent his fourteen-year-old son Charles Edward as a volunteer to the siege of Gaeta, to which he sailed with Don Carlos at the end of July. After five days the walls were breached, and the Austrian garrison, diminished by death and disease, was forced to surrender. The Spanish and Scottish Princes entered it together on horseback, and then returned to celebrate in

Naples. Charles Edward was treated as if he were the true heir to the crown of Great Britain; apart from which the young men were most congenial. It was pleasant for Charles to have so high-spirited a companion after an overdose of Spanish gravity, and both had shared the excitement, if not the perils, of the adventure. On board the galley from Gaeta the Young Pretender's hat fell into the sea, and when the sailors were about to rescue it, Don Carlos cried out: 'Never mind, it floats towards England, and the owner will soon go fetch it; and that I may have something to fetch, too, mine shall accompany it.' Whereupon he threw his own hat into the sea, while the whole retinue of both Princes did likewise with a lusty cheer, shouting: 'To England! To England!'

When this was repeated in London, King George II felt outraged. Though the Spanish ambassador was profusely apologetic—'he absolutely denied that Spain had countenanced this measure, and said to the Duke of Newcastle that orders were sent, as soon as the thing was known, to have the boy recalled'—this excuse, as Lord Hervey wrote, 'was a very insufficient recompense, the affront having been public and the reparation private'. Fortunately Sir Robert Walpole was in power. 'He said Their Majesties' situation was such, that, if they had a mind to quarrel with Spain, this incident no doubt gave them a handle to do it; but if they had no mind to it, he thought the excuse that had been made for the impertinence of Spain was sufficient to justify their honour in overlooking it. The latter was the part they took.' George II swallowed his resentment and nursed his revenge. His sympathies were entirely Austrian, and all Walpole's tact was required to keep England out of war.

Capua, defended by Traun, was the last of the forts to yield. With copious munitions and 6,100 men, Traun managed to hold out until November 24. This is hardly surprising when we consider the exaggerated military courtesy of the Spaniards, of which the Austrians took ample advantage. On September 14, for instance, Traun sent word to the Spanish commander that he even lacked oil for the Blessed Sacrament, and he soon received two pack-saddles of oil, fifty pounds of wax candles, another fifty pounds of chocolate, fifty more of coffee, a hundred lemons, besides other useful provisions.

The conquest of Sicily proceeded as smoothly as that of the mainland. Montemar sailed for Palermo, and Marsillac for Messina. The Sicilians rallied gladly to their support; only the citadels of Messina, Trapani and Syracuse offered serious resistance. Prince Lobkowitz held Messina for nearly six months, until his water and victuals ran out, and he was allowed to retire to Trieste with all his garrison. Syracuse and Trapani fell soon after. During the siege of the former the commander of the citadel, Marchese Orsini, wanted a day's truce to restore his defences and refresh his men. With characteristic urbanity he sent his opponents a message, expressing great admiration for their skill in conducting the siege and begging permission to inspect their trenches and batteries. If this were granted, he promised to suspend hostilities while he was outside the fort. The Spaniards were duly flattered and agreed to a truce. Orsini examined and praised the excellence of their earthworks, and was hospitably entertained by the Spanish general till nightfall. The siege continued, until a bomb happened to fall into the room where Orsini was dining. He promptly vowed to the patron saint of the city that he would surrender the citadel if he survived. The bomb failed to explode and Orsini kept his vow.

While his army was subduing hostile elements in Sicily and the Tuscan Presidi, Charles made a leisurely tour of his provinces, where he could indulge his weakness for hunting to his heart's content. He would enter each town on horseback and dine in public, charming all who saw him with his flow of youthful spirits and natural courtesy. At Nola he sat with evident enjoyment through a long rambling comedy by Baron de Liveri, a local grandee who devoted himself to theatricals. At Montescaglioso the monks presented him with relics of Saint Philip the Apostle, Saint Elisabeth, Saint Januarius and Saint Charles, after which he set off with his falcon and gun and shot a few birds before supper. There are many anecdotes about his generosity to the natives during his country expeditions. On one occasion he took shelter from a downpour of rain in a poor hut, where he found a young woman who had recently given birth to a boy. Telling her that he wished the babe to be christened Charles and become his godson, he gave her a hundred gold doubloons. The boy was to receive twenty-five ducats a month until the age of seven, when he was to go to the royal palace for employment.

Before the conquest of Sicily was completed Charles sailed to Messina, and Prince Ruffo provided him with a flotilla of gaily decorated boats which accompanied him all the way. Five of these were manned, or womanned, with brightly costumed girls selected for their beauty, some rowing, others steering, singing and playing joyful melodies. But the sirens sang in vain as far as Charles was concerned, for besides having little ear for music he was incorrigibly chaste. He would have stayed longer in Messina had he not been recalled to Naples by his parents, who were afraid that the climate of Sicily might be bad for him at this season. Two months later, though the citadel of Trapani had not yet surrendered, Charles sailed to Palermo, where he was crowned in the cathedral on July 3. His arms and shoulders were anointed with consecrated oil by Archbishop Basile, the Primate of Sicily, and he was the nineteenth king to be crowned in the first See of the Two Sicilies: *prima sedes coronæ regis, et regni caput*, since the foundation of the monarchy by Roger the Norman. Gold and silver coins with the inscription *Fausto coronationis anno* were showered among the people when he left the cathedral. The festivities lasted four days; on July 8 the King sailed back in an imposing convoy of galleys.

On his arrival the bay was thronged with the gorgeous barges of the nobility who had come to greet him. The whole sea was in gilded and beflagged gala, resounding with songs, cheers, trumpets and guns. The sunburnt young King stood in gleaming satin on the poop, very proud to be the centre of so much commotion. Even the effigy of San Gennaro had been brought out to welcome him when he landed from the royal launch with Santo Stefano, the new Cardinal Archbishop Spinelli, Prince Corsini and Don Lelio Carafa. A covered bridge had been built from the wharf to the palace. Hung with tapestry, chandeliers and cornucopia of wax tapers, it culminated in a spacious balcony with allegorical statues and poetical inscriptions, where two orchestras vied with each other. From his new throne the King graciously received the congratulations of his subjects.

II

Matrimonial projects—Charles's betrothal to Maria Amalia of Saxony—The kingdom of Naples becomes independent—The King under tutelage—Santo Stefano, Montealegre and Tanucci—The first Committee of Distrust—Embellishment of the capital—The San Carlo—Opera, singers and drama—The arrival of the royal bride—Public rejoicings—The Cuccagna—Foundation of the Order of San Gennaro.

The War of the Polish Succession petered out in October 1735, when France signed peace preliminaries with Austria behind Spain's back. Tuscany was assigned to Duke Francis of Lorraine as an indemnity for his own duchies of Lorraine and Bar, which in turn were to indemnify Stanislaus Leczinski for renouncing his claim to Poland. Parma and Piacenza were allotted to the Emperor of Austria, while the young King of the Two Sicilies was merely confirmed in his possessions. Elisabeth Farnese was most reluctant to surrender her patrimony, but for the nonce she could find no alternative. After much hesitation, Spain acceded to the preliminaries of Vienna in February 1736, and the Two Sicilies did likewise.

During the negotiations Elisabeth tried in vain to arrange a marriage between Charles and a sister of Maria Theresa of Austria. The French wished him to marry one of their princesses, but the oldest available was barely ten and Elisabeth had cause to be prejudiced against such a match. A scalded cat, she retorted quaintly, fears cold water. In other words, once bitten, twice shy. The Infanta Anna Maria Victoria, who had gone to France at the age of three as Louis XV's future bride, was sent back to Spain before she was seven because the French were in a hurry for Louis to beget an heir since he had turned fifteen. Luis I of Spain's girl-widow, the French Regent's fourth daughter, born Mademoiselle de Montpensier, and her sister, Mademoiselle de Beaujolais, who had been betrothed to the Infante Charles, were packed home to France as a reprisal. Spanish pride had been wounded by this broken engagement, but Elisabeth was not sorry to be rid of the French princesses, the former of whom had never ceased to shock the Court by her outlandish behaviour. Her own grandmother described Mademoiselle de Montpensier as the most disagreeable person she had ever seen. Apart from her sulks and her gluttony, she had taken to running out of doors in an open dressing-gown and thought nothing of pulling her skirts up to her thighs in public.

When his parents consulted Charles about various marriage proposals, he said he relied entirely on their choice, but he hoped they would soon decide—'since time was passing'. The final choice was not calculated to please the French. Maria Amalia was the daughter of the Saxon King Augustus III of Poland, the successful rival of Stanislaus Leczinski. The engagement was signed when Charles was twenty-one, but as Maria Amalia was under thirteen a dispensation of age would have to be procured from Rome. This would cause some delay.

In 1737 both Philip V and Charles ceded Parma and Piacenza to the Emperor of Austria, and Tuscany to Francis of Lorraine. However, Charles was authorized to remove all the personal property and securities of the Farnese family from Parma and Piacenza. The collection of works of art, the ducal library and archives, the cannons of the forts, even the marble staircase of the palace, were removed to Naples. Though the Parmesans lamented this spoliation of their city, it turned out well for Italy in the long run. The treasures would have been sent to Austria otherwise. The Emperor renounced all claim to the Two Sicilies and the Tuscan Presidi, but these were never to be united with the Spanish crown. Should Charles succeed to Spain, he was to relinquish the Two Sicilies to his next-of-kin.

The benefits of independence were soon visible in Naples, in spite of the family link with Spain. A royal Court with its prestige and stimulating influence; a council of ministers instead of viceregal secretaries; foreign ambassadors instead of dim commercial agents; a tremendous increase in building activity; a separate financial administration; an army for self-defence instead of fighting in the service of Austria—these changes convinced the Neapolitans that their state was autonomous indeed. But Charles was the son of his parents, whom he had been brought up devoutly to obey. He could hardly be expected to break loose from them suddenly. After all, it was to them, especially to his mother, that he owed his kingdom.

The first years of his reign were a period of tutelage. Santo Stefano was omnipotent at Court as chief councillor of state and chief major-domo, who interpreted the Queen Mother's wishes. But while he organized the royal household in accordance with Spanish etiquette, he had the good sense to conciliate the Neapolitan nobility by distributing coveted posts among them. He appointed 115 gentlemen-in-waiting to the King, fifty of whom were admitted into every part of the palace, and had gold keys as symbols; the rest could not penetrate beyond the fourth antechamber. Santo Stefano was jealous of rivals winning the King's confidence, and Charles could only see those whom he had introduced. At night his own son slept in the King's bedroom.

Next in importance came the Marquis Montealegre, Secretary of State, a handsome intriguer who had been a favourite of the Spanish minister Patiño. Count de Charny was chief adviser on military affairs; the others were typical courtiers of average ability, with the exception of Bernardo Tanucci, who soon came to the fore as Minister of Justice. The King's attendance at Council was purely formal. Santo Stefano heard the reports of each minister or secretary and decided what measures to take, and he filled his post with dignity. He remained the royal tutor.

Less noticeable at first was the blunt and rugged Tanucci, but he was to outlast all his colleagues and play a considerable role in the government for the next forty years. Born in 1698 at Stia in the upper valley of the Arno, known as the Casentino, he had won his early laurels as professor of law at Pisa University. In 1730 the Spanish government had applied to the Grand Duke of Tuscany for a skilled jurist to confute Austrian claims of investiture to Siena, and Tanucci had been recommended. Santo Stefano was impressed by his erudition combined with a forthright manner, and these men, so different, were to become firm friends. Some twenty years later Tanucci wrote: 'The heroic period of this Court ended with the departure of Santo Stefano.'

Tanucci went to Parma as a legal adviser to Don Carlos, and accompanied his army south during the conquest of Naples. When Santo Stefano formed his cabinet at Aversa on April 29, before Charles's entry into Naples, he appointed Tanucci Minister of Justice. The magistrature then formed a state within a state, composed of lawyers and their hangers-on, who wallowed in an atmosphere of privileged corruption. Petitions against the whole tribe were showered upon the King; they had been so perverted by antiquated abuses that the public had lost faith in them. Tanucci's first task was to cleanse these Augean Stables, and he set to work with great energy and persistence. Intieri often praised his reforms in despatches to Florence, and related the following anecdote as a sample of his vigour. A certain protégé of the Duke of Berwick and Liria, the first Spanish ambassador to Naples, had been banished for various thefts, as well as for robbing and murdering the mother of his mistress. After escaping to Venice, where he also robbed the famous composer Porpora, who had innocently befriended him as a compatriot, he made his way back to Naples under a false name, as a petty officer in the Bourbon regiment. Here he swaggered about the streets, deaf to his former mistress's appeals for compensation. At last she appealed to the King. The case was tried by Tanucci, who had the culprit arrested and banished perpetually from the kingdom; his money and goods were consigned to the injured woman.

'The whole city,' wrote Intieri, 'is astounded at this verdict, so unusual, unheard of, and incomprehensible, that Signor Tanucci has had the greatest difficulty in inducing his subordinates to carry out their duties. They let the criminal roam at large without forcing him to obey, so hard is it to uproot long-established prejudices.' Intieri extolled Tanucci as 'the man who in a few hours has restored law and order to this city and to most of the kingdom, so that one does not hear of a brawl, let alone a murder'. In spite of rhetorical exaggeration, this throws some light on the condition of the law courts when Charles arrived in Naples. In the teeth of powerful opposition Tanucci restricted the arbitration of the feudal barons, whose tribunals hampered justice and oppressed their wretched vassals. This started an underground warfare between the barons and the ministry which was to become endemic.

Under the Austrian regime a great magnate like Prince Michele Imperiali di Francavilla had been able to take the law into his own hands. When he disagreed with the verdict of an honest judge called Cito, he had him exiled to Ischia. After the Bourbon conquest, some of Francavilla's retainers happened to kill those of a neighbour. Tanucci ordered him to arrest the culprits. Instead of doing so he rode to Naples, 'expecting to receive the same facilities he had enjoyed from the Court of Vienna'. But the King refused to see him. When he went to Tanucci, he was told to arrest his men or remove himself from Naples. Francavilla was already exasperated, and this interview with the Minister of Justice, an outsider and a commoner, cut him to the quick. While on his way to make another appeal for a royal audience he died of apoplexy on the steps of the palace. His grandson, who succeeded him, was weaned from his feuds by appointments to the highest dignities at Court, a policy which curbed potentially obstreperous barons.

Tanucci antagonized the clergy even more than the nobility, as the leading champion in the struggle between the monarchy and ecclesiastical power. Religion had nothing to do with this: Charles was intensely devout, and Tanucci was sufficiently so to detest Voltaire and ban his works. Religion had only an indirect bearing on the pretensions of the Neapolitan clergy. Their excessive number, their ever-increasing property, their immunity from taxation and their separate jurisdiction were some of the obvious causes of economic hardship in the South of Italy.

The political relations of Charles and the Holy See had been strained from the beginning. Pope Clement XII wavered between Austria and Spain, and he had appointed a Committee of Cardinals who decided to back the former. Charles had been eager for a papal legate to attend his coronation, but this wish had not been granted. Since the reign of the Angevins it had been customary for the King of Naples to send a *chinea* or white palfrey with 7,000 gold ducats to the Pope on Saint Peter's Day. This had become a question of obtaining papal recognition rather than of paying tribute to a feudal lord. In 1735 both Charles and the Austrian ambassador presented the *chinea*, and Charles's was rejected, although his conquest of the Two Sicilies was a *fait accompli*.

Austrian propaganda was still strong in Naples, especially among the feudal barons who had never enjoyed such independence as under the Austrian regime. One of Santo Stefano's first actions was to get rid of malcontents and confiscate their property. A special commission called *Giunta d'Inconfidenza*, or Committee of Distrust, was appointed to investigate the activities of traitors. Its extreme severity has been much criticized, but under the circumstances most governments would have done likewise.

The numerous reforms in the administration so suddenly following the King's arrival were bound to cause unemployment and discontent. The British Consul, Edward Allen, reported to the Duke of Newcastle in July 1734: 'The Chamber of Finances, which consisted of one Head President and twelve Assistants, is now reduced as to power in the person of the Intendant-General. And the whole civil government and disposition of all payments from the Treasury, which was before divided and subdivided into an infinite number of Ministers and Officers, is already in the hands of three persons only: viz. the Count of St Stefano, Prime Minister, the Marquis of Montealegre, Secretary of State, and Don José Campillo, Intendant-General; and it is apprehended that in a short time the major part of the offices will be reformed or abolished. This great change, which affects so many thousand dependants on the Robe, occasions loud complaints and heavy disgust among all that set of people, which has been very prevalent, and have still a great influence... In other respects it is certainly for the advantage of this city and kingdom to have the Sovereign reside among them, who brings money into the country from Spain and carries none out, as the Germans did in the most excessive degree, and had drained them of all their gold, and almost their whole silver coin, by the large donations to the Emperor, infinite pensions to the Spanish Ministry at Vienna, and by the venality of all offices both civil and military, which circumstances under the bad management of the Catalans have been the chief cause of the Emperor losing Naples. Now it is certain that a greater circulation and plenty of money is already visible, but this is not sufficient in the opinion of the Neapolitans for the restraint of their liberty, which they enjoyed in the greatest latitude before; whereas a new Court of Enquiry has been now erected, called *La Giunta d'Inconfidenza*, which is a sort of State Inquisition, and gives great umbrage to all sorts of people. ... The Count of St Stefano never leaves the Prince one moment, and seems as if his whole thought and attention was engaged and occupied about his person. None ever speak to him unless the said Prime Minister be present, and the Prince hardly ever answers anything, and never but in general terms. The Secretary executes and despatches all affairs, is very difficult of access in general, and I am sorry to say that in all his actions, notwithstanding his fair words, does not discover any sort of partiality for our Nation, rather a prejudice against us.'

Charles soon displayed more than one of Louis XIV's characteristics. Besides his passion for hunting, he had an acute sense of royal decorum. Wishing everything about his Court to be worthy of a Bourbon, he immediately began to beautify his capital. The royal palace had been designed by Domenico Fontana in 1600 with a handsome three-storied façade and a magnificent staircase, but it had been left in a wretched condition by the last viceroy. Charles had it enlarged and redecorated by such painters as Solimena, De Mura, Bonito and Fischetti, and the spacious apartments were further enriched by the Farnese collection from Parma.

Throughout the eighteenth century Italy was pre-eminently the land of music, and Naples was the most brilliant centre of musical culture. Rousseau, in his famous article on *Genius*, advised the aspiring musician to repair to Naples to perfect himself. 'Music is the triumph of the Neapolitans,' wrote Lalande. 'It seems that in this country the fibres of the ear are more sensitive, more harmonic, more sonorous than in the rest of Europe; the whole nation sings; gestures, the inflection of the voice, the cadence of the syllables, conversation—everything there expresses and exhales music. Naples is the principal source of music.' Its *Conservatori* were the great market for singers, instrumentalists, virtuosi, and composers, and the demand for these was insatiable. Though the King cared little for opera personally, it was the favoured entertainment of all the Courts of Europe, and as it was much concerned with the glorification of monarchy he felt obliged to provide his capital with a worthy opera house. Carasale, an enterprising organizer of festivities on a grandiose scale, was to assist the architect Medrano as contractor and impresario, and the theatre was built with prodigious speed. Begun in March 1737, it was finished in the following October and opened to the public on November 4, the King's saint's day, after which it was called the San Carlo.

The whole Court flocked to the first performance, which began at eight o'clock before a packed house. There were six rows of boxes, and the first four were qualified as noble: the competition for the nearest position to the royal box in the centre had been intense, and all rallied round the King in gorgeous gala. Every owner of a box received its key and could furnish it to his taste, so that each resembled a miniature drawing-room. The theatre was lighted with oil lamps and candles, and the number of candles in each box varied with the rank of its holder—hence the Neapolitan expression: 'He's only a one-candle gent!' Among the regulations, no member of the audience might trespass on the stage, clap hands or light candles for applause, or call for an *encore*—the King reserved that right for himself—and servants in livery were excluded from the pit. Refreshments were sold in the corridors. Two bodyguards stood sentry at the main entrance of the pit, and two others on the stage throughout the performance.

The first three *libretti* to be chosen were by Metastasio, who was then in his zenith. Though he was actually the Imperial Court Poet of Austria he had started his career in Naples and, as the manager of the San Carlo declared, 'he might be said to dwell amongst us now', so great was his popularity. Such supreme art was above political considerations. Elisabeth Farnese pronounced him the greatest poet of the age, and the majority agreed with her. Voltaire said his dramas were 'worthy of Corneille, when Corneille is not declamatory, and of Racine, when Racine is not insipid'. Doctor Burney, who published his life and letters in three volumes, considered that his writings had probably contributed more to the perfection of vocal melody and music in general than the united efforts of all the great European composers. Yet after a conversation with him he noted: 'Metastasio laughs at all poetic inspiration and makes a poem as another would make a watch, at what time he pleases and without any other occasion than the want of it.' This may help to explain why nobody reads his poetry today. His *libretti* were set to music by the finest composers of the age, from Handel to Mozart, many of them several times. *Achilles on Scyros*, which provided splendid opportunities for impetuous action and scenic display, was selected for the opening night; its elaborate plot has been analysed by Vernon Lee in *Studies of the Eighteenth Century in Italy*. On this occasion Domenico Sarro was responsible for the music, but there were the usual rifts in the lute. The first *prima donna*, Anna Peruzzi, nicknamed 'The little hairdresser', refused to sing with a second *prima donna*; she was only persuaded to relent because her rival, Vittoria Tesi, was to personate Achilles. The contrast between these ladies must have been amusing, for the Tesi was as massive as 'the little hairdresser' was minute.

Magnificence, Glory and Speed addressed Royal Genius in the Prologue:

'Behold the new, sublime and spacious theatre,
Vaster than which Europa hath not seen!'

and the chorus shouted: 'Long live Charles!' A baroque temple with two lofty flights of steps, surrounded by porticoes forming an open piazza, filled the stage. A sacred wood was visible between the colonnade on one side, the coast of Scyros on the other. Bacchantes began the chorus; and the faded charm of the ensuing dialogue with its neat rhymes can only be appreciated by nostalgic lovers of the rococo. When the ships of Ulysses appeared, Deidamia exclaimed: *'O Dei! Vien meco!'* ('Ye Gods! Come with me!'). And Achilles, in female garb, replied: *'Di che temi, mia vita? Achille è teco!'* ('What fearest thou, my life? Achilles is with thee!'). Great attention was paid to the battle-scenes, directed by fencing-masters, and the scenery was as complicated and surprising as Vincenzo Re could make it. The King, who preferred dancing to singing, gave orders that there were to be at least two ballets to every act of an opera, so that during the intervals there were ballets of sailors and gypsies, of the four seasons, and of acrobatic butlers. *Achilles* was given fourteen nights running, and was followed by *Olimpiade* and *Artaxerxes*, both replete with 'pathetically developed situations'.

The speed with which the San Carlo was built gave rise to a legend. While congratulating Carasale on the opening night, the King is said to have remarked that it might be convenient to build a private passage from the theatre to the palace. After the opera, Carasale invited the King to return by the corridor he had mentioned, which had been completed in three hours, with tapestry to cover the wet plaster.

Since the original structure was destroyed by fire in 1816, we must rely on the descriptions of contemporaries.

'The King's Theatre, upon the first view, is, perhaps, almost as remarkable an object as any man sees in his travels,' wrote Samuel Sharp in 1765. 'The amazing extent of the stage, with the prodigious circumference of the boxes and the height of the ceiling, produce a marvellous effect on the mind... Notwithstanding the amazing noisiness of the audience during the whole performance of the opera, the moment the dances begin there is a universal dead silence, which continues so long as the dances continue. Witty people, therefore, never fail to tell me, the Neapolitans go to see not to hear an opera... It must be confessed that their scenery is extremely fine; their dresses are new and rich; and the music is well adapted; but, above all, the stage is so large and noble, as to set off the performance to an inexpressible advantage... It is customary for gentlemen to run about from box to box between the acts, and even in the midst of the performance; but the ladies, after they are seated, never quit their box the whole evening. It is the fashion to make appointments for such and such nights. A lady receives visitors in her box one night, and they remain with her the whole opera; another night she returns the visit in the same manner. In the intervals between the acts, principally between the first and second, the proprietor of the box regales her company with iced fruits and sweetmeats... The seats have elbows, which circumstance, I believe, is peculiar to this theatre. The pit here is very ample: it contains between five and six hundred seats, with arms resembling a large elbow chair, besides an interval all through the middle and a circuit all round it, under the boxes, both of which, I judge, in a crowded house, will hold between one and two hundred people standing. The seat of each chair lifts up like the lid of a box, and has a lock to fasten it. There are in Naples gentlemen enough to hire by the year the first four rows next to the orchestra, who take the key of the chair home with them when the opera is finished, lifting up the seat and leaving it locked. By this contrivance they are always sure of the same place at whatever hour they please to go to the opera; nor do they disturb the audience, though it be in the middle of a scene, as the intervals between the rows are wide enough to admit a lusty man to walk to his chair, without obliging anybody to rise. The usual payment for the season, or the whole year, in which they give four operas, is twenty ducats, about three pounds fifteen shillings; the people who do not hire their seats by the year pay three carlines, about thirteen pence halfpenny, for their place in the pit... The three lower ranges of boxes are hired either by the season, or the whole year, by the ladies of distinction; the price of a box for the whole year is two hundred and forty ducats, equal to about forty-six or forty-seven pounds sterling. The other three ranges are let by the night... Each of the six ranges, consisting of thirty boxes, would make one hundred and eighty in all if the King's box, in the front, did not occupy the place of four of them... The boxes are large enough to hold twelve people standing, but their largeness is owing to their depth, for they are so narrow that only three ladies can sit in front, and the three next behind them must stand up, if they would see all the stage and the actors... It is the custom in Italy to light the stage only... but on gala nights it is illuminated in every part... I must not omit a foolish singularity in relation to the women dancers at Naples, that in consequence of an order from Court, in the late King's (Charles's) time, they all wear black drawers. I presume it was from some conceit on the subject of modesty, but it appears very odd and ridiculous.'

The King talked through half the opera and slept through the other half, when Président de Brosses heard *Parthenope* in 1739, which was also by Domenico Sarro. The music struck de Brosses as dry and dreary, but 'to make amends, the performance was perfect. The famous Senesino took the first role; I was enchanted by the taste of his singing and dramatic action. However, I perceived with astonishment that the people of the country were not at all satisfied with it. They complained that he sang in an antiquated style. For the musical fashion here changes at least every decade. All the applause was reserved for the Baratti, a new actress both pretty and self-assured, who recited in male disguise... The structure of the *libretto* in Italian operas is very different from ours... They pander much to the taste of the lower orders. An opera would not please at all unless it contained, amongst other things, a mimic battle. Two hundred urchins on either side take part in this, but they are careful to put in the foreground a number of bravos skilled in the use of weapons. This cannot fail to be amusing; at least it is less absurd than our combats between Cadmus and Theseus, who kill each other while dancing. In this opera of *Parthenope* there was an effective cavalry charge which gave me infinite pleasure. Before coming to blows the two regimental commanders on horseback sang a contradictory duo in perfect harmony.'

None of these 'serious operas' with such sonorous titles—*Artaxerxes, Themistocles, Semiramis, Demetrius, Zenobia, Hadrian in Syria, The Triumph of Camillus*, etc.—have been revived in our time; it would be almost impossible to evoke, let alone reconstruct, so obsolete a form of art or synthesis of arts. They depended largely on a type of vocalization long extinct. The *castrato* or male soprano, who 'combined the high range and sweetness of the female with the power of the male voice' was their mainstay, and such *castrati* as Senesino and Caffarello were the rage in every European capital.

Lalande relates that the San Carlo orchestra was larger and more varied than the Parisian, since musicians were neither scarce nor expensive. At first it contained forty-five musicians and was conducted by the first violinist: eventually it was increased to a total of fifty-five. Three or four *castrati* or women sang soprano to one tenor or 'natural male voice'; usually there were no bass voices except in comic roles. This convention led to a certain monotony. 'The ear grows tired of five similar voices all singing in the same style, the *bravura*, which is unnatural to man and only suited to birds. The leading actors and *virtuosi* greet their acquaintances in the middle of the performance without fear of displeasing the public, whose indulgence permits this abuse.' Unless the King were present, the din of the audience was apt to be intolerable. Lalande also complained that the singers were too obsessed with musical flourishes. While their light roulades in falsetto were admirable, they gave no thought to declamation, and their acting was worse than mediocre; but Italians considered French acting as extravagant and artificial as the French considered their *castrati*. As for the ballets, he concluded that the Italians only liked mime dancing with fantastic steps, contortions and *tours de force*. An element of the grotesque was required to titillate a San Carlo audience.

The contractor-impresario Carasale became a sort of royal factotum after the rapid completion of the San Carlo. The son of a humble blacksmith, he was made a lieutenant-colonel and entrusted with most of the King's important building operations. His profits were said to be enormous, as the King was constantly acquiring new estates for his favourite pastime. The courtiers were shocked to see this plebeian chatting familiarly with the King in the royal coach. Success turned his head; he gave extravagant entertainments and lavished large sums on gambling and women. Many became envious of the wealth that flowed through his hands, and clouds began to gather about his reputation. But he made abundant hay while the sun shone, and at the beginning of Charles's reign the sun shone with a splendour reminiscent of Louis XIV.

Among the leading singers at the San Carlo Caffarello was considered indispensable, and he was constantly employed there until he went to Paris in 1753. He was more arrogant and temperamental than most *castrati*, and is said to have scorned a jewelled snuffbox presented to him by Louis XV because it did not contain the King's portrait. When it was explained that the King only gave snuff-boxes with his portraits to ambassadors, he retorted: 'Then let His Majesty make the ambassadors sing!' In 1741 he was arrested because, after frequent warnings, he had joked with the audience from the stage at the expense of his rivals and ogled another singer in a lascivious manner. Often he bewildered fellow performers by suddenly altering the music; sometimes he would strike them. But the caprices of *castrati* were usually tolerated, for they were recognized as a rare species who could provide vocal thrills impossible to recapture. In the intervals between their musical pyrotechnics, the audience chattered as at a social rout.

Above his palace in Naples, Caffarello had inscribed '*Amphion Thebas, ego domum*' ('As Amphion raised the walls of Thebes with the sound of his lyre, I built this house with my voice'), to which a wag added: '*Ille cum, tu sine*' ('He with, you without!'). Metastasio preferred his famous rival Farinelli, to whom he wrote that Caffarello seemed like an old nun in recitatives, and that a perverse tone of lamentation prevailed in all he sang; but Metastasio was prejudiced, as he owed a large share of his success to Farinelli's interpretations. Dr Burney, who heard Caffarello sing when he was over sixty, wrote: 'Though Caffarello and Barbella are rather ancient and in ruin, yet what remains of them is but the more precious.' And the genial Irish singer Michael Kelly, who came to Naples in his youth, related in his lively *Reminiscences*: 'The young and beautiful daughter of the Duke of Monteleone, the richest nobleman in Naples, was destined by her family to take the veil; she consented without a murmur to quit the world, provided the ceremony of her profession was performed with splendour; and a *sine qua non* was that Caffarello, the great soprano singer, should perform at it. It was represented to her that he had retired with a fine fortune to his estate in the interior of Calabria, and had declared his determination never to sing again. "*I* declare *my determination* never to take the veil unless he does. He sang six years ago, when my cousin was professed, and I had rather die than it should be said that she had the first singer in the world to sing for *her*, and that I had not." The fair lady was firm, and her glorious obstinacy was such that her father was obliged to take a journey into Calabria, when, with much entreaty, and many very *weighty* arguments, he prevailed on Caffarello to return with him to Naples. He sang a *Salve Regina* at the ceremony; and the signora, having gained her point, cheerfully submitted to be led, like a lamb, to the sacrifice, to eternal seclusion from the gay and wicked world. In justice to her taste, however, it must be said that Caffarello was one of the greatest soprano singers Italy ever produced.'

The King, who was bored by opera, could sit enthralled through the seven-hour comedies of Baron de Liveri. These had extremely intricate plots and a horde of characters; their appeal was due to the meticulous naturalism of the scenes, diction, miming and gestures. Baron de Liveri thought that dramatic expression counted more than the words. As a contemporary recorded: 'A sigh (and I speak as an eye-witness), a sigh which one character had to exhale, as rehearsed by the late Marquis de Liveri of ever glorious memory, was repeated thirty-two times in an evening without achieving the effect he desired. The actor's brow ran with cold sweat to satisfy the distinguished producer, who wanted a hundred things to be expressed in that single sigh.' The King summoned him from his native Nola and created him a Marquis. He succeeded Carasale as manager of the San Carlo, in spite of scruples as to whether he, a noble, should sign contracts with singers and dancers. Every year he produced a new comedy in the Court theatre until his death in 1757. 'Who shall ever see again,' wrote a nostalgic admirer, 'so great a gathering of knights as in the *Contessa*, or a meeting of two mighty lords with such large retinues as in the *Solitario*, or a scene like that of the pavilion in *Enrico*, when a royal Court waits in expectation of a historic event? The characters were all appropriate and picturesque but supremely natural.' These comedies have gone the way of the great *castrati*.

Before the King's marriage the Countess of Santo Stefano was the mistress of ceremonies at Court, and she organized a series of masked balls for the carnival. To the first each couple came as peasants of different countries; to the second in various Oriental costumes, and as night and day, dusk and dawn, and the four seasons; to the third as the months of the year; to the fourth as a medley of ballet dancers, huntsmen, pilgrims, shepherds, fishermen, innkeepers and characters from the *Commedia dell' Arte*; on subsequent evenings as mythological couples, Venus and Adonis, Pluto and Proserpine, Bacchus and Ariadne, etc., with scores of nymphs, naiads, satyrs and bacchantes. The fifty-four musicians wore pink and blue uniforms. No more than sixty guests were bidden, so that the heat was never oppressive. At the first ball two of the gentlemen created a diversion by appearing in feminine disguise: the Prince of Roccella seemed 'almost too graceful as a country lass', and little Count Gaetani captivated everybody with his flirtatious airs. The King arrived after dinner with his face masked, in a Roman court costume of crimson hue, trimmed with white lace, a wondrous diamond in his hat and another in the mask's mouth. When all the guests had kissed his hand he opened the ball, dancing a minuet with the Marchioness of Solera. After dancing, he bowed to his partner and the assembly while the whole orchestra played.

At the second ball the King appeared as an African potentate seemingly naked, but actually covered with a very fine glove-skin which fitted him perfectly, and a mask to match. At the other balls he was garbed as a Hungarian in blue-black velvet and silver Spanish embroidery, as a Janissary, a Greek peasant, an Indian, and as Neptune. At the seventh and last a horse-shoe table with some eighty covers was laid in an anteroom. Among the decorations there was a statue of the King in sugar. 'When all were seated His Majesty entered, and everybody wished to rise, but the Count of Santo Stefano told them at once that the King was not dining, whereupon they sat down again with obedient indifference. His Majesty stood inside the horse-shoe where there were no covers or chairs, with a few attendants and the French ambassador, who remained standing while the King conversed with them. Sometimes the King walked round the table, now pausing to speak to a guest, or accepting some refreshment... By half-past ten all went home satisfied and happy, full of love for the Prince who had entertained them with so much kindness.'

The papal dispensation for Maria Amalia's wedding arrived in December 1737, and the marriage was solemnized by proxy in Dresden next May, with the bride's crippled brother Frederick Christian, Electoral Prince of Saxony, representing Charles. The bull of papal investiture was signed the day after, and the Princess left for Naples. The Duke of Sora, accompanied by the special court which Santo Stefano had selected to wait on her, joined her at Palmanuova on the frontier between Austrian and Venetian territory, where they replaced the Saxons and Poles who had escorted her so far. She was much fêted along the journey; everywhere she was met by important dignitaries and loaded with gifts. A spacious pavilion had been erected for the nuptial rendezvous at Portella on the Neapolitan border. The King rode from Gaeta on the morning of June 19, reaching Portella at half-past nine. Here he had to wait two and a half hours with the French ambassador, the Modenese minister, the commander of the Maltese galleys and a hundred knights of Malta in full-dress uniform.

The royal bridegroom was burning with all the impatience of youth and pent up chastity, and happiness had almost made him handsome. When the girl-Queen arrived she advanced to kneel before him as was customary, but he promptly raised her in his stalwart arms and led her to his coach, and off they drove to Fondi.

Charles was twenty-two, and his bride just under fourteen but overdeveloped for her age; both were supremely conscious of their royalty, of their duties to the Church and to each other. They were expected to fall in love, and they did so beyond expectation. Maria Amalia was tall, fair and blue-eyed, a typical Saxon; she was dignified but vivacious, a euphemism for hot-tempered; she knew French and Italian besides Latin, and shared the King's taste for riding and hunting. Her complexion was soon marred by smallpox, and many considered her ugly, but she never ceased to charm her husband, a natural monogamist impervious to other women.

The poet Thomas Gray considered Charles and Maria Amalia 'as ugly a little pair as one can see,' and this opinion is somewhat corroborated by de Brosses, who was presented to them in 1739: 'That day there was a grand gala at Court to celebrate the King's birthday, when he offers his hand to be kissed by all his gentlemen. These were dressed with great magnificence, but His Majesty wore an old suit of brown drugget with yellow buttons. He has a long narrow face with a very prominent nose, a sad and timid expression, and a mediocre figure which is not free from blemishes. He attends to little, does not speak at all, and only has a taste for hunting... The Queen also gave her hand to be kissed which, to my mind, was far more of an honour than a favour. Both of them dined in public and were served in accordance with Spanish etiquette which prevails at this Court, the King by a gentleman of his chamber, the Queen by Countess de Charny, who is lame, but the deuce, how pretty!... Her jealous old husband is ripe for cuckoldom, the son of the Charny of whom one hears at such length in the memoirs of Mademoiselle de Montpensier. As you know, he was the natural son of Gaston, Duc d'Orléans, and of Mademoiselle Saugeon, Madame's maid of honour. They kneel to offer drink to the King and Queen, and they do not rise until the glass is restored to them. On this account I was a little prejudiced against the Queen who, to the great scandal of the knees of my divine Charny, amused herself for half an hour with making a soup of Canary wine in her glass. This worthy Princess has a malicious air, with her bullet nose, her crayfish features and magpie voice. 'Tis said she was pretty when she arrived from Saxony, but she has recently had smallpox. She is still quite young, and has not yet grown up. (At the time I wrote this she was a month or five weeks with child, which happened to her before any sign was apparent.)'

Charles had had to wait long for his *suspirada esposa*, and when she arrived the whole of Naples exploded into a series of festivities. A traditional element of these was the *Cuccagna*, which varied according to the fantasy of the designer. Usually it was a structure representing a castle, 'built according to the rules of fortification, and faced all over with pieces of beef, bacon, hams, geese, turkeys and other provisions, with which the imaginary country of Cockaigne is said to abound'. Fountains of wine gushed from either side, and it was guarded by soldiers to restrain the ardour of the populace till the King gave the signal for assault.

Lady Anne Miller described one of these entertainments in 1770, when they had become more humane: 'A hill appears exactly opposite the palace, from the centre of which bursts forth a fountain, and falls into a bason at its foot; the base represents incrustations of rocks and shells like grotto-work; such is the appearance from the windows of the palace; but this grotto-work is composed of nothing else than dried fish varnished and gilt, and intermixed with loaves of bread so well placed as to deceive the eye. On the sides of the hill (which is covered with green boughs), appear living lambs ornamented with ribands and artificial flowers; in another part are calves and some oxen: amongst the boughs geese and pigeons are nailed fast by the wings. On the top stands a figure of Apollo playing on the lyre. Formerly all the creatures were placed here alive, and tied fast to the wood-work; but now, by this amiable Queen's particular command, the oxen are killed before the sport begins. The guards are drawn out round this artificial hill to prevent mischief; and at a signal given, the mob fall on, destroy the building, carry off whatever they can lay hold of; and fight with each other, till generally some fatal accident ensues. The court are frequently in the balconies of the palace, with most of the nobility of Naples, to see the *Cuccagna*. When the Queen (in this case Maria Carolina) first saw this barbarous amusement, she was shocked at the cruelty of tearing the wretched animals to pieces, whose cries reached the palace, and commanded, as I have already said, that the cattle should not be exposed alive to the brutality of the populace; but the lambs, geese, pigeons, and some other poor birds, fall a living sacrifice to their amusement: they tear them away unfeelingly from their fastenings, so as often to leave their wings behind. We have been to see this sight... and we saw it in the most complete manner, being permitted to occupy one of the royal balconies. In the midst of the riot and confusion, a *Lazzarone* dropped, and was carried off by his comrades; he had received a stab in the breast by a knife from one of his brethren, who disputed with him somewhat taken off from the *Cuccagna*. As such events are common upon this occasion, no notice was taken of it; but the man died on the spot.

'This *amusement* was so far from proving such to us, that I believe our curiosity will never again induce us to partake of it: for my part, I was so sick in the stomach, that all eatables went exceedingly against me; and it was with difficulty that I could sit down to table at my return. Were it possible to be insensible to the cruelty connected with this *fête*, the ingenuity of the contrivance and workmanship with which the *Cuccagna*, etc., is constructed, would excite admiration. A great deal of taste is displayed in varying the scene every week (during the Carnival). The architects are no other than the *Lazzaroni* themselves: sometimes they represent Mount Parnassus, at other times Orpheus charming the brutes by his harmony, varying these by representations of other fables taken from the heathen mythology. It is surprising how these poor people can have acquired any knowledge of this nature.'

In honour of the Saxon Queen a gigantic wooden structure had been set up on the shore of the Chiaia to represent the city of Dresden, and the surrounding walls, towers, belfries and roofs, all in skilful perspective, had been hung with the usual trophies. Troops had to defend the citadel, denoted by a red flag, against some sixty galleys containing 1,600 men who rowed from a considerable distance to attack it. Mock bombs were hurled from either side, and cannon were fired with apples and lemons as ammunition. The bombs were made to explode under water and spurt it high into the air, to the delight of the crowds by the shore and on the house-tops. After a feigned attack, the men from the galleys began to plunder the fortress, seizing the eatables and filling their boats with them. The whole apparatus was then transformed into a 'tower of fireworks', but, as often happened, parts of it caught fire prematurely and several spectators were injured.

A second *Cuccagna* represented the garden of the Hesperides, since Hesperia had been a name common to both Italy and Spain in antiquity. The fruit, replaced by more substantial victuals, were duly plucked by the daring amid much merriment. Nine chariots, symbolizing different virtues and allegories, were driven down the Toledo towards the palace, and on each sat four Neapolitan damsels distinguished for beauty and breeding, radiantly costumed, besides eight knights and eight musicians playing instruments, escorted by pages and preceded by cavalry. At the palace the knights and ladies dismounted to kiss the hands of the King and Queen, who invited them to partake of some refreshments.

What was called the Queen's Fair was opened on the Largo del Castello. This was a square palisade with two large entrance gates and several obelisks and fountains in the centre designed by Marchese Ferdinando Sanfelice; each side was lined with shops where samples of all the arts and crafts of Naples were exhibited for sale, and they made a fine show at night lit up by hundreds of tapers. The triumphal arches, the fantastic fountains, the fireworks and illuminations on a scale not seen before—all these gave even more pleasure to the masses than to the royal couple. After a few days the King marched his crack regiments into the country for manoeuvres to impress his bride. An attack was staged on the fort of Granatello, which surrendered to the King with the usual formalities.

A new order of knights, that of San Gennaro or Januarius, was founded in honour of the King's marriage. It is remarkable that such an order had not been founded before. Where else is a saint so ubiquitous? His effigy is visible on the oldest coinage; his hand in coral is one of the safest guards against the evil eye; his blood preserved in two crystal vials liquefies annually on September 19, December 16 and for a week in the beginning of May; and he is the city's special protector against eruptions of Vesuvius. No name is more frequent at Neapolitan christenings. Yet all that is known of him is that he was a Bishop of Benevento in the third century who went to Naples to encourage the persecuted Christians. He was seized and thrown to wild beasts in the amphitheatre of Pozzuoli, and when these refused to harm him he was cast into a furnace. Immune to the flames, he was beheaded at the Solfatara, an extinct volcano, where a Capuchin monastery was built in his name.

Wondrous are the legends of San Gennaro and worthy of the Neapolitan imagination. Samuel Sharp relates that the Saracens in one of their expeditions had wantonly defaced the saint's statue at Pozzuoli, 'by breaking off his nose and putting it in their pockets; upon which storms arose, and continued blowing so violently that they could never put to sea till, providentially, some of them thought it was owing to the resentment of the image, who would not be appeased so long as his nose was in their possession; upon which they threw it into the sea; and fine weather immediately succeeding, they sailed prosperously to their havens. In the meanwhile, the artists endeavoured to repair the image with a new nose, but neither art nor force could fasten one on. At length, some fishermen took up the original nose in their nets, but disregarding it, because they did not know what it was, they flung it again into the sea; nevertheless, the nose continuing to offer itself to their nets in whatever place they fished, they began to conceive it must be something supernatural; and one, more cunning than the others, suggested it might be the nose of the Saint, upon which they applied it to the statue to examine whether it fitted, and immediately, without any cement, it united so exactly as hardly to leave any appearance of a scar; in which state we see it.'

Since this order's foundation on July 3, 1738, the investiture of a knight was one of the most solemn functions at the Court of Naples, and the honour was highly coveted. The chief duties attached to it were: to defend the Catholic Faith; to reconcile enemies; to swear loyalty to the Grand Master, the King; to hear Mass daily, communicate at Easter and on the saint's anniversary; to celebrate Mass, recite the office of the dead, and communicate on the death of a fellow knight; neither to offer nor accept any challenge to a duel, but to submit all offences to the Grand Master's decision; and to worship at every chapel where the saint was venerated. Its badge was a cross bordered with four lilies and an image of the Bishop Martyr with the motto *In Sanguine Fœdus*, hanging on a crimson sash to symbolize his martyrdom. The number of knights was limited to sixty. Later on Pope Benedict XIV granted them absolution and plenary indulgence if they visited three churches thrice a year on his miraculous days, as well as dispensations from fasting.

III

New palaces—Portici and Herculaneum—Royal hunting preserves and regulations—The Queen's first offspring—Montealegre succeeds Santo Stefano—The Neapolitan Fine Arts—The Sultan's ambassador—War of Austrian Succession—Commodore Martin's Expedition—A new Family Compact—The King decides to march—The Battle of Velletri—A formal visit to Rome—Disgrace of Montealegre—Fogliani succeeds him—Death of Philip V of Spain—Final emancipation of Charles.

When Maria Amalia arrived the royal palace was pullulating with painters and workmen; but magnificence mattered more than comfort. The corridors and stairways were probably as dirty and evil-smelling as at Versailles; Président de Brosses observed that many of the Farnese treasures had been left for three years to moulder on a dark staircase where everyone went to relieve nature—'Yes, sir, they made water next to Guido and Correggio!' On the other hand, he praised the recent decorations: 'All the furniture is rich and modern, and the doorframes are of marble. I noticed that there was no bed in the King's apartment, so punctual is he in sleeping in the Queen's. No doubt this is a fine example of conjugal assiduity...'

At a period when love was regarded as a pastime in Court circles, an amusement independent of marriage, the King's uxoriousness struck most foreigners as eccentric. But in this respect he took after his father, who was inseparable from Elisabeth Farnese at all times. And like Louis XIV, Charles enjoyed being surrounded by his architects, painters and builders. To a certain extent the palaces he began to build at Portici, Capodimonte, and later at Caserta, owed their origins to his mania for hunting: they were admirably situated for shooting parties on a majestic scale. Medrano was commissioned to build Capodimonte on the wooded hill north of the city commanding one of the finest views of the bay with all its islands, and Carasale was again put in charge of the works in August 1738. The houses already standing there were demolished: four hundred soldiers a day were employed on the task, and these were supplemented by galley-slaves. But various disadvantages soon became apparent: Medrano had disregarded the numerous caves of Christian catacombs, dating from the first century, under the hill, which began to collapse when the massive building was started. Moreover, there was a complete absence of water, so that eight hundred barrels had to be brought up daily from the Capuan Gate. Eventually Medrano confessed that he could not cope with so many problems, and Antonio Canevari, a Roman architect who had been employed in Spain, was called to collaborate with him. The palace was left unfinished, but it served as a spacious hunting lodge, and later its apartments were used as picture galleries. Charles established a porcelain factory in the grounds to please his bride, who had inherited her father's love of ceramics.

When Charles selected Portici as a residence, he was warned that it was dangerously near Vesuvius. 'God Almighty, the Immaculate Virgin and San Gennaro will tend to that', he is said to have replied. On one side it was open to the sea, on the other to a large garden and wilderness of evergreen oaks planted on volcanic soil: a situation convenient both for hunting and fishing, but it was also near Herculaneum, a quarry of more subtle fascination. While digging a well, some labourers had unearthed a statue there in 1711. This came to the notice of Prince d'Elbeuf, who started secret excavations with fortunate results, filled his neighbouring villa with the statues, pillars and fragments he continued to find, and sent some choice statues to Vienna, where they were much admired. But he left with the Austrian regime and the digging ceased. Charles acquired his house and ordered Alcubierre, an engineer he had brought from Spain, to proceed with the excavations. The difficulties were considerable, for the old city was buried from fifty to sixty feet under petrified mud, and the houses of Resina stood over it. In spite of Alcubierre's clumsy methods, it is remarkable that so much of value came to light, and survived not only damage from pick-axe and gunpowder but also the ruthless manipulation of Canart, the sculptor mistakenly commissioned to restore broken statues. Besides removing the fine patina of bronzes, this vandal did not hesitate to melt down those with which his deadly fingers could not grapple; amongst others thus destroyed was the splendid torso of a Grecian charioteer.

Charles watched his collection grow by leaps and bounds, and housed it in a wing of his palace at Portici, where he spent many a delightful hour with the Queen and his learned curator, Marchese

Venuti. A small band of sculptors, painters, engravers and scholars were employed to copy, restore and describe these amazing discoveries. But special permission was required to visit the underground ruins, which were not open to the general public. The privileged had to creep through holes from house to house with torches to light up the gloom. Among these was Horace Walpole, whose enthusiasm still has a breathless accent: 'This underground city is perhaps one of the noblest curiosities that ever has been discovered... You may walk the compass of a mile; but by the misfortune of the modern town being overhead, they are obliged to proceed with great caution, lest they destroy both one and t'other. By this occasion the path is very narrow, just wide enough and high enough for one man to walk upright... except some columns, they have found all the edifices standing upright in their proper situation. There is one inside of a temple quite perfect... It is built of brick plastered over and painted with architecture: almost all the insides of the houses are in the same manner; and, what is very particular, the general ground of all the painting is red. Besides this temple, they make out very plainly an amphitheatre: the stairs of white marble and the seats are very perfect... They have found among other things some fine statues, some human bones, some rice, medals, and a few paintings extremely fine... There is nothing of the kind known in the world; I mean a Roman city entire of that age, and that has not been corrupted with modern repairs... 'Tis certainly an advantage to the learned world that this has been laid up so long. Most of the discoveries in Rome were made in a barbarous age, where they only ransacked the ruins in quest of treasure.' But the interest of Herculaneum was somewhat eclipsed by the later discovery of the more extensive and approachable Pompeii.

Until the new palace of Caserta was built, Portici was the favourite residence of the royal family. Its peculiarity is that the old high road passes through the middle of the palace, so that everyone going to Calabria, or even to Torre del Greco and the coastal towns, had to enter at one gate and go out at the other. 'So ill suited with rural stillness,' remarked one traveller, 'that I should never fix on this bustling solitude for my recreation.' But the King and Queen were inured to living in public: privacy was as unfamiliar to them as to their humblest subjects, who like to look and be looked at, and no doubt they slept soundly while the coaches rattled through their courtyard.

While Charles had an exalted idea of his regal dignity, he was irked by the trappings of royalty and disliked standing on ceremony. His boredom at state functions was apparent to all his courtiers, one of whom wrote: 'When he had to dress for a ceremony, he would sulkily wear a costume of rich material, sometimes with diamond buttons, over his hunting suit. This was intended to conceal his under-garments, but occasionally it displayed a portion here and there. Thus garbed he appeared at Court, in Chapel, at a kissing of hands, and when the ceremony was over he returned to his closet with a great sigh of relief, exclaiming: "Thank God that is over!" as if he had been delivered of a heavy load... It was martyrdom to His Majesty to wear new clothes or shoes or even a new hat. These objects would often remain a whole week beside the old ones on his table, until the King slowly got used to them.'

The royal routine revolved about hunting and shooting to an inordinate degree. The first three months of the year were spent at Caserta, with alternate visits to Torre di Guevara, Bovino and Venafro. Holy Week was invariably spent at Naples; spring and part of the summer between there and Portici. In mid-September the King sailed to the island of Procida for the pheasant-shooting, then back to Portici, with a visit to Ottaiano for the partridges; All Saints in the capital; then to Persano for more game.

Minute regulations protected the King's sport. An official report on Procida in 1735 states that the pheasants had greatly diminished there owing to the former proprietor's neglect, but that the first step to remedy this had been to count all the pheasants on the island. Veteran sportsmen made a tour of inspection for three consecutive days, and with the help of the rangers were able to count ninety-nine. This number was registered by the keepers, who were to be fined twenty ducats apiece for any pheasant missing. A proclamation declared that nobody save the King was allowed to shoot on the island. The penalty for killing pheasants, rabbits or any other wild creatures was a fine of 50,000 ducats and seven years of confinement in a fortress for nobles, 200 ducats and seven years in the galleys for commoners. Firearms were only to be used if the place were invaded by pirates or enemies. The same penalties were ordered for those who molested or frightened animals and birds with clubs, poles, whether pointed or not, rings, ropes, stones or any other weapon, or dug holes for them, apart from those already existing, which were to be supervised by the head gamekeeper. If ecclesiastics infringed these rules, the penalties would apply to their nearest relations. The testimony of one eye witness and two 'ear-witnesses' sufficed to convict a defendant. Pheasant feathers found in a private house provided sufficient evidence for torture, likewise a gun found on any person after the sound of gunfire. Half the fines exacted were to reward the informers; and head rangers were to see that nobody in the neighbourhood kept dogs or cats which might disturb the game. Similar rules applied to the King's other hunting preserves.

Since no cats were allowed at Procida, there was soon a plague of rats and mice, whose havoc was picturesquely exaggerated by Dumas Père and other anti-Bourbon writers. The governor of Procida, however, was pitiless in carrying out the letter of the law. For instance, he wrote to the minister Fogliani that three kittens had been concealed and brought up as pets by the girls of a local orphanage. Through their confessor Don Tomaso Ferrara, he had ordered the Mother Superior to surrender the prohibited pussies, but Don Tomaso, moved by the orphans' tears, replied that he thought it too cruel to deprive them of their pets, which could hardly cause much damage as they were shut up inside the house. For this brazen contempt of the law, continued the governor, he had banished him from the island for two months, and suspended the Mother Superior from her duties for the same period. A few hours later the three kittens were delivered to him in a sack, and he had shot each of them in turn. Fogliani replied that without exiling the priest and suspending the Mother Superior, the mortification already inflicted on them seemed adequate. Subsequently the same governor wrote to Fogliani that one of his spies had discovered that the Dominicans of Santa Margherita were hiding a white cat with a spot on its head. The friars denied this, but after a thorough search it was caught and killed by one of his agents. This edict, after being carried to absurd lengths, was eventually revoked.

The intendants or rangers of royal parks were given large salaries as well as the use of a carriage with two horses and a coachman in livery. A petition from one of the King's gamekeepers relates the happy increase of pheasants on Procida: the petitioner had promised not to marry before the King had done so, and since this had happened he now begged for permission to take a wife; in the meantime his whole family were 'praying for the continued good health of the King and Queen with abundant offspring for the major consolation of his realm and most faithful vassals, *ut Deus*'.

The old feudal castle of Procida was finely situated on the north-eastern summit of the island, and Charles had it enlarged, repaired and redecorated. The journey from Naples took roughly three hours by boat, and towards the end of the century the castle was open to foreign visitors. 'In this palace, which is always cool,' wrote Mariana Starke in 1792, 'you are permitted to dine [a cold dinner having been brought from Naples], the *custodi* finding you a table-cloth, plates, dishes, and a machine for icing water, the ice to fill which may easily be procured in the town. From the landing-place to the palace is a short mile; and if you visit Procida on Sunday, or on any other *festa*, you will be recompensed from the fatigue of walking through the town by a view of its inhabitants, the women being dressed in the Greek style, while the men wear Phrygian caps, and waistcoats ornamented with buttons resembling little bells, such as the Turks now wear. The people of Procida are rich, and it is said they maintain the Grecian customs as well as dress—they have one remarkable quality, instead of importuning strangers for money, and never being satisfied give what you may, as is common in the environs of Naples, they show you everything worth seeing, allow you to examine their dresses, and appear fully recompensed by the pleasure of asking you questions. This island is famous for grapes, figs and wine; the houses are flat-roofed, with terraces on the top—the staircases chiefly on the outside of the houses.' An idyllic spot, though the castle has been converted into a gloomy prison. Most of the King's shooting lodges were more remote.

Meticulous arrangements were made in advance for the mass migration which these royal excursions involved. The chief chaplain provided a list of those who were to tend the King's spiritual welfare, and similar lists were drawn up for the royal kitchen, pantry, stables, etc. Private houses were rented when accommodation for the King's suite was insufficient. Santo Stefano, who could enjoy a greater sense of power in the King's absence, encouraged this mode of existence with the Queen Mother's warm approval. It was all in the Bourbon tradition. Louis XIV had divided his time between various châteaux, and like him Charles preferred palaces surrounded by plenty of space where the gardens merged into hunting parks. His extravagance gave employment to many and benefited the country. Fine new roads were laid out to his distant estates, the large

Pozzuoli grotto was restored, solid bridges were built as on the road from Capua to Venafro, and the important highway to Salerno, known as the Via di Calabria, was prolonged as far as Persano. These were constantly improved and extended by his successors.

In 1740 the news of the Queen's first pregnancy was celebrated with much gaiety at Court and in the provinces. On September 6, before she was sixteen, she gave birth to a daughter. The attendance of the Queen of France's surgeon on this occasion was extremely shocking to Neapolitan notions of modesty. It was said that Doctor Peyrat invented non-existent complications to enhance his reputation, and that he alarmed the Queen with his collection of surgical instruments. Four more princesses were born before the advent of a son and heir, but after her first delivery the Queen insisted on having a midwife. 'The Queen has received great presents from Dresden upon the late occasion,' wrote the British consul in October, 'and has much influence in many affairs, and by the most discerning it is thought will have more hereafter.'

Charles went to the shrine of Saint Nicholas of Bari to thank him for her safe delivery. After investigating the gifts of former sovereigns, he decided to offer the saint a baldaquin and monstrance of pure silver designed by Canevari. During the three days he spent in Bari he chanted among the canons in the choir, and behaved with a somewhat priggish devoutness. Some nuns at Barletta were so anxious to catch a glimpse of him that they clustered round the convent gate and chatted with members of the royal bodyguard. A pardonable peccadillo, but the King was scandalized. The inquisitive sisters were severely admonished for their breach of discipline.

From distant Spain Elisabeth Farnese kept a sharp eye on her son's activities, including the religious processions he followed on foot; every week she received a detailed account of them from Montealegre. She intended to control Italy through Naples and Naples by ministers dependent upon herself. It was not yet time for Charles to declare his independence. He achieved this gradually by surreptitious means, spurred on by Maria Amalia, who had political ambitions, and assisted by the internal combustion of palace cabal and Court intrigue. He had grown thoroughly tired of Santo Stefano, who treated him as if he were still his pupil. The Queen objected to Santo Stefano's wife and daughter for similar reasons. For four years these haughty dames had swayed the Court, and they resented being dispossessed by the girl-bride from Saxony. They would not even show her proper respect, and spoke of her as a mere child, of which she was angrily aware. Montealegre and the Duke of Sora, the Queen's major-domo, bore grudges against the too powerful minister, apart from the lesser courtiers who had been offended by his arrogance; and since Montealegre's wife had become lady-in-waiting to Elisabeth Farnese she did much to undermine his influence at home. Both Charles and Maria Amalia wrote to Spain urging his recall. Santo Stefano submitted his resignation, believing that he was indispensable. But the cabal against him had crystallized, and in August 1738 he was granted 2,000 gold doubloons for his return journey.

Montealegre succeeded him as virtual Prime Minister for the next eight years, and his first aim was to reverse the system of his predecessor. From now on the King attended Privy Councils, which increased his experience of state affairs and enabled him to control his ministers in future. But Montealegre proved no more popular than Santo Stefano; soon many were complaining that he promised far more than he could fulfil and forgot his promises. The fundamental reason, which could not be spoken, was that he was just another Spaniard. So long as he kept on good terms with the Queen of Spain, his position was invulnerable. He referred everything to her, and consulted her about the King's most trivial amusements, such as whether she approved of his playing *biribissi*. His vigilance over the King's associates exceeded that of Santo Stefano, and those who roused his suspicions were quietly eliminated. There was the seductive Princess of Belmonte, for instance, whose husband was still in Vienna. Although she had been exiled to a distant castle, she had contrived to ingratiate herself with the Queen and win her way back to Court.

Card games were even more popular in society than they are today, and the Princess's house was open every night to a mixed company of gamblers. The great impresario-contractor Carasale was one of her most assiduous guests, and it was an evening at her house that led to his ruin. He seemed at the height of his prosperity: tens of thousands of ducats were being lavished on the building and embellishment of Portici, Capodimonte and the castle of Procida, and his profits were so large that he made considerable loans to various members of the nobility without demanding interest. Unfortunately he lost his temper while gambling with a prominent lawyer, Andrea Vignes. A scuffle ensued, and Carasale sent a lamp crashing to the floor. The Princess took the lawyer's side, and as she stood high in the Queen's favour it was easy to prejudice her against the impresario. Insinuations were followed by accusations. Though the King appreciated his talents, he was naturally inclined to listen to his spouse. The Board of Accounts was ordered to inquire into Carasale's expenditure of 266,860 ducats which had been paid him for various ventures, and several rushed forward with claims, including some Jesuits who said that they had not received their share for some land he had bought near Capodimonte. His affairs were found to be in a hopeless muddle. A complicated lawsuit culminated in his arrest and imprisonment. While further evidence was being collected against him, the broken man died of apoplexy in the Castle of Sant' Elmo.

The Princess of Belmonte's disgrace was swift to follow. Montealegre accused her of corresponding secretly with Vienna, an accusation supported by the Marquis de l'Hôpital, the French ambassador, and his friend the Duchess of Maddaloni. The Queen of Spain obliged her son to remove this scheming lady, and as Maria Amalia was devoted to her she took a violent dislike to Montealegre in consequence. The Court painter, Antonio Sebastiani, was one of his more innocent victims. The King and Queen often watched him at his easel, and remained to chat with him on various topics. Moreover, Charles had remarked that a King would be happy if he could always find such friends. As Sebastiani was related to a bishop and other Church dignitaries, Charles appointed him an adjutant of the royal chamber; he also gave him a lucrative sinecure in the customs. Such favours to a mere picture dauber roused Montealegre's deepest suspicions: no doubt the fellow was a spy, employed behind his back to report on the state of public opinion. He, too, would have to be exiled. To save appearances, Sebastiani begged leave to retire to Rome with the continuation of his pension, fees and emoluments, a petition which was readily granted.

Sebastiani had specialized in 'official' portraits of the King, which were distributed among the embassies abroad. At least eleven of these had been commissioned by Montealegre for the modest sum of six ducats apiece: though 'painted by hand', no doubt these were mass-produced. Like many of our Royal Academicians, Sebastiani's gifts seem to have been social rather than artistic.

Solimena, still indefatigable in his eighties, was the venerable doyen of Neapolitan painters, and he had countless imitators, most of whom exaggerated his mannerisms to the point of caricature. He took pride in his 'universality' of style extended to every branch of art; history, portraits, landscape, animals, fruit and architecture; and as he worked with great speed, he may best be compared with his friend and competitor Luca Giordano. He believed in rendering nature 'noble and stylish', so that even his drapery was endowed with 'ideal folds'. Eventually facility and elegance became his weaknesses: his success came too easily. The King posed to him for a full-length equestrian portrait which was much admired, except by Président de Brosses, who mentioned with disapproval that he had amassed a million and a half ducats in the exercise of his profession. 'Oh, what a shame!' was his comment, 'when Messer Annibale [Carracci] had to drag his cart like a horse to earn 1,500 crowns in six years. If there had only been Solimena and I in the world, he would never have earned fifty *sous* with his insipid manner, and his compositions devoid of energy and genius.' This censure is surprising when we examine such a typical sample of Solimena's work as 'Heliodorus Driven Out of the Temple' in the Gesù Nuovo. He could be rhetorical and over-emphatic, but this vigorous delineator of mass-movement was seldom insipid. His best pupils were Francesco de Mura, Sebastiano Conca, Corrado Giaquinto and Giuseppe Bonito, who were almost as prolific as their master. Solimena died at the age of ninety in 1747.

The King had a preference for Bonito at this time; later on he was captivated by the neo-classical style of Raphael Mengs, and always travelled with one or two of his pictures. Bonito was appointed a royal *pittore di camera* and director of the first Neapolitan Academy of Art, founded by Charles. The King had already founded a factory of tapestry in 1737; of *pietre dure* (engraved stones, cameos and mosaics) in 1738; and of porcelain in 1739; which supplied a growing demand for these long-neglected luxuries and flourished accordingly. The Royal Academy of Design was started in 1752 to encourage the development of figurative arts in a practical manner. An Academy of Architecture was added in 1762, but this was chiefly concerned with stage design and the decoration of Court festivals. These schools were installed next to the tapestry and *pietre dure* factories at San Carlo alle Mortelle; eventually they were moved to the Palazzo degli Studi, the former seat of the university. Bonito had too many lucrative private commissions to devote much time to teaching. So seldom did he attend the academy that there were loud complaints from the students, but when De Mura was appointed assistant director, the autocratic Bonito evidently made him regret this, as he soon tendered his resignation. In spite of grumblings and rivalries, Bonito retained his directorship until he died in 1789. Recently some of the most spirited paintings attributed to him have been fathered on his pupil Gaspare Traversi, and the pupil seems to have excelled the master. The pictures which made Bonito's early reputation represented a schoolmaster and a mistress teaching girls to sew; he had little aptitude for decorative composition.

Caravaggio's realism and Piazzetta's glowing contrasts of light and shadow appear to have influenced his literal and business-like brush. He was one of the first local *genre* painters of the period, and his huntsmen, musicians, surgeons and other vivid types are rollickingly realistic in contrast with the prevalent theatricalism. Besides a set of pictures illustrating the life of Don Quixote, which were reproduced in tapestry in the King's factory, he painted some curious groups to commemorate the embassies from Turkey and Tripoli.

The behaviour of the Sultan's ambassador had caused some embarrassment to his hosts in 1741. He was so pleased with the apartment which had been furnished for him in the Prince of Teora's palace that he declared he would take all the furniture back to Turkey, and was with difficulty dissuaded from doing so. Then at a banquet given for him by Montealegre he consumed immoderate draughts of champagne, which he would call lemonade. 'But I assure Your Excellency that this is pure champagne!' 'I say it is lemonade, and beg you not to contradict me.' This insistence may have been due to the fact that his religion forbade him wine. After his departure an elephant arrived from Turkey. It was said to have been sent by the Sultan, but it had actually been acquired by the Neapolitan envoy for the sake of prestige. The animal was kept at Portici and fully described by the naturalist Serao in a booklet which includes its portrait. When 'Alexander in the Indies' was being rehearsed at the San Carlo, the manager proposed to bring it on the stage, 'since such a sight would attract a larger audience during the Carnival season and spread His Majesty's fame abroad'. Though the King was at first reluctant, fearing that the elephant would take fright, he was persuaded to consent, so that the opera's success was assured.

While relations with Turkey were improving, the differences with the Holy See had become serious. 'I cannot deny', the Venetian ambassador Mocenigo had written in 1737, 'that there is something unnatural in the sight of the collected body of Catholic sovereigns ranging themselves against the Court of Rome, and the altercations are now so violent that there can be no hope of any reconciliation by which that Court would not be injured in some vital part.' The new Pope, Benedict XIV, elected in 1740, resolved to make timely concessions. One of the first acts of his pontificate was the Concordat he concluded with Naples in 1741, which allowed the taxation of some ecclesiastical property, and limited clerical jurisdiction and immunities, besides restricting the number of clergy in the kingdom. A mixed tribunal of ecclesiastical and secular judges was to settle controversies arising from the Concordat, which gave an impetus to further reforms.

While Charles was concerned with domestic affairs and the improvement of his capital, the War of the Austrian Succession broke out between Spain and Austria. On the death of the Emperor Charles VI in 1740, Philip V of Spain, spurred on by Elisabeth who was determined to recover the central Italian duchies, sent an expeditionary force under Montemar to Italy. Though Charles declared himself neutral, his father ordered him to send as large a force as he could muster to support Montemar. While employing Neapolitan troops, Spain also expected to enjoy the advantages of Neapolitan neutrality, a point of view that betrays Elisabeth's feminine reasoning. Charles had to submit: he sent 12,000 troops to Pesaro under the Duke of Castropignano. But this time Montemar's luck turned. Charles Emmanuel of Savoy was now an open enemy, and England supplied him with money to defend Lombardy against the Bourbons. He occupied Parma, Reggio, Modena and Mirandola; while Montemar, who had hesitated too long, was driven back to Rimini and Foligno. The partisans of Austria were greatly encouraged.

On the night of August 18, 1742, Naples was rocked by an earthquake which caused more alarm than damage. Many fled from their houses, and the criminal element exploited the calamity. The King and Queen spent the whole night in the garden of the royal palace. Those who had been suborned by the pro-Austrians to foment an insurrection regarded the earthquake as a warning from Heaven. Next day an English squadron appeared off Baia. Reports of its strength were exaggerated; actually it consisted of thirteen ships under Commodore Martin, which anchored without saluting in full view of the city. Crowds watched them in amazement and dread. The pro-Austrians who tried to make trouble met with no response. Many hot-heads ran to the royal palace shouting for arms to destroy the hostile squadron. The King was distracted by conflicting emotions. The city was lamentably unprepared, for the Nuovo, Ovo and Sant' Elmo castles were no defence against a naval force. Besides, as Addison had remarked, 'the sea which lies near it is not subject to storms, has no sensible flux and re-flux, and is so deep that a vessel of burthen may come up to the very mole. The houses are flat-roofed, to walk upon; so that every bomb that fell on them would take effect'. Even so, the King had no desire to be called a coward.

Two months previously Montealegre had been warned that a British squadron was due, and the Neapolitan ambassador in Paris had even described it as consisting of fourteen ships of about eighty guns. The French ambassador in Naples had also advised him to be prepared. But Montealegre paid no attention to these repeated warnings. Perhaps he imagined that the British would bow to his professions of neutrality. With an air of injured dignity he now asked Mr Edward Allen, the British consul, to find out the squadron commander's intentions, and tell him that the King would be glad to receive them as friends. The consul went to see Commodore Martin, who read him the message he had ordered Captain de l'Angle to deliver to the King:

'That, as His Britannic Majesty was in alliance with the Queen of Hungary and the King of Sardinia, and the King of the Two Sicilies, having joined his forces with those of Spain, in declared war with England, to invade the Queen of Hungary's dominions, contrary to all treaties; he, the Commodore, was sent to demand that the King of the Two Sicilies should not only immediately withdraw his troops from acting in conjunction with those of Spain, but that His Sicilian Majesty should, in writing, promise not to give them any further assistance of any kind whatsoever... If His Sicilian Majesty refused to comply with this message, the Commodore would make the necessary dispositions to bombard the city, and press his demand by the force of arms.'

At five o'clock the captain and consul were in Montealegre's office. The King was still at church, but Montealegre told them that when he returned they would receive an answer. In the meantime he issued orders to prevent a landing. That evening the King presided over a stormy Council; personally he was in favour of refusal, but he was finally induced to yield, so as to save the city from bombardment. Accordingly Montealegre told Captain de l'Angle, who had been waiting with a truculent air, watch in hand, that the demand would be complied with, and in writing, as required; but he wished to have some answer also in writing, stating that upon such a compliance no hostilities should be committed on either side. Captain de l'Angle and the consul returned to the Commodore, but he said his orders were absolute and did not authorize him to give any answer; but that he expected compliance in an hour after the consul and captain had been on shore, where they both returned to deliver the Commodore's reply to Montealegre. It was two hours past midnight when the consul was back on board, and the Commodore was so far satisfied as to promise he would not commence any hostilities; next morning a letter was written in the exact words required, upon receipt of which the Commodore ordered all the ships to prepare for sailing. But they did not sail very far. They anchored near Capri for the next ten days and withdrew on August 30.

Momentary relief was no sop for the King's mortification. The incident provoked equal resentment at Madrid and Versailles, which led to mutual recrimination. The Spaniards said that the English would never have been so bold had France been ready to support her ally. The French retorted that the King should never have grovelled to an English pirate; he should have replied firmly, refusing to believe that the King of England had given such orders. Elisabeth rebuked her son for his indecorous retreat, but Montealegre had been to blame for his improvidence. The lesson had been deserved, and the shock roused the administration to a sense of danger.

Charles hastened to repair fortifications and coastal defences. New regiments were recruited from the provinces: nine were raised by 1743, to which a tenth was added and a company of 'mountain fusiliers'. Don Michele Reggio, Captain-General of the Galleys, created a small marine of two men-of-war with sixty-four and sixty guns, two frigates of thirty cannon, and six xebecs of twenty cannon. A new mole was built, and a new road from the arsenal to the Carmine fort. The special magistracy called *Giunta d'Inconfidenza* was revived to nip conspiracies in the bud. These had been inspired by Austrian victories in the north: a plot for a rebellion to coincide with the arrival of an English fleet was found to have extensive ramifications. Tanucci was energetic as president of the new *Giunta*, and he proved that many nobles, government officials, priests, soldiers, lawyers and merchants were among the disaffected. An Augustinian monk had been one of the ringleaders in Calabria, where it was said that the loss of one battle would have driven the Bourbons from Naples. More than eight hundred were arrested owing to the discovery of secret documents at Portella. An astute lawyer had been sending exact reports to the Austrian ambassador in Rome about the state of public opinion, events at Court, the scarcity of troops, besides plans of fortifications; he had also drawn up an inflammatory manifesto, which was published under Maria Theresa's name. A certain Abate Gambari had reaped a handsome profit from the sale of coupons or promissory notes for posts in the new government, with faked seals of the Austrian Empress. A few suffered arbitrary arrest, but the *Giunta* achieved its purpose.

Charles sent Marchese Fogliani, his ambassador to the Hague, on a special mission to England in March 1743, but nothing came of it. The British government disowned Commodore Martin's action, but would not acknowledge the neutrality of the Two Sicilies. When Charles heard that Naples and the Presidi had been allotted to Austria and Sicily to Charles Emmanuel of Savoy at the Treaty of Worms in September, he realized that he could not stay neutral if he wished to keep his throne. This treaty drew Spain and France together again: a new Family Compact was signed, and France was pledged to maintain Charles in the Two Sicilies while his brother, Don Philip, was to conquer Milan, Parma and Piacenza. Montemar was recalled after a series of reverses and replaced by the Flemish Count de Gages, who proved a more able commander.

Maria Theresa sent fresh troops under the Prince of Lobkowitz to advance on Naples. The proclamations distributed in her name promised the feudal barons and ecclesiastics to restore all their privileges, to expel the Jews and lower the cost of provisions, but such promises meant nothing to the majority, whose memories of Austrian misrule were still green.

Montealegre was in favour of clinging to neutrality, and his timorous advice had reduced Charles to a state of despondent lethargy when he was roused by furious letters from his parents. These compared his shameful inertia with the gallant resolution of his younger brother, Don Philip, who had invaded Nice and captured Villafranca and Oneglia; and they urged him to attack Lobkowitz before he reached the Neapolitan frontier. With the superior advantage of two united armies, he should easily rout the Austrians, they concluded. But Gages had been forced to retreat with the unhappy Duke of Modena, who had lost his states owing to his alliance with the Bourbons and been rewarded by the King of Spain with the honorific title of generalissimo of his armies in Italy. In early March 1744 they were driven as far as the Neapolitan frontier, and the promised protectors appealed to Charles for protection. Montealegre still wavered, but Charles could not refuse, and the Spaniards were quartered in various towns of the Abruzzo.

Harassed by his parents on the one hand and by Montealegre on the other, the King was much comforted by an interview with his Jesuit adviser Father Pepe, who not only inspired him with confidence but gave him a bag full of holy charms called 'tickets of the Immaculate' to wear continuously and swallow in time of danger. He issued an edict, too mild to please his mother, declaring that the Austrians had forced him to defend his kingdom against attack. The government was entrusted to a committee under Don Michele Reggio, Captain General of the Galleys. The Queen, who was again an expectant mother, was sent to Gaeta with her ladies-in-waiting. On March 25, 1744, the King set out with 20,000 troops for the Abruzzo amid the cheers of the people, who had implored the Queen not to leave them. Consul Allen wrote: 'This City has addressed the King for the Queen's stay in the most earnest manner, which has been very agreeable, and the people in general have shown such marks of affection and regret upon this occasion as will hardly be believed, running in crowds this afternoon, and stopping the coach to beg that the Queen and Infants might remain.' To show his people that he had complete faith in their loyalty, the King had released all political prisoners.

Fortunately Lobkowitz dallied near Ancona, waiting for his orders from Vienna. After the usual vicissitudes of an unusually tedious war, Charles and Gages met in the Papal States, and eventually confronted Lobkowitz at Velletri. For six weeks the two armies bombarded each other spasmodically across the valley. Charles hoped that a victory in Piedmont, where his more martial brother was attacking Charles Emmanuel, would force Lobkowitz to withdraw; Lobkowitz was hoping for more active assistance from the British fleet under Admiral Mathews. Sickness and desertions were reducing the Austrian camp, so General Brown, an Irishman in Austrian service, proposed a surprise attack on Velletri by night. The King and all his staff were to be captured at a swoop and the war rushed to a lightning end. A deserter was to guide the Austrian regiments through the difficult by-paths. Some were to attack the city on the opposite side to their camp; others were to spread an alarm towards the east.

At first the stratagem seemed successful. At dawn on August 10 the Irish regiments in Spanish service, which were quartered outside the Neapolitan gate, were cut to pieces by their compatriot Brown and his cavalry; the few that survived were taken prisoners. Brown made a bonfire of all their tents and equipment. The town gate was forced open while Charles was asleep and Gages was inspecting his outposts.

Awakened and warned, Charles leapt out of bed half dressed and escaped from a window of the Ginetti Palace where he was staying. There are several versions of what happened in the next few hours. Certain it is that he found a horse and rode to a neighbouring monastery, where he met the Duke of Modena and the French ambassador, for whose safety he had been anxious. Rallying the right wing of his troops, who were encamped on that side of Velletri, he exhorted them to victory.

The Austrians were so intent on sacking the city that Gages had time to muster his forces outside the walls and return the attack, which he led with great skill and vigour. In this brief engagement the enemy lost 2,600 men and the Bourbons less than half that number. Afraid of being encircled, the Austrians thought only of escaping as fast as they could. Many were killed by jumping down the steep ravines surrounding the city. The Spaniards and Neapolitans pursued them so effectively that the road to the Austrian camp was strewn with corpses. A few Austrians, however, still remained in Velletri. These barricaded themselves in various houses, from which they were able to snipe at a great many Hispano-Neapolitans with impunity. The latter could not easily bring their cannon to play upon them in the narrow streets; besides, they were short of artillery. Eventually Gages's Walloon guards cut down the doors with hatchets and, with some loss, killed or captured them. In the meantime Charles held a conference about pursuing the Austrians with all the forces at his command, but his generals disagreed about the direction they were to take, which allowed the enemy time for an orderly retreat.

The Battle of Velletri was a decisive victory for Charles, who showed courage and leadership throughout the confusion of that day. The King of Sardinia, who understood such matters, in secret instructions to his ambassador after the war, wrote that on this occasion the King of Naples 'had revealed a constancy worthy of his blood and had acquitted himself gloriously'—a testimonial from one who could not be accused of partiality. But instead of pursuing the foe, Charles allowed his troops to rest. The battle had begun at dawn and lasted till nine o'clock. Next day the King gave public thanks to all his army, congratulating Count de Gages and the Duke of Castropignano. He distributed praise and rewards between the Spaniards and Neapolitans, telling them not to be discouraged by their losses but to rejoice in their defeat of a nearly victorious foe. The losses of arms, horses and equipment were soon repaired. Every province was ordered to send recruits and horses, and Spanish reinforcements had the luck to reach Gaeta in spite of the British fleet.

Lobkowitz, while planning to retire to Lombardy, pretended that he had won a great victory. He had suffered heavy casualties, and those who had not been wounded were prostrated by the torrid August heat, to which they were less accustomed than their freshly fortified opponents. As usual in adversity, his officers began to quarrel and criticize his competence. Both armies had drained the country dry and autumn was advancing. The King of Sardinia appealed for reinforcements which Lobkowitz needed himself, and he was obliged by orders from Vienna to send them. He was thus placed in a dilemma: he wanted to march, yet he lingered two months longer in sight of the Spanish army, as if he were ashamed to admit defeat or hoped for a change of fortune. Both camps remained face to face till the end of October. On the first of November Lobkowitz stealthily crossed the Tiber, destroying the bridges behind him, and withdrew to Viterbo.

Before returning to Naples, Charles entered Rome with the Duke of Modena, Gages, Castropignano and his other generals, and received a public ovation hardly less enthusiastic than that which had greeted the Austrian army some months before, when the Romans had said that no nation, much less the Neapolitan, could withstand the look of such troops, overawed by their barbaric uniforms and guttural speech. Now the balconies were brimming with people who acclaimed Charles as 'liberator of the country'. The guns of Sant' Angelo boomed in his honour, and the Pope embraced him and called him a true son of the Church. During his conference with Benedict XIV, he begged him to curtail the number of religious holidays in Naples as they proved a serious nuisance to the working classes. After visiting Saint Peter's, the Lateran and the chief sights, he returned to Velletri and distributed compensations among the loyal inhabitants. At Portella he met the happy Queen and his infant daughter, whom he accompanied to Naples on November 5. His people gave him a hero's welcome, but this time he forbade extravagant demonstrations. Charles was satisfied that he had checked the invasion, and being a quiet man he was determined to enjoy the blessings of peace. The Battle of Velletri had avenged Commodore Martin's insult and ensured the independence of Naples under the Bourbons. The pro-Austrians realized that their cause was lost and belatedly came to terms with the government.

Montealegre still appeared invincible at Court. But the Queen hated him and, watching him retire with a pompous retinue, she remarked aloud: 'There goes the King of Naples!' Gages had quarrelled with him, as any impatient man of action would; the Duke of Sora and Cardinal Acquaviva had long been scheming for his downfall. The unexpected blow fell on him in the spring of 1746, when he was recalled to Spain. Marchese Fogliani was appointed to succeed him in June, and this was a notable advance towards greater independence.

Fogliani was an accomplished courtier, but mediocre in every other respect. After two Spanish prime ministers, the fact that he was Italian had a certain importance. Born in Piacenza, he had gone to Spain with Elisabeth Farnese, and he owed his good fortune to his wife's influence on the Queen Mother. He had returned to Italy as one of the King's first gentlemen-in-waiting, and he had been his first envoy to Genoa and The Hague. The Sardinian ambassador described him as 'tall, fair, with a long face, an average mind, and a strong bias towards France. He was long-winded and inconclusive, and [like Montealegre] he was apt to ignore his former promises'. Now, at the age of forty-nine, he was placed in charge of foreign affairs, the army and navy, commerce and the complicated administration of the royal household.

The death of Philip V in July brought an even more momentous change, not only to Naples but to the whole of Italy, since it involved the retirement of Elisabeth Farnese. The new King of Spain, Ferdinand VI, was indifferent if not hostile to his fierce stepmother's ambitions. As a son of Marie Louise Gabrielle of Savoy, he preferred his maternal relations, and he was tired of war. Don Philip wrote to his mother, the Queen Dowager: 'What is terrible is that we nourish a serpent in our bosom.' The serpent in question was lazy and good-natured. Like Philip V, he was governed by his wife. The singularly plain Maria Barbara of Braganza stepped into Elisabeth Farnese's shoes.

His father's death completed Charles's emancipation. Now he was his own master, and from this moment his character seemed to change. Everybody noticed that he had acquired a deeper sense of responsibility, a greater energy and a broader range of vision. He began to control his ministers, whose councils he attended regularly. Not only did he hold private audiences; he conferred privately with foreign ambassadors, who remarked that with all his affability he was disarmingly firm. He hunted as much as before, but he worked according to a strict time table. As he told Monasterolo, the Sardinian ambassador: 'I rise at five in the morning, read and attend to memorials till eight, when I dress and proceed to the State Council. I hope to make this kingdom flourish again and relieve it from taxes, especially since this year [1750] I have finished paying all the debts contracted during the last war and still have 300,000 ducats in savings to put in my treasury. To prove this I have refused the usual voted tax [*donativo*] from the Sicilian Parliament, a larger sum than any voted previously, telling them I had no present need of it, and that they were to save it until it was required. Apart from which I have revoked a tax, and devote all my attention to improving the welfare of my subjects, since I wish to save my soul and go to Heaven.' This ingenuous statement rings true, and nothing in his life contradicted it.

IV

The birth of an Heir Apparent—A cruel disillusion—The Queen's ambitions—Squillace—Naples, France and Sardinia—The gorgeous Prince Esterhazy—The Inquisition nipped in the bud—The building of Caserta.

Ever since the King's marriage the learned academicians had been arguing about a suitable title for the Heir Apparent, but so far the heir had failed to appear. The Queen had only given birth to five princesses, four of whom had died in infancy. On June 13, 1747, while the Court was at Portici, another royal delivery was expected; surely this time a little prince would answer the people's prayers. All the chief ministers, magistrates and courtiers were to hasten to the palace as soon as they received notice of the Queen's first pangs, whereupon the two monasteries of the Cappucinelle and Eremite were to pray for divine mercy and a happy result at whatever hour of the day or night the delivery occurred. Sentries and bodyguards were doubled; all embarkations were suspended for the time being. The Duchess Miranda Caracciolo stood by to swaddle the babe.

The event occurred late at night. At last a plump, soft, rosy son was born, and he was christened immediately with eight names, of which the first was Philip. The King, beside himself with joy, seized the infant in his arms and embraced him, lifting him up for all to admire and thanking Heaven again and again.

Three wet-nurses were allotted to the child, with the approval of the royal physicians. His title was discussed at a special Council of State, which decided that he was to be called the Duke of Puglia, 'since Divine Providence had revived the genius and fortunes of Roger in the royal parent'. But the academicians of Cosenza sent in so eloquent a plea for him to be called the Duke of Calabria that these won the day. His godfather Ferdinand VI made him an Infante of Spain with an annual pension of 4,000 piastres. A month later the King and Queen went to render public thanks at the shrine of San Gennaro, and a hundred thousand ducats in *carlini*[1] were coined with the royal pair on one side and Fortune dandling the new-born prince on the other, inscribed '*Firmata securitas*' above and '*populi spes nat.* 1747' below.

As well as illuminations on land and sea, from the summit of Sant' Elmo to the galleys gleaming in the bay, there were two weeks of public celebrations, including balls, serenades, masquerades, fireworks and a *Cuccagna* on the square before the palace. 'The Dream of Olympia', a dramatic poem set to music, alluding to the dream of Alexander the Great's mother about his future triumphs, was performed in the Court theatre. The poet Calzabigi and the composer Giuseppe di Maio have long been forgotten, together with the stars who lighted the performance. But an old engraving still evokes it: a palatial hall with the usual baroque accessories, dome, arches, balustrades, porticoes, statues, formal garden and fountain of Neptune with tritons and dolphins. Above the stage floats a goddess surrounded by cupids; in the foreground Vittoria Tesi in a billowy crinoline stands beside Caffarello, while Angela Conti sits in rapt melody, and other singers descend the formal staircase on the right. Beside the King and Queen an empty chair is set apart for the Prince, still lying in his cradle.

Two incidents marred the festivities. An elaborate structure for the display of fireworks, symbolizing a Temple of Victory on the Largo del Castello, caught fire prematurely, and many were trampled on and suffocated in the ensuing stampede. And there was an unfortunate episode at the grand reception given by the Duke of Medinaceli, who stood godfather for the King of Spain to the Hereditary Prince. One of the guests, Count Carafa of Policastro, was searching for his wife, who happened to be among the ladies in another room, but two armed guards refused to let him pass. The Count indignantly asked them why. 'Those are our orders,' they answered, barring the way with their halberds. The Count lost his temper completely. He shouted that not only was the order absurd, but the persons who had issued it and carried it out and the whole Spanish nation as well; that nothing of the sort would happen if the aristocracy were all like himself and insisted on prompt satisfaction for every insult. When the King was informed, he sent the Count to cool his choler in the castle of Messina.

[1] A ducat was equivalent to ten carlini, three shillings and fourpence sterling at the same period.

The subject of these rejoicings was to cause his parents much sorrow. In compensation, the Queen continued to be prolific. Next year a second son was born, Charles Antony, the future King of Spain, followed by a princess who lived only five months. A third son, Ferdinand, who succeeded to the Two Sicilies, was born in 1751, and a fourth, Gabriel, in 1752. After a miscarriage caused by too strenuous exercise while hunting, the Queen gave birth to another princess who died ten months later, and to a fifth son, Francis Saverio, in 1758.

Before the Prince Royal was weaned, it was said that his nurse had been summoned to feed him while she was having a quarrel, and that he suffered from epileptic fits in consequence. The nurse was discharged, as were several who succeeded her. Finally, one was found under whose care he seemed to recover, but after a while she refused to stay in spite of every possible inducement. As he grew up the most dismal rumours about him were confirmed. Although the prince suffered from 'a great heaviness of head, which makes him gloomy and ill-humoured', he was often present at Court galas, when he would offer his hand to be kissed; he was even taken to the opera. 'The Prince Royal does not appear to enjoy good health,' reported the Sardinian ambassador, 'there is something in his eyes that does not harmonize with the rest of his features. I have been assured that although he is seven years old he does not speak, and that he can scarcely utter a word. The second prince seems sturdier, with an agreeable face and a sprightly manner; the other, too, seems pretty and in good health. As for the princesses, they are amiable without beauty; they are also extremely thin...' And again: 'The Prince Royal has been violently attacked by his usual convulsions and does not look as if he will reach maturity.'

His parents tried to conceal his deficiency from the public as well as from themselves. Until the age of seven he remained with his sisters and younger brothers under the care of a governess and a bevy of discreet ladies, but in 1755 the two elder sons were placed under the tutorship of the Prince of San Nicandro and had separate apartments and retinues. The third son, Ferdinand, was destined for the Church; he, too, had a separate apartment in due course. When the King and Queen went hunting some distance from Naples, reports about their children reached them daily—whether they took exercise or stayed indoors owing to cold weather, their increase or loss of appetite, the vicissitudes of a fluxion, etc.

After the birth of her first son the Queen was admitted to the Council of State, which gave her an itch to meddle in politics. To avoid embarrassing the ministers, who were not used to a feminine presence at their meetings, she listened to their discussions behind a curtain. Perhaps she aspired to rival her mother-in-law, but the difference between the bold Parmesan virago and the prim, bigoted Saxon was rather pathetic. Maria Amalia could never extricate herself from the tangled web of Court intrigue around her. In appearance she had become increasingly masculine and she looked almost kingly on horseback. Her features, pitted with smallpox, were sharply accentuated by lines of chronic ill-temper, and her voice was strident and scolding. Her impatient character and habit of command could brook no contradiction, and when she lost control she boxed her pages and slapped her ladies-in-waiting. Charles, who was genuinely fond of her, bore her tantrums with equanimity. He was aware that she was easily influenced by the Duchess of Castropignano, her favourite lady-in-waiting, whom he detested but had to tolerate for her sake. His propitiatory tactics were mistaken for weakness, but in reality his was the stronger will.

Fernan-Nunez relates an anecdote which points the contrast between the King's placidity and his spouse's petulance. When the Queen was in an advanced state of pregnancy an order was issued that as soon as she was seized with the first pangs all courtiers were to don full-dress uniform to celebrate the baptism which, in the case of Infants of Spain, immediately followed their birth. A certain Spaccaforno was waiting on their Majesties at dinner, and while serving a dish he upset a little gravy. The Queen let out a piercing shriek, as usual whenever she was vexed. Spaccaforno dropped the dish and ran out of the room. 'Where are you going, you lunatic?' the King called after him. 'Sire, I was hurrying to change my uniform,' he replied, 'for I thought Her Majesty was about to be delivered.' The King burst out laughing and told him to stop playing the fool. Then glancing roguishly at his wife, he whispered: 'You see, you see what happens!' And he readily pardoned the servant who had been so daring as to give the Queen a lesson.

The Queen's clique had engineered the downfall of Santo Stefano and Montealegre and was preparing to trip up Fogliani. Tanucci managed to steer clear of it, though he complained of the excessive intrigues at Court in his letters to Florence, pretending that they often made him yearn to retire from public life. 'The heroic period of this Court,' he wrote, 'ended with the departure of Santo Stefano.' Since then everybody had plunged headlong into the 'ministry war'; ministers were chiefly concerned with clinging to their positions, and many a wise project fell by the wayside. The Queen's caprices inspired a certain apprehension.

Foreign ambassadors blamed the King's mania for hunting, but Charles had a secret dread of insanity and believed that outdoor exercise would preserve him from it. His father's melancholia had verged on madness; his half-brother was similarly afflicted; and his eldest son was a victim to the family curse. Whenever he grew despondent he escaped into the open air, and this escape had bred its own conventions and become compulsory. To go for a single day without riding or shooting was out of the question. He suffered from restlessness, moodiness and physical discomfort when he was kept too long indoors. Rain or shine, he went out immediately after his twelve o'clock dinner, except in summer when he rested for an hour, and he did not return till dusk. The foulest weather could not deter him, and when it rained he would often repeat, 'Rain breaks no bones'—a maxim which must have broken the spirit of his dripping courtiers. All his superfluous energies were absorbed in this extravagant pastime; in other respects he was frugal, even austere, in his personal habits. But he was aware that he was criticized for devoting so much time to sport, and he confided to a gentleman–in–waiting: 'If they only knew how seldom I really enjoy myself while hunting, they would pity rather than envy me this innocent diversion.'

His servants were so used to his jocularity that they considered his silence as a serious rebuke. Few realized the melancholy of the inner man. That he did exert control over his wife and ministers and that he had a policy of his own, became increasingly clear after Montealegre's disgrace. It was owing to his confidence in Tanucci's honesty and ability that this pedantic ex-professor rose steadily to power; and Leopoldo di Gregorio, better known as the Marquis of Squillace, owed his promotion entirely to the King's favour. Squillace was a Sicilian of obscure origin who had begun his industrious career as an accountant in a commercial firm and caught the King's eye as purveyor to the army. He was said to have made a fortune by none too scrupulous means, but Charles was impressed by his spirit of enterprise. In 1746 he was put in charge of the customs, and eventually he was appointed Minister of Finance. Both

Fogliani and Tanucci were jealous of this slick Sicilian, but nothing could alter the King's affection for him, and after rewarding him with titles and estates he took him to Spain. Charles liked familiar faces as he liked old clothes; his loyalty to Tanucci, Squillace and his crony Miranda, who became Duke of Losada, was as steady as his devotion to the cross and ugly Queen. Sometimes he squabbled with Losada, especially in the evenings when they played *reversis* together, a card game where the winner is the one who makes the lowest score. Being a pernickety player, Losada was an easy butt, and the King could seldom resist a temptation to chaff him. When he went too far Losada relapsed into a glum silence and retired pouting. Next morning he would fail to appear at the usual hour, and the King would say to his valet: 'Losada was upset yesterday. Go and fetch him.' The Duke arrived, still crestfallen, but after a few kind words in which the King would almost excuse himself, his old friend's sulks would melt into a wrinkled smile.

The King's mildness, like his cheerful manner, was deceptive, for he could be severe when principle was involved. But his method of dealing with offenders was often oblique. When he heard that the Duke of Castropignano, Captain-General of the army, was tainted with corruption, and that the Duchess, his wife's favourite, was said to be in French pay, he said nothing about the subject in Council. The same evening the Duke was ordered to discharge his secretaries, who were arrested and sent to prison. 'This example,' wrote the Sardinian ambassador, 'with regard to a pampered Captain-General whose wife continued to enjoy the highest credit with the Queen, has made a great sensation, to the delight of most people and to the honour of this monarch.' The Duke's private secretary was ordered to submit all his master's accounts to be examined by the Marquis of Squillace. A French tutor to the Duke's son was found to have received 6,000 *livres* from his ambassador, which looked suspicious as the tutor was in Paris at the time. An officer on the Duke's staff, Don Sanches de Luna, was proved to have collected bribes from 370 convicts, who had been set free after payment. As they had been employed on defence works, the money for their maintenance had been pocketed by de Luna and his colleagues, no doubt with the Duke's connivance. When the Queen persisted in defending her protégés, the King told her to stop meddling in his affairs.

The Spanish minister was very frank in discussing the King and Queen with his English colleague Sir James Gray, who reported (January 15, 1754): 'The King of Naples, he said, is of a very reserved temper; a great master of dissimulation, and has an habitual smile on his face, contracted by a constant attention to conceal his thoughts; has a good understanding and a surprising memory, as his father had; is unread and unlearned, but retains an exact knowledge of all that has passed within his own observation, and is capable of entering into the most minute detail. He is in many things his own Minister, passing several hours every day alone in his cabinet; has too good an opinion of his own judgement; and is so positive and obstinate, that he is seldom induced to alter his resolutions. He has very high notions of his prerogative and his independency, and thinks himself the most absolute monarch in Europe.

'The Queen is haughty, fond of power, has violent and quick passions; and in this, the reverse of the King, that she always discovers by her countenance the impressions things make on her mind. She has a great influence over the King, who is very fond of her, and by her assiduity and complaisance is capable of biasing him, and even sometimes of making him change a resolution he has taken.

'The Duchess of Castropignano is the Queen's favourite, and governs her in many things. She is corrupt, and at present entirely in the French interest. He gave her the worst of characters, and called her the Serpent in the Fable. The King knows and hates her.

'He expressed a very low opinion of the Marquis Fogliani's talents and capacity. His inclinations are French but he has not resolution to adhere to any party, which, he added, was some merit. The last person he mentioned was the French ambassador, who is of a grave and serious turn and moderate parts, constantly attends the King a-hunting; by this means is liked by him more than his predecessor; but Mr Clementi is persuaded this favour is merely personal and that the King retains the same aversion for the French he has ever had.'

Diplomatic relations with the two elder Bourbon dynasties were far from cordial. Though there was a Neapolitan ambassador in Spain, Ferdinand VI did not trouble to send a representative to Naples until 1753, and for seven years France sent no successor to the Marquis de l'Hôpital, who had been recalled in 1744. Charles was annoyed by Ferdinand's indifference to Italian affairs, and he was disgusted when he betrothed his sister Maria Antonia to the son of his arch-enemy Charles Emmanuel of Savoy. The treaty of Aix-la-Chapelle, which Charles refused to ratify, embittered him against France, for it postulated that his younger brother Don Philip should have Naples when Charles became King of Spain, and he was determined that one of his sons should inherit the Two Sicilies. Don Philip, who had married Louis XV's daughter Louise-Elisabeth, considered that Parma was too unimportant for him; and his wife intrigued at Versailles for additional territory. Maria Theresa of Austria had a covetous eye on Parma; Charles Emmanuel wanted Piacenza, and France even proposed that he should get it. Nobody was satisfied. When a Neapolitan messenger announced the birth of Charles's third son to Louis XV, that monarch merely exclaimed: *'Morbleu, morbleu, morbleu!'* They keep on having sons and I have none.' And he turned his back on the messenger without offering the usual gratuity. A commercial treaty with France had long hung fire as a result of all this friction. A French ambassador, the Marquis d'Ossun, was finally sent to Naples in 1752, but although he joined the King's hunting parties he did not achieve much in his official capacity.

The French Foreign Minister d'Argenson, who shared Mazarin's and Richelieu's ideal of an autonomous Italy independent of Austria, an ideal which could be traced back to Henri IV, complained that 'the Italians seem obsessed with the chimerical fear of seeing the King of Sardinia grow too powerful'; but the fear was not chimerical. Whether in alliance or in opposition to the Bourbons, the House of Savoy had always frustrated their plans. In 1740 the Président de Brosses penned an exact appraisal of Charles Emmanuel: 'He is not really strong enough to invade much at a time, but he expands little by little. His father King Victor used to say that Italy was an artichoke which had to be eaten leaf by leaf. His son will follow this maxim as much as he can, and will ally himself successively, regardless of the past, with all the great princes who will ameliorate his condition, always preferring the House of Austria to the Spaniards or ourselves, though he can only enlarge himself at Austria's expense, since the duchy of Milan is the real object of his greed. But in troublous times he will hook something from her, and with patience he may hook everything; whereas if he let a prince of the Spanish branch establish himself in Lombardy, like

Don Carlos or one of his brothers, it would be a power at least equal to his own... which would always serve him as a stumbling-block.' If this was the impression of a dispassionate observer, is it surprising that the Bourbons of Spain and Italy were wary of their Piedmontese rival? A league between Naples and Savoy might have rendered Italy independent, but as the Chinese say, 'you cannot clap hands with one palm'.

Elisabeth Farnese had declared that she would rather give Austria half the peninsula than cede a yard of it to Sardinia. Charles had the same prejudice which Charles Emmanuel's foxy diplomacy did nothing to dispel. Consequently, in spite of lingering mutual suspicions, Neapolitan relations with Austria began to improve. At first it was not easy: many of the nobility were pro-Austrian because they were anti-Bourbon. These welcomed the new Austrian ambassador, Prince Esterhazy, with such perfervid manifestations of joy that the government took umbrage. 'The Court has noted the leading demonstrators,' wrote the Sardinian envoy, prophesying that tears would follow such tactless rejoicings, as silver medals of Maria Theresa had been widely distributed and the ambassador's servants had bragged of their greater military power; they had even spread a rumour that 30,000 Croats would land at Manfredonia. Once more a 'Committee of Distrust' was formed to deal with treasonable activities.

Prince Esterhazy was even richer than his name, and his love of ostentation seems to have been whetted by the Neapolitan climate. He was too flamboyant an individual for a diplomatist. When he was told that the Court did not relish his popularity with the masses, he remarked that it was not his fault if a crowd of *lazzaroni* followed his carriage through the streets with jubilant cries. The government should try to win the people's love instead of organizing 'Committees of Distrust', which were an open insult to Vienna.

Another difficulty arose because the Prince's credentials did not give Charles the title of Majesty. The ambassador was admitted to a private audience, but for a whole year crotchety controversies were exchanged between Naples and Vienna about this delicate point, apart from some tricky questions of ceremonial, such as the procedure during a special audience, the persons who were to accompany the ambassador, the manner of doffing his hat, etc. These were further complicated by the arrival of Princess Esterhazy, since the wives of envoys had not accompanied their husbands heretofore. The

Princess took offence because when she visited the Queen she was admitted by the chief major-domo, but 'received no compliment' before retiring: nobody escorted her to the door. When the Queen's ladies-in-waiting went to call on the ambassadress they were escorted by hussars with torches instead of by pages on their departure, as tit for tat. Then Prince Esterhazy gave a sumptuous banquet for Maria Theresa's birthday, but none of the high Court officials accepted the invitation. Yet none were so fond of a feast. 'Nowhere else in the world, I think,' wrote the Sardinian envoy, 'will you find such greed and gormandizing as among the Neapolitans, the most distinguished of whom did not blush to call out [at a party given for the Prince of Piedmont's anniversary]: "Will there be enough iced refreshments? Will supper be served?" And such questions were asked repeatedly... I should have liked Your Excellency to be present on this occasion, and I doubt if you would have laughed more in wonder or admiration at the spectacle of these Princes and Dukes giving a perfect imitation of the national *lazzaroni* during the pillaging of the dessert, which was treated like the cars of their *Cuccagna.*'

When a Tunisian ship was captured by a Neapolitan galley near the island of Giglio, the Austrian ambassador protested against this aggressive incursion in Tuscan waters. These differences were patched up after 1752, when a Neapolitan *chargé d'affaires* was sent to Tuscany. Barbary pirates continued to interfere with Naples's none too prosperous sea trade, and the marine's chief task was to protect her merchant ships, which were often seized half-way to Palermo. The King appealed in vain to the Pope to contribute a few galleys for their common defence. Relations with the Holy See had improved little since the Concordat of 1741: there were endless disputes over bordering territory as well as ecclesiastical reforms, and there was a violent popular reaction against the Cardinal Archbishop Spinelli's attempt to introduce the Inquisition by stealth in 1746. As in the time of the viceroy Pedro of Toledo, the King was met by a large deputation near the Carmine church. He dismounted from his carriage and asked what had happened. On being informed, he entered the church and, kneeling before the altar, he touched it with his drawn sword and swore as a knight, not as a king, that there would never be an Inquisition in Naples. Charles kept his word, and thanked the deputation for the vigilance and zeal they had shown on this occasion. The archbishop had to renounce his see and leave the capital.

Later on Sir James Gray reported (February 19, 1754): 'Cardinal Spinelli was on Sunday at Caserta, to thank the King for having permitted him to resign the Archbishopric of Naples, in which he is to be succeeded by Monsignor Sersale. The Cardinal was formerly a favourite of His Majesty's, and had a great share in his confidence. He was also esteemed and beloved by the people, but having made some attempts to introduce the Inquisition, he lost the favour of both. Upon his disgrace he retired to Rome about three years ago, where he has continued till now with the hopes of making his peace at Court and keeping his preferments, which he is at last constrained to resign, though he affects to do it as a voluntary act. It is scarcely to be believed how much the aversion to the Inquisition is rooted in the hearts of the Neapolitans, and how vigilant they have ever been in guarding against all the artifices which the Court of Rome has made use of... so that the King's conduct on this occasion... is looked upon as the most popular act of his reign.'

According to tradition, Charles chose to build his largest palace at Caserta, about sixteen miles north of Naples, because it was a safe distance from both Vesuvius and the sea: there was always the danger of eruptions from the former and of hostile raids, like Commodore Martin's, from the latter. But he had had a hunting-lodge there since 1735, and had always been partial to this fertile stretch of level plain lying at the foot of the hills. No doubt it reminded him pleasantly of the Spanish landscape where his father had built the palace of San Ildefonso. Versailles may have also been present in his thoughts, for this was to be the culmination of his building activities, as magnificent in conception as in execution.

Neither Medrano nor Canevari seemed equal to such a task; Sanfelice and Vaccaro were too old. The best architects had gravitated to Rome, where they could be sure of regular employment. Nicola Salvi and Luigi Vanvitelli were the most famous of these, and Charles negotiated through his ambassador for both of them. Just then Salvi was employed on the Trevi fountain, but Vanvitelli was free to accept the King's commission. He had been born in Naples in 1700, the son of Gaspar Van Wittel of Utrecht, a meticulous painter of the Dutch architectural school who had italianized his name and married a Roman; and he had studied under Juvara. Now, at the age of fifty, he had achieved mastery of a superb classical style. His plans for Caserta were ready in 1751; they were presented in the form of sixteen engravings, including not only the palace and grounds but also a map of the new city which was to rise near them and the roads radiating from them. The palace dominates the composition with its immense square pile, like an eighteenth-century version of the Escurial. Charles required winter and summer apartments for himself and the Queen, great halls for public ceremonies, belvederes, galleries, a library, even a court of justice with dependent offices, a church, a seminary, a theatre with rooms for the actors, an astronomical observatory, a royal secretariat, and 136 private apartments besides those for Court retainers.

The first stone of this colossal structure was laid on the King's thirty-sixth birthday, January 20, 1752. Its perimeter was marked by several regiments of infantry and squadrons of cavalry; two cannons were placed with artillerymen at each angle; and a handsome pavilion was raised in the centre of this area. Together with the foundation-stone, the King and Queen placed some gold and silver medals with their portraits and a view of the palace, inscribed *Deliciæ Regis, Felicitas Populi.* The King presented the silver trowel and hammer which he had used during the ceremony to Vanvitelli, who sent them as *ex votos* to Saint Philip Neri in Rome.

The army of workmen engaged on the building was increased by convicts and galley-slaves. It was like a monstrous bee hive where blocks of stone and marble were accumulated instead of honey. Vanvitelli supervised the works until he died in 1773, when the crowning cornice was completed. In dedicating his engravings to the King and Queen, he described them as 'so many truthful mirrors in which your royal grandeur may recognize itself... My own merit was restricted to the execution of the sublime ideas conceived by the magnificence of Your Majesties.'

While making allowance for the conventions of courtly address, it is evident that the architect was exhilarated by his task, which was to rival the greatest monuments of antiquity. Charles was an active collaborator who gave him constant encouragement. His interest in every detail is mentioned by the Sardinian ambassador, who visited Caserta in its second year. 'What do you think of this fine discovery?' the King asked him, noticing that he paid special attention to some small marble columns with unusual colours and markings. 'I have never seen marbles of such beautiful quality. Those little columns seem worthy to adorn tabernacles,' he replied. 'They are merely samples of all the marbles found in the mountains of this kingdom and in Sicily. The best are reserved for the chapel. Only the Verona yellow was lacking, but by chance I found some buried pieces which are fairly large and thick, and if these are cut skilfully I shall have enough to inlay the chapel walls according to the design. The rest will serve for the pillars and ornaments of my palace, the vestibule of which will contain thirty-two columns of a single piece. This is not the only luck I have had in my mountain quarries, since a rich mine of lead has been found and a tolerable quantity of very fine silver... which is being worked into chalices and other small ornaments for my chapel, as I should offer the first fruits to God.' But he also told the ambassador, alluding to the odious treaties his King had signed, that 'he did not count on building for others'.

The palace has been called a megalomaniac construction by some: 'The smaller the monarchy the larger the palace.' But we live in an age antagonistic to palaces. Most contemporaries regarded it as 'one of the noblest edifices of the kind in Europe for magnitude and elevation'. 'The vast dimensions of its apartments,' wrote Henry Swinburne in the 1770's, 'the bold span of their ceilings, the excellence and beauty of the materials employed in building and decorating it, and the strength of the masonry, claim the admiration of all beholders, who must confess it is a dwelling spacious and grand enough to have lodged the ancient masters of the Roman world. It is a pity that its enormous bulk drowns the minuter members of its architecture, and gives too much the idea of a regular monastery, where the wealthy chief of some religious order presides over long dormitories of segregated monks; by the gigantic range, and the number of windows, too great a sameness is produced, the few breaks in the front become imperceptible, and the lines too long and uniform, consequently fatiguing to the eye; the colonnades sink into the walls, and variety is in vain sought for in the prodigious expanse; bolder and greater projections, massive towers, arcades or porticoes, would have shown the parts of this great building to more advantage, and formed those happy contrasts that are so necessary in works of so very large a dimension. Upon a nearer approach, the parts and proportions are better distinguished, and the objection ceases.

'The two principal fronts are seven hundred and eighty-seven feet in length, and contain five stories of thirty-seven windows each. The two other sides are six hundred and sixteen feet long, and consist also of five stories, in each of which are twenty-seven windows. The interior is divided into four courts, and in the centre of the palace is a superb staircase, crowned by a circular hall which affords a communication to every set of apartments. The richest marbles are displayed with profusion, most of them dug out of quarries within the realm.'

The gardens, which have suffered much since the departure of the Bourbons, extend to the north, east and west sides of the palace; on the south side the high road from Naples approaches an oval courtyard enclosed by barracks and stables. On the north the grand parterre terminated in a huge semicircle of groves, originally designed with box scroll-work in rococo patterns, with a vast fountain and four pools in the centre, leading eventually to the grand cascade. The water for this is led by a winding aqueduct, twenty-one miles long, from Monte Taburno, crossing an immense bridge over the Maddaloni valley formed of a triple row of lofty arches; the first row consists of nineteen arches, the second of twenty-seven, and the third of forty-three, a monument altogether Roman in spirit, though the arches of the upper row are the highest. 'Solidity has been more attended to than ornament,' wrote Swinburne, 'the work is plain, but built to withstand the insults of time.' Eventually the water falls some fifty feet into a basin, whence it is conducted by a succession of leaps down the middle of a wooded hill-slope. At the foot of the cascade are marble groups of Diana surrounded by nymphs and Actaeon being turned into a stag, attacked by ferocious hounds.

Other parts of the garden were laid out subsequently in the so-called English style; there are more modest fountains and romantic groves of evergreen oaks, artificial ruins, a spacious fishpond and a more intimate garden surrounding the *Castelluccia*, a miniature fort for Prince Ferdinand's mimic battles, a swan lake, an apple orchard, a classical temple, a bath of Venus, covered walks and greenhouses. But the grand cascade, which can be seen clearly from the palace two miles away, is the axial summit of the garden's glory, the perennially cool and glittering cynosure. This without and the palace staircase within leave abiding impressions of wonder and surprise even on those familiar with Versailles and other great European palaces. The staircase ascends to the upper vestibule, an octagon surrounded by twenty-four pillars of yellow marble. This peristyle is the central trunk, as it were, uniting all the branches of the stupendous whole, distributing space with precise yet prodigal genius.

The usual strictures on Caserta have been answered with sense and sensibility by Joseph Forsyth in 1802. 'The situation of this palace is often condemned as flat,' he wrote, 'but is this a disadvantage? A convent, a Gothic castle, a villa, a hunting-lodge may, like ordinary men, seek distinction from eminence of station; but this august pile, like a true hero, involves all its dignity in itself. It depends on no accessories, nor tricks of the picturesque: it challenges inspection near or remote: it demands an immense plain, and solitude.

'The late king [Charles] sought grandeur here from every dimension. The plan which he prescribed to the architect must have astonished the world. A common elevation, on such a length of front, would present only the idea of barracks. The elevation rose proportioned to the plan, and the result is a palace.

' "But the elevation is also too flat," say the critics; "it wants contrast, life, movement, relief: it should start out into pavilions; it should rise into towers, and break up the immensity of the front". Yet this very immensity was the effect sought; an effect more sublime than all the diversities of aspect, and all the play of *chiaroscuro*. The very flatness which they blame promotes this effect; it amplifies every dimension, it unfolds the general design, at one view, in all its symmetry and expansion.'

V

The Reale Albergo dei Poveri—*Father Rocco— The* Presepe—*A ministerial reshuffle—The rise of Tanucci—The antiquities of Herculaneum—Ferdinando Galiani—Genoa and Corsica—The fatal hypochondria of Ferdinand VI of Spain.*

King Charles's passion for building was not consummated with Caserta. He also wished to build a colossal palace for the poor, and Ferdinando Fuga was commissioned to start work on the Reale Albergo dei Poveri in 1751. The actual building, of which the front is 354 metres long, only represents half the original project, as the work on it was interrupted periodically until 1829. Here vagabonds and helpless orphans, the unemployed and unemployable, were to be housed, fed, educated and, if possible, converted into useful citizens.

The foundation of this enormous hospice was partly inspired by the Dominican Father Rocco, the popular preacher and 'city missionary', one of the most curious Neapolitan characters of the eighteenth century. Born in 1700, he died in 1782; and he spent his long dedicated life among the populace, fulminating against vice, settling petty lawsuits, beating the quarrelsome into peace and fighting sinners with a stout stick or with a heavy crucifix he carried in his belt when his floods of eloquence failed. The *lazzaroni* responded to one who could express himself masterfully in their language, who could thrill their impressionable minds with the images of his own religious ardour, who fearlessly thrust his way into their lowest haunts, startling the taverns and brothels with apocalyptic visions of woe. 'Now then,' he shouted, 'I want a sign of your repentance and good intentions. Those who are well determined lift your arms!' Every arm was duly raised, and Father Rocco remained silent. After gazing long and expressively, first at the crucifix, then at the image of the Madonna before him, he exclaimed: 'Oh my God! would that I now had a sabre to cut off those hands which have offended you with forgery, with usury, with thievery, with homicides, and with sins of the flesh, so that they may no longer commit these evil actions!' And immediately every hand went down and hid itself, and there was a general outburst of sobbing. Tanucci joked with Galiani about the effect of these sermons, 'which made those rabid propagators of the species laugh and set to work more merrily than before'.

Father Rocco was a valuable intermediary between the King and the populace and vice versa. 'The court understands his importance,' wrote Swinburne, 'and has often experienced the good effects of his mediation; though of late years an attention to the plentiful supply of cheap provisions, and a strong garrison, have kept the populace quiet, to a degree unknown in former times, yet particular circumstances may yet render a Neapolitan mob formidable to government. During a late eruption of Vesuvius, the people took offence at the new theatre being more frequented than the churches, and assembled in great numbers to drive the nobility from the opera; they snatched the flambeaux from the footmen, and were proceeding tumultuously to the cathedral to fetch the head of San Gennaro, and oppose its miraculous influence to the threats of the blazing volcano: this would undoubtedly have ended in a very serious sedition if Father Rocco had not stepped forth, and after reproaching them bitterly with the affront they were about to put upon the saint by attending his relics with torches taken from mercenary hands, ordered them all to go home and provide themselves with wax tapers; the crowd dispersed, and proper measures were taken to prevent its gathering again.'

Father Rocco's influence on Charles, and later on his son, led to the foundation of many charitable institutions, of which the Albergo dei Poveri is the most striking. Naples was also indebted to him for the first experiment in lighting the streets. All previous attempts had failed when he suggested setting up holy shrines at every convenient corner, beginning with the darkest and most dangerous; and he soon roused a general competition for supplying the lamps before these shrines with oil. They are kept burning to this day in many a sombre alley, and until 1806 they provided the city's only regular illumination. Father Rocco began a vigorous campaign against gambling, which had become a general epidemic. To persuade the King to support it, he is said to have compiled a list of the noble families ruined by this vice, so that Charles exclaimed in horror: 'Father Rocco, I do not wish to be a king of beggars !'—hence the decree against gambling of November 24, 1753.

Nowhere else has the pious custom of the *presepe*, or Christmas crib, assumed so many delightful forms, and Father Rocco did much to popularize it. He wished to bring the Mystery of the Nativity to the people and make them visualize it. Half his cell was filled with a *presepe*, which he constantly improved with additional figures and effective details. The figures were usually about six inches high carved in sycamore wood. Before Christmas he bustled about the shops of sculptors and artisans, such as still exist in the Vico dei Figurari, to criticize and encourage their work. A realist himself, he persuaded them to avoid the rococo mannerisms of the sculptors then in vogue. He set up a Nativity scene in a grotto near Capodimonte, which the King often stopped to admire on his way to the hunt.

Charles himself designed and modelled the settings for the Christmas crib in the royal palace, dabbling in clay and cutting up cork for the manger, while the Queen and Princesses sewed and embroidered costumes for the figures, each according to scale. The aristocracy and wealthy merchants followed the King's example, so that the *presepe* increased in gorgeousness and variety, and this was the period of its highest artistic development.

The most elaborate consisted of three scenes, the Annunciation, the Nativity and the Tavern (or *diversarium*); occasionally the Massacre of the Innocents was added. The skyborne angel waking the shepherds was more or less conventional, but fancy ran riot in the Tavern scene, where peasants were gathered in cheerful gossip or sang to the guitar, while a rubicund innkeeper prepared a feast to satisfy the most ravenous appetite. Palestine was conceived in terms of the Neapolitan landscape; often Vesuvius erupted boisterously in the background. Hundreds of figures were scattered across the scene; except for the Blessed Virgin, Saint Joseph and the angels, who wore the traditional robes, all were clad in contemporary costume. The Magi wore long cloaks like the knights of San Gennaro. Their retinue were decked in the trappings of Africa and Asia; Mongols and Kaffirs mingled with Circassians and Hindoos; pages, cup-bearers, grooms, guards, slaves were loaded with precious caskets, besides the gold and frankincense and myrrh. The peasants and shepherds wore the festive apparel of Ischia, Procida and other parts of the Two Sicilies. Some were portraits of well-known personalities like Father Rocco; occasionally Pulcinella and characters from the *Commedia dell' Arte* were introduced.

Such famous sculptors as Sammartino, Celebrano and the Bottiglieri brothers devoted much time and skill to this form of art. Some specialized in domestic animals; others in fish, fruit, vegetables and groceries. Exuberance and profusion flourish; most of these tableaux interpret the jovial, sensuous, expansive aspects of the Neapolitan temperament. The artisans shared the faith of the simple shepherds.

The King was at one with his people in exalting the family cult by this outward symbol of the sacred mystery. As long as the Bourbon dynasty ruled Naples, the *presepe* was the centre of Christmas rejoicings. The whole Court accompanied the King and Queen from church to church to visit the Nativity scenes which were their special pride. Soft organ music and the light of candles helped to foster the illusion of reality. The crib in the Jesuit Church of Gesù Nuovo always attracted a large crowd, as its Babe was said to have spoken to a Moorish slave and converted him. A hymn commemorated the miracle: 'The Infant Jesus in the manger speaketh to a slave.' Outside in the streets, Calabrian bagpipers, like the Biblical shepherds, wailed poignant melodies. In private houses the Babe was usually removed from the manger before Christmas Eve. Then a party would be given, enlivened with music and impromptu poems until midnight, when a priest recited prayers, after which the Babe was consigned to the youngest girl in the family, who restored it to the crib.

'In many houses a room, in some a whole suite of apartments, in others a terrace upon the house-top, is dedicated to this very uncommon show,' wrote Mrs Piozzi. 'One wonders, and cries out it is certainly but a baby-house at best; yet, managed by people whose heads, naturally turned towards architecture and design, give them power thus to defy a traveller not to feel delighted with the general effect; while if every single figure is not capitally executed and nicely expressed beside, the proprietor is truly miserable, and will cut a new cow, or vary the horse's attitude, against next Christmas, *coûte que coûte*. And perhaps I should not have said so much about the matter if there had not been shown me within this last week presepios which have cost their possessors fifteen hundred or two thousand English pounds; and rather than relinquish or sell them, many families have gone to ruin. I have wrote the sums down in letters not figures, for fear of the possibility of a mistake. One of these playthings had the journey of the three kings represented in it, and the presents were all of real gold and silver finely worked; nothing could be better or more livelily finished.

'"But, sir," said I, "why do you dress up one of the wise men with a turban and crescent, six hundred years before the birth of Mahomet, who first put that mark in the forehead of his followers? The eastern magi were not Turks; this is a breach of costume." My gentleman paused, and thanked me; said he would inquire if there was nothing heretical in the objection; and if all was right, it should be changed next year without fail.'

Charles became so addicted to this Neapolitan custom that he introduced it into Spain, whence he continued to order figures of shepherds and other Nativity properties from Naples. Besides this hobby, the porcelain factory he had started at Capodimonte in 1743 was winning a reputation. Though the secrets of the Saxon china were jealously guarded—'Secret to Death' was written over the factory doors at Meissen—King Augustus had permitted a few of his craftsmen to go to Naples on his daughter's account, and these helped to develop the Capodimonte ware, which was to assimilate many local characteristics like the *presepi*. A white earth like kaolin was discovered in Calabria, and talent was not lacking to infuse it with the warmth and colour of Naples. Soon those precious groups of figures and table decorations were produced which have outlasted more solid creations; and many reflect the masks and merrymakings of the people, their dances and carnival antics. They can still be seen in the palace of Capodimonte, above all the *Chinoiserie* boudoir, whose mirrors wreathed with flowers and pseudo-Oriental conceits are as delicious in their harmony and detail as any in Saxony.

The porcelain factory was one of the King's most expensive luxuries, and it was only after much trial-and-error that the right composition of paste was found. He could not resist a gentle dig at the King of Sardinia when he discussed the subject with the Sardinian envoy. He said he was not yet satisfied with the whiteness of his porcelain, since he could not find a material capable of resisting the proper degree of heat for more than forty-eight hours, whereas the Saxons had one which could resist it for a whole week. The Sardinian envoy suggested that it would be only too easy for the King to obtain the secret as well as the material, referring to his father-in-

–law. 'Oh, as to that,' replied Charles, 'no, I shall do nothing. I shall not even attempt it, though some have advised me to do so. Everybody should keep what he has, and should not demand or grab what belongs to others. I shall always be content with my own possessions.' All the same, an attempt to buy the secret was made, and his agents tried to entice some Viennese craftsmen who had been engaged by Francis of Lorraine. When Charles left for Spain, he removed all his workmen and dismantled the Capodimonte factory.

The Prime Minister Fogliani had been so inept that it was easy for the Queen's clique to get rid of him. His failure to make the slightest impression on the negotiators of the treaty of Aix-la-Chapelle and the League of Aranjuez hastened his downfall. In June 1755 he was dismissed, and the post of Prime Minister was abolished. He was appointed Viceroy of Sicily as a consolation. From now on the King decided to rule through the secretaries of departments. He realized that a legal expert, supported by an able financier, would suit his purposes best. The administration was divided between Tanucci, who was put in charge of Foreign Affairs as well as the department of Justice and the Royal Household; Squillace, Secretary of Finance, War and the Marine; and Brancone, who was oddly put in charge of theatres as well as ecclesiastical affairs.

Tanucci soon came so much to the fore as to make his colleagues seem dummies. His coarse features and blunt manners produced a disagreeable impression, but even those who disliked him were forced to admit that he was honest and industrious. Croce, who has written a sympathetic study of the man, depicts him as a hypochondriac who took refuge in strenuous toil as Charles took refuge in strenuous exercise. Perhaps their inherent melancholy made the King and his minister congenial.

From Tanucci's correspondence, some of which has been published, a fussy old don emerges. He wrote in an involved pedantic style, stiffening his paragraphs with classical quotations. Often he gazed back wistfully to the University of Pisa. But his professions of weariness with the thankless burdens of office should be taken with a pinch of salt. 'My father,' he wrote, 'used to argue with his brother about my career, whether I should apply myself to study or farming. "Farming," said my father; study, said my uncle, whose counsel unfortunately prevailed, since I did not derive that wisdom from study which I might have gleaned from country life... whereas in study I found that wind which swells according to Saint Paul, and which transported me tempestuously to Court, in other words to the tragi-comedy and confusion of nature.'

Croce remarked that he was truly Tuscan in his hatred of the abstract and love of the concrete. His conception of government was domestic and paternal, and he had no sympathy for parliamentary or democratic systems. He regarded sovereigns as different from other mortals. While he admired his own King and Frederick II of Prussia, 'two great and different originals', he did not think that a monarch need be an extraordinary man or do extraordinary things. 'The sovereign,' he wrote, 'should always be cool and collected, which he cannot be when he wants to see and do everything himself. Public affairs are like a woman or a kitchen; both nauseate, if you see them being cleaned up and prepared. The woman should be seen dressed, the table laid.' Princes should enjoy the leisure of the gods without any of their fatigue; excess of zeal should be avoided, and their glory should be the practice of virtue. To his friend Viviani, who had entertained the Grand Duke of Tuscany at dinner, he wrote: 'Sovereigns are too mighty to associate with poor little private individuals with mutual pleasure. Pleasure lies in the horizontal: it is uncomfortable having always to lift one's head and eyes in conversation with a sovereign. They differ too much from ourselves, and that is all as it should be. In a tolerable joke the King of Prussia remarked that he loved virtue, but his sovereignty prevented him from practising it. Your historian Segni wrote a eulogy of Cosimo I, attributing several virtues to him which we hold in good repute. Cosimo having read it remarked to Segni: "Bernardo, that is what I should be if I were a private citizen; but with these virtues of yours I should make a paltry prince".' 'To the eyes and minds of sovereigns,' he wrote again, 'we private individuals are as flies, butterflies, and sometimes food. We are far more valued by God, who came down to live and die in the world for us, than we are by sovereigns.'

These quotations show that Tanucci's opinions were in harmony with his master's, though Charles wanted to see and do everything himself as he grew older. Steeped in the classics, which 'continually counselled, comforted and upheld him' during his career, the ex-professor fully realized the importance of the recent discoveries at Herculaneum.

The King had not been fortunate with Monsignor Baiardi,

whom Fogliani had foisted upon him to compile a catalogue of the antiquities. Baiardi was Fogliani's cousin, and a caricature of the most flatulent pedantry of the age. He could not approach the excavations on account of his asthma, so instead of producing a catalogue he compiled an endless series of introductory volumes called *Prodromi*, laboriously describing the labours of Hercules and the mythical origin of Herculaneum. Nor would he allow others to poach on what he considered his exclusive preserve. When Venuti and Gori published their account in 1748, he got it banned by his cousin the Prime Minister. By 1752 he had produced five *Prodromi* of 500 pages each, packed with quaint Hebrew, Arabic and Greek quotations; the only reference to the discoveries was in the preface. As Marchese Caracciolo commented: 'So far Monsignor Baiardi has delighted to bury the antique world of Herculaneum beneath a much denser shroud than that spread over it by the lava.'

Eventually the long-suffering King insisted on having his catalogue, and the pedant reluctantly complied. This appeared in 1755, and its chief merit was its handsome production. Baiardi retired to Rome the same year when his cousin fell from power. Owing to his ineptitude, the Florentines were saying that Herculaneum was just a Neapolitan hoax. The Tuscan Tanucci, who took a possessive pride in his adopted country, was put on his mettle. He proposed that future publications of the antiquities should be entrusted to a body of learned Neapolitans, and on the strength of his advice the Royal Herculanean Academy was founded in 1755. The fifteen members met once a fortnight in Tanucci's office for general discussion; and the first folio of *The Antiquities of Herculaneum* was issued two years later. This book, which contained engravings of the most important paintings and cost the King 12,000 ducats, was to influence taste from St Petersburg to Edinburgh for the next half-century. Furniture and interior decoration, costume and jewellery; hardly any art or craft was not affected by this publication. Others followed; altogether nine volumes illustrating the discoveries left the royal printing press, and these were eagerly sought for by kings and collectors abroad. The King and Tanucci supervised their production, and both were highly sensitive to criticism. When Winckelmann, who visited the jealously guarded museum of Portici in 1758, wrote his famous *Letter* ridiculing the excavators and denouncing their clumsy methods, Tanucci took it as a personal insult; and he demanded a withdrawal and amends from Baretti, who imitated Winckelmann in the *Frusta letteraria*. As archaeology was in its infancy, it was easy for others to scoff, but, considering their clumsiness, the excavators had not done too badly.

The youngest and liveliest member of the Herculanean Academy was Ferdinando Galiani, nephew of the King's first chaplain, the Archbishop of Taranto. Born in 1728, the precocious Abbé had won local celebrity with a treatise 'On Money' (*Della Moneta*), published in 1750, which is still readable though it might be described as a paean to good King Charles in terms of political economy, then an exciting new science only recently introduced to the university curriculum. The treatise concludes: 'I am pained and afflicted, however, that while the kingdoms of Naples and Sicily rise again… the rest of Italy wanes from day to day, and visibly declines.' For Galiani, who came to be regarded as a Parisian, was intrinsically Neapolitan. 'The most Parisian wit that France has had', wrote the Goncourt brothers, 'is the French wit of foreigners, of Galiani, the Prince de Ligne, and Henri Heine.'

Long before his treatise 'On Money', he had set Naples laughing with a book of parodies. His elder brother was to have addressed a pompous academy on the Immaculate Conception, but he was unable to appear at the last moment and begged Ferdinando to replace him. Galiani was four and a half feet high and he looked even younger than his age: so that when he presented himself the president of the academy, the lawyer Don Antonio Sergio, refused to let him address so dignified a gathering. Since one of the functions of this society was to publish panegyrics on the distinguished dead, Galiani devised an ingenious revenge. Assisted by a friend, he composed several panegyrics on the public executioner, who had died recently. The collection was entitled 'Divers Compositions on the Decease of Domenico Jannacone, executioner to the High Court of the Vicaria, compiled and published by Don Antonio Sergio, Neapolitan advocate, dedicated by an Arcadian Shepherd to the illustrious Feet-puller, faithful companion of the Deceased'. (The duty of the feet-puller—*tira-piedi*—was to cling to the feet of the hanged while the executioner 'climbed up from behind and seated himself firmly, like the Old Man of the Sea, upon their shoulders, where he was swayed to and fro by the victim's convulsions till at last the vertebrae were broken', as Norman Douglas described it.) Each item was in the style of one of the academicians; the production was a replica of the academy's publications, and it was widely distributed as such. There was a shrill outcry from the victims, who sent a complaint to the King. Galiani went straight to Tanucci, and told him the whole story. Tanucci was charmed and amused by the young man's wit; but to placate the outraged members he condemned Galiani and his collaborator to ten days' spiritual exercises in a monastery near Naples.

Even Pope Benedict XIV wanted to hear about this literary prank. 'Since I asked no favours of him,' wrote Galiani to his uncle, 'we remain the best of friends.' In due course he had taken holy orders and received various benefices from the King. As well as being a polished Latinist, he was an able political economist, geologist and expert on numismatics. He formed a collection of curious stones from Vesuvius, which he sent to the Pope with a scholarly dissertation and the touching request: '*Beatissime Pater, fac ut lapides isti panes fiant*' ('Most Holy Father, let these stones be turned into bread'). And the appreciative Pontiff added another lucrative benefice to those Galiani had received from the King. After the death of Benedict XIV, Galiani wrote the funeral oration which he considered his best composition; Diderot described it as '*un morceau plein d'éloquence et de nerf*'.

He had a genius for deciphering obscure inscriptions and for composing clear ones. In later years Grimm was to write: 'I only met one man who really knew Latin in Paris, and he was an Italian, the Abbé Galiani. You could pound the whole Academy of Inscriptions in a mortar sooner than make it compose an inscription comparable with those of the Abbé.' His wit enlivened the Herculanean Academy and put the quarrelsome members in a better temper.

Among his humorous productions was a treatise on giants, inspired by the appearance of an extraordinarily tall young Irishman named Cornelius Magrath, and a serio-comic essay proposing to draw lots for *cicisbei*, the fashionable gigolos of the period, on New Year's Day. But his expenditure outstripped his income owing to his collection of rare coins, antiques and editions of the classics. Tanucci kept a fatherly eye on him, however, and at the age of thirty Galiani was appointed secretary to the Neapolitan Embassy in Paris. The post was apparently modest, but he was secretly instructed to do the ambassador's work without rousing his suspicions. For the Count of Cantillana was no more than a figurehead, and since relations with France were delicate Tanucci required an envoy he could trust to carry out his policy.

Galiani aspired to become ambassador, and he left in a cheerful mood. The next ten years were the most brilliant of his life. His intellectual vivacity, his Neapolitan gifts of mimicry and gesticulation, his blend of scholarship and pungent wit, were to endear him to the leading *salons* of the French capital, which was then, in his own phrase, 'the café of Europe'. It was by conversation rather than by literature that the Encyclopaedists launched their ideas, and it was in conversation that Galiani glittered. His *mots* were repeated and his acquaintance was eagerly sought.

His friendship with Mme d'Épinay resulted in a correspondence thanks to which we may breathe the air of the eighteenth century as naturally as our own. 'The letters of Galiani', wrote the Goncourts, 'are just what the man was; they were written with a simplicity of apt expression which we have lost. Their great charm is that they are letters pure and simple... One is conscious neither of effort nor pretension, yet they aim at and capture everything, men and systems; they have rods for monarchs as well as for the Encyclopaedists... The Abbé goes from one subject to another, always daring, always thoughtful, and he thinks aloud, sometimes bursting into flashes of lightning, into revelations of the future.' These will outlive the writings which established his fame among his contemporaries.

Tanucci's letters were turgid in comparison: most of them oozed pessimism, fatigue and disgust. He hated the Roman Curia, the Jesuits and the Jansenists, 'equally lying, slandering and seditious', the House of Savoy, the French, and especially Voltaire, whose works he caused to be banned under penalty of five years' hard labour. 'If only Voltaire had never been printed!' he exclaimed, whereas the more tolerant Pope Benedict XIV had graciously accepted the dedication of Voltaire's *Mahomet*. As for women, he was constantly inveighing against them, 'machines denied to virtue and prone to vice'. 'The nations differ because of their males,' he wrote, 'but the females of every country are alike.'

His antipathies exceeded his sympathies, which accounted for his sensible choice of collaborators. More intelligent Neapolitans were drawn into the administration and these began to form a cultural *élite*, very different from the Spanish courtiers who had come over with Charles. Besides Galiani there was Marchese Domenico Caracciolo, whom Tanucci sent as envoy to Turin and later to London and Paris. 'You say that Caracciolo is my henchman,' he wrote. 'I have always served the King alone, and I have never been *servus servorum*. Caracciolo has derived some benefits from me, such as his embassy in France; but my chief object has not been the welfare of Caracciolo, but the service of the King, hence Caracciolo owes me nothing.'

Tanucci was determined not to let Naples be dragged into the Seven Years War. He dreaded the ambitions of Piedmont, nominally Sardinia, the only other kingdom in the peninsula, and feared that 'the Prussian example might seduce the Italian Frederick, whose power had increased by usurping his neighbours' land'. Charles Emmanuel coveted Piacenza, and seemed to have designs on Corsica. Caracciolo wrote that he was greatly impressed with the fine, well-disciplined troops he saw in Turin: 'and what I consider to their advantage, this sovereign's army is composed of natives who form the backbone and major part of it, and is packed with the nobility and the most florid youth of the country, whose constitution has become entirely military, whence proceeds the chief source of the real strength and power of a State.' Words unpleasing to the peaceful Tanucci's ears.

Relations with Genoa were strained by Genoese suspicions that the Corsican rebels were receiving support from Naples. The Genoese government begged Charles to prevent this, and he agreed. But the revolt continued, and when Gianpietro Gaffori, the commander of the rebels, was assassinated in 1755, the Corsicans sent for Pasquale Paoli, the son of an exiled leader, to succeed him. Paoli was an officer in the Neapolitan army; he applied for six months' leave, and as soon as it was granted he sailed to Corsica.

The Genoese urged Tanucci to recall him, and their written protests were passed on to Squillace, the Secretary for War, who promised to order Paoli back to his regiment. But Paoli had become a general in the meantime; he was to rule Corsica for the next fourteen years. Further complaints followed. Squillace answered that 'the King has decided that unless Pasquale de Paoli presents himself here within fifteen days he shall be dismissed the service'. Nothing more could be done about it in Naples, though Genoa continued to protest that Paoli was being assisted by his Neapolitan friends.

Tanucci's fears that Sardinia would grab Corsica were not allayed by Caracciolo, who wrote: 'It does not seem probable that this Court is thinking of Corsica, because it has not yet taken the first step to establish a foothold on the coast and open up trade with the country, which is the main object.' So anxious was Tanucci to avoid any pretext for a quarrel that he removed the Neapolitan envoy from London because he had been too outspokenly pro-Austrian; and when Maria Theresa presented a diamond aigrette to Marchesa De Maio, the wife of the Neapolitan ambassador in Vienna, Tanucci rebuked him for letting her accept it, since it might be construed as a sign of partiality. Another *Giunta d'Inconfidenza* was organized.

William Pitt proposed the formation of an Italian league to drive the Austrians from Italy, but nobody could induce Charles to co-operate with Sardinia. The far-sighted Caracciolo deplored this, and wrote from Turin: 'This situation of Italian affairs is not happy, but it is aggravated by the circumstance that the King of Naples and the King of Sardinia, who have greater strength than all the others, if united in some manner could oppose the designs of their neighbours and defend themselves against disturbers of the peace, but they happen to be distant and separated by so much territory and perhaps their respective systems are too dissimilar.'

Sardinia was placed in a quandary by the second Treaty of Versailles (1757) between the Hapsburgs and the Bourbons; neither Austria nor France courted Charles Emmanuel as before, and he was cut off geographically from the opposing league of England and Prussia. But he was determined to get Piacenza, regardless of its present owner, Don Philip, as soon as Charles succeeded to Spain. That prospect seemed to be hastened by the death of Queen Maria Barbara on August 27, 1758, when the too-uxorious Ferdinand VI, always liable to fits of depression, gave way to hopeless melancholy.

Ferdinand, being without issue, made a will declaring Charles his universal heir, and shut himself up in the castle of Villaviciosa about five miles from Madrid. Here he would either prowl up and down his room like a caged animal or sit motionless for eighteen hours on end. Not even the roulades of Farinelli, which had soothed him for so many years, could distract him from his misery. With maniacal obstinacy he refused to be shaved or to change his clothes; he would alternately starve and stuff himself for months together. The Spanish Minister of Foreign Affairs, Richard Wall, kept Charles informed of all the gruesome details of Ferdinand's protracted agony. Consequently the state of the King of Spain's health was a burning topic in Naples. Sir James Gray reported in

October 1758: 'The Council here, I am told, are divided in opinion about measures expedient to be taken in these circumstances. Some of them think it absolutely necessary that His Sicilian Majesty should go immediately to Spain, but others look upon this as a hazardous step, and that the King ought not to leave these kingdoms till his presence in Spain is formally requested. As far as I can penetrate, His Sicilian Majesty inclines to adhere to the last opinion, and which to the best of my judgement, seems most conformable to His Majesty's temper and way of thinking.'

VI

An architectural transformation—Reforms—Genovesi—The Prince of San Severo—Death of Ferdinand VI of Spain and succession of Charles III—Exclusion of the imbecile Heir Apparent—Ferdinand becomes Heir to the Two Sicilies—A treaty with Austria—Charles abdicates and embarks for Spain—Death of Queen Maria Amalia.

The King's passion for building proved to be contagious. All the wealthier nobles had begun to enlarge and embellish their palaces. Between Portici and Torre del Greco many new mansions sprang up in harmony with the landscape. Unwearied by his labours at Caserta, Vanvitelli seemed to find them a stimulus to greater activity, and his designs, advice and criticism were in constant demand. New bridges, city gates, church altars, military defence works—he switched from one to another with astonishing versatility. In Naples he built the noble façade and staircase of Palazzo Calabritto, the magnificent hemicycle of the *Foro Carolino*, now in Piazza Dante, the serene and spacious convent of San Marcellino with its surprising sunken courtyard and garden, flanked by a classical façade; Villa Campolieto at Resina, perhaps the most poetical of all his inventions, true 'frozen music', with its peristyle against the background of green orchard and blue sea. But his activities were not confined to Naples: he carried out other projects at Milan, Brescia and Cesena; he was also consulted by the Pope and the Republic of Genoa.

In twenty-five years Charles had so transformed Naples that it had become one of the finest capitals in Europe. The population had been 270,000 on his arrival; by the census of 1742 it numbered 300,000. The extravagance of his Court, which spent three times as much as that of Turin, had not been wasteful. The state revenue was almost doubled, and taxation had been steadily diminished, in spite of the barons and lawyers who tried to cling to old abuses. Many of Charles's best efforts had been thwarted by the obstinate conservatism of his subjects. It was the delegates of the people, the *eletti*, who had insisted on abolishing the Magistracy for Commerce, which he had specially founded to revive home industry and stimulate foreign trade. Though he had encouraged the Jews to settle in Naples, bigoted friars and jealous merchants had excited the populace against them. The Jesuit Father Pepe had assured Charles that he would not have a son so long as they remained, and he had yielded to popular clamour. Many a promising seed had fallen on barren ground. Reforms that seem simple and easy to later generations were impracticable under prevailing conditions. Twenty-five years are a moment in the history of a kingdom. But this had been a creative moment, a wonderful efflorescence, even if some petals were scattered and others blighted. Charles had brought with him a salutary breeze of optimism, an intellectual freedom which was luminous in comparison with other Italian states. In Piedmont, as a diplomatist wrote, 'to think is a twitch, to write is almost ridiculous'. The most talented members of the Neapolitan nobility were thinkers and writers who accepted posts in the government and the diplomatic service.

Some of the deepest scholars were among the clergy; the reform of the university, now installed in the Palazzo degli Studi, was chiefly due to Monsignor Celestino Galiani, the famous Abbé's uncle. Superfluous chairs of jurisprudence and scholastic theology were suppressed, and more modern and practical subjects were introduced to the curriculum, such as experimental physics, astronomy, botany, chemistry and political economy The Abbé Antonio Genovesi was the first to lecture at a European university on political economy (in 1755), and in Italian instead of Latin, attracting hundreds of pupils, who spread his doctrines. Under a despotism these would have been forbidden, for he persistently fought civil privileges, economic monopolies and intellectual prejudice. He taught that the supreme duty of the state was to educate the people; science should permeate every class and be applied to public welfare; the nobles should turn to useful activities and become 'masters and fathers' of the people as in Tuscany and in England. He stressed the reform of agriculture and the redistribution of property. A socialist would find much to approve in his lectures, the tone of which was often revolutionary. 'Those who do not know us,' he wrote, 'would not believe that the conditions of property among us are such that, if all the families of the kingdom were divided into sixty portions, only one would be rich and the other fifty-nine would not have enough ground to bury themselves.' He compared the people to savages, who could hardly be considered Christians except that they were baptized. We must make allowance for the rhetoric without which he could not have captured the attention of a Neapolitan audience in the eighteenth century, or even, perhaps, today. But it is significant of the new spirit of liberalism under Charles that Genovesi kept his chair at the university for sixteen years. Croce described him as an evangelist of reason.

He laid down no special system, but he promoted a spirit of philosophical inquiry which extended to other branches of knowledge. Giovanni Battista Vico had been his master, whose teachings he was one of the first to interpret and popularize. But it is doubtful if the solitary Vico was understood by his contemporaries, though many of them borrowed opinions and theories from his *Scienza nuova*. Vico, who had lived in relative obscurity, stood far in advance of his age. Indeed it is remarkable that he should have been able to publish so many far from remunerative books whose importance could scarcely have been guessed. His views were to influence Herder and Turgot, Comte and Schelling.

Genovesi also lectured on Montesquieu and d'Alembert and other contemporary philosophers, and had a number of foreign books translated. His variety of knowledge, the novelty of his subject matter and his vivid manner of explaining it drew large audiences, until he wore himself out with overwork and was forced to stop teaching. 'My lessons have given birth to a great movement,' he wrote, 'and all classes are asking for books on economy, the arts, and agriculture, and this is a good beginning.'

It was as a teacher of political economy that he left his deepest mark. In founding this chair at the university, Intieri had imposed one condition—that Genovesi was to hold it during his lifetime. Intieri's confidence in him was amply justified by his *Lezioni di Commercio, o sia d'Economia Civile*, wherein he expounded free trade and the laws that govern prices. Galiani was another champion of free trade, but he was then at the embassy in Paris, and his essay on free trade in corn was written in French. We hear more of him after his return to Naples during Ferdinand's reign, and of that great legal reformer Gaetano Filangieri, who owed much to Genovesi's inspiration.

Francesco Serao, who lectured on medicine, was another light of the university. His account of an eruption of Vesuvius, printed in

1738, was one of the first scientific books on the subject; and his treatises on the tarantula of Puglia and other zoological subjects were widely read at the time. Alessio Mazzocchi was the most learned of Neapolitan philologists, and he refused a bishopric in order to devote himself to his favourite branch of study.

Outside the university, Raimondo di Sangro, the Prince of San Severo, better known as a patron of the arts, was a versatile scientist to whom several discoveries and inventions were attributed. A German critic has dismissed him as 'a Neapolitan charlatan', perhaps because he failed to appreciate his blend of recondite fantasy and showmanship. His family chapel, for which he commissioned the statues, remains his most famous monument. To some, these marble groups seem precursors of the worst perpetrations in Carrara to commemorate a loved one in a popular cemetery. But none can deny their hallucinating technical skill, and they will ever appeal to those who cherish realism, though in this case it is oddly mingled with eighteenth-century rococo.

Corradini's figure of 'Modesty', so immodestly revealing her fleshiness under a too-clinging veil, seems to betray a latent cynicism; Queirolo's 'Undeception' (*Il Disinganno*) represents a weary-looking man who, with the aid of a hovering cherub, breaks out of the net in which he has been caught like a great white fish, a symbol obvious to the simplest; Sammartino's 'Dead Christ' lies under a transparent shroud, the hideous crown of thorns beside Him; another 'Dead Christ' by Celebrano seems to be melting like tallow over the altar; and all these effects are gruesomely disturbing.

How did they strike near contemporaries? 'The art with which the sculptor has surmounted the difficulty of representing human bodies wrapped up in cloths or entangled in the meshes of a net is truly wonderful,' wrote Henry Swinburne, 'but the piece of statuary which appeared in my eyes to have the most real merit, is a Christ in the shroud, by Sammartino, a living Neapolitan artist; undoubtedly a fine performance.' The Prince of San Severo's personality is reflected in this oratory, which kindles our curiosity about the bizarre speculations seething in his brain.

Among his inventions described by the French astronomer Lalande in 1765 were: successful new methods of colouring glass and marble; a solid stucco or cement, much harder than that used for paving Neapolitan terraces, guaranteed against cracks and crevices; a method of tinting precious stones, especially amethysts, and of brightening those that were pale and dull; a white porcelain which he polished with a wheel; paper resembling that manufactured in China; a textile refined from coarse oakum and hemp, which resembled fine white silk; a waterproof coat for the King when he went hunting; a stuff which was woollen on one side and silken on the other; and an ingenious and simple method of plating kitchen utensils.

Other more unusual discoveries which the Prince mentioned to Lalande were: 'a natural palingenesy of vegetables and animals [one wonders which], especially with ashes of fennel; wood and coal which produce no ashes after burning, and are so slowly consumed that after long exposure to the violence of fire they only split and break up; a sort of paper for artillery cartridges which does not catch fire and leaves no sparks, but is promptly carbonized; a lamp which he assured me is inextinguishable and perpetual: his letters on the subject to Abbé Nollet [who discovered endosmosis and was a pioneer of electricity] were printed in 1753'.

What damned him chiefly in the eyes of the bigots was that he attempted to reproduce the miracle of San Gennaro. He designed a monstrance or reliquary similar to that containing the saint's blood, with phials of the same shape, filled with a mixture of gold, mercury and cinnabar, whose colour resembled coagulated blood. To make this fluid, there was a supply of running mercury in the hollow rim, with a valve which opened to let the mercury enter the phials when the reliquary was turned about. The Prince used to entertain his guests with such conjuring tricks.

A hydraulic machine which could be used for extinguishing fires and watering fields was another of his inventions. He compiled a 'military vocabulary' whose sixth volume had reached the letter O in 1741, but this was discontinued; and a *Manual of Military Exercises*, which was said to have been praised by Frederick the Great of Prussia and introduced into the French army by the Maréchal de Saxe. The glow of his ovens, the grinding of wheels and the groaning of his printing press helped to foster his reputation as one in league with the devil. He printed his own writings on silk as well as paper and in various colours, and when the King warmly congratulated him on one of these, the *Lettera apologetica* (1750), the Prince begged his sovereign to accept his printing machines and equipment as a gift. This was the origin of the royal press, installed on the ground floor of the royal palace.

Naples could also boast of a coterie of philosophical and scientific ladies, one of whom, Giuseppa Eleonora Barba-Picciola, published a translation of Descartes, and another, Maria-Angiola Ardinghelli, kept up a learned correspondence with the Abbé Nollet on the subject of electricity. The Prince of Tarsia opened his fine private library to the public, and Giovanni Carafa, Prince of Noja, founded a museum of antiquities and coins, so there was no lack of public-spirited Mæcenases. But the university was the natural centre of intellectual movements, and these stemmed from Genovesi, who was 'the soul of all that was great and honourable in the academic world'.

He appreciated what Charles had done for Naples, and his gratitude was without courtly adulation. 'We, too, are beginning to have a fatherland,' he wrote in 1754, 'and to understand what an advantage it is for the whole nation to have a prince of our own. Let us take our national honour close to heart. Foreigners realize and say clearly what we ought to do, if we had better heads. Our august sovereign does as much as he can to rouse us. In 1740 he concluded a treaty of peace and navigation in our favour with the Ottoman Porte; recently he has concluded another with the Dutch; now he is negotiating one with the English; he is increasing the marine to repress the audacity of the Africans; he has supported the foundation of a chair of commerce. What more do we need? I know what we want, but unless we wake up, we shall never obtain it.' Genovesi's constant refrain was: 'We must do it ourselves.'

Little or nothing had been done under Austrian rule, whereas Charles had created the conditions favourable for reform, and paved the way for a stable government. He was now in the prime of life; the most virtuous of contemporary sovereigns. His only fault was that he gave too much time to hunting, but this could not harm his subjects, who dreaded the prospect of his departure.

The King of Spain had fallen into a state of complete lunacy. His fits of rage were increasingly violent; he attacked his servants; he tried to hang himself with sheets and strangle himself with napkins, and after blood-curdling screams and contortions he collapsed, torpid and inert. Accounts of his medical treatment—a 'light and fortifying regime' of emollients, lenitives, asses' milk, quinine, white decoction of Sydenham, hartshorn jelly with fresh vipers, and occasional cordials—were sent to Naples, and the opinions of Neapolitan doctors were consulted. In his rare, lucid intervals he would only discuss his illness; no other subject interested him.

As he lingered on in this pitiful plight, there were various intrigues to make Don Philip, Duke of Parma, his successor. By the Treaty of Aix-la-Chapelle, from which Charles had abstained, Don Philip was to succeed to the Two Sicilies, and his duchies of Parma, Piacenza and Guastalla were to be shared between Austria and Sardinia. But it suited Austria to conciliate the heir to Spain and the Indies, and in the fourth Treaty of Versailles (1758) Austria renounced its claim on Parma and Guastalla. Charles Emmanuel, however, continued to cry out for Piacenza.

Louis XV was in a dilemma. He had foolishly guaranteed Charles Emmanuel's claim, yet he did not wish his daughter and son-in-law, Philip, to lose half their territory. And Charles had no intention of letting his younger brother inherit the Two Sicilies. Nobody could trust Sardinia, least of all Charles. 'It seems to me useless,' wrote his envoy Caracciolo to Tanucci from Turin, 'to recommend me to cultivate peaceful sentiments at this Court; it has been a sheer waste of effort. These gentlemen have ambition rooted in their bones, and they will not rest until they find an opportunity to improve their own interests.' Charles massed troops along his frontiers. It looked as if war could not be averted, but Louis XV made strenuous efforts to reach a compromise. Eventually Charles Emmanuel was persuaded to accept financial compensation.

As the King of Spain's death drew near, it is said that in a moment of lucidity he called for a sergeant-major of his bodyguard to whom he was particularly attached. On being told that the man was in church, praying for the health of His Majesty, he replied: 'My health? Say rather for the happy journey of my brother Charles.' He expired on August 10, 1759, and the Queen Dowager, Elisabeth Farnese, became temporary Regent.

The news reached Naples on August 22, and was broken to the King 'with exquisite delicacy' by his devoted Losada. Since the two crowns were never to be united, he assumed the title of Charles III of Spain, and until the succession was settled, Lord of the Two Sicilies. The deepest mourning was observed in Naples. In spite of Richard Wall's despatches, Charles had never discussed his half-brother's illness. Though he must have been prepared for the news of his death, he fainted and remained speechless all the rest of the day. His grief surprised those who had been deceived by his apparent cheerfulness; the cloven hoof of constitutional melancholy betrayed itself as soon as it could find no outlet in hunting. For nine days he never left his rooms, to which very few were admitted.

The declaration of his successor to the Two Sicilies was the last and most painful duty of an otherwise happy reign. Charles had to appoint a committee of the highest officials and magistrates, supported by six physicians, to examine the mental state of his eldest son and pronounce on his capacity to govern. The Prince was kept under close observation for two weeks, and the committee's verdict was that his complete imbecility should exclude him from the succession. Thus the second Prince, Charles, became heir to Spain, and the third Prince, Ferdinand, to Naples. Both were impatient to hear what had been planned for them, and plied their tutors with embarrassing questions. When all was settled, each prince was perfectly satisfied with his share. 'I am destined to rule the largest dominions in the two worlds,' said the Prince of the Asturias. 'Yes,' said the King of Naples, 'perhaps you will rule one day, but I am a King already.'

The succession of Charles III was proclaimed in Madrid on September 11. All mourning ceased in Naples, and there were three days of illuminations and public festivities. On October 3, Tanucci and the Austrian ambassador, Count Neipperg, signed a treaty which guaranteed the succession to the Sicilies, in return for the surrender of the Presidi to Tuscany, now under an Austrian Archduke. Charles could depart with an easy conscience: Naples was ensured the protection of another great Power. Caracciolo considered this 'a fatal blow to the hopes and designs of the King of Sardinia', and wrote to Tanucci: 'It is the seal of Your Excellency's great achievement.' Such a reversal of foreign policy was all the more fantastic considering how recently the Bourbons and Hapsburgs had been at loggerheads. Its aim was to preserve Italian peace and check the ambitions of Sardinia, but its result, which neither Charles nor Tanucci had foreseen, was to substitute Austrian for Spanish influence in Naples. The new alliance was to be cemented by Ferdinand's marriage to one of the Empress Maria Theresa's daughters.

The negotiations might have been wrecked, since Maria Theresa's son, the future Emperor Joseph II, was to have married one of Charles's daughters and the betrothal had been discussed since 1757. But Charles's French sister-in-law, Louise Elisabeth, Duchess of Parma, had arranged with the Austrian ambassador in Paris to substitute her elder daughter Isabella for the Neapolitan princess—

a marriage which would gradually bring Parma and Guastalla under Hapsburg sway. Charles was too canny to allow this rebuff to affect his new policy, but Maria Amalia was cut to the quick and visited her resentment on the French Court, including her own sister the Dauphine. On leaving Naples, she had intended to travel to Spain via France and meet her sister in Lyons. Now she changed her mind and, though she was a wretched sailor, decided to travel by sea.

The most lavish of Neapolitan kings was very scrupulous about removing nothing that belonged to the Two Sicilies. Before leaving, he consigned the crown jewels and other treasures to the ministers of his heir; he even returned the ring which he had found himself at Pompeii—though the discovery had probably been prearranged to please him, a polite archæological fraud. Slipping it off his finger, he said: 'Even this ring is the patrimony of the state.' It was long pointed out to visitors as a proof of his delicacy of feeling. 'The famous cameo the King of Spain left here on his quitting Naples', wrote Lady Anne Miller, 'is of a smaller size than most of the other antiques: it represents the face of an old man of grotesque countenance with a long beard (I take it for a Silenus) and is highly finished; every curl and wave of the beard appear distinctly.'

A Spanish fleet was waiting to transport Charles and his family to Barcelona. Just before embarking, on October 6, Charles sat on the throne of Naples for the last time with Ferdinand on his left, and in the presence of the Council of State, the deputies of Naples, Palermo and Messina, and other high officials, announced his intention to abdicate the Crown of the Two Sicilies in favour of the eight-year-old Prince. The act of abdication was read by Tanucci and signed by Charles and Ferdinand, then Charles presented his son with a sword, the same which had been given by Louis XIV to his father, Philip V, when he went to Spain, and by his father to himself when he left for Italy; and in handing it to him he repeated their exhortations, that he was to use it to defend his religion, his person and his subjects. Sir James Gray reported that the speeches of the city deputies were so pathetic that the Queen burst into tears. 'The same morning there was a chapter held of the Golden Fleece, at which the King invested the young Prince Don Ferdinand with the collar of the Order. The Queen was present at the ceremony, which was a natural cause of renewing her grief, and indeed the tears ran down her cheeks during the whole function.' The King retired visibly shaken, saying, 'I am still a man'. Alone with the

Queen he broke down; both were overcome with emotion and tried to comfort each other. In leaving Naples they realized that they were leaving all the associations of their happy if not carefree youth, and a prolonged honeymoon. For the Saxon Queen Spain had all the terror of the mysterious unknown.

Charles appointed a Council of eight Regents to govern during Ferdinand's minority, which was to cease at the age of sixteen, but all important questions were to be referred to Spain, so that the final decision still rested with himself. As Tanucci was far the most powerful of the Regents, the government of the Two Sicilies was really entrusted to him. The Prince of San Nicandro assumed the title of chief major-domo, but remained the King's tutor in fact. The choice was lamentable—how lamentable could not yet be realized, since the King was only eight years old. His parents were preoccupied with his physical well-being, and this was all that interested San Nicandro.

A trifling incident at the first meeting of the Council of Regency seemed portentous to all observers. The position of a table had given rise to a discussion. Tanucci wanted it in one part of the room, San Nicandro in another. The latter yielded to the former, wrote the Venetian envoy, in order to gain credit for moderation in the report that would inevitably reach His Catholic Majesty.

Amid the triple discharge of guns from twenty-one frigates, as well as from all the castles and Maltese galleys in the bay, Charles was rowed by twenty-four sailors in a richly decorated barge to the ship *Phoenix*. Queen Maria Amalia, the two Infantas, Maria Josepha and Maria Luisa, and the second and fourth Infantes Charles and Gabriel, sat beside him, while Navarro, the Captain-General of the Spanish fleet, sat at the rudder wearing the red cordon of the Order of San Gennaro, which he had received two days previously, blowing his whistle ever and anon to the children's delight. The two youngest had embarked on another ship, since the *Phoenix* could not accommodate all the royal family, and Spanish etiquette was to be as strictly observed as on land. The Duchess of Castropignano, the King, the Duke of Losada and Navarro had starboard cabins on the upper deck; the Queen, the Princesses and Squillace had smaller cabins on the port side, while the Princes Charles and Gabriel were accommodated on the lower deck.

Public prayers had been ordered in all the churches for their safe voyage. As a strong wind sprang up soon after they embarked, Navarro decided not to sail till early next morning. Ten days later they landed at Barcelona, where they met with so uproarious a welcome that the Queen was frightened. Accustomed as she was to the outbursts of Neapolitan crowds, these struck her as barbaric. She expressed her distaste for the country and climate in her letters to Tanucci; she was homesick for her dear Naples, 'the pupils of my eyes, the city I bear in my heart'. The Duchess of Castropignano took a perverse pleasure in provoking her discontent with everything. Contrary to expectation, however, the Queen enjoyed the bullfights.

Charles entered Madrid *incognito* and stayed at the Retiro Palace, which Maria Amalia again compared unfavourably with those she had left behind. Decrepit, corpulent and almost blind, Elisabeth Farnese was carried in a litter into the King's apartment. It was twenty-eight years since she had seen her eldest son, and she rose with effort to welcome him. Both wept as they embraced. The old autocrat's ambitions had been justified; she had cause to be proud of Charles. She had brought sumptuous gifts: a sword studded with diamonds for the King; for the Queen a dressing-case of gold and Chinese porcelain—a looking-glass, a jewelled watch and an ivory fan were contained under the lid. The Infantas received necklaces, bracelets and ear-rings; and the Queen Mother overflowed with affection for her plain and gawky grandchildren.

Maria Amalia had always been jealous of her mother-in-law, and she was afraid she might yet recover her former influence. These fears were groundless. Charles treated his mother with exquisite deference, but he had no intention of letting her interfere in politics. He, too, had become an autocrat, in spite of his apparent mildness and simplicity. Besides, his mother's physical energy had begun to ebb, and her whole routine of life was different from his. Having adapted herself to Philip V's eccentric habits—his sleeping in the daytime and rising at night, his closely shuttered rooms—she clung to them as a widow. She rested while Charles was working, and vice versa. They did not meet often enough for her to regain her ascendancy over his mind after so long a separation. Accustomed to the open air, Charles felt suffocated in her heavily curtained and carpeted rooms, where the windows were never opened and large stoves were usually burning.

Charles rose early and spent his morning transacting business, as at Naples, and he went hunting every afternoon. Maria Amalia's health deteriorated ever since her arrival. A fall from her horse brought on a chronic cough, and she died on September 27, 1760, at the age of thirty-six. Charles was inconsolable. His mother, the Duc d'Ossun (who had followed him from Naples as French ambassador by special request, since he disliked new faces even among the diplomatists accredited to him) and his old friend the Duke of Losada, united in coaxing him to marry one of Louis XV's daughters, but he was determined to remain faithful to Maria Amalia for the rest of his days. No scandal ever attached itself to him. His austerity became proverbial. Whenever the slumbering embers of his temperament were stirred, he would jump out of bed and pace his room barefoot until the chill of night had calmed his fever. He became morbidly methodical, a slave to his rigid timetable, with hunting and a card game before supper as his only distractions. Every year on the same date he changed residence: as formerly he had moved from Portici to Caserta and from Venafro to Procida, he proceeded from Madrid to the Escurial, from San Ildefonso to Aranjuez. Neither illness nor accident was allowed to hinder his plans.

He believed passionately in the sacred character of his mission. 'Beside his father and his brother,' wrote a distinguished historian, 'Charles III appears to be a genius.' It is certain that he had an infinite capacity for taking pains. If he was no genius in other respects, he was a wise man among fools.

VII

Tanucci and the Abbé Galiani—Baiting the Pope—The famine of 1764—Ferdinand's education—The arrival of William Hamilton as British Minister—Ferdinand's coming of age, 1767—Expulsion of the Jesuits—The Tutor of the Two Sicilies—The hapless Archduchess Josepha—Eruption of Vesuvius—Ferdinand's betrothal to Archduchess Maria Carolina.

'We have no pretensions,' Charles had written to his ambassador in London in 1756, 'we lack ambition.' Tanucci took his cue from the King. In foreign policy he was a rigid isolationist; the Two Sicilies ought to be self-sufficient. What had France and England to contribute? Their fashions and luxuries he considered detrimental to morality and economy. The French wanted to search all Neapolitan ships, but would not allow the Neapolitans to search theirs; they wanted to import timber from Calabria for shipbuilding when this was required at home. Tanucci inveighed against the French style of courtesy, which 'ends in words and bows... without any obligation to act, rather with a deliberate intention to do nothing for others.' And their superior attitude towards Italian literature exasperated him.

Galiani, as secretary of the embassy in Paris, was alarmed by the excessive frankness of his letters. He warned him that these were intercepted and might annoy the authorities. Tanucci replied that if his liberty displeased them, their displeasure displeased himself; he was used to being frank, and was so grateful to those who reciprocated that he even learnt by heart the satires composed against him. He would rather not write at all than resort to a cipher. 'Whoever opens my letters,' he wrote, 'will find them all unction, spirit, zeal for the Bourbons, and disgust that the French disgust those countries which are friendly to the Bourbons, quite unnecessarily and uselessly. I have spoken from the abundance of my heart, of a heart which I know to be Bourbonic, and with so clear a conscience that I have spoken and written without cipher.' Dreading lest France should drag Naples into war, he had been secretly opposed to the

Bourbon Family Compact, and had consistently deferred signing it. Consequently his protégé Galiani had to bear the brunt of the Duke of Choiseul's resentment.

Instead of showing his dislike of the too clever secretary, Choiseul suggested that he should be promoted elsewhere: 'If the Marquis Tanucci could find him a post as Minister of the King of the Two Sicilies, I believe the Abbé Galiani would consider himself most happy; and if the Count of Cantillana were to remain here alone, I would undertake to second him in promoting His Majesty's interests.' Tanucci smothered this proposal with the politest expressions of gratitude, and Galiani continued to haunt the *salons* of Paris. 'In his person,' wrote Marmontel, who met him with Mme Geoffrin, 'he was the prettiest little Harlequin Italy had produced, but with the head of Machiavelli on his shoulders. Epicurean in his philosophy, yet with a melancholy soul, having discerned all the ridiculous side of nature, there was nothing either in politics or in moral philosophy about which he had not some good story to relate. His stories always had the precision of perfect aptness and the salt of an unexpected and artful allusion. Imagine an extremely naïve grace besides, in his manner of telling and gesticulation, and see what pleasure we derived from the contrast between the profound sense inherent in the story and the comical, roguish manner of the story-teller. I do not exaggerate in the least when I say that people forgot everything to listen to him for hours together.'

Some of these stories have crept into print, but they are incomplete without Galiani's musical voice and vivid gestures. There is his famous fable of the cogged dice, for instance, with which he regaled the agnostic *philosophes* of Baron d'Holbach's circle, sitting cross-legged in a huge armchair after dinner. 'Please suppose, gentlemen, that one of you, who is quite convinced that this world is the result of chance, is playing at dice, not in a gambling den but in one of the best houses in Paris. His opponent, casting one, two, three, four, many times, always throws number six. After the game has continued a while my friend Diderot, let us say, who is losing money, will be sure to call out: "The dice are cogged! This is some swindler's den!" What ho, Master Philosopher! Because you lose half a dozen francs after ten or twelve throws of dice, you are positive that this is the result of some clever plan, an artificial combination, an elaborate trick; and yet, seeing in the world innumerable combinations a thousand times more difficult, more complicated, and more useful, do you not suspect that Nature's dice are also cogged, and that above there is a great Arranger?'

During a discussion on law, Galiani compared the legislator to a painter commissioned by the police to paint on a wall in bold letters: 'It is forbidden to commit any nuisance here under penalty of a fine or corporal punishment.' He sets to work, but in the middle of it he wishes to relieve nature. So he runs down the ladder and, while breaking the law, he admires the beauty of his own inscription.

After meeting Galiani the Duchess of Choiseul remarked: 'In France we only have wit in small change; in Italy they have it in bullion.' But her husband was itching to get rid of this bullion purveyor, who found so many pretexts for evading the Bourbon Family Compact.

If Tanucci was anti-French, the naval bombardment threatened in 1742 had made him even more anti-English. As for Austria and Piedmont (or Sardinia), he mistrusted both as potential devourers of the whole peninsula. He was disgusted to hear of a ballet given at the French Court in 1762, in which dancers representing England, France, Spain and Portugal were symbolically reconciled by one representing Sardinia. Having refused to act as mediator, he protested to Charles against Sardinian intervention. 'They will only sow discord,' he wrote; 'dealings with vipers and tigers are never profitable. I know that all Sardinian diplomats poison everything they touch.'

As a temporal state, the Papacy was weak, and therefore vulnerable; it was easier to attack ecclesiastical than lay abuses. Tanucci, supported by the influential class of lawyers who hated the encroachments of the clergy, joined eagerly in the popular sport of baiting the Pope. His jeremiads against Rome are wearisome in their monotony. According to him, Rome was 'that city of atheism which it has sometimes been believed could not exist'. 'When have priests ever loved their country, their sovereign, their religion?' he asked rhetorically. His particular hatred was concentrated on the Jesuits. The Concordat of 1741 had already allowed the taxation of some Church property and limited its jurisdiction, but he wanted to go farther, to claim the revenue of vacant benefices, to separate religious Orders from their Roman superiors and place their property under government control, to forbid legacies to the Church or wills in favour of 'the soul' or for the celebration of masses.

Decree after decree struck at papal rights and privileges, to such an extent that King Charles ordered him to relax. But Tanucci was indefatigable, and he had to have a finger in every pie. His chief merit was that he cut down useless expenditure. Squillace had made Charles believe that his treasury was inexhaustible, whereas Tanucci reduced the King's expenses from 324,000 to 169,685 ducats a year. He refused to allow the purchase of a costly diamond for the King, because 'the value of an acquisition must always have some element of public benefit in proportion to the sweat and pains that have produced it. And what proportion is there between that diamond and the toils of seven thousand families for a whole year, which the Crown would exchange with that stone?' Noble sentiments; but he was unable to prevent the great famine of 1764, caused by a shortage of corn, and his measures to counteract it were scarcely successful.

'The famine is appalling,' wrote the Sardinian ambassador; 'accompanied by riots and pillage. One man tears the bread from another's mouth, and there is killing and wounding whenever bread is distributed. The aristocracy hide their silver in convents, and the foreign ministers do likewise. Between eight and ten thousand women have gone to ask the Archbishop to expose San Gennaro's relics, and public penances are all confused with the Carnival. Many have perished in the provinces. White bread is an exquisite gift worth a marzipan... The processions of women with crowns of thorns and crosses on their backs are pitiful and gruesome. The famine is thought to be a chastisement from God. Images work miracles in abundance, except that of multiplying bread. A crucifix which opened and shut its eyes has been cut to pieces because everybody wants a relic. And in the meantime work has come to a stop. There is dread, desolation and despair, and corpses lie in the streets. The terrified Court has fled to Caserta; and the lives of San Nicandro and Jaci have been threatened. The King left between two files of soldiers in echelon all along the road, at an unaccustomed hour: it is called "the flight into Egypt". No member of the Regency wishes to remain in Naples, except that old stalwart, the General of the Galleys... Bread can only be obtained at the point of a pistol; it cannot be bought in peaceful fashion, but must be torn from the seller... The King is ready to escape to Gaeta, and the roads are being repaired in consequence. Frightful diseases accompany the dearth, and the list of the dead increases daily. Processions of haggard women wander from village to village begging for bread...

'The King, on returning from Caserta for Holy Week between a double hedge of soldiers, was received in lugubrious silence, except for the voices of the dying calling out for bread. Struck with terror, he has not gone out of doors. Tanucci has received orders from Spain to deal solely with provisions. In the Hospital of Incurables which contains two thousand sick, between sixty and seventy a day are dying of hunger... Three millions of ducats have been allotted to the import of cereals from abroad and nearly all the communes are ruined. It has been a great financial disaster. The Bishops of Isernia and Trivento have written to the Regents for permission to burn the corpses, since the graves are glutted and plague has been reported. The Regents have written to Madrid; but until now this has not been carried out so as not to alarm the public.'

Tanucci tried to minimize the calamity, which was falsely attributed to monopolists. On April 14 he wrote to Galiani: 'We are not so afflicted by famine as the world reports at present. We have enough grain for the whole of May, and we have contracted for enough to last us through July. This provision is for the capital and its neighbourhood. High prices, which the poor cannot afford, cause distress in the provinces. This calamity is all the greater because there is no remedy for it... The deputies [*eletti*] of Naples perpetrate this villainy most foully because they profit by it both in public and in private.' The latter controlled the bake-houses which dispensed bad bread. 'They accepted bribes from the bakers to keep silent about their monstrous frauds, such as mixing marble dust with flour... I am old, dear Abbé, I have served your country for thirty years or more with zeal, good-will and attention. But I have not been able to extinguish theft, inertia and iniquity. Of these eruptions I leave little less than what I found.'

Foreign supplies of corn arrived to the rescue, but the famine was followed by an epidemic which killed off between twenty and thirty thousand inhabitants. 'The doctors are brothers of astrologers,' wrote Tanucci. 'The bakers of the Neapolitan *eletti* have sold abominable bread: the substance mixed with it has perhaps caused several deaths from gangrened intestines. It is certain that the vast number of beggars coming into the cities, especially Naples, dirty, squalid and putrid, have brought much death and disease into the charitable houses to which they repaired, with lamentable results. But it is also certain that not a few were infected who did not eat the city bread or come in contact with the horde of beggars. The symptoms have differed... Soothing drugs have saved many, but more were killed by the doctors, who used emetics, leeches, blistering ointments, strong purges, etc. Here as all the world over the doctors are ignorant brazen impostors. But they have not even saved appearances. They have not opened or dissected a corpse, and I have preached on this subject in vain. Worms and gangrene have been noted. Recently the good King of Spain sent me a balsam called Salazar's, and I had experiments made with it in a hospital built at Posillipo at the King's expense, under my direction. It cured those with intestinal trouble, but was useless for those whose chests had been attacked.'

Dr Michele Sarcone wrote a lengthy treatise on the subject which is dedicated to Tanucci, but which is scarcely enlightening to the layman, who will only wonder that any of his patients survived. Among the recipes given is that of Salazar's balsam, which consisted of incense, mastic gum, soccotrine aloes, and hard rosin dissolved in alcohol, hermetically sealed in a small bottle. Every three hours a few drops of this compound were to anoint the stomach and stricken parts. With cooler weather the epidemic decreased, but it had taken a severe toll. At least the cemeteries benefited. Thanks to Father Rocco, funds were collected for a new burial ground on a hillside near Poggio Reale, half a mile from the city; this was divided into three hundred and sixty-five deep vaults, one of which was opened every day of the year, and the bodies to be interred were deposited in order. Each vault was covered with a slab of lava which fitted it exactly. The bodies were brought there at night, and all expenses defrayed by public charity. But many corpses were still buried in churches. As Tanucci wrote: 'The monks are avaricious of corpses, from which they derive great profit. Burial in churches means perpetual masses, anniversaries, *dies iræ*.' But the new cemetery was due to the strenuous campaign of Father Rocco, a Dominican friar, rather than to Tanucci, who groaned that he was 'nauseated by the ministry and the human species'.

In the following years the export of grain was banned. The population soon increased by leaps and bounds, and the careworn Tanucci was able to return to his anti-clerical crusade.

From his letters it would appear he never lost interest in education. 'The true culture is that of Athens and Florence,' he wrote, 'where artists were philosophers.' He wished to encourage serious literature, 'not the rhyming, amorous and facetious literature of Petrarch and Berni, which made all cultivated nations laugh at the Italians'. He disapproved of the 'low tone of modern prose and conversation'; and he was amazed that the Neapolitans disparaged literature in comparison with politics.

What prevented him from applying his principles as the young King's mentor? As we have seen, he believed that the monarch belonged to a race apart, but need not be extraordinary in any way: Providence did wondrous things through unworthy instruments. And he quoted with approval a remark of Frederick of Prussia (borrowed from Lucian) that some men were so stolid that Providence had to make sovereigns of them lest they should die of hunger. Yet Ferdinand showed signs of intelligence as a child, and most of the foreign ambassadors were impressed by his bright appearance. The Sardinian minister described him when he was thirteen as tall for his age, with a fine head, fair hair, blue eyes, and a very white skin, which accentuated the gentleness of his features. His body was covered with herpes, which the doctors considered an indication of good health. He seemed delicate, but he had a robust constitution; he was high-spirited and alert, and he had a roving eye. Like his mother, he noticed everything, especially its ludicrous aspect. He had a decided taste for hunting, fishing and mechanics, and talked of little else. His father used to call him the *paglietta*—Neapolitan slang for a lawyer—since he always acted as spokesman for his brothers and sisters.

Under wise tuition, his natural gifts might have had a chance to develop. But his health seems to have been the sole preoccupation of his tutors. All agree that his chief governor, the Prince of San Nicandro, was stingy, hypocritical and grossly ignorant, except where his privileges were concerned. He had the conviction, then shared by many of his class, that physical culture was quite sufficient for a gentleman, especially for a King. Croce has called him the prototype of the plebeian noble who flourished till 1860 or later, 'with plebeian speech, habits and gestures; totally different from an active thinker; with a close affinity to his coachman, being a fine driver himself, good-natured with all and beloved as a *buon signore* for his improvidence, admired for his pomp and luxury, easy to compete with in jokes and gibes'. Under his ægis the young King was moulded in similar fashion.

Ferdinand was wakened at seven in the morning, and he spent

the next hour dressing and saying his prayers. At eight o'clock Father Cardel, a Bohemian Jesuit, came to teach him Latin, French and German for a couple of hours but, as the Sardinian minister remarked, 'His Majesty profits little by it, for he only speaks Neapolitan'. This adherence to his native dialect was one of the causes of his popularity. He spent most of his time with people who could speak no other language. Father Cardel was more of a courtier than a teacher, determined not to risk displeasing his royal pupil. He paid more attention to his conduct than to his lessons, and little enough to that. From ten till midday the King amused himself with childish games in which there was a great deal of rough horseplay. At midday he dined, after which he addressed a few words to his Captain-General and the foreign ministers assembled in the adjoining gallery for fifteen minutes; then he was obliged, against his will, to lie down for an hour. At 4 p.m. his writing master arrived; as he had to write to his father once a week and occasionally to his other relations, he paid more attention to this lesson, and his calligraphy was fair. Next came his mathematical teacher, but he never advanced beyond the simplest arithmetic. Once a week he had a dancing lesson, for which he showed no enthusiasm; nor did he care for fencing. Riding was his favourite pursuit. Two hours before sunset he went out in his carriage to shoot or fish. In winter this routine was slightly varied.

The young King often visited his imbecile brother, for whom he had a touching affection. The Infante Don Philip seems to have been looked upon rather as a mascot, and as a justification for not burdening the King with any sort of mental problem. 'He is rarely visible,' wrote Samuel Sharp, 'but the Regency think proper to exhibit him a few times in the year, namely, when the King removes from Naples to Portici, and from Portici to Naples. I took the opportunity, when the family came to town, of entertaining myself with that spectacle... The administration acts wisely in exposing him now and then to the eye of the public, as the very sight of him is a full vindication of their conduct in regard to the sentence of idiotism and disinheritance passed on him some years since. The Court was in mourning, but he was as well dressed as a youth in mourning can be, and his hair as well combed and as well powdered. With all these advantages, however, the very first glance of him convinced me that he wants every one faculty of the mind. He has that wandering roll of the eye which is peculiar to idiots and new-born infants, who, not having the endowment of thought and reflection, consequently cannot fix their attention to one object. There are some knavish quacks, and some silly doctors, who say the cure is not impossible, and that he may be restored to his senses... The opinion, however, might in future times be attended with pernicious consequences. A faction in opposition to the King, his younger brother, might possess themselves of his person; affirm he had, by virtue of some remedy, recovered his understanding, and attempt to place him on the throne... By what I can learn, he leads a happy kind of animal life. He eats and drinks with much pleasure, is subject to no gust of passion, and enjoys such infantine amusements as a child in arms may be supposed to enjoy.'

Every ship from Spain brought Ferdinand more hunting dogs and guns; regularly San Nicandro sent Charles III lists of the game shot by his pupil. For the present his sporting expeditions were limited to Capodimonte, Portici and Caserta. Thus San Nicandro's policy was to encourage the King to amuse himself and to keep him away from those who might cultivate his mind; he was allowed to waste his time with servants and illiterate boys of his own age, from whom the tutor-chamberlain had nothing to fear. The King always spoke of him as 'the friend': perhaps he had a bantering regard for him, but he laughed at him behind his back. San Nicandro's wife curried favour with Ferdinand by allowing her pretty ten-year-old daughter to play with him at all hours; she kept him company at the opera, and even visited him in bed. He seldom saw Tanucci except when the special messengers arrived from Spain. His attendants tried to undermine the minister's influence by ridiculing his gravity of manner, but the gravity was effective, for the young King stood in awe of him.

William Hamilton, the new English minister, had arrived on November 17, 1764, little realizing that he would spend the best part of his life in this position. The Abbé Galiani, who met him on his way to Naples, imparted to Tanucci: 'I was enamoured of him. Either I am grossly deceived or Your Excellency will love him greatly, even more than Gray. He has more innocence and candour, and no less ability.' Galiani was not deceived, for Hamilton made the best of impressions on Tanucci and the whole Court. Thanks to his seeming innocence and candour, he inspired confidence, which is proved by his letters home, a refreshing contrast with those of his predecessor. In September 1766, he wrote: 'Mr Tanucci lately received an order from the King of Spain to acquaint His Sicilian Majesty that, unless he would readily answer His Catholic Majesty's letter himself, he must not expect any more confidentially from him. Previous to this message, the King of the Two Sicilies employed his confessor, in concert with the Prince San Nicandro, to answer his letter; now he writes to His Catholic Majesty with his own hand, with the utmost difficulty as I am informed; His Sicilian Majesty's education in every respect having been most shamefully neglected.' Observing that his letters were being opened, he resorted to cipher when he wrote in the same month: 'The members of the Regency which will expire in January next lose no time in winding up their bottom and making themselves rich; and I am well assured that such a scene of bribery and corruption can be scarcely paralleled in history. Mr Tanucci is alone excepted. His character in that particular is unblemished. I have frequent proofs that Mr Tanucci alone here is in possession of the entire confidence of the King of Spain.'

Ferdinand's coming of age on January 12, 1767, made little difference to his government. The Papal Nuncio reported: 'The Regency has ceased, but it has been succeeded by a Council of State. The members of the former will attend the latter, with the name of Regent changed to Councillor. They have the right to speak but not to vote, except in the Council of Justice, which the King is unwilling to attend, or, as others allege, has been dissuaded from doing so. The councillors will have a decisive vote... It is difficult to understand why, at the beginning of his reign, this King wishes to deprive himself of a prerogative which seems the most important... It is said to be at the King of Spain's suggestion.' And again: 'In the time of His Catholic Majesty all royal diplomas and patents were signed with the King's name by an engraved stamp, which was kept in the secretariat from which the favour issued. Now by the King of Spain's order this stamp must be kept by Marchese Tanucci, to whom other secretaries must apply for the royal signature on all occasions... It is generally inferred that Marchese Tanucci has obtained a key by which he can control all the ministers, as in the period of Regency, and keep them under subjection.' All the ministers were Tanucci's creatures, even Cardinal Orsini the ambassador to the Holy See, who 'applauded all his proposals and accepted them as oracles'. Nobody was to speak at the Council unless questioned by the King. Ferdinand kept his eyes fixed on Tanucci, and according to the tone of his voice or movement of his head expressed his own sentiment.

Tanucci was thus responsible for the King's first act upon attaining his majority. This was the expulsion of the Jesuits from Naples, following the examples of Portugal, France and Spain. Pombal had accused the Portuguese Jesuits of plotting to assassinate the King; the French Parliament had declared that the Society of Jesus was opposed to all authority, spiritual and temporal, and was scheming to usurp the government by means direct and indirect; while Charles III of Spain was convinced that it was plotting to put his brother Don Luis on the throne in his stead.

So elated was Charles at getting rid of this imaginary thorn that he exclaimed he had conquered a new world. Tanucci proceeded with the same determined secrecy as his patron, though in Spain the Jesuits seem to have had a premonition of their fate, since they had removed their money and papers. In Naples they were taken by surprise. At midnight on November 3, 1767, every Jesuit house in the kingdom was confiscated by royal officials: the doors were opened, the cells closely guarded, the bell-ropes cut, and the priests and their servants were all collected in a single room, from which they were escorted to the nearest harbour and embarked for the Papal States. They could take away nothing but their clothes; not even the old and the sick were allowed to linger. Tanucci wished to avoid exciting public sympathy—not that he had much faith in the populace. When Father Spinelli warned him of the disorders likely to follow the expulsion of the Jesuits, he retorted: 'Father, you do not know the Neapolitans. If I hanged you tomorrow in the middle of the market-place, nobody would move.' As an extra precaution he revived the Committee of Distrust, but for once this proved unnecessary.

The Jesuits, condemned without a trial or any proof of guilt, left calmly and quietly, and saw their life work destroyed with Christian resignation. They had educated the flower of Neapolitan youth, and their schools had been free, without any expense to the state. Tanucci crowed over his easy victory, still he would not rest until the Order was abolished. In the meantime he drafted edicts transferring all their possessions to the state, adapting them to communal use, reorganizing their schools and charities. The wealth derived from this mass confiscation was immense, but Tanucci took care not to publish the exact figures. Though most of the Order's revenue was to be devoted to public education, a great deal of it found its way into private pockets.

A thousand copies of the Pope's protest were distributed, and Tanucci asked the minister to the Holy See to reply 'very simply and modestly'. Naples was also flooded with satires and libels, and when his attention was drawn to them, he asked if the King had been attacked. When he was told that himself and a few ministers were the only targets, he said: 'Then let them be', and changed the topic of conversation. The Nuncio continued to appear at Court and to dine with Tanucci as if nothing untoward had happened. The King's Jesuit confessor, Father Cardel, was sent back to Bohemia with a small pension.

At this point Parma also took a hand in ecclesiastical reform. The young Duke Ferdinand, whose chief minister, Du Tillot, was Tanucci's equivalent, went so far as to forbid recourse to the Roman tribunals, as well as the nomination of foreigners to the benefices of his duchy. The Pope thought he could safely retaliate against this princeling, threatening excommunication and renewing the Papal claim to his estates. The Duke retorted with unexpected vigour, and the whole house of Bourbon supported him. While France occupied Avignon, Naples seized Benevento and Pontecorvo and marched troops into the Papal States. The Bourbons now insisted on the total suppression of the Jesuits. Clement XIII was spared this final humiliation by sudden death in 1769. The election of his successor, Clement XIV, was largely due to Bourbon influence. As a Franciscan, he was unfavourable to the Jesuits; and from this moment the Order was doomed. He suspended the 'monitorium' against Parma, and his concessions, like those of Benedict XIV, evinced a spirit of conciliation. But Tanucci refused to be won over.

In January 1768 Tanucci was formally appointed First Secretary, though he had, in fact, been Prime Minister since Ferdinand's succession: he was invariably referred to as the 'Tutor of the Two Sicilies'.

William Hamilton sent Lord Shelburne the following 'succinct account of the King and the Ministers who govern here,' in March 1767: 'His Sicilian Majesty is of a constitution extremely delicate, which with his brother's most probably he inherited from the great-grandfather of his mother. Unhappily for himself and his people, he has neither had masters capable of instructing him nor governors who have studied to inspire him with ideas worthy of his rank. He is beloved by the vulgar Neapolitans merely from his having been born amongst them, and if he loves them, as he seems to do, it is perhaps because by the distance they have always carefully placed between him and the nobility of his own age, he has been drove rather to seek the company of menial servants and people of the very lowest class than those of a better education, and indeed it is in the company of the former that he is best pleased, whilst he treats the latter as if there was no difference between the one and the other. It is easy to imagine what sort of principles he must have imbibed in such a school, and to what low flattery he has been accustomed. Whilst he was yet a minor they had great hopes from him; those hopes were neither founded upon the goodness of his education nor upon any word or remarkable action of his, but having felt all the weight of the past bad administration, they imagined that as they could not be in a worse state, any change would lead to a better. As yet, however, they have not found it so. Ambitious to come out of his minority, the young King who had been counting the days to it for a year past, seems to have been more desirous of becoming his own master to follow his caprices, than to govern his kingdoms, neither has he given the least attention to business, wholly giving himself up to his pleasures, which he shares with people of the very lowest class, whose manners he imitates. His most intimate friend and favourite is, as I am credibly informed, one who serves in the palace, even below the degree of a livery servant. He is thought not to have a great share of sensibility, is choleric, obstinate, and capable of bearing resentment; yet from a child he was always thought to have a better temper than any of his brothers...

'The Regency being changed into a Council of State, the Marquis Tanucci has united in his person all the authority that was divided amongst the Regency and by that means is become Prime Minister, for one cannot say that the King sees through him, but that he sees for the King... His honesty is unsuspected, and all the world agree that he has taken more pains to raise than to enrich himself; he seems to think at present that his elevation may supply the place of his want of talents for governing which nature has refused him, and which he has never been able to acquire by study. He wishes to do well, but as he has learnt policy from books of law only, he sees too much with the eyes of a lawyer and wants the means of doing better, besides he has not a friend about him of experience enough to point out those means, which occasions his acting with very confined views. He hates monks and does not love the Court of Rome, but instead of taking the true method of setting bounds to the avarice of the clergy and the ambition of the priests, he contents himself with openly mortifying them, and showing them the contempt he has for them. He piques himself more upon his being a learned man than a statesman; his flatterers praise, and he himself applauds his skill in letters. The idea of his knowledge renders him obstinate and occasions his doing business with a harshness that, even with a good heart, one contracts by having too good an opinion of oneself. When he finds himself embarrassed, he seeks to gain time and has recourse to palliatives, and is satisfied in finding expedients, without troubling himself with the consequences they may have, which has often proved of great detriment to the kingdom as in the time of the famine three years ago.

'The Marquis Tanucci hates the French, because their Ministers have shown too openly that they have not that good opinion of him which he has of himself, and if he agrees with us, it is perhaps because we agree so little with the French; indeed, I believe he rather fears than loves us, but I believe him capable of doing much in our favour provided that taking advantage of the fear he has of our power, one has always the precaution of showing a great regard for him in his private capacity. He is more jealous of his power than taken up with his affairs, but he loves to appear to have great application to them, and requires being treated by foreign Ministers with a gravity that can give him no room to believe that he has an ascendency over them.

'He is, however, the only one who knows anything of business, and at present his credit is independent of the will of the King of Naples, but not of that of the King of Spain, who places entire confidence in him and who would have great need of him should any accident happen to His Sicilian Majesty. After the character I have been giving, Your Lordship may well imagine that bribery, the common and almost avowed channel to preferment in this kingdom, can do nothing with him, but it is certain that his wife and those about him think in that respect very differently from him, and I am well assured that they attend much more to their own interest than to his reputation.'

The King remained a boisterous boy, with hardly any sense of responsibility. His democratic manners gained him an easy popularity: he was a Neapolitan by birth, and in many ways representative of his people. It was without any lack of respect that he came to be called the *Lazzarone* King. He changed little with age and experience. As Mrs Piozzi wrote of him some fifteen years later: 'He rides and rows, hunts the wild boar, and catches fish in the bay, and sells it in the market—as dear as he can, too—but gives away the money they pay him for it, and that directly; so that no suspicion of meanness, or of anything worse than a little rough merriment, can be ever attached to his truly honest, open, undesigning character.'

He could endure any amount of physical exertion, but reading and writing were so obnoxious to him that he had a stamp made with a facsimile of his signature, which he entrusted to Tanucci. Thus no document could fail to pass through the Prime Minister's hands. But omnipotence had its penalties, and Tanucci often groaned to his Tuscan friends. Accustomed to a sedentary life, he was obliged to follow the King at all seasons to his various hunting resorts. 'I take as much air as I can: at Persano, where I had to do the work of all the secretaries combined, I rose from my bed at five o'clock in the morning; from six to seven I despatched business with the King, after which I heard Mass, then worked at my desk until midday. An hour after dinner I went five or six miles by carriage over the most beautiful road through that extensive wood, either towards the Silaro or the Calore, which including the return journey amounted to ten or twelve miles; at six in the evening another session with the King until eight; and after that I worked until midnight at my little table. Such is the repose I get in my old age.'

And Tanucci, who had never had any *joie de vivre*, felt prematurely old. The wealthy Prince Francavilla, King Charles III, the late King Philip V, were all hypochondriacs, he observed; so were Tiberius and others vested with worldly power. 'Old age,' he wrote, 'has added to my hypochondriac and despairing temperament. I have always had more fear than hope...' Gout had become his 'irrevocable and indivisible concubine'. After following so many royal hunts at a distance, their bloodthirsty futility increased his gloom: 'To hunt without shooting signifies movement and humanity. Not having made the poor beasts ourselves, we have no right to kill them. This was the dogma of Pythagoras, to whom David is not opposed, if you observe. Meat for nourishment was an invention of the priests.'

What Mrs Piozzi called a little rough merriment was often carried too far. On one occasion at Portici when Ferdinand was playing *pallone*, the old forerunner of football (in which one party throws the ball as far as possible and the other side returns it till it is driven beyond one or the other boundary, usually with a heavy leather armlet), a couple of young seminarists appeared upon the scene. They had come from Florence and were dressed in travelling clothes, perhaps too foppishly, for it seems that they struck Ferdinand as grotesque. He and his companions seized the protesting youths and tossed them up in a blanket again and again, in the presence of many spectators who roared with laughter. One of the victims belonged to a noble Florentine family, the Mazzinghi. He took this public insult so much to heart that he felt he could neither stay in Naples nor return to Florence. He went to Rome, where he brooded on the incident until he died of melancholia shortly after.

Bonechi, the Florentine agent who reported the case to the Grand Duke, said he would have been treated in the same manner, but luckily he was absent. Both the Tuscan and Spanish Courts complained to Tanucci, who had much ado to throw water on the fire. In trying to defend the royal culprit, he attributed his prank to the odd appearance of the seminarists, as if they could help it. With characteristic pedantry, Tanucci concluded that even the old Greeks and Romans, in spite of their seriousness, were addicted to the game, which was called *la manta*. But this was slender consolation to the sufferers, and their fellow-Tuscans were very indignant. It was said, however, that the Prince of Butera had been the real instigator. No doubt Tanucci lectured the King, who was moved to tears by his eloquence. Did it occur to him that if Ferdinand wasted his time with bullies and buffoons, encouraging their familiarities and horseplay, and assuming undignified disguises, it was partly through his fault?

'It is amazing that they dare discuss these matters even in the public coffee-houses,' the Florentine agent wrote. To protect his dignity, Tanucci had obtained an order from 'the Patriarch' forbidding all except courtiers on duty to attend the King's meals, as he was particularly liable to be rowdy at the dinner table.

During the last ten years there had been delicate negotiations for Ferdinand's marriage to an Austrian Archduchess; the Marchese de Maio, Neapolitan minister in Vienna, had persevered through thick and thin. One of the first set backs had been the choice of a

Princess of Parma, instead of an Infanta of Spain, as a bride for the Emperor Joseph. Charles III had been nettled, and Tanucci bristled with his master's irritation. De Maio made plausible excuses for the Empress Maria Theresa. Had she not honoured him with an audience lasting almost half an hour, in which she stressed her anxiety for a family alliance, 'the most solid, if not the only, means of ensuring peace in Italy'? It was half understood that the eleven-year-old Archduchess Joanna would be betrothed to Ferdinand, but nothing definite had been settled when the Duke of Santa Elisabetta replaced De Maio in 1761.

The Archduchess Joanna died of smallpox, so Ferdinand was formally engaged to the fifth Archduchess Maria Josepha when he was nearly thirteen. His father had left the choice to the Empress Maria Theresa, and the Neapolitan minister had reported that Josepha, who was three months younger than Ferdinand, had a comely figure, agreeable and vivacious features, flourishing health and unusual intelligence. She was the Emperor Joseph's favourite sister, and the Empress Maria Theresa, who was fully informed about Ferdinand's unprepossessing ways, confessed that her heart was very uneasy. 'I look upon poor Josepha as a sacrifice to politics,' she wrote. 'If only she fulfils her duty to God and her husband and attends to the welfare of her soul, I shall be content even if she is not happy.'

After Ferdinand's coming of age there were minute preparations for the bride's journey. A magnificent trousseau was ordered, including a hundred dresses from Paris, and a miniature portrait of Ferdinand set in diamonds was pinned to her corsage in token of betrothal. At the end of June the Archduchess complained of fever and a sore throat, and it was feared that she, too, had caught smallpox. But it was a false alarm, and the nuptial preparations continued. The Austrian minister in Naples and the Neapolitan minister in Vienna were promoted as ambassadors extraordinary. Arrangements were made in the Venetian state and in Lombardy to welcome the bride, and these were complicated by the Emperor's decision to accompany his sister *incognito* as far as Florence. Count Zinner left Vienna to supervise the itinerary and investigate the roads. For the first time since her widowhood Maria Theresa appeared in public at the Court balls given in honour of Josepha's marriage.

In Naples there were special theatricals at the San Carlo, and wooden towers were erected for the *Cuccagne*. Hymeneal verses poured in from every part of Italy: the Duke of Belforte offered his future Queen an ode of eighty-two octaves, calling her magnanimous, a sublime genius, a polyglot and the very perfection of beauty. On receiving further compositions in the same strain from the Virgilian Academy and the Israelite University, the Prince of Kaunitz was forced to reply that the Empress had had a surfeit of them. Thirty-four royal coaches, nine one-horse carriages, four luggage waggons, fourteen litters and accessories were all ready for departure on October 16.

The late Emperor and other members of the imperial family were buried in the vaults of the Capuchin Church at Vienna, and on solemn occasions Maria Theresa went down to these dismal depths with her children to weep and pray beside her husband's tomb. Josepha had a horror of these pious visits, and when her mother insisted upon her doing this for the last time before leaving Vienna, she begged to be spared such an ordeal. The Empress had said that the only fault of this otherwise blameless daughter was a slight tendency to obstinacy. But the Empress could be more obstinate, and she forced the sobbing Josepha to go down to the vault, where the coffin of the Emperor Joseph's widow, who had died of smallpox four months previously, was also exposed. Soon Josepha showed symptoms of the virulent disease, and she succumbed on October 15, the day before she was due to start for Naples.

Simultaneously there was a violent eruption of Vesuvius, with dense clouds by day and crimson flames by night, accompanied by showers of ashes.

William Hamilton was irresistibly drawn to Vesuvius. 'It is impossible,' he wrote, 'to describe the glorious sight of a river of liquid fire, nor the effect of thousands of red-hot stones thrown up at least 200 yards high and rolling down the side of the mountain when they fell.' After examining this eruption at close quarters he reported: 'I thought proper to acquaint the Marquis Tanucci with what I had seen upon the mountain, and gave it as my opinion that His Sicilian Majesty would do well to remove from Portici. However (I believe on account of the smallpox being at Naples) the Court did not remove till two o'clock this morning when the explosions of the volcano shook the palace so much that His Sicilian Majesty was obliged to quit it hastily.' The lava was flowing only a mile and a half away. In the meantime the streets of Naples were full of processions. 'On Tuesday the mob set fire to the Cardinal Archbishop's gate, His Eminence having refused to bring out the relics of Saint Januarius, and the same night the prisoners in the city jail, having wounded the jailer, attempted to escape but were prevented by the troops. On Thursday the mob was so increased and so tumultuous that His Sicilian Majesty thought proper to order the procession of Saint Januarius: it was attended by twenty thousand people at least. ... After having loaded their Saint with the grossest abuse for having suffered the mountain to give them these alarms, this riotous mob fell on their faces and then returned to the Cathedral singing the praises of the Saint for the late miracle.'

Tanucci and Monsignor Latilla, the King's confessor, found Ferdinand rather dazed when they broke the news of his bereavement, but never having seen Josepha, he was soon consoled with the hope of a substitute. In his *Historical Memoirs*, Sir Nathaniel Wraxall repeats a story he heard from Hamilton about this melancholy occasion. A circumstance which increased the King's chagrin was that he was prevented from hunting or fishing on the day that the news reached Naples. 'Ferdinand reluctantly submitted to such a painful and unusual renunciation; but, having consented to it from a sense of decorum, he immediately set about endeavouring to amuse himself within doors, in the best manner that circumstances would admit; an attempt in which he was aided by the noblemen in waiting about his person. They began therefore with billiards, a game which His Majesty likes and at which he plays with skill. When they had continued it for some time, leapfrog was tried, to which succeeded various other feats of agility or gambols. At length one of the gentlemen, more ingenious than the others, proposed to celebrate the funeral of the deceased Archduchess. The idea, far from shocking the King, appeared to him, and to the whole company, as most entertaining; and no reflexions, either on the indecorum, or want of apparent humanity in the proceeding, interposed to prevent its immediate realization. Having selected one of the chamberlains, as proper, from his youth and feminine appearance, to represent the Princess, they habited him in a manner suitable to the mournful occasion; laid him out on an open bier, according to the Neapolitan custom at interments; and in order to render the ceremony more appropriate, as well as more accurately correct, they marked his face and hands with chocolate drops, which were designed to imitate the pustules of the smallpox. All the apparatus being ready, the funeral procession began, and proceeded through the principal apartments of the palace at Portici, Ferdinand officiating as chief mourner. Having heard of the Archduchess's decease, I had gone thither on that day, in order to make my condolence privately to His Majesty on the misfortune; and entering at the time, I became an eye-witness of this extraordinary scene.'

In his letter of condolence to the Empress, Ferdinand begged for one of Josepha's sisters. The choice lay between Maria Amalia and Maria Carolina; the former was five years older than Ferdinand and the latter was nineteen months younger. Their portraits were sent to Madrid, and Maria Carolina was chosen. After a seemly interval, preparations for the marriage festivities and the bride's journey were picked up at the point where they had been dropped. The Abbé Galiani, writing to Tanucci from Paris, exclaimed: 'I am delighted by the nuptials, but how will the King reach Gaeta without risk of being overturned? I hear no mention of roads, and the time is too short to make something durable and good. The double expense incurred by mending the road in a hurry, and doing it well, is one of the services which the thrifty San Nicandro has rendered the King.' Tanucci replied: 'The King is tired of the Council's opposition and annoyed by the complaints of travellers and the impropriety, now notorious, of our barbarous lack of roads: he has sacrificed his postal revenue in giving me the task to repair them.'

Galiani also proposed that he should acquire for the King a small writing-desk of Chinese lacquer mounted in gold. Besides being an object of choice and delicate luxury, it would be a graceful gift to the Queen on her arrival. While presenting it, the King might suggest that she use it for writing letters to her august mother. Tanucci replied that there were plenty of such desks in Naples; even card-tables were now made of lacquer. Moreover, 'that compliment about writing to her mother might be taken amiss and for more than one reason. The alphabet of sovereigns was extremely frugal'. Little did Tanucci know Maria Carolina, whose propensity for letter-writing was to exceed her mother's.

VIII

Maria Carolina's journey to Naples—Her reception—The Emperor Joseph's account of his visit in 1769—His description of Ferdinand: speculations about his future development—An unfavourable analysis of Tanucci's character—Joseph's summary of his impressions.

The Archduchess Maria Carolina was very unlike the gentle, submissive Maria Josepha. She was wilful and impetuous, convinced that she had been born to rule. Until the age of fifteen she was brought up with her younger sister, Marie Antoinette, to whom she was deeply attached, but the girls were separated when it was noticed that they were getting into bad habits, such as 'playing childish tricks, making improper remarks, and longing for unsuitable and unreasonable amusements'. 'I shall now treat you as a grown-up person,' the Empress wrote to Maria Carolina, in a long letter full of practical advice. Of all her daughters, the Empress had said, she was the one who most resembled herself.

Maria Carolina had heard enough about Ferdinand to dread the prospect of marrying him, but she had no voice in the matter. Her mother was set on a family alliance with the Bourbons, and she lavished instructions on her royal and domestic duties. 'Avoid coquetry... Remember that many things harmless in a girl are not so in a married woman, although contemptible in either... Love your husband and be firmly attached to him; that is the only true happiness on earth.' The Empress demanded a great deal and made little allowance for human nature. She had been fortunate in her own husband, whereas Ferdinand offered no comparable attractions.

In March Maria Carolina fell ill, and she even feared she would share Josepha's fate. Ferdinand seemed to bring bad luck, she remarked. But she was only suffering from a 'slight fluxion', and soon recovered. On April 7 she was married by proxy in Vienna, where Ferdinand was represented by her homonymous brother. It required some courage for a highly strung girl of sixteen to face long separation from all that was dear to her. She could not conceal her dejection, and said 'they might as well have thrown her into the sea'.

Though Tanucci groaned that he was dizzy with a thousand matrimonial preparations ('my brain has never produced festivities!'), the Austrian ambassador, Count Kaunitz, was none too pleased. Having rented an additional palace on the Chiaia, he expected the King to order celebrations, or at least to announce his betrothal with the discharge of guns. Why had his colleagues received no official notice? Tanucci replied that nothing was to be done until the Queen's arrival. 'This need not cause surprise,' wrote the Venetian resident, 'since for several years there has been nothing but chaos and no system of well-ordered government. Naples remains a Spanish province, or a kingdom in a state of pupilage.' But the Austrian ambassador made such a fuss that Tanucci was induced to search the records. On finding a precedent in the archives of the Royal Artillery, he ordered the nobility to assemble at Portici to kiss the King's hand on April 24. A triple discharge from the fortresses would announce the event to the people, with a solemn *Te Deum,* a universal gala and three evenings of illuminations throughout the city.

In the meantime there were plentiful banquets, balls, concerts and festivities to distract the young Queen on her journey. Her brother Leopold, the Grand Duke of Tuscany, awaited her at Bologna, and his warm reception made her feel almost at home. The whole Florentine Court was kept standing for six hours without food in anticipation of her arrival, but the unusual rejoicings that followed were ample compensation. 'She is a most amiable little Queen,' wrote the English minister Horace Mann to his friend Horace Walpole, 'but it is feared that her extreme delicacy and good sense will only make her feel the more the want of both in her Royal Consort, whose deficiency in both has made many people interpret it as an organical defect approaching madness on some occasions. But Lord Stormont assures me it proceeds totally from the want of education; and that he is now what many school-boys are in England at ten years old. If so, the scandalous neglect may be repaired by his most excellently well-bred Queen, whose great propriety of behaviour and most sensible questions and replies raised admiration in everybody.

'The Duke of Parma went to make her a visit at Mantua, and among others of his suite, presented to her his late preceptor, "who had care," said the Duke, "of my education." "And everybody says," was her reply, "that he may well be proud of it." It was really astonishing to see how well she held the circle here in Florence.'

Maria Carolina wrote home frequently during the journey. To her governess she confessed: 'I remain true to my dear Vienna. Things are more beautiful here than there, but for me they lack the charm and strong attraction of Vienna.' As she approached her destination she became increasingly nervous lest her husband might not be pleased with her.

Owing to the hostilities between the Pope and the Bourbons, she was to avoid Rome; but this was a polite age, and hostilities were often suspended for civilities. 'They could not resist the temptation to see Rome; and therefore suddenly took the resolution to drive through it, taking all the principal streets to St Peter's, where only they alighted. They were complimented on the part of the Pope by his two secular nephews, and were saluted three times by the Castle of St Angelo. They afterwards dined at Villa Borghese, and lay that night at Marino, from whence they sent Prince Schwartzemberg, a chamberlain, to thank the Pope for his civilities.'

While the Grand Duke and Grand Duchess visited the lovely villas of Frascati, 'the Queen was forced to stay at Marino, to receive the homage of her new subjects settled at Rome; not the purpled ones, for the Cardinals were all prohibited going there, on account of the etiquette in regard to their dress'. Ferdinand, prompted by Tanucci, had ordered the Neapolitan prelates to pay their court to her in full canonicals, whereas the Pope had told them to wear travelling costume. Consequently all except the Neapolitan minister to the Holy See failed to appear.

On May 12, 1768, the whole party arrived at Terracina, where Maria Carolina's Austrian suite were to leave her. The young Queen had such a violent fit of trembling that her brother feared she would faint, yet she made an affectionate speech to her attendants, who were all in tears. After this her brother escorted her to the palace occupied by the Austrian minister, where she was introduced to her new suite and presented with a casket of jewels from the King. The old Prince of San Nicandro had come from Naples to welcome her, with the Duchess of Andria as her chief lady-in-waiting and a select body of courtiers. The King was to meet her at Portella, the first Neapolitan town across the border, where an imposing pavilion had been erected as for his parents' first meeting. Into this she was ushered with the Grand Duke and Grand Duchess of Tuscany; and on seeing her bridegroom enter she knelt to kiss his hand, but he soon raised her and escorted her in another carriage to Caserta which they reached shortly before midnight. The stupendous palace had been illuminated, and the so-called 'family ministers', Austrian, French and Spanish, had assembled to greet her, a privilege not shared by the envoys of other Powers.

William Hamilton told his friend Wraxall that though the young Queen could not by any means be esteemed handsome, yet she possessed many charms. 'Ferdinand manifested on his part, neither ardour nor indifference for the Queen. On the morning after his nuptials, when the weather was very warm, he rose at an early hour and went out as usual to the chase, leaving his young wife in bed. Those courtiers who accompanied him, having inquired of His Majesty how he liked her; "*Dorme come un' ammazzata*," replied he, "*e suda come un porco*" ("She sleeps as if she had been killed, and sweats like a pig"). Such an answer would be esteemed, anywhere except at Naples, most indecorous; but here we are familiarized to far greater violations of propriety and decency. Those acts and functions which are never mentioned in England, and which are there studiously concealed, even by the vulgar, here are openly performed. When the King has made a hearty meal, and feels an inclination to retire, he commonly communicates that intention to the noblemen around him in waiting, and selects the favoured individuals, whom, as a mark of predilection, he chooses shall attend him. "*Sono ben pranzato*," says he, laying his hand on his belly, "*Adesso bisogna una buona panciata*" ("I have dined well, and now I need a good easing of the belly"). The persons thus preferred then accompany His Majesty, stand respectfully round him, and amuse him by their conversation during the performance.'

The young Queen, always voluble with her intimates, made no secret of her first impressions. Her bridegroom was indeed very ugly, she wrote to her governess, but no doubt she would grow accustomed to that. His character was better than she had been led to expect, but he thought himself handsome and clever, which was irritating. She confessed that she did not love him, but with tact and gentleness she tried to win his affection. Her efforts were rewarded, for Ferdinand was convinced that she had fallen in love with him. But it was a struggle to feign pleasure when she was often disgusted, bored and homesick.

'Do not always be talking about our country, or drawing comparisons between our customs and theirs,' her mother had written. 'In your heart and in the uprightness of your mind be a German; in all that is unimportant, though in nothing that is wrong, you must appear to be Neapolitan.' But comparisons forced themselves upon her; and Ferdinand must have appeared a savage after the society of her cultured brothers.

Fortunately she had little time for introspection. The foreign envoys outside the 'family clique' had also gone to Caserta to be presented to the Queen, and they were peeved by Tanucci's mismanagement. The Venetian resident wrote that when all the diplomatic corps were assembled, Tanucci informed them that this was neither the right time nor place; he would confer with the King and study some alternative. So they were told to wait in the passage between the Queen's apartments and the chapel, where her chief major-domo would present them to her. They were kept waiting in vain. Finally their doyen, the Papal Nuncio, decided to leave and not return until he had received a written notice confirming the exact place, day and time. This was not the only hitch caused by Tanucci's determination to supervise every finicking formality. 'As all his knowledge is confined to law and the law-courts, he is very bewildered at this juncture... Neither the Queen nor the Grand Duke and Grand Duchess of Tuscany appear to relish their visit to Caserta. Their reserve is attributed to the confusion of the Court, and chiefly to the effect of the King's education, which since his coming of age has been contemptible and ill-suited to one who should hold the reins of government.' Fireworks, concerts, a performance of *The Chinese Idol*, a comedy by Lorenzi, excursions to the great aqueduct, the Capuan monastery of Saint Gabriel, and the waterfall of Mount Briano, filled the five days before the solemn entry to Naples, where public festivities continued for a month.

'During the fêtes,' wrote Hamilton, 'as Their Sicilian Majesties and the Great Duke and Duchess have been continually in the eye of the public, every one is struck with the contrast in the behaviour of His Sicilian Majesty and that of the Queen and Great Duke. The Neapolitan nobility do not conceal their indignation at the lack of their Sovereign's education, and the foreigners, of which there are many here at present... are struck with amazement. The Prince San Nicandro, His Sicilian Majesty's late governor, hangs his head; and those very courtiers who lately encouraged their master in his youthful behaviour, I see are shy of appearing near His Majesty in public, lest his familiarity with them should convey (which is but too true) that they have had a share in His Majesty's education. Your Lordship may easily conceive how much the Queen and Great Duke, whose good sense and good education are conspicuous in every word and action, must suffer upon this occasion; however, they seem to be calmer than they were the first few days of their arrival... The people in general are likewise at the moment greatly discontented, the price of corn having been injudiciously raised; they follow the Great Duke wherever he goes, and cry aloud for bread and redress of their grievances. The Marquis Tanucci is not spared, and the neglects in his administration are the topics of discourse in every coffee house.' During one of their excursions the royal party had a narrow escape from drowning: 'Their Sicilian Majesties with the Great Duke and Duchess went to the island of Procida on Friday last and on Saturday evening as they were taking the diversion of fishing between the islands of Ischia and Procida a sudden wind caused so great a swell that they were in some danger, the boat being small, and it was with difficulty that they reached the island of Procida. His Sicilian Majesty has promoted the two sea-officers who steered the boat, and has ordered a reward of thirty ducats to each of the boat's crew, with a pension for life of twenty-four ducats.' The King's frantic shrieks and gesticulations made a painful impression on his more dignified guests, who contrived to keep their composure.

The Grand Duke of Tuscany wrote to his mother that Maria Carolina's behaviour in public, except a little childishness, was excellent, though she should have stayed another year with her last governess. But Ferdinand was far more childish. As Samuel Sharp observed in 1765: 'It has always been said, that the guardians of a pupil King endeavour to keep their ward in ignorance as a means to preserve their own power when he comes of age. The Neapolitan Regency seems to have adopted this golden rule. Would you believe, that though the King be turned of fifteen, and is contracted to a daughter of the Queen of Hungary, his tutors suffer him to play with puppets, and are not ashamed to let strangers and all the world see in what his principal amusements consist? In one of the chambers of the palace, you find Punch and the whole company of comedians hanging upon pegs, and close to them is a little theatre, where they are exhibited, not to the Monarch but by the Monarch. During Holy Week the King here, because he cannot with propriety partake of the public communion has, just by Punch's theatre on the same floor, a little piece of scenery as long as a dining table, which is to be lighted up with candles as thick as pack-thread; and here the function of burying our Saviour is to be performed, for his entertainment and devotion, for a few days.' How unlike the elaborate tuition Maria Carolina had received in Vienna, which still seemed incomplete to her polished brother! 'The affability and goodness of the Queen of Naples gives universal satisfaction here,' wrote Hamilton in June. But she was slightly indisposed owing to so many junketings, while the Grand Duchess of Tuscany had the misfortune to miscarry.

Though Ferdinand was one year older than Maria Carolina, he was still like a country bumpkin whose instincts had had no other outlet or stimulus apart from physical exercise. He enjoyed drilling his pet regiment of Lipariotes and practising mimic warfare. This was mere playing at soldiers though some took the game seriously, as if he might develop into a militarist. 'It is very strange,' wrote the Abbé Galiani, 'that our young King has the same amusements as the Czar Peter the Great at the same age... War must be an instinct of princes, as it is of kittens to catch mice. There must be a keen relish in extinguishing this evil human race. But if the King enjoys waging war for fun, why does he not capture the castle of Sant' Angelo, which is certainly no stronger than his little toy fort?' 'If we consider the intrigues which provide amusement in popular dramas,' Tanucci replied, 'why should not the young King amuse himself with war and soldiers? May God will that this is the only war his people may have to suffer!' His letters to his father were merely accounts of his sporting activities, whereas Maria Carolina's to her mother reveal an alert, impressionable mind. Education had encouraged her ambitions. Maria Theresa had been careful to stipulate in the marriage contract that her daughter was to take part in the state council as soon as she gave birth to a son. Though she had to wait seven years, Maria Carolina never lost sight of this aim. In the meantime the fact that she could dominate her husband reconciled her to her new life. Before she had been married a year she wrote to her governess: 'I passionately love my dear country and my good countrymen, and I have so strongly inspired my dear husband with the same taste that he has a great desire to go there, and if it only depended on him we should be there already.'

Ferdinand was dazzled by this very self-possessed young woman, whose energy contrasted with his own lack of enterprise. Maria Carolina followed her mother's instructions to the letter; she would always remain an Austrian at heart. She appeared to sympathize with her husband's pursuits, flattered him about his athletic prowess and made him think he had originated her own suggestions, congratulating him when he had carried them out.

Next year the Emperor Joseph went to Naples as he had promised, and his account of his visit is all the more fantastic because it is true. He arrived on March 31, 1769, and stayed in the Austrian ambassador's villa near Portici, declining the magnificent apartment prepared for him in the palace. Noticing that Ferdinand was embarrassed at their first meeting, the Emperor put him at ease by lying on the floor to peer through a telescope and inviting him to do the same. The ice was broken: 'This was the first sign of my favour,' the Emperor remarked; 'my natural tone, but even more my playful and jesting manner, which sometimes made him laugh, removed all his embarrassment, and we became intimate from that moment.' After a while some twenty ministers and courtiers were presented to him; Tanucci stood behind them at the end of the hall. The Emperor saluted the whole assembly without addressing anyone in particular, and later on the King made three remarks that struck him as significant. As they were passing the famous porcelain cabinet (since transferred to Capodimonte) Ferdinand drew attention to its beauty. 'I praised it highly and asked if it were not from Saxony, but he answered no, it came from a local factory, which his father had destroyed, removing all the workmen to Spain, and not even allowing it to be re-established, to his great regret.' The Emperor went on to discuss porcelain factories, especially that of Vienna, and Ferdinand replied that he had promised to take Maria Carolina to Vienna 'as soon as the Pope died'. The Emperor, rather shocked, noted that he said this without any change of expression. 'Then he asked if I had seen Tanucci, whom he described as "a bear that walks on two feet". To sound his opinion on this subject, I told him I was very sorry not to have been able to penetrate the crowd of courtiers so as to pay Tanucci my particular respects. He replied with fervour: "You did well, because he only put himself behind the others to make you bring him forward; and you pleased me by not distinguishing him above the rest."'

Soon the Emperor and the King were calling each other Don Fernando and Don Pepe. After a copious dinner, too highly seasoned for the Emperor's palate, the King led him to his room, where he was surrounded by a motley crowd, including a sculptor in wax who had just finished a caricature of Tanucci which amused the King and Queen; he was also shown some engravings which the King had 'illuminated' not too badly, and the royal collection of guns and whips, which he cracked very smartly in a variety of ways. Then a hunting party was proposed in the walled thickets of Portici, through which the King rambled with a sort of shepherd's crook; accompanied by half a dozen shabby gamekeepers and a band of beggarly beaters-up. The King ran about making a lot of noise, pursuing some wretched deer which had been enclosed there, while the Emperor followed with the Queen, surprised by his antics. At last they came to a place where a camp had been held for manoeuvres, which the King described with gusto, especially the kitchen, where food was available at any hour, and the small cabin for prisoners. From here they proceeded to a ball game; the King took off his coat, tucked up his sleeves, and played with eight bodyguards, valets and ragamuffins. He played tolerably well, but as soon as the Emperor proposed joining him he stopped; as he was afraid of royal competition he became a spectator. He was vastly amused when anybody was hit, so his courtiers did not fail to oblige him, hurling themselves at the ball with mimic frenzy and tumbling about on purpose. But the game seemed interminable to the Emperor.

During the evening Ferdinand had much to say about his forests, hunts, dogs and Court etiquette, and the Emperor noticed that he often complained of the latter, as if it had never occurred to him to change it. In reply to the Emperor's questions he was able to name his government departments, the number of employees, some of their salaries and what their duties were, but in so muddled a manner that the Emperor could not make out if he only had a rough idea or if he knew nothing about it and had invented all this for his benefit. He also described his regiments and where they were quartered. 'Some of his general principles are good enough,' the Emperor concluded. 'He loves his country and admires it to excess, believing that all he has is excellent. He wants everything to be manufactured here, and particularly hates French products, which also applies to his officials. This might have wide repercussions...'

At least the Emperor could assure his mother that the King was deeply in love with Maria Carolina, who was quite aware of her growing influence. So eccentric was Ferdinand's behaviour, that it amused rather than distressed her; fortunately she had a sense of humour. She would have been ashamed to admit loving a person so obviously her inferior, but in describing him to her brother she used the German expression: '*Er ist ein recht guter Narr*' ('He is a right good fool'). The Emperor thought it would be hopeless to try to educate him; she should aim at fostering his affection and leading as respectable and agreeable a life as possible. He asked her if there were any truth in the tales he had heard about the King's punching and slapping her. She admitted that she had received a few kicks, and perhaps a few punches, half in temper and half in fun, sometimes in bed, sometimes in their carriage, but that he had never been really violent, even when she had been cross with him.

As for Ferdinand, he often repeated that he could not be more contented with his wife. His only complaint was that she was too fond of books; he detested reading and did not approve of it in others. She had little opportunity to indulge this vice, which was constantly interrupted by the King's comings and goings. In unbosoming herself to her brother, she told him of various inconveniences which she hoped to remedy. Whenever she accompanied the King on his hunting expeditions she was obliged to sit in his shooting-box without any lady-in-waiting for hours together, in rain, cold or heat, surrounded by pages, equerries, adjutants and huntsmen. These would sit on the ground beside her without ceremony, and as the King's conversation had taught them familiar habits, they were apt to talk loosely to the Queen. She would either have to spend the whole day with the King and his hunting companions, or stay indoors with one of her ladies, in whom she would confide all her thoughts out of sheer boredom, hearing much unsavoury gossip in return. The tone of Court conversation was frivolous in any case, and the King and Queen were well versed in local intrigues and petty scandals.

The Emperor suggested that she should form a salon and invite a select number of ladies to visit her every evening. On the whole, considering that she was barely seventeen, he was impressed by her intelligence and poise. Her character had an excellent foundation, he decided. 'She has not the slightest germ of coquetry, or desire to fascinate, either with her familiars—although she has frequent opportunities, being surrounded by young people—or in her dress, which is very simple and devoid of affectation.' She always wore a scarf and was only slightly *décolletée*; her skirts were so long that you could not even see the tip of her foot; and at balls she wore a hat in the English fashion, or a plume in her hair. The King wanted her to display more bosom, but to this she objected. She had grown a little plumper, which suited her, and she had lovely round arms and milky hands, but unfortunately she had the bad habit of biting the cuticle and tearing it with a pin. Though she could speak fluent Italian, she had picked up all sorts of Neapolitan expressions from her husband, many of them far from polite, and Joseph urged her to apply herself more to the Tuscan.

The Emperor's description of Ferdinand is meticulous. 'He must be five feet seven inches, and therefore a good inch taller than me, very thin, gaunt and raw-boned... his knees always bent and his back very supple, since at every step he bends and sways his whole body. The part below his waist is so limp and feeble that it does not seem to belong to the upper part, which is much stronger. He has muscular arms and wrists, and his coarse brown hands are very dirty since he never wears gloves when he rides or hunts. His head is relatively small, surmounted by a forest of coffee-coloured hair, which he never powders, a nose which begins in his forehead and gradually swells in a straight line as far as his mouth, which is very large with a jutting lower lip, filled with fairly good but irregular teeth. The rest of his features, his low brow, pig's eyes, flat cheeks and long neck, are not remarkable.

'Although an ugly Prince, he is not absolutely repulsive: his skin is fairly smooth and firm, of a yellowish pallor: he is clean except for his hands; and at least he does not stink. So far he shows no trace of a beard. But he is very oddly dressed: his hair smoothed back behind the head and gathered in a net; he wears a large white collar, cuffs of embroidered muslin, and sometimes lace, a grey coat of mixed cloth which we call pepper–and–salt in Vienna, a waistcoat of yellow leather with a little gold braid and copper buttons across his chest, lined with green satin, of which he also wears a sleeveless doublet over his shirt, large yellow deerskin breeches with designs round the button-holes, grey silk stockings and heavy leather shoes with copper buckles; and he never wears a hat, sword or hunting knife indoors, not even when he dines in public, or goes to church or the theatre... But his hunting garb is even more peculiar. He wears a large hat let down on every side, a shaggy grey coat with pockets hanging half-way down his legs, an old leather waistcoat, breeches of the same, a large pouch containing his bags of small shot and a hunting knife like a bayonet, heavy grey stockings of beaver and wool, which not being suspended fall in thick folds over his shoes, a long and heavy Spanish gun on his shoulder, a powder-horn dangling beside it with a knitted green game-bag, and various whistles attached to his button holes. Thus attired he goes hunting every morning. We asked him if he had had good sport and he drew five domestic pigeons and several other small birds he had shot from his pockets, where he had kept them with tender care. Two or three big pointers followed him. These enjoy the privilege of entering everywhere, lying on all the furniture, which at Portici as at Naples is superb and in excellent taste, and filling all the rooms with their filth. After a few minutes' talk the King went to change his clothes. Several courtiers were in attendance; a chamberlain put on his shoes and stockings and a valet combed his hair, to the accompaniment of much tickling and childishness.'

Nothing daunted, the Emperor persisted in his efforts to draw Ferdinand into serious conversation and submitted him to intelligence tests of which he was unconscious. He told him funny stories, but he could only appreciate those about hoaxes and drubbings; anything with a double meaning was beyond him. 'At last I emptied my whole bag and did not know what else to say,' he confessed. 'I happened to see the Grand Mistress and other Court ladies waiting in the ante-chamber and persuaded the King and Queen to let them join us. As they were reluctant I made a joke of it, opened the door and coaxed them in. I wanted to attempt a general conversation, but the King proposed some parlour games. I agreed, but as he had to despatch the Spanish mail I had all the difficulty in the world to make him attend to this and even refused to play until he wrote his letter, whereupon he went off; to return within a quarter of an hour. Then five or six Court ladies, my sister, the King and I began to play blindman's buff and other games... Throughout these the King distributes blows and smacks the ladies' behinds without distinction... There is a continuous tussle with the ladies, who are inured to it and throw themselves sprawling on the floor. This never fails to amuse the King, who bursts with uproarious laughter. As he seldom speaks without shouting and has a piercing voice like a shrill falsetto, one can distinguish it among a thousand...'

The Emperor complained of earache as well as headache. His brother-in-law was positively deafening when he exercised his battalion indoors. 'Some thirty officers, several aged forty, have to play this comedy and submit to daily fisticuffs, kicks and even canings from the King who commands them. The battalion is really an assemblage of all the wretched knaves and rogues surrounding this Prince. I could see no sense in their exercise... The drums and fifes keep up an incessant noise, to which the King's piercing cries are added. He commands sword in hand, shouting, scolding, laughing and striking those who miss. They all wear red and blue uniforms, like the King. In the middle the sutler is announced. They down arms and everybody rushes to eat, without sitting, without knives or forks, tearing the meat with their fingers, drinking from bottles without glasses, and all in order to have a more martial air. On this occasion I saw the King drink a quantity of unmixed wine without any ill effect.'

In religious matters Ferdinand seemed grossly material: he heard Mass every day because his father did likewise; he also confessed and took communion on the same days as his father. Between confession and communion he saw no harm in rough horseplay with his valets. The Emperor doubted if he knew the ten commandments, but he did know that the devil was black and angels were white; he believed in ghosts and spirits, and that Saint Januarius was a superlative saint. Apart from Ferdinand's irresponsibility, his brother-in-law concluded that he was amoral in most respects: 'He explained that he only thought it wrong to sleep with another woman, to steal, murder and lie. I tried to find out if he had any feelings of love and gratitude which the very nature of our Supreme Creator inspires, but I could not discover the slightest vestige, or even any fear of Hell or desire for Heaven.'

The intellectual Emperor must have felt a fish out of water in this environment, but he hoped to persuade his young sister to rise above it. There was material for her to work on: her husband was already chafing under the restrictions of Spanish etiquette. It was for her to set the example: to domesticate the boor by her feminine subtlety and kindle his sparks of native pride.

After sitting four hours through an improvised comedy at Portici, the Emperor exclaimed that he had never sat through anything so tedious and insipid. The actors were mostly courtiers, and the men took feminine roles, repeating the same coarse jokes *ad nauseam*, while the King and the whole audience roared with laughter. Joseph was exasperated with those who were responsible for such rubbish, instead of providing him with civilized entertainment. But curiosity overcame his disgust; and he stayed on purposely to watch the King retire for the night; which he did immediately after supper, donning a purple velvet dressing-gown and red slippers. 'He made no ceremony about going to bed before us, when etiquette demands that the Grand Mistress must fetch his sword, leather breeches, handkerchief and tie, and put them together on an adjacent table. The King would not sleep without his sword, not for all the gold in the world.'

When the Emperor called on Ferdinand and Maria Carolina in the morning he found the former in an amorous mood. 'He fondled her in my presence very tenderly, even voluptuously. She responded coolly, and seemed to tolerate rather than reciprocate his caresses.'

The Queen's patience was often tried in unexpected ways. Before going to the opera, for instance, the King seized one of her gloves. When she begged him to return it, he pretended to hide it, making her search the room in vain when he had thrown it out of the window. 'My sister behaved with great moderation,' wrote the Emperor, considering that a few days previously Ferdinand had also thrown her best muff into the fire. And when Maria Carolina wished to drive along the Mole and the Strada Nuova, the King refused, as he was afraid of crowds. So accustomed was he to being surrounded by his guards, running footmen and equerries, that he lost his nerve when he found himself alone. He was also afraid of the dark, and on returning from the opera, he required torches before and behind his carriage as well as beside each door. When they went to see the aqueduct of Caserta, some peasants gathered round him. 'He had a horrible scare and always kept well behind my sister, not daring to advance until he had called his runners, whom he scolded for leaving him in the lurch.'

In fact, he never wished to be alone. The Emperor relates that when Maria Carolina was singing at the harpsichord after dinner, 'he begged us to keep him company while he was sitting on the close-stool. I found him on this throne with lowered breeches, surrounded by five or six valets, chamberlains and others. We made conversation for more than half an hour, and I believe he would be there still if a terrible stench had not convinced us that all was over. He did not fail to describe the details and even wished to show them to us; and without more ado, his breeches down, he ran with the smelly pot in one hand after two of his gentlemen, who took to their heels. I retired quietly to my sister's, without being able to relate how this scene ended, and if they got off with only a good fright.'

Evidently the Emperor's curiosity was insatiable, for he asked to see the mad Infante, Ferdinand's eldest brother, 'a fairly small child, his head all twisted, with startled eyes, eating all day long, uttering few words, without memory, walking with great difficulty, and truly besotted and pitiful'. But Ferdinand's behaviour seemed to him almost as pathetic. At a Court ball he appeared in a domino of white taffeta; knowing that he was a poor dancer, he escaped, after a couple of quadrilles with the Queen, to play *vingt-et-un* with his chamberlains. 'From a distance,' wrote the Emperor, 'I could see him leaning with his elbows on the table, and he often sent the tapers, counters and cards flying at the other players and spectators. My sister asked him to start another quadrille, and I admired his good nature, as he rose immediately and went to dance, though he certainly dislikes it. My sister seldom plays cards and then for very small stakes. At present *vingt et-un* is in vogue and they play it for high stakes in Naples.'

At another Court ball, the Emperor was selected for special favour. 'The King gave me a great salute with all his might on my behind at the moment I least expected it, in the presence of more than four people. For an age I had the honour of carrying him on my back, and more than twenty times he came and put his arms over my shoulders, slackening his whole body so that it dragged after me. When I got rid of him he prowled round the hall with two of his favourites, clutching them by the collar or by the breeches, laughing and joking with them but noticing nobody else. Our departure for this ball was truly singular. We proceeded in great ceremony to the ante-chamber, where all the courtiers and high officials were waiting for us. The march began with solemnity and good order, the King and Queen both accompanied by two chamberlains with lights, but apparently the King was bored with this procession, for he began to shout like the postillions and kick bottoms lustily right and left, which seemed the signal to start galloping. The whole Court, big and small, ministers, old men, galloped away while the King chased them in front of him, always shouting at the top of his voice. The French ambassador Choiseul unhappily found himself in the King's path and received a punch in passing. Weak as he is, his nose collided with the wall. In this manner they passed the first and second ante-chambers, saloon and corridor, while I remained with the Queen on my arm, leading the ladies. I had almost lost sight of the galloping troop, when we finally met them at our normal pace at the door of the theatre, which was packed with a dense crowd: owing to the ticklings and cries it was appallingly noisy. I asked what the ladies usually did on these occasions, and they assured me that when the King gallops they gallop too, so that all these good old dames follow the procession out of breath. I doubt if I have ever seen anything more ludicrous.'

At one Court ball given in the Emperor's honour, William Hamilton told Wraxall that he witnessed 'a scene truly original, as well as comic... While his Imperial Majesty was standing near the dancers, engaged in conversation with me; Ferdinand having gone down the set and being in a most profuse state of perspiration, pulled open his waistcoat: then taking Joseph's hand, he applied it suddenly to his own shirt behind, exclaiming at the same time, "*Sentite quì, fratello mio*" ("Feel here, brother mine"). The Emperor instantly withdrew his hand, not without manifesting great discomposure; and the two Sovereigns remained for a few seconds, looking in each other's faces. Surprise was equally painted in the features of both; for, as the one had never before been invited to try such an experiment, so the other had never found any individual who did not esteem himself honoured by the familiarity. I had no little difficulty to restrain the muscles of my countenance on the occasion.' Swinburne relates that when the King was standing at a balcony with his brother-in-law he made a very unwarrantable noise, and by way of apology said: '*E necessario per la salute, fratello mio!*' ('It is necessary to the health, brother!').

During a visit to the Certosa of San Martino 'the King seized Mr d'Aliano by the collar and Kaunitz by the arm and scoured the innermost recesses of the monastery, committing a thousand childish follies which ended in the kitchen, where he started to cook an omelette, and urged the good fathers to prepare one which he ate with Dietrichstein, Kaunitz and a few other favourites. They made a singular uproar. I only looked in for a moment and soon left them, foreseeing that this would take a very long time. I advised my sister to sit in the refectory with some of her ladies, and we stayed there talking more than an hour before the King left the kitchen. All the gentlemen of the party had the honour of being treated, either to water which he flung in their faces, or to ices which he spilled in their pockets, or to marmalade which he put in their hats. Even the ambassador Kaunitz was not exempted. He has the misfortune to be ticklish, which amuses the King, who makes him yell and calls him Don Cristofano. From there we went to the university. I was very anxious to speak to the professors and learn their methods, but that did not interest the King in the least; he only went to see a stuffed elephant and a skeleton which were kept there.'

Even the King's hunting seemed pointless to the Emperor. 'Never was country less suitable for hunting than the environs of Naples, especially Portici, which is built on the lava of Vesuvius. They have to blow up rocks and fill the holes with earth to plant a tree; and it is in artificial woods like these that the King has fenced in some wretched deer and wild boars. More than two hundred men, who are invariably the same and whose names and surnames are familiar to the King, are employed as beaters-up. He orders them about, cudgelling them at random and shouting at them in Neapolitan. When the enclosure is entirely surrounded by people... about thirty dogs of all species and sizes are let loose, which run hither and thither chasing whatever they can find. All the beaters-up begin to shout simultaneously, advancing with continuous cries towards the centre where the King stands when he chooses, but usually he prefers to go with the beaters-up and make a noise with them instead of firing. A net is spread to catch the game, which the hunters or peasants take to the King who sets it free and then fires from about ten paces off. The King shoots very recklessly, and I believe he would not be too scrupulous about shooting those in his way. I have seen him fire into the midst of his people; besides he is always playing with his gun, which might easily cause an accident. He was very proud of having shot two boars which had been brought to him by hand, indeed there was no sense in it, since they observe neither rule nor order, and kill game at all seasons of the year. After this the King went fishing in a well-stocked reservoir beside the sea. He should have been successful, but he had no patience and broke all the lines and hooks. Then he showed me a small place about the size of a room filled with sea water and containing a boat which could hardly turn round. In this he is capable of rowing a couple of hours with his chamberlains, thirty paces at most, as the place is no larger than that. I returned to my lodging quite numbed with all the tedious jokes and childishness I had witnessed throughout the day.'

The Emperor thought he could detect some glimmerings of intelligent interest during a visit to Pompeii. 'Having found a spot where they were just digging up some pots and antique vases, he seemed to take infinite pleasure in it and was amused. I did not fail to encourage this inclination and explain all the advantages and prestige connected with it. He expressed a wish to return there more often and ordered the director to advise him whenever there were new discoveries. Seeing that he was well disposed, I spoke to him about the duties of state, glory, reputation and liberty; in fact, I tried to find out if there was any hope or probability of his shaking off his present degradation, and the subjection and constraint in which he is kept by Spain. I could detect germs of all these sentiments, but so definite an aversion from all innovation, so great an indolence of mind and a distaste for all reflection, that I almost dare assure you that the man has never reflected in his life either about himself or his physical or moral existence, his situation, his interests, or his country. He is quite ignorant of the past and present and has never thought about the future; in fact he vegetates from day to day, merely engaged in killing time…'

Joseph's attempts to rouse Ferdinand from his lethargy were admirable. He lectured him on the blessings of matrimony and the importance of keeping his wife's affection; he suggested that instead of receiving oral reports from Tanucci he should demand them in writing, and that if he did not sign his name he should at least take charge of his own private stamp. What would he do, Joseph asked, when he lost Tanucci? He answered that he would never have another Prime Minister, but would make each minister responsible for his own department. Joseph agreed that this would be the best solution, after he had selected the most competent men. He also tried to rouse Ferdinand's resentment against paternal interference. Ferdinand told him that his father had even forbidden him to shoot in a wood near Persano which had been his favourite preserve. Without being able to enjoy it himself, he prevented his own son from doing so.

The Emperor saw Tanucci as the villain of the piece, and his account of the Prime Minister was prejudiced in consequence. After a three hours' interview, in which he shrewdly let Tanucci say his say, airing all his grievances against Rome and the rascalities of the Jesuits, and quoting at least fifty pundits, chapter and verse, to display his erudition, the Emperor probed the man's character with remarkable insight. He granted that Tanucci was learned and a man of talent, but he was also an arrant pedant full of quibbles and cunning, altogether too preoccupied with trifles. Extremely jealous of his authority, he juggled with the distribution of Court favours and posts, however small. He kept the King's and Queen's privy purses, and was their only channel of information about home and foreign affairs. The King had to apply to him when he required money for his private pleasures or when, encouraged by the Queen, he wanted to alter Spanish etiquette, of which Sir Horace Mann wrote: 'The King of Naples gives great balls at Caserta, and to eat, too; but as, by a most rigorous order from Spain, he cannot admit people to his table, he has no table at all. He and his Queen, as well as the whole company, eat off their knees; a strange and very slovenly way of serving a great supper.' A concession in writing from Tanucci was necessary if the King wished to dine in the garden.

But Tanucci's close contact with Spain made him formidable. He was as much Charles III's minister as Santo Stefano had been Elisabeth Farnese's. 'The King of Spain realizes how monstrous it is that he should still dictate despotically from Madrid, and interfere in the minutest affairs of this kingdom, after ceding it fully to his son, who is now a major. But his love for this country, and above all his ambition, prevent him from relaxing his grip. Tanucci is the only man to carry out his wishes: his maintenance is therefore of the utmost consequence, as he sees clearly that if he should lose him, the King of Naples would escape from his cage and act independently. On the other hand, the King of Naples is constantly intimidated by Tanucci, who threatens him with his father's anger and writes to the King of Spain whatever he pleases. The King of Naples, who is timid and irresponsible by nature, is charmed to have an apology for doing even what his reason disapproves, and uses the pretext of his papa whenever it suits him... Tanucci abandons him, after carefully excluding from his circle everybody who could offer him good advice, and surrounding him with a swarm of rogues who are all his creatures and therefore his tools, he obliges the King to consult him. In short, Tanucci is an accomplished shuttle between the two Kings: he knows how to exploit both, and render himself equally necessary and agreeable to both to preserve his own credit, which in my opinion he will keep as long as the present King of Spain is alive, and possibly after his death. Good moral qualities and disinterestedness are attributed to him. He accepts no favours, but his wife does; he is a great worker; being all-powerful, he must do everything, and being jealous of his authority, every trifle must pass through his hands. He is a Tartuffe, outwardly humble and punctilious in unimportant matters that might rouse comment, but otherwise a scoundrel, caring little about the two Kings, his benefactors, or the kingdom, making trouble between father and son, flattering both and muffling them in the ignorance which serves his ends; while keeping truth and honest people at a distance. He only thinks of himself, and turns all means lawful and unlawful to his personal profit. He has seen with his own eyes the King's infamous education, and he alone could have changed this. Every day he has had opportunities to wean him from his childish amusements and persuade him by degrees to take an interest in work and application. But this did not suit his plan; and although when I discussed it with him he pretended to be eager for it, I had no difficulty in perceiving that the wretch was trembling for fear I should open the King's eyes.

'After we had discussed one thing and another, and his loquacity was somewhat exhausted by two hours of conversation, when midnight struck and he wished to go home I began to talk about my sister, otherwise he never sticks to the subject and jumps from branch to branch, beginning with stories dating from the deluge. He answered me with precision, as I had also taken the precaution to make him rise and keep him standing, in spite of his gout. He assured me that he was satisfied with the Queen, but he could not conceal that he feared her, since she did not seem so infatuated with his merit or blind about his integrity as he would wish. I reassured him on this point and promised my assistance, because I believe this would serve the Queen at this particular moment.'

Tanucci professed to be charmed by this enlightened monarch, so simple in his manners and dress, little guessing that his sympathy was not returned. But their political difference was fundamental, for Tanucci was determined to uphold Spanish against Austrian influence. He was doggedly devoted to his old master, 'the patriarch' as he affectionately called him. When Galiani told him about the cordial reception he had been given by Count Firmian, the Austrian governor of Milan, 'who is equally kind to all Neapolitans who come here,' Tanucci retorted: 'The Germans' love is pastoral, like the Pope's: they feed sheep and lambs in order to fleece and devour them.'

According to Hamilton, who, already in demand as a cicerone, escorted the Emperor to Vesuvius and Pompeii, 'Joseph, who held his brother-in-law's understanding in great contempt, endeavoured to assume over him the sort of superiority, arrogated by a strong over a weak mind. But Ferdinand, though confessedly his inferior in cultivation and refinement, was by no means disposed to adopt his political opinions or ideas. He even manifested, in various conversations and on many occasions, that, defective as his education had been, he possessed as much plain sense, and even acute discernment, as the Emperor, or his brother Leopold, Grand Duke of Tuscany. Joseph did not, indeed, inspire any very high admiration by his deportment or general conduct, while he remained at Naples. He was irritable, and even irascible, where he should have shown good humour or command of temper. I accompanied him to the summit of Vesuvius, and with concern saw him break his cane over the shoulders of the guide, Bartolomeo, for some slight offence he had given His Imperial Majesty.'

The Emperor Joseph's verdict on Tanucci was undoubtedly biased by his sister, who saw him already as the chief obstacle to her ambitions. She had told him soon after his arrival that she believed Tanucci was false and unfriendly to her. 'I calmed her as well as I could on the subject,' he wrote, 'and by force of reasoning persuaded her to see him more often and consult his advice. Her pride suffered from having to burn incense like others before the idol of the day.' At the moment Tanucci had nothing to fear from her, whereas she had plenty to learn from him.

After nine days of playing the courtier, as the Emperor described his Neapolitan visit, he confessed that he had never been saddled with a more arduous occupation. Ferdinand remained boisterous till the last. Seeing his wife burst into tears before her brother's departure, he made fun of her by aping her emotion. Joseph had much ado to pacify her. 'She was on the point of getting very angry, and it was only after preaching to her in German that his behaviour was due to mere childishness and bad education that she mastered her feelings and said nothing. On the other hand, I preached to the

King to leave her alone today and not torment her. He assured me that he regretted my departure and the pain it caused her; at the same time he said he had never wept from sorrow in his life, but often from anger, that he had lost his mother without caring much, and that his father might go the same way without causing him the slightest twinge, since he could not remember having seen either of them. He would be sorry to lose his wife, but he could never wait through six weeks of mourning before taking another...

'My last words to the King were jocular: "*Ma qui si piange, Addio!*"—as in the opera *Regulus*. And he repeated two words which he often applied to me, and which will ever be engraved on my heart: "*Pazzo Briccone!*" ("Mad Rascal!").'

Summing up his impressions, the Emperor wrote: 'The Court has an air of grandeur and magnificence, the town palace and that of Portici are superb; among the copious nobility are several men and women of wit who could make life very agreeable. The lower orders pullulate, and you cannot walk into an ante-chamber without finding a dozen of them. There is a cohort of game-keepers, whippers-in, beaters-up, etc., and all the palaces swarm with the most infantile amusements. The palace of Naples contains five or six frescoed and marble rooms filled with chickens, pigeons, ducks, geese, partridges, quails, birds of all sorts, canaries, cats, dogs and even cages full of rats and mice, which the King occasionally sets free and enjoys the pleasure of chasing. One day he seized a live mouse and carried it among the Court ladies, and after thoroughly tormenting them he threw it in their faces. Women make no impression on him, and he takes as little notice of them as of a running footman. Those who surround the King's person are mostly wretches, and it would be useless to get rid of some, as has been done already, since they are like a hydra: by cutting off one head ten others will grow. The King is amused by every street urchin, and the only thing he ever writes is a list of the nicknames he has given his beaters-up, as an aid to memory. No Court employee, however important, lacks a nickname, which the King used in presenting them to me. The King is an indefinable being. Even if he had not been neglected in the past, he could never have reached distinction. About his future I dare not prophesy, but if he ever changes I am greatly mistaken. But as I also do not foresee that he will deteriorate and my sister is satisfied, the present situation is likely to last. She, dazzled by the grandeur of the Court, the honours paid her, the beauty of the country and the freedom she enjoys, will become ever more accustomed to it, and I am quite at ease about her fate.'

IX

Maria Carolina and the Freemasons—Court life rejuvenated—Large influx of foreigners—Casanova—The Prince of Francavilla—Sarah Goudar—Galiani's reluctant return—Piccinni—William Hamilton becomes a Neapolitan institution—A paternal government—English visitors—Maria Carolina's firstborn—The Queen enters the Council of State—Fall of Tanucci, 1776.

The Emperor Joseph's visit had thrown many a provocative pebble into the clear pool of Maria Carolina's impressionable mind, and while her husband was amusing himself she began to save time for more serious occupations. As the daughter of a great Empress, as the sister of the Co-Regent of the Hapsburg realm and of the Grand Duke of Tuscany, equally patriotic and industrious, she expected to play a role in world affairs. If she could not enlarge the kingdom of Naples, she hoped to increase its importance. To be independent it would have to be strong. But she would have to wait in the wings until she produced a son. The Abbé Galiani had suggested to his friend Mme d'Épinay, who took a modish interest in education, that she should come to Naples and educate the royal children, but before that event the Queen would have to be pregnant. 'I am working for that end,' he wrote, 'by my prayers to Heaven and by my sincerest wishes. If our Queen were the wife of a private individual, I should try to work for it even more efficaciously, for she has one of the most interesting faces I have ever seen. She is the most beautiful woman in Naples, and it is a great pity that she should be Queen.' Knowing that his letters were read to a wide circle, he was aware that the compliment would be repeated. Later, when the Queen gave birth to a daughter, he described her more truthfully as having 'a delivering air', and prophesied that she would fill the royal nursery with little princes. In the meantime she rehearsed; she gathered a sympathetic group around her. Making the most of her Viennese education, she set out to win the confidence of the cultured *élite*, coquetting with the fashionable 'philosophy' of the period.

Maria Carolina had been brought up in a Masonic environment: her father, her brother Joseph II and two of her sisters were Freemasons. Consequently she took an interest in the fraternity, which began to flourish in Naples under her protection. The various lodges provided modern entertainment, gay suppers, balls and literary discussions of the lighter sort. Many joined them to get in touch with foreigners, and most were attracted by the mysterious mumbo-jumbo of signs and symbols combined with a carefree, sceptical atmosphere.

Pope Benedict XIV had warned Christianity against the social and religious dangers of their secret meetings, and Charles had banned the sect in 1751 when the miracle of San Gennaro had failed. The Prince of San Severo, Grand Master of the Neapolitan lodges, wrote a letter to the Pope declaring that Freemasonry, as he knew it, was merely concerned with charity and innocent amusement, but that he was ready to sever all connexion with it. However, the meetings continued, and after Maria Carolina's arrival the lodges multiplied and spread through the provinces. The pillars of Neapolitan society were known to belong to them. The Prince of Caramanico, a favourite of the Queen, became Grand Master of all the national lodges; the Duke of San Demetrio, Grand Master of the lodge of Equality, the Prince of Ferolito, of the lodge of Peace; the Duke of Serracapriola, of the lodge of Friendship. There was also a feminine lodge over which the Princess of Ottaiano presided as Venerable; her sister-in-law the Marchesa di San Marco, the Duchess of Termoli, and other leading ladies of the Court belonged, and the Queen enjoyed the novelty of their banquets. During an opera at the San Carlo the *prima donna* Bernasconi stopped on the middle of the stage and made the Masonic sign of recognition. She was greeted with general applause. Thus, though Freemasonry had been condemned by the Pope and Charles III, it continued to thrive in Naples. Tanucci never took it seriously. He saw the Pope, the Jesuits and the Roman Curia as a far greater menace.

With her youthful vivacity and the aura of Viennese glamour still clinging to her, it was easy for Maria Carolina to charm. Since her arrival the Court had become a livelier social centre and far more cosmopolitan. Not so amusing by Parisian standards, perhaps, but a refreshing change after the dull, Tanucci-ridden Regency, as we may judge from Lady Anne Miller's account of a Court ball given in the theatre of Caserta in 1771: 'Her Majesty is a beautiful woman, she has the finest and most transparent complexion I ever saw; her hair is of that glossy light chestnut I so much admire; it is by no means red; her eyes are large, brilliant, and of a dark blue, her eyebrows exact and darker than her hair, her nose inclining to the aquiline, her mouth small, her lips very red (not of the Austrian thickness), her teeth beautifully white and even, and when she smiles she discovers two dimples, which give a finishing sweetness to her whole countenance; her shape is perfect: she is just plump enough not to appear lean; her neck is long, her deportment easy, her walk majestic, her attitudes and action graceful; she is a beauty so much to my taste, that I must say no more of her person, etc., lest she should fill up too much of my paper.

'As soon as her Majesty, etc., were come into the pit, the Queen immediately danced a minuet, and to the highest perfection; both their Majesties were dressed *en Savoyarde*, the stuff was striped satin. Neither gold, silver, jewels, lace, or embroidery are permitted to be worn at these *fêtes*.

'At the time I was presented, the Queen and all the company in the box were unmasked; but when her Majesty descended into the ballroom (the pit) she entered masked, as did the others. A small black mask which covers half the face is what everybody must wear.

'There is no precedence observed at these balls; the King and Queen go in and out promiscuously, which is the reason why the company is not so numerous as one might expect to find it. None but such as the Queen esteems proper to receive and converse with *sans cérémonie* are ever admitted; and there are many of the Neapolitan nobility, even to the rank of dukes, who are allowed only to see the ball from the upper boxes... Any of the company may dance at the same time as their Majesties. There are three or four sets of English country-dances, and when the Queen is tired of them, minuets are danced, as many as can be at the same time. The Queen calls out those she chooses to dance with; she did M— the honour to order him more than once that night to dance with her. His Majesty is not fond of this amusement; however, he danced a country-dance in a set he commanded, consisting of men only, that he might, I suppose, dance as high and as violently as he pleased; but he met with one young Englishman who was more than his match, the Lord L—, who gave him such a twirl in return, as both surprised and pleased his Majesty.

'The theatre is in the palace; it is approached through spacious courts, and then through large passages lined with a double row of guards under arms. The plan is circular, the proscenium appeared to me to cut off about a third from the circle; the boxes are larger than those in any other I have yet seen; they are lined, gilt, and decorated with a profusion of ornaments... The stage was covered with the musicians upon benches, rising pyramidically one above the other, the top of the pyramid is crowned by the kettle-drums. The musicians are all in a livery, their coats blue, richly laced, their waistcoats red, and almost covered with silver, small black hats, with long scarlet feathers stuck upright in them: large wax candles are placed between, so that they form a striking *coup d'oeil* upon your entering the theatre; the whole is so artfully illuminated that the effect is equal, and seems as if the light proceeded from a brilliant sun at the top... The pit (which is more like an antique arena) is floored with a composition coloured red, very hard, and rather slippery; here it is they dance. The boxes are appropriated to the foreign ministers and great officers belonging to the Court. At twelve the Queen unmasks, as do all the company in the same moment: they then adjourn to supper, those who happen to be near the door going out first, thus it may happen that their Majesties may be last, so completely is the *etiquette* annihilated here. When the Queen is near the door, all the courtiers crowd about her on their knees to kiss her hands, which she lends on each side in the most gracious manner.

'After mounting a staircase, you enter several large rooms, hung and adorned in the Italian taste with crimson damask, velvet, etc., and amply illuminated. The chairs are placed all round against the walls, and each sits down where they choose. These rooms were so full, that there was a double row of chairs placed back to back down the middle. Accident placed me exactly opposite the Queen, who took the first chair she found empty. There are no tables in any of the rooms; but every person being seated, the supper is served thus: The best looking soldiers, chosen from the King's guards, carry about the supper with as much order, regularity, and gravity as if they were performing a military manoeuvre. First appears a soldier bearing a large basket with napkins, followed by a page, who unfolds and spreads them on the lap of each of the company as they happen to sit; but when it comes to the Queen's turn to be served, a lord of the Court presents her Majesty's napkin. The first soldier is immediately followed by a second, bearing a basket of silver plates; another carries knives and forks; then follows a fourth, with a great *pâté*, composed of macaroni, cheese, and butter; he is accompanied by an *écuyer tranchant*, or carver, armed with a knife a foot long, who cuts the pie, and lays a large slice on the plate (which has been placed on the lap of each of the company); then a fifth soldier, with an empty basket, to take away the dirty plates: others succeed in the same order, carrying wine, iced water, etc.; the drinkables are served between the arrival of each eatable: the rest of the supper consisted of various dishes of fish, ragouts, game, fried and baked meats, perigord-pies, boar's-heads, etc. The dessert was formed into pyramids, and carried round in the same manner; it consisted of sweetmeats, biscuits, iced chocolate, and a great variety of iced fruits, creams, etc. The Queen ate of two things only, which were prepared particularly for her by her German cooks; she did me the singular honour to send me some of each dish.

'As soon as the Queen perceived that all the company had supped, she arose and proceeded to the coffee-room, as did those of the company who chose coffee. This room is furnished like the coffee-houses of Paris precisely: the walls covered with shelves, on which are placed all kinds of liqueurs and Greek wines. Here are tables, behind which stand young men in white waistcoats and caps, who make and serve the coffee and other refreshments, of which there is a profusion. The Queen was most gracious to me, and distressed me by her goodness; for there being a great crowd, and finding a chair empty, I sat down upon it, when turning my head I perceived her Majesty close to me: I arose; she took hold of me and obliged me to sit down; and having a dish of coffee in my hand, it was with the utmost difficulty I could prevent the contents of it from falling upon her clothes—I have often observed that Princes are exceedingly sudden in their motions. She was so gracious as to commence a conversation; but quickly perceived how much she embarrassed me by her commands, as I was sitting and her Majesty standing close to me, she most kindly relieved me, by giving me an opportunity of rising, pretending she wanted something.

'The ball lasted till seven in the morning; we quitted it at four, being much fatigued with dancing. I was determined to follow the example of the Italian ladies in one instance, that of drinking iced water and iced lemonade when very warm; and what is surprising, so far from feeling any bad effect, I found myself considerably relieved from my fatigue, and not the least chilliness succeed. We returned back to Naples without any accident, and slept profoundly for ten hours. We are invited to a grand *Bal Paré* at the French ambassador's, Monsieur de Choiseul's, and to a second at the Princess Potero's (Butera's).'

As an Italian historian expressed it, this was an Austrian Carnival after the Spanish Lent. At the same time Naples became the favourite resort of distinguished and opulent foreign travellers, drawn by Vesuvius, Pompeii, the classical scenery, the benign climate, the agreeable society and the dramatic picturesqueness of it all. The tourist was supplemented by the foreign resident, and so many of these published their impressions that the life of the metropolis may be reconstructed from several points of view. A horde of adventurers followed in their wake who have also left records: of these Casanova and Sarah Goudar were the most garish specimens.

As usual, Casanova was to be found wherever the votaries of pleasure were assembled. During the reign of Charles he had consorted with the prodigal Carlo Carafa, Duke of Maddaloni, a lavish patron of the theatre. His palace on the Toledo was a club for amateur actors and dramatists, and the Duke himself invented plots for improvised plays and excelled in the lover's role. But off the stage he was less successful as a lover. He is said to have vowed to Saint Francis that he would build a fine church next to the Capuchin Convent at Maddaloni if he was granted a son and heir, and eventually this blessing, which proved deceptive, was vouchsafed.

Casanova happened to call while he was dining, and the Duke rushed to meet him with open arms, introducing him to the Duchess and his guests. One of these exclaimed: 'You must surely be a bastard of my father's!' 'More likely of your mother's,' Casanova retorted. But instead of taking offence, the speaker rose to embrace him. It was the Duke of Casalnuovo, who had misunderstood the surname. Maddaloni had his three-year-old son brought in and shown to Casanova, who exclaimed that he was the image of his papa. But a waggish monk protested that he did not resemble the Duke in the least. The Duchess gave him a resounding slap, which he accepted with a burst of laughter. She impressed Casanova as beautiful, but 'as tall as time, and always the mistress of her eyes'. Casanova failed to seduce her—'which was perhaps as well, and I abandoned her to her pride'.

He describes the Duke's vast stables, his magnificent Arab, Andalusian and English horses, his precious picture gallery and library, which contained a choice collection of 'forbidden books'. While pointing to the latter, the Duke said mysteriously: 'Promise me the strictest secrecy about what I am going to show you.' Casanova expected something extraordinary, but the Duke with great caution produced a satire ridiculing various personalities at Court, of which he could understand nothing. 'Never was it easier for me to keep a secret,' he wrote. The Duke took him to the San Carlo and the Fiorentini theatre, and introduced him to a young woman whom he advertised as his mistress, 'for the sake of appearance'. Of course Casanova took advantage of this opportunity to plunge into another love affair, eventually to discover that Leonilda, as she was called, was his own daughter. The Duke also took him to several houses, such as that of the Duke Monteleone Pignatelli, where Casanova first lost and then won back several thousands of *ducats* at faro, and to the Prince of Cassaro's villa at Posillipo, where he was even luckier. Maddaloni also presented him at Court when King Ferdinand was only nine years old, and he kissed a little hand 'all covered with chilblains'.

On his next visit to Naples the Duke had died, after a short but merry life, at the age of thirty. His son turned into a typical ne'er-do-well, whose marriage was annulled for impotence in a cause *célèbre*, and who 'democratized' himself as Citizen Carafa Maddaloni under the Republic of 1799. Casanova found another distinguished prodigal to entertain him in 1770. This was Michele Imperiale, the Prince of Francavilla, whose grandfather had died of a fit after an interview with Tanucci. He had rented the Palazzo Cellamare, magnificent even now as a shadow of its former self, which he restored and redecorated in the French taste. Cochin described his picture gallery, valued at 30,000 ducats, which contained a Virgin and Child by Titian, a 'Magdalen anointing the feet of Jesus' by Paul Veronese, many romantic scenes of ruins and architectural panels by Pannini, and a lively 'Bacchanal of Boys' in the manner of Rubens, besides his rare furniture, porcelain and tapestry as fine as anything in the royal palace. Lalande described the terraced gardens as among the most splendid in Naples, and admired the quantities of pineapples flourishing in the conservatory.

The stables were almost as valuable as the picture gallery, and their keeper, Gaetano Pezzella, was so highly esteemed that a book was dedicated to him, entitled *The Pride of Neapolitan Coachmen, or Of their very noble Art of taming horses and guiding them under carriages, superior to that of any other Nation*, adorned with the hero's portrait, a burly fellow of forty with a wig and embroidered waistcoat. The Prince's retinue of stewards, secretaries, butlers, valets and pages included a dwarf who had been presented to the Princess by Cardinal Valente. At the age of twenty-seven he was only three feet three inches high, wrote Lalande; however, he was not so remarkable, nor was his figure so well-proportioned, as Count Borowloski, a Pole only twenty-eight inches high, whom Lalande had seen in Paris, as well as King Stanislas of Poland's dwarf, called Baby, who was three feet high. 'As for intellectual faculties, the Princess's fell between these two, of whom the first had much wit and talent, and the second was almost a fool.'

The Prince of Francavilla used to entertain between seven and eight hundred guests almost every other day. Casanova was among these in 1770, with the British ambassador and the notorious Duchess of Kingston, at a party in the Prince's casino at Santa Lucia. After dinner, says Casanova, 'the Prince led us to a pool beside the sea, where we were shown a prodigy. A priest jumped stark naked into the water and without making any movement he floated like a pineplank. There was no trick in it; and this marvel must have been due to some special quality in his organs of breathing.' The priest was Don Paolo Moccia, one of the curiosities of Naples, and an excellent Greek and Latin scholar, who taught in the royal school of pages. 'After this truly astonishing immersion,' Casanova continues, 'the Prince treated the Duchess to a very interesting spectacle: he made all his pages dive into the pool together. These were boys ranging from fifteen to seventeen, as comely as cupids, and on leaving the breast of the waves almost simultaneously, they swam up under our eyes, developing in strength and grace, and performing a thousand evolutions. All these Adonises were the minions of this amiable and magnificent Prince, who preferred the love of Ganymede to that of Hebe.' The Englishmen of the party asked the Prince for a diversion of the opposite sex, and accordingly a beauty chorus of sirens gave a brilliant swimming display in the marble pool of his country house near Portici—a spectacle, adds Casanova, which the

Duchess of Kingston pronounced to be tedious, whereas she had thought the other delicious.

Nearly all visitors to Naples at this time refer to the Prince's splendour. According to Casanova, 'he was in favour in Spain, but the King allowed him to reside at Naples because he foresaw that he might easily initiate the Prince of Asturias, his brothers, and perhaps the whole Court, into his peculiar tastes'. In a description of the Carnival festivities, Sarah Goudar mentions that he contributed two gorgeous chariots in the form of a ship drawn by superb horses. The first contained an orchestra which played melodious symphonies; the second was filled with posturing characters from the *Commedia dell' Arte*. These elaborate coaches paraded in the middle of the Toledo, and Swinburne mentions that sledges of hunters with horsemen and hounds attended them in 1777, when the last carriage was an English packet-boat, manned by the royal cadets.

Sarah Goudar was a feminine counterpart of Casanova, who had met her as a sixteen-year-old maid in a London tavern and had magnanimously waived the rights of seduction to his friend Goudar, a Frenchman with a versatile pen. Goudar was quick to exploit the collaboration of his brains with her beauty. The couple drifted to Naples, where Goudar offered Tanucci an economic plan to improve Neapolitan trade, and when this was rejected, he published a provocative book on the subject. Sarah was more successful. When Casanova met her again the tavern wench had blossomed into the elegant hostess of a mansion at Posillipo, frequented by the cosmopolitan aristocracy. Although a Catholic, her husband passed her off as an Anglican, and posing as such she was 'converted' with loud publicity. To camouflage her real activities she published letters on theatrical subjects, which were penned by her husband in the pert style of a female gossip columnist: 'As for me, I am always gloomy in dark weather. If I chose what they call a *cicisbeo*, which merely means a lover in good French, I would ask him only to enter my apartment with the sun, for if he appeared when the sun was hidden, I think he would fail to make the best of me.' And speaking of the singer Pacchierotti, who sent so many dilettanti, like Beckford, into raptures: 'I know not if it is because I am a woman, but I dislike eunuchs.'

A clue to the real activities of the Goudars is to be found in a curious little book called *The History of the Greeks, or of those who correct luck at gambling*. 'This is not a history of cheating,' wrote

Goudar. 'It is only the history of cheats.' Their old friend Casanova struck up acquaintance with rich and gullible tourists at his inn and took them to the Goudar casino to be plucked. 'The lovely Irishwoman had every quality to please,' he wrote, 'beauty, grace, wit, youth, talent, and gaiety; above all, an easy distinguished manner which made her irresistible. Oh, how worthily this tavern wench would have occupied a throne! But Fortune is blind.' All those who came to Naples for amusement rather than instruction were bound to meet this adventurous couple, who were accommodating to a fault.

There were two classes of nobility: the great families connected with the Court, holding appointments in the royal household, and the larger feudal clans living on their country estates, accumulating wealth and clinging to their privileges, often in defiance of royal jurisdiction. King Charles had enticed many of these to the capital, where they rivalled each other in extravagance, like the Duke of Maddaloni and the Prince of Francavilla. Some ruined themselves, but it is absurd to dismiss them all as frivolous. Many were conscientious landlords who improved their property and saw to the welfare of their peasants. They were probably more enlightened than any other class except the clergy and denizens of the law. Many were eager to absorb the new ideas on philosophy, politics and economy which were filtering in from France and pervading the Court, where Maria Carolina welcomed them, hoping they would destroy Tanucci and Spanish influence.

Galiani's letters to Madame d'Épinay describe the sensational success of the first French company of actors to visit Naples in 1773. Other theatres were deserted for the Fiorentini, where these were performing, and the popular enthusiasm even affected the King, who was seen to weep copiously at Voltaire's *Zaïre*.

Poor Galiani hated to return to Naples, but he had to pay for a diplomatic indiscretion. His enemy Choiseul had watched and waited till a compromising document fell into his hands, a despatch from the Danish minister reporting a conversation: 'The Abbé Galiani, secretary to the Court of Naples and close confidant of the Marquis Tanucci, informed Baron de Gleichen that the King of Naples had never acceded and would probably never accede to the Family Compact, whence the lack of agreement between the Ministries of France and Naples; that the Court of Naples would choose the first convenient opportunity to differ from the Courts of Versailles and Madrid...'

Choiseul wrote indignantly to Madrid demanding Galiani's recall, and Grimaldi, the Spanish Minister of Foreign Affairs, was all the more eager to oblige him since he loathed Tanucci. 'I regret,' he wrote ironically to the latter, 'that Your Excellency must suffer such a reprimand from the King owing to the light words of a subordinate, and to his greater frivolity in communicating his private notions as if they emanated from his Court. However, this reprimand can only recoil on the author of the speech.'

Galiani was stunned when he was ordered back to Naples at three days' notice. 'Save death, nothing worse could have happened to me,' he exclaimed. Feigning illness, he contrived to linger in Paris another month and finish his *Dialogues on the Corn Trade*, which he flung as a parting bomb into the enemy camp. Though he returned to Naples, he left his heart in Paris; though he received more lucrative posts, he refused to be consoled. He tried to recreate the atmosphere in which he had gloried. 'I have arranged a sample-specimen of Paris here,' he wrote. 'Gleichen, General Kock, a Venetian resident, the secretary of the French embassy and I all dine together; we meet and play at Paris much as Nicolet plays Molière at the fair. But our Fridays will revert to Neapolitan Fridays, remote from the character and tone of those in Paris, unless we can find a woman who will guide us, who will Geoffrinize us.' For he missed above all the *salons* of Mme Geoffrin, Mme Necker and his devoted Mme d'Épinay. 'Nobody electrifies me in this unhappy country,' he complained. 'I cannot accustom myself to this diet and this air, formerly my native air, which is so no longer. My eyesight gets worse every day, and I continue to lose my teeth... My mother is dead, my sisters are nuns, and my nieces are idiots.' He could only enjoy the society of his cat, which inspired him to write—since Mme d'Épinay was much interested in elementary education—a facetious book entitled *Moral and political instructions of a cat to its young, translated from cat language into French by Mr Scratchy* (Égratigny). He became a devourer of travel literature, to 'expatriate himself as much as possible'.

Gradually he was acclimatized. He was appointed fiscal advocate and president of the council which administered the King's domain: 'I write masterpieces of advice for the King which nobody reads and will never be printed, but these rob me of the time to do anything else.' The fact was that in Naples his erudition was more appreciated than his wit, which was local currency with a higher polish, while absence enhanced his Parisian prestige. Voltaire had been so delighted with his *Dialogues on the Corn Trade* that he remarked: 'No man has ever made famine so amusing. Even if the book does not lower the price of bread, it will give pleasure to the whole country... Plato and Molière might have written it together.' And Grimm called it the product of a statesman and of a sound philosopher, adding that if he were Controller-General he would attach Galiani to France, even if it cost the King forty thousand *livres* per annum—'without any other stipulation except that he should amuse himself and come twice a week to chat with me about the affairs of my Government'.

Sweet incense; but alas, his King was incapable of savouring the subtleties of a Galiani. The Queen realized that he was a social asset, but she was disconcerted by his scepticism. 'I have all the vices,' he said, but he was extremely kind to his family and took endless trouble to marry off his nieces, one of whom was hunchbacked. 'Half the human species has far greater need of a good husband than of a good book,' he wrote, 'and if this is true in Paris, judge how true it must be in Naples, where at the most there are only twelve people who can read.'

His favourite relaxation was the comic opera; nowhere else had it reached such perfection. 'Of all musicians my favourite is Pergolesi,' the Président de Brosses had written. 'Ah, what a charming talent both simple and natural! It is impossible to compose with greater facility, grace and good taste.' Galiani was equally enthusiastic about Piccinni and Paisiello, an enthusiasm which even the King was able to share. Whiffs of it reach us in his letters to Mme d'Épinay: 'I am sending you an *aria* of Piccinni's which is, in my opinion, one of the most agreeable pieces of music I have heard in my life, but you should hear it with all the instruments, as the author composed it, not omitting one... I am also sending another *aria* from the same opera: the words are French, which may surprise you, though they are somewhat mangled. The plot is that Scapin, to deceive a jealous old husband, introduces himself into his house as a foreign nobleman travelling for his health. He pays very dear for his lodging, but he declares that he cannot endure the sight of a woman, even less the smell of one, without feeling sick. In the husband's presence, his mistress arrives and he pretends to faint, then he jumps up and cries "Murder and Assassination!" and threatens the jealous old man who escapes, thus giving him an opportunity to elope with his mistress. This last *aria* is fine too, but requires the accompanying action.'

Piccinni went to Paris, where his conflict with Gluck divided society into Gluckists and Piccinnists. Queen Marie Antoinette led the Gluckist party, which eventually won the day. Mme d'Oberkirch wrote in her *Memoirs* that the quarrel started with the Abbé Arnaud's remark that Gluck had composed an Orlando and Piccinni an Orlandino. 'Marmontel, who had written Piccinni's libretto, became infuriated and the battle broke loose. Women as well as men joined in the fray... Even families were divided, and I know a very pretty woman who gave as the reason for her conjugal infidelities: "How can one endure such a man and be faithful to him? He is a Piccinnist and grates on my ears from morning till night." "Then you repay him from night till morning," somebody retorted.'

Galiani exerted himself from a distance in support of Piccinni who, as Vernon Lee wrote, 'did more than any composer of his day to bring about the gradual transition to the softer, brighter, less tragic, more richly accompanied style, which, twenty years later, was to attain to perfection in the hands of Paisiello, Cimarosa, and, most resplendently unheroic of all, Mozart'. In 1775 Galiani was collaborating with Paisiello. 'I am seriously engaged in directing a comic opera,' he told Mme d'Épinay. He described the plot as an imitation of Don Quixote: it was entitled *The Imaginary Socrates*. 'A worthy provincial bourgeois suddenly becomes obsessed with the idea of reviving ancient philosophy, ancient music, gymnastics, etc. He imagines himself Socrates and makes a Plato of his barber, the Sancho Panza of the piece. His wife is Xantippe, a shrew who always beats him. He goes into his garden to consult his dæmon; finally he is persuaded to drink a soporific, which he believes to be hemlock. Thanks to the opiate, as soon as he wakes up he finds himself cured of his folly.'

The plot and many of the scenes were invented by Galiani, but they were versified in the Neapolitan dialect by Giambattista Lorenzi. The Socrates in question was a burlesque of the Calabrian Saverio Mattei, a carping critic and Greek scholar who had attacked Piccinni and his influence as frivolous and effeminate. In Galiani's words: 'It has enjoyed the most sublime success. After six public performances and one at Court, it was banned by His Majesty's express command. This has not happened in Italy before, and in

France only *Tartuffe* has deserved such an honour. Thus *Socrates* may be compared with *Tartuffe* owing to the clamour it has caused, the cabals, intrigues and malice it has engendered. Such is my position here, and the terror my wit excites in the heads of imbeciles. Envy rather than pity me, for this affair has done me no harm. You cannot imagine all the explanations which have been tacked on to this comedy, all the allusions it was said to contain. Since the Apocalypse nothing has been so drolly interpreted. Let me perish if I ever knew anything of what has been attributed to me in this opera. However, its publication has not been forbidden.'

Galiani maintained: 'It was really impossible that this style of music should cross the French border since it had not even reached Rome. One had to be a Neapolitan to appreciate the masterly perfection to which Piccinni had brought comic opera in Naples.' Yet the gushing Lady Craven asserted that Piccinni was her favourite composer, whose sweet simplicity could never be too highly estimated, though he excited more laughter than tears; and Dr Burney was commissioned to engage him to compose operas for the King's Theatre, London, so he evidently appealed to the English.

Under the ægis of Sir William Hamilton, the British embassy in Naples had become a musical centre where all artists were assured of a cordial welcome. Hamilton was the ideal eighteenth-century dilettante. Nearly all visitors to Naples agreed with Sir Nathaniel Wraxall that he 'constituted in himself the greatest source of entertainment, no less than of instruction, which that capital then afforded to strangers... In his person, though tall and meagre, with a dark complexion, a very aquiline nose, and a figure which always reminded me of Rolando in *Gil Blas*, he had nevertheless such an air of intelligence, blended with distinction in his countenance, as powerfully attracted and conciliated every beholder... Endowed with a superior understanding, a philosophic mind, and a strong inclination to the study of many branches of science, or of polite letters, which, as is well known, he cultivated with distinguished success; he was equally keen as a sportsman, in all the exercises of the field. After being actively occupied in studying the phenomena of Vesuvius, like the Elder Pliny; or in exploring the antiquities of Pompeii and of Stabia, with as much enthusiasm as Pausanias did those of ancient Greece; he would pass whole days, and almost weeks, with the King of Naples, either hunting or shooting in the royal woods; or more laboriously engaged in an open boat, exposed to the rays of a burning sun, harpooning fish in the bay of Castellammare... Though a finished courtier, he preserved such an independence of manner, without any mixture of servility or adulation, as seemed eminently to qualify him for the diplomatic profession. His conversation offered a rich diversity of anecdote. With these qualifications, it cannot excite wonder that he formed the delight and ornament of the Court of Naples. No foreign Minister, not even the *family* ambassadors of France and Spain resident there, enjoyed in so eminent a degree the favour or affection of His Sicilian Majesty.' Already he had become a Neapolitan institution; and the *lazzaroni* often lamented that so good a man must be eternally punished, since he was a heretic. His first wife, according to Michael Kelly, was considered the finest pianoforte player in Italy, and William Beckford has left eloquent tributes to her charm and talent.

When the indefatigable Dr Burney, collecting materials for his *History of Music*, visited Naples in 1770, the Hamiltons did everything possible to assist him. While Lady Hamilton received him informally in her dressing-room, she asked her Sicilian maid to sing her native songs, accompanied on the tambourine, and Burney transcribed them in his journal. Hamilton, himself a pupil of the great Giardini, had two pages who were gifted performers on the violin and violoncello, and he organized concerts to enable Burney to meet the best local talent. His box at the opera was also at the Doctor's disposal. Another patron of music, Lord Fortrose, was equally hospitable; and Burney heard the veteran Caffarello sing with a full orchestra at his house after dinner. He attended the rehearsal and first performance of Jommelli's serious opera *Demofoonte*; he also heard a new operetta called *Le Trame per Amore*, by the budding composer Paisiello, whose fresh vitality and spontaneity captivated him. He investigated the famous music schools which, having bred a galaxy of genius, now seemed to have passed their zenith; the classic era was declining, and the romantic had not yet dawned. Hamilton helped him to study ancient instruments from Etruscan vases and other remote sources.

His scientific interests are often reflected in Hamilton's official despatches. Thus on March 16, 1773, he wrote: 'I hope Your Lordship will forgive me if I finish this despatch with some account of a curious accident that happened last night here, at Lord Tylney's house. His Lordship usually receives company on Monday nights, and last night about half-past ten o'clock whilst most of the nobility of this country, the foreign Ministers and the English (I suppose near three hundred people in all) were assembled there in nine rooms, playing at cards or conversing, an explosion as loud as of a pistol was heard, and a bright light was seen in every room at the same instant. The confusion was great. Many thought that a pistol had been discharged, but it was soon discovered to have been occasioned by lightning, the effects of which were very visible and extraordinary indeed. Fortunately the fashion of this country is to have very broad cornices gilt with false gold in all their rooms, and from the cornice in the corner and round the hangings, usually a gilt frame; their chairs and sofas likewise are massive, and charged with the same sort of gilding as is seen in no other country, and it plainly appears by the damage done to it in almost all the rooms, that this circumstance with the assistance of the bell wires saved the company. The lightning was conducted by their means from where it entered from the upper storey to the further room, where it seems to have exerted its collected force, having melted the bell wires and jumping about thirteen inches from a picture frame to a gilt door case, which it damaged and burnt, went through a room underneath, damaging the wall, and lost itself in a well underneath that. Again I observed that some of the sofas and chairs which were occupied at the time of the explosion had been likewise conductors, as the gilding is damaged, as is likewise the damask in contact with it. A servant of the French ambassador was struck down in the hall, and has the mark of a slight stroke on his arm and thighs. It is really wonderful when including servants we were certainly at least five hundred people closely surrounded by lightning and not one essentially hurt. Many of the company were sensible of a stroke, like a smart one from an electrical machine, and a Polish Prince feeling the stroke and hearing a report, as he thought of a pistol, laid his hand on his sword, and was thinking of defending himself. Your Lordship may well conceive the confusion that such an event must have occasioned in a great assembly consisting chiefly of those whose ideas were not... very philosophical.'

In a later despatch of March 30, Hamilton continued: 'The extraordinary accident which I took the liberty of mentioning... in my last will, in the end, be productive of good to this city. The priests did not fail to represent it as a warning for true believers to avoid the company of heretics, and indeed Lord Tylney's next assembly was very thin. However, by the means of an electrical machine little known in this country, I have been enabled to represent exactly in miniature many of the phenomena occasioned by the lightning in Lord Tylney's house, and which I have fully described in a letter to the Royal Society. The nobility who were present at Lord Tylney's, and have now seen the electric fluid spread itself in the like manner over the gilt cornices of two of my rooms (with some other experiments by which I demonstrate the efficacy of Dr Franklin's pointed conductors in preserving buildings from the bad effects of lightning) are perfectly convinced that the accident was not preternatural, and several are resolved to erect conductors on their houses.'

These were halcyon years of peace and prosperity for Naples, fish and game excepted. More and more English flocked to the bay. On February 21, 1775, Hamilton wrote: 'Their Sicilian Majesties upon every occasion are remarkably gracious to the subjects of Great Britain, of whom there were no less than forty-three at the Court ball on Sunday last. The King of Naples, looking over a card table at which Lord Monson, Lord George and several other English were at play, was pleased to tell me (who was looking on also) that he liked the English manner of playing so well that he would play with them, and actually did for two hours with the greatest affability and good humour. The play was deep for this country and ended by His Sicilian Majesty's having won all the money at the table, about two hundred and fifty pounds sterling.' Later he reported that 'the English party in three nights lost about two thousand pounds sterling, most of which was won by the King'. Small wonder that His Majesty liked the English manner of playing! Hamilton attended most of the King's shooting parties, and dined with him four days in a week. 'The affability and goodness of heart in this Prince is every day more and more conspicuous,' he wrote, but in the long run he had to confess that he found this existence wearisome. 'His Sicilian Majesty is really indefatigable. We have been here [at Persano] eight days, and every day employed totally in shooting in different quarters of the forest... Above one thousand deer, one hundred wild boars, three wolves and many foxes have fallen already, and twice that number will probably die before His Majesty returns to Naples... Notwithstanding all these honours, it is impossible for me to continue this life of continual dissipation and carnage rather than sport the twenty-six days the Court will remain here, and I propose to return to Naples on Friday next if I can get away with any degree of propriety.'

Hamilton told Wraxall that at these royal hunting parties he had frequently seen a heap entirely composed of offal or bowels, reaching as high as his head and many feet in circumference. 'The King rarely misses a shot; but when he is tired with killing, then commences another operation. He next dissects the principal pieces of game, of which he sends presents to favoured courtiers, or distributes it among his attendants. In order to perform this part of the diversion, he strips, puts on a flannel dress, takes the knife in hand, and, with inconceivable dexterity cuts up the animal. No carcass-butcher in Smithfield can exceed him in anatomical ability; but he is frequently besmeared with blood from head to foot before he has finished, and exhibits an extraordinary spectacle, not easily to be imagined. The Queen herself is sometimes obliged to be present at the scene, though more, as may be supposed, in compliance with the King's wish than from her own inclination. He is equally indefatigable on the water, in harpooning or in catching fish; particularly the *pesce spada,* or sword-fish; and he neither regards heat, nor cold, nor hunger, nor danger. On these occasions, he is usually or always attended by a number of chosen Liparots, natives of the Lipari islands, who have been in all ages most expert sailors, divers, and fishermen.'

In 1775 Hamilton wrote that he had found a greater facility of late years in the execution of any little business at Court than had any of his colleagues. 'I have long been the *Doyen du Corps Diplomatique*... I have the greatest reason to be pleased and flattered with my situation at this Court, having the honour of being distinguished very particularly indeed by Their Sicilian Majesties who are often pleased to call me *Paesano Nostro.*' But having also acquired the reputation of the best cicerone of Naples and its environs, this honour was attended with some fatigue, for he was constantly asked to show the sights to royal visitors.

Tanucci was satisfied, perhaps too complacently, with things as they were. 'I do not know why you consider this government confused,' he had written to his friend Viviani in 1768. 'Every week I survey nearly all the other governments of Europe, and I doubt if there be any more tranquil and orderly than this. Envy, slander, Court cabals are common everywhere, and here... even Court quarrels are more innocent than elsewhere, although, even when they are at boiling-point they exert little or no influence on governments, which are run by the ministry, not by courtiers.' And again, in 1771, he wrote: 'Here I see arts and letters and civilisation increase... I refer to the male population, for the females should not be counted in any country: they are all either Agrippinas or Messalinas devoid of virtue, and only through fear converted in old age to the materialistic religion of priests and friars.' He took it as a personal compliment when 'the wise and valiant Prince of Brunswick told the King of England that he had found Naples the metropolis of Italy'.

With all his faults, Tanucci had some cause for self-congratulation. A general spirit of tolerance reigned; the university was expanding, with new chairs of agriculture, architecture, geography, natural history and chemistry. If the King remained ignorant, at least his subjects were becoming enlightened. Scholars were consulted and given posts in the government. Of these Galiani, Domenico Caracciolo and Gaetano Filangieri won fame even outside Italy. Galiani was too caustic to be popular in Naples, but his opinions were respected; after a brilliant career in the diplomatic service, Caracciolo was to apply his reforming zeal as Viceroy of Sicily; Filangieri's great work, *La Scienza della Legislazione*, had almost as powerful an influence on legal reform as Beccaria's *Dei Delitti e delle Pene*, and as a comprehensive treatise on education and political science as well, with its diatribes against prevalent abuses, it had a wide appeal. Giuseppe Maria Galanti's *Descrizione delle due Sicilie*, an impressive landmark in statistics which was translated into French and German, still remains the standard work on Neapolitan institutions and economic life under the Bourbons.

During this peaceful period, even those who ended as revolutionaries sang the praises of Ferdinand's 'paternal government'. To read the Metastasian rhapsodies of Eleonora Pimentel or the dithyrambs of Luigi Seno, so famous for his lyrical improvisations, nobody could foretell that these would become the King's fiercest detractors. Eleonora Pimentel's epithalamium for Ferdinand's marriage was followed by a series of sonnets to celebrate the births of his children. Luigi Serio wrote the libretto for Cimarosa's *Oreste*, performed at the San Carlo in honour of Maria Carolina's birthday, and he was soon given the post of Court Poet, which had long been vacant. As a poetical improviser he seldom failed to enchant and astonish his audience. The King and Queen invited him to the royal dinner table, and foreigners of note made a special point of hearing him. Serio would ask for a theme, and in one case he was given 'the second childhood of a great man as a result of old age' with special reference to the nonagenarian scholar Alessio Mazzocchi. The novelty of the subject suited Serio, we are told, and he proceeded to chant for a whole hour while a guest accompanied him on the harpsichord. The decay of the nerves and tissues, the fading of memory and impoverishment of ideas, were described with mournful gusto, culminating in an appraisal of Mazzocchi's past achievements, which he recommended as a model to the younger generation. It was a series of verbal fireworks depending largely on the author's voice, gesture and personal magnetism for their effect. But the printed works of this prolific versifier, who held the chair of Italian rhetoric at the university for over twenty years, are cold and dusty with a few exceptions. Croce has drawn attention to his *Bacchus in Mergellina*, an imitation of Redi's *Bacchus in Tuscany* in the Neapolitan vernacular, half serious, half facetious, defending the fine landscape and happy-go-lucky existence of the people against critics who compared Naples with more progressive cities. 'It is true that in London you never find a man bare-footed,' he wrote, 'but I'll be hanged if you ever find a man there who laughs.'

That English visitors were fascinated by Naples is proved by the throngs who arrived in continuous relays. 'It is really a serious consideration for our country,' wrote Sir William Hamilton in 1786, 'the enormous sum of money spent abroad by subjects of Great Britain. I had the curiosity to enquire of the two principal bankers here what was the amount of the money they had furnished the English travellers with at Naples this year, and can assure you it is very nearly fifty thousand pounds.' In 1777 Swinburne mentions, among those he knew, Lord Dalrymple, Lord Graham, Lord John Clinton, Lord Tylney, Messrs Osbaldeston, Dillon, Tierney, Molyneux, Stanley, Pelham, Crosbie, Lady Catherine and Miss Murray, Lady Anne Severino, the eldest daughter of the second Lord Derwentwater, who had married a Venetian, and Lady Orford, the daughter-in-law of Sir Robert Walpole, who was separated from her husband. Doubtless there were dozens more. They gave frequent dinners and entertainments, especially Lady Orford and Lord Tylney. After the strenuous excursions and Court balls, they relaxed as cosily as if they were at home.

Lady Orford, wrote Swinburne, 'is very fond of whist, and is peculiar for always saying at the end, "*and two by honours*," by which declaration, if not always investigated, she often makes two more on her score than are her due, unless playing with those who are accustomed to her pranks. She is at the same time very severe with regard to others, and scolds famously both her partner and her antagonists.

'We were amused the other night at Lord Tylney's card party by a *scena*. A Mrs Sperme, who is a sort of toady of Lady Orford's, and generally makes up her whist party, happened to have thirteen trumps dealt to her. She was in great dismay, being frightened to death at Lady O., and feeling sure she would accuse her of cheating, at least by innuendos, if not openly. In her agitation she got up and asked leave to speak to Lord Tylney, to whom she told her distress, and asked him what she should do.

' "Do, madam," said he; "why play them out, to be sure." '

At the Court balls there were more English than other foreign guests, and Swinburne relates that a Mr Spence and Miss Snow— so fat that she was called 'Double Stout'—entertained the King prodigiously by their furious dancing. 'He was in roars of laughter, bravoed, clapped his hands, and encouraged them to skip and jump about. Each of them was conscious how much the other was laughed at, and took care to tell it to all the company, without suspecting that their own figure and performance could be the object of merriment.'

'Nothing can be gayer than the town, nor kinder than we find its inhabitants,' was Swinburne's verdict, and most Englishmen agreed with him. The morose Tanucci wrote to a friend: 'Here you will find the best of hearts, a more human hospitality.' But in his opinion it was not a country to cure hypochondria. 'The climate in which one can be cheerful is either very hot or very cold. A temperate climate effeminates the fibre.'

Though Tanucci was addicted to grumbling, the relations between sovereign and minister were excellent as far as he was concerned. He gloried in the sensation of being indispensable. As William Preston, acting as Hamilton's substitute, wrote in 1772: 'He is equally powerful and equally jealous of power; nor is it likely that he will think of quitting the helm till age and infirmities disqualify him for holding it, or the conclusion of all things wrests it from him. These, it may be supposed, can be no distant events to a man who is already advanced beyond the age of seventy and who in the course of last winter was subject besides to frequent indispositions. Neither his health, however, nor his understanding seem hitherto to have undergone any violent revolution, and he is so far capable of the exertion of both as not to feel any necessity for retrenching his labours. He superintends every department of state with an authority that suffers little or no control, and hardly anything is done in any (but military perhaps in some few instances excepted) beyond the ordinary form and business of office, without his inspection or order. Hence it follows that while his eye is endeavouring to extend its view to, and would take in the whole, some of the parts are overlooked, or but imperfectly distinguished. Little or nothing effectual has been done of late years for the improvement of their commerce and manufactures, or multiplying the internal resources and riches of the kingdom; and the justice of the country, as well from the number and venality of its officers as from the want of order and precision in the laws, continues to be administered in a manner that is dilatory, oppressive and precarious. On the other hand many useful, though in some instances perhaps harsh, regulations have been made by the present Minister for lessening the wealth and prerogatives of the Church; and by effectually circumscribing the insolent and capricious authority of the nobles, which rendered the property and even lives of their vassals, and sometimes their own, precarious, he has given to industry its object and consulted the peace and good order of society, as well as the interests of humanity in general.'

The following anecdote illustrates Ferdinand's respectful attitude towards him. One of the royal bodyguards, the Duke of Lauria, happened to shoot at one of the King's equerries, Count Cantelli of Piacenza, with whom he had exchanged high words from a balcony of the palace. Luckily the bullet went astray. Lauria was put under arrest, but his many influential relations and the feminine clique, which consisted of the Queen's ladies-in-waiting, did everything possible to obtain the King's pardon, with the excuse that the culprit was prone to fits of absent-mindedness. Heckled from both sides, Ferdinand was much embarrassed, perhaps because, as usual, he had promised to satisfy everyone. 'Call Tanucci and leave me in peace,' he said. And the King explained that he had been bombarded with petitions—what was he to do? 'What did Your Majesty reply to them?' Tanucci asked. 'I told them that justice would have to take its course.' 'Did your Majesty speak firmly, without making any promises?' 'Yes, I said exactly what I believed was right.' Tanucci kissed his hand, saying: 'God keep these sentiments in Your Majesty's mind. I should be the first to plead for clemency in case of need, but this is a matter which should be left to justice.' And the lawsuit continued without royal interference.

After so many years of unchallenged power Tanucci underrated the young Queen's influence. In his letters he often inveighed against women, their vanity, their caprices, their lack of syllogism (his pet word for common sense), and above all their recent mania for government, which was becoming contagious, though he could admire the intelligence of Catherine the Great and Maria Theresa. 'Women at Court are the very devil,' he wrote, 'envious, irascible, and intolerant. *Non est ira super iram mulieris*, said Solomon, who knew the sex well.' But Maria Carolina seemed too flippant to take seriously. Laughing and joking as she stepped off a galley after dining *al fresco*—the King having retired early so as to hunt soon after dawn—she had fallen merrily into the sea with the two Kaunitz brothers. The commander of the royal galleys and several sailors had dived in to assist her, and the incident had given rise to malicious gossip. When the King heard of it he was furious, and Tanucci shook his head. What a contrast with the stiff and staid Maria Amalia! It was all very shocking, but he reassured himself that he had little to fear from this high-spirited young woman.

So far their differences had been limited to questions of Spanish etiquette, of which he remained the staunch umpire. Maria Carolina's first child was born in 1772, but it was a daughter; so was the next one. The heir presumptive[1] was not born until 1775, but Maria Carolina was fully prepared for that event. The public rejoicings had scarcely subsided before she claimed her right to enter the Council, as stated in her marriage contract.

Tanucci now had to face a headstrong opponent at Council meetings. He was the last bulwark of the Spanish regime, and apart from a personal itch for vengeance she wanted a radical change of policy.

Her support of the Freemasons had become embarrassing, since Tanucci had been ordered by the Patriarch to suppress them. In April 1775, General Pignatelli discovered that the royal battalion of cadets had a lodge and reported it to the King. Ferdinand duti-

[1] This first son, Prince Carlo Tito, died in 1778, hence the second son Francis, born in 1777, became Heir Apparent.

fully informed his father and asked his advice, since 'the country was full of them; they were like the renascent hydra'. Charles suggested that he should catch them by surprise and arrest the leaders, so Tanucci revived the edict of 1751, obliging all Freemasons in the kingdom to renounce their connexion with the fraternity. Most of Ferdinand's letters to his father were written with the Queen at his elbow, but she was surely somewhere else when he confessed that she was fostering the hydra. She made scenes when she was thwarted, and Ferdinand must have been henpecked when he wrote on August 1, 1775: 'Until now I did not like to mention it, but since Your Majesty is acquainted with my woes, I may tell you that it is my wife who has played the devil in order to have them [the masonic meetings]...and I for the sake of peace had to allow it, protesting all the time that this was against my wish, as Tanucci is well aware. When I knew that this would displease Your Majesty, I begged her for charity's sake to avoid giving offence, especially when Your Majesty wrote that I paid more attention to others' advice than your own. She found me weeping and asked what was the matter. I showed her the letter and she replied: "So this is why you are upset? What difference can it make? He is a stubborn old blockhead who will not listen to reason and has got this bee in his bonnet. Cheer up, and do as I tell you." And because I told her that this was no way to talk, knowing the respect due to a father, she said: "Rave, despair, either burst or die, both of you together, I do not care a fig." This was in the presence of certain ladies and gentlemen who are all intriguers, and the Duchess of Termoli leads then, as Tanucci will bear me out.'

On September 12 the King signed an edict against Freemasons which was announced by the public herald to the sound of trumpets and posted up in the streets. They were to be considered as enemies and rebels. But the edict was removed or torn down, and the secret meetings continued. As soon as Ferdinand had signed it, he wrote his father about the masonic banquets to which the Queen had been escorted by the Prince of Cattolica and the Duchess of Termoli, and about her excessive intimacy with an officer of the guards called Capece Galeota. 'Not that I am jealous,' he added, 'but I do not think he exerts a good influence, as he is very friendly with the Termoli and also a Freemason. I know too well how often my wife tried to induce me to become a mason and have had to excuse myself again and again, saying that I took no pleasure in such things. As regards my wife's duty, she has been better since the incident of August 13, but as regards her caprices she is always the same.' The incident referred to was a row about her pregnancy, described in a previous letter: ' "For at least a year, whether you die or burst, I refuse to be pregnant," she cried. In the evening she became a fury. She jumped at me like a dog and even bit my hand, of which I still bear the scar. At table she was even worse, calling all the ladies–in–waiting who are spinsters, who could only see that she was screaming like an eagle and using expressions that were far from decent. I stood with head bowed listening to these compliments, never opening my mouth; then I calmly left the table without a word, to avoid giving further scandal to the spinsters.' On October 1, he announced to his father: 'The Freemasons are protected by my wife, and it is only too true, as Your Majesty wisely says, that she wishes to govern at all costs, instigated by Vienna and those who surround her, which I must bear with patience, because otherwise, as you know, she might trouble me for the same cause... Assuredly I do what I can, but I like to have peace at home and try to disturb it as little as possible.' He went on to say that the wily masons had managed to avoid capture, but 'what must be done, will be done by the care and zeal of Tanucci, who is persecuted to death by her'.

Tanucci could no longer wink at the activities of the Freemasons when they supported the Queen against himself in return for her protection. Aware that his power was ebbing, he dug in his claws. He wished to avoid pitched battle with the fraternity and placate the autocrat in Spain at the same time. So he warned his masonic friends to lie low and ordered his henchman Pallante, Chief of the Tribunal, to surprise a masonic meeting excluding nobles. Pallante took him seriously, and through his spies caught a small gathering *in flagrante*. Entering in his scarlet robes with a squadron of police he called out 'Long live the King!' In a room called 'the chamber of reflection' he found 'a lighted oil-lamp, eleven figures of black paper cut out in the form of heads upon the walls, and under them the picture of two crossbones, a bloody shirt hanging over a chair, a plate full of blood on the table, and a wooden skull with a ticket inscribed: "Ponder on death, tremble because he is dead." The novice was blindfold, ready for initiation. In the "chamber of light" were tables for the Venerable and the Secretary, four "tackle" of white leather, eight or ten pairs of white kid gloves for men and others for women, the masonic catechism, etc.' All were arrested, and Pallante hurried off to Persano, where the King was concerned with other quarry, to announce his successful catch. The King ordered an immediate trial. Although Pallante collected their depositions, signed under oath, proving that they had broken the royal edict, although Madrid wanted a quick decision, the case hung fire and Tanucci prevaricated with sibylline sentences. For all the friends and relations of the prisoners, besides the local and foreign Masons, came to visit them in jail with hampers of food and legal advice. 'A horde of powerful protectors,' wrote Tanucci to Charles III, 'from the army, the nobility and the Court, goes about to confuse, tempt and terrify the judges.' It became obvious that the Queen was behind them. The Prince of Caramanico, Grand Master of the national lodge, had sent her a petition in their favour through her bosom friend the Marchesa di San Marco, with the result that 'she pleaded with the King, who was touched'. Then came a swarm of exalted Masons, the Duke and Duchess of Saxe-Teschen, Maria Carolina's sister, the Duchess of Chartres and her lady-in-waiting the Countess of Genlis, known as 'mother of the Church', all of whom declared that the honour of the sect was compromised by this case. Tanucci was out-manoeuvred, and Pallante discredited as the author of a trumped-up charge. The meeting was declared to be innocuous, and the Masons were absolved.

Ferdinand's letters to his father assumed a different tinge. They became eloquent in their repeated attacks on the old Prime Minister, who wished to control everything; as for himself, 'he was only the statue of the King of Naples.' Under his wife's dictation he accused Tanucci of ruining the country, and he assured his father that this was an impartial opinion, the voice of his own conscience. In spite of continuous pressure he had never been able to obtain a clear account of Tanucci's expenditure, and he had ordered an inquiry into his management of Jesuit properties since the time of their expulsion. He could never forgive Tanucci's carelessness in promoting so many costly enterprises without examining if he had sufficient funds, etc. His confessor had told him that unless he dismissed Tanucci he would have to bear the responsibility before God.

Charles answered him firmly but sadly. Reminding him of Tanucci's long and loyal service, he refused to consider his dismissal. The distant father inspired a certain awe, but he was no match for the resolute young wife at Ferdinand's elbow. The conventions had been observed; the King of Spain had been dutifully consulted; but it was also the duty of the King of Naples to consult his own interest. Tanucci had often begged to resign. Again and again he had said that he would sooner enjoy the peace of private life, but he had never meant it. When resignation was forced upon him he was taken by surprise.

A contemporary recorded: 'Last Saturday morning [October 26, 1776] the sudden change took place, and Marchese de Marco brought Marchese Tanucci the order in the King's own hand while he was still in bed. Tanucci read it and exclaimed: "But the Catholic King has written me nothing about this!" To which De Marco replied: "Your Excellency has requested it often and the King has just granted your wish." Whereupon he was dumbfounded. This news has produced the same sensation as when the Jesuits left... I must tell you confidentially that all this has been our Queen's trick.'

Charles III had not written to Tanucci because he could not believe that Ferdinand would do anything so drastic without his permission. When he heard of it he wrote at once to his faithful henchman: 'Believe me, nobody sympathizes with your misfortune more than I do. Let us help each other to bear all the disgusts and trials which God has wished to send us in our old age... You may be sure that I shall not cease writing to you, unless God sends me some infirmity which prevents me, for I know how you have always served me and I esteem and love you...'

Tanucci was stunned. 'I thank the King's clemency,' he wrote, 'for relieving me of so great a burden, and Divine mercy for granting me leisure to think of my soul, to which I have not been able to give thought in the tumult of so many affairs. I have loved the King and his Kingdom too deeply. I do not repent, that if I had loved him less, this blow would not have fallen on me, or it would have done so much later.' Colletta describes him as like an exiled monarch retiring to the country from the odious sight of man. He regarded his downfall as a symptom of modern decadence. But he remained a Councillor of State, to be consulted on special occasions. His successor, the Marchese della Sambuca, had won his laurels as ambassador in Vienna. The choice indicated a new political trend; he was essentially the Queen's minister, and he fell from grace as soon as he forgot it.

Galiani, in one of his sprightly letters to Madame d'Épinay, reflects the point of view of the advanced minority: 'After forty-two years, we have had a sort of change in the ministry here. Marchese Tanucci has been discharged from his departments, which have been handed over to Marchese della Sambuca, a Sicilian, and he remains a minister of state without portfolio. He would resemble M. de Maurepas, if his successor were his creature, but the latter has been chosen by the King without his knowledge, which makes a difference. Such an event in a land of lethargy and slumber like ours is an event indeed. It would cause no sensation in Paris. For us, however, it is considerable; and I, who have an infinite love of bustle, noise and variety, am enchanted by the spectacle. It has roused me somewhat from the depression in which the illness of my angora cat, reputed to be incurable, had plunged me, and I see that this world is only a perpetual chain of pleasures and sorrows.'

Grimaldi had fallen at the same time in Madrid, and the Spanish and Neapolitan Court messengers happened to meet at Saragossa. The Spaniard said to the Neapolitan: 'I have a mighty piece of news in my bag, brother.' 'What news is that?' asked the Neapolitan. 'The resignation of Grimaldi.' 'You must take me for a lame duck,' retorted the Neapolitan, 'I have Tanucci's resignation in mine.' Both were equally amazed, wrote Galiani, and, after embracing each other and thanking God that they were messengers, departed convinced that they would find somebody to receive their despatches on arrival.

Galiani had long ceased to care for his former patron. 'As everybody knows that Tanucci did not like me at all and employed me even less, I cannot be enveloped in the disgrace of his creatures. Sambuca is my old and true friend, but he will make nothing of me and will consequently do nothing for me, for the same reason as Tanucci's. A minister is only attached to people who devote themselves, and I am incapable of it; I could not even devote myself to the devil. I belong to myself. I shall neither experience great fortune nor great persecutions. So long as I obtain a year's leave to see Paris again, I shall be content.'

Henry Swinburne describes Sambuca as 'a creature of Prince Jaci's who looks very unlike a genius: his aspect is heavy and inanimate: his first manoeuvre was very impolitic and blundering, in laying a tax upon oil, which he was obliged to take off...'

Soon after Tanucci's retirement a question came up before the State Council which perplexed his successor: the French maintained that only their ambassador in Naples was entitled to arbitrate in local disputes with their citizens. As the Queen did not know what to decide, the King summoned Tanucci. When the matter was explained to him, he said the solution was simple: if the King of France granted the same jurisdiction to the Neapolitan ambassador in Paris with regard to Neapolitan disputes, he would agree to the French demand. Ferdinand interjected: 'Haven't I always said that San Nicandro, Sambuca, the other ministers and myself, are only donkeys? Tanucci knows more than the lot of us put together.' And when Sambuca wanted to interrupt Tanucci at a Council meeting, the King shouted: *'Zittati tu. Isso è lo maestro; noi siamo li ciucci'* ('Be silent! He's the master and we are the donkeys').

Though Tanucci was consulted now and then, this was generally out of compassion for his past.

X

Death of the imbecile Infante Philip—Dr Gatti introduces inoculation against smallpox—The advent of John Acton—The Queen's reputed gallantries—Conflict with Spain over Acton—Sambuca's disgrace and Acton's triumph.

The Queen soon turned her victory to advantage. After Tanucci's fall Ferdinand wrote to his father (November 12, 1776): 'Regarding my wife, instigated by her country she has plucked up courage with this change and makes every effort to enter the Government... I shall try to prevent her from succeeding though she may threaten me in every street, declaring that she will show me who she is and who her parents are, and that it has been a great favour and fortune to receive her in our family. In Your Majesty's reply please do not show that you are acquainted with this, or, if you wish to warn or command me, do so in a separate letter, for if she came to hear of this I should be troubled as long as I live, as she preaches nothing else but the closest confidence between husband and wife and wishes to see and know all my affairs and read all my letters. But when I speak of wishing to see some letter she writes home, or know what she is writing, there is a fight; and if I insist she loads me with abuse, so I keep silent for the sake of peace.'

In September 1777, the imbecile Infante Don Philip, by birth heir to the Spanish monarchy and the King's eldest brother, caught the smallpox. 'Our learned doctors could not decide whether it was smallpox or a malignant fever causing skin eruptions,' wrote the Abbé Galiani, 'so that the King and Queen fled to Caserta in dismay.' According to Hamilton, as recorded by Wraxall, the unfortunate Infante 'was treated with certain distinctions, having chamberlains placed about him in constant attendance, who watched him with unremitting attention; as otherwise he would have committed a thousand excesses. Care was particularly taken to keep him from having any connexion with the other sex, for which he manifested the strongest propensity; but it became at last impossible to prevent him altogether from attempting to emancipate himself in this respect. He has many times eluded the vigilance of his keepers, and on seeing ladies pass through the apartments of the palace, would attack them with the same impetuosity as Pan or the Satyrs are described by Ovid, when pursuing the Nymphs; and with the same intentions. More than one lady of the Court has been critically rescued from his embraces. On particular days of the year, he was allowed to hold a sort of Court or Levee, when the foreign ministers repaired to his apartments to pay their compliments to him: but his greatest amusement consisted in having his hand held up by his attendants while gloves were put upon it, one larger than another to the number of fifteen or sixteen. His death was justly considered as a fortunate event, under such circumstances of incurable imbecility.' He died on September 19, and his body was exposed on a catafalque in Santa Chiara.

'There is to be no mourning, the King of Spain having disapproved of it, which is a rare comedy,' remarked Swinburne. But the King of Spain also disapproved of inoculation against smallpox, on theological grounds. Ferdinand and Maria Carolina, however, had taken fright. They begged the Grand Duke Leopold to send Dr Gatti immediately to Caserta to inoculate the Hereditary Prince and his sisters. Gatti, who was now lecturing on medicine at Pisa University, was an old friend of the Abbé Galiani and had frequented the same *salons* in Paris, where he had acquired a distinguished if eccentric reputation. He was considered a specialist on the smallpox, though his method of treatment was highly unconventional. When Mme Helvétius suffered from it he ordered her fire to be extinguished and all the windows to be opened, although the month was January. During the stage of eruption he obliged her to get out of bed and walk about her chilly room. On every visit he would play pranks and dance with her daughters in the bedchamber; but the patient was cured. He had already practised inoculation in Naples with some success. As Galiani wrote to Mme d'Épinay (March 28, 1772): 'If you saw how the mothers offer their children to be inoculated, their mixture of tenderness and stupidity, it would strike you as very odd. Of all the arguments raised in Paris against inoculation, not one is mentioned here. The only one you hear occasionally is that it seems opposed to destiny and divine omnipotence. How true it is that fatalism is the only system suitable to savages! And if one understood the language of animals, one would see that it is their only system. Fatalism is the father and son of barbarism: it is first begotten by it, then proceeds to nourish it, and do you know why? Because it is the laziest system, consequently the best suited to man. No Neapolitan thought of sending for Gatti, but since he is here they get themselves inoculated.'

When the King and Queen sent to Pisa for him, inoculation became a burning topic. 'Gatti arrived a week ago,' wrote Galiani on October 4. 'On Wednesday he inoculated the Prince and two Princesses. Everybody except himself is trembling about the result. Public prayers are offered. The Queen herself, who wanted the inoculation, already repents of it. Seeing others tremble, I begin to tremble too. Within a week we shall know for certain.' Everything turned out happily. Gatti was magnificently rewarded, 'and what is worse for him,' wrote Galiani, 'is that the Princes and Princesses are all enamoured of him.' On April 11, 1778, Galiani wrote: 'Gatti has won the heart of the sovereigns. They have asked him to settle in Naples. He has consented; but without charges, titles or appointments: such are his conditions. In the meantime he has obtained a pension of 4,200 *livres* and nearly 10,000 francs in gifts and ready money for inoculating the King.'

The Tuscan Tanucci had been forced to retire, yet it was still to Tuscany that the King and Queen looked for men of fresh talent and ability.

Maria Carolina was most anxious to reorganize the marine. A fleet was necessary for commercial as well as military purposes, but Naples lacked both naval and military experts since Tanucci had always relied upon Spain. Again the Queen applied urgently to her brother the Grand Duke of Tuscany, who had an officer with ideal qualifications.

John Acton, an expatriate member of 'that ancient and loyal family of Shropshire Baronets' of whom their cousin Edward Gibbon was so proud, was described in the latter's autobiography as 'a very pretty sensible young man'. That was in 1762, when Acton was already a Captain of Foot and Lieutenant of a man-of-war in the Austrian (nominally the Tuscan) service. He had had a curious career for an Englishman. Born in Besançon in 1736, after serving in the French navy he had joined his uncle, Commodore Acton, who commanded the fleet of the Grand Duke of Tuscany. There he soon distinguished himself with the scanty means at his disposal. The light, swift ships he designed proved invaluable in Charles III's ill-fated expedition against Algiers in 1775. The Spanish troops under General O'Reilly had been tricked and enveloped by superior forces, and they would have been decimated if Acton had not sailed close to the shore to protect their retreat and re-embarkation with well-aimed fire. At least 4,000 troops were saved by his manoeuvres, and Charles III presented him with a snuff-box containing his portrait set in diamonds in token of gratitude.

Most of the Neapolitan galleys were unserviceable, and the merchant marine consisted chiefly of tartans which, owing to the Barbary corsairs, seldom ventured far from the coast. While dining on board one of Ferdinand's frigates anchored before the palace of Portici, the Emperor Joseph II had remarked: 'If I were King of Naples I would have fewer soldiers, but I would give everything to form a navy. This would in fact be a source of new wealth for Naples. Though the kingdom is superbly situated, it is exposed to attack from any maritime power, and would derive the greatest benefit from a fleet.' These words made a deep impression on his sister.

Tuscany was too small for a man of John Acton's ambitions. Did the Grand Duke realize this when he allowed him to go to Naples? On August 4, 1778, Hamilton recorded: 'Captain Acton... who has been honoured with the rank of a General Officer by the Great Duke of Tuscany, is arrived here in one of the Great Duke's frigates in order to give his advice and assistance towards the putting His Sicilian Majesty's marine (hitherto neglected) on a respectable footing.' The Queen was more than obliged: she was enchanted. Acton expressed her own ideas in unequivocal language: he seemed to interpret her thoughts. He was forty-two, an experienced man of the world, enterprising, cosmopolitan and a bachelor. After a few conversations with him, Maria Carolina was convinced that she had found a perfect collaborator, and with her usual impulsiveness she was carried away by her enthusiasm. She regarded him as her own discovery. Together they would create a really independent kingdom. Acton set to work with cool thoroughness, patience and a systematic energy almost unknown in Naples.

The advent of this mysterious sailor-soldier of fortune aroused much misgiving at Court. Without being handsome, he had a fine presence, magnetic, penetrating eyes and a slim, agile figure; his appearance was dignified and self-assured. From the beginning he incurred the jealousy of the corrupt and incompetent old officials, who had never made a practical suggestion in their lives. Indifferent to their backbiting, he persevered with his task, in closest consultation with the Queen. As for the King, he was only too grateful to be relieved of greater responsibilities by this capable new comer.

Hamilton was delighted to discover a new ally at Court who furnished him with much valuable information. 'General Acton,' he wrote in October 1778, 'comes frequently to my house, and I flatter myself I have had the good fortune to gain his confidence and esteem. He is certainly a very sensible man, and has the character of an excellent sea officer. His services have been earnestly sought both by France and Spain with the most tempting offers, but he has constantly declined quitting the service of the Great Duke of Tuscany. He is but too well acquainted with our marine and its regulations, having served under Lord Bristol, and having since resided some time in our greatest sea-port. He is likewise perfectly acquainted with the present state of the French navy. He was at Brest about a year ago, for M. de Sartine not having been able to tempt him into the French service solicited his attendance in France for some months to advise with him in order to form a complete set of new regulations.' After giving a summary of these and some information about French naval commanders, Hamilton proceeded: 'I can perceive him to be still an Englishman at heart. He is quite persuaded that France is now in earnest in aiming at rivalling us upon the sea, but if a hard blow was given to its marine now, the active Minister at the head of it must fall, and that it would be many years before they could recover themselves. On the contrary, should peace be now made, and time given for the completion of their well-judged plan, they would in six years become formidable indeed.'

In January 1779, Acton's plan for reorganizing the Neapolitan marine was approved by the King, and though he would not leave the Grand Duke of Tuscany's service, he was appointed *pro tempore* Secretary of State for the Marine with the rank of Lieutenant-General. From now on Hamilton's despatches were full of naval and military intelligence 'from the usual good quarter'. Thus in May he repeated the substance of a letter from the King of Spain declaring that he had determined on war with Great Britain, 'which was told me by General Acton, to whom His Sicilian Majesty actually read the letter... The Queen of Naples on Wednesday last said with a very significant look at me, that the Prime Minister of Spain was very ill.' In July he wrote: '1 have reason to believe that Their Majesties' Prime Minister [Sambuca] has a strong bias to the Court of Versailles; however, that Minister's power is now greatly on the decline; it is the Queen of Naples that actually governs this country, with the advice of her favourite Prince Caramanico and of my friend General Acton, who is now greatly esteemed at this Court.'

As the Queen's relations with Acton became more intimate, she could not escape the innuendoes of a malicious Court. These innuendoes were converted into positive statements by the libellous Count Gorani, by Lady Morgan and other anti-Bourbonists. 'His first attraction in the eyes of the Queen,' wrote Lady Morgan, 'was apparent indifference to her charms, to which none save him, in the Sybarite court of her husband, had appeared insensible. His second, was his being a foreigner, and his coincidence, real or affected, with her deep and genuine hatred, her profound contempt of the people, over whom she was called to reign... The Princess—, an old friend of the Queen's, and one of the first ladies of her court, assured me that she could trace the passion of the Queen for Acton to his natural insensibility to female charms: his inexpressive countenance was as cold as his heart; and, when the Queen conversed with him in the circle, his eye alone did not sparkle at the distinction. *Piquée au jeu*, she began to play off those coquettish arts, in which, like her sisters, she was an adept, and Acton, flattered, though not subdued, was about to yield, when a friend suggested to him that, if he submitted, he was lost; that, instead of being the sovereign of Naples, he would be but one of the Queen's *mille et un*. Acton took the hint, and the Queen, unused to such cruelty, became devoted, as she was hopeless. She at last irremissibly committed herself, by writing to this ministerial Adonis. From that moment she became his slave; and through her, the King was but the agent of his plans, which nearly ended in the ruin of all, but mostly in that of the unhappy and oppressed people.' This is a typically Latin explanation, and it is superficially plausible. *Se non è vero è ben trovato*. But it should be remembered that throughout these early years of marriage the Queen was an expectant mother, a condition unpropitious to amorous intrigue; she complained frequently of its discomforts and often vented her spleen on Ferdinand when she was feeling sick and miserable. No doubt Acton appealed strongly to her imagination: he encouraged her ambitions and showed her distant horizons; he evoked the fascination of sea-power. In his company she breathed a more bracing, intellectual air than with her lubberly husband. Certainly he was far more than a friend. Even Ferdinand regarded him as a precious acquisition, a person he could safely trust.

Of course the Queen had her favourites. It was an age of so-called gallantry, and even the Abbé Galiani, on his return from Paris, was amazed at its crude manifestations at the Neapolitan Court after the sophisticated society he had left behind him. There is no dearth of contemporary descriptions to revive its atmosphere. Thus Mme de Saussure confided to her diary: 'On Thursday we visited Princess Ferolito, who is much more amiable since Tuesday, when her lover Count Colione had to leave. But during this time she has made no effort to hide the sorrow caused by his departure: everybody mentions him to her as if he were her husband or brother. I heard a very funny conversation this evening. She called the Duchess of Castel Pagano by her lover's name, Count Wurmbrand [the Austrian envoy]. The Duchess replied: "*Mon Dieu*, one has such fits of absent-mindedness. All morning I have been calling Count Wurmbrand, Count Kaunitz!" And Kaunitz had been her previous lover. It was comic to see the old Duchess Duro, who is as fat and red as a *vivandière*, with a superbly handsome officer continually by her side.'

Another day Mme de Saussure went to the Princess of Belmonte's to watch a procession in which the King and Queen were taking part. 'What amused me as much as the show was the rapture, the cries, the gestures of the ladies with whom I shared the balcony, and whom I see almost daily at the houses of Princess Ferolito and the Belmonte. As soon as they recognized one of their friends or lovers they would scream: "There's your beloved! There's mine! Oh, how handsome he is! my son, my joy! God bless him!" And what beckonings and bursts of laughter! Having nobody to beckon to, I caught a bad cold. All the women, old and young, ugly or pretty, have lovers. The Princess of Belmonte usually has three: the gentle Don Felice, the pretty Niccolino, and a dark fellow whose name I forget; and their Neapolitan chatter and gesticulations are very laughable. Since the Court has been in Naples we have seen Princess Ferolito's husband at her parties every evening; he appears to be on excellent terms with her lovers. The customs of this country are very strange, and my husband and I amuse each other vastly, discussing the various things we have observed.'

Monsieur de Bérenger, the French *chargé d'affaires*, gave the following appraisal of Neapolitan society in a letter to Choiseul, January 26, 1770: 'The husbands are far more tolerant than those of other nations. Marchese Santo Marco, a man in his sixties, captain of the royal bodyguard, decided to claim exclusive rights to his wife when he married, but he soon became aware that this was unreasonable. "Since I must inevitably change my category," he said, "I would rather be inscribed in the same class as the Viennese ambassador." So he treats him as his bosom friend. The Prince of Belmonte, first equerry, deals no less frankly with my Lord Fortrose. The Duke of Palma, who was sorry not to have an heir, is enchanted now that the Chevalier Lomma has taken care to provide him with one. Knowing this, he receives congratulations on his wife's pregnancy, though he is also aware that his impotence is generally established.

'That Galingo who made an impression on the Queen's heart, still parades his fatuity, to the great scandal of those who fear the consequences. He was the regular lover of the Princess of Aliano, who seemed unconscious that the Queen was a rival. Finally the Princess broke with her paramour, but their liaison was too genuine for the rupture to pass unnoticed. The Queen, who was certainly the cause of it, was afraid of the sensation it was bound to create. She begged the Princess to reinstate her lover; she even stooped to entreaties, but that woman stood firm. Since his salary as equerry was insufficient and he could no longer count on financial assistance from the Princess of Aliano, the Queen has assigned him a secret monthly pension, and it is the Princess Butera who pays it.

'The tone of brazen familiarity, indecency and licentiousness prevailing at this Court is inconceivable. It is necessary to hold a certain rank to be admitted to the balls of Caserta. "Allow me to bring my lover," said the Duchess La Tripalda to the Queen. "We dote on each other, and I get bored wherever I do not see him." "I want to take a lover," said the little Princess Pietra Persia to her sovereign, "and Your Majesty must choose one for me"—in spite of the fact that she has had lovers of every hue since her marriage.'

Seven years later Swinburne reported: 'Ill-natured people say the Queen's gallantries are numerous, and that her confidante was the Duchess of San Severo, whose husband was at one time a great favourite with the King. For some unknown reasons, the Queen has had a quarrel with the Duchess, who, to revenge herself, persuaded her husband to inform His Majesty of his wife's conduct, upon promise of his never divulging the name of his informer. The King, who was just then worried to death by the Queen's real or affected jealousies, was quite enchanted with this discovery, and could not help telling her of it the first time she upbraided him with going astray. This attack made her furious, and she never rested till she learned from him the name of the person who had given him this information. The Duke of San Severo was banished from Naples, and his vexation brought on a fever of which he died.

'The King once carried his jokes so far as, at a grand supper at Posillipo, to take Guarini by the hand, and bring him up from the end of the table to the seat next the Queen, saying that was his place: she boiled with anger, but was forced to swallow the affront and, as soon as she could, had him removed to Turin, there furnished a house for him, and gave him a magnificent set of porcelain, which she had received as a present from the Emperor, besides a very fine diamond star and cross. Her present favourite is an officer in the guards, son of the late Prince of Marsico. They are much together at the masquerades, etc. She is only allowed 50,000 ducats a year for every expense, therefore cannot be very generous.'

Ill-natured people were numerous; and the Queen's gallantries were probably no more than flirtations, the fleeting fancies of an exuberant young woman. Her brother, the Emperor, had noticed that she was free from coquetry, and she had little time for serious love affairs. She was always expansive, but the King was even more so. He was incapable of keeping a secret; bubbling over with bonhomie, he could not help telling her everything.

Swinburne's account of the King, 'good-natured, boyish and romping', has been amply corroborated: 'He has no very strong passion for women, and what country girls and others he has taken a fancy to has been at the instigation of those about him, who put him up to it. He has no jealousy about him. His intrigues have lain in the sphere of *contadine*, except a Madame Goudar, wife to a French author on economy, and an English woman. But he found out she had a cancer, and she and her husband were banished immediately. He has had some flirtations with ladies of rank, one of whom was exiled, from the Queen finding a note of hers to the King, with some extraordinary expressions. His present views are upon the Rossi, first dancer at the opera, and late mistress to the Duke of Arcos. She always comes to the balcony, when the King appears at his, to see the masks. They say he was in love with the Duchess of Lusciano, daughter of the Marquis de Goyzueta, secretary of state.

'The Queen has something very disagreeable in her manner of speaking, moving her whole face when she talks, and gesticulating violently. Her voice is very hoarse, and her eyes goggle. She has acquired a roundness in her shoulders, and is very fond of showing her hand, which is beautiful. If she sees or suspects the King to be taken with any woman, she plagues her life out, is in horrid humour, and leaves no stone unturned to break off all connexion between them; whether from real jealousy, or apprehension from losing the power she has over her husband, which is very great, since she has got quit of old Tanucci. The King cries out in vain that his case is very hard, that he cannot go where he pleases, etc.'

It is true that the Spanish faction, to counter-balance the Queen's influence, had tried to exploit the charms of Sarah Goudar, but a cancer was not the cause of her banishment. The King met her, apparently by chance, when he went hunting; he saw her again at the theatre, where she had taken a box which could not escape his eye. After their first interview, says Casanova, the Queen caught her husband roaring with laughter over a letter which he refused to show her. Her curiosity roused, she insisted so strongly that he finally handed it to her. 'I shall await you at the same place and at the same hour,' she read, 'with the same impatience as a cow yearning for a bull.' 'How infamous!' she cried. And the Goudar couple were ordered to leave Naples within three days. Referring to the fall of the French Chancellor Maupeou, Galiani wrote to Mme d'Épinay: 'We have banished the beautiful Mme Goudar, and this banishment is quite equal to that of a chancellor.'

The King's intrigue with the Duchess of Lusciano seemed a potential source of danger to the Queen, as she had political affiliations. Indignant at the King's betrayal, the Duchess disguised herself as a man and upbraided her royal lover, who could not save her from being exiled. The Duchess of Casalduni and the Duchess of Cassano, whose son became a rebel, were banished for the same cause. The latter lady, as Ferdinand told his wife, had rejected his advances, but her virtue seemed all the more suspicious to Maria Carolina, who had no objection to mere dancers and country wenches.

The Queen preferred power to pleasure, and her appetite for it grew under the stimulus of Acton. Realizing that he was losing every vestige of influence, Charles III blamed the Englishman for it. Though Ferdinand showed him the same filial respect, he paid little or no attention to his advice. Hearing that Maria Carolina accused him of wishing to govern Naples solely in the interest of Spain, Charles retorted bitterly: 'Is it not natural that a father should advise his son? For a long time, seeing how my advice was received, I have shut myself up in silence.' When Acton was appointed Minister of War as well as Minister of the Marine, he exploded. He had never forgotten the British threat to bombard Naples in 1742. As a Bourbon he had sympathized with the French in the Seven Years War and his relations with the British government were under a constant strain for a number of reasons, such as the British contraband trade on the Mississippi, the Gulf of Mexico and elsewhere, a dispute about the Falkland Islands, and others with the Spanish governors of New Orleans and Buenos Aires. Above all, he hoped to recover Gibraltar and Minorca. When further diplomatic efforts seemed futile, he declared war against Great Britain in June 1779. The choice of an English Minister of War and the Marine in his former kingdom offended him deeply in consequence. What administrative talents had Acton shown to justify such honours, he demanded. Why had Ferdinand not chosen Don Antonio Otero, a reliable Spaniard?

Ferdinand replied with some equivocation: 'Mr Otero was of all men the most inefficient, and the Marquis Tanucci, who promoted him, has declared a hundred times that he felt ashamed of him. Mr Acton is not English: he was born in Franche-Comté and his mother was French. His father settled in Besançon, and has never returned to England since leaving it for religious reasons. His two brothers are in the service of France. This Minister was appointed on the first of January 1779, when Spain was at peace with Great Britain. It should be remembered that before war was declared Acton furnished the Court of Madrid with all the military munitions that were in the royal stores. It is true that no more have been provided since then, for the simple reason that not a bullet remains in the arsenals.'

The conflict was really between Charles III and his daughter-in-law, both equally headstrong, but what could a distant father do against a determined young wife? Since he could not strike at the Queen directly, Charles struck at Acton instead. His clumsy thrusts only helped to consolidate Acton's position.

Honours were showered on the indefatigable foreign minister: he was awarded the rank of Field-Marshal and was called General from now on. In May 1780 Hamilton reported: 'His integrity is already conspicuous here, having in less than two years saved in his department half a million of ducats of this country, at the same time that the Marine is stronger and better regulated than when he came to the head of it; but as Your Lordship may well imagine he has not been able to make such a reform without creating a great number of enemies, and I do not think his life quite secure. The Queen of Naples herself told me once that she was apprehensive that he would be poisoned.' And in November: 'General Acton's favour augments daily, he has become in a manner for some time past Prime Minister, and made such alterations, particularly in the administration of the finances, as must in a short time be productive of the most happy effects for this country. He is sensible, steady and honest.' His maxim was: *Si vis pacem para bellum*; and he prepared for war with all his might. His projects were broadly conceived and broadly executed. The shipbuilder's yard of Castellammare was modernized, so that it soon compared with the Venetian arsenal, the largest in Italy. Skilled engineers and technicians were engaged from abroad, while the most was made of local talent. Six new ships of the line were launched from Castellammare within six years, and an impressive number of frigates, corvettes, brigs, brigantines and gunboats, until the war fleet had about a hundred and fifty ships large and small. Nor were these idle. In Charles III's second campaign against the Algerine pirates in 1784, a Neapolitan flotilla rendered an excellent account of itself.

Four naval colleges were founded with the best instructors available; one of these published the first correct nautical chart of the Mediterranean, which was adopted by other nationalities. During the Franco-Spanish war with England of 1779 Acton sent a number of qualified naval cadets to serve in whichever fleet they chose so as to gain experience of actual hostilities. Among these were Francesco Caracciolo, Giovanni Bausan and others who were to win renown. A new spirit of enterprise filled the merchant marine, and the skill of Neapolitan pilots became proverbial. Greater security and the revival of sea trade were assisted by sensible treaties, especially with Genoa and Russia. The pollacks of Sorrento were models of their kind, and sailed to France, Spain, Portugal, England and even to America. The feluccas of Positano and the pinnaces of Procida traded with France and Spain.

To improve the army, Acton engaged a number of foreign officers and drill-sergeants, since the Neapolitans had had scant experience of war. This influx of aliens did not add to his popularity, but it is worth noting that among the sergeants was Pierre Augereau, who became a Maréchal de France and Duc de Castiglione, while the future French General Jean-Baptiste Eblé, who perished gloriously in 1812, served in Naples as a mere lieutenant. The Swiss Baron de Salis and the French Colonel Pommereul were Acton's chief military collaborators, and had to share the brunt of envy in and out of Court. The pro-Spanish faction, secretly supported by Sambuca, kept them under a raking fire.

The Sardinian minister, Marchese di Breme, reported in November 1782: 'The Queen... sees all officials on business and listens to them, especially to Acton, who is mixed up in almost everything... discusses all his plans with her and spends a great many hours in her company, to such a point that town gossip credits him with being her acknowledged lover, which is not true, though it is probable that in private the severe Minister of War softens at the will of his sovereign, who desires to be ogled, for that is her dearest delight. One is easily convinced of this when one sees her in high society, that is in the midst of her courtiers. Then all vie in sending her the most languishing glances; both young and old compete and, attentive to all, it is obvious that she feeds on them with pleasure. I have often observed this at hunting parties... especially when she is only surrounded by fifteen or twenty people... Then all glances are aimed at her, and each is jealous of his neighbour if he gets a favouring glance in return.' The Queen expressed her opinions before all, but 'not with the frankness that characterizes the King, rather to exhibit that subtlety of discernment on which she prides herself'. During dinner the Queen said she wanted to give a certain post to the husband of one of her children's governesses. The King replied: 'But Acton wishes to suppress this post, *maestra mia*' (the name he usually gives her). 'In that case,' she remarked, 'I shall say no more about it, for that is the most certain proof that it ought to be suppressed.' Di Breme concluded that 'Acton is neither a Colbert, a Sully or a Walpole, which is what this country needs, and it is the system of finance and all that pertains to it that should be reformed here before anything else. He may be ideal for the marine and military affairs, but he can only have little experience of finance. In this respect his sole virtue is a large foundation of honesty and impartiality... and his hands are untainted, a rarity here. His honesty makes him very reserved about matters outside his province; by this laudable delicacy it is certain that he will agree with the sentiments of those whom he can trust.'

The Abbé Galiani seemed to Di Breme the most eligible of economic advisers, but not without reservations. 'He appears to have much wit, and it cannot be denied that he has knowledge, but he is a perfect egoist, ready to sacrifice a whole state to his private interest, and even his private interest to a witticism. This last tendency has often risked arousing the enmity of Chevalier Acton, whom he ridicules in spite of the familiarity with which this minister treats him, admitting him almost daily to his table. Lately he received a retort which imposed silence on him for a while. They were discussing national constitutions at his dinner table. Galiani maintained that the people of these kingdoms had certain ancient conventions with their kings which limited the authority of the latter. Acton maintained the contrary. Galiani, who does not care to be contradicted, stubbornly defended his thesis in too cosmopolitan a style, to the extent of formally attacking the King's authority, so that the minister told him that although there was no Bastille in Naples to punish the foolhardy, there was an Orlando's tower (at Gaeta).' Eventually Galiani's friend Dr Gatti interceded for him with Acton. The Abbé was soon forgiven and appointed first adviser to the Council of Finance. He was also an adviser on more frivolous matters as when, during the Carnival of 1784, the visiting King Gustavus III of Sweden organized 'a bearhunt in the style of his country to celebrate his triumph over those animals [the Russians] as a masquerade with a gallant compliment for the Queen,' and the Queen wished to return the courtesy. 'We may torture our wits,' the Queen told Acton, 'but we will only do something insipid unless we consult Galiani.' So the Minister wrote the Abbé to devise 'a quick and easy masquerade... to compliment the author of the revolution in Sweden, the friend of the arts and men of letters, also the patron of those "liberal arts" which are ever on his tongue, next Sunday or Tuesday evening. In fulfilling this commission, I wish you good day.'

Di Breme described Sambuca as 'a plunderer' who accepted large bribes yet was always in debt. The Prime Minister, while filling his pockets, was seldom at ease. 'We dined yesterday with the Marquis of Sambuca,' wrote Swinburne. 'During the whole time of dinner he never opened his lips, either to eat or speak, and looked quite planet-struck. I thought he was seized with some mad fit, or hypochondria, but it came out afterwards that his dismayed appearance was caused by Carlino, the intendant of the King's bakehouse who had been put in prison for cheating, having made his escape from thence, and was just retaken as he was endeavouring to get to the King to make a discovery of everything; which it is believed would have strongly implicated Sambuca.' But he was more deeply implicated in the plot to ruin Acton, whom he depicted to Spain as an unscrupulous adventurer who had seduced the Queen body and soul. Ferdinand scoffed at such rumours, but his father warned him that there was no smoke without fire.

'Open your eyes, my son,' wrote the King of Spain on July 20, 1784, 'and recognize those who blind you, whose intention is to affront me so that I may turn my back on you. Having transformed you into a pasteboard king, they have now made you lose your honour, the welfare of your children, and your soul. Do not think I exaggerate, for if you take cognizance of it without the weakness to show this letter to those who are ruining you, you will discover what even the children sing, not only in Naples but at the chief courts of Europe, from where they write me things I must not repeat. Everybody is amazed at what is happening, not excepting your own relations and those of your wife. Cease your artful speeches... You know well what I told you when you appointed Acton, although with a discretion which I must not keep today, for I suppose that he himself does not keep it. He talks and behaves with such lack of restraint in all that concerns me that there is not a foreign visitor or resident in Naples who does not know or report to his own country what you should know and correct... If you wish to please me... you must get rid of Acton at once, or send him out of your kingdom. Unless you do this I shall not believe that you are a good son, and I shall pray God for further enlightenment...'

Viscount La Herreria, the Spanish ambassador who presented this letter to Ferdinand, was aware of its contents since he had been the chief source of the information it contained, but Florida Blanca, the Spanish prime minister, was the leading spirit in the cabal against Acton and the Queen, and probably had a hand in its composition. After reading it, Ferdinand became almost hysterical. He rushed to the Queen's room, shouting and waving the letter in her face, and repeated his father's accusations. Maria Carolina, who was only too familiar with his failings, turned the tables on him completely. Her immediate reaction was that of the outraged wife; she, the mother of his children, the daughter of the great Maria Theresa, to be so injured and insulted! Was he not man enough to defend her honour—apart from his own—against such gross calumny? Acton's departure would mean a return to the Spanish yoke. Did he still want to be dictated to by his old papa, or rather by his papa's sycophants? After appealing to his pride she appealed to his affection, and in her wounded dignity she seemed a superior being, drawing herself up majestically, her bosom heaving, flashing her large blue eyes which filled with tears as she reminded him that she was again with child. Paroxysm by paroxysm she worked herself up to a crisis, until Ferdinand cursed himself for his indiscretion. The King and Queen remained locked in their chamber for twenty-four hours. When they left it, Ferdinand was convinced that his wife was entirely justified. His confidence in Acton, momentarily shaken by his father, was fully restored. He refused to be bullied by Madrid. Sambuca was forbidden to hold any further communication with La Herreria, who was recalled.

Count de Las Casas, the next ambassador, fared no better than his predecessor. On May 15, 1785, Hamilton reported: 'Monsieur de Las Casas, the new Spanish minister, having been on board the ship in which the King and Queen of Naples went to Leghorn... was very much offended at seeing the state room furnished with English prints representing the defeat of Langara and Monsieur de Gras by Sir George Rodney, and the destruction of the floating batteries before Gibraltar; he was weak enough to reproach His Sicilian Majesty with the impropriety of such furniture and to threaten to complain to His Catholic Majesty. The Queen of Naples sent for him, and in a very spirited manner warned him to be on his guard and rather to endeavour at diminishing than increasing the coolness which unfortunately subsisted between the father and the son, owing to the cabals of ill-designing persons.

'I have been credibly informed that M. de Las Casas and Monsieur de Talleyrand, the new French ambassador who is expected here very soon, have it in their instructions to act in concert and do all in their power to remove General Acton from the service of Their Sicilian Majesties. General Acton himself told me that he did not doubt of the truth of this report as the Emperor had informed the Queen of Naples that the French minister had applied to him to join this league, and that he had answered that he would readily do so when they should have pointed out to him any just cause of complaint against the General. The party here likewise in opposition to General Acton is certainly very strong, but it appears to me that Their Sicilian Majesties are determined to support him, and indeed it is for their own interest so to do, as he is the only one of their ministers who is active and indefatigable in their service and whose character is free from blemish.' The Queen accused Las Casas of stealing Acton's papers, which caused a panic in diplomatic circles. The Austrian minister begged Acton to burn all documents compromising his Court and that of Russia. Baron de Talleyrand, the French ambassador, tried in vain to pacify the Queen. She was determined to extract a personal confession from Las Casas, but he would only speak to the King, which she was able to prevent. Las Casas was kept at bay and snubbed by the whole Court. In his secret correspondence he called the Queen a viper.

Finally, negotiations with Algiers afforded him a pretext for an audience. While he was closeted with the King, the Queen burst in and delivered a tirade against the Spanish ambassador, which ended in convulsions. The ambassador retired in confusion. Promptly recovering her self-possession, the Queen rose and taunted her husband. By playing a double game the ambassador hoped to dupe him. These secrets, which he pretended were only for the King's ears, were already known to her. The hypocrite had already spoken to her about his father, in very different language from the sentiments he had just professed. Overwhelmed by her vehemence, the King yielded to his wife as usual. He wrote a letter under her dictation, accusing Las Casas of deliberate deception and refusing to see him unless he could justify his statements and hand over the written proofs against Acton which were said to be in his possession.

A copy of the King's letter was brought to Las Casas on October 4, 1785: 'I would not have delayed granting your wish to speak to me without the Queen's knowledge, if you had not prevented this by playing two opposite roles at the same time. After having informed me in the morning that you desired to speak to me secretly, so that the Queen should know nothing about it... you went on to broach the same subject with the Queen, trying to persuade her to facilitate Acton's dismissal by saying: "His Catholic Majesty is seventy years old and only has a few more years to live. Therefore this satisfaction might be given him for the present, and the person could be reinstated, with all due honours, as soon as the King expires..." From this it is clear that your language is unworthy of a loyal servant. If the person is bad he should be dismissed for ever. But when you declare that, after granting this satisfaction for the time being, he could be reinstated with all honours in the future, it becomes obvious that, fundamentally, you realize he is a man of merit who could be useful in my service. Instead of quashing this intrigue, you speak like one indifferent to law, honour or conscience so long as he does his business, seeking to ruin an honest man and upsetting both my father and myself.'

Prince Pignatelli was sent post-haste to Madrid as a special envoy to explain what had happened, and orders were sent to Capua to permit nobody else to pass, so that he should arrive before the Spanish courier. A letter in cipher from Sir William Hamilton throws further light on this murky intrigue; it is dated October 25, 1785. 'The cabal excited by the favour which General Acton has long enjoyed at this Court seems now likely to come to a crisis and, as I have reason to believe, a very serious one. At first his enemies accused him only of acting upon Austrian principles and not those of the House of Bourbon, and by these means induced the Courts of France and Spain to join in their application to this Court for the removal of this Minister, but their Sicilian Majesties were firm in the support of the only Minister in whom they have entire confidence, hence proceeded the coolness that subsisted some time ago between their Catholic and their Sicilian Majesties. The new Spanish minister last week renewed the attack, and finding His Majesty firm in the support of his Minister, was so rash as to insinuate that the attachment that the Queen of Naples had to the General was not supposed by His Catholic Majesty to be of the purest nature.

'The King received this calumny (for such I believe it to be) with the utmost indignation—informed the Queen thereof, and has dispatched Marshal Pignatelli to Madrid to clear the character of the Queen of Naples, and the Minister from so vile an accusation, but as I know for certain (and of which in all probability His Sicilian Majesty is ignorant) that the opposition party have, by very unfair means, obtained four original letters in the Queen's own handwriting, proving too clearly a former weakness, and have communicated those letters to the Court of Madrid, I believe it will not be an easy matter to alter the opinion of the King of Spain, and that this affair must end in ill-humour.'

Charles III remained inflexible; he asked if Acton was still in office, and turned his back on Pignatelli when he answered in the affirmative. Nothing less than complete submission would satisfy him. He even thought of asking the Emperor Joseph to intervene, but his innate distrust of Austria deterred him. Florida Blanca was in favour of less civilized tactics, if indeed he was serious when he wrote (September 28, 1784): 'Mr Acton is odious to the people and to nearly all the aristocracy of Naples. We have several regiments in this capital which we could muster at the first signal. There would be nothing easier than to seize this Minister in the evening on his way home, gag his mouth to prevent him from crying out, and carry him off in a felucca which would transport him immediately to the nearest Spanish port. We would arrest and imprison him and thus be rid of him for ever. But how could we persuade so loyal and scrupulous a prince as the King of Spain, a monarch so opposed to any infringement of sovereignty, to approve of such an expedient? In vain he believes he has rights over this son who owes his crown to him. In his eyes this son is no less a sovereign than all the rest! Besides I would never dare propose this violent measure, though I believe it would be easy to execute and would be the only quick and effective means of eliminating our difficulties.'

So far Sambuca, intriguing with Spain in the background, had managed to keep out of trouble. In June 1783, Hamilton had written: 'A baron of Sicily has accused the Prime Minister here of having cheated His Sicilian Majesty of a sum equivalent to one hundred and fifty thousand pounds... The accusation has been clearly proved, yet from the universal corruption that prevails here it is most probable that that Minister will not be punished nor the King... recover his money.' The German Philip Hackert, who had been appointed Court painter to the King, has related the circumstances leading to Sambuca's disgrace. While the Court was at Caserta many sent their letters to Naples furtively by the kitchen messenger instead of by the official courier. It was noticed that whenever the Spanish despatches arrived this kitchen messenger carried a box to Caserta, of which several courtiers, including Sambuca's secretary, possessed the key. He was arrested by a colonel of dragoons and twenty men, and the Spanish box, as well as a quantity of other letters, were seized and brought directly to the King, who sat down with the Queen and Acton to read them. The letters from Spain contained enough evidence to convict Sambuca of treason. After examining these, says Hackert, they read those intended for the ladies-in-waiting and others who had something to conceal. They contained many an amusing surprise. Among them, however, the King found one addressed to the Queen's Austrian cook, and the writer, apparently a Neapolitan friend, asked if pheasant eggs took longer to hatch than those of an ordinary hen, since hers had been brooded on for twenty days without any result. The King was more affected by this than by all the other letters. 'What! so they have taken to stealing my eggs!' he exclaimed in a fury. To save her cook the Queen replied that she had ordered her to send the eggs to Naples, as she wanted to hatch some pheasants there for the children. The King got angrier. 'So you even meddle with my sport? I have had enough of this. Read the rest yourself. I shall read no more this evening as I wish to be spared further annoyance.' And he retired to play billiards.

Next day the cook was forced to accompany the King to the coverts and show him exactly where she had found the pheasant eggs in question. All the while she grumbled against the King in broken Italian for making such a fuss about a few paltry eggs. When this matter was settled the King proceeded to the State Council, where severe sentences were meted out to all those who had plotted against the Queen. Sambuca was dismissed, but he was allowed to retain his large salary and retire to Palermo. As he had always lived extravagantly, he left vast debts behind him, but having acquired very cheaply all the property of the suppressed Jesuits in Palermo and its neighbourhood, he was assured of a handsome revenue. Acton had triumphed; he was given the Order of San Gennaro and appointed a royal Councillor. The Queen wished him to be Minister for Foreign Affairs, but the King was unwilling to defy his father too flamboyantly. Ferdinand still hoped for a reconciliation, blaming his father's ministers for the present deadlock. As he wrote to the Count of Vergennes, French Minister of Foreign Affairs: 'It seems that their plan is to alienate my august father from me, and destroy his paternal affection. An infernal cabal has reduced me to the cruel alternative of displeasing my father or of acting against my own conscience and honour.'

About this time the Queen began her voluminous correspondence with Marchese di Gallo which lasted for over twenty years.

Her letters, written in fluent but faulty French, were never intended for publication: she constantly urged him to burn them, an injunction which, happily for historians, is seldom fulfilled. Gallo was far too cautious to destroy such precious documents, which were published in 1911. He was a supple courtier who had a special way with the ladies. Evidently Maria Carolina was susceptible to his charm. His uncle Marchese Caracciolo, the most intelligent and jovial of Neapolitan ambassadors, treated him as a son, and helped him to rise in his profession. Now, at the age of thirty, he was minister to Turin.

One of the Queen's first letters to Gallo announced his uncle's promotion and Sambuca's disgrace: 'The frigate left five days ago with the King's orders to fetch the Viceroy Caracciolo, your worthy uncle, to be Secretary of Foreign Affairs. I count on his integrity and talents, and hope he will have the necessary dose of patriotism to sacrifice himself for the good of his country without afterthought or personal considerations. You know my heart well: it was painful to come to these extremities. But all that has happened has been too outrageous not to lead to decisions which, considering the circumstances, should be regarded as lenient compared with what they deserved, when the infamous plot miscarried.'

XI

Marchese Caracciolo becomes Prime Minister—The Queen's vendetta against the Spanish faction—More royal offspring—Abolition of the Chinea—Mrs Piozzi's impressions—Goethe on Naples—Emma Hart—Filangieri and his sprightly sister—Tischbein, Angelica Kauffmann and Hackert—Death of Charles III, 1788—Bereavements and betrothals—Death of Marchese Caracciolo—Acton becomes Minister for Foreign Affairs.

After a leisurely decade as ambassador in Paris, where he had been even more popular than Galiani, Caracciolo had spent five arduous years as Viceroy of Sicily (1781-6) attempting to put his theories into practice. When summoned to succeed Sambuca as Prime Minister, he was a bachelor of seventy-one, corpulent and rheumatic, but his intellect was as alert as ever.

The French memoirs of the period are full of tributes to his social talents. The Duc de Levis wrote that 'he had the wit of four, the gestures of eight, and made a noise like twenty. He alone filled an entire salon; but his gaiety was so natural that it disturbed nobody; he had an original way of seeing and expressing things and an inexhaustible fund of good jokes, in which there was no trace of bitterness or malice.' Mme Necker said that 'his conversation was always linked to that of others: whereas that of the Abbé Galiani only dealt with the extraordinary, Caracciolo always saw things as if under a new aspect.'

Marmontel's sketch of him is the most detailed: 'At first sight, Caracciolo had the heavy, massive look which might denote stupidity. To kindle his eyes and features it was necessary for him to talk. Then, as his keen, piercing, luminous intelligence became roused, it was as if sparks flew out of him; and the acuteness, gaiety and originality of his thought, the naturalness of his expression, the charm of his smile, the sensibility of his glance combined to give an amiable, clever and interesting character to his ugliness. He had some trouble in speaking our language but was eloquent in his own; and when the French term failed him borrowed the word, the turn of phrase and the image he required from Italian. Thus, at every moment he enriched his language with a thousand bold and picturesque expressions which made us envy him. These were accompanied with that Neapolitan gesticulation which enlivened the Abbé Galiani's expression so graciously, and it was said of both of them that they were witty to their finger tips. Both also had excellent stories to tell, mostly with a subtle, moral and profound significance. Caracciolo had made a philosophical study of mankind, but he had observed men more as a politician and a statesman than as a satirical moralist... With inexhaustible wealth of knowledge and a very agreeable, spontaneous manner of distributing it, he had the additional merit of being an excellent man.' Galiani's verdict on him was less kind: 'Caracciolo is always Caracciolo: useless to society, agreeable in society.' But as Marmontel remarked: 'None of us would have thought of making a friend of the Abbé Galiani, whereas all of us aspired to the friendship of Caracciolo.'

He had been so reluctant to leave France that he had postponed his departure till the Sicilians were offended. As viceroy he had been more useful than agreeable to a feudal society which had changed little since the Spanish domination. He had abolished the Inquisition and reduced the power of the barons, but the ultra-conservative Sicilians were none too sorry when he left them. His reforms were more applauded in Paris than in Palermo, for Sicily could never be converted into a country of Encyclopædists. With his contempt for local religious beliefs, he had tried to suppress the annual festivities held on July 11-15 in honour of their patron saint, Rosalia. Even the chief magistrate opposed this, and the people wrote on his palace gate: '*O festa, o testa*' ('Either the holiday or your head'). The people won, and he was obliged to let them celebrate with the usual processions and illuminations. Throughout these five years he had kept up a close correspondence with Acton, instead of with the Prime Minister Sambuca; he realized where the true power lay and his letters, like those of a civilized exile in a savage land, betray a sincere respect for 'the foreign adventurer', as well as a desire for sympathy in his uncongenial task. Having spent eight years in London and ten in Paris, he could appreciate the rare qualities of this Englishman born in France.

Like Tanucci, who had launched him on his career, he believed in the divine right of kings. 'The King of Naples,' he wrote, 'is no less a king than those of France and Spain, nor less a sovereign than the Emperor, hence there is no reason why he should not enjoy the same prerogatives and attentions.' With all due deference for Charles III, he too objected to his overbearing attitude, but as a friend of the Encyclopædists he felt more bitterly against the Pope's 'pretensions'. Many years ago he had said: 'If ever I am Minister at Naples, I will make the King independent of that Grand Mufti at Rome.'

Congratulating his uncle on his promotion, Gallo wrote him an almost avuncular letter: 'It worries me to think that the political situation will oblige you to spend most of the winter in the severe and none too healthy climate of Caserta or Venafro... As I fear that Your Excellency might suffer from it and especially from so sudden a change, I fervently implore you to prefer your own precious preservation to any form of heroism, a virtue which in a charming letter Your Excellency once compared to sodomy and other unnatural things. Perhaps without staying at Caserta Your Excellency could go there two or three times a week while residing in Naples, and this continual movement would help to stimulate your circulation and give energy to the system. Another important consideration is not to let yourself be overburdened by affairs, or by the intrigues and cabals of courtiers: it would be difficult to find a country more corrupt than ours in this respect. As a friend of justice, merit and truth, Your Excellency will surely find most troublesome obstacles in the bad faith, disorder and trickery of this Court...'

Such advice was scarcely needed, but no doubt his old uncle was touched. Marchese di Gallo was one of the first to benefit from the change. Soon the Prime Minister informed him: 'I have some good news for you. His Majesty of his own accord has ordained that you are to receive the same salary as his minister and your colleague in London, that is to say 10,000 ducats... This will be useful to you, but what redounds to your highest honour and should win your eternal gratitude was the sympathy, graciousness and affectionate tone of his expressions when he charged me to inform you of this... Great fortune is yours, and of all who have the honour to serve such adorable masters, so grateful, appreciative and loving...'

The government consisted of four departments, the first three under secretaries of state, the fourth under a supreme council of finance, consisting of the same three secretaries, a director and a body of councillors. The Prime Minister was Secretary for Foreign Affairs, the royal household and the postal service. Acton was Minister for War, the Marine and Commerce. Carlo de Marco, described by Tanucci as a declamatory Jansenist who believed in canon law rather than in sound judgement, was Minister for Justice and Ecclesiastical Affairs, a post he had held for twenty-seven years.

Each minister or secretary submitted his proposals to the King, who heard the opinion of the Council of State before making his decision. This was almost invariably the Queen's decision. Unless their presence was demanded, the ministers did not attend the Council of State, which met three times a week. The Queen had attended it regularly since 1775. Since she had wanted Acton to succeed Sambuca, she tended to disparage Caracciolo. According to Baron Thugut, the Austrian ambassador: 'The Queen deigned to inform me that Marchese Caracciolo's part in the administration is absolutely null. Her Majesty went on to say that he had only been given his present post because it was not yet feasible to add this department to the others which had been entrusted to Mr Acton... It is a fact that, enjoying the Queen's whole confidence... this Minister, even now, disposes almost arbitrarily of all the affairs of the kingdom.'

This is confirmed by Hamilton, who wrote that the Queen was well aware that, unless she took a personal interest in the affairs which the King avoided, the whole state would fall into confusion. She gave up most of her time to looking minutely into every paper, and preparing matters for settlement when she met the King in Council at night, more or less weary with hunting or fishing since sunrise. In spite of difficulties and delays owing to the King's jealousy of others acting for him, she usually carried every point at last. Since Acton was the only minister she trusted, 'his channel is become the universal one for the despatch of every business, even what is foreign to his department, and he may truly be esteemed the Prime Minister of this country. I really believe that the General is worthy of the entire confidence that is reposed in him: he has already given ample proofs of his integrity, diligence and ability in the two departments allotted to him, and His Excellency is indefatigable in the despatch of the business of the finances and of other departments which have been forced upon him; but the fatigue of so much business together with the vexations which malicious and envious opposition are ever throwing in his way, appears to me to be too much for his weak constitution, and at times he visibly sinks under the weight.' As for Caracciolo, he seemed well contented in his old age to be relieved from the onus and have time to mix in the gay societies of Naples, to the mirth of which he greatly contributed. The Prince of Caramanico had succeeded him as Viceroy of Sicily, 'and would probably, in case any accident should happen to General Acton, be placed at the head of the affairs of this country'.

Although Acton did most of his work, even as a figure-head Caracciolo found his post no sinecure. 'Here I am home again after a long absence,' he wrote to a friend, 'and although I had hoped to find peace and tranquillity, I am kept more than ever on the trot, exposed to winds and tempests.'

After the withdrawal of Las Casas only a *chargé d'affaires* acted as Spanish representative in Naples, though Ferdinand retained an ambassador, the Prince of Raffadale, at his father's Court. That the Queen persisted in her reprisals while Caracciolo tried to soften them is apparent from his note to Raffadale, February 14, 1786: 'Last week the King arranged that his chief major-domo was to invite all the members of the diplomatic corps and several foreigners of quality to a hunt at Carditello. The King saw that Clemente de Campos, the Spanish *chargé d'affaires*, was placed on the list of guests, but owing to a mistake the invitation failed to reach him. The King was very vexed. Having ordered the major-domo to exert more vigilance in future, he has charged me to tell Your Excellency to express his keen regret for this incident to his august Father.'

Caracciolo laboured for a better understanding with the senior Bourbons. He hoped to induce the King of France, as head of the family, to intervene with Charles III. Instead of applying to the Neapolitan ambassador in Paris, his own subordinate, he decided to send a special envoy. The choice was unfortunate. Chevalier de Bressac, a French colonel in the Neapolitan army, and therefore a subordinate of Acton, went to Paris to confer with the Minister of Foreign Affairs, Comte de Vergennes. A face-saving solution was finally found: Ferdinand was to declare his readiness to dismiss Acton in order to gratify his father, and Charles III was to reply that he had no objection to that worthy and zealous minister. In all good faith Ferdinand wrote this letter and the French government sent it to Madrid, but no reply was vouchsafed. It was even rumoured that Charles intended to change the order of succession established by Philip V, to the disadvantage of the Bourbons of Naples.

Ferdinand continued to write to his father once a week about domestic trifles, while the Queen pursued her vengeance. The slanders which the Spanish party had published about her relations with Acton were all the more galling because there was an element of truth in them: she had fallen under his spell. Her enemies had procured several compromising letters which she had been able to recover except two or three, the most indiscreet. It was suspected that the Princess of Jaci had stolen these, and she was involved in Sambuca's disgrace. Though her husband was a Councillor of State and a Grandee of Spain, she was banished from Court, but her applications to leave the country were all refused. However, she secured a passport under another name and embarked from Sorrento with a few retainers. A former secretary who had been expelled for the same reason was waiting for her at Civitavecchia, whence a ship was to take her to Spain. But the secret had leaked out. Less than a mile from Sorrento she was arrested and brought back to Naples by sea. On arrival she had to wait eight hours exposed to a broiling sun in her little boat, while a crowd of onlookers gathered on the mole. Their rude comments about the runaway dame may be imagined. Finally she was bundled off to a convent, where she was kept under close confinement. When this was known in Madrid, Florida Blanca sent a tearful appeal to Caracciolo; Charles III had ordered him to plead for clemency, out of regard for the long service, old age and high rank of her husband, and compassion for both. After a week Caracciolo reported that the Princess had been set free.

These were the prolific years of the Queen's life. In 1786 she gave birth to her sixth daughter, Maria Clotilde, and in 1787 to her seventh, Enrichetta Maria Carmela. Her father-in-law forgot his resentment so far as to send her a message that if she bore another son he would present him with the Golden Fleece and Grand Cross of Charles III. Her third son was duly born in 1788, soon after the Queen had returned from the theatre, and Charles was the first of the seventeen names he was given at the christening.

To offset this exchange of domestic courtesies, Charles III insisted on the reinstatement of Quiñones, who had lost his post of Court physician owing to his intrigues against Acton and the Queen. Florida Blanca assured Caracciolo that Quiñones had behaved with the greatest discretion and impartiality, 'and had done everything to promote the King of Spain's goodwill and benevolence for his beloved son'. Ferdinand replied that the Quiñones case was *sub judice,* therefore he would not interfere with the course of justice. Regarding the man's conduct, His Majesty had no need of any private individual's services to promote the benevolence of his august and beloved father. But Quiñones still hoped to recover his lucrative post. Armed with recommendations from Florida Blanca, he left Madrid, but his journey was delayed by an accident: his carriage broke down and he was thrown into a ditch not far from the capital. Eventually he reached Florence, where he heard that the Queen had ordered his arrest if he crossed the frontier. He was still agitating in high circles when his royal patron died, so that he could only return disconsolately to Spain.

The King himself took part in the tortuous negotiations for a new Concordat with Rome. As a devout, even a superstitious, Catholic he would have welcomed an understanding with the Pope. Though Caracciolo had been a lifelong anti-clerical, he began to draw a distinction between the Holy See and the Roman Curia, saying that he only loathed the latter. Age and responsibility had modified his views: the sceptical doctrinaire was coming to attach more importance to men than to measures. His old friends attributed this to senility. But the Queen did not really want a Concordat: she needed the vast ecclesiastical revenues to enrich the treasury and defray the expenses of her Court. The chief points of the controversy concerned the nomination of bishops, the dependence of regular clergy on their superiors in Rome, the Nuncio's jurisdiction and the bestowal of monasteries, benefices, etc. Though the King had no grasp of history or theology, he had been steeped in the knowledge of his royal privileges since boyhood. He saw these as rights received directly from God. Thus the negotiations with Cardinal Buoncompagni and Monsignor Caleppi were doomed, and in 1788 Caracciolo went further than Tanucci: he obliterated the last feudal connexion with the Holy See. This was the presentation of the white palfrey called the *chinea,* accompanied by the payment of 7,000 gold *scudi*; an act of homage dating from the thirteenth century, when Charles of Anjou declared himself a vassal of the Pope and promised a yearly tribute to legitimize his conquest. Ferdinand said he would pay a 'devout offering' instead of the 'customary tribute', but this did not satisfy Pius VI, who delighted in the picturesque ceremony.

Miss Cornelia Knight, who watched it on June 28, 1780,

described it as follows: 'The procession commenced with the Pope's light horse, sent to escort the Constable Colonna. Then came the servants of several cardinals and princes in their liveries, in attendance upon some of their gentlemen on horseback with black mantles. The Constable's was the last, with their mantles turned back with gold stuff. Next followed the horse, richly caparisoned, the present—a silver flower—being carried on his back. Behind the animal came the Constable, preceded by his pages in lilac and silver, and by his first gentlemen. He was dressed in light brown, with a mantle, and was mounted on a beautiful horse: he himself was a pretty figure. His state carriages followed him. The first was a chariot, which belonged to his uncle, Cardinal Pamfili, when he was nuncio in France, and the second was a coach, richly ornamented, belonging to the King of Naples, whom he represented as ambassador; the rest were of various colours, but all drawn by fine horses. When they arrived at St Peter's, the guns of Sant' Angelo were fired, and after them a volley of musketry. We entered St Peter's a few minutes before the Pope came in to receive the Constable. He was carried on men's shoulders down the body of the church, attended by the cardinals. The horse was then brought in and led up to the altar, when he received a slight tap with a wand, and immediately knelt down, and the Pope gave him his benediction. The statue of St Peter was dressed in gold stuff with a ring on its finger, rare jewels on its breast, and a tiara on its head. Large candlesticks with lighted tapers were placed in front, and a guard of soldiers stationed to check the indiscreet devotion of the saint's votaries; but the black face and hands of the statue had a comical effect. The church was hung with crimson velvet and gold, the great altar finely arranged, and festoons of artificial flowers hung round the silver lamps that surrounded it. The throne of the Pope was set out for next day's mass, and the whole building in perfect *fiocchi* [equivalent to 'gala costume'—from the tassels with which horses were ornamented in state processions]. The Constable returned in his state coach, drawn by six horses.'

'I thought I was watching a parody of some Mexican or Peruvian rite,' said a French observer.

It is difficult to understand all the bother about this pretty function, which Neapolitan patriots considered so humiliating. Caracciolo was congratulated as if he had won a great victory, and Mirabeau wrote fulsome eulogies of this master-stroke of statesmanship. He deserves more credit for improving the university, founding a number of new schools, including one for the dumb, reviving the Herculanean Academy and introducing various postal reforms.

Goethe visited Naples at this time; so did the more volatile Mrs Piozzi; and their impressions, though diverse, are complementary.

As the wife of an Italian, Mrs Piozzi had a certain advantage over other English travellers, and she could describe the *Lazzarone* King without prejudice: 'This prince lives among his subjects with the old Roman idea of a window before his bosom, I believe. They know the worst of him is that he shoots at the birds, dances with the girls, eats macaroni, and helps himself to it with his fingers, and rows against the watermen in the bay, till one of them burst out o' bleeding at the nose last week with his uncourtly efforts to outdo the king, who won the trifling wager by this accident—conquered, laughed, and leaped on shore, amidst the acclamations of the populace, who huzzaed him home to the palace, from whence he sent double the sum he had won to the waterman's wife and children, with other tokens of kindness. Meantime, while he resolves to be happy himself, he is equally determined to make no man miserable.

'When the Emperor and the Grand Duke talked to him of their new projects for reformation in the Church, he told them he saw little advantage they brought into their states by these new-fangled notions; that when he was at Florence and Milan the deuce a Neapolitan could he find in either, while his capital was crowded with refugees from thence; that in short, they might do their way, but he would do his; that he had not now an enemy in the world, public or private, and that he would not make himself any for the sake of propagating doctrines he did not understand, and would not take the trouble to study; that he should say his prayers as he used to do, and had no doubt of their being heard, while he only begged blessings on his beloved people. So if these wise brothers-in-law would learn of him to enjoy life, instead of shortening it by unnecessary cares, he invited them to see him the next morning play a great match at tennis.

'The truth is, the jolly Neapolitans lead a coarse life; but it is an unoppressed one.'

Goethe, who owed so much to Winckelmann and felt the same wistful attraction towards the south, almost succumbed, but with a northerner's uneasy conscience, to the Circean magic of the place.

'When I would write words, only images start before my eyes—the beautiful land, the free sea; the hazy islands, the roaring mountain; powers to delineate all this fail me.' But they could not really fail so great a poet. His pages about Naples in March 1787 are as alive as when they were written. 'Naples is a paradise,' he exclaimed, 'in it every one lives in a sort of intoxicated self-forgetfulness. It is even so with me; I scarcely know myself—I seem quite an altered man. Yesterday I said to myself: either you have always been mad, or you are so now.' And again: 'If in Rome one can readily set oneself to study, here one can do nothing but live. You forget yourself and the world; and to me it is a strange feeling to go about with people who think of nothing but enjoying themselves... Were I not impelled by the German spirit, and desire to learn and to do rather than to enjoy, I should tarry a little longer in this school of a light-hearted and happy life, and try to profit from it still more.'

Sir William Hamilton struck him as the pattern of an intelligent epicurean. His wife had died in 1782; and recently Amy Lyon, better known as Emma Hart, his nephew's mistress, had come to live with him, a creature of sensational beauty. From Romney's numerous portraits of her she would seem to have been the prototype of the modern 'pin-up girl'. The author of *Faust* was fascinated by this association of age and youth. 'Sir William Hamilton has contrived highly to enjoy a long residence in this city, and now, in the evening of his life, is reaping the fruits of it. The rooms which he has had furnished in the English style are most delightful, and the view from the corner room, perhaps, unique. Below you is the sea, with a view of Capri, Posillipo at your right, with the promenade of Villa Reale between you and the grotto; on the left an ancient building which belonged to the Jesuits, and beyond it the coast stretching from Sorrento to Cape Minerva. Another prospect equal to this is scarcely to be found in Europe—at least, not in the centre of a great and populous city.

'Hamilton is a person of universal taste, and after having wandered through the whole realm of creation, has found rest at last in a most beautiful companion, a masterpiece of the great artist—Nature... She is an Englishwoman of about twenty years old... The old knight has had a Greek costume made for her, which becomes her extremely. Dressed in this, and letting her hair loose, and taking a couple of shawls, she exhibits every possible variety of posture, expression, and look, so that at the last the spectator almost fancies it is a dream. One beholds there in perfection, in movement, in ravishing variety, all that the greatest of artists have rejoiced to be able to produce. Standing, kneeling, sitting, lying down, grave or sad, playful, exulting, repentant, wanton, menacing, anxious—all mental states follow rapidly one after another. With wonderful taste she suits the folding of her veil to each expression, and with the same handkerchief makes every kind of head-dress. The old knight holds the light for her, and enters into the exhibition with his whole soul. He thinks he can discern in her a resemblance to all the most famous antiques, all the beautiful profiles on the Sicilian coins—aye, of the Apollo Belvedere itself. This much at any rate is certain—the entertainment is unique. We spent two evenings on it with thorough enjoyment. Today Tischbein is engaged in painting her.'

Tischbein acted as Goethe's Baedeker in Rome and Naples, but in Naples, as Sir Max Beerbohm divined in one of his most subtle essays, the cicerone became bored with his too solemn and illustrious companion and recommended him to a young painter called Kniep, who accompanied him to Sicily in his stead. Tischbein's portrait of Goethe draped in a white mantle, sitting on a fallen obelisk and surveying the ruins of the Roman Campagna, remained unfinished. Having set eyes on the dazzling Emma, he seems to have become infatuated, like all the other painters.

Among the memorable figures described by Goethe are Gaetano Filangieri and his vivacious sister Teresa, Princess Ravaschieri di Satriano. Filangieri's *Scienza della Legislazione* had been published in 1780, and Goethe had corresponded with him before meeting him in the flesh. He was then thirty-five, and had married Countess Caroline Fremdel, who had come to Naples as governess to one of the royal princesses. 'In his bearing', wrote Goethe, 'you recognize at once the soldier, the gentleman, and the man of the world; but this appearance is softened by an expression of tender moral sensibility, which is diffused over his whole countenance, and shines forth most agreeably in his character and conversation; he is, moreover, heartily attached to his sovereign and country, even though he cannot approve of all that goes on. He is also oppressed with a fear of Joseph II. The idea of a despot, even though it only floats as a phantom in the air, excites the apprehensions of every noble-minded man. He spoke to me without reserve of what Naples had to fear from him; but in particular he was delighted to speak of

Montesquieu, Beccaria, and of some of his own writings—all in the same spirit of the best will, and of a heart full of youthful enthusiasm to do good.'

He introduced Goethe to Vico's *Scienza nuova*, which had not reached Germany; and a few days later he introduced him to his sister, who seems to have made a deeper impression on the poet. 'As I came back from Capodimonte, I paid an evening visit to Filangieri, and saw sitting on the sofa, beside the mistress of the house, a lady whose external appearance seemed to be at odds with the familiarity and easy manner she indulged in. In a light striped silk gown of very ordinary texture, and a most singular cap by way of head-dress, but of a pretty figure, she looked like some dressmaker who, always busy adorning others, had little time to bestow on her own appearance... My entrance did not interrupt her gossip, and she went on talking of the ridiculous adventures which had happened to her that day, most of which had been occasioned by her own sprightliness. The lady of the house wished to help me to get in a word or two, and spoke of the beautiful position of Capodimonte, and of the treasures there. Upon this the lively lady sprang with a jump from the sofa, and as she stood up seemed still prettier than before. She took leave, and said, as she ran past me to the door: "The Filangieri are soon coming to dine with me. I hope to see you too." She was gone before I had a chance to accept. I now discovered that she was the Princess—, a near relative of my host. The Filangieri were not rich, and lived in a becoming but moderate style; and such I presumed was the case with my little Princess, especially as such titles are anything but rare in Naples. I noted the name, the day and the hour, and decided to be there on time.'

When he set out for dinner with the Princess, Goethe was astonished to find that she lived in a splendid palace: 'I entered a spacious court, silent and solitary, empty and clean... The architecture was the usual gay Neapolitan style, as was also the colouring. Right before me was a grand porch, and a broad but not very steep flight of steps. Both sides of it were lined with servants in rich liveries, who bowed very low as I passed. I fancied myself the Sultan in Wieland's fairy-tale, and tried to live up to this role. Next I was received by the higher domestics, till at last the most courtly of them opened a door, and introduced me into a vast hall, which was as splendid, but also as empty of people as all before. In passing to and fro I observed, in a side room, a table laid for about forty guests, with a splendour harmonizing with all around. A priest now entered, and without asking who I was or whence I came, took my presence for granted, and conversed on commonplace topics.

'A pair of folding doors were thrown open and immediately closed again, as an elderly gentleman walked in. The priest went straight up to him, so did I; we greeted him with a few words of courtesy, which he returned in a barking, stuttering tone, so that I could scarcely make out a syllable of his Hottentot dialect. When he had taken his place by the stove, the priest and I moved away. A portly Benedictine entered, accompanied by a younger member of his order. He went to salute the host, and after being also barked at, retired to a window... In the meantime the hall had filled: officers, courtiers, secular ecclesiastics, and even some Capuchins had arrived. Once more a set of folding doors opened and shut; an aged lady, somewhat older than my host, had entered; and now the presence of what I took to be the lady of the house made me feel certain that I was in a strange mansion, where I was wholly unknown to its owners.

'Dinner was now served, and I was keeping close to my friends the monks in order to slip with them into the paradise of the dining-room, when all at once I saw Filangieri enter with his wife, apologizing for being so late. A minute later my little Princess hopped into the room, and with nods, and winks, and bows to all as she passed, came straight to me. "It is very good of you to keep your word," she exclaimed; "mind you sit next to me, you shall have the best helpings,—but wait a minute! I must first choose my place, then you must sit immediately beside me." Thus commanded, I followed her meanderings, and at last we reached our seats: the Benedictine opposite and Filangieri on my other side. "The dishes are all good," she observed, "all Lenten fare, but choice: I'll point out to you the best. But now I must tease those priests, the scamps! I cannot abide them. Every day they are pecking another slice off our estate. What we have, we should like to spend on ourselves and our friends."

'The soup was now handed round—the Benedictine was sipping his very deliberately. "Pray do not stint yourself," she cried. "Perhaps the spoon is too small? I shall tell them to bring you a larger one. Your reverences are accustomed to big mouthfuls." The good father replied that in her house everything was so well arranged that many a more distinguished guest would find everything to his heart's content. Seeing that the Benedictine took only a single pie, she called out to him: "Pray take half a dozen. Pastry, your reverence surely knows, is easily digested." With good sense he took another, thanking her for her kind attention as if he had not seen through her mockery. A solid tart gave her a further opportunity to joke at his expense, for as he helped himself to a piece, a second rolled off the dish towards his plate. "A third, your reverence!" she cried. "You seem anxious to lay a good foundation." "When such excellent materials are offered, the architect's labours are easy," he retorted. She continued in the same strain, only pausing, conscientiously, to point out to me the best dishes.

'All this while I was conversing with my neighbour on the most serious topics. Positively, I have never heard Filangieri utter a commonplace sentence...

'During the whole of this time my naughty neighbour allowed the clerical gentry not a moment's truce. Especially the fish, which is prepared during Lent in imitation of meat, gave her inexhaustible opportunities for remarks neither pious nor moral, to justify a taste for meat, observing that one might as well enjoy the appearance, even when the reality was forbidden.

'I noticed several other jokes of the same kind, but am not in the humour to repeat them. Falling freshly from beautiful lips they may be tolerable, but set down in black and white they lose all charm, at least for me...

'The dessert was brought in, and I feared that my fair neighbour would continue in the same strain, when suddenly she turned to me quite calmly and said: "Let the priests gulp their Syracusan wine in peace, for I shall never succeed in worrying them to the point of spoiling their appetites. Now let us have some rational conversation. What were you discussing with Filangieri? The worthy man; he gives himself a great deal of trouble for nothing. I often say to him, if you make new laws, we must again set our wits to discover the means of transgressing them, just as we have done with the old ones. See how beautiful Naples is! The people have lived contented and free from care for so many years, and if now and then some poor wretch gets hanged, all the rest still pursue their own merry course." She then proposed that I should pay a visit to Sorrento, where she had a large estate; her steward would feast me with the best of fish and delicious suckling calf. The mountain air and the wonderful panorama would cure me of all philosophy; then she would come herself, and not a trace would remain of all my precocious wrinkles, and we would lead a truly gay life together.'

The Princess was less strange than she seemed to the solemn northerner. With her pagan delight in worldly blessings, her lack of constraint and her laughing mockery, she remains typical of her nationality. She respected her brother without being unduly impressed by his reputation; all the same he struck her as something of a freak. Why bother to change the laws when men were bound to break them? And she had taken to Goethe instinctively as a human being, regardless of *Werther* and his philosophy. He had appealed to her as *simpatico*, in spite of his wrinkles. How could the poet help being flattered? She was so completely natural, a pure product of the Neapolitan soil and climate.

He was unable to see her when he returned from Sicily in May: 'I shall not see my capricious little Princess. She had gone to Sorrento, and before leaving did me the honour to chide me for preferring stony and savage Sicily. A few friends told me more about this strange little person [whose real name he did not print]. Born of a noble but not affluent family and brought up in a convent, she was married off to an old and wealthy Prince. It was easier to induce her to take this step because, though her character was good she was incapable of falling in love. In spite of her wealth she was greatly hampered by her social rank, so she tried to help herself out with her wit; unable to behave. as she pleased, she wanted at least to give free rein to her tongue. I was told that her conduct was irreproachable; on the other hand, she would like to break all respectable conventions with her unbridled talk. A wag remarked that if her conversation was set down in writing it would not pass the censorship, because she never says anything that does not offend religion, the state or morality. The most charming and fantastic anecdotes are told about her, of which I shall repeat one, although it is not the most proper.

'Shortly before the earthquake which struck Calabria, she had gone to her husband's estates there. A shed had been built near her castle, a simple wooden hut, but otherwise furnished and well arranged. At the first sign of the earthquake she took shelter there. She was sitting on a sofa, embroidering, with a little work-table beside her, and an old priest, a member of the household, sat opposite. Suddenly the earth rocked, the shanty fell on her side and rose on the other, so that the priest and the table were hoisted on high.

"Shame on you!" she cried, while her head lay against the toppling wall. "Is this a seemly posture for so venerable a man? You look as if you intend to fall on top of me. This is against morality and decency!" In the meantime the hut had swayed back into position, but she could not stop laughing at the indecent attitude of the good old man, and this joke seemed to make her oblivious of all the calamities and heavy losses, which struck her own family and so many thousands of others. An admirably happy character, who can afford to joke when the earth is about to swallow her!'

Two years later Tischbein was appointed director of the Neapolitan Academy of Painting, where he exerted a healthy influence by insisting on studies of the nude when improvisations *à la Solimena* were still in vogue. 'A thorough and original German,' Goethe called him, but while his German thoroughness is only too apparent his originality is hard to perceive. He was a student of Lavater, steeped in Winckelmann's *History of Art* and the classical glories of Rome; consequently a practitioner in the 'historical' style. His first noteworthy picture, thanks to which he obtained a pension from the Duke of Weimar allowing him to return to Italy, represented 'Conradin receiving his death-sentence while playing chess with Frederic of Austria'. But for Goethe's friendship he would probably be forgotten: 'In his company,' wrote Goethe, 'all my enjoyments are more than doubled.'

The bard had to confess that he puzzled the Neapolitans: 'Tischbein pleases them far better. This evening he hastily painted some life-size heads, and about these they disported themselves as strangely as the New Zealanders at the sight of a ship of war... Tischbein has a great knack of etching with a pen the shapes of gods and heroes, of the size of life and even larger. He uses very few lines, but cleverly puts in the shades with a broad pencil, so that the heads stand out roundly and nobly. The bystanders looked on with amazement, and were highly delighted. At last an itching seized their fingers to try and paint; they snatched the brushes and painted—one another's beards, daubing each other's faces. Was not this an original trait of human nature? And this was done in elegant society, in the house of one who was himself a clever draughtsman and painter! It is impossible to form an idea of this race without having seen it.'

Tischbein joined Sir William Hamilton's circle, and besides painting Emma as Iphigenia at the Sacrificial Altar, he published an album of drawings of Greek vases from Sir William's collection. Both the King and Queen had the highest opinion of his gifts. Thanks to Maria Carolina's encouragement, there was a prevalence of German and German-Swiss painters in Naples at this time; besides Tischbein, there were the Hackert brothers (Philip the painter and George the engraver), Angelica Kauffmann, Christopher Kniep and Henry Füger. Their precursor and father superior had been the frigid Raphael Mengs, who had portrayed the King at the time of his succession.

Angelica Kauffmann depicted various members of the royal family in 1782, and her portrait of Ferdinand and Maria Carolina surrounded by their children, now at Capodimonte, is one of her most graceful compositions. The Queen persuaded her to give drawing lessons to the little princesses and showered her with gifts, but Angelica preferred Rome, where she had a larger coterie of admirers. She also painted Emma Hamilton's favourite portrait as the Comic Muse, to which the model clung in adversity. Goethe wrote of her: 'The good Angelica has a most remarkable and, for a woman, really unheard-of talent; one must see and value what she does and not what she leaves undone.' Fuseli was more severe: 'She pleased, and desired to please, the age in which she lived and the race for which she wrought. The Germans, with at least as much patriotism as judgement, have styled her the Paintress of Minds (*Seelen Mahlerin*); nor can this be wondered at for a nation who, in A. R. Mengs, flatter themselves that they possess an artist equal to Raphael.'

Philip Hackert was the pioneer of those topographical views of Naples which were to become stereotyped in the nineteenth century. Obsessed with scrupulous exactitude, he attempted to portray photographic truth. No doubt his painstaking efforts seemed fresh and novel to a generation glutted with the cascades, caves, castles and rumbling rockeries of Salvator Rosa and his progeny. The prosaic Ferdinand admired his meticulousness, but so did the poet Goethe. Another typical German, we decide, after reading Goethe's description: 'Today we visited Philip Hackert, the famous landscape-painter, who enjoys the special confidence and peculiar favour of the King and Queen. A wing of the Francavilla palace has been assigned to him which, having furnished it with true artistic taste, he feels great satisfaction in inhabiting. He is a very precise and prudent personage who, with untiring industry, manages to enjoy life nevertheless.' He visited him again at Caserta, 'in his highly agreeable apartments, which have been assigned him in the ancient castle... Constantly busy with drawing and painting, he is also very social and easily attracts people to become his scholars. He has won me over by putting up patiently with my weaknesses, and insists, above all things, on distinctness of drawing and a clear distribution of light and shadow. When he paints in water-colour, he has three colours always ready; and as he works on and uses one after another, a picture is produced one knows not how or whence. I wish the execution were as easy as it looks. With his usual frankness he said to me: "You have capacity, but you are unable to accomplish anything. If you stay with me a year and a half, you will produce something that will give pleasure to yourself and your friends." Is not this a text on which one might preach eternally to dilettanti? We shall see what profit I derive from it... The special confidence with which the Queen honours him is shown not only by the fact that he gives lessons to the Princesses, but still more so by his being frequently summoned in the evening to talk with and instruct them on art and kindred subjects.'

The King showered commissions on him, for here was a man whose craft he could understand. He ordered him to paint his best-loved hunting-grounds for his study at Caserta, and chatted with him while he worked, criticizing and offering suggestions. One day he said to Hackert with a sigh: 'I would willingly give thousands to know only a tenth part of what you do. They even wanted to teach me to draw, but I was taught this like everything else, so that I know very little. God forgive my old teachers, who are now in Heaven.'

Hackert followed the King when he went hunting to make studies for his huge canvases. These got larger and larger: vast skies and stretches of sea monopolize more than half of them, for an excellent reason: Hackert was paid for them at the rate of fifty ducats a *palmo*, or span. As painter to the King he received a pension of twelve hundred ducats a year, besides the magnificent lodgings mentioned by Goethe, while his brother George received eight hundred ducats as second engraver to the King.

Those who entered the royal service were supposed. to swear an oath of allegiance, but Hackert as a Protestant was dispensed from this. Some courtly busybody asked the King if he realized that the painter was not a Catholic. 'I know it,' he replied; 'I also know that he's an honest man with a highly respectable character, and that he serves me faithfully without any oath. I wish my Catholic subjects would serve me as well!'

Hackert was consulted on all sorts of matters: when some new lamps arrived from Paris, he had to show the major-domo how to clean them and put in the wicks. These were left at Caserta during the summer without being cleaned. When the King returned in October he found that the wicks were finished. He tried to replenish them, but they failed to burn. After he and an equerry had bespattered their clothes with oil, he shouted: 'Take them to Hackert; he's sure to put them right!' The painter was also asked to supervise the transportation of the Farnese collection from Rome with Cavaliere Venuti. Somebody had told the King that many of the statues were worse than mediocre, suggesting that he should sell these and spend the proceeds on restoring the good ones. Hackert objected so strongly to this that the King told Caracciolo: 'Send twelve hundred ducats to Rome to pay the statue-restorer Albicini. Hackert is a stubborn Prussian and will never yield, but he knows what he's talking about.' It was owing to Hackert's advice that the King employed the picture-restorer Anders, in whose technique he took unusual interest. All the while Hackert was dabbing away at his series of vast canvases. Quaint as topographical records, they are singularly lacking in the light and colour of the Neapolitan landscape. The launching of the *Parthenope*, a ship of war with seventy-four guns; the King's return from Leghorn viewed from the *Granili*; the Neapolitan squadron sailing back from Algiers; views of Gaeta and Ischia; the ports of Puglia and Sicily; military manoeuvres and hunting scenes: all were stiffly recorded like daguerreotypes by Philip and engraved by his brother George. Once the King gave Hackert a gold snuff-box and repeating watch. 'God forgive me,' the Queen exclaimed, 'I fear he's at the end of his tether, for he never gives presents.' While the Queen was lavish with snuff-boxes, for which she paid twice their value, occasionally the King was profuse in gifts of money.

The German element introduced a simple *gemütlichkeit* into Neapolitan Court life. When Lady Craven stayed at Caserta she saw only German maids in the Queen's apartments, and she was told that there were at least forty-five of them, who performed the functions of pages and valets. The Queen's domestic existence among her growing children seemed the epitome of boredom to her Neapolitan courtiers, who preferred Spanish pomp and French frivolity. They resented this Nordic invasion.

With the death of Charles III, the last trace of Spanish influence vanished from Court. That excellent monarch had been sorely tried towards the end of his existence. First his daughter-in-law Dona Mariana, then her infant, and last his favourite son Don Gabriel, had died from smallpox in rapid succession; and the behaviour of his other daughters-in-law, Maria Luisa in Spain and Maria Carolina in Naples, had intensified his gloom. As usual, he tried to fight off melancholy with hunting, but he caught a feverish cold and was forced to retire to his bed. Even so he refused to consider himself ill. He allowed his faithful valet Pini to rub him with hot deer's grease, but would take no other remedy. As the deer's grease failed to warm him, not wishing to disturb anybody during the night, he asked Pini to wrap him in the covers which were put over his parrot cages. The doctors disagreed about the nature of his fever, but he was in his seventy-third year and soon his condition was hopeless. He died 'with great firmness and piety' on December 14, 1788.

The news of his death and of Charles IV's succession was announced to Ferdinand and Maria Carolina when they were mourning their nine-year-old son Gennaro, who had recently died of smallpox. Their youngest son Carlo, only five months old, succumbed to the same disease a few days later. So violent was the Queen's grief that many feared for her sanity. In her frenzy she cursed the Spaniards, and accused them of infecting her family with smallpox in order to kill them off. The consequences of these wild accusations might have been serious, but the new King of Spain was too placid to take much notice of them. Charles IV resembled Ferdinand in many ways: he shared his passion for hunting and was dominated by his wife, who was dominated by the predatory Manuel Godoy.

On February 10, 1789, Maria Carolina wrote to Marchese di Gallo: 'Overwhelmed by anguish and deep despair at the loss of two beloved sons, my fondest hopes, I only have time to assure you that I am still the mother of eight children, and that I shall fulfil to the utmost all the duties of motherhood. It is only to accomplish these that I wish to prolong a life which a thousand sorrows has rendered so distressing.'

Ferdinand was either more stoical or more phlegmatic. Marchese del Vasto had been sent to Spain with official condolences and congratulations. Ferdinand attached great importance to the receipt of an autograph letter from his brother, and in several despatches Caracciolo complained on his King's behalf that Charles IV had not yet written. So eager was Ferdinand for this token that before he went hunting at Mondragone he left orders to have it forwarded to him immediately, and kept a special messenger waiting for that purpose. At last towards the end of February Charles IV wrote to his brother; a letter from Maria Luisa followed; and a regular correspondence began, in which the King of Spain proposed to send his fleet to Naples to salute the King and Queen. He also offered one of his daughters in marriage to the Hereditary Prince. Ferdinand might have consented: he had been delighted with the gift of some Spanish fowling-pieces. But the Queen recoiled with horror from such a suggestion. She regarded her sister-in-law of Spain as no better than a harlot; besides, she intended to marry her children into the Hapsburg family.

Maria Carolina was to have two more sons: Leopold, born in 1790, who became her favourite, and Albert, born in 1792, who died in childhood. In the midst of child-bearing she was anxious to arrange marriages for those who were growing up, and her dearest wishes were granted when her brother, the Grand Duke of Tuscany, proposed his second son for her eldest daughter, and his daughter the Archduchess for the Prince Royal. When the portraits of the betrothed were exchanged, the Queen wrote to Gallo that her son Francis was delighted with that of Clementine: he smiled with pleasure whenever he looked at it and showed it proudly to his tutors and entourage. 'There is only one thing that humiliates him: this is the difference in height between them, as his fiancée is four or five inches taller. He hopes to grow, and in order to reach her height, he rides assiduously and takes more exercise... He has a fairly good presence, an excellent heart, is little interested in Latin but very much in geometry. He has a fine memory and a taste for history and music; but Latin, reading and application do not appeal to him at all.' Of her two eldest daughters, who eventually became Empress of Austria and Grand Duchess of Tuscany, she wrote: 'They are neither beautiful nor agreeable, but I hope they will make good wives.'

The Prime Minister Caracciolo died on July 16, 1789, two days after the Fall of the Bastille: some said that his end was hastened by the ambassador Circello's reports from Paris, 'which he feared must sound like nightmares'. Caracciolo was not the only reformer to be shocked by the news from France. 'His Sicilian

Majesty has for the present appointed General Acton to execute the office of the Foreign Department,' wrote Hamilton.

From this moment Schipa and the so-called 'liberal' school of Neapolitan historians date the ruin of the Bourbon dynasty in Naples. Acton has been blamed for all the misfortunes that followed, a rather superficial interpretation of events, since his succession to Caracciolo coincided with the outbreak of revolution in France. Always the same old cry: blame the foreigner! But as Nicola Nicolini remarked, whoever examines the political situation of Naples at the end of the eighteenth century must realize that the kingdom was too small for a wholly independent foreign policy, yet too large to rely on its moderate scale for security. Freed from the Spanish harness, it had to steer its foreign policy towards that of the great powers, and among these the greatest of sea powers.

Acton's was the broader view. His Neapolitan adversaries, who would have yoked their country to France, were as short-sighted as most doctrinaires. He wanted an independent policy, but he had to measure the means at his disposal. Naples was still in the midst of its growing pains when it was surprised by the French Revolution. Acton had not had time to complete his programme for defence and offence. Strong allies were necessary, and it is unlikely that any other statesman devoted to the dynasty would have chosen a different course.

XII

Acton's reforms—The Colony of San Leucio—Tragic news from France—The first émigrés—Carnival in Naples—Death of the Emperor Joseph and succession of Leopold III—Betrothal ceremonies—The King and Queen visit Austria—Their return journey through Rome—Pleasure versus duty—Luigi de' Medici and his sister the San Marco.

Acton had been in Naples ten years as Minister of the Marine and of War; he had worked strenuously to build up the army and navy in spite of popular apathy and the cabals of political enemies. He had plenty to show for his pains, but there was still a yawning gap between appearance and reality: the unknown personal equation. The impressive new fleet he had built was a source of proud satisfaction to the King and Queen. Even so there were cases of sabotage, as when a new seventy-four-gun ship was burnt at Castellammare. 'Opinions seem to be divided between negligence and treachery,' wrote Hamilton, 'was I to hazard mine I should attribute the event to both. A ship of such consequence completely ready for the sea... having been left without a guard, and not even an officer of so high a rank as midshipman on board, sufficiently proves the neglect; and it is not improbable that some treacherous persons, envious and jealous of the very great power which the Minister of the Marine has acquired in this country, may have taken advantage of such neglect to mortify him, which it has done indeed to a high degree.' He had summoned experienced French, Swiss and Austrian officers to reorganize the army; the infantry were clothed and partly equipped in the Austrian style; the artillery were modelled after the French and the cavalry after the Prussian. But the strict methods of foreign instructors caused many desertions, and recruiting was not easy, for the Neapolitans did not take kindly to any form of discipline. The officers of the privileged corps raised a howl when their fat sinecures were threatened; consequently these corps, including the King's favourite Lipariotes and battalion of cadets, were abolished. Swinburne described the *Volon-*

tari della Marina, or Lipariotes, as a 'most complete and handsome regiment, commanded by all the young men of the highest rank at Court. The uniform is green, lined and cuffed with scarlet, and yellow buttons. The soldiers perform their evolutions wonderfully well. The King has been their major, and takes infinite pains with them. He always wears their regimentals. All summer they row his galliots, and in the winter follow him out shooting. I am sorry to add, that this brilliant set of soldiers is composed of the most abandoned wretches under the sun. Scarce one but has several murders upon his head, and I do not suppose all these rascals together would stand the charge of one company of resolute, cool grenadiers.' By abolishing these, Acton deprived the King of his last youthful toys. He, too, had come to the conclusion that they were more decorative than serviceable. To console the officers, the King allowed them to wear their uniforms after they had been excused from military service.

The foundations were laid but the building was far from complete. The Royal Military Academy was handsomely housed in the Nunziatella on Pizzofalcone, and the courses were greatly improved. Picked artillery officers were sent to Bologna to polish their mathematics; others were sent to France and Austria to study army administration and the latest inventions in engineering. A military hospital was installed at San Giacomo degli Spagnoli with an anatomical theatre, laboratories, a pharmacy, etc. An important new arms factory and ironworks were established at Torre Annunziata; and the arsenal was one of the best in Italy.

The Engineer Corps had done remarkable work in restoring the port of Brindisi and rebuilding Messina after the earthquake of 1783; fortifications had been improved, and there was a scheme to rebuild the old ports of Baia and Miseno, reclaim the waste land nearby, and connect Lakes Averno and Lucrino. New high roads, such as that to the Abruzzo; great constructions in the capital, such as the *Granili*, the vast grain deposits erected by Fuga in 1779 near the Maddalena bridge; the sloping bulwark to strengthen Pizzofalcone on the Chiatamone side; and an embellishment we may still enjoy, though but a wayward offspring of the original design by Vanvitelli, the public garden then called Villa Reale along the shore of the Chiaia: these were among the notable achievements of the last decade.

The three years of Caracciolo's premiership have been described as an idyll between the monarchy and the politically minded aristocracy (as distinct from the regular courtiers), but even then Acton's influence on the Sovereigns was paramount, for he had been the outward and visible bone of contention with Spain. The King's growing dependence on him did not altogether suit Maria Carolina. If there be any truth in Gorani's gossip, the Queen had won her ascendancy by choosing the psychological moment to obtain whatever she wanted. Acton was kept informed of all that happened, even in the privacy of the King's bedroom, and was in constant touch with the Queen, who sent for him as soon as the King was in a frame of mind to sign edicts and other documents. It was said that his privileged regiments were abolished in this manner: he was urged to sign the unpalatable edict when he was in a passive mood after a good day's shooting. Although he might grumble, experience had taught him to value Acton's advice. As Maria Carolina wrote to Gallo: 'Six years ago the name of the King of Naples was ignored or at most regarded as a viceroy sent from Spain to a subordinate province. Now he plays a fine role with glory and distinction... My first aim... is to render service to my adored brother the Emperor, for whom I would willingly shed my blood.'

If the King was not glorious, he was at least the monarch of all he surveyed and master in his own house—as far as the world was concerned. A practical hobby which absorbed more and more of his attention was the little colony of silk manufacturers at San Leucio, near Caserta. His enemies accused him of founding this for his sexual satisfaction, as he was partial to sturdy country wenches, and of using it both as an escape from his wife's supervision and as a rustic harem. But it was his first and only social experiment. After a tour of Northern Italy in 1785, where his progressive brother-in-law had surfeited him with moral lectures, he was inspired to embark on an enterprise of his own. He had always been fond of San Leucio, and even if he did not originate the idea, such ideas were in the air. He took a personal interest in the smallest details of its management, and continued to add more buildings, hoping to convert it into a modern industrial city. Galanti wrote in 1790 that 'no expense was spared to improve it with better machinery and more useful instructions, and they have now reached such a high standard that they can be compared with the best in foreign countries.' The families of the workmen received good salaries, medical care and education, and Ferdinand himself drew up a special code of laws for them.

The code was published and lauded to the skies by contemporary doctrinaires, who attributed it to Gaetano Filangieri and Tanucci. But as Signor Tescione, the historian of the colony, pointed out: 'Its perfect religious and dynastic orthodoxy, the personal records in the narrative, the heavier emphasis on the religious element, the economic instructions and strong accent of paternalism, even some of the stylistic details, reveal Ferdinand's own imprint.' The laws may have been written by Antonio Planelli of Bitonto, but they were examined and revised by the King. Affairs of far greater moment he left to the Queen and Acton, but this was his own pet project, of which he was the proud Lycurgus and patriarch. The code was prefaced with a brief outline of the colony's origin and progress: having chosen San Leucio for meditation and repose, the King wished to provide the inhabitants, who, thanks to the pure air and tranquil existence, had been prolific, with a school for their education and a silk factory for their sustenance, so that they should be useful to the state, to their families, and to themselves. As the population increased it became necessary to give them rules, more as a father to his children than as a legislator to his subjects. These were to be considered as a fundamental declaration of immutable principles, susceptible to later changes. They were reminded of the decalogue, love of God and their fellow men, their positive and negative duties, 'to do the utmost possible good to all', and return good for evil, since men were equal, only governed by God and those He had chosen to govern them, such as the law-giving Prince who had conceived the plan of founding a colony of artisans in order to transform the products of prodigal nature for the happiness of his kingdom. Virtue and skill in trade were the only means of acquiring merit. They were to dress alike without sign of distinction, and cleanliness was imposed as a condition of health. The servile title of *Don* was to be reserved for priests only in token of respect. Funerals were to be simple, and mourning was to be abolished, except black arm-bands for men and scarves for women, to be worn not longer than two months. Five elders were to be elected annually on San Leucio's day, January 11, by secret ballot, from the oldest, wisest and most experienced members of the community, who were to settle controversies together with the parish priest, supervising local commerce, hygiene and public morals. Marriage was to be preceded by an engagement with an exchange of flowers in the parish church at Pentecost: the bride had to be at least sixteen and the bridegroom twenty; dowries were forbidden but the King would provide each married couple with a little house and two looms. Wills were abolished, and children inherited by natural right from their parents. Skill in work was to be rewarded with gold and silver medals and a special place in church called 'of merit' on the left of the altar in front of the elders. The parish priest and elders administered a charitable fund to support the aged and infirm and prevent mendicity, 'the most infamous and detestable condition on earth'. Among the health regulations, inoculation against smallpox was compulsory. Work was guaranteed for all, and outsiders could only become 'naturalized' after one year's probation. Penal sanctions consisted of fines for minor offences and expulsion for those against morality. The code winds up with a definition of Christian duties and an elaborate time table. 'A monarch's caprice,' was Croce's comment, 'which reminds me of the "menagerie of happy men" which the Marquis of Argenson once intended to found.' The spirit behind it was humanitarian, and shows that the King was far from indifferent to the welfare of his subjects. 'When the code appeared', wrote Colletta, 'it aroused universal wonder and delight among the Neapolitans, who, although they knew that the King had not originated these conceptions, hoped to see the governing principles of the colony extended throughout the kingdom.' Panegyrists, drunk with enthusiasm, saw it as a return to an imaginary golden age: most of these in due course became the rebels and martyrs of the Parthenopean Republic. Subsequent detractors were equally exaggerated. San Leucio expressed the better side of Ferdinand's nature, a side which would have had a chance to develop if it had not been warped by fear as a result of the French Revolution. Apart from which he deserves some credit for reviving the silk industry: the products of San Leucio soon became famous even outside the kingdom, and the colony thrived, in spite of the King's lack of experience, until the chaos of foreign invasion. But the industrial city which was to be called Ferdinandopolis remained an Arcadian dream.

Since Acton stepped into the place left vacant by Caracciolo, a place he had really shared, he had no intention of letting Austria dictate as Spain had done. Maria Carolina did not suspect this. In her heart and soul she remained an Austrian. She longed to go to Vienna to strengthen the family alliance. The news from France became more alarming. She was worried about her sister Marie

Antoinette and blamed the weakness of Louis XVI for their misfortunes, but neither she nor anybody else in Naples could foresee the tragedies that were impending.

Many French refugees had arrived with disturbing accounts of all they had seen and suffered before their escape. Two of them, the Comte d'Espinchal and Mme Vigée Le Brun, the painter, left records of their visits. D'Espinchal had been a prominent figure in Parisian society: 'his business, his pleasures, in a word his whole existence was limited to knowing all that happened in Paris day by day.' Exile was bitter for so parochial a butterfly, but even in Naples his curiosity made him flutter from flower to flower. He arrived on January 22, 1790, and stayed till March 15. Carnival was in full swing, so he was able to see the Queen in her box at the San Carlo and note her resemblance to Marie Antoinette, though she was three years older and looked even more so: her face was more serious. She appeared to be tired and ill-humoured owing to her state of pregnancy. The King was away hunting.

D'Espinchal remarked that a great many French businessmen had settled in Naples, of whom the majority were strongly infected with the 'democratic spirit'. One of the masked figures at the San Carlo ball declared in a loud voice while looking at the Queen: 'If I weren't afraid of a fuss, I would wear my national cockade.' D'Espinchal's companions stared at him so indignantly that he lost his nerve and escaped among the dancers. He was followed, but he was not fast enough for his pursuer, who caught up with him on the third floor of a neighbouring house and gave him a thrashing.

D'Espinchal was hospitably entertained by the pro-French section of society, many of whom had not made up their minds about the Revolution. The Duke of Coscia invited him to a delicious dinner served in the French style; he had lived in Paris and, like Galiani and Caracciolo, loved the French, their manners and customs. Then there were those charming sisters, the Duchess of Cassano and the Duchess of Popoli; the former, with whom he felt quite at home, had stayed a year in France and sent her sons there to be educated. The French ambassador's box at the San Carlo, or two communicating boxes, served as the drawing-room of the French community, so that even here D'Espinchal was able to collect the latest news. No doubt he echoed his ambassador's opinions, as English travellers echoed Sir William Hamilton's. Though he had an introduction to Acton, he was deterred from 'swelling the court of this favourite of fortune, who did not love the French'.

Carnival this year was feverishly gay. Among the chariots full of masks which thronged the Toledo, the King appeared in a simple one-horse carriage, revelling like his subjects in the uproar; he could easily be recognized by his escort of *lazzaroni*, with whom he bandied jokes along the street. All the windows and balconies were crammed, and there was barely space for the two interminable rows of carriages, whose occupants pelted each other with sugar-plums. The King provided a tempting target, and he replied with magnificent gusto. The Queen, too, in spite of her interesting condition, was driving in the thick of the throng, but to avoid the hail of sugar-plums, a placard was attached to her carriage with the words: 'Peace, not war.' The battling masks were armed with shields, as the missiles, unlike modern confetti, were hard enough to hurt. To complain of these attacks was to invite their repetition, as happened to the King of Sweden when he came to Naples. D'Espinchal remarked that there was only one mounted guard on police duty, who seemed sensible and efficient, and everybody was in the best of humour. This struck him as a favourable comment on the population, for he had never seen, not even in Paris, so dense a traffic and so many crowded balconies over a distance of about three miles.

After dining with Baron de Salis, he was thrilled by Emma Hart's performance of the *tarantella*: she danced with a grace and voluptuousness that would inflame a Laplander. Like Goethe he paid tribute to her beauty and admired the classical illusions she could conjure with her 'attitudes'. 'If I were Sir William Hamilton,' he mused, 'I would review the whole of Olympus. I should often see Hebe, or Venus and the Graces, occasionally Juno, but Minerva very seldom. To vary my pleasures, sometimes a rich boudoir would disclose a vision of Cleopatra giving Mark Antony an ardent reception, or a summer-house that of Alcibiades frolicking with Glycera.' While he enjoyed the cosmopolitan company, d'Espinchal disapproved of his host. Baron de Salis had won a military reputation in France, under the ministry of the Duc de Choiseul, though too much of a martinet to be popular with the troops. At present he was a Field-Marshal commanding the de Salis-Grisons regiment, with a salary of about sixty-thousand *livres*. But he had disgusted the aristocracy and antagonized the Neapolitan officers with his innovations. He was about to reform the King's bodyguard, and d'Espinchal regarded this as a pernicious measure; were not the nobility the throne's strongest support? He prophesied (quite correctly) that Baron de Salis would not be able to hold out against his many powerful enemies. But he could not deny that the troops showed a vast improvement since his arrival.

D'Espinchal was presented to the King at a royal hunt, some twenty-seven miles from Naples. At five o'clock on a cold windy morning he set off in a carriage with three compatriots. After three and a half hours' drive, he found the King breakfasting under a tent with only seven or eight gentlemen in attendance. He behaved without ceremony, like an amiable country squire, inviting them to a breakfast consisting of coffee, chocolate, bread, butter and liqueurs, but not a drop of wine. He offered them mounts, but all declined, not knowing what sort of hunt it would be, except a French abbé who was proud of his horsemanship.

The hunt he described as 'no more than a beat-up of wild boars'. The huntsmen assembled in a plain surrounded by brushwood, from which hundreds of boars were driven. Dogs were set upon them, and each rider was armed with a long pike to throw at any boar which tried to escape the hounds. Sometimes a clumsy huntsman hurt himself or one of the dogs with his pike, which infuriated the King. The beat-up was continued at irregular intervals until the whole plain was strewn with dead or dying animals.

After four hours of this dubious sport, the King sat down to dinner and invited his guests to join him. Those who had been presented were entitled to sit at a table laid for about thirty. A second table was prepared for the officers of his suite and less pretentious folk. D'Espinchal was placed near the King, whose jovial humour put everyone at ease. The meal seemed mediocre to the Frenchman, and it lasted a whole hour. But Ferdinand seemed to him 'a true King of Cockaigne'. In spite of his popularity with the masses, d'Espinchal remarked that 'democracy has made considerable progress'. His note of warning is dated February 6, 1790: 'Beware of a revolution! The government wants to appear energetic, but betrays its weakness. The high nobility are discontented with the Court, which follows the false and pernicious maxim of all the sovereigns of Europe, tending to degrade and even destroy an order which has always been the bulwark of the throne. Kings will only escape from the lethargy into which they have been lulled by perfidious ministers when the dreadful example of France warns them of the danger, probably too late. Moreover, Ferdinand lets the French Revolution proceed without paying much attention to it. His ministers appear to take extreme precautions, by refusing passports to persons of note whose principles are under suspicion, while they have the weakness to allow the French merchants and artisans, who are very numerous here, to found clubs and patriotic assemblies. Everywhere the same flabbiness and treason are apparent. And the same principles are spreading everywhere.'

On February 10, 1790, the Emperor Joseph died, leaving Flanders and Hungary in revolt and a fine army almost defeated by the Turks. With the noblest of intentions, he had lacked common sense: his reforms had been tactless and ill-timed. His brother, the Grand Duke of Tuscany, succeeded him as Leopold II. He shared Joseph's ideas but fortunately had greater discretion, all of which was required to save his tottering throne.

As Leopold's eldest son, the Crown Prince Francis, had been left a widower soon after Joseph's death, it was now arranged that he should marry Maria Carolina's eldest daughter Maria Theresa; while his second son Ferdinand, Grand Duke of Tuscany, was to marry her second daughter Luisa. At the same time Maria Carolina was expecting another child. She wrote to Gallo: 'I'm in the fifth month of my fifteenth pregnancy. I yearn for a son who might partly repair my cruel losses.'

She was full of excitement at the prospect of revisiting Vienna, but she would not be able to travel before her babe was born. All her letters throb with solicitude for her daughters. She wished to assure her brother that he need not regret his choice. 'The betrothed are flourishing and very happy. Louise [engaged to Ferdinand] has become quite different... Happiness has completely transformed her. She has a very good heart and will succeed admirably if she is well advised and guided in the beginning. Theresa is very sensible: she is delighted with Francis's affection for her brother and his solid qualities. She assures me that she will try to satisfy him in every particular. I have not dared to read her the verbal portrait which their August Father has drawn of his sons with so much fidelity and kindness because, although it matters little, if she knew that Francis had spat blood there would be no consoling her. The other day she said she had prayed God to let her die rather than become a widow; she hopes that she and her husband will reach the age of Philemon and Baucis, to end their lives together. From this you may judge how she thinks and hopes to become attached to her husband... May God protect them and make them content their parents-in-law!... The eldest girl prays that the Archduke will be pleased with her: she is always afraid of being compared with his first wife [the Princess of Württemberg who had died on February 18]. Already she feels a great tenderness for him. If he gives her a good reception, she will love him passionately. Louise will be more absentminded, less deeply attached but more cheerful.'

Absorbed as she was by her growing family, she devoted much time to politics while her husband continued to amuse himself out of doors. Gradually her family and politics became inseparable: she identified the claims of her children with those of the Two Sicilies. On July 3 her prayers for a son were answered. The King wished Benjamin to be added to the infant's seven other names as a token of his joy, and ordered three days of festivities and illuminations.

On August 12 Prince Ruspoli, the Austrian ambassador, presented the formal demands for the marriages of the Archdukes with their portraits set in jewels. The betrothal ceremony followed in the Royal Chapel: the fourteen-year-old Prince Francis stood proxy for the bridegrooms and the Cardinal Archbishop officiated, with Paisiello conducting the choir. The city offered the King a donation of seventy thousand ducats, but he ordered this sum to be distributed as dowries for poor unmarried girls and alms for needy families. Many prisoners were pardoned and favours conferred all round.

There were touching demonstrations of popular affection when the King and Queen set out on their journey to Austria. The *lazzaroni* reproached them for leaving, and begged them to return as soon as possible. They sailed from Barletta on August 21, the King on the frigate *Sibilla*, and the Queen and Princesses on the *Pallade*. For Maria Carolina this was a well-earned vacation. She had done her best for the future of her eldest daughters, and she had procured a dependable daughter-in-law instead of a strange Infanta. The marriages were celebrated in Vienna with the utmost splendour, but as the Hereditary Prince and the Archduchess Maria Clementina were only fourteen their union was deferred. The Queen's instincts and affections were ineradicably Austrian, and she had taught Ferdinand to regard Austria as his second home. At Schönbrunn he could almost enjoy the illusion of being in Italy, for most of it had been decorated by Italians. The ceilings by Gregorio Guglielmi, the mirror- and tapestry-rooms, the formal gardens with their high clipped hedges and groups of statues, had many points in common with Caserta. And the baying of hounds, the blowing of horns, the belling of deer were as loud and exhilarating as at home: the same kind of massacres, so necessary to his health, continued in this cooler clime.

After the marriages of their daughters, Ferdinand and Maria Carolina attended Leopold's coronation as Emperor at Frankfurt and as King of Hungary at Pressburg, the seat of the Hungarian Diet. The Magyars honoured the King and Queen of Naples with a Latin panegyric on their reforms, among which the silk-weaving colony of San Leucio was selected for special praise. Altogether they stayed eight months, a blissful holiday for Maria Carolina, who adored her brother and basked in the scenes of her childhood. As mother of the future Empress, and as a Queen who had raised the dignity of Naples, she felt worthy of the great Maria Theresa.

Alas, politics would creep in to spoil Ferdinand's fun. During the festivities at Frankfurt, Leopold complained that he had been left more and more in the dark about Neapolitan affairs. Ferdinand answered that having put his trust in the minister he had recommended, he was surprised and sorry to hear this. Leopold said that when he had applied to him for a good naval officer, he had sent him the best available, but that a good sailor and a good statesman were two very different things. A long discussion followed, in which Acton's conduct was criticized severely by the Emperor.

The cause of the Emperor's annoyance was that Acton had succeeded in conciliating his old enemy, the Spanish prime minister. Since Naples had become independent of Spain, he wished to counterbalance the increasing power of Austria in Italy. He was also anxious to improve relations with Rome. As the Sardinian ambassador in Naples had written, 'this minister's enthusiasm for the reigning Emperor has totally disappeared'. He tried to restrain Gallo, whose popularity at the Court of Vienna had gone to his head like wine, advising him to be cautious with Leopold, who was 'jealous and reserved by nature'; and to practise more reserve himself, since 'any other conduct might prejudice the King's interests'.

Petted by Maria Carolina and her brother, Gallo had become infatuated with the Austrian alliance. Perhaps he thought it would repay him to be indiscreet. The Sardinian ambassador Di Breme wrote from Vienna: 'It is certain that the Queen complains much of her Prime Minister. She alleges that he has completely gone over to the King's side and is capable of the blackest ingratitude towards her. If he did not possess certain documents of the highest consequence which might compromise herself, she declares that she would have tried to remove him from the Ministry.'

No doubt the Emperor had kindled this explosion. He suggested that the Queen was being brushed aside. It was intolerable that Acton should swing the foreign policy of Naples on his own initiative, but this was one of the penalties of absence. The situation would be remedied as soon as she returned. In the meantime she was deeply concerned with the plight of France, involving her sister. Maria Carolina was in favour of prompt intervention, but Leopold was lukewarm. A war with France would leave Poland at the mercy of Russia, and he had other reasons to wish for peace, as he was negotiating with Prussia and hoping to end hostilities with Turkey. He would make no promises yet; all depended on a coalition of the other Powers.

While in Vienna, Maria Carolina told the Apostolic Nuncio that she and Ferdinand would like to spend Easter in Rome, but in that case was the Pope prepared to make any concessions? The Nuncio replied that His Holiness would be delighted to welcome Their Majesties and concede everything they pleased, except his conscience and his honour. It was arranged accordingly that they were to visit Pope Pius VI, arriving earlier than expected so as to emphasize their eagerness to see him.

The Roman Court consulted the Bishop of Salerno as to the best method of tackling Ferdinand, and the bishop replied: 'The King's character is excellent; he likes to hear that sovereigns have a favourable opinion of his talents, and it does not displease him when one of his bishops explains with reverent submission that his conscience forbids him to execute one of his commands. Then he does not use compulsion, but is rather inclined to respect him on that account.' He proposed that the Pope should speak to him in short concise sentences, explaining the difference between royal privilege and despotism.

The King and Queen duly arrived at the Vatican ahead of time, and the Pope received them with polite surprise. The audience passed in apparent harmony, but Ferdinand repeated his former claims, and for the sake of appeasement the Pope resigned to him the nomination of bishops to vacant sees. Both realized the danger of leaving the flocks of vacant dioceses to their own devices: now that France had declared war on religion and royal rights they saw that they had a common cause to defend. Ferdinand returned to Naples with enhanced prestige. He had not yielded an inch, yet he had come to terms with the Pontiff. The honours paid him were correspondingly impressive at a time when papal splendour could hardly be surpassed, and he and Maria Carolina were presented with gorgeous gifts on their departure: a gold and lapis lazuli crown adorned with cameos representing the Annunciation and San Gennaro for the King; a more jewelled one for the Queen and the Golden Rose with a brief, addressed to 'Our dearest daughter in Christ Maria Carolina', besides tapestry, rich mosaics and holy relics.

Mesdames Adelaïde and Victoire, the aunts of Louis XVI, had recently taken refuge in Rome, and they increased the Queen's alarm about her sister. All the fugitives streaming into Italy had some pitiful story to tell, and many, like d'Espinchal, were prophets of woe who did not mince their words: 'Beware of a revolution in Naples!' Ferdinand scoffed at such an idea, but Maria Carolina, who had patronized the Freemasons, was disconcerted by what she had heard of their activities in France.

Was it possible that she had been misled by her desire for progress? So far she had only seen the benevolent side of those masonic meetings. Her most intimate friends, the Princess of Belmonte and the Marchesa di San Marco, had both been ardent votaries; surely these could not be accused of treachery! The Prince of Belmonte was the King's chief major-domo; the San Marco's brother Luigi de' Medici was a royal counsellor and one of the highest magistrates in the kingdom. Yet before the Queen's journey to Austria, the Emperor had written to her: 'I beg you to bring only people who are necessary. Allow me to tell you that I believe it would be advantageous if, in choosing the ladies of your suite, you exclude both Mme Belmonte and the San Marco.' Maria Carolina regretfully took the hint.

Beckford, who had met both these ladies at Sir William Hamilton's ten years since, described them as 'the determined San Marco, and the more nymph-like, modest-looking, though not less dangerous Belmonte.' D'Espinchal, who spent an evening at her villa near Posillipo, described the Princess of Belmonte as a lady who had been and was still conspicuously gallant in an amorous sense, although well over fifty. 'She is tall and well proportioned and has a very noble bearing. No foreigners arrive in Naples without an introduction to her. She entertains them to perfection and is always rewarded by tokens of their gratitude. At present she is in charge of a handsome Pole, of whom she never loses sight for a single instant. She is apt to retire with him from the assembly now and then. This young man seems a little exhausted by his duties. It is he who does the honours of the house; her two sons, Counts Francesco and Giuseppe Pignatelli, most amiable youths, do not seem to belong there at all. Very few Neapolitan ladies were to be observed. Although the Princess is a friend of the Queen, she is considered ill-bred. Prince Belmonte, her husband, is grand master of the King's household. He never appears at these gatherings, and as he is never mentioned he might as well not exist. The guests were numerous and nearly all distinguished foreigners: the Margrave of Bayreuth; the Duchess of Saxe-Weimar, his sister; the Primate of Poland, the King's brother; the Margrave of Anspach, accompanied by Milady Craven, who has succeeded Mme Clairon and who, it is said, will marry the Margrave; the Crown Prince of Brunswick, son of the reigning Duke, an uncommonly awkward, callow youth albeit very decent; all our French ladies, etc. First we had music and were obliged to listen to the Princess, who decided to sing. She wants to do something of everything, even to paint. For instance, she has presented her portrait to the gallery of Florence, painted by herself: it is a veritable daub, for I remember noticing it there. After the concert a collation was served, ices, refreshments and sweetmeats in the greatest profusion. The evening ended with faro, and all the guests retired an hour after midnight, leaving the Princess in undisturbed possession of her Pole.'

It was owing to her partiality for such ladies that the Queen's morals were assailed by hostile critics. But the most respectable are often attracted to natures contrasting romantically with their own. These vivacious dames who triumphed over age and the social conventions had a rejuvenating effect on the Queen when she was burdened with family cares: they reminded her that there were pleasures as well as duties; they were full of bright gossip and suggestions for novel entertainment. The King's pleasures had always bored her: in her presence or absence he would continue to enjoy the same open-air routine. As Beckford had written: 'Though people have imagined him a weak monarch, I beg leave to differ in opinion, since he has the boldness to prolong his childhood and be happy, in spite of years and conviction. Give him a boar to stab and a pigeon to shoot at, a battledore or an angling rod, and he is better contented than Solomon in all his glory, and will never discover, like that sapient sovereign, that all is vanity and vexation of spirit.'

The Queen's pleasures were represented by the Belmonte and the San Marco; her duties, by Acton and the care of her large family. There was a tug-of-war between them. This comes out clearly in the correspondence of the Sardinian ambassador, which contradicts the oft-repeated assertion that Acton encouraged the Queen's extravagances. Referring to Acton's conflict with the San Marco, he wrote: 'Two persons of a character diametrically opposed could not march in step; one strove to moderate the Queen's passions, the other to inflame them. One was concerned with the royal prestige and its reflection upon himself; the other merely thought of inducing the Queen to squander right and left, in order to gain power and form a party which could restore the reign of dissipation and disorder.'

The San Marco's brother, Luigi de' Medici, was so jealous of Acton that he would have stopped at nothing to ruin him. He was a sceptical opportunist, an aristocrat who despised the aristocracy though proud of his descent from the Princes of Ottaiano, and by far the most ambitious of the younger politicians. Having fallen under the influence of the French *philosophes*, he was one of the first Neapolitan nobles to open a *salon* for political discussion. Inevitably he was surrounded by clever young professors and lawyers with revolutionary opinions who flattered him into believing that he could play a dominant role in a new regime. At the same time he could 'run with the hare and hold with the hound', for he was a major-domo and gentleman-in-waiting to the King. To him, as to many other Neapolitans of his class, Acton was a foreign interloper, selfish and sinister, and his hatred drove him into the opposite camp. Youth is apt to be intolerant, and Luigi de' Medici was only thirty-two. In his sister he had a nimble collaborator. The San Marco could not wait for the Queen's arrival in Naples; she rushed off to Tuscany to give her own biased account of all that had been happening during her absence.

The Queen, always voluble with her intimates, described in return the glorious diversions and gay society she had left behind in Vienna. She confessed that she missed such amenities in Naples, and almost dreaded the old round of monotonous duties. The San Marco promised to help her organize a more cheerful and varied existence. But she hinted that Acton would be a stumbling-block; he was forever preaching economy; he was becoming a regular despot. She implied that a younger man should be at the helm; her brother had remarkable qualities, and nobody could be more devoted to the Queen. Remembering the Emperor's complaints about Acton, Maria Carolina was inclined to agree. She had always been kindly disposed to Luigi de' Medici, and she decided to speak to the King about him. He deserved a higher office.

The San Marco had been smart in seizing the initiative. But the Sardinian ambassador predicted that 'further reflection must redound to Acton's advantage, as the Queen would be forced to realize that she could find in none of her courtiers the honest character, zeal and strenuous assiduity of Chevalier Acton'. None could deny that he had kept perfect order during the long absence of the King and Queen. Calm and aloof from the chattering mob of courtiers, he stood by while the Princesses rushed forward to embrace their parents at Capua. After a clamorous reception they drove on to Naples. From Capodichino the royal coaches were escorted by three ornate chariots, preceded and followed by a cavalcade of splendid youths, the most comely disguised as nymphs. The first chariot was filled with gardeners scattering flowers and bakers scattering flour; the second with burgesses releasing flocks of doves, quails and smaller birds; the third with fishermen distributing ballads and sonnets. More birds were let loose by a horde of *lazzaroni* garbed as Turks. It was a baroque spectacle dear to the Neapolitan heart; magnificence and squalor, melody and sheer noise, combined to celebrate the royal return. Other festive paraphernalia, specially designed 'machines', illuminations and triumphal arches, delighted the populace for the next three days.

'I recollect,' wrote Mme Vigée Le Brun, 'that when the Queen returned [from Vienna] she said to me: "I have had a successful journey. I have just arranged two very satisfactory marriages for my daughters." '

XIII

Effects of the French Revolution on the King and Queen—Medici as chief of police—Hamilton marries Emma Hart—Death of Emperor Leopold and succession of Francis II—Relations with France—Mackau, Bassville and Sémonville—Latouche-Tréville's expedition—Bassville's murder—Execution of Louis XVI—Treaty of alliance with Great Britain—Jacobin conspiracy—Nelson arrives and Mackau departs.

Most of the so-called liberal Neapolitan historians seem to be naïvely surprised that the King and Queen loathed the French Revolution and that this loathing affected their characters and future policy. They portray Ferdinand as a Jekyll and Hyde: 'In Ferdinand there are two distinct men, the one we have known until now [kindly and tolerant], and the other we shall see develop [a vindictive tyrant].' As for the Queen, words fail them: she was an absolute gorgon. According to these pundits a sudden change came over the sovereigns after their return from Vienna, as if the Emperor Leopold had given them some magic potion. But whereas the American Revolution had been too remote to affect them, the events following the fall of the Bastille were nearer home. The very lives of the Queen's sister and brother-in-law were in danger, and the contagion of revolt had crossed the Alps.

Though Ferdinand and Maria Carolina had encouraged many wise reforms during the last thirty years, it would be strange to expect them to promote reforms which threatened their ultimate existence—strange to us, but not to Lomonaco, Cuoco, Arrighi, Colletta and their parrot successors. According to these, it was selfish and unreasonable of the King and Queen not to have appreciated the French Jacobins and afforded every facility to those who wished to emulate them in Naples. But the majority of the population had a horror of revolutionary ideas and refused to be 'enlightened'. Perhaps they realized instinctively that the French Revolution could effect no fundamental change in human nature. Their attachment to the King was genuine, and they had no desire for any other regime. The republics of Italy had not been fortunate, while

Naples had enjoyed the blessings of peace since the battle of Velletri.

Of course there was a minority hoping to benefit by a change of government. The best-intentioned of these believed in the possibility of a bloodless revolution imposed from above, instead of a bloody one from below. At Court there was a clique whose politics were swayed by resentment against Acton. They resented him chiefly as a foreigner who had filled important posts in the army and navy with other foreigners. They forgot their own lack of military experience. To get rid of Acton they would have called in the French, forgetting that these were aliens, too. Luigi de' Medici was prominent among this disgruntled group, but he was no idealist. On a lower level were the demagogues who had begun as Freemasons and ended as Jacobins: these were to be found among the university professors and students, the lawyers, and renegade priests who lived upon their wits. These met in secret, and so far few suspected the extent of their ramifications.

Largely owing to the Marchesa di San Marco's intrigues, her brother Luigi de' Medici was appointed 'Regent of the Grand Court of the *Vicaria*', equivalent to chief of police. By devious methods the brother and sister attempted to hamper Acton's programme of economy. The San Marco embarrassed him by encouraging the Queen's extravagance: Maria Carolina had always been generous, and was more so than ever now that so many French refugees appealed to her for assistance. She distributed pensions and presents with sublime disregard of her own and the kingdom's finances.

The Marquis de Bombelles, for instance, who had been the French minister in Venice, was dismissed because he would not swear to the oath of allegiance demanded by the Constituent Assembly, though his family were impoverished in consequence. Maria Carolina said she respected him far more than if he had clung to his post: 'He has sacrificed everything to his duty. Sooner or later he will reap his reward, as is only just, but in the meantime he ought to enjoy all the honour he deserves.' And she granted him a pension of twelve thousand francs until he was reinstated. Thanking the Queen, Bombelles remarked that he did not deserve so much kindness, since he had never rendered any service to the Court of Naples. 'You have served the cause of all sovereigns,' she replied. Her gratitude did not stop with the pension; through the

Austrian Court she secured positions for his children. This was characteristic of her generosity, and she was equally lavish in other ways. The Sardinian ambassador, Castellalfer, wrote that 'Acton never fails to remonstrate with her most pathetically on these occasions, reminding her that the terrible *deficit* which caused the present abysmal plight of France was mainly due to her sister's similar conduct'.

The Queen did not relish such home truths; she paid more attention to the San Marco's insinuations against Acton's motives for economy. The old hypocrite must be feathering his nest, providing for the day when he would sail to England. But according to Castellalfer the King was convinced that 'no minister had ever served him like this one... He thinks him the only man capable of governing his kingdom well, and he is probably not mistaken. But the great inconvenience is that Acton finds himself forced to devote much valuable time to this struggle which he might employ more usefully in attending to the multiple affairs of the departments under his charge.'

Sir William Hamilton wrote: 'This upright Minister has certainly done a great deal of good in this Court, but much remains to be done. There is a general want of good faith at Naples, and every department of the State is more or less corrupted. The next generation may perhaps be better...' Though the constant cabals 'excited against him by the discontented nobility and gentry' had made him extremely irritable, he concealed this under a mask of tired courtesy. Only the contrast between his polite pursed lips and gimlet eyes betrayed his ingrowing exasperation. No moral reformer, he was forced to make use of available talent and overlook the rest. He could not afford to wait for the next generation.

On the surface he was on amicable terms with the chief of police. Luigi de' Medici was refreshingly enterprising: he had studied the police methods of Sartine and Lenoir. Among other reforms he had street signs put up; he had shops and houses numbered systematically; he improved the lighting of the city and started penal colonies on the islands of Tremiti and Lampedusa. He also employed spies for political purposes on his own account. At the same time he courted popularity with a shifty group of pseudo-Jacobins, two of whom, the Giordano brothers, lived in his house; and he was the patron of the Academy of Chemistry, a crypto-Jacobin club whose aim was to spread revolutionary propaganda.

His apologists have portrayed him as a genial broad-minded aristocrat who, despising the vanities of his caste, took refuge from boredom in the company of 'cultured representatives of the middle class, the intellectual élite of the city'. But it is absurd to pretend that the Giordano brothers and their associates were men of superior endowments. Annibale Giordano was a teacher of mathematics at the Nunziatella Military College and his political ideas were borrowed from French revolutionary pamphlets. As for his character, he turned against his old patron in a dastardly manner, and it is no thanks to him that Medici escaped conviction for high treason.

Was it merely through careless tolerance that the chief of police kept open house for the leading rebels of 1799? Or was he playing a double game? It has been alleged that his sympathy for revolutionary France was quickened by reaction to the Prime Minister. While this is possible, it does not show his character to advantage. He owed his appointment to the Queen's friendship and to Acton's goodwill. So long as he was an efficient functionary, Acton overlooked his underhand thrusts against himself.

Maria Carolina felt, like most other sovereigns, that the French Constitution had been extorted from Louis XVI on September 14, 1791, and that it had reduced him to the position of a puppet. That all sovereignty resided in the nation was a contradiction of monarchy as she understood it. She wrote to Gallo in a mood of profound pessimism: 'The King of France having accepted and signed what was imposed on him has finished playing his part. All sovereigns will have to do likewise sooner or later: that is my conviction.'

She complained of her wretched nerves; she suffered from fits of dizziness; all the blood rushed to her head, and the doctors did nothing for fear of bringing on a miscarriage. For she was pregnant again, though she had just become a grandmother. 'I sincerely hope that this will be my last child,' she admitted. However, she was too busy with her daughters' problems to brood upon her own. Like her mother, she wrote them copious letters of advice based on personal experience. When her eldest daughter gave birth to the future Empress Marie Louise, she wrote: 'I should like her to be pregnant again within two months and continue in this state for five or six years... That is, in my opinion, the best remedy for the frivolity of youth.' She asked Gallo for all the details, sent her thanks and a little souvenir for the physician in attendance, distributed gifts all round to the maids and nurses, and told Gallo to hand her daughter twenty thousand florins from the King. (Ferdinand had promised this sum on the birth of her first child, as the Archduchess had been quick to remind him.) 'Francis is well,' she continued, 'and on all occasions gives proof of his good heart. I hope he will be the comfort of my old age, and I shall be relieved when all my children are happily settled. The others are growing and flourishing to my great satisfaction... Do not forget to tell me if Theresa was pleased with her present... It seems to me that I am relieved of a heavy burden, and since my daughter's delivery I have felt much lighter.'

No foreign ambassador was more of a *persona grata* than the doyen Sir William Hamilton, whose second wife was therefore introduced to the Queen. Sir William had finally married the dazzling young Emma, who had been living with him for the last five years, though she had kept her mother as chaperon to save appearances. Sir William had had her taught French and Italian, singing and dancing, and since she was a born actress as well as a striking beauty, she could play almost any role with charm, even that of ambassadress. She did not have to talk much when her features were so eloquent. She could raise her eyes to heaven with such an expression of purity that an abbé, moved to tears, told her that God had sent her into this world with a special design. She had every reason to be pleased with herself. Usually she was dressed in virginal white with her long hair rippling loose, and among the dusky Neapolitans her fair English complexion shone with an exotic lustre to which men, women and children paid demonstrative tribute. For her theatrical and musical gifts we must rely upon the impressions of contemporaries, but her portraits still convey her physical glamour.

Sir William Hamilton was sixty-one, but he did not look his age: he was tall, thin and athletic. Emma was about twenty-six, and she bore no trace of her humble origin and chequered past. In spite of a convention that only ladies who had been presented at their own Courts could be presented at that of Naples—and the Queen of England had refused to receive her—she was received very graciously by Maria Carolina. This was no moment to fuss about private morals: to please the British ambassador was a matter of political expediency, for the Queen wanted an alliance with Great Britain. A little royal favour went a long way with Emma Hamilton, who was flattered to the marrow by the Queen's attentions. Soon she was singing duets with the King and dining *en famille* with the royal family, 'but at the drawing-room', as she told her former lover Greville, 'I kept my distance, and paid the Queen as much respect as if I had never seen her before, which pleased her very much. But she showed me great distinction that night, and told me several times how she admired my good conduct.'

Compared with the determined San Marco and the no less dangerous Belmonte, Emma Hamilton was almost respectable, and she had the advantage of superior beauty and youthful spirits. The proud Queen could not help being charmed by this bird of paradise, and diplomatic reasons drew them closer together. Mme Vigée Le Brun, who painted her portrait at this time, wrote that 'Lady Hamilton, being very indiscreet, acquainted the Queen with many little diplomatic secrets which her Majesty turned to account for the affairs of her kingdom'. Emma applied to Greville for titbits of political gossip: 'Send me some news, political and private; for, against my will, *owing to my situation here* I am got into politicks, and I wish to have news for our dear much-loved Queen, whom I adore. Nor can I live without her, for she is to me another friend and everything. If you could know her as I do, how you would adore her! For she is the first woman in the world; her talents are superior to every woman's in the world; and her heart is most excellent and strictly good and upright...'

The sudden death of the Emperor Leopold on March 1, 1792, was a disaster for Austria and for all who hoped to maintain the established order by peaceful means. Only King Gustavus III of Sweden was eager to lead a crusade in the cause of French monarchy, and he was murdered on March 29. Maria Carolina would have been tempted to follow the King of Sweden's crusade; but Leopold, whom she loved and revered, had curbed her aggressive instincts. She poured out her grief to Gallo: 'Tell me, in God's name, how did they leave my poor dear brother to die without the Sacraments, without telling him of his condition. Delirium, his swollen stomach and four bleedings indicated the inflammation, yet nobody was charitable enough to warn him. Alas! how rare are true attachment and devotion! Here they talk of poison. I think those infernal Frenchmen capable of anything, but you will tell me the sad truth frankly about the cause of this unexpected and unforeseen misfortune. Send me all the details. All my life I shall never cease mourning my brother and friend. I cannot yet persuade myself that he is dead and that we shall be parted for ever. This idea overwhelms me. I was already very ill from violent attacks of headache and nerves: only this blow was missing... A copious bleeding saved me; I had many fainting-fits, and today an appalling headache forces me to end.'

Leopold's successor, Francis II, was young and inexperienced, and he was soon swayed by the party in favour of war. Maria Carolina's eldest daughter was now Empress, so that the bonds between the two countries appeared stronger than ever, but Naples could not render much assistance to Austria when France declared war on April 20, 1792. Active hostilities did not break out till later, since neither France nor Austria was mobilized.

Baron de Talleyrand's position as French ambassador in Naples had become more and more difficult; after the arrest of Louis XVI he resigned and stayed on as a private resident. His secretary Cacault, who had no such delicacy, was appointed *chargé d'affaires*, and although the Court would not recognize him he refused to leave. In his rage he threatened reprisals and urged his government to send a punitive expedition. The country, he said, lacked strength, courage, ability and the proper means of defence, and in spite of much native wit the Neapolitans, on the whole, were not inspired by any sentiment that was noble and estimable. Acton, while flattering his masters with an appearance of military strength, would never fire a shot unless he was solidly supported by an anti-French coalition.

But France still had a thriving trade with the Two Sicilies, and had nothing to gain from such a drastic step. Acton complained that Neapolitan ships had been searched illegally at Toulon and Marseilles and that Neapolitan coral fishers had been molested in Corsica. Promising satisfaction, the French government sent Citizen Armand de Mackau as minister to Naples, accompanied by Citizen Hugou as his secretary, who added de Bassville as a flourish to his name. Mackau was the son of a former assistant governess to the French royal family, and had been minister to Württemberg under the *ancien régime*, but he was among those careerists who welcomed the Revolution. Hugou de Bassville was the son of an Abbeville dyer, and had been a priest, a *protégé* of the Prince de Condé, a tutor to the children of a rich American who gave him a pension, and a sub editor of the *Mercure politique*: an ambitious fanatic whose death brought him posthumous fame.

This pair arrived under the worst auspices. Mackau had left his passport behind; perhaps he imagined that it was not necessary. After browbeating the police with threats of immediate war, he was allowed to cross the frontier, but the officer in charge was punished for not sending him back. When he presented his credentials on August 24, the French monarchy had ceased. The King and Queen refused to recognize his diplomatic status. He had stormy interviews with Acton, yet he dug himself in, conscious of a special mission. Bassville felt that the Legation was too small for both Mackau and himself, and applied to Lebrun, the Minister of Foreign Affairs, for a post in Florence or Venice. 'While I am writing to you,' he told Lebrun, 'a painter beside me is painting our coat-of-arms. Where the Bourbon lilies flowered, stands a beauteous Minerva with her lance and the sacred cap of liberty, as on your last despatch which the local Argus has not torn or seized [a reference to the prevalent tampering with diplomatic mail]. Tomorrow it will be put up, and I know this will be a festival for many people who will come out on purpose to admire it. I also count on showing my uniform of the national guard at the San Carlo theatre. It will be the first time it has been seen in Naples, and perhaps in Italy. I implore you to send us the *Marseillaise* with music. Everybody is asking for it.' And he ends: 'I am terribly bored here.' Later he boasted that he had gone to the San Carlo in his blue uniform 'to defy the Queen in public, or at home', and that all Naples had admired the beauty, with the red cap on the tip of a spear, whom some [no doubt the great majority] had mistaken for the Madonna. It is hardly surprising that Mackau and his secretary were shunned by society and watched by the police. The Queen had written: 'M. Mackau, who arrived three days ago, already betrays his character and causes us vexations: he is a bad piece of furniture. There is another reason for us to abhor Spain, which nearly persuaded us to accept him.'

The French Revolution had flooded into Savoy and Piedmont, and its agents had caused riots in Turin. Though order was restored, these were the first sparks of a bigger blaze. To oppose a French invasion the government of Turin urged all Italian states to join a defensive league. This was to consist of the King of Sardinia, the Emperor of Austria, the King of Spain (representing Parma), the Pope, the Republic of Venice and the King of Naples. Acton was wholly in favour of it, and promised to send substantial forces to Lombardy and Tuscany. But Spain hung back after the fall of Florida Blanca, with whom Acton had made peace; the Pope would only use spiritual weapons; and Venice, afraid of Austria, voted for neutrality. Acton sent Micheroux to Venice with the draft of a treaty, but the Committee of the *Savi* remained obstinate, though as merchants they could not resist selling corn to the Austrians. The league foundered against so many obstacles. However, Acton kept his promise to the King of Sardinia, despite strong opposition at the Council. But instead of the Neapolitan troops, who were needed in Sicily and Central Italy, he offered four hundred thousand ducats a year to enrol a force of five thousand Swiss mercenaries, a more practical suggestion. Vittorio Amedeo III sent Acton a message of thanks 'for the promptitude and energy with which this firm and enlightened Minister was able to persuade his Court to take a resolution conforming to the difficult circumstances and the true interest and dignity of the King, his master.'

Though Acton worked hard for an Austro-Spanish reconciliation, he shared Tanucci's distrust of Family Pacts. Nor did he believe in the sincerity of the Austro-Prussian alliance. While Gallo was gushing about 'the brave Austrians and Prussians who do not desert and do not understand philosophy', both were demoralized after the battle of Valmy, and there was growing friction between them, which the French were able to exploit. From this moment the French seized the offensive and maintained it with devastating success.

The battle of Valmy which 'taught the world that France was still a nation', was fought on September 20, 1792: two days later the French Republic was proclaimed. Mackau announced that he would serve it as he had served the King. The Neapolitan Court's refusal to recognize him increased the tension between the two countries. Maria Carolina was goaded to fury by the activities of French revolutionary agents, and to desperation by the news of French victories; she could not control her impatience to go to war. Yet the retreat of the Prussians, with whom the Neapolitan troops could hardly compare, should have cooled her ardour. The French armies had overrun most of the Rhine country and the Austrian Netherlands.

Until he could count on England as an ally, Acton tried to pacify the Queen on one hand and smooth Mackau's ruffled plumage on the other. At the same time, he tried to prevent French agents from stirring up mischief. He knew that Mackau was in close correspondence with Huguet de Sémonville, who as French minister in

Genoa was one of the most dangerous firebrands, translating seditious literature and scattering it throughout Italy. After being transferred to Turin, where the King of Sardinia would not receive him, he was assigned to Turkey. But Acton warned Ludolf, the Neapolitan minister at Constantinople, about Sémonville's true character. Ludolf warned the Sultan, who also refused to have him. All this was explained by the Count de Choiseul, former French ambassador in Constantinople, to the Count d'Artois, in a letter which the republicans intercepted. The National Convention swore to avenge this insult.

Early in November Acton heard that Sémonville had held a council of war in Genoa which had decided to attack Naples, but he did not know the details. He was aware that a fleet of fifty-two ships under Rear-Admiral Truguet had been concentrated in the Mediterranean for an assault upon Sardinia. Defence measures were intensified, but no help could be expected from England yet. Mackau was recalled by the Convention, and he was about to shake the dust of Naples from his feet when lo! the Court reluctantly decided to recognize him.

According to a Roman correspondent, the long-postponed audience was distinctly chilly. 'The King merely asked Mackau how the air of Naples agreed with him, and the Queen asked him if his wife, who was in an advanced state of pregnancy, would be confined in Naples. Hitherto Mackau had not been entertained by anyone, but since his appearance before the sovereigns I hear he has been admitted to the *conversazione* of the Prince of Butera, but I believe merely as a foreign gentleman, like the Pasha of Damascus who is also here... On Monday, after the Queen had spoken to Mackau's wife she smashed her fan as soon as the visitor's back was turned...' The strain of being civil to the emissaries of the French Republic had been too much for her nerves. Recent events in France, anxiety about Marie Antoinette, physical exhaustion, the knowledge that she was personally disliked and that the Court was full of potential traitors, all combined to upset her. A temporary truce with France, however insincere, seemed the only solution. Acton has been blamed for this *volte-face* and its consequences. But the letters of the Sardinian ambassador, and of Maria Carolina to Gallo, throw more light on the confused situation.

Castellalfer wrote on November 20, 1792: 'The Sunday courier brought us the minutes of the war council held at Genoa the eighth of this month at M. de Sémonville's house... It was decided unanimously that the French squadron should sail to Naples and Civitavecchia to attack and pillage these places... This squadron, which is now supposed to be at Leghorn, may reach Naples within two days, and the defence preparations... will only be completed on the 10th or 12th at the earliest. This has sufficed to create indescribable alarm in a country which at bottom could not be less military. The Chevalier Acton certainly has great qualities and he has shown them clearly on this occasion, for it can be stated categorically that only he did not lose his head. But he is very poorly supported. He has done everything possible to send the Queen to Castellammare so that she should not add to the general alarm... but he has not succeeded. He would have liked the King to show himself often to the people who cherish him, and encourage by his presence the workmen at the docks, the troops and militia; but that could not be managed either. His Majesty repairs daily to the hunt as if nothing was happening; most of the minister's subordinates are of a revolting mediocrity. He has to arrange everything and struggle incessantly against intrigue, ignorance and ill-will. In the meantime everybody is so terrified that each thinks of saving his property and running away... Upon the appearance of the enemy the Court has decided to retire to the Castle of Sant' Elmo, which owing to its position on the hill dominating the city is safe from insult.'

The Sardinian ambassador concluded that whether energy or weakness prevailed 'depends on the greater or less influence of different cliques on the King and Queen... All these are united under two leaders, and the first is Chevalier Acton. The whole marine is for him as well as the majority of wise and sensible people who only desire the country's welfare and the King's prestige. At the head of the second, called the favourite's party or Mme de San Marco's, is her brother the Chevalier de Medici, chief of police, a young man whose cleverness and knowledge of his own department is indisputable, but whose overweening ambition could only be satisfied by his elevation to the first place in the ministry. This is far the most numerous party, and consists of people who have nothing in common but hatred of Acton. They are ignorant, conceited courtiers, disgruntled through not obtaining some coveted post, ladies-in-waiting who resent any curb on their wasteful extravagance, people to whom all order is intolerable. These approach their Majesties in turn. Watching for the opportune moment, now they inspire an abnormal fear by exaggerating the dangers of the situation, now they blame the minister by disparaging his subordinates. Thus it often happens that when a wise resolution is passed at the Council, the Cabinet decides on a different policy. This continual fluctuation has the worst possible effect, and the panic of the Court is certainly not calculated to kindle energy in the least martial of nations.'

The Queen's letters to Gallo register a crescendo of agitation. On November 18 she wrote: 'This year the dearth of corn and provisions of all kinds has been general. Even water has become scarce. God has wished to chastise us in all things. As for me, I wish to live in order to save my children and the country. Otherwise I can only see trouble and woe.' On November 20: 'Doubtless you have been informed of the council of war at Genoa... We have preferred to accept Mackau rather than have him forced upon us by a superior squadron. God knows what this has cost me. Finally the sacrifice has been accomplished. If this squadron makes unjustifiable claims when it arrives, we will retort with vigour, and I expect the best results from the good disposition of our people. We have got rid of our silver. We have not even a chandelier between the children and ourselves. Not even coffee-pots, all is gone. The King has given up 392 horses and 300 dogs, and reduced his hunting grounds. He is selling Roccabella at Posillipo. Yesterday he had the wild beasts of the menagerie killed... He has practised the strictest economy to defray his heavy expenses. I am writing you by the light of a tin lamp. *Apropos* of this, buy me four toilet sets of black varnished tin and send them to me when you can. My poor children have cheerfully deprived themselves of everything...' On December 4: 'My health is bad: my mind is mortally troubled and I do nothing but weep. Six little children to look after and the state in danger... From one minute to the next we expect the French squadron of fifty-four sails. They assure us that they are coming as brothers and friends. This squadron is strong in artillery, pontoons, ammunition, etc. Finally the crisis has come: we have stipulated the number of ships we can receive. If the French exceed this number, we have informed them that the surplus will be regarded as hostile. As for us, we shall have to see what fate has in store for us. I only weep on account of my poor children, for if we suffer a real defeat all is over, and we can consider ourselves irretrievably lost... The King gives proof of extraordinary courage. If we perish, I recommend myself to your services and zeal on my children's behalf. They are so small, especially the two little boys. Farewell, if I could only fly to Vienna! I had tears in my eyes when my daughter offered me hospitality in her capital, but duty compels me to live or die here, too happy if I may be of some service to the state, which is now in imminent danger.'

These brief extracts from the Queen's voluminous letters show what Acton had to contend with. He continued to speed up mobilization and rearmament, while the King's 'extraordinary courage' seemed to consist in hunting and fishing as usual. He cut down a few expenses, but nothing was allowed to interfere with his favourite sport. True, he wrote to Gallo: 'When we are put with our backs to the wall we shall defend ourselves desperately and fight like brave Neapolitans, and I shall be the first to set a good example.' No doubt he believed it. Mackau protested—he spent his life protesting—against military preparations which appeared to be hostile to France. Acton silenced him with a report of the recent council in Genoa which stated, among other friendly aims, 'the sacking of churches and the public treasury'.

As soon as Mackau was recognized officially, he sent a messenger to inform his government and urge Admiral Truguet to send his entire squadron to Naples. Yet he coolly maintained that the squadron was coming on a mere visit of courtesy. In that case, Acton told him, no more than twenty-two ships could be admitted, the quota for friendly powers. Already Mackau must have known that instead of Truguet's fleet, only a small squadron was to be sent under Admiral Latouche-Tréville, but he kept this to himself. After much bargaining, Acton conceded that six ships might be admitted at Naples; the rest were to anchor off Baia. At the same time Mackau bombarded Acton with diplomatic notes, proposing an alliance between France, Spain, Prussia and Naples, thanks to which Naples might annexe part of the Papal States. Acton was evasive, reminding him that the Neapolitans were Catholic to the core. Perhaps Mackau could not realize this, hobnobbing with the local Jacobins.

When Mackau announced that Latouche-Tréville's squadron was sailing to Naples, Acton ordered Medici 'to persuade the people of its peaceful intentions and to behave in a friendly manner', but also to guard against unpleasant surprise. The ships appeared on December 12, when Mackau sent word to Latouche that the Republic had been recognized, and that the Neapolitan government did not expect him to enter with more than six vessels: the rest could anchor off Baia. Latouche refused to divide them and drew them up in line of battle, nine ships of the line and four frigates. Towards midday the largest dropped anchor near the Castel dell' Ovo. Anxious to prevent a rupture now that so much had been gained by negotiation, Mackau and a party of French merchants boarded the flagship to parley with Latouche. The Admiral wished to hand the King an ultimatum, that Acton be sent to France as a hostage until Sémonville had been received by the Ottoman Porte—'within an hour General Acton must be in my power or Naples will be destroyed'. Mackau expostulated that this was untimely, and after a heated argument in which all the merchants and officers joined, a milder ultimatum was substituted. The Neapolitan envoy was to be recalled from Constantinople and an ambassador was to be sent to Paris on a French frigate. All Naples watched the squadron from the shore, and the sea was dotted with little boats bobbing about the new comers. Some contained Jacobins longing to fraternize, but these were outnumbered by the *lazzaroni* who made 'signs of derision' with obscene gesticulations, so that the French called out to them: 'We are your friends, good people, we are your friends!'

Mackau and Redon de Belleville, the Convention's special representative, landed from a launch flying the symbolical red cap, and were greeted with piercing whistles and shouts of 'Long live our King!'

After three hours, the Council of State decided not to resist. All the conditions were approved except the despatch of an ambassador on a French frigate; instead the Prince of Castelcicala was to proceed from London to Paris. Acton pointed out that the squadron had little chance if they came to grips, but the King was determined to avoid war and the Queen's nerve gave way. He was tempted to resign, but he would not afford his enemies that satisfaction. Medici scoffed that if he had been Latouche he would have insisted on Acton being sent to Paris to apologize for the Sémonville affair. And if the King had been asked to dance a minuet on the mole, he said, His Majesty would have done so without demur. These sarcasms were uttered when the coast was clear. Only the Queen realized the depth of Acton's frustration. 'I fear,' she wrote, 'that this worthy man will succumb to the weight of his worries. He deserves to be pitied, especially by those who know thoroughly as I do, all that he feels and suffers, and all that he would like to achieve and is hindered from achieving. This existence is intolerable to those who think, see and foresee.'

Since their conditions had been so easily accepted, the French tried to foist Belleville on the King at a farewell audience. To avoid this form of recognition Latouche and all his officers were invited to Court, but they excused themselves with the pretext that they were preparing for departure. Consequently Belleville, rigged out as a grenadier of the French national guard, was introduced by Mackau to the King. Later he boasted of having delivered a revolutionary tirade, but his actual words were these: 'Sire, the bad weather has not permitted the Admiral and his officers to land; they propose to sail at once, taking advantage of a favourable wind, which within thirty-six hours should carry the squadron to its destination. I shall tell the Republic about Your Majesty's kindness: I am sure it will be fully gratified; I am also sure that it will attribute Your Majesty's friendship to its excellent fortune.'

After twenty-eight hours the squadron sailed for Sardinia. Mackau, for whom the visit had been a triumph, scattered ribald anti-Acton pamphlets among the citizens of Naples. Belleville, on his arrival in Paris, made a speech before the Convention, extolling Latouche as a new Brutus who had anchored under the royal palace. Had a single shot been fired, said he, Latouche would have returned a thousand. The Neapolitans had been dazed by the formidable display of might. On landing he had been met by a cheering crowd. 'Courage, brave Frenchmen, persevere!' they had cried. 'Here are fifty-thousand comrades ready to uphold you!' The King had instantly yielded to all his demands, etc. And the president of the assembly replied: 'Another Bourbon among the vanquished! The honour of the nation has been repaired without bloodshed: you could not bring happier news to the National Convention. She applauds the valour of Latouche, the public spirit and fine conduct of the crews,' etc. Bassville, who had been transferred to Rome, published another inflated version of the incident.

Later the King regretted that he had not been in a position to fight because then, as he wrote: 'I should have been able to vent my rage against them, and it would have given me a chance to cut up all the Frenchmen in Naples...'

The unwelcome guests had scarcely gone ere they returned. Buffeted by a storm off Civitavecchia, they staggered back to

Naples for repairs and provisions. Latouche's ship, the *Languedoc*, had to be towed in with her mainmast broken, but her plight was cold comfort to Ferdinand. 'To avoid war,' wrote Maria Carolina, 'a detestable misfortune, but far less dire when the nation is in favour of it, we caress the serpent which will poison us.' The French officers, each a republican missionary, were now free to land. They visited theatres, museums and private houses, where they were entertained by all the Jacobins, who threw discretion to the winds and welcomed them with transports of joy. Latouche attended three meetings of the Academy of Chemistry, at one of which he made an inflammatory speech urging the people of Italy to emulate the French. Dinners were given by the Abbé Cestari and other sympathizers, at which the guests wore Phrygian caps and sang toasts to liberty.

On January 12, 1793, the King's birthday, Latouche invited his Neapolitan hosts to a banquet on the *Languedoc*. The table was not large enough for all the guests, many of whom remained standing or strolled about the deck. A Neapolitan officer toasted the French Republic and the Abbé Jerocades, a Calabrian Freemason, declaimed an ode to the assassin of Gustavus III of Sweden, 'the Tyrant of the Goths', and led a general sing-song. Then the French gazettes were read aloud and a sailor solemnly passed round a 'cap of liberty', which each wore in turn while another chanted a republican anthem. As a climax Latouche urged his guests to swear to exterminate tyrants. He proposed the foundation of a Society of Friends of Liberty and Equality, like that of Marseilles, to make the people realize that they were enslaved. For there was one hitch to the 'democratization' of the Two Sicilies: the people 'loved their chains' and were fond of their tyrants. Without the support of the people, how could the despot be destroyed? Latouche selected a French resident, Jean Pécher, to organize the new society with the assistance of Carlo Lauberg, a Neapolitan priest, despite his surname, who kept a private school which became a nursery of Jacobinism. Lauberg was a conspirator by vocation, a precursor of the professional agitators who were to become the bane of South Italy.

While the *Languedoc* was being repaired, one of her most pugnacious officers, La Flotte, was sent on a mission to Rome. The Nuncio had left Paris since Pius VI had been burnt in effigy; Avignon had been wrenched from the Pope amid scenes of massacre and anarchy; and since the resignation of Cardinal de Bernis, France was only represented by a consul in the Eternal City. The Pope's Secretary of State, Cardinal Zelada, refused permission to set up the republican arms on the French consulate for reasons of public security. Mackau sent La Flotte with an insolent letter to the Cardinal, telling him that he had ordered the consul to raise the arms within twenty-four hours. Bassville had already made himself obnoxious with his bullying ways, and La Flotte was equally rash. They threw down Louis XIV's statue in the French Academy which he had founded, collected a subscription for the repair of the *Languedoc*, were seen everywhere flaunting their tricolour cockades, exasperating everybody except their few partisans.

The republican arms were duly hoisted outside the consulate. As in Naples, Bassville predicted that it would be a day of public rejoicing. He drove swaggering along the Corso with his wife, son, secretary and La Flotte in a carriage bedizened with the tricolour. An excited crowd, shouting 'Kill those rags of Frenchmen!' followed them all the way to Bassville's lodgings. As the crowd grew more menacing Bassville fired his pistol and barricaded his party in the Palombara Palace. The infuriated mob proceeded to batter down the doors, shouting: 'Long live Saint Peter, the Pope, the King of France! Down with the tricolour! Death to the Jacobins!' La Flotte managed to escape over the roof, but Bassville was fatally gashed by a razor while defending himself with a stiletto. The crowd went on to attack the French Academy, where they destroyed the revolutionary emblems and shattered the furniture. An epic poem called *Bassvilliana*, by Vincenzo Monti, dedicated to Pope Pius VI, commemorated the incident.

Mackau preached war against the Pope 'to punish the crime'. But the Neapolitans sympathized with the Romans, and one night the arms over the French legation and consulate in Naples were broken and befouled. A printed manifesto signed by 'the people of Naples' begged the King not to deal with men who 'no longer have the right to be called such' and concluded: 'We prefer death to the false friendship of a nation which is only proud because of the weak resistance it has encountered so far.' Mackau continued to protest, but none of the culprits were caught or punished. He proposed a joint expedition against Rome; the Republic would let the King take any part of the Papal territory he chose. Acton replied with a promise of strict neutrality and offered to mediate between Rome and France. Mackau repeated that this was not a case of neutrality or mediation but of a joint campaign from which Naples would benefit. Acton then assured him that public opinion would be outraged by any act hostile to the Pope.

The murder of Bassville was overshadowed by the news of the execution of Louis XVI (on January 21, 1793). It was the eve of Carnival, but all Naples went into mourning and a requiem for the guillotined monarch was attended by the whole Court. Even Citizen Mackau was upset when he broke the news to Acton, who replied:

'General Acton has been gratified to learn that M. de Mackau takes part in his present sorrow. This Court has been plunged in the deepest grief and horror.' But as he refused to wear mourning, he was identified with the regicides. In spite of snubs and humiliations, he clung to his post.

The Queen's hatred of France became a burning obsession. She poured out her feelings to everybody on the subject. To Gallo she wrote: 'Knowing your upright mind, I can imagine your emotion on hearing of the appalling crime perpetrated against the unfortunate King of France in all solemnity, tranquillity and illegality. We knew it from the Gazette, and as I am always impatient I fell upon the article of January 22 and read the account of the tragedy set down in terms of such indifference that I had to read it three times over in order to recover. We have gone into mourning for four months. He was the head of our family, our kinsman, cousin and brother-in-law. What an atrocious example! What an execrable nation! I know nothing about the other wretched victims in the Temple. If sorrow does not kill them, other horrors may be expected from this horde of assassins. I hope that the ashes of this good Prince, of this too good Prince who has suffered shame and infamy for four years culminating in execution, will implore a striking and visible vengeance from divine Justice, and that on this account the Powers of Europe will have no more than a single united will, since it is a matter in which they are all involved.'

She would have severed relations with France had Ferdinand allowed her this expensive luxury. She longed to avenge, help, save her sister, whose sufferings continued to keep her in suspense. On March 5 she wrote: 'I hear horrible details from that infernal Paris. At every moment, at every noise and cry, every time they enter her room, my unfortunate sister kneels, prays and prepares for death.

The inhuman brutes that surround her amuse themselves in this manner: day and night they bellow on purpose to terrorize her and make her fear death a thousand times. Death is what one may wish for the poor soul, and it is what I pray God to send her that she may cease to suffer... I should like this infamous nation to be cut to pieces, annihilated, dishonoured, reduced to nothing for at least fifty years. I hope that divine chastisement will fall visibly on France, destroyed by the glorious arms of Austria.'

During the first months of 1793 the French armies met with reverses and had to evacuate the Netherlands. General Dumouriez went over to the Austrian side, but the Austrian and Prussian generals failed to agree and therefore lost many a golden opportunity. Latouche left Naples on January 29, having sown the seeds of rebellion against the government. But his ultimatum proved barren, for Prince Castelcicala, the Neapolitan ambassador in London, refused to go to Paris, and Sémonville together with Maret, the future Duc de Bassano, was kidnapped by Austrian agents and imprisoned in the Tyrol. The execution of Louis XVI was a final challenge to England; and Danton's phrase about hurling the head of a King at the feet of crowned brigands reflected the mood of the faction governing France, which declared war against England and Holland on February 1. If the declaration was 'highly agreeable' to George III, it was even more so to Maria Carolina.

Reviewing present conditions to Lord Grenville in February 1793, Hamilton wrote: 'The King of Naples by the goodness of his heart and great affability has certainly gained the love of all his subjects, but they regret his not trusting more to his own judgement, as whenever he does take upon himself to decide, it is always on the right side, as His Majesty is not deficient in understanding and is, on all occasions, remarkably inclined to do justice. The Queen of Naples is by no means popular, but as her power is evident she is greatly feared. No one doubts the capacity or integrity of General Acton, but they complain, and I fear not without reason, that having taken upon himself almost every department of the state, he has not time (although a perfect slave to business) to transact the half of that he has undertaken, and which being left to the corrupt clerks in his offices, causes much clamour and discontent. His uncle, a British baronet, died last year and left him the family seat and a part of his estate, and being the immediate heir to the title he is now Sir John Acton, of which he is not a little proud, and I have reason to think that he is meditating his retreat from an elevated but perilous situation to his quiet family seat in Shropshire.'

In May Ferdinand and Maria Carolina heard that the Empress of Austria, their eldest daughter, had borne a son, so they decided to interrupt their mourning in honour of the event. All the foreign ambassadors were invited to a Court reception, including Mackau, who should have realized that this was a mere formality. He attended it, however, and the King and Queen turned their backs on him when he approached. His presence had evoked the guillotine, and the sneers of the courtiers showed him his mistake. The French foreign minister rebuked him for his want of tact and ordered him to stay at his post until his successor arrived. As this was Maret, who was kidnapped by the Austrians in July, he had to wait some time. A treaty of alliance with England had long been in the air, and it was signed on July 12, before Mackau's departure. The King of Naples was to provide six thousand soldiers, four ships of the line, four frigates, four small ships of war, for operations in the Mediterranean. His subjects were forbidden to trade with France; English ships were to protect Neapolitan merchantmen; the King could not make a separate peace without British consent, when, if England continued fighting, he was to remain neutral. England was pledged to maintain a fleet in the Mediterranean throughout the period of emergency and, upon the conclusion of peace, promised to give special consideration to the interests of the Two Sicilies.

During Latouche's long visit the King and Queen had been mortified by reports that some of their subjects had gone out of their way to cultivate his friendship. It was suspected that a conspiracy was brewing. The Queen hoped to protect her family, and employed spies of her own as a precaution. She has been much abused for doing so, but what other weapon had she against those who were plotting to destroy the monarchy? Spies were also employed by her enemies, and their technique was perfected under Bonaparte. Unfortunately she had no Fouché. For a reason not apparent at the time, the most dangerous conspirators were allowed to slip through the hands of the police. Medici sent them warning, so that when Latouche sailed only the smaller fry were caught. Their trials were delayed until more evidence could be collected, and as Medici was secretly on their side very little could be done. Renegade priests like Cestari and Jerocades, who had started as Jansenists and Freemasons, were sent to cool their ardour in distant monasteries; but Lauberg was still at large. He continued to address the Academy of Chemistry on liberty and the rights of man, revolutionary style; he translated the French Constitution of 1793 and had it clandestinely printed; and he induced many aristocratic young Freemasons to cross the Rubicon. His aim was to transform the masonic lodges into Jacobin clubs. How lightly this was done, as if they were acting in a charade, can be seen from the records of the charges brought against them.

Ferdinando Pignatelli, Prince of Strongoli, decided to found a masonic lodge in his house, and his friend Ettore Carafa, Count of Ruvo, promised to provide the equipment for the initiation of five friends 'whose eyes were still closed to the true light'. They were to meet at the San Carlo theatre and go separately to the Strongoli palace. After founding the new lodge, they were to return to the theatre before the end of the performance. This was to avert suspicion, since the aristocracy used the San Carlo as a general rendezvous.

On the appointed evening, Carafa produced a sheet of black cloth on which a trowel, a compass, a triangle, an apron and two columns were depicted with chalk and paper. Three lighted candles were placed in a triangle on this cloth, while the five neophytes were kept in an adjoining room with the doors closed. The six Freemasons, wearing handkerchiefs round their waists as official aprons and brandishing keys as substitutes for hammers, proceeded to elect Pignatelli, Lauberg and de Marco, the old minister's nephew, as introducer and treasurer, 'master regent' and 'grand orator' respectively, and the following rite was repeated five times running. Each neophyte blindfold knocked thrice at the door and Lauberg inquired: 'Who's there?' The introducer Pignatelli replied: 'A blind man whose sight is regained, seeking the light.' Lauberg said: 'Come in!' The door was opened and the neophyte was led by Pignatelli to the centre of the room. Lauberg asked: 'You seek the light, but have you strength to keep the secret?' The neophyte having said yes was conducted to the master regent, who sat at a table with a book, with the other masons beside him. The bandage was removed and he had to swear with his hand on the book. After the last initiation Lauberg, who had expounded the mystery of the emblems on the cloth, announced: 'Brothers, the veil is rent; the deception is revealed. Believe this: Freemasonry is nothing but pure Jacobinism.' The grand orator, de Marco, delivered a lecture about the origin and development of masonry, winding up with an assertion that the French Revolution had been its culmination. He exhorted them to imitate their good French brethren and shake off the yoke of tyranny in Naples. Two candles were then lighted before a portrait of Voltaire on the chimney-piece to which a red cap with a tricolour ribbon and rosette was attached, and the *Marseillaise* was sung in chorus. The manuscript of de Marco's lecture was burnt and some paper lilies were thrown into the flames to symbolize the destruction of the Bourbons, after which all retired in haste to the San Carlo. At a dinner given later by Pignatelli the Queen's portrait was substituted for Voltaire's and the guests sang the *Marseillaise* before it. While de Marco spat at the picture each contributed another insult.

There was an element of snobbery in all this mumbo-jumbo; it was considered smart and modern by young men of good family holding 'advanced' views. There was also an element of adventure: they loved rhetoric and melodrama; their brains had been heated by Alfieri's *Brutus* and *The Pazzi Conspiracy*, of which they knew chunks by heart: they were assiduous readers of the *Moniteur*, and it was fun to play with fire when there seemed to be little risk of getting scorched. The ignorant masses would have to be educated of course, but it never occurred to them that this would be a long and arduous process, if not an airy illusion. For the most part they were not interested in the masses: they were more concerned with self-dramatization, with striking heroic attitudes. Many of them were fascinated by conspiracy for its own sake. They were exalted by the Terror, and having sworn 'to liberate their country, to fight tyranny and hate tyrants', the King and Queen in the first place, they felt rather foolish for having achieved so little.

In August 1793, Lauberg organized a meeting of the leading Neapolitan Jacobins on the beach of Mergellina, and plans were discussed for the future. No club was to contain more than eleven members, to ensure strict secrecy. Each was to choose a president, a deputy and a secretary to collect funds. It was all intensely complicated and bureaucratic, and at the end of the meeting the others laid their hats at Lauberg's feet, to show that they had elected him as chief. Medici's police were strangely tolerant. So far, the committee in charge of public safety had only found eight persons guilty of making seditious speeches. After a short term of imprisonment all were released except a Piedmontese priest and a Roman duke, who were banished. A great many suspects, however, were still awaiting trial. It was known that Mackau took every advantage of his position to encourage the rebels, and that he probably had a list of them in his house. On August 29 unknown persons removed a pile of papers from his study, but nothing incriminating was found among them. Mackau protested for the hundredth time; it was rumoured that one of the Queen's agents called Luigi Custode was the culprit, but nothing could be proved against him. In any case, Mackau's mission was ended. On September 1 Acton told him about the treaty with England and urbanely pointed to the article which had been inserted by the King's wish, enabling him to cease hostilities whenever he desired. While this left a loophole for reconciliation, it did not soften the blow. His official note was worded: 'The Court of Naples, no longer able to tolerate the faction which has usurped power in France, has determined to inform M. de Mackau that within a week he must leave the states of His Sicilian Majesty.'

On September 8 Mackau embarked with sixty-eight compatriots on the *Ark*, a British ship which had been chartered for that purpose; he did not reach Marseilles till October 29, after many vicissitudes. By then Marie Antoinette had been executed; the Terror had run amok.

Captain Nelson, in H.M.S. *Agamemnon*, sailed into Naples on September 11 with despatches for Sir William Hamilton. To quote a famous passage from Southey's *Life of Nelson*: 'Sir William, after his first interview with him, told Lady Hamilton he was about to introduce a little man to her who could not boast of being very handsome, but such a man as, he believed, would one day astonish the world. "I have never before," he continued, "entertained an officer at my house; but I am determined to bring him here. Let him be put in the room prepared for Prince Augustus."'

XIV

Naples and the Siege of Toulon—Execution of Marie Antoinette—'Lomo' and 'Romo'—The Giunta di Stato—Jacobin excitement—The thirty-third eruption of Vesuvius—Medici and the Giordano brothers—Public execution of three conspirators—Medici's disgrace—Revolt at Palermo—Political arrests.

Nelson had come to ask for troops to help garrison Toulon, which had been occupied by the British fleet in league with French Royalists and Moderates on August 28. He had only been twice on shore in the last nineteen weeks, during which his men had been without fresh meat and vegetables. 'We are absolutely sick with fatigue,' he wrote. But he was elated by the view of Vesuvius, and even more so by the graciousness of his reception, for at a dinner in the royal palace he was placed on the King's right hand in spite of the presence of the ambassador. Since he could speak only English, Lady Hamilton acted as his interpreter. The King was exceedingly affable and called the British navy the saviours of Italy. Acton, 'whose activity is beyond all expression', as Hamilton wrote, promised to send six thousand troops to Toulon; and Nelson was so pleased with Hamilton's exertions 'that he is said to have exclaimed: "Sir William, you are a man after my own heart!—you do business in my own way"; and then to have added, "I am now only a captain: but I will, if I live, be at the top of the tree."'

Historians have tried to date the origin of Nelson's passion for Lady Hamilton; most agree that it did not begin till five years later. But after the rough celibate life of the *Agamemnon*, the perfumed proximity of this radiant beauty must have had a disturbing effect on his emotions, and her image must have haunted him at sea; he was thirty-five years old. The first dart had flown, and it had ample time to sink into the flesh. Nelson was all prepared to entertain the King on board his ship when he heard from Acton that a French man-of-war and three sail had anchored off Sardinia. Nothing could detain him; at once he set off in pursuit.

'The brief occupation of Toulon by the British fleet,' as G. M. Trevelyan wrote, 'only served to identify the Jacobin cause with that of the nation, and to elicit the genius of Bonaparte, the young captain of artillery.'

The British were joined by seventeen Spanish sail of the line, besides Neapolitan and Sardinian detachments, but the presence of these different nationalities did not contribute towards unity, which the French alone possessed. The French besieged Toulon on the land side and received daily reinforcements. In December Bonaparte stormed Fort Mulgrave, which dominated the harbour. The allied commanders, deciding that it was untenable, towed away or destroyed half the French ships-of-war before the Republicans entered the city on December 19. Nearly 15,000 French Royalists and Moderates escaped with the allied fleet; those who remained were slaughtered with extreme ferocity.

It had been a dismal baptism of fire for the Neapolitan troops, who had been among the last to defend the city walls. The Neapolitan squadron sailed for Spezia, towing the French ship *Gabare* as a trophy full of royalist refugees. The Commander Forteguerri sent a brigantine in quest of missing troops, presuming they had embarked on English ships. Waiting for these and detained by foul weather, the whole squadron did not return to Naples before February 2, 1794. Altogether they had lost six hundred men; two hundred dead and the rest wounded or prisoners, besides horses, provisions and fifteen guns. Distance and imagination magnified their gains as well as their losses, but the episode had been a bitter disappointment, especially for Maria Carolina.

Throughout 1793 the fate of Marie Antoinette had preyed constantly on her mind. She had been prepared for the catastrophe, as her letters to Gallo show. In July she wrote: 'They have taken away my unfortunate sister's son and moved him into the apartments of his late father with a certain Simon, a shoe-maker, and his wife. This blow must have been terrible for my unfortunate sister. I could have wished it to end her life. For a long time I have been wishing her a natural death as the best thing that could happen to her. But Providence has decreed otherwise and we shall have to submit. Certain it is that she is made to suffer all the sharpest pangs, at such intervals as to drain the full bitterness of each. And just when time and resignation seem to have formed a protecting crust, her wounds are torn open again.' In August: 'I am increasingly anxious about the fate of my wretched sister and long for it to be over; my imagination always anticipates reality. I do not know what to hope or fear for her and her family. What I wish is that France could be pulverized with all its inhabitants.'

The news of her execution prostrated her none the less. Pale and weeping, she led her children to the palace chapel, where they repeated her sobbing prayers with tremulous voices. A yearning for vengeance was mingled with her grief, and left a permanent scar on her character. Under a picture of Marie Antoinette in her study she inscribed: *'Je poursuiverai ma vengeance jusqu'au tombeau.'*

As she was in an advanced state of pregnancy, her health was seriously affected by this torrent of emotions. Marchesa Solari, an Englishwoman by birth who had waited on Marie Antoinette, was in Naples at this time and the Queen wished to see her. For a moment Maria Carolina's likeness to her dead sister struck her as so uncanny that she hesitated with a startled air, as if she had seen a ghost. The Queen gave a piercing shriek and, as soon as she could find the words, said hoarsely: 'Good God! Did you ever imagine that the French would treat my sister and her husband so horribly?' Then, as the Marchesa began to reply in French, she continued: 'For God's sake do not, I beseech you, let me hear any more of that murderous language! You speak Italian and German: please address me in either of those languages in future.' But as the Queen grew calmer she relapsed into French from mere force of habit.

In December she gave birth to another princess, and although this event was celebrated in the midst of Court mourning, nothing could relieve her gloom. 'My health is feeble and poor,' she wrote on December 28, 'and I think it will never be otherwise. They talk of sending me to breathe the air of Pozzuoli for some forty days, to strengthen my nerves. But to leave the King, my children and the whole train of business at this time seems to me rather unfair, and I cannot make up my mind, though I am useless in my present condition. To tell you the plain truth, my constitution was already weakened, but these last events have dealt me a blow from which I shall never recover... I should like to establish my children, either in Paradise or in this world... May God chastise the French and grant us soon a lasting general peace... Brigadier Micheroux has arrived with the news that after three days' fighting the cursed French captured all the forts and recovered Toulon. Our men, who embarked with infinite trouble and confusion, are now at Spezia, and they assure me they set fire to the arsenal and the squadron at Toulon...'

Almost four hundred French royalists landed with the Neapolitan squadron, and these were an extra burden on the state. Many found employment, but others needed government support. Their accounts of the Terror did not endear the Republicans to their hosts. Yet at the same time the Neapolitan Jacobins were prating of their passion for liberty. Except for a handful of forgotten Bourbon loyalists, Neapolitan historians have tried to dismiss these as gentle utopians whose only crime was to discuss the French Revolution with their mistresses and barbers. According to Colletta they merely 'praised republics, read the foreign gazettes and copied French fashions of dressing'. In fact, they were militant conspirators who defended the French Terror and revelled vicariously in its ferocity.

While the Court was in mourning for Marie Antoinette, the Neapolitan Jacobins made merry; straining at the leash, they hoped to imitate Robespierre. In February 1794, the 'Patriotic Society', or central club of Jacobins, was split by clashes of opinion between the moderates and extremists; the new clubs were called *Lomo* and *Romo*, from the initials of *Liberta o Morte* and *Repubblica o Morte*. The former wanted liberty under a constitutional monarchy; they did not consider the republican system suitable to the Neapolitan people. The latter were all for a republic, and were led by a demagogue whose slogans appealed strongly to the sailors and *lazzaroni*. This was Andrea Vitaliani, a watchmaker who had learnt no subtlety from his trade.

Though the *Lomo* and *Romo* clubs differed about ends, they agreed about means: both were to co-operate until the revolution was completed. They were to capture the castles, rouse the rabble, burn the arsenal and docks, and massacre the royal family and their ministers in the general confusion. The plot spread to the provinces: March 30 was to be the day of reckoning. Orators began to preach in the most populous parts of the city, money was distributed among the small artisans and the conspirators were ready for action. The arms had been collected, the roles of individuals and groups allotted, their rallying-points determined, the time table, signals, tactics for surprising the castles—all was set.

Neither the police nor the Queen's much-talked-of spies seem to have had an inkling of what was in the air. The Queen herself, still ailing, was on the track of Gorani, who had slandered her viciously. His *Memoirs of European Courts* (1793) are the source of all the scurrilous anecdotes repeated by her enemies. To Gallo she wrote: 'I enclose an extract from an infamous book by a certain Gorani, a Milanese. In this opus he openly incites people to embrace the cause of the revolution. I shall say nothing of his abominable calumnies about the King, and mainly about myself, in the first volume dealing with Naples. The two others deal in similar fashion with the other Princes of Italy. So long as they are limited to personal attacks one can only scorn such filth, but where the matter becomes really dangerous and intolerable is when he urges the people to revolt... Closely connected with Hébert, a member of the infernal Convention, he was warned that he might be guillotined and fled to Geneva. To recover favour he proposed to write memoirs on all the governments and sovereigns of Europe, designed to draw upon them the contempt of their subjects. As a sample he offered the work in question, asking them to pay his printing expenses. The Convention accepted his proposal and allotted him 80,000 francs as a reward. If possible, I should suggest having this Gorani taken to Switzerland. The Emperor could then claim him as one of his subjects, quoting the edict published recently by the Swiss, in which they promise to extradite agitators.' Gorani only avoided being kidnapped by the skin of his teeth. The agitators just round the corner continued unmolested, and grew bolder in anticipation of March 30.

On March 16 the cabinet-maker Vincenzo Vitaliani, the watchmaker Andrea's brother, was walking along the mole with two fellow conspirators, who were joined by a voluble priest. With an eye to increasing their membership they started a political discussion: French victories and efficiency were contrasted with Neapolitan ineptitude and the folly of waging war on so mighty a nation. They went on to speak of the misery of the Neapolitans, governed by a lazy King, a rapacious Englishman and a capricious Austrian female. An acquaintance, Donato Froncillo, joined the group. Hoping to convert him, Vitaliani declared that the time had come for the people to govern themselves. He urged Froncillo to join the party and look out for the signal to rise against the tyrant. Froncillo protested that he was quite satisfied with the present government, had no faith in revolutions and heartily disapproved of the whole idea. Realizing his blunder, Vitaliani lost his temper and proceeded to threaten and insult the stupid reactionary. Friends tried in vain to pacify him: he cursed on.

Vitaliani's words rankled: relieve yourself or burst, as they say in the south. After five days' brooding Froncillo denounced Vitaliani to the chief of police. Medici had already been warned of the plot by Patarini, a priest from Bari, and another source had confirmed it, yet he was still slow to act. His defendants maintain that he was too good-natured to take it seriously. On March 26 he had Vitaliani and several other conspirators arrested and reported the case to the King. By royal decree a Committee of Inquiry under Medici was to conduct an investigation. The civil and military authorities were to arrest all suspects and watch the frontiers and outgoing ships lest any sneaked away. The ringleaders had been allowed to escape, however, except for Annibale Giordano, the teacher of mathematics, who thought himself immune as Medici's protégé. Vincenzo Galiani, who had organized the university students since 1792 and volunteered with three hundred others to capture the forts, got as far as Terracina, but was arrested and sent back.

The Committee of Inquiry brought all that was despicable in the so-called 'patriotic' movement to the surface. At least twenty-seven of the fifty-three prisoners tripped over each other to denounce their comrades and reveal all they knew about the conspiracy. One of them, Doctor De Falco, went so far as to denounce Medici as an accomplice, but this was considered a spiteful fabrication. When the preliminary investigation was over, the prisoners were tried by a special *Giunta di Stato*, or High Court of State, a modern version of the old *Giunta d'Inconfidenza*. It consisted of seven magistrates whose loyalty to the Crown was above reproach, and though it has been compared with the French Committee of Public Safety, which had powers to deliberate in secret over the life and death of citizens, the *Giunta di Stato* of 1794 was strictly fair by contemporary standards.

Such propagandists as Carlo Lauberg and Annibale Giordano had exploited their acquaintance with Medici to persuade faltering converts that he was behind the conspiracy. Most of the clubs were convinced that he was their guardian angel. It was therefore a shock when this amiable chief of police presided over the board of investigation. Giordano, who had lived in his house, continued to assert that his heart was with the accused: he would do his utmost to save them. Certainly it was due to Medici's scrupulous 'respect for procedure' that over two months elapsed before the results of the inquiry were known. As the King complained, 'they dragged it on with the usual formulas, not appreciating the seriousness of the case'.

Andrea Vitaliani, the founder of the *Romo* club, was able to escape because Medici had been too kind to issue a warrant for him so soon after the arrest of his brother. And Medici's influence swayed most of the magistrates. He had known several of the defendants in private life; even so his affability towards them was remarkable. When one of them was acquitted, he took him home in his carriage. 'How do you do, my little Jacobin?' he would ask ('*Giacobiniello mio, come stai?*'). Or he would make signs with his eyes, 'as if he wished him to be silent'. But in spite of his efforts, the Jacobins were hard to help. Their denunciations and confessions had revealed the whole plot, but the evidence was confused by contradictions.

During the inquiry a certain Tommaso Amato rushed into the crowded church of the Carmine on a Sunday morning shouting obscene blasphemies against God and the King, and urging the congregation to revolt against the government. After a struggle he was seized, and in less than three days he was sentenced to the gallows. Relays of priests tried to persuade him to repent; he was exorcised; the Cardinal Archbishop Zurlo in person went to admonish and cajole him. But nothing could stop his torrent of blasphemy. The harassed priests had to acknowledge their failure, yet they persevered. At last he said he wanted to confess, but after a contrite beginning he returned to his ravings. By dint of extraordinary patience one priest managed to soothe him, and in another lucid interval he begged for Holy Communion. But when the priest told him to wait—for he must prepare to receive it in a true spirit of contrition—he got into a rage and said he would spit out the Host and trample it on the ground. 'Such impiety cannot be described without trembling,' adds the recorder. From this moment the wretch grew more obstinate. While denying God, he demanded the death penalty with maniacal persistence, saying he was quite content to go to Hell. The sentence was carried out to the accompaniment of hymns and orisons, after which his tongue was torn out with pincers, his corpse was burnt and the ashes were scattered. A few days later the governor of Messina sent word that the man had escaped from a mad-house in that city. His brain had been addled by Jacobin talk, and he was the first victim of the panic created by the conspiracy.

There was another scare on May 26, 1794, when some deserters from the camp at Sessa having plundered some houses, the peasants thought they were French and the alarm bell was rung accordingly from village to village. 'The report soon arrived in Naples, and until the truth was known caused the utmost confusion at the palace,' wrote Hamilton; 'however, it has shown how much the French are detested by the people of this country, for thousands turned out immediately, surrounded the palace with every sort of weapon they could meet with, and declared they would lose the last drop of their blood in defence of their religion and sovereigns.' The panic was increased by the thirty-third eruption of Vesuvius in the middle of June. On the night of the 12th a violent earthquake shook the capital, accompanied by a hollow rumbling. The inhabitants of the suburbs fled from their homes and spent the next three days in the open air. Three more earthquakes followed, a dense cloud over the volcano darkened the sky, and the noise of rumbling increased. 'A very smart shock took place in the evening of the 15th and, immediately afterwards, the mountain burst open... Lava in great quantities instantly boiled out with a noise like the discharge of heavy guns, and rolled down the mountain in copious waves with great velocity towards Resina, but suddenly turned and rushed upon Torre del Greco, overwhelming four-fifths of the town and flowing 650 feet into the sea, having passed a distance of 6,000 yards in the short space of eight hours. On the 19th a discharge of ashes, greater than had yet occurred, took place; a portion of the southern and western edge of the crater having fallen in during the night, lowering the summit of the mountain in that part about a ninth of its whole height above the sea. Quantities of ashes fell in Naples and the neighbourhood.'

The subterranean sounds, the sensations of the earth undulating and splitting, the pervading darkness and gloom, the fiery columns rising and falling down the mountain, the zigzag flashes of lightning and balls of fire hurled into the distance, the succession of flames from the crater, the vineyards consumed and houses engulfed by molten lava, and then the black shower of ashes for many miles around, had an apocalyptic effect on the people. Instinctively they turned to religion for consolation. Bare-footed processions tramped the streets in penitential garb, with halters round their necks, wailing lugubriously, and in their midst the Cardinal Archbishop and all the clergy followed the golden statue of

San Gennaro and the phials of his blood, which were carried as far as the Maddalena bridge, where another statue of the saint commands the volcano to be still. At the bridge they paused, and turning the golden statue towards the flaming mountain, invoked the mercy of God. Night could only be distinguished from day by the ringing of the church bells. When Vesuvius was visible again, it had lost its summit; Mount Somma soared above it.

Bands of robbers flocked like vultures to Torre del Greco and the stricken towns, adding to the general misfortune. Thirty-three men and two thousand four hundred animals had perished. The royal family and Acton were all at the military camp in the plain of Sessa to encourage the army's manoeuvres. Help was immediately organized for the victims of the eruption and, as Colletta wrote: 'While the ground was still warm, a new city rose upon the ruins, house upon house, street upon street, and church upon church.' Nothing could weaken these people's attachment to their treacherous native soil.

The trial of the conspirators dragged on, and volume after volume of evidence against them was slowly compiled: eventually there were 124 of these. Medici's intimacy with Annibale and Michele Giordano compromised his reputation when it became clear how deeply they were involved. Why had he not warned them to escape like Lauberg and the other leaders? The fact that he ordered their arrest has been considered the best proof that he believed in their innocence. But as chief of police he could not tear up the denunciations against them. Since they were clients of his in the old feudal sense—they had been born and bred in his family fief of Ottaiano, where their father was the local physician—they considered themselves immune. Both had lived under his roof and been treated like members of his family. He had confided in them, airing his grievances and aspirations, ridiculing Acton and the Court, and discussing state affairs as if they were in the Cabinet. He had introduced them to disgruntled aristocrats who shared his views. A couple of ambitious young provincials were bound to be excited by such an atmosphere. In theory Medici was on their side. But they were not content with theory; since the visit of Admiral Latouche they became eager for practice.

Annibale seems to have been the favourite, a Balzac hero in embryo, and one can only conclude that his imagination ran away with him. He misinterpreted Medici's sympathy, and came to believe that he was his intermediary with the Jacobin clubs. Medici must have known that Annibale had been active as a revolutionary propagandist, yet he had never remonstrated with him. A special service kept him informed about events in France four days before the gazettes arrived. Annibale exploited this advance information among the educated converts, while his brother Michele cajoled the illiterate with bribes in Medici's name.

Gradually the Giordano brothers had built up a legend about their patron. His tacit encouragement persuaded them that he was aware of the conspiracy. They were so sure of themselves and of their mentor that their arrest was a double shock. Medici instantly summoned their father from Ottaiano to urge them to write an affidavit which would secure their freedom. He drafted it himself, a tissue of fact and fantasy, exculpating them from the most serious charges. Old Doctor Giordano had but one idea: to save his sons at all costs. He could not forgive Medici for arresting them, and he held him responsible for their fate. Medici tried to soothe his anxieties: after they had signed the affidavit he would see that all would end well. But the indignant parent thought that Medici should have exerted himself more strenuously on their behalf.

In the meantime everything was done to mitigate their captivity. They were moved into better rooms, and supplied with wholesome food and other comforts by Medici's valet. But as the months wore on their self-confidence waned, and as the evidence piled up against them Medici grew more embarrassed. In August he arranged for them to be transferred to the Castel dell' Ovo, from which it would be easier to escape. On the night of September 3 they climbed down the nearest wall by means of knotted sheets and jumped into the sea. There can be little doubt that Medici connived at this plan; later it was alleged that he had promised Annibale a liberal reward if he succeeded. But it was Michele who swam to a boat and rowed to safety; Annibale hurt himself in falling so that he was captured by one of the guards.

This failure drew attention to one who, in any case, had received preferential treatment. He was shut up in the castle dungeon, and when he was tried on October 3, he was prominent among those for whom the Public Prosecutor demanded the death penalty. He was found guilty of making a false deposition and of attempted escape. Owing to Medici's influence, he was sentenced to life deportation on the island of Pantelleria, which was commuted to the castle of Aquila. Even so Medici dared not face Annibale's father; he asked his own mother and sister to break the news to the old doctor. To console him they said that the French would arrive within a couple of months; if not, his son would find a way of escape. But Doctor Giordano refused to be consoled. He blamed Medici for his family misfortunes. He had given them his moral support, supplied them with revolutionary literature and introduced them to 'fellow travellers' too clever to be snared. Why should Annibale rot in prison while Medici sat among the judges? Father and son both meditated revenge.

The verdict of the High Court has been attacked in chorus by anti-Bourbon writers, but only three of the accused were condemned to death; two were acquitted and the rest were imprisoned or exiled. The three condemned, Emmanuele De Deo, Vincenzo Vitaliani and Vincenzo Galiani, have been portrayed as patriotic martyrs. They were all young, but old enough to be responsible for their actions. Galiani was one of the most garrulous denouncers of his comrades; Vitaliani's rashness had betrayed the conspiracy; only De Deo behaved with dignity throughout his trial, silent and proud to the end. There is probably no truth in the story that the Queen promised to procure his pardon if he revealed other conspirators. Writing to Gallo with her usual frankness, the Queen declared: 'I have done everything possible to obtain the King's pardon but in vain. He has always replied to me: "If they only wanted to take my life and wipe out my family, I might easily have pardoned them, but I cannot forgive their oath to destroy religion, the government and the state. It is our magistrates who have condemned them unanimously, and I owe it to the state and to the public safety to execute them." I suffer for it, but I cannot blame him. I think that even the magistrates have been very arbitrary in saving a great number of them.'

The three young men went to the gallows with Christian resignation. While their fate was lamentable, we must bear in mind the verdicts of the French Revolutionary Tribunal of which they and their accomplices had approved. Between April 6 and July 28, 1793, it sent 2,625 persons to the scaffold: during that period 80 per cent. of those accused before it were sentenced to death. The *Giunta di Stato*, which Cuoco called the Tribunal of Blood, only sentenced three persons, and the Jacobins spread a rumour that 50,000 armed 'patriots' were ready to raise an insurrection to save their lives. Anonymous letters threatened the public prosecutor, Palmieri, with poison and the guillotine. But the Largo del Castello, now Piazza del Municipio, was well guarded and the execution was orderly, with a vast crowd in attendance. In the hush that followed a horse took fright and a musket shot was heard, nobody knew from whence. Suddenly there was a frantic stampede in all directions. More shots were fired at random by the patrol, leaving six dead and thirty-five wounded. Shoes, buckles, hats, wigs and fragments of clothing soon littered the deserted square. Medici remarked that the Neapolitans never had a better chance of starting a revolution than on this day, but that they had missed it because they were incapable of decision.

He continued to insist on the harmlessness of the Neapolitan Jacobins, but their conspiracy against the Crown had been proved, and it had been hatched behind his back. The question arose: had he turned his back to oblige them?

Medici had made so much political capital out of the Latouche episode, for which he blamed Acton, that it had looked as if he might become the next Prime Minister. He had been championed by his sister, the Marchesa di San Marco, and by his friend the Prince of Caramanico, the Viceroy of Sicily, who could never forgive Acton for replacing him in the Queen's favour. But now the tables were turned: the Queen began to consider Medici more dangerous than useful. 'I cannot express to you', she wrote from Caserta to Gallo in September, 'what a relief it is to be far from the capital, especially from the Court... which was a *café* of the blackest and most atrocious slander.'

Acton was convinced that Medici had been intriguing with the Jacobins. He conducted a personal investigation, and found that the plot had been far more extensive than he had suspected. Desperate at the prospect of life imprisonment, Annibale Giordano diverted his resentment towards his former patron. He composed another detailed indictment in which he accused Medici of ordering him to create a Jacobin organization, of secret correspondence with the King's enemies, of urging Latouche to declare war, promising the support of his friends, and of consigning to him the plans of the fortifications interlarding these statements with authentic state secrets which he had heard as a guest in Medici's house. Doctor Giordano, even more embittered because he believed that Medici had used his son as a scapegoat, went to Acton and told him all he knew and imagined about his subversive intrigues. There was no dearth of material. Appearances were against the chief of police, even if he was innocent. On January 24, 1795, the Queen wrote to Gallo: 'We are on the verge of discovering a Jacobin plot and of imprisoning the leaders. This is good for our safety, but it is painful to see such falseness and ingratitude, bringing sorrow to so many families. Already the idea makes me ill.'

As soon as Medici was forbidden access to the royal palace he sent a memorial to the King and Queen, asking to be relieved of his duties and confined in a fortress until his innocence was proved. On February 28 the Queen wrote: 'Last Wednesday a great Council of State of eleven members was held: the four secretaries, Vasto, Gravina, Migliano, Cardinal Ruffo, Pignatelli, the King and myself. It lasted from eight o'clock in the morning till eleven at night with only one interruption of an hour and a half. All the wretched papers received from outside as well as from inside were read, in fact all that concerns the accursed Jacobin sect. When these had been discussed it was decided to imprison, provisionally at Gaeta, the Regent of the Vicaria, Don Luigi Medici, and dismiss him from his posts, as well as Giuseppe Daniele, Nicola Fasulo, Father Caputo and several lesser men. It is a light beginning, but they will have to increase the number and I admit this makes me very unhappy...'

A new *Giunta di Stato* was formed, of which Marchese Carlo Vanni, a fanatical royalist, was the leading spirit. Vanni declared that the whole kingdom was riddled with Jacobins; he felt sure of Medici's guilt. The Prince of Caramanico, Viceroy of Sicily, had died suddenly in January; some said that he had committed suicide because he was involved in the conspiracy, others that he had been poisoned at the instigation of Acton. He was known to have shared Medici's opinions, and his death at this juncture seemed to confirm the suspicions against him. Subsequently a young naval lieutenant returning from France after two years as a prisoner of war, reported that the French had regretted Caramanico, but had shown little sympathy for Medici, whom they considered weak and vacillating.

Michele Rossi, who wrote the most scholarly analysis of the events preceding the republic of 1799, has defined Medici's character as a combination of instability with a highly exaggerated notion of his own merits, and such boundless ambition that he could not bear anybody being placed above him. 'To dominate was his whole purpose. He served the monarchy with the same indifference as he would have served a republic, and his own country no better than the Chinese Empire. He flattered himself that he was shrewd, but he only succeeded in deceiving himself and the few who trusted him.'

It was three and a half years before he could be acquitted with the help of a forged document. Besides Giordano's denunciation, signed by nearly all those who had been arrested, Acton produced an intercepted letter from Tilly, the French minister in Genoa, to Medici. Tilly deplored the severity of the Neapolitan government and begged the chief of police to take pity on the political prisoners and alleviate their distress. He assured him that 'times would change and that the impetus of the revolution was irresistible'. The tone of this letter was confidential and helped to support allegations that Medici had been corresponding with the enemy. The Marchesa di San Marco arranged with Trequatrini, one of the High Court advocates, to have an obvious forgery substituted during the trial. All paper manufactured in Naples had a watermark with a date which was visible when held against the light. Trequatrini pointed triumphantly to this 1795 watermark, and said it was improbable that a letter from Genoa should have been written on Neapolitan paper. It was examined by experts and declared to be spurious.

Medici's disgrace was attributed to Acton. To gloss over his indiscretions, he posed as the victim of an unscrupulous Englishman. Being a Neapolitan, whose geniality contrasted with Acton's cold reserve, he was readily believed by most of his compatriots. But the destruction of Tilly's letter is significant. Acton had merely performed his duty; cautious at all times, his behaviour was logical. A chief of police who had allowed seditious societies to flourish and the ringleaders of a vast conspiracy to escape was incompetent, to say the least. His relations with Annibale Giordano could not be lightly dismissed. The Prime Minister had to lay all the evidence before the King and Queen. It is therefore unjust to accuse him of sacrificing an innocent man to his personal ambition. After so many years of uninterrupted power, he had little to fear from the petty intrigues of a Medici. His own position was not easy to assail just because he was an Englishman. Michele Rossi, who underrated his abilities, was not far wrong when he wrote that much of his credit was due to the Anglomania with which he had injected the King and Queen, so that the prestige of England became greater than that of Austria at Naples. His compatriots did not always appreciate this; some even complained of his lack of zeal, forgetting that as Prime Minister he could not sacrifice Neapolitan interests to his private feelings, though he tried to balance them. He had always lived on the continent: his mother was French; after Tuscany, Naples had become his land of adoption; as a Roman Catholic he could not hold a British commission, yet he was English to the backbone. Therein lay his secret strength. This consciousness gave him an armour difficult to pierce. He was more concerned with the war against France than with local conspirators. Heartily sick of plots and counter plots, and of what would now be called the 'smearing campaign' of the Medici clique, his health at a low ebb, he wished to resign and retire to his estate in Shropshire. Few believed that this wish was sincere. The King insisted upon his remaining to superintend affairs in the Cabinet.

The Queen could only think of summoning Gallo from Vienna. Having lived far from this turmoil, he might bring a more dispassionate point of view to cope with the present crisis. Besides, he had the virtue of being Neapolitan. 'Your coming,' she wrote on March 4, 'your elevation to the highest posts decided by the King, are no longer a secret and are the topic of general conversation, as usual in this country... Heaven will help you. Acton, as an upright man who sincerely wishes to promote our welfare, will assist you with all his experience, will acquaint you with all the facts, and will ease your difficult task. His desire, which is also mine, would be to leave immediately for eight months or a year to prove to this ungrateful country that he did not seek undue influence; even had he sought it he could not have gained it. But on the one hand it is impossible to obtain the King's consent, and on the other he believes that his honour is at stake, that he would be considered a coward if he retired in the midst of the war. Therefore he will remain to fight on land or sea because he is less apprehensive of cannon fire and its effects than of continual injustices and calumnies. As soon as the war is over he will ask the King for leave of absence, which is necessary to his health and private affairs.'

But even the promise of rich remuneration could not lure the wily Gallo into this wasps' nest. He was far too comfortable in Vienna, so he procrastinated with a thousand pretexts. In the meantime Annibale Giordano denounced 259 persons of treasonable activities, and on March 5 an edict promised free pardons to those who confessed that they had been 'seduced', revealing their seducers and accomplices. Thirty-four stepped forward with further denunciations, and 113 were accused of taking part in last year's conspiracy. A large proportion of these belonged to the aristocracy. Among the denouncers were the republican bard Jerocades and the two brothers Ferdinando and Mario Pignatelli di Strongoli, who took advantage of their indemnity to escape with 30,000 ducats. These were to return to Naples with the French army under Championnet and 'wipe out their shame with blood' in 1799.

Another conspiracy was nipped in the bud at Palermo. A lawyer, De Blasi, had tried to exploit popular discontent on account of a bad harvest and taxation to overturn the government. 'The discovery was miraculous,' wrote the Queen to Gallo, 'in my opinion it was far more dangerous in Sicily, for there it might have succeeded and become established. Here there is never more than a massacre or pillage. Either one escapes a massacre and it comes to nothing, or else one is its victim and one's sufferings are over. I consider that the business in Sicily required great attention. Until now it seems that their nobility has not been implicated, but here it is the most depraved and vicious class, which wants a King without strength or authority, without power or rights, a mere doll, in order to shine with borrowed lustre, and curry favour with its inferiors. If they are slightly thwarted they become vipers. The worst are the lawyers, the corrupted young students and soldiers; the people are good; the class which comes in contact with the nobles (servants, etc.) bears their stamp. That is the real truth as you will find it... Acton, the unfortunate Acton, awaits you like the Messiah. He will do his best to help you... I am and shall always be attached to him till I die.'

After a brief exile from Court, the Marchesa di San Marco had returned to favour. Her party gained strength and volubility, protesting that Medici was innocent, the victim of a jealous autocrat. Acton was about to resign in disgust when Giovanni Caviglia appeared on the scene with fresh revelations. These led to further arrests, confessions and indictments, liberally besprinkled with Medici's name. Caviglia was a Ligurian ship's pilot who had met Antonio Belpulsi and other Neapolitan revolutionaries in Genoa and knew of their dealings with General Masséna and various French agents. He was to have smuggled a shipload of munitions into Naples with a crew of exiles, including Andrea Vitaliani; instead he thought it more profitable to turn informer. All this added fuel to the official inquiry. The Jacobins dreaded discovery, the Royalists assassination. 'I go nowhere without wondering if I shall return alive,' wrote the Queen. Among other precautions, the bedrooms of the King and Queen were frequently changed and their diet was strictly supervised. Acton was implored to stay at his post.

The political structure was modified, with Acton placed above the secretaries of state as Grand Chancellor. When Gallo finally arrived, expecting to be greeted as a man of destiny, he was merely invited to collaborate with Acton. The alternative of serving under Acton or of leading the opposition did not appeal to him. He was too subtle to accept the invitation. After a month's visit, during which the Emperor made repeated demands for his recall, he went back to Vienna sadder but richer, with a gratification of six thousand ducats.

Prince Castelcicala was appointed Minister of Foreign Affairs and General Manuel y Arriola Minister for War. Castelcicala has been described as the 'double' of Acton, whose passions and prejudices he shared. He was as pro-British as he was anti-French; and he had felt perfectly at home as ambassador in London, which he had been reluctant to leave. 'Not a word or gesture,' it was said, 'betrayed his real feelings.' A single-minded monarchist, more rigid than Acton, he despised Medici whose seat he now occupied on the reformed Committee of Inquiry. He had no patience with disaffected members of his class; their ancestry meant nothing to him if they were traitors to the King. Among those to be arrested were Ettore Carafa, Count of Ruvo, the Duke of Andria's eldest son; Gaetano Coppola, son of the Duke of Canzano; Giuliano Colonna, youngest son of the Prince of Stigliano; Gennaro Serra, third son of the Duke of Cassano; and Giuseppe Riario, sixth son of the Marquis of Corleto. Even the Queen, who was attached to his mother, her chief lady-in-waiting, could not save the young Count of Ruvo from arrest. Eventually he escaped from Sant' Elmo by bribing his guards, and joined the French army in the north.

'This infamous revolution has made me cruel,' wrote the Queen, yet as if to contradict this she continued: 'Recently I saved a whole club where many of the nobility spat upon, reviled and finally pierced my portrait with knives, inciting each other to repeat these gestures to the original... Personally I scorn the madness of these people, but when it rages against their King—and what a

King!—an affectionate father, devoted to them, just and good, such as they do not deserve, I cannot forgive them for it.' The Royal Bodyguard, which consisted entirely of nobles, had to be reformed, since it had been infected by revolutionary ideas. From now on it was called the Royal Corps of Guards, and its 248 officers were carefully selected from other regiments to protect the King and his family. The Marchesa di San Marco was banished again, 'for reasons of economy, I think,' wrote the Queen, 'lest she win me over, but they are mistaken... I know Medici better than they suppose, and even if all the tribunals declared him innocent he would not be so in my opinion. For *I know him*. But he will not lose his life, only his liberty.'

XV

Spain and France—Bonaparte and the Army of Italy—Belmonte's negotiations with Bonaparte—Armistice of June 5, 1796—Peace treaty of October 10—Treaty of Tolentino, 1797—Leoben—The Queen's rift with Acton—Prince Augustus Frederick—Marriage of the Hereditary Prince—The Queen's opinion of Bonaparte.

Disillusioned by the republican recapture of Toulon, worried by republican conspirators at home, King Ferdinand would have preferred to stand by and watch the course of events from one of his hunting lodges had not the Queen persisted in goading him on. 'I must leave for one whole day at Carditello,' she wrote wearily to Lady Hamilton. This was one of the King's favourite resorts, where wild boars and stags abounded. 'My health and fragile physique do not relish these long excursions, but one must obey...'

By feigning an interest in her husband's amusements, she kept her influence over him. Left alone, he might have turned neutral, for he resented the cost of increased mobilization and regretted the loss of his remunerative trade with France. He had tried secret negotiations through his resident in Venice, Micheroux, who had met the French minister Lallement in a secluded garden to discuss restoring the *status quo*. But the Queen had got wind of this, and frightened him with Austrian and British reprisals unless the negotiations were dropped. Micheroux was not punished, but his secretary was dismissed. To compensate for this lapse, the King sent four of his best cavalry regiments to join the Austrians in Lombardy. The *Tancredi*, a ship of seventy-four cannon under the command of Francesco Caracciolo, and the *Pallas* and *Minerva*, frigates of forty guns, were sent to support Vice-Admiral Hotham's blockade of French ports.

Thanks to the adroit Gallo, the Court of Austria understood Ferdinand's difficulties; he had to defend himself from treachery at home as well as from the danger of French invasion. That danger drew nearer when, without warning, his brother the King of Spain made peace with France on July 22, 1795. Two days before this peace was signed, Charles IV had mentioned it in a letter to Ferdinand as a remote contingency, and his gigolo minister Godoy had been superciliously cool to the Neapolitan ambassador Belmonte when he demanded an explanation.

By one article in the treaty the French Republic accepted Spanish mediation with the Two Sicilies: what were His Catholic Majesty's intentions? Godoy replied that Charles would enter into further details as soon as his brother was ready to be reconciled with France; he had offered to mediate in a purely friendly spirit. Spain was peeved with Naples for keeping on good terms with England. On October 6 Belmonte was recalled to Naples, and Godoy told him that Ferdinand's rejection of Spanish mediation had offended his brother, who saw this as a British manoeuvre. As for himself, in spite of political differences he wished to preserve Bourbon harmony, but Belmonte doubted his sincerity. This treaty, which was to subordinate Catholic and monarchist Spain to revolutionary France, was regarded as a triumph by the fatuous Charles IV and Maria Luisa. Manuel Godoy was now created Prince of the Peace. 'They have created him the god Janus,' wrote Maria Carolina, 'allowing him an equerry on horseback and on foot who always precede him with a hat bearing the arms of Aragon and other follies of the kind... In fact, it seems that these sovereigns are doing everything possible to dishonour themselves, and all this will end badly.'

Consequently Ferdinand was drawn closer to his son-in-law of Austria, who was appealing to him for more military aid. The Emperor's brother, the Grand Duke Ferdinand III of Tuscany, had been the first sovereign to recognize the French Republic. Although the Emperor had asked him—and this was practically a command —to admit Neapolitan troops in Tuscany 'to succour the common cause of Italy, and especially of Lombardy', the Grand Duke had refused—a refusal most gratifying to France.

As soon as peace with Spain was settled, Bonaparte urged the Directory to reinforce the Army of Italy, and at the end of March 1796 he arrived at Nice to take command of it. His harangue to the troops is memorable, for the Italian Jacobins overlooked the fact that he came as a conqueror: 'Soldiers, you are starving and in rags. Government is in arrears with your pay and has nothing to give you. Your patience and your courage amidst these rocks are admirable, but they bring you no fame: no ray of glory shines upon you. I am about to lead you into the most fertile plains in the world; fruitful provinces and large cities will soon lie at your mercy; there you will find honour, profit and wealth. Soldiers of Italy, have you the needful courage and perseverance?' Fertile, fruitful, large; honour, profit, wealth: these simple adjectives and nouns went straight to the solar plexus. No republican catchwords here; these were held in reserve for his Italian dupes. The prospect of wealth above all, of infinite facilities for plunder, appealed to his ragged *sans-culottes*. The treasures of Italian art were to enhance the prestige of the Directors in Paris, whose commissioners followed the army collecting spoils.

The speed of Bonaparte's conquest is startling even today. Within a month he had forced the King of Sardinia to hand over his strongest fortresses and surrender Nice and Savoy. Next he overran Lombardy, and granted armistices to the Dukes of Parma and Modena for exorbitant ransoms. The Directors wished to divide the Italian command: while General Kellermann milked the Milanese, Bonaparte was to march against Tuscany and Rome, 'in order to chase the perfidious English, so long masters of the Mediterranean, from Central Italy'. But Bonaparte insisted on having his own way, and the arguments of so triumphant a general were unanswerable. The liquidation of the Austrians came first; Leghorn and Rome could wait.

In Naples Ferdinand exhorted his people to resist: 'Our holy Religion, the State and the Throne are in danger; they require defence and defenders. Ready to spill our blood and perish for our subjects, we expect them to reciprocate.' A new crusade was preached from pulpits and public squares. The whole Court attended a three days' ceremony in the cathedral, where the King invoked God's aid in a loud voice and the multitude wept and cheered with frantic emotion. In the last few months the army had been increased by more than a third. Volunteers were so eager to join it that the Jacobins were disconcerted. Young Prince Leopold was appointed Commander of the Royal Corps of Nobles, four hundred cavalry volunteers between the ages of sixteen and forty-five who provided their own mounts. These were a gallant sight on parade in their white uniforms with blue velvet borders, plumes aflutter, like the paladins of Tasso come to life. Their morale was high, for the Neapolitan cavalry had done well at the battle of Lodi, rallying again and again when they were outflanked and outnumbered. But the Queen, who had a touching faith in the Austrian army, was alarmed by the news of its consecutive defeats. If Spain became France's ally, the British fleet would be dwarfed in the Mediterranean.

The King realized that he had better make terms with the enemy while his forces were still intact. He continued to prepare for war: at the same time he ordered the Prince of Belmonte to meet Bonaparte wherever he could find him and sue for peace. On May 17, when Belmonte received these instructions, the Queen wrote to Gallo: 'Only the absolute necessity of avoiding pillage and devastation could make us swallow the ignominy of peace with those monsters. We are arming ourselves for defence with all our might, but Italy, little experienced in arms, believes this enemy invincible, and it will be difficult to mobilize her for the task. Every means will be employed, money, religion, promises and personalities, with the King at their head. Finally God will help us. But the moment is very critical owing to the enemy without and within. All the letters we receive are full of fear and bewilderment. We have begun our *Triduum* in all the churches, and yesterday we went to the cathedral. More than twenty thousand *lazzaroni* accompanied us, shouting: "Long live the King! Long live our Holy Faith! We are ready to die for it." But only the populace expresses these sentiments. The nobility maintains a complete silence.'

Belmonte went to Florence to see Miot, the French representative there, who had the reputation of being moderate. Miot understood the advantages of an armistice with Naples: he hoped it would close the ports to the British and separate the Neapolitan cavalry regiments from the Austrian army. He promised to support Belmonte's proposals. A strenuous hunt for Bonaparte ensued. The few available horses were exhausted; the French had seized the rest. Belmonte's carriage broke down outside Modena, and he was slightly injured. On May 27 he reached Piacenza, where he heard that the French headquarters were not at Cremona, as he had been told, but at Crema in the Veneto. Off he went to Crema, arriving the next morning, but Bonaparte had already left for Brescia. Belmonte ran after him, but only found some of his staff; the General had joined his vanguard at Borghetto. To save time, Belmonte left his carriage at Brescia and drove on in a sort of gig towards Calcinato, where the headquarters had been transferred. He arrived the same morning and asked for Bonaparte, but he was with his outposts and Belmonte was not allowed to proceed. As he had to remain incognito he could only wait all day and night, when he heard that the Neapolitan cavalry had suffered heavy losses after covering the Austrian retreat. Their brave commander, the Prince of Cutò, had been wounded and taken prisoner. The French headquarters were moved to Valeggio, two miles beyond Borghetto, and Belmonte followed through battlefields strewn with corpses. But Bonaparte was hotly pursuing the Austrians northwards up the valley of the Adige. As the French had consumed all provisions, Belmonte and his courier could not even find any bread. May 31, as he wrote, was a day of fasting. That afternoon he heard of other French successes: they had occupied Peschiera and crossed the Adige. The small French garrison at Pavia, however, had been overpowered by the local peasants, and the French had returned to sack the city, shoot its chief citizens, send two hundred hostages to France, and burn the whole village of Binasco. A swarm of these peasants had robbed the Spanish minister Azara on his way to Milan; they would have killed him if a detachment of French dragoons had not come to his rescue.

At last, after many hardships, Belmonte was able to meet Bonaparte on June 1; he had been waiting more than two hours when he was ushered into the General's room at nine o'clock in the morning. Bonaparte received him with an air of polite superiority, but Belmonte held his own in the long discussion which followed. He pointed out that his King was in a different position from the King of Sardinia or the Dukes of Parma and Modena—'he would sooner perish sword in hand, supported by his troops and faithful subjects, than consent to a dishonourable peace'. Besides, would it not be an advantage for the French to have four regiments less fighting against them?

'This might be an advantage if the Austrian army were still on the plains of Lombardy,' Bonaparte replied. 'But the Austrians have been forced to withdraw among the mountains, where I keep them blockaded. Cavalry is useless among the mountains.' Spreading a map of Italy, he delivered a glowing lecture on his military situation. 'My army is twice as strong as the Austrian; it is victorious and full of courage... The Austrians are confused and demoralized, they have an incompetent General, they flee whenever they meet us... Beaulieu has hardly eighteen thousand troops capable of fighting. I know he expects seven battalions to reinforce him, but I am credibly informed that they will not arrive yet, or even collectively. Moreover, I am expecting Kellermann's army of twenty-five thousand strong at any moment, all fresh troops, whose vanguard of three thousand is already in Milan; the rest are on the march. I am expecting other troops from Nice. Within a few days I shall have more than eighty thousand fighting men ready for service, excluding the garrisons of fortified towns. These are not gasconades, but well-known facts. I shall leave half this force to oppose the Austrians and besiege Mantua; with the rest I shall march to Rome without opposition. I am aware that the King of Naples has gathered about twenty thousand troops on his frontiers. But I shall bring three times more, and all victorious, hardened by five campaigns. I know that another forty thousand militia, volunteers, etc., are being levied in the kingdom of Naples, but how can such people be relied upon, especially in a country which has been on the verge of revolution for the last three years? Believe me, sir, in three weeks' time I shall be at Bologna, in a month perhaps at Rome. Now when I get there, will the King of Naples risk everything in a battle?'

Belmonte retorted with an ironical smile: 'This picture of yours, General, is easier to describe than to verify. During this military walk you may meet more obstacles than you suppose. The King still has troops intact and subjects ready to give their blood for him... and you should know that war is a game in which the person who thinks he holds the best cards may lose the round. Your colleagues on the Rhine have experienced this; and the same might happen in Italy.'

But Belmonte's eloquence was drowned by the facts which Bonaparte poured over him: 'I agree that the fortunes of war are always uncertain, but let us examine things a little closer. If I lose a battle against Neapolitan troops in the Roman State or on the frontiers of your kingdom, France would only incur the sacrifice of a few thousand soldiers. I should then fall back on Lombardy or Piedmont where I should have nothing to fear; I should promptly find reinforcements and all I require, and in a few days repair my loss. But if the King of Naples loses a battle... he will probably lose his states. Is there not a vast difference between his risk and mine?' After a spate of cogent arguments, threatening harder conditions unless he arranged an armistice immediately, Bonaparte wound up: 'Your Court could have made an advantageous and honourable peace six months ago, and perhaps as late as March, before we entered Piedmont. It has missed that opportunity. Today there is still time to make a respectable one, but not without sacrifice. If you wait, and if you do not send a negotiator to Paris at once, you will make a worse one, as a difference of fifteen or twenty days might involve considerable changes. Your government must open its eyes to the true state of affairs and to its actual situation. It can no longer treat with France on terms of equality. The immense superiority acquired by France has destroyed this equality, and you will have to conform to it.'

Belmonte replied with dignity: 'General, I shall never make any sacrifice on behalf of my Court to obtain the armistice, nor have I the authority even if I desired it. Besides, I cannot go to Paris... All you have been saying does not alarm me, and it will not alarm my Court... I repeat it is resolved to perish rather than dishonour itself. This is my last word.'

Bonaparte pondered, then took out his watch and said: 'We have been talking for four hours: it is one o'clock past midday. Let us go to dinner, and return to our conference later.'

Belmonte's calm had saved the armistice, point by point of which was chiselled during the afternoon. It became obvious that Bonaparte thought he would get better terms after winning more victories, so Belmonte repressed his eagerness, especially when he proposed expelling the French refugees and closing the ports to the British. 'What! In a mere suspension of hostilities to raise claims which would even be inadmissible in the final peace treaty! We are to expel the refugees while you drag a horde of our conspirators along with your army?... How can these be compared with the honest, unhappy victims of loyalty to their own Sovereign, and to a constitution which has ruled France for fourteen centuries!'

Bonaparte replied that this would have to be thrashed out during the peace negotiations, the conditions of which would be the following: first, to renounce alliance with Great Britain; second, to close the ports to British ships of war; third, to supply the French army with provisions and hemp; fourth, to expel all the *émigrés*; fifth, to arrange a commercial treaty wherein France would be treated as the most-favoured nation.

The discussion continued all afternoon, Belmonte insisting again that there was no question of his Court 'capitulating'. Bonaparte arranged to meet him at Brescia, where the armistice was signed on June 5. Hostilities between France and Naples were to cease from the day when the four Neapolitan cavalry regiments were detached from the Austrian army; all the ships fighting with the British were to be sent back to Naples. In sending a signed copy to Naples, Belmonte said he hoped that the King would approve, 'as it was the only armistice concluded until now, in which there was no positive sacrifice of interests or decorum; he had obtained the primary object of checking the invasion by these new Goths or Vandals'. In his announcement to the Directory, Bonaparte congratulated himself on having detached another member from the Coalition.

Mantua contained the last Austrians left in Italy: General Beaulieu had at least prepared it for a long siege. Another septuagenarian, Marshal Wurmser, was to replace the vanquished commander. Before he could move, Bonaparte attacked Leghorn in spite of Tuscany's neutrality; having confiscated British merchandise there, he occupied the Roman Legations of Bologna and Ferrara. Pope Pius VI begged the Spanish minister Azara to mediate with the twenty-seven-year-old General. Bonaparte granted a truce on condition that he paid a sum of twenty-one million francs, besides the thirteen millions which his soldiers had levied from the occupied cities, and surrendered five hundred manuscripts and one hundred works of art to be selected by French commissioners. The French were to garrison the Citadel of Ancona.

After conferring with Gallo and Barthélemy at Basle, where there was some indefinite talk of Austria signing peace, Belmonte went on to Paris, arriving on July 27. His negotiations with the Directory were tightened or relaxed according to the shifting military situation. Hope revived in Rome and Naples when Wurmser started his offensive on July 29. His advance was rapid, but so was his retreat. Within a week he had lost some 17,000 men. Cacault, the French envoy to Rome, irritated Bonaparte against the Neapolitan Court by repeating rumours not wholly without foundation. Anticipating a French reverse, he said, 30,000 Neapolitan troops were ready to invade the Papal States, recapture Leghorn, march to Ferrara, and relieve the garrison at Mantua, having received a subsidy from England. In fact only 2,000 Neapolitan troops had occupied Pontecorvo as a precaution. 'We need a more powerful protector here than Saint Peter and Saint Paul,' he wrote to Bonaparte. 'It will be a rare joke; at the same time you are general of the Holy See and of the French Republic.' He even wrote to Acton saying he was sure that Naples would break the armistice as soon as the Austrians won a victory. Bonaparte vented his spleen to the Directory on August 26: 'The English have persuaded the King of Naples that he is something. I shall convince him that he is nothing. If he persists in mobilizing in spite of the armistice, I swear in the face of Europe to march against his visionary 70,000 troops with 6,000 grenadiers, 4,000 cavalry and 50 pieces of artillery.' He told his generals to disarm the Neapolitan cavalry at the first opportunity. As the Directory had heard that the Emperor was dying, it warned Bonaparte to prevent the Grand Duke of Tuscany from leaving for Vienna.

The Emperor was in perfect health, according to Gallo, but he was thinking of withdrawing his troops from Italy and concentrating them on the Danube. All this was discouraging to Ferdinand and Maria Carolina. And on August 18 a treaty of alliance was signed between France and Spain, which would deal a blow to the British in the Mediterranean. Belmonte, who was kept kicking his heels in Paris by the Directory, dared not threaten to break off negotiations. In London Lord Grenville had told the Neapolitan ambassador Circello that if his Court could obtain as honourable a peace as possible there was not a moment to lose; since the Austrian army had been reduced to impotence, His Sicilian Majesty could not hope to save Italy. French agents continued to report that Naples had no intention of making peace, and that Belmonte had secret orders to spin out negotiations until the Austrians won a victory.

These reports impressed the Directory, so that two months were wasted in futile discussion. Among the first proposals of Delacroix, the French foreign minister, political prisoners were to be amnestied, their trials abolished, their property restored, with the right to sell out and emigrate if they desired; no French citizen in the kingdom could be arrested without the written consent of his minister or consul; all French refugees were to be banished forty-five miles from the ports and coast; an indemnity of sixty million francs was to be paid; fifteen millions at once in ready cash, fifteen within three months, and five millions annually during the next six years. One hundred statues, pictures or manuscripts and two thousand stallions were to be sent in addition; the right to excavate at Pompeii, Herculaneum and Portici was to be conceded, as well as the restitution of prisoners and taxes, and a number of commercial privileges. Among the secret clauses were more indemnities: three ships of the line and three frigates, twenty gunboats all armed and equipped; the cession of Trapani and a slice of neighbouring territory; and of the island of Elba and the Presidi. The Republic would induce the Pope to cede the Duchy of Benevento to the King as a form of compensation. The property and ships of Powers at war with France were to be sequestrated, and Acton was to be dismissed and banished.

Belmonte pointed out the absurdity of these proposals, substituting alternatives here and there, such as that both parties should extradite each other's subjects who had been proved guilty of disturbing the public order. As for the dismissal of Acton—'...this would be to punish a minister for having served his master for twenty years with the greatest zeal, honesty, intelligence and loyalty. How could the King consent to this without forgetting his dignity and interests?'

The Queen, who had written to Gallo that the morale of the provinces was excellent and the troops appeared to be in fine condition, made the following comments: 'The second clause [ports closed to the English] means war with the latter, and if Naples is to undergo such great expense and humiliation to insure herself against French bombs, English bombs have the same effect and are equally hard to digest. Moreover, this would be the height of ingratitude, as we owe four years of tranquillity to their presence in the Mediterranean. The third clause [release of our criminals] would sow the seed of rebellion... As to the fifth [reparation for insults in expelling Mackau from Naples] this is ridiculous. Mackau left at his own convenience by sea. He even wished to attend the Piedigrotta festival and was allowed to do so. He left overwhelmed with attentions. With regard to the expulsion of *émigrés*, that is what I should welcome, but honesty and charity forbid it. The other clauses are not yet divulged. I imagine these will coincide with what Azara is preaching in Rome, to put me back in my place as a woman outside the Council. But even that will not suffice, because owing to my credit and influence with my husband, I shall have to be pensioned off and sent to my native land, after serving thirty years and bearing nineteen children. [*Sic.*] Acton will have to be pensioned and driven out. I do not know what they are planning for him, but I think it will be loss of life or liberty. I am curious to learn whether the Directory will dare to make an official pronouncement or will be content to publish it abroad like Cacault and Azara in Rome...

We have already given orders to redouble armaments and recruits, but in this we have had serious setbacks. The people are cowardly, lazy and soft, and will not comply. Compulsory recruiting is not feasible for fear of revolts, emigration or flight. Volunteers receive 25 grani a day [a little over a shilling]. In spite of this few join up. They desert, steal, and in my opinion are not to be trusted. We have hardly 40,000 men. And these may decamp and have not yet experienced fire... Nobody is willing to make the slightest contribution. The tax on the barons, which is entirely legal, makes them cry out and raise incredible obstacles... P.S. The King has called for Acton to discuss plans. My own idea is to arm and co-ordinate all means of defence as much as possible. If the Emperor withdraws from Italy, we must continue to arm while negotiating peace, subscribing to no degrading conditions which would ruin us as much as the loss of a battle, and disgrace us as well. We should declare that if the French pass Bologna and Ferrara by a certain line, the Neapolitan army will assume the defensive in the Papal States. In a word, we should carry out in action: Death rather than dishonour... I shall see what the King and Acton decide; but I think that if we show faint hearts in a crisis, we shall fall under the French yoke. Five million inhabitants can defend themselves if they wish, especially with sea protection. I can answer for the King and the Ministry, but the country makes me tremble. The general fear, inefficiency and selfishness are incredible.'

In the meantime a treaty with the Pope miscarried as he refused to declare a religious war against the French. The King and Acton considered this an opportunity to embark on a new crusade, using spiritual as well as material weapons, for it seemed that otherwise the papal power was doomed. The Directory made no secret of their intention to destroy the rule of priests. Godoy was scheming to enlarge the duchy of Parma: his plan was to transfer the Papal States to the Duke and send the Pope to Sardinia.

Cacault's agents were already inciting the Romans to revolt. At the same time he informed Bonaparte that the King had made an alliance with the Pope. Consequently Bonaparte advised the Directory to come to terms with Belmonte: 'The King of Naples has sixty thousand men under arms and can only be attacked and dethroned by eighteen thousand infantry and three thousand cavalry ...Rome has the force of its fanaticism. If Rome and Naples combine against us we shall need reinforcements... At present we cannot wage war on Naples and Austria simultaneously.' When he heard of the French reverses on the Rhine, he said he thought peace with Naples indispensable.

Peace was therefore signed on October 10 without the most objectionable clauses, but in a secret clause Naples had to pay an indemnity of eight million francs within a year. It might have been much worse. Compared with other treaties, the Directory regarded it as 'the reverse of the medal', and it was not ratified until November 27. The Queen took no pains to conceal her disapproval. 'I am not and never shall be on good terms with the French,' she wrote to Gallo on November 8. 'I shall always regard them as the murderers of my sister and the royal family, as the oppressors of all monarchies, as the villains who have seduced and put poniard and poison into the hands of all classes and peoples against legitimate authority, and who have consequently blighted my existence. Apart from which, I have always considered that the French nation, even under their King, intended to dominate and oppress the Two Sicilies... encouraging the Barbary pirates, hampering even our paltry coral fishery, destroying our manufactures, and wishing to monopolize our products, without leaving our subjects any scope for trade. It was thus under a King! What will it be under the scoundrels of the present system, who are mostly the money-grubbing tools of merchants? I foresee a dreadful series of mortifications, vexations and sorrows.' The peace was published in Naples to the sound of the trumpet on December 11, and the *Te Deum* was chanted in all the churches. Neither Naples nor France had any intention of observing the treaty whenever it suited them to break it. 'Nominally neutral but never in our feelings,' wrote the Queen to Lady Hamilton, 'we shall give proof of this on every available opportunity.'

General Canclaux, the new French ambassador to Naples, had been a cavalry officer under the old dispensation and still retained a refinement which the new school of diplomatists lacked. He was surprised by his friendly reception, but this was chiefly due to his own good manners. The peace so laboriously patched up in Paris was strained by the threatened invasion of Rome. Ferdinand again massed troops on the frontier and promised to protect the Pope. All the same, he thought that the Pope had invited disaster by not listening to his advice. It was too late for him to take up the offensive now. But the Romans, except for a few Jacobins who had nothing to lose, were driven to desperation by the extortions of the new Attila, and all were grieved to see their city despoiled of its venerable monuments. Most of the aristocracy, especially Prince Doria Pamphili, Duke Braschi and Don Filippo Colonna, made heavy sacrifices to pay the peace tribute. Holy relics were exposed in all the churches and miracles were on every tongue. Images of the Blessed Virgin were reported to have wept copious tears. The streets were thronged with religious processions, and the populace was excited by visions of celestial vengeance. The Pope had been negotiating secretly with Vienna, and it was rumoured that the Emperor had promised 6,000 troops to help him recover his lost legations. Most of the Cardinals voted for war.

The French envoy Cacault fled from Rome on January 27. After Mantua's surrender on February 2, Bonaparte marched to chastise the Pontiff, whose troops melted away at the sight of his bayonets. Belmonte rushed to Ancona and pleaded with Bonaparte to spare the Eternal City; he even threatened him with Ferdinand's reprisals. After a four hours' conference he persuaded him to renew negotiations for peace, if the Pope adhered to the preliminaries, which were being discussed with Cardinal Mattei, Archbishop of Ferrara. The Pope sent his nephew, Duke Braschi, Monsignor Caleppi and Prince Camillo Massimo to join the Cardinal as representatives of the Holy See, and the treaty was signed at Tolentino on February 19, 1797. At one point Cacault wanted to break off negotiations as he was nettled by Braschi's Roman pride. The wretched Cardinal threw himself on his knees to make the pugnacious envoy change his mind. The war indemnity was fixed at 32,700,000 francs to be paid within four months. The papal army was to be disbanded; Bologna, Ferrara and the Romagna were to be ceded to France; the port of Ancona was to be occupied by the invaders until the treaty was implemented. A large collection of art treasures and manuscripts were to be sent to Paris, and the Roman ports were to be closed to allied shipping.

Bonaparte wrote to the Directory: 'My reasons for concluding this treaty are... that thirty millions are worth Rome ten times over, from which we could not have extracted five millions, since everything of value has been removed to Terracina. My opinion is that Rome, shorn of Bologna, Ferrara, the Romagna and the thirty millions we are taking, can no longer exist; this old machine will disintegrate.' In sending the treasures from the shrine of Loreto to the

Directors he noted with disappointment that 'the Madonna is of wood', but that the art treasures from Ravenna, Rimini, Pesaro, Ancona and Perugia, together with those of Loreto and Rome, would supply France with 'almost every fine object in Italy, except a few things at Rome and Naples'. To Belmonte he wrote that this was a fresh proof of the Republic's friendship and esteem for the King of the Two Sicilies. But the Directory frowned upon the treaty: nothing less than the extinction of the papacy would satisfy them.

The preliminaries of peace between France and Austria were signed on April 18, 1797, at Leoben, with Gallo as the Emperor's plenipotentiary, a flattering testimony to the favour he enjoyed in Vienna. At first Bonaparte was unwilling to accept him in this role, which seemed incompatible with that of Neapolitan ambassador, but on both sides there were reasons for a speedy signature. Bonaparte was now in the heart of Austria and anxious about his communications. The Austrian Chancellor Thugut was exasperated by the withdrawal of the British fleet from the Mediterranean, which he blamed, above all, for the Austrian reverses in Italy. The peace treaty was not concluded till six months later.

The two old aunts of Louis XVI, Mesdames Adelaide and Victoire, who had been living in Rome under the Pope's protection, had now sought refuge at Caserta, much to the Queen's annoyance. 'I have the awful torment of harbouring the two old Princesses of France with eighty persons in their retinue and every conceivable impertinence,' she complained. This was due to the fact that the unfortunate Princesses refused to discard any of their former etiquette: 'The same ceremonies are observed in the interior of their apartments here as were formerly at Versailles.' More than fifty families had to be turned out of the old palace of Caserta to make room for them and their suite.

Acton talked of going to England to rest and recuperate—'but he cannot make up his mind... I believe Castelcicala to be an upright man, but he is muddled and fretful and his manners make him unpopular... Ascoli has military talents, but he is irascible, stubborn and full of self-importance. I strongly doubt his loyalty... for he leans towards Spain. In fact, I regard him as dangerous and necessary to watch. The others are mere machines... perambulating corpses. All the strings are held by Acton, who forgets them... He refuses to admit that he has undertaken more than he can manage, grows desperate, and is killing himself with overwork. Nothing goes well: it is a complete Babel.'

Hamilton noted that there was little harmony at present between the Queen and Acton. 'No one,' he said, 'can have a greater respect than I have for the Queen of Naples. Her talents are certainly very great.' But—'all the daughters of Maria Theresa had very tender hearts, subject to sudden and violent impressions. Now I have reason to believe that such an impression took place lately in the heart of the Queen of Naples, for she showed for some time past a remarkable attention to the Prince of Saxe, son of Prince Xavier of Saxony, who has a regiment of cavalry in Her Sicilian Majesty's service. He is a young man of a very good figure and does not seem to want talents. It is highly probable that General Acton, perceiving this growing attachment, dreading its consequences and not being able to conquer it, let His Sicilian Majesty into the secret, who immediately ordered the Prince of Saxe to go to Vienna... If... my conjecture should prove to be well-founded and that the General has actually sided with the King, the Queen's influence would be entirely lost, and indeed from the remarkable coolness in the behaviour of His Sicilian Majesty to the Queen I should judge it to be so.' The conjugal rift was only temporary; that with Acton went deeper, but the Queen, having learnt to fear him, contrived not to make it obvious.

The social life went on as before. Twice a week the royal gardens in the Favorita at Portici were thrown open to the public when the Court moved thither. 'There is a band of music, and all sorts of rural diversions, such as swinging and wooden horses that run round, the riders running at the ring or firing pistols at a Turk's head.' Besides, there were the usual magnificent balls. 'Alas! with all this I cannot say that there are many gay faces,' wrote Hamilton. Almost all the British travellers in Italy were now collected in Naples—'from whence, in case of necessity, they might be able to get off by sea'. Prince Augustus Frederick, the sixth son of King George III, who was later created Duke of Sussex, was the most prominent member of the British community in rank as well as stature, for he was a burly six foot three inches high. But all those inches suffered acutely from asthma so that he was forced to spend much time in milder climates. That of Naples suited him to perfection; he enjoyed the music as well as the sea-bathing. In one respect he considered he had no rivals. 'I have the most wonderful voice that was ever heard,' he said, 'three octaves.' He took a villa for the season at Portici and attended most of the concerts. From one of these he retired in dudgeon on discovering that no seat had been reserved for him, but realizing that this was due to a Court official's mistake, the matter was cleared up. The King invited him to join the least fatiguing chases, and he lived with their Sicilian Majesties quite *en famille*. His health improved since Dr Cotugno had taken him off the vegetable diet to which he had long been accustomed. When he was uneasy about the political situation, Hamilton assured him that if the French had any evil intentions against Naples it would not be difficult for him to escape by land or sea.

Hamilton expressed amazement at the latest French fashions. In July 1797 he wrote: 'General Acton gave a great dinner on Thursday and another on Sunday last to all the diplomatic corps and the principal officers of the Court. Monsieur de Canclaux was dressed in a handsome embroidered uniform and a rich sash round his waist, Madame Canclaux in a simple *chemise* that scarcely covered her shoulders, the rest of her arms being quite naked, and Mademoiselle Canclaux came to that formal dinner with a blue silk bonnet on her head. There were also four secretaries of the French legation whose appearance was very mean indeed, particularly that of the first secretary Monsieur Trouvé, the person that formerly had the direction of the *Moniteur* at Paris. His hair, very black, was cut short all round and stood up on end in all directions. He wore a pair of large spectacles through which he constantly stared every one full in the face, a dark blue coat with brass buttons and buttoned up close to his chin, a pair of black leather buskins with a narrow gold lace at the top, and a huge scimitar hanging to a broad black leather belt going over his coat. Your Lordship may imagine the effect of such a figure in the midst of a great company dressed in the highest gala. However, as they call it the uniform of the first secretary of the French legation, he will, I suppose, be received everywhere in this extraordinary dress.'

The Hereditary Prince of Naples had been engaged to the Archduchess Clementine since 1790; he was now nineteen and his fiancée fifteen years old, and the truce with France enabled her to travel. A frigate was sent to fetch her from Trieste while the royal family waited at Foggia, where the marriage was to be celebrated quietly, for, as the Queen said, 'luxury and ostentation are not proper at a time when all pay taxes which must last many years, even after the war'. She had taken every precaution for her daughter-in-law's comfort. 'I flatter myself that I shall be a tolerable mother-in-law,' she had written. 'Every day by persuasion and advice I shall try to stimulate her young husband's good nature, sincerity and desire to be loved for his worth rather than from a sense of duty, a subject about which he feels keenly and reasons sensibly. The young man is not at all amiable; he has little social sense and no style, caring neither to take trouble nor to hold himself well, and he is completely innocent. This does not give him an engaging appearance, though he has a pleasant face. But his principles and character are estimable, and if the young bride disregards his exterior she will be able to cherish and respect him, for he wishes to be loved. He will be passionately attached to her, at least in my opinion.' In a postscript marked 'Very Private' she added more in the same strain: the Prince had so much physical exuberance that she dared not leave him alone with his sisters for a minute. He liked agriculture and machines and preferred country to town life. He had a tendency to avarice, but the Queen and his sisters hoped to tease him out of it. Altogether it was not a glowing picture.

The Archduchess was strongly pitted with smallpox, but her walk was that of a Queen, said Baroness du Montet. Though she had been very homesick on the journey, she managed to conceal this when she arrived on June 18. 'My son loves her passionately and she reciprocates,' wrote the Queen. 'It is a pleasure to see them harmonize so well... I am delighted with the Princess, gentle, fresh, sensible and accommodating.' But a few weeks later she was puzzled by her sullen reserve. 'Her husband is her husband two or three times in twenty-four hours, a matter which interests her. In spite of this there is a sadness, a boredom, an invincible disgust. I think it must be due to her health. For it is unnatural, she has no taste for anything at all. It is not that she regrets her life in Vienna... I will do everything for her happiness, although I am sowing amid brambles and on thorny soil. But she is my son's wife. Thanks to my training, the young man is very much in love with her as a woman... But this may not last with so much disgust, boredom and no charm of feature, which he is fortunately too nice to notice... I shall try to win her confidence, but I am not sure of succeeding. All her wants are anticipated; nothing is lacking; she is quite independent; but she is discontented and everybody notices it. I can read into her soul better than I can tell you.' As time went on the Princess Royal still remained an enigma to her mother-in-law, who wrote: 'I hope she will have at least one child a year for twelve years running, and rather difficult pregnancies. Without this effective remedy the young woman will make us anxious about her happiness. She is gentle and good, but very reserved and rather suspicious. One can see that she is playing a part which is not natural to her... The essential is that her husband adores her in every sense of the word. She says she loves him, and assuredly shows and demands many proofs of love, to such an extent that Dr Cotugno scolds and expostulates in vain, for Francis is quite besotted.'

While the health of the Princess improved, the Prince was losing his colour. 'He has a flabby fleshiness that looks unhealthy. I think it is due to excess in certain exercises. (She is ill-humoured and sulks when Francis does not respond to her continuous provocations and oglings.) A painful pregnancy would be useful to both of them and would fulfil all our desires. But I am afraid that we shall not see this until they become more moderate.'

Always reserved with her mother-in-law, Clementine was wilful in dealing with Francis and, like Maria Carolina herself thirty years since, she was too familiar with the members of her household and prone to tittle-tattle. She fondled her husband incessantly before his sisters, and these caresses were so suggestive that the Queen had to separate them from the young couple 'so as not to rouse certain desires in two pure and placid young girls aged sixteen and nineteen.'

'The only thing that pains me,' the Queen concluded, 'is that my son is completely altered. She has drawn his attention to his parents' faults and foibles which he had never noticed before.' The Princess cared as little as her husband for Court life. She preferred family games, moonlit walks on the terrace and frivolous conversation. 'This little girl has arrived so well trained in everything, in theory and in practice, that it really makes one shudder. But we must be silent, live quietly together, and ask Heaven to calm their overexcited senses by sending them children.'

Maria Carolina's restless temperament drove her back to politics. She followed Bonaparte's career with increasing astonishment and reluctant admiration. She could not understand how the ragged French army had beaten the Austrians, the best equipped in the world. She could not understand Neapolitan apathy. She saw everything in black or white, but mostly in black: treachery at home and the French menace from abroad. Shortly before the treaty of Campo Formio she wrote to Gallo: 'War would ruin us, but the neutrality they imagine is a chimera. Under this name Bonaparte will make mealy-mouthed demands for all sorts of supplies, for horses and cattle, and if we refuse (as we ought to, cost what it may), he will cry out and try to revolutionize Naples... Our shortage of currency, banks and public funds discredited, provisions exorbitant, the new spirit, the general unrest, all classes, especially the best educated, entirely corrupted, the King's apartments having become, like the cafés, hothouses for running down the government... all this will make it easy for him to stir up trouble. That is our sad but real situation... Peace could only give us a brief respite, time to take certain measures, form a new ministry, put things in better order. If war breaks out now, we are lost. We lack the vigour, firmness, energy and will to set to work and do everything on a big scale; we lack a true political sense, more impossible to acquire than grabbing the moon with one's teeth... Personally I abhor the part that Bonaparte serves and plays. He is the Attila, the scourge of Italy, but I have a genuine esteem and deep admiration for him. He is the greatest man several centuries have produced. His force, energy, constancy, activity and talent have won my admiration. Happy the country with such a sovereign; for it need not fear conquest or defeat. Happy the prince with such a minister or general!... I prefer him to Frederick who, apart from his talents, had much meanness and absurdity. In this man everything is great.

'I admire him, and my sole regret is that he serves so detestable a cause. I should like the fall of the Republic, but the preservation of Bonaparte. For he is really a great man; and when one can only see ministries and sovereigns with petty and narrow views, one is all the more pleased and astonished to watch such a man rise and increase in power, while deploring that his grandeur is attached to so infernal a cause. This may seem strange to you. But while I loathe his operations, I admire the man. I hope that his plans will miscarry and his enterprises fail; at the same time I wish for his personal happiness and glory so long as it is not at our expense... If he dies they should reduce him to powder and give a dose of it to each ruling sovereign, and two to each of their ministers, then things would go better.'

After the peace of Campo Formio (October 17, 1797), where

Gallo again represented the Emperor, Maria Carolina sent him a similar eulogy: 'In spite of all the harm he has done to us in Italy, I must admit that I hold a high opinion of him, as I love the great in all things and everywhere, even when I find it turned against myself. I wish this rare and extraordinary man to succeed and distinguish himself outside Italy. I foresee that this world will resound with his name, and that history will immortalize him. He will be great in all things, in war, diplomacy, conduct, resolution, talent, genius: he will be the greatest man of our century... Cultivate in him friendly sentiments for Naples and the desire not to injure us.'

XVI

Envoys of the French Directory—The Marquis of Gallo—General Duphot and the French occupation of Rome, 1798—Citizen Garat—Release of Medici and political prisoners—Aboukir—Nelson's enthusiastic reception at Naples—General Mack—The King's disastrous expedition to Rome—A belated appeal to the Neapolitan masses.

Canclaux was far too polite and conciliating an ambassador to please the Directory, who chose their envoys for their revolutionary opinions. Of Citizen Gassé, for instance, who had been recommended for the French consulate in Naples, Canclaux wrote to his chief: 'Perhaps you are unaware, as I have been until now, that this citizen, who may deserve to be appointed to any post elsewhere, has been General Acton's cook. Would it be suitable for him to reappear in Naples, where his wife still keeps an inn, as a public representative of the French Government?'

No doubt the Directory branded Canclaux as a reactionary snob; according to Sir William Hamilton, one of his secretaries had complained to Paris of his being 'too much the courtier to represent the French Republic', and that he had requested at the same time to be recalled. At first they thought of sending Treilhard, an astute lawyer and ex-member of the Convention who had voted for the execution of Louis XVI, to replace him. The Queen wrote indignantly: 'I could never regard that knave who voted for the King's death as anything but a monster soiled with the blood of his masters... Let them send us a descendant of Cartouche, but not a member of the Convention, for I should be afraid that his shoes had come from that famous tannery of human skin invented by their villainy.' But Treilhard became one of the Directors and Citizen Trouvé, no less fanatical, was appointed to Naples in his stead. Trouvé's behaviour was scarcely calculated to inspire confidence in his government's goodwill. He refused to kiss the King's hand, and remained seated when the King and Queen entered the theatre, to proclaim his contempt for monarchist servility. On all occasions he insisted on being addressed as plain 'Citizen'.

As England and France were still at war, Acton's ill-health gave him a pretext for withdrawing from the arena; he was relieved to pass the Foreign Minister's portfolio to Castelcicala and watch the strange comedy from the wings. But the ex-ambassador was equally pro-English, and he was unable to cope with a ruffian like Citizen Trouvé, who refused to accord him the title that was his due. Neither the Queen nor Acton had any faith in the Peace of Campo Formio, but they decided to test a policy of appeasement. Gallo was consequently recalled from Vienna and appointed Councillor of State in charge of Foreign Affairs, the Marine and Commerce, Grand Courier and General Superintendent of Posts and Secretary to the Queen, with the privilege of using the royal coaches and livery and a salary of 14,400 ducats. 'In my opinion we should continue to be suave and prudent,' the Queen wrote to him, 'prevent all cause of serious disorder, condescend to little kindnesses, but always remain on guard and never become their ally. Tanucci, the creature and worshipper of the King of Spain, would never let him sign the Family Compact on account of the disadvantages it would incur, for which no advantage could compensate. These are still the same, not to speak of how monstrous an alliance would be with the assassins of our family, the demolishers of thrones...'

Gallo was suspicious of England and saw Acton as its unscrupulous emissary. His distrust was reciprocated; perhaps he could not conceal his bias. Nelson for one could not bear him. He described him as a supercilious fop elaborately studying his snuffbox, decorations and ring to convey an impression that 'he has been bred in a Court, and I in a rough element'. On the other hand, he had gained the confidence of the great Corsican. Bonaparte had taken a liking to him at Campo Formio: he had spotted a potential satellite. Gallo also managed to mollify Trouvé. Under all Trouvé's bluster he detected a jealous plebeian smarting under an inferiority complex. He made flattering inquiries about his wife, and encouraged him to unburden himself of his troubles. These were many, for he had made himself so disagreeable that he was shunned by Neapolitan society. His first interview with Gallo ended in effusive embraces, but these did not lead to happier official relations. On the contrary, Trouvé became more crotchety and exacting. He complained bitterly because a biography of Louis XVI, in which the Convention was dubbed 'regicide', was on sale in a local bookshop, and he demanded its instant withdrawal. For all his talk of freedom he evidently did not approve of a free press. He harped continuously on the release of political prisoners, as if these were French citizens for whom he was responsible. Gallo had never dealt before with so difficult a customer.

France's intentions in Italy were increasingly transparent to impartial observers. Bonaparte's brother Joseph had come to Rome as ambassador and his residence was a hive of subversive activity. Pius VI was old and ailing: the Directory ordered that no Pope was to be elected after his death. But the aged Pontiff refused to oblige them by dying. Ironically, a young French officer was to serve their purpose better. General Duphot, aged twenty-seven, was on Joseph Bonaparte's staff, a republican extremist who had composed a popular ode to 'The heroes who died for liberty'. The local Jacobins, stiffened by Neapolitan exiles and agitators from other cities, wished to provoke an immediate rupture. On December 27, 1797, they raised an outcry for the Republic at the Villa Medici, where the French Academy was installed, but this tumult was dispersed by papal cavalry. Next day they swarmed before the French embassy and noisily demanded the ambassador's protection. Again a detachment of cavalry rode up, and General Duphot with some French officers went into the street—according to the ambassador's report to pacify them, according to the Roman, to lead an attack on the papal patrol. His orders, shouted in French, were not understood. Seeing him advance with drawn sword, a Roman corporal shot him dead.

The ambassador would not hear the Vatican's explanations and left for Florence, whence he sent a biased account of these events to the Directory. He alleged that one of the most brilliant French generals had been assassinated at the instigation of the priests. This provided the Directory with an excuse all ready-made. General Berthier was ordered to march on Rome and occupy the city, which he achieved without opposition on February 10, 1798. On February 15 the new republic was proclaimed at a mass meeting in the ancient Forum, surrounded by a strong detachment of French cavalry under General Murat. General Berthier made a triumphal entry into Rome, and received a crown of laurel, which he sent to Bonaparte. A republican deputation invited him to preside at a pompous function on the Capitol, where he saluted the 'independent' republic in the name of France: 'Shades of Cato, Pompey,

Brutus, Cicero and Hortensius! Here on the Capitol you made famous, where so often you defended the rights of the people, receive the homage of free French warriors. They have come, these sons of the Gauls, holding the peaceful olive, to raise the altars of liberty where the first Brutus raised them of yore.' Another tree of liberty was planted, and the rabble danced around it with drunken song.

The Pope, with gentle dignity, refused to abdicate, and was barbarously treated by the French commissioner Haller, who even tore the rings from his fingers. When the Pope asked to be allowed to die where he had lived, as he was eighty years old, Haller retorted that he could die anywhere. The room he sat in was plundered; he was even deprived of the trifles for his personal comfort. Without further ceremony, be was bundled off in a carriage, first to Siena and finally to France, where he died in August 1799.

'In sending me to Rome,' wrote Berthier to Bonaparte, 'you appoint me treasurer to the expedition against England. I will try to fill the exchequer.' After the Vatican, the palaces and country houses of the nobility were looted. Nor were the churches spared. Between the commissioners and military marauders the sack of Rome was as complete as in the heyday of the Goths. Yet Bonaparte had assured the people of Italy: 'The French Army is coming to break your chains... Your property, your religion, your customs shall not be touched. Every one shall enjoy his possessions in security and, under the protection of virtue, exercise his rights.' Soon the people of Rome were starving. Even the French had mutinied, and the workmen of the Trastevere had pillaged their arms depots and started a massacre, with cries of 'Long live the Pope!' But this and other popular risings were quickly crushed.

In spite of the peace treaty with France, the presence of such neighbours across their frontier alarmed the King and Queen, and all Naples was outraged by the persecution of the Pope. Why should the Two Sicilies be spared when all the rest of Italy had been overrun? Bonaparte's seizure of Malta in June seemed another preliminary to the encirclement of Naples. As Nelson was to reiterate: 'Malta is the direct road to Sicily.' The Queen had no illusions: even before Malta was occupied she had been secretly negotiating with Austria, and a defensive treaty between Austria and Naples was signed on May 20, 1798. Sir William Hamilton assured her of British co-operation. She began to grow bolder in consequence.

Citizen Garat, who succeeded Trouvé as French ambassador in May, was scarcely a more tactful choice, for he had announced the death sentence to Louis XVI. The Queen wrote to Gallo from Caserta: 'You may easily imagine that I have no ardent desire to see this representative whose former embassy is ever before my eyes. But since it is a question of duty, I am ready to drain the chalice however bitter.'

At his first audience Garat praised the virtues of republican government in a long-winded homily to the King and Queen: 'When revolutions and a Republic sent me to Your Majesties, invested with a title and charged with a mission which might benefit many peoples, imagination recalls those periods of antiquity when philosophers, who were only famous because they could think, came from the Republics of Greece to these same shores, on this same continent, to these same islands, bringing their good wishes for the happiness of mankind.' The fatuous ambassador interpreted the smiles of the King and Queen as a token of appreciation. 'You will see,' he wrote to Paris, 'that without lowering the lofty tone of republican language I have softened it considerably. It was quite impossible for me to win the affection of a King and Queen, but I have cause to believe that at least I have won their esteem.'

Garat had been sent to negotiate a commercial treaty, but he seems to have considered the release of the political prisoners as his special vocation. It is surprising that Gallo did not retort with a plea for the amnesty of French *émigrés* whose possessions had been confiscated. When a few young men were locked up for parading in Jacobin togs, Garat protested that this was an insult to France.

After the treaty of Paris (October 10, 1796), the political prisoners had hoped for a general amnesty, but only two Frenchmen were released. There was a wave of public sympathy for all the captives who had never been brought to trial. Various members of the aristocracy, like the Duchess of Canzano and Princess Colonna, appealed on behalf of sons and kinsmen to the Queen, who was moved by their entreaties. Perhaps some of them were as innocent as these ladies, dressed in blackest mourning and hardly audible for sobs, maintained. The delay was becoming a scandal. The Queen gave orders to expedite proceedings. Garat announced that he would consider the execution of these prisoners as a renewal of war. Thanks to his vociferous threats, he gained the credit when the majority were set free in the summer of 1798. Among them were many who won brief notoriety under the Parthenopean Republic. Luigi de' Medici was not released without prolonged deliberation. Three of the judges, Vanni, Bisogni and Guidobaldi, voted for his death; one abstained; and two, Ferreri and Chinigò, voted for his release. When one judge abstained it was customary for the president of the High Court, who pronounced the final verdict, to support the merciful party. The president, Mazzocchi, passed judgment in Medici's favour.

The King, convinced of Medici's guilt, was so enraged that he wrote an order for the arrest of Mazzocchi, Ferreri and Chinigò. But Acton feared that this would alienate public sympathy and lead to more trouble with France. From the very beginning one judge, Marchese Vanni, had steadily maintained that the prisoners were guilty, and that Naples pullulated with traitors. He had therefore done much to discredit the High Court of State. Acton and the Queen persuaded Ferdinand that Vanni had misled them, so the warrant against the three judges was torn up and Vanni was banished 'with all honours' to his native Abruzzo. Medici retired to his estate of Ottaiano, but he never lost sight of his ambition. What the King and Queen felt about the High Court's verdict may be deduced from one of Lady Hamilton's letters: 'The Jacobins have all been lately declared innocent, after suffering four years' imprisonment, and I know they all deserved to be hanged long ago; and since Garat has been here, and through his insolent letters to Gallo, these pretty gentlemen, that had planned the death of their Majesties, are to be let out on society again.'

Baffled in his pursuit of the French fleet to Alexandria, Nelson returned to Syracuse on July 20 in a desperate frame of mind. A month previously Acton, 'a true man of business' as Nelson described him, had provided him with an informal order in the King's name, authorizing all port governors of the Two Sicilies to give the British admiral every necessary assistance and supply, 'under the rose'—since Gallo was resolved not to endanger peace with the Directory. He needed assistance now if he were to continue his chase, for some of his ships had not been watered since early May. Though his correspondence on the subject was ambiguous, possibly, as Miss Carola Oman suggested, to exonerate those who had helped him surreptitiously, Nelson wrote from Syracuse to Sir William Hamilton of 'this delightful harbour, where our present wants have been most amply supplied, and where every attention has been paid to us'. Thus revictualled he sailed in four days to Alexandria, and on August 1 he destroyed the French fleet in Aboukir Bay.

Citizen Garat was spared further protest, for he had left Naples declaring that 'the infamous behaviour of the Court was not due to barbarity but to ingrained hostility, because the Queen's sister and brother-in-law perished on the scaffolds of the Republic'. His secretary Lachèze remained in charge of the embassy, and he had little to do but complain. A new edict forbade passports to foreigners; this was obviously aimed at his compatriots. Fearing espionage, Acton wished to close Neapolitan ports to the French army occupying Rome. Having seized Malta, of which Ferdinand was suzerain, the French asked him to send supplies to its garrison. Since that island had withdrawn its allegiance, he pointed out that this was unreasonable. No Maltese ships were allowed in Neapolitan ports.

The news of Nelson's great victory reached Naples on September 3. 'After England, no country was more enthusiastic,' wrote a Frenchman bitterly. An English lady then in Naples has left a candid record of this enthusiasm. Miss Cornelia Knight, who later became governess to Charlotte, Princess of Wales, had escaped from Rome with her invalid mother, the impoverished widow of a Rear-Admiral, and had been taken to the bosom of the British colony. 'Our telescope,' she wrote, 'was constantly directed towards the entrance of the beautiful bay, the prospect of which we so perfectly enjoyed from our windows.' She happened to be reading to her mother when they noticed a sloop of war in the offing. Both rushed to the telescope to watch it draw nearer; soon they saw the blue ensign and a shimmer of gold epaulettes, and the commotion as two officers got into a boat and were rowed to shore, the gestures of the sailors to indicate the sinking and blowing up of ships, the appearance of Captain Hoste and Captain Capel with despatches from Nelson for Sir William Hamilton and for England.

'The battle of the Nile had been fought and won. Never, perhaps, was a victory more complete!... Old General di Pietra... lived in a house adjoining our hotel, and there was a door of communication between them. He had been very attentive to us and we met excellent society at his table, for he delighted in giving dinner-parties. We knew his anxiety to receive the earliest accounts of the meeting of the two fleets, and my mother desired me to give him the first intelligence. I ran to the door, and the servant who opened it, and to whom I delivered my message, uttered exclamations of joy which were heard in the dining-room, where the General was entertaining a large party of officers. The secretary was instantly sent to me, and I was obliged to go in and tell my story. Never shall I forget the shouts, the bursts of applause, the toasts drunk, the glasses broken one after another by the secretary in token of exultation, till the General, laughing heartily, stopped him by saying that he should not have a glass left to drink Nelson's health in on his arrival.

'The first care of Sir William Hamilton was to take Captain Capel to the palace. The King and Queen were at dinner with their children, as was their custom, for they dined early. As soon as the King heard the good news he started up, embraced the Queen, the Princes, the Princesses, and exclaimed: "Oh, my children, you are now safe!"'

After her long depression the Queen was delirious with joy. Lady Hamilton, now her favourite companion, wrote: 'It is not possible to describe her transports: she wept, she kissed her husband, her children, walked frantically about the room, burst into tears again, and again kissed and embraced every person near her, exclaiming, "Oh, brave Nelson! Oh God! bless and protect our brave deliverer! Oh Nelson! Nelson! what do we not owe you! Oh conqueror—saviour of Italy! Oh that my swollen heart could now tell him personally what we owe to him!"' Caution was thrown to the winds, and the city was illuminated for three days. 'Come here, for God's sake, my dear friend,' wrote Sir William Hamilton to Nelson, 'as soon as the service will permit you. A pleasant apartment is ready for you in my house, and Emma is looking out for the softest pillows to repose the few wearied limbs you have left...' Emma told him that she was dressed from head to foot '*alla* Nelson. Even my shawl is Blue with gold anchors all over.'

Nelson's spectacular entry into Naples on September 22 has often been described. What setting could surpass it for a hero's return from victory? People joyous by nature grabbed this opportunity for expressing their elation. More than five hundred boats and barges packed with singers and guitar-strummers rowed towards the *Vanguard*, badly battered by a recent squall. The British Anthem, 'Rule Britannia' and 'See the Conquering Hero' were repeated by various bands across the bay. The British ambassador's barge was the first to come alongside, greeted by a salvo of thirteen guns. Lady Hamilton, ever a mime in the grand manner, now enacted a scene which was to conquer the conquering hero. She had had three weeks to rehearse it. In a much-quoted letter to his wife Nelson described the performance as terribly affecting: 'Up flew her ladyship, and exclaiming, "Oh God, is it possible?" she fell into my arm more dead than alive. Tears, however, soon set matters to rights...'

To moderns, accustomed to a different school of acting, the scene is hard to visualize without a smile. Lady Hamilton was considerably plumper than when Nelson had last met her, and she must have incurred the risk of knocking over the one-armed hero, who was short and spare, and not in the best of health. But 'a fine figure of a woman' connoted *embonpoint*, and this full-blown, highly coloured rose expanding with patriotic fervour must have thrilled the simple-hearted sailor. An hour later the King himself climbed on board, saluted by twenty-one guns. His huge nose shone like a friendly beacon above his black velvet and gold lace, as he wrung Nelson's hand, calling him his deliverer and preserver. Among other compliments, he said he wished he could have served under Nelson at the battle of the Nile. The Queen was indisposed, having recently lost her youngest daughter, but the Princess Royal represented her though in an advanced state of pregnancy which caused her to swoon in the heat. With boyish curiosity the King wished to see everything, including the sick-bay where a seaman was reading to a wounded mate, a sight which appealed to his sentiment, and the hat which Nelson had worn when his head was wounded. A lavish breakfast had been prepared for the guests. Even Commodore Caracciolo, most distinguished of Neapolitan sailors, came to congratulate Nelson, although he bore him a grudge. Miss Knight, who was of the party, recorded that a small white bird was also in attendance. She was told that it had alighted on the *Vanguard* the eve before the battle and had preferred to settle in the Admiral's quarters, though fed and petted by all.

From the moment Nelson stepped ashore he was fêted on a tremendous scale. Myriads of caged birds were released by fishermen, a symbol of rejoicing since time immemorial; and after dusk Nelson's name blazed from three thousand lamps on the British Embassy. 'Between business and what is called pleasure,' he observed, 'I am not my own master for five minutes.' Acton gave a sumptuous official banquet in his honour, after which the nine-year-old Prince Leopold presented a letter from the Queen, regretting that ill-health had prevented her from giving 'Our Saviour' an audience. The Queen had commissioned his portrait, and the little Prince said he would stand beneath it with the daily prayer: 'Dear Nelson, teach me to become like you.' The King felt he could not publicly entertain a British admiral while at peace with France, but he suspended Court mourning for the anniversary of Nelson's fortieth birthday on September 29. Every detail of this grand climax had been thought out by Lady Hamilton, from the buttons and ribbons with his initials distributed among the eighteen hundred guests to the rostral column, engraved with the names of his captains under the words *Veni, vidi, vici*, which was unveiled by the hostess with a Boadicean air. Miss Knight had composed an extra verse to the British Anthem in Nelson's praise. Wherever he moved he met with an ovation. When he visited the porcelain factory he was presented with the royal busts which he had intended to buy. But Lady Hamilton was worried by his meagre appetite. He was inwardly fretting to fight on against France.

At last the Queen gave him a private audience, and he could not help being impressed. 'She is truly a daughter of Maria Theresa,' he decided. 'This country, by its system of procrastination, will ruin itself: the Queen sees it, and thinks as we do.' Nelson, who never ceased railing at the French as 'enemies of the human race', had met a feminine partisan. After his audience Nelson sat down and wrote a letter which was intended for the Queen, although it was addressed to Lady Hamilton, in whose house he was staying. This letter proves that he was not, as many have supposed, the innocent tool of a termagant in league with a Circe. After a review of the general situation he urged an immediate attack on France, ending with the words underlined: '*The boldest measures are the safest.*' These words were soon dinned into the King's ears by Sir William Hamilton, Acton, and the Queen.

In spite of the strenuous honours Nelson had received in Naples, his fundamental frustration was expressed in the well-known outburst to Lord St Vincent: 'What precious moments the Courts of Naples and Vienna are losing! Three months would liberate Italy: but this Court is so enervated that the happy moment will be lost... I am very unwell, and the miserable conduct of this Court is not likely to cool my irritable temper. It is a country of fiddlers and poets, whores and scoundrels.' His native Puritanism revolted against the pagan, pleasure-seeking, procrastinating Neapolitans; his conscience struggled against his growing infatuation for Lady Hamilton, whose virtues he was ingenuous enough to extol in letters to his wife. As he could speak no foreign language Lady Hamilton acted as his interpreter; she shared his thoughts and emotions and attended to all his wants. Yet he said he longed to be at sea. 'We are killed by kindness,' he sighed.

Though the Queen's detestation of the French was second to none, she had every reason to temporize with the Directory until Austria was ready to support her in the north. Her husband still listened to Gallo, but Nelson had won her over to his own point of view and the Hamiltons, especially Emma, kept on striking while the iron was hot. Nelson's victory had revived the Queen's hopes. She saw him as the protector of the throne and chief bulwark against republicans. Indignation against the French was growing in northern Italy, for Berthier soon 'purged' the nationalists who had dared to object to the political and commercial treaty forced upon them by the Directory, and the Cisalpine Republic had ceased to be independent. In Rome the French had antagonized both populace and peasantry. This wave of discontent seemed to favour a general rising to arms. The Queen implored her imperial son-in-law to move. The French were bound to invade the Two Sicilies, she repeated: it was wiser to strike first. But the Emperor refused to be hustled, and the King shrank back beside Gallo. The Queen could rely on the British fleet, but she was worried by the lack of a first-class general to take command of the army and appealed for one to her son-in-law. This was the only prayer of hers he deigned to answer. General Mack, whose reputation as a fine strategist will ever remain a mystery, arrived on October 9. The Queen interpreted this as a sign of encouragement. When Mack was introduced to Nelson, she exclaimed: 'General, be to us by land, what my hero, Nelson, has been by sea!'

In London Lord Grenville warned the Neapolitan ambassador of the risks of attacking France; he also wrote to Hamilton about 'the danger which must attend such a resolution, if taken without the fullest assurances of support from the Court of Vienna'. But in Naples the die had been cast. At the same time (on October 16) Hamilton wrote to Grenville that 'the conferences we have had with General Acton have certainly decided this government to the salutary determination of attacking rather than waiting to be attacked'.

Nelson and Mack agreed to place their confidence in the Queen and Acton alone as soon as the war began. 'Acton was going down, but we have set him up again,' wrote Nelson. 'This evening I shall have in writing the result of last night's "Session", the Queen calls it—not a Council, as in that case *Gallo* must have been at it; but he is tottering, and the Queen has promised he shall not be the War Minister.'

At first Mack struck Nelson as active and intelligent, but on his return from blockading Malta in November he was assailed by doubts. 'General Mack,' he wrote, 'cannot move without five carriages! I have formed my opinion. I heartily pray I may be mistaken.' During the military manoeuvres he witnessed with the Hamiltons at San Germano, the Austrian general's own troops were surrounded instead of those of 'the enemy', and Nelson remarked that the fellow did not understand his business. Mack spoke little but promised victory at every word. He told the King and Queen that he was sorry so superb an army should not encounter an enemy more worthy of its prowess. While Nelson conceded that the troops looked promising, he observed privately that they were wretchedly officered. His return from Malta coincided with the Princess Royal's delivery of a daughter, the future Duchesse de Berry. The whole Court had migrated to San Germano where the army was encamped. A little daughter had died; a granddaughter was born; but Maria Carolina had caught fire from Nelson's spirit. In a blue riding-habit with gold *fleurs-de-lis* at the neck and a general's hat with a white plume, she rode through the lines to encourage the troops. Stirred by the pageantry of military reviews, she began to share Mack's optimism. In the last six weeks the army had been increased from fifteen to fifty thousand by forced levies. This looked well on paper, and the troops may have looked well on parade, but according to General Roger de Damas, a French *émigré* formerly in Russian service whom Acton had engaged for the Neapolitan in February, though fifty thousand men had been armed and equipped, the raw recruits added nothing save confusion and impediment to the basic fifteen thousand. 'I was distressed to see that three-quarters of the troops were only peasants in uniform who, never having been drilled, hesitated during firing exercises and barely satisfied the requirements for a simple review.'

At a council of war it was agreed that four thousand infantry and six hundred cavalry were to be landed at Leghorn in the enemy's rear, and that Nelson was to transport the infantry while Mack invaded the Roman State. But next day there was a setback, for the King had received news from Vienna which made him falter. The Emperor would promise no help unless the French attacked first, and the King did not wish to be branded as the aggressor. Nelson, exasperated by such timidity, for which he blamed the weakness and treachery of Gallo and the Austrian Minister, exploded in most uncourtly fashion: 'he told the King in plain terms that he had his choice, either to advance, trusting to God for his blessing on a just cause, and prepared to die sword in hand, or to remain quiet and be kicked out of his Kingdom'. The shaken King replied he would go on, trusting in God and Nelson. The Queen had failed to force the Emperor's hand, but Nelson had forced the King's. The campaign was irrevocably decided and a holy crusade was preached from all the pulpits. On November 21 Ferdinand issued a proclamation as Defender of the Faith and champion of Italian liberty: he would lead an army into the Roman State to restore the head of Christianity and peace to his own kingdom, which had been threatened by the political upheavals in Northern Italy and the close proximity of the enemies of monarchy and peace.

On November 22 Mack's army marched at dawn from San Germano. Damas, one of the few able generals in the Neapolitan service, has left a trustworthy account of the campaign which damns Mack's incompetence from the beginning. During the last month he should have foreseen that his army would have to cross the river Melfa, and built a bridge as a precaution. Instead of which he gave orders to ford it. Damas tested it on horseback and saw that the troops would be up to their necks in water; so strong was the current that his horse could only wade with difficulty. But the order had to be obeyed: two squadrons of cavalry tried to dam the current while the infantry platoons crossed in serried ranks. Many of them stumbled and all were soaked to the skin; as they churned up the mud it was worse for the rear columns. Besides, it was raining steadily. Both the King's and Acton's carriages were bogged in the mire, and relays of mules were harnessed to extricate them; but none of the regimental wagons were able to move. They bivouacked for the night on the other side of the river, but as the wagons lagged far behind, the officers were unable to change their clothes till the end of the campaign. This was not an encouraging start for fresh troops. 'On the third march,' wrote Damas, 'the vanguard met the French, who could not yet be called the enemy, as we had been warned by an authentic army order to ask them to withdraw, and only to use force in the case of their refusal, which they were careful to avoid, preferring with good reason to take advantage of this inconceivable complaisance...'

As the Neapolitans advanced the French retired without opposition. General Championnet only protested that the treaty with France had been violated, but in that treaty the Directory had promised not to march troops into the Roman State beyond Ancona, and not to promote political innovations in Southern Italy. Rome was evacuated except for a garrison of four hundred in the castle of Sant' Angelo. The King entered it as a conqueror on November 29, accompanied by Mack and Acton. Trees of liberty were torn down by the dozen amid cries of '*Evviva il Re di Napoli!*' 'After so many fears and disillusions, we have had a moment of satisfaction,' wrote a Roman diarist, rejoicing at the spectacle of Ferdinand's entry on horseback beside his Grand Constable, Prince Colonna, to the pealing of bells and plaudits of the people. The King stayed in the splendid Farnese palace, inherited from his grandmother, where he held a reception for the prelates and Roman nobility. The Pope was invited to return; victorious messages were sent to Naples; thanksgiving ceremonies were ordered. It was all too good to be true.

While Mack had mistaken Championnet's withdrawal for a confession of weakness, he was blind to the sorry condition of his own troops. In his *Memoirs* Damas has shown the reverse of the medal: 'When the army reached Rome it was in such a state of distress that no general, except Mack, would have believed it possible to continue the campaign without reorganizing it. Weapons were rusted by the continuous rain, boots were lost, artillery dispersed, many of the mules dead or straggling on the roads, convoys five marches in arrears. The Seven Years War had not exhausted any of the armies in action as much as these six days' march had exhausted the Neapolitan army. Having thus proved the part they could play in general operations by the occupation of Rome, they should have awaited Austrian developments, repaired and strengthened all the details of the army which had suffered so prodigiously. But instead of this wise and indispensable measure, they were ordered to march the next day...' In the meantime Nelson had sailed to

Leghorn with the regiments under General Naselli, and the governor had surrendered unconditionally to their summons. Nelson returned to Naples on December 5 to find that all of a sudden everything had gone wrong.

The raptures of the Romans and Neapolitans were followed by swift disillusion. Championnet had merely withdrawn to concentrate his forces and spring on Mack's scattered columns from a better strategic position. The King had been cruelly misled by his Austrian commander. On December 7 he had to slip out of Rome to avoid capture; two days later the French returned. Division after division of Mack's army collapsed at nearly every point of contact with the foe. Generals de Damas, Macdonald, Bonnamy, Pignatelli Strongoli and others have left varied accounts of the rout that followed. On one point all agree: the ignorance, inexperience, incapacity and even treachery of the commanding officers were chiefly to blame. These had mostly been selected by Mack himself. Under such wretched leaders, very few of whom were Neapolitan, the troops suspected that they were being betrayed, as indeed they were. Mack's first order to Damas was intercepted by Manthoné, an officer who became Minister for War under the Parthenopean Republic. Mack's *aide-de-camp* Orazio Massa was singled out for praise by Colletta and others of his persuasion for suppressing vital despatches. Years hence many were to boast to their children of similar acts of sabotage. Small wonder if the soldiers called their officers Jacobins. Under resolute leadership like that of Damas the troops fought well, but Damas was a rare exception.

Though Mack's despatches were either intercepted or reached him much too late, Damas managed to slip through General Kellermann's hands like a piece of soap, as the latter expressed it, with a force of some six thousand men and all their equipment. Kellermann pursued and attacked him at Montalto. During the battle, described by Championnet as '*des plus vifs et des plus sanglants*', Damas's lower jaw was shattered, but he would not leave the field until the French had retreated. 'Fortunately I did not fall off my horse,' he remarked. 'Had I not been wounded I might have tried to cut off their retreat... but I had no confidence in any of our chiefs: the oldest brigadier [General Ferrola] had been captured while mistaking a French battalion for his own troops. I could not articulate another word and was swallowing bowls of blood: if I had been attacked on the morrow I could not have taken command.'

He retired to the stronghold of Orbetello, where he hoped to be joined by the five thousand Neapolitans at Leghorn, but timid old General Naselli refused to co-operate.

Two weeks after the King's departure from San Germano he was back at Caserta. No doubt he was thoroughly alarmed and despondent, but it is improbable that he exchanged clothes with his equerry, the Duke of Ascoli, on the way, though it seems a pity to spoil a funny story. Apart from their different physiques—Ascoli was short and slim—the King's features were so well known that he would have had to wear a mask: even then his too prominent nose would have betrayed him. The Prince of Migliano Loffredo, who rode beside the King until a carriage was found, used to mimic his Pulcinella accents imploring him: 'Keep your knee stuck close to mine! Don't leave me alone!' In later years 'the King himself used to laugh at his own terrors as well as Ascoli's during their flight from Rome. *Paura* was a subject that never ceased to amuse him in retrospect, and his candour about it was one of his most disarming characteristics.

The Queen, whose hopes had but recently risen to a pinnacle of exaltation, became a tragic figure. She who had set her whole heart on victory and had seen it as a distinct possibility when Mack reassured her about 'the finest army in Europe' and the victorious Nelson repeated 'the boldest measures are the safest', now saw her husband return as a fugitive quaking with fear. Her breathless notes to Lady Hamilton express her rage, bewilderment and mortification. She, the daughter of Maria Theresa, had been brought up to dream of military glory, and many of her own family had distinguished themselves in war. She had always admired courage, and considering her poor health, undermined by an endless series of pregnancies, and the constant strain of living with so incompatible a husband, she was not without courage herself. Now Mack's troops were behaving like rabbits, as she said. The glittering vision had faded, and the nightmare had returned. Instead of military glory, she saw cowardice and treachery. Soon the French would be in Naples: 'the scenes of Varennes with all their sequels' might be repeated here.

The most extraordinary part of the King's predicament was that he had not declared war on France. Even when he entered the Roman State he never thought of himself as an aggressor. As the Queen put it: 'Championnet wrote very politely that he was evacuating Rome—all in order not to be beaten in detail. We faithful (and unhappily too faithful to our engagements), in order not to be the aggressors, allowed them to retreat, and thus lost the chance of destroying or paralysing seven to eight thousand men, which would have encouraged our raw troops. We wished, you see, to be punctilious, and we believed in the word of those wretches.' Such reasoning is subtly *naif*. After the King's entry to Rome, all Frenchmen were banished from Naples for having broken the peace treaty. The last French ambassador, Lacombe Saint-Michel, who had only arrived in late September, was sent off in a Genoese pink: an ill-fated journey, for he was captured by pirates and taken to North Africa. All French property was sequestrated, and the embassy was stoned by *lazzaroni*. Even so Ferdinand had not declared war. But when the French were sweeping the wreck of Mack's army to the banks of the Volturno he issued an edict of extermination, antedated from Rome: 'While I am in the capital of the Christian world to re-establish Holy Church, the French, with whom I have done everything to live in peace, are threatening to enter the Abruzzo. I shall hasten with a mighty army to exterminate them; but in the meantime let the people arm, let them succour the Faith, let them defend their King and father who risks his life, ready to sacrifice it in order to preserve the altars, possessions, domestic honour and freedom of his subjects. Let them remember their ancient valour...'

This belated summons proved more effective than Mack's army. The masses rose in defence of their beloved King, but they displayed their loyalty with such violence that they frightened the King away.

XVII

Preparations for the flight of the royal family—Complete demoralization of Mack—A rough passage with Nelson to Palermo—The Vicar General Pignatelli—Armistice with Championnet—Mack's resignation—Resistance of the Neapolitan masses—Moliterno and the 'patriots'—The brave lazzaroni—*Betrayal: the Parthenopean Republic.*

The large majority of the people, including the sturdy *lazzaroni* who lived from hand to mouth, were united by certain quasi-religious sentiments, of which the most intense was the love of home. Naples was their home, associated with all that makes life beautiful and sacred. Those who had no private property and who could neither read nor write were bound to Naples by a deep spiritual and poetic tie. They belonged to this land, this sea; here they multiplied and luxuriated in the benign climate, accepting their lot without questioning the inequalities of fortune any more than the caprices of Vesuvius. Havelock Ellis has called patriotism 'a virtue—among barbarians'. The *lazzaroni* were generally regarded as barbarians, and it is certain that they possessed this virtue. A touching example of it was noted by Goethe on his return to Naples from Sorrento in 1787: 'We now reached an eminence. The most extensive area in the world opened before us. Naples, in all its splendour: its mile-long line of houses on the flat shore of the bay, the promontories, tongues of land and walls of rock; then the islands and, behind all, the sea—the whole was a ravishing sight.

'A most hideous singing, or rather exulting cry and howl of joy, from the boy behind, frightened and disturbed us. Somewhat angrily, I called out to him; he had never had any harsh words from us—he had been a very good boy.

'For a while he did not move; then he patted me lightly on the shoulder, and pushing between us both his right arm, with the forefinger stretched out, exclaimed, "*Signor, perdonate! questa è la mia patria!*" ("Forgive me, Sir, for this is my native land!").

'And so I was ravished for a second time. Something like a tear stood in the eyes of the phlegmatic child of the north.'

The King had appealed to this instinctive emotion, which was to explode with terrific force against the republican invasion. At first he announced that he would await the French surrounded by his loyal subjects, who gathered below the palace and roared until he appeared. But as the exulting howl had frightened Goethe, on a magnified scale it was to frighten the King.

As ever in time of misfortune, there were penitential processions and special prayers and vows to San Gennaro. The Court went into mourning. The blood of the patron saint remained congealed throughout the morning of December 16—a bad omen—and only began to liquefy after a long day of incessant entreaties. Rumours thick as confetti flurried through the panic-stricken air. The Minister for War, Arriola, was arrested, as well as other officers suspected of treachery. Deserters were disarmed by the *lazzaroni*, or were inspired by new courage now that they had no officers to mislead them. The Jacobins and political prisoners were longing for the French to set them free.

'If Mack is defeated this country is lost', Nelson had written. Consequently he had made preparations to evacuate the British colony and the royal family. While the King seemed unwilling to move, the Queen had been packing clothes and valuables since December 15 and sending them by night to the British Embassy, where Lady Hamilton collected and consigned them to Nelson's seamen.

Although she saw her daily, the Queen bombarded Lady Hamilton with letters which betray the turmoil of her mind. As usual, it was she who had to make the decisions without any support from her vacillating husband. 'Dear Miledy,' she wrote on December 19, 'I abuse your goodness as well as that of our brave Admiral. Let the great cases be thrown into the hold, the smaller ones are easier to dispose of. Unfortunately I have such a large family. Such distress drives me to despair, and my tears flow unceasingly, the suddenness of the blow has distracted me, and I do not think I shall ever recover from it, but it will strike me down and the shock will lead me to the grave. Pray send me, my dear friend, all available information, and rely on my discretion. My son has returned from Capua with dreadful accounts of the flying troops and unheard-of misfortunes. Adieu, my dear, this horrible calamity shortens two-thirds of our existence...' On December 21 she wrote breathlessly, without punctuation, which we have supplied: 'The dangers increase. Aquila is taken with six hundred men, to the everlasting shame of our country. Mack writes in despair. The weather seems to be clearing, so the King is urgent. I am stunned and in despair, as this entirely changes our condition, life and situation, all that formed my ideas, and those of my family for life. I do not know where my head is. This evening I will send some other boxes and clothes for my numerous family, for it is for life...' Next day she wrote again: 'I tremble at the errors that will be committed by a people who do not defend themselves against the enemy, but allow themselves all the horrors of the most unbridled licence. The preparations are being made with our liberator. I count on them and entrust myself to him with ten innocent members of my family... The wretched Vanni killed himself with a pistol this morning. How I reproach myself for it!'

Vanni, the over-zealous inquisitor of republicans, had applied for transportation to Sicily and been refused. He left a note saying: 'The ingratitude of the Government, the certainty of not finding asylum anywhere, have determined me to kill myself. Lest my death be attributed to others, I leave this memorial.' This seemed another sinister omen.

On December 18 Mack wrote urging the King to move before the French captured Naples. With the forces of Damas and Naselli still intact, besides other provincial regiments and the remnants of his own division, Mack could have organized another army to outnumber that of Championnet, but he was too demoralized. On the 20th another large mob gathered before the palace, shouting for arms to defend the King and themselves, and for permission to kill the Jacobins and the French. The spectacle of such mass excitement was far from reassuring to the royal family, who began to regard their palace as a prison. Next morning the royal messenger Ferreri was mistaken for a French spy and dragged under the King's balcony where he was butchered by the mob, howling 'Death to the Jacobin!' The King was horrified to recognize this innocent victim, whose bleeding corpse was held up to him as a proof of his people's loyalty. Republican writers allege that the Queen and Acton had instigated this atrocity, first to get rid of an accomplice who might betray secrets, and secondly to persuade the King to leave. This is mere party journalism, but the incident would have unnerved a braver man than Ferdinand. As for the Queen, she was haunted by what had happened to her sister. 'They want to keep us as hostages,' she wrote, 'and force us to make terms with those villains.'

Nelson, who was always braced by a crisis—'my mind never better and my heart in the right trim'—had given minute instructions for the embarkation of their Majesties and household. The *Vanguard* with one Portuguese and two Neapolitan men-of-war, the *Archimede* and *Sannita*, commanded by Caracciolo, besides some twenty merchant-men and two Greek polacres chartered by Sir William Hamilton for the French *émigrés*, all loaded with Court treasure, jewels, plate and specie to the value of £2,500,000, had cast anchor at a great distance from the city, 'to be beyond the range of the forts in the event of treachery or surprise'. The weather was so rough that the transfer from the Vittoria landing-stage to the men-of-war was a laborious undertaking. The royal family, escorted by Nelson, left the palace by a secret passage at nine o'clock on the night of December 21. It is probable that Caracciolo was mortally offended at their choosing to embark on Nelson's ship instead of his own, which would help to account for his subsequent behaviour. But the crew of the *Sannita* was short of as many as three hundred sailors, and not even the promise of double pay could persuade them to return. Their excuse for this desertion was anxiety about their families. At the last moment they were reinforced by twenty-five English sailors. Caracciolo himself described his crew as *poco e cattivo*—scanty and bad. His royal master and mistress, however proud of their fleet, could hardly be blamed for preferring the *Vanguard* under the circumstances. Boat after boat brought more shivering refugees, including Lady Knight and her daughter, who left an account of their experiences: 'When we came alongside the Admiral's ship, the captain, Sir Thomas Hardy, stepped into the boat, and told my mother that the ship was so full there was no room for us. In vain we entreated to be taken on board. The thing was impossible. We must take our passage in a Portuguese man-of-war, commanded by an Englishman, who had been a master in our navy, but had now the rank of commodore.

'There was no alternative, but we were some time before we reached the ship to which we had been consigned. The young midshipman who conducted us was constantly jumping about in the boat to keep himself from falling asleep, for during the last forty-eight hours he had been unceasingly engaged in getting the baggage and numerous attendants of the royal family on board.

'We reached our destination about two in the morning, and were ushered into the chief cabin, where we found many ladies of different countries. Only one, a Russian lady of high rank and great wealth, had a bed to sleep on, the others being obliged to content themselves with mattresses on the floor. We now learned that we were bound for Palermo, and it was a great satisfaction to us to receive this confirmation of our previous hopes.'

The royal family were safe, but in what conditions! The ladies and children were given the admiral's quarters; the gentlemen were packed in the wardroom, while the ship rolled at single anchor in the freezing night. The pain of parting from Naples after thirty years was more poignant for the Queen than for her husband. Sicily offered no consoling prospects to a woman of her temperament. She would be isolated, cut off from the rest of Europe and from everything that made life tolerable. In the meantime Naples would probably be lost, she might never see it again. But she could not reproach herself or even Mack.

Next day the Neapolitans were shocked to discover that their King had left them. A royal edict announced that he was going to Sicily to gather reinforcements, leaving General Francesco Pignatelli in charge of the government and General Mack in command of the army. But the *Vanguard* was still at anchor, and it was hoped that the King might be induced to stay. Such a storm arose that communication between the ships was impossible; as soon as it died down the *Vanguard* was besieged by boatloads of deputations. The Cardinal Archbishop, the municipal councillors and magistrates, all pleaded for an audience with the King. Never had Ferdinand doubted his popularity, but recent events had filled him with distrust. It had been difficult for him to make up his mind, but having done so he was obstinate. The steady routine of his sporting life had been monstrously disturbed. His subjects had behaved like wicked children. Very well then, he would teach them a lesson and punish them with his absence. He would only receive the Cardinal Archbishop, who begged him in vain to return. After recommending himself to his prayers and reminding him of his pastoral duties, the King said he had gone to sea because he had been betrayed on land. The harsh words attributed to him by the diarist De Nicola were probably a garbled version of Acton's remarks to the other deputations. Weary of their rhetoric, Acton said it was too late to make excuses: the King would return when they had proved their loyalty with deeds. De Nicola's comment, however, naïvely reflects the sentiment of the majority: 'That a prince who is idolized by the entire nation should have been heard to speak so will lead posterity to believe that the King's trust in the Neapolitans has been ill requited, and yet it is most certain that each one of us is devoted to him and would lay down his life for him. Who could have prejudiced him so deeply against a people most attached to him and deserving the title of *fedelissimo*—most faithful!' The answer inferred is that the Queen was responsible.

The squadron remained at anchor on the 23rd, some said on account of the weather which failed to improve. Apparently the King wished to see Mack before sailing. At last he came on board the *Vanguard*. 'My heart bled for him,' said Nelson,'he is worn to a shadow.' He could only confirm his defeat; all that remained of his army was cooped up at Capua. At a gloomy conference it was decided that if Naples could not resist the French invasion his troops were to withdraw to Salerno or march through Calabria towards Sicily, from which they would receive support. In the last extremity he was to cross over to Messina and reorganize his army there. Nelson wished to prevent the Neapolitan men-of-war from falling into enemy hands. As these had been abandoned by most of their crews, it would be difficult to send them to Sicily. Naturally the King and Queen were opposed to their destruction. Nelson could only order his Portuguese ally, the Marquis de Niza, to save as many as possible, but those which could not be saved were to be burnt if Naples was captured.

After two days and two nights in the rough bay, the *Vanguard* sailed with a large convoy on the night of the 23rd. According to an English fellow-passenger: 'The King seemed quite reconciled to his fate when he embarked, continued on deck till midnight, and conversed familiarly with the officers who knew Italian or French. Shortly after they got under weigh, the wind shifted to the *tramontana* (north), when His Majesty observed to Sir William Hamilton, "We shall have plenty of woodcocks, Cavaliere; this wind will bring them—it is just the season, and we shall have rare sport. You must get your *cannone* ready," and summoning his principal game-keeper, the two entered into a long discussion about woodcocks. The wind, however, increased with heavy squalls, accompanied by vivid flashes of lightning, the sure forerunner of a storm in the Mediterranean. At length it blew so hard that the sails were split into atoms, the sea rose mountains high, and the ship was considered in such danger during the hurricane, that preparations were made to cut away the main-mast, after the loss of the fore-yard.' It was an appalling voyage, the worst in Nelson's experience. The passengers were prostrate except Lady Hamilton, her mother and one of the Queen's stewards. The ambassadress tended the Queen and the royal children in turn, supplying them with her own bedding and linen, as if Venus had sprung from the foam to their assistance. Nelson's pride in the splendid Emma as she soared above panic and physical squalor with indomitable exuberance is comprehensible. In his own words, she had put him and the whole royal family under an eternal obligation; she had 'become *their slave*, for except for one man, no person belonging to Royalty assisted the Royal Family, nor did her Ladyship enter a bed the whole time they were on board'. Sir William, who had also 'made every sacrifice for the comfort of the august Family', was found during the height of the gale with a loaded pistol in each hand.' In answer to her Ladyship's exclamation of surprise, he calmly told her that he was resolved not to die with the "guggle-guggle-guggle" of the salt-water in his throat; and therefore he was prepared, as soon as he felt the ship sinking, to shoot himself'. Count Esterhazy, the Austrian ambassador, tossed his jewelled snuff-box overboard, which was adorned with a miniature of his mistress in the nude, 'for he considered it highly impious to keep about his person so profane an article, when (as he thought) on the verge of eternity'.

Christmas Day was nearly as rough, and the British officers apologized for not being able to offer some seasonable entertainment. After heart-rending convulsions, the six-year-old Prince Carlo Alberto died of exhaustion in Lady Hamilton's arms the same night. At two o'clock next morning the *Vanguard* reached Palermo. The Queen did not wait for dawn to land. So ill was she during the next few days that her life seemed to be in danger. Yet she was soon committing her sombre thoughts to paper. 'I have lived long enough,' she wrote, 'even two or three years too long. Consequently I do not fear death, and the storm which threatened to bury us all did not frighten me.' Worn out and cruelly bereaved, her courage rallied: 'But I must perform my duty, and mine at this moment is to reconquer the property of my dear husband and beloved sons. Only when this has been done shall I be able to consider returning, my sole desire.'

Accommodation for the sudden influx of some two thousand refugees was not easy to find in Palermo. The Colli Palace, damp, gloomy and sparsely furnished, was ill prepared for the royal family. Nearly all succumbed to the effects of anxiety, cold and fatigue. Sir William Hamilton was confined to bed by a bilious fever, and his wife was prone to hysteria after twelve sleepless nights. Even Nelson complained of the detestable air and climate. He was fuming over the appointment of his bugbear, Sir Sidney Smith, to conduct operations in Egypt. 'Is it to be borne?' he wrote to his Commander-in-Chief. 'Pray grant me permission to retire, and I hope the *Vanguard* will be allowed to convey me and my friends, Sir William and Lady Hamilton, to England.'

Only the King seemed impervious to recent shocks. He had chosen to land at the more convenient hour of nine in the morning after a substantial breakfast, and he was much gratified by the joyful manifestations of his subjects. Neither the loss of Naples nor that of his little son could be allowed to upset his balance. He maintained that all would come right in the end; in the meantime there was variety of sport to be had on the island. His favourite dogs had accompanied him, and he was determined to make the best of his visit, which he did not think would last very long.

Next to the King, perhaps Lady Knight and her talented daughter were the most placid of the refugees. Having escaped the full fury of the storm, they arrived in an appreciative mood, and were lucky to find nice apartments on the Marina, the long promenade. 'Accustomed as I had been to the lovely and magnificent scenery of Italy,' wrote Miss Knight, 'I was not less surprised than delighted at the picturesque beauty of the Sicilian coast. Then, when the prospect of the city opened upon us, with the regal elegance of its marble palaces and the fanciful singularity of its remaining specimens of Saracenic architecture, it was like a fairy scene...'

All seemed African to the shuddering Queen, even the inhabitants. Ill though she was, she poured out her woes in a long letter to Gallo, who had been sent to plead her cause in Vienna: 'The most unhappy of Queens, mothers and women, writes you this. I say the most unhappy because I feel so keenly and I doubt if I shall survive all I have experienced these last forty days. Here I am at Palermo. We escaped on Friday. Arrangements to burn the ships and other matters detained us in the roads until Sunday, when deputations came to harangue us and urge us to return, but never mentioned arming to defend us. Mack came on board Sunday morning half-dead, weeping, explaining that all was lost, that treachery and cowardice had reached their limit, that his only consolation was to see the family safe on board Nelson's ship, that the royal family of Piedmont had been dragged to Paris, and that the whole of Italy was irremediably lost—in short, news to freeze one's blood; that he had reached Capua with the vanguard and the French were at Terracina. If these advanced with reinforcements and our troops fled, he expected them to be in Naples within three days. Forteguerri (the Minister of the Marine) arrived and begged to be saved, as his life had been threatened, the galley-slaves had mutinied, etc. The sailors deserted the ships: English and Portuguese seamen had to replace at least 1,500 who had fled in a night, in order to save the *Sannita* and the *Archimede*s, without which Nelson would not leave. The Portuguese stayed in the roads to burn our fine fleet which has cost us so much, to my lasting sorrow. We sailed at eight o'clock at night... To describe the most essential, the people of Palermo seemed pleased to see us, but without frantic enthusiasm. The nobility are on the alert and never leave our apartments... My heart tells me that unless the Emperor hastens to act or puts a stop to his quarrels, within four months we shall be driven from Sicily, perhaps even more tragically. Let us offer these vultures all the jewels, liveries, gold lace, everything, and may they let us return to live and die in peace. As for me, my scene is sorrowfully ended. If I am granted the happiness of returning to Naples, I have decided to retire to Linz or Graz or Salzburg, or if that is not feasible, to Sorrento, to end my miserable days. I have lived too long and grief is killing me... In short, I feel desperate. I am sure I cannot continue to live in this way and doubt if I shall survive. For God's sake let them allow my unfortunate daughters to go to Vienna until husbands can be found for them or they can become canonesses. My daughter-in-law has consumption and will not live. Concerning their father I should be silent. He feels nothing but self-love and he hardly feels that. He should realize that he has lost the best part of his Crown, of his revenue; but he is only aware of the novelties which amuse him, without thinking that we are reduced to a quarter of our income, dishonoured, unhappy, and dragging others into the same misfortune... Everything here repels me. Our provinces, Sorrento—I would prefer any other place. Either I succumb or I shall have to leave this country which is alien to my nature... I implore you to adjust our affairs. I have ceased to believe in grandeur, glory, honour. This self-conceit has been my ruin. My sole aim is to live retired in a corner, Sorrento or Pozzuoli, to see the few friends left me in misfortune and die in peace... Adieu. May Heaven give you happiness... Count on my gratitude, useless, it is true, but sincere. Think occasionally of our eighteen years of friendship, and remember with compassion the unhappiest of mortals. Speak, if you judge it opportune, to the insensible souls where you are.' The insensible souls were her imperial daughter and son-in-law.

Ferdinand and Maria Carolina have been endlessly abused for seeking refuge in Palermo instead of risking humiliation and expulsion, like Pope Pius VI and the sovereigns of Sardinia, or perhaps violent death. But even if they wished to act heroically, had they the right to sacrifice their dynasty? Was it likely that their troops, so crushingly defeated by inferior numbers in a brief campaign, would rally to their defence at the last minute? Even if the populace were loyal, what could they hope to achieve against a better organized phalanx of traitors plotting from within and without to deliver them to the enemy? By going to Palermo, the King and Queen were exchanging one capital for another: they were still on their own territory, which they could use as a base for recovering the rest of their realm. Nelson had advised this course, and he was no coward. Had they waited to be driven out by the invader, their dynasty would have been doomed. They have also been castigated for removing as many valuables as possible. The simple alternative was to leave them for the French, who had already grabbed half the treasures of Italy.

The choice of General Francesco Pignatelli as the King's Vicar or Regent proved as disastrous as the choice of Mack. He was prematurely old at sixty-five, and all his actions were defeatist. In the tremulous lull that followed the royal departure much precious time was wasted in futile debate. The delegates representing the municipal government proposed the formation of a city guard to keep law and order, but Pignatelli told them haughtily not to interfere. After more than a week he was induced to consent and some 14,000 militia were conscripted. When these applied to him for arms he said that none were available. Yielding to pressure, he distributed muskets in driblets: eventually some 500 were collected. A semblance of calm was maintained.

Fortress after fortress surrendered to the enemy, Civitella, Pescara, and finally Gaeta, with a garrison of 4,000, 12 mortars, 70 cannons, 20,000 muskets and provisions for a year. The Swiss governor Tschudy opened the gates to the enemy without a skirmish. Mack had one belated flicker of self-confidence as the French advanced on Capua. The Duke of Roccaromana forced the French back from the Volturno near Caiazzo with some 400 casualties. General Boisregard was killed and General Mathieu lost an arm. Roccaromana was wounded, but he might have inflicted a greater defeat had the Prince of Moliterno galloped with his two cavalry regiments to his assistance. The whole countryside was swarming with armed bands of peasants who harried isolated French columns, seizing their transports, blowing up an artillery park and destroying the bridges over the Garigliano.

In spite of the effective resistance at Capua, Pignatelli was growing more and more discouraged. Everybody distrusted everybody else, and there was nobody with sufficient character to dominate the situation. Many of the city deputies were in favour of a republic, and these used every available stick to belabour the wretched Regent. Public opinion was exasperated when he ordered all the powder and ammunition stored at Mergellina to be dumped into the sea, and the destruction of more than a hundred gunboats moored at Posillipo. One blaze begot another. On January 8 the English-born Commodore Mitchell in Portuguese service, who distrusted Pignatelli, decided to burn the Neapolitan ships of war in anticipation of the French. The *Partenope, Tancredi, Guiscardo*, each of seventy-four guns, the *San Giovacchino* of sixty-four, the frigate *Pallade* of forty, the corvette *Flora* of twenty-four, besides several smaller vessels were set on fire. 'It was a pitiful sight,' wrote the diarist Marinelli, 'while the nation was robbed of its strength, and so many tears, so much substance and wealth of the citizens were consumed. All night they went on burning, keeping the whole bay ablaze.'

On January 11, when alarm and despondency reached a climax, Pignatelli negotiated a two months' armistice with General Championnet. The terms were ruinous: Capua was to be evacuated; the French were to occupy all the land north of the Volturno from the Mediterranean to the Adriatic, cutting the high road to Naples; all the ports were to be closed to the British; and an indemnity of ten million francs was to be paid to the Republic, half on the

15th and half on the 25th of January. From a military point of view there had still been a good chance of defending Naples, of contesting the ground inch by inch and making the French pay dear for their invasion. All that was lost with Capua. To summarize the judgment of Count Roger de Damas, the French at Capua were without supplies, harried from the rear by armed peasants, and if Gaeta had not been cravenly surrendered, they would have been in a worse plight than the Neapolitan army. A Neapolitan force of 14,000 men under General de Gambs was still intact in the provinces between Naples and the Abruzzo. This could be sent to defend the capital, and even if it failed to arrive in time, it could march into Calabria and await the junction of Damas's column with that from Leghorn, and preserve that valuable province. But such an idea had never occurred to Mack. In Damas's words, he had lost his head, and nobody else could remedy that deficiency. 'The French had everything to fear in their advance on Naples and could find no provisions at Capua. It has been discovered since that they were ready to come to terms which would result in their withdrawal, but the folly of the Neapolitan government forestalled this by proposing an armistice. The delegates sent to Championnet met his *aide-de-camp* on the road. He had also come with instructions, but instead of waiting for him to speak they hastened to blurt out their own. Seeing what he was likely to gain, the *aide-de-camp* kept silent and introduced them to his general. Their preamble enabled him to discern that they thought their situation critical without realizing his. He took advantage of this to increase his demands and their consternation...'

When the armistice was announced in Naples the people felt that they had been betrayed; a period of anarchy began. On the 14th the French commissioners arrived for the first instalment of the indemnity. Pignatelli summoned the city deputies and proposed taxing merchants and property owners to pay it. When they refused, he declared he would wash his hands of the whole business. The rumour that the French were in their midst caused riots among the *lazzaroni*, who burst into the theatres in quest of them. The curtain of the San Carlo was lowered in a hurry and the audience promptly scattered. The French were smuggled out of the city in the early hours of the morning while a mob shouted outside the palace for the traitors who had sold them to the enemy. The urban militia were assaulted and disarmed wherever they appeared, and the women were just as violent as the men. Next day the *lazzaroni* boarded the ship which had brought Naselli's regiments back from Leghorn and forced the troops to hand over their arms and ammunition. Thus strengthened, they attacked each of the forts in turn. The commandant of Castel Nuovo asked Pignatelli for instructions and was told to defend the castle without harming the assailants. 'Must we not even fire?' 'Yes, but with powder only.' Then a messenger was sent with orders not to fire. The mob scaled the outer gate; the second was opened by some of the garrison; the royal flag was hoisted; the officers were driven out; and the *lazzaroni* were soon in possession of the castle. The same happened at the Sant' Elmo, Carmine and Ovo castles. The arsenal was seized and the prisons thrown open, so that the Jacobins were set free besides some six thousand common malefactors. An armed band went to Casoria to arrest Mack, but he was warned in advance. Dressed as an Austrian general, he presented himself to Championnet and applied for a passport to Austria. Championnet gave him one, but refused the sword he offered with the remark: 'Keep it, General; my government forbids me to accept presents made in England.' Subsequently the Directory had Mack arrested and sent to Paris as a prisoner of war.

Marshal Macdonald relates in his *Souvenirs* that Mack paid him a visit on his way through Capua. 'It was five o'clock in the morning and I was asleep. Soon up, I said to him: "General, a fortnight ago you would not have surprised me in bed." "Ah!" he replied, "you broke my neck at Calvi." Talking of past events, he told me that they had poisoned him at Capua and tried to murder him at Naples; he was in fact very ill, and I saw him again in the same condition in Paris, a year later. During this first interview I asked him: "How could a general so distinguished for his talents thus risk his military reputation as a great tactician by putting himself at the head of such an army?" "I was summoned by request of the King of Naples," he replied. "I declined, but my sovereign commanded me and I was forced to obey. Then, when I saw this army I was seduced, as it was well kept, organized and trained, showing a great devotion and above all a great zeal to fight you and deliver Rome and Italy." "And also no doubt," I added, laughing, "to come to France and Paris." "Ah!" he exclaimed, "this army only lacked officers and the leadership of a French general." After this compliment he took his leave, and I recommended him to the attentions of all our commanders.'

At the last moment Mack had resigned his command to the old Duke of Salandra, who had to pay the penalty. A group of citizens mistook him for the Austrian, wounded him in the head and broke one of his arms; he was lucky to have escaped with his life. Pignatelli, frightened out of his wits by the anarchy he had done so much to produce, dressed up in his wife's clothes and fled to Sicily on the 16th. As soon as he landed he was imprisoned in the fortress of Girgenti. 'We regard him as criminal for leaving and for making the armistice,' wrote the Queen. But for a long time she continued to sympathize with 'the worthy and unfortunate Mack', and begged Gallo to save his reputation in Vienna.

The people decided to appoint a leader they could trust. Their choice, influenced by some of the nobility and abetted by bribes, fell on the Prince of Moliterno, who had lost an eye while fighting the French in Lombardy. The flashy young Duke of Roccaromana was appointed his second-in-command, and four nobles were put in charge of the castles. It was a delicate task to subdue those who had chosen him, but at least Moliterno made a strenuous effort. The events of the next few days are difficult to disentangle from the general chaos: the diarists Marinelli and De Nicola noted as many false rumours as facts. An intercepted letter from Giuseppe Zurlo, the Minister of Finance, was said to prove that he was parleying with the enemy: according to some it was addressed to Mack, according to others to Championnet, informing him that the indemnity could not be paid under the circumstances. His house was sacked by the mob, and he would have been executed in the market square if his friend the Duke of San Valentino had not urged them to take him to the neighbouring castle of the Carmine to stand for public trial. The mob was still malleable since Moliterno had published severe edicts and erected gallows in various parts of the city.

Having failed to raise money, the French considered the armistice broken. Championnet laughed at the deputation of citizens who tried to delay his advance by further negotiation. 'Do you suppose that you are the victors and we are the vanquished?' he asked them. When they got wind of this secret mission the populace ran riot, destroyed the gallows, dragged cannons to such strategic points as Capodichino, Capodimonte and the Maddalena bridge, and appointed bold leaders in the Masaniello tradition, such as Paggio, a flour-merchant, and Michele il Pazzo—Mad

Michael. Priests and friars, crucifix in hand, inveighed against the French heretics and blessed the weapons which the people held up to them. Those who were known to be Jacobins or whose short hair and unconventional attire stigmatized them as such went in terror of their lives, and many innocents were massacred by mistake. The mob broke into the palace of the scholarly Duke della Torre, whose barber had spread a rumour that he was in touch with the enemy. The house, which contained a valuable library and a collection of pictures and scientific instruments, was looted from top to bottom; the harmless Duke and his brother Don Clemente Filomarino were tied to chairs and shot, after which their bodies were burned. This was but one of several outrages which inclined law-abiding citizens to wish for the French to restore order since nobody else could do so.

A committee of ardent republicans, the remnants of the old 'Patriotic Society', managed to elude the vigilance of the *lazzaroni*. They held clandestine meetings in the house of Luigi de' Medici's old friend, the lawyer Nicola Fasulo, and sent Championnet an urgent message begging him to hasten his advance and assuring him of their complete co-operation. He replied that he would not attack the city until the castle of Sant' Elmo was safely in their hands. At this point it seems that they won over Moliterno and Roccaromana, whose brother was in command of Sant' Elmo, garrisoned by *lazzaroni* who were determined to resist to the end. The problem was how to get rid of these embarrassing comrades. The self-styled 'patriots', as von Helfert observed, were those who did everything to collaborate with the foreign invader. Those who were ready to sacrifice their lives for king and country were the genuine patriots.

Moliterno's deception of the simple folk who had trusted him was far from gallant. Knowing their psychology, he induced the Cardinal Archbishop to have all the church bells tolled at ten o'clock at night, whereupon the miraculous blood of San Gennaro was to be exposed and borne in procession through the streets. Hearing the bells at this unusual hour, some imagined that the French had arrived, others that they had been routed, but all rushed to the cathedral, where the Cardinal Archbishop sat among his clergy in a blaze of candles. Dazzled, they fell on their knees, invoking their patron saint with frantic fervour. Moliterno and Roccaromana appeared in penitential garb; with dishevelled hair and bare feet they accompanied the winding procession of men and women who implored forgiveness for their sins aloud. At midnight they returned to the cathedral for the Archbishop's blessing, and Moliterno harangued them with the sobs and tears of an inspired orator, urging them to trust San Gennaro and return quietly to their homes. They were to reassemble at dawn to fight the enemy. The people were calmed by his hypocritical words, and it was by a trick scarcely more chivalrous that the Republicans seized Sant' Elmo. Groups of renegade officers, in league with Nicola Caracciolo, Roccaromana's brother, who commanded the castle, volunteered to reinforce the defenders, and were invited in as brothers. Luigi Brandi, the *lazzarone* chief, grumbled that he did not like the look of these dandies: evidently his suspicions had been roused. But Caracciolo reassured him with talk about a vigorous defence. Brandi was sent outside on patrol with a party of some eighty *lazzaroni* while those of the garrison who were known to be loyal were disarmed. When the republicans felt themselves sufficiently strong, Brandi was summoned for fresh instructions. Once behind closed doors, he was pounced on, his eyes were bandaged, and his hands and feet were bound. The republicans could congratulate themselves that they had gained the key to the capital without bloodshed.

Sant' Elmo also became a place of refuge for those 'patriots' who longed to deliver their country to the French. Many groups of reforming idealists, including that exalted blue-stocking Eleonora Fonseca Pimentel, came to join the garrison. One of them, disguised as a hermit, brought the glad news to Championnet, promising to attack the populace from the rear as soon as he entered the city. The tricolour was hoisted on the 21st and Championnet marched on the city from Capodimonte. But the populace refused to be cowed by this act of treachery. Though ignorant of military tactics, they inflicted severe losses on the invaders, who were guided and assisted in every way by their Neapolitan partisans. Fired upon from the rear by their fellow-citizens at Sant' Elmo, sniped at from above and below by 'democratic' students, mown down by the charging French, they fought on with wild courage at the Maddalena bridge, at the Capuan gate and at Capodimonte. 'How unlike their ancestors,' remarked Schipa, 'those who had offered cakes and kisses to the Austrian soldiers in 1707 and given the Spaniards an ovation in 1734! In half a century the Bourbons had transformed sheep into heroes: their resistance did honour to the monarchy.'

For three days the struggle continued from street to street and house to house. It had become a civil war in which a growing number of citizens backed the winning side. They fired on the *lazzaroni* from the house-tops and threw stones and flower pots at them; the entire street of Toledo, now Via Roma, as far as the turning into the Chiaia, was densely littered with objects hurled at the frantic defenders. From his house near the museum, then called the Palazzo degli Studii, the German painter Tischbein watched the street fighting between the *lazzaroni* and the French: 'The *lazzaroni*, who until then had been dragging cannon through the city every night, shouting, "Look out, look out! The enemy are near!" had fortified themselves in a street off the big square called Largo del le Pigne. The French, on the other side, just under my windows, had placed a battery, and the explosions now began. Among the high houses, built of stone, these made a reverberation as if the world were about to collapse. One was almost deafened. The door of my house was strongly barred; all the windows were hermetically closed; and there was nothing to do but wait patiently for death. However, one gets used to everything. When the terrifying noise had continued a while I called my cook and said: "Come what may, I do not wish to die of hunger. Get ready." Dinner was brought to the table, and we ate to convivial strains which it is not easy to enjoy... Then we were prompted by curiosity to see what was happening outside. We searched for a hole to peep through, and it was certainly worth the effort. Not far from my house a joiner had placed a pile of beams from the wrecked mansion of the Duke della Torre, who had been shot with his brother, then cut to pieces and burnt. With those beams the French had made a kitchen fire, and began to roast ribs of pork. A large crowd stood round it. When one finished eating he rose and fired on the *lazzaroni*. Others who had no more cartridges turned and ate, were given fresh ammunition, and began to shoot again. Before the Studii, there was a lofty flight of steps on which the bullets beat incessantly like hail. Whoever stood behind it was safe, because the bullets bounded high up, flying over the houses. Among the French I noticed a fine young grenadier, who was remarkable for his unusual stature; it would be difficult to see a more magnificent soldier. Like the others, he shot assiduously. I thought that the snipers from Solimena's house, facing the door, would take aim at him, because all those who barely put their heads over the steps disappeared. As soon as his bearskin cap and a fraction of his forehead were visible a bullet came: he fell over backwards full length, with his arms outstretched, and never moved a limb.

'A large cannon, found at the port, had been placed by the *lazzaroni* under a door in front of my house. After its first discharge the French began to fire at it, and it was soon abandoned. A youth leapt forward and tried to rescue it, but he was immediately struck dead by a hail of bullets; the others escaped. On this occasion an image of Christ was miserably shattered; only the arms and legs hung from a few splinters. The previous day I had observed that handsome youth, who tried to save the cannon, busily throwing down the signs by which the enemy were to distinguish the houses to be burnt. Soon after I heard a Frenchman cry out in agony, and I saw that, struck by a bullet, he had fallen flat on the ground. The weight of his knapsack, crammed with stolen goods, had carried him in the same direction. His comrades ran to his assistance, but he said "*Adieu, camarades!*" and died.'

Suddenly Tischbein's stable-boy announced: 'The French are here. They want to shoot the master of the house and all of us.' Two of his pupils volunteered to go in his stead, but he would not let them. While he was going downstairs, he thought he would never need to be shaved again—'a thing which has always been most painful to me'. Eventually he was saved by declaring his German nationality and fraternizing with a French officer. Among other anecdotes in his *Memoirs*, the following typifies the strange illusions which the Neapolitan Jacobins cherished about their prototypes: 'One of my pupils was a sculptor. Passionately pro-French, because he believed that they wished to convert the whole of Italy into a Republic, he set out in the direction of Aversa to welcome them. At Capodichino he was arrested by the *lazzaroni*, but when they searched his carriage they found a breviary. "After all," they said, "we see that you are a good fellow, and not a traitor!" Thus his best passport was his prayer-book, and he returned safely to the city. During the night my pupil Ludovic Hummel came to see me. Although he disliked anything that remotely resembled a political idea, and detested revolts, tumults and warfare, he was always in touch with what was happening, because everybody, of every shade of opinion, liked him and enjoyed his company. The sculptor told him enthusiastically in my presence what splendid people the French were, with what courtesy they would receive him, and what happiness they would diffuse through Italy, and especially Naples. "Imagine," he said, "I saw one of their soldiers carrying a nestful of wood-pigeons in his knapsack. Between marching, fighting and capturing cities, he feeds his pigeons! Such gentle souls are to be found among these republican heroes!" And he went on to say that the French had no other desire but to introduce liberty into Italy; therefore they should be supported at all costs. But they did not come as soon as he expected. Hearing that he had consorted with the enemy, the *lazzaroni* wanted to kill him, so that he was forced to go into hiding. He concealed himself in the vast building of the Studii, where he could not be discovered. At last when the French arrived he emerged from his shelter, and rushed with open arms towards his liberators. But these pointed their guns at the chest of their enthusiastic admirer and stole his watch.'

The *lazzaroni*, too, had their illusions. When one of them was taken off to be shot he laughed and said: 'What do you want to do to me with your guns? Look here!' And he twirled his cap in the air to show an image of San Gennaro and the Madonna, which he had stuck on his forehead as a means of protection, like most of his fellows. 'The French made short work of him and his amulet: they levelled their guns and his brains bespattered the wall.'

Gradually the *lazzaroni* were forced to realize that further resistance was futile. Castle after castle surrendered and hoisted the tricolour flag; French detachments occupied the strategic points of the capital on the 23rd. There were a thousand French casualties and three thousand Neapolitan. Sporadic fighting continued in the back alleys, but most of the populace began to concentrate on plunder. Even if luck had turned against them they might as well wrest the spoils from the enemy. To break up further opposition, a rumour was started that the French permitted them to sack the royal palace. Why had they not thought of it before? Rather than the enemy, the King would prefer his loyal subjects to enrich themselves at his expense. Hordes of men, women and children invaded the palace like locusts, and in less than three hours they had stripped it bare. A couple of cannon-bursts from Sant' Elmo scattered the looters, many of whom dropped their prizes in a scramble for safety; a priest and a peasant were killed. Championnet, who described the *lazzaroni* as heroes, wrote: 'If I had not succeeded in dividing them and concentrating all their fury on the pillage of the royal palace, the occupation of the city would probably have entailed sacrifices of men far greater than the immense advantages resulting from it.' Michele il Pazzo fought on valiantly until he was taken prisoner. Appreciating his potential value, Championnet treated him with special consideration, explaining that he had come to bring peace and liberty to Naples and that he would always respect religion and San Gennaro. The *lazzarone* leader soon raised a cheer for the Republic, the French and San Gennaro, which was echoed by his flock. When Championnet sent a guard of honour for the Saint, the populace were reassured. But the guard was really to keep the old Archbishop and the clergy in order, who were made responsible for the good behaviour of the populace. A new flag, blue, red and yellow, was seen to flutter over Sant' Elmo—the flag of what was to be called the Parthenopean Republic. Proclamations to the people were published by Moliterno and Roccaromana as well as by Generals Championnet and Kellermann, all variations on the same theme: the French had come as liberators pure and simple. 'Your liberty is the only reward France wishes to claim from her conquest... The French army assumes the name of the Neapolitan army, and is solemnly pledged to maintain your rights and wield arms for the cause of your freedom.'

Already on the 22nd the 'patriots of Sant' Elmo' had planted a tree of liberty in the castle yard, proclaiming the Neapolitan Republic One and Indivisible under the protection of the great French nation, and Eleonora Pimentel had declaimed her latest effusion, a 'Hymn to Liberty' with a chorus in which everybody joined. On the 23rd they sent Championnet a list of candidates for the provisional government. Most of these had cropped up in the Jacobin trials and Annibale Giordano's denunciations. Prominent among them was Carlo Lauberg, the renegade monk who had fled to France and returned, a married man, in French uniform.

A French officer remarked that if Bonaparte had occupied Naples after encountering such fierce resistance, most of it would have been wiped out. Fortunately Championnet was humane and moderate, and he showed rare finesse in dealing with an alien people. Doubtless he realized that without the support of the Neapolitan republicans, those who had accompanied him from exile as well as those who had seized Sant' Elmo, he could not have entered the capital so soon, and he might not have entered it at all. The Parthenopean Republic was installed by conquest, and the French army of occupation was its only solid prop. Championnet tactfully tried to persuade his collaborators, so sensitive on this sore point, to forget about it. Very nearly he succeeded. Those who had opened Sant' Elmo to the invader came to believe that they had accomplished a revolution. The expression stuck. The events that took place in Naples in 1799 are, as Croce said, among the best known in modern Italian history. Copious publications deal with them in many languages, and all of them speak of the 'Neapolitan Revolution', though some, like Cuoco, discriminate it with a qualifying adjective, in his case 'passive'. But as General de Damas wrote: 'It was absurd to call this a revolution. The united will of the people or the postulate of popular suffrage forms what is usually called a revolution: this was merely an invasion, which force invested with revolutionary trappings to sustain it.'

The Citizen Cardinal Archbishop was ordered to have the Blessed Sacrament exposed for ten days in all the churches 'for the most happy entrance of the French army into this capital', and in announcing this the prelate related an extraordinary miraculous liquefaction of the blood of San Gennaro the same evening. As Croce observed, it appears that the saint was indifferent to political changes, and continued to smile on his devotees and reassure them with his supernatural conjuring. At any rate, the saint showed no hostility to the French, which was all they required of him. A *Te Deum* in the cathedral was also ordered, after which a tree of liberty was planted in front of the royal, now called the national, palace. This was a large pine with a cap of liberty on the summit and the new flag tied to it with tricolour bands. On the same night some of the populace attempted to burn it, and even when they failed it was hung with satirical scrawls. On February 1 sentinels and guns were posted around the tree to protect it from insult. All the crowns, lilies and other royal emblems on the palace were destroyed. The city was illuminated for three nights; the theatres were reopened under different names. At the San Carlo, now the National Theatre, an opera by Tritti called *Nicaboro in Jucatan*, originally composed for the King's birthday, was performed 'to celebrate the expulsion of the tyrant, with an analogous hymn and ballet'. After the hymn the audience cried out 'Long live Liberty! Death to the Tyrant!' ('He will return in spite of you!' one voice rejoindered), and the names of Acton, Castelcicala and other satellites of the tyrant were singled out for special obloquy. Liberty! Henceforth the word was on everybody's lips, and in the beginning it seemed to work like a magic spell. 'Three days after the French entry into Naples,' wrote Hackert, 'the *lazzaroni* were transformed into lambs.'

XVIII

The Court of Palermo—Treaties with Russia and Turkey—Sicilian pride and prejudice—Cardinal Ruffo and the Calabrian Crusade—The Queen's disgust with Mack—The cost of frenchified liberty—Eleonora Pimentel and the Monitore Napoletano—Republican doctrinaires—General Macdonald and the recall of Championnet.

'Ah, if only I were there,' exclaimed the Queen, 'I should certainly save Naples or perish, and that surely, for to live as I do now is worse than death...' If only she were a man, instead of an ailing middle-aged woman! Ferdinand's placidity exasperated her. 'The King is delighted to be safe, makes petty economies at our expense, torments us terribly, goes forth on excursions, attends theatres, hunts, and is the least affected. The Prince and Princess Royal are ill. My daughters and Leopold suffer but try to comfort me. But nothing can console me, I am in despair. My advice is that the King should convoke the Sicilian Parliament, address them as their sovereign and father, tell of his requirements and the need to defend ourselves, using every means available, grant a few favours and privileges of minor consequence and rouse their enthusiasm to great sacrifices. But I have not been able to obtain this unique and urgent measure. Nothing is done; and soon, in spite of our privations, we shall be in financial straits, for we must create everything anew, marine, artillery, everything... Alas, the thought of being dishonoured and disparaged throughout Europe kills me even more than my losses and misfortunes.'

The truth was that the King blamed his wife. He had always looked up to her as a superior intellect. But it was she who had plunged him into this premature campaign; it was through her that he had been saddled with the egregious Mack. His confidence in her judgment had cracked. After thirty years of married life she could not fail to notice it, but she refused to be shelved. On January 1, 1799, she wrote to Lady Hamilton: 'Many compliments to our excellent Admiral. I am anxious to have a quiet conversation with him about the defence of this island, for everything that I see, foresee, hear and feel does not give me the slightest tranquillity. I am neither consulted nor even listened to, and am exceedingly unhappy...' News of the destruction of the fleet and of Pignatelli's armistice reached Palermo on January 12, the King's birthday, yet there was a gala reception at Court, followed by a performance at the theatre, and the whole city was festively illuminated. 'There is death in my heart,' wrote the Queen, 'but in order not to give offence I have to be present at all this. The weather is perishingly cold and it snows continually, so that all the streets and roofs are white, which is very extraordinary for Palermo. I have never been so cold in my life. Not a window or door can be closed, and there is not a fireplace or carpet in our rooms... I live in a new apartment never inhabited before, which lacks furniture and upholstery. My feverish chill only yields to opiates, which benumb me during the evening. The King is in good health. I envy him. He is not at all afflicted, and it annoys him to see me always in tears.'

Ferdinand was the last person to don sackcloth and ashes, but he showed signs of unwonted activity and his temper became more irritable. He had suspended the viceregal government and appointed the viceroy, Prince de Luzzi, Secretary of State for Internal Affairs. Acton remained his chief adviser, mingling firmness, sympathy and tact when he gave way to tantrums. The Queen was bitterly jealous; she taxed him with ingratitude. Was not Acton her own creation? To spare himself the tedium of the Queen's tears and tirades, he used ill health as a pretext for seeing as little of her as possible. In spite of her resentment, the Queen had to realize that without Acton she, too, stood alone. Whom else could she trust? Gallo? Had she followed his advice, she might have been able to remain in Naples, but for how long? Gallo was more concerned with the present than the future, like most Neapolitans. Besides, Nelson and the Hamiltons abhorred him. He could be useful as an intermediary with her son-in-law the Emperor, who had an exalted opinion of his merits. But it was disquieting to hear that he was still at Brindisi on January 21, a month after he had left Naples. What could he be doing there—waiting to see the turn of events? Moreover, he had sold all his furniture in Palermo, which looked suspicious. Then Commodore Caracciolo applied for permission to return to Naples to look after his property, which the Republic had threatened to seize. It seemed a strange request from a loyal officer.

In granting it, the King sent him warning: 'Beware of meddling with French politics, and avoid the snares of the Republicans. I know I shall recover the Kingdom of Naples.' But he was determined to go. These were 'so many dagger-thrusts', as the Queen expressed it. At least she could trust Acton. That close intimacy which had long been the centre of her existence, which had caused so much scandalous gossip and trouble with Spain, had ended some years ago. Though shrivelled and ageing he was imperturbable; he had never lost his grip.

An offensive and defensive treaty had been signed with Russia on December 29, by which Russia promised to keep a fleet in the Mediterranean and send nine battalions and two hundred Cossacks as soon as the season allowed them to travel. A similar treaty was signed with Turkey on January 21. Unfortunately Nelson did little to conceal his dislike of the Russians and his impatience with the Austrians, but Hamilton's blandness made up for Nelson's bluntness, and Acton worked hard to maintain goodwill between the allied envoys in Palermo. As Captain-General of the kingdom, Acton started to reorganize the military forces of the island, raising three infantry and three cavalry regiments with good pay and a royal corps of artillery and engineers. Prince della Cattolica and other notabilities toured the provinces to encourage recruiting.

Republican agents had sneaked into Messina, but they could make little progress among people whose hatred of the French had been smouldering ever since the Sicilian Vespers. This hatred blazed up with all the old fury on January 20, when a French ship from Egypt appeared in Sicilian waters. Mr Charles Lock, the new British Consul-General, described the event as follows: 'Figure to yourself, my dear Sir, 120 fugitives from Alexandria, ignorant of the state of warfare between the two countries, arrived at Augusta. Amongst them was General Souci, a young man of considerable talents. They were immediately secured, and coming from an infected place were lodged in quarantine in a house on the sea-shore without the walls. The sight of all these men was more or less affected by the reflection of the sun on the burning sands of Egypt, and between forty and fifty of them were nearly blind. They were looked upon with an evil eye from the moment of their arrival, and as it was soon after the flight of the King from Naples, they could the less bear the jokes and reflections these Frenchmen impudently threw out upon that sore subject. Their contempt for their religion which some of them did not attempt to conceal was a heavy aggravation in the minds of superstitious men, and the display of gold with which they played at chuck farthing was a further incitement to the tragedy which followed. On the 20th day of their confinement and the day before they were to be removed to a house within the walls, some of them were playing at bowls, and the boys of the town who were standing round proving troublesome, one of them said: "Get you gone, or I will make bowls of your heads!" This is the only immediate cause of provocation I ever heard assigned. A report was spread that they had threatened to murder the boys, the people assembled round the house, and the officer commanding the guard growing apprehensive that they might commit some violence upon the prisoners, sent to the Governor asking for a reinforcement of regulars as he had no dependence upon the militia of which his guard was composed. His request was slighted and he sent again and again, saying it was no longer in his power to restrain the people from laying their hands upon the prisoners as his soldiers sided with the populace; a few men were at last sent, but too late, as the Governor was in danger of being sacrificed himself for attempting to protect them. The Captain of the Vessel who brought them, coming out of his house with a sword and pistol in his hands, was instantly shot dead by a sentinel, and as others ran out endeavouring to escape they were butchered by the militia and mob together. As the French upon this shut and barricaded their doors, the people got upon the roof, removed the tiling, and from thence fired among them. Finding they were thus exposed they again opened the doors, and about thirty of them who could best see ran out, gained the seaside, got into a boat and effected their escape to the opposite shore. In this number was a young woman. The guns of the fortress were fired by the garrison upon these poor wretches and they were fired at without remission as long as they were within reach. The major part, however, among whom were the blind, who remained within doors, were murdered without mercy; eighty-four were killed upon their knees. Souci was the last who was sacrificed; he was pulled out from under some straw and dead bodies and counterfeited death. But as they began to strip him they perceived the deceit and tho' the officer who had had charge of him, and whose esteem he had conciliated by his generosity and amiable manners, exerted himself to the utmost to save him, he was torn to a thousand pieces. The rage of the populace went so far as to roast and eat their livers.'

So violent was the Sicilian prejudice against the French that the King had to get rid of the unfortunate *émigrés* who had followed him from Naples. 'Unless they find their way over from Calabria, I think we are not likely to be disturbed,' wrote Mr Lock. But the Sicilians had no love for the Neapolitans either, and these predominated in the administration. The Queen's first impression was that Sicily would soon follow the fate of Naples; Hamilton and Nelson apparently thought the same. Writing to Lord Minto on January 19, Nelson anticipated Bentinck's opinions on the subject ten years later: 'These people are proud beyond any I have seen and, in fairness, I think they ought to be consulted on the defence of their own country. They may not have the experience of the others, but they cannot act worse than the *foreigners* [meaning the Neapolitans] have done.'

Early in February there were riots owing to the high cost of provisions, and the Queen described the situation to Gallo in the darkest colours: 'Palermo is in full ferment and I expect grave events. Having neither troops nor arms, lacking everything, I am ready for anything and quite desperate. Here the priests are completely corrupted, the people savage, the nobility more than uncertain and of questionable loyalty. The people and clergy might let us leave if we promised to agree to the establishment of a republic. But the nobility would oppose our departure because then they would be ruined, and they dread the democratization of the country. They would prefer to rise and put themselves at the head of the movement and have us massacred, ourselves and all Neapolitans. The dangers we run here are immense and real. You may imagine what I suffer. Before forty days revolution will have broken out here. It will be appalling and terribly violent. My daughters are all ill. As for my daughter-in-law [the Princess Royal], she is dying of consumption... As the climax of misfortune, nearly all the English ships have been detached to Malta and Alexandria: there is only one left at Palermo. The villainous tricoloured republic, vassal and tributary of the French, arms frigates and schooners and pushes on armaments with feverish activity. Salerno has been for some time in French hands. The Calabrians are revolutionized. The poison spreads everywhere and we shall be the victims. I am only waiting for the return of the English ships to send my daughter-in-law and daughters to Trieste. But everything, even the season, is against it, and I am afraid of losing other children at sea. As if this were not sufficient, I suffer yet another torment: the King will not hear me speak of going to Germany. In case of extremity he seems resolved to settle in England. Irritated with good reason by what has happened, he is convinced, as I am, that we are not at the end of our troubles. As for me, I wish to retire to Germany because I am a mother, because life is less expensive there than in England, and we could lead an existence more compatible with our feeble resources, and I would sooner live modestly there than beg for my bread in England... I should be satisfied with bread and onions rather than live at others' expense... Here are some of the kindnesses they tell us to our face: "Down with the treacherous and cowardly Neapolitans! Out with the Neapolitans!" The upper classes excite the populace, and I live in dread and constant alarm. The King, so as not to give these Sicilians a pretext for complaint, has ceased going to the hunt or to the theatre, and boredom and melancholy devour him. I live in such terror that I no longer dare to say: "Tomorrow I shall still be in this world." Imagine my plight, which would even make stones pity me. The only thing which still sustains me, is the thought that I have not deserved these misfortunes and that I cannot reproach myself with cruelty or anything else. I am simply a victim. I recommend my children to you, if I succeed in saving them and sending them to my own country.

'As regards politics, we must try to make the Emperor and England adhere to the alliance and insist that our devastated realm is restored to us at the peace. At present we only have the Turks in sight, between thirty and fifty thousand of them, plundering everything but sparing those who have remained loyal to us. These, sword in hand, could drive out the French and the Republicans...'

To propitiate the Sicilians, the Prince of Trabia was appointed Minister of War and the Prince of Cassaro Minister of Police, Justice and Supplies; both appointments were popular. Acton remained in charge of foreign affairs, like a pillar of weather-beaten porphyry. But a person more daring and dynamic was required to lead a counter revolution, and he stepped forward from an unexpected quarter. Cardinal Fabrizio Ruffo had been treasurer to Pope Pius VI, but his various reforms had been too radical for the Roman aristocracy. Consequently he had retired to Naples, where the King had appointed him superintendent of his utopian colony and silk factory at San Leucio, a position scarcely compatible with his dignity. As a Prince of the Church he had followed the Court to Palermo, where he immediately proposed a plan to save Calabria. Himself a Calabrian, he had confidence in his people and in his own powers of leadership. He volunteered to defend that part of the country which had not been revolutionized and recover the rest of it, as a first step towards the re-conquest of Naples. A bold undertaking for a white-haired Cardinal of over sixty, but Ruffo was a survival of the militant churchmen of the Renaissance. This was to be a crusade against the enemies of God and the Church. Naturally the sovereigns and Acton were in favour of this project, which combined slight risk with a reasonable chance of success. Acton's detractors say that he schemed against this enterprising rival as soon as his back was turned, but most of his correspondence with Ruffo has been published, from which it is evident that he supported him sincerely, though finances were low and sufficient arms were lacking. On January 25, two days after the proclamation of the Parthenopean Republic, the King signed a decree authorizing the Cardinal to act as his Vicar and *alter ego* on the continent. This would not have been signed with Acton in opposition.

The royal treasurer, Marchese Taccone, had been ordered to supply Ruffo with funds; the governor of Messina, General Danero, with arms and ammunition; but neither were forthcoming. Taccone made the excuse that the funds in question had been consigned to Pignatelli, who had left all his documents in Naples. Danero protested that he had no arms to spare; he had the professional soldier's distrust of the amateur in clerical garb. 'How I wish,' he wrote, 'that instead of Cardinals, Bishops and Abbots, there were as many Generals, and military officers of integrity and experience who might share with me the burden of affairs…' Ruffo observed bitterly that there was a wide discrepancy between giving orders and carrying them out. But he had no time for controversial correspondence. Councillor Di Fiore had warned him that four important coastal districts opposite Messina—Palmi, Bagnara, Scilla and Reggio—were on the verge of being revolutionized, and his family estates were at Scilla and Bagnara. He sent Di Fiore ahead of him to muster as many armed men as possible from the latter places.

With only eight companions, including Marchese Malaspina, as adjutant, two clerical secretaries, a chaplain, and two retainers, Cardinal Ruffo landed at Punta del Pezzo on February 7.[1]

---

[1] His biographers differ in detail; on the whole we concur with the scholarly Sansone. The *Memorie* of Sacchinelli, Ruffo's devoted secretary, were written in after years and published in 1836.

'His sole equipment was a banner with the royal arms on one side and the cross on the other, inscribed *In hoc signo vinces.*' His brother, the Duke of Baranello, had a country house nearby which he made his first headquarters, hoisting his flag from the balcony. From here he sent an encyclical letter to all the local bishops and clergy, magistrates and prominent citizens, saying that it was the duty of every Christian to defend his Religion, his King, his Fatherland, the honour of his family... The clergy should set the first example. And he exhorted all to take up arms and assemble at two places—Mileto for those from the mountains and Palmi for those from the plain.

According to his secretary-biographer Sacchinelli, after sending this encyclical the Cardinal went out on the beach, where he saw Commodore Caracciolo and a Frenchman called Périer landing from a small boat. Périer was 'one of those *émigrés* who pretended to hate the Revolution but were secretly in favour of it while living at the sovereigns' expense'. The Cardinal asked them what they were doing in these parts, and they replied frankly that they were returning to Naples by way of Calabria, since the English had not allowed them to embark at Palermo. The Cardinal invited them to dinner, promising them some excellent fish, but they declined as they were in a hurry. Caracciolo inquired about the Cardinal's plans and he cautiously replied: 'Do you see that boat on the shore? It is ready to take me back in case of need.' Doubt has been cast on this anecdote, since Sacchinelli made several chronological mistakes in the first part of his biography, before he became the Cardinal's secretary. But it is improbable that it was a complete fabrication. Indeed, it is likely that Caracciolo brought the first news of the Cardinal's activities to Naples.

Rumour and fantasy were to serve as valuable propaganda throughout his expedition. Above all, this Cardinal, who had landed with little else but the Sign of the Cross, appealed strongly to the popular imagination. From the small band of eighty armed ruffians who joined him soon after his arrival, 'persons of no good intention and stability,' as he described them in a letter to Acton, his followers rose to 17,000 before the end of the month, and these were more than doubled by hearsay. He had to take what came; he could not afford to be particular. 'There was every kind of ecclesiastic; there were rich landowners, artisans, and field labourers; there were upright men impelled by religious fervour, attachment to the King and to good order; and unfortunately there were assassins and thieves, thirsty for plunder, vengeance and blood.' Some wealthy monasteries and proprietors supplied them with money, arms and provisions; and Ruffo sequestrated the revenues of landowners living in French-occupied territory, beginning with those of his brother, the Duke of Bagnara, to prove his impartiality. These forced loans, together with the sale of oil and other produce, provided for the maintenance of what was to be called the Christian Army of the Holy Faith.

The Calabrians and natives of the Abruzzi were warlike by nature. As Paribelli wrote later in a report to Bonaparte, they loved arms better than women. The first and sometimes the only thing they learned was the use of fire arms, and their average skill in hitting the target was high. When they had no chance to fight the enemies of their country, they fought each other. They were fiercely jealous of their women, capable of every sacrifice for a friend, and they never forgave an injury, pursuing their vengeance till death, and dying impenitent if their vengeance had not been consummated. They knew no half-measures.

Sacchinelli wrote that in 1799 not the most miserable peasant in Calabria but had a crucifix on one side of his bed, a gun on the other. 'The Cardinal, knowing these characteristics, sought to win their confidence and friendship from the start. He treated them with the utmost familiarity, ate the same food as they did, commanded them more with his example than with words, and did not allow them to talk of other subjects but *guapperie* in his presence—a Calabrian term for deeds of valour. A plucky fellow was said to be a *guappo*. In this manner he inspired so much attachment and courage in his troops, that in spite of all the hardships of hunger and half-nakedness in that very severe season, they followed him willingly wherever he bade them. In that army there was no fear of treachery, because all were animated with the same spirit and pledged to the same cause; and if anybody joined them whose behaviour was suspicious, he was immediately discovered, arrested or killed.' Their greatest disadvantage was that they were totally undisciplined, and it was the Cardinal's triumph that he was able to manipulate such refractory material. They were promised rewards in Heaven, but they expected loot on earth.

The primitive roads became bogs in the pouring rain; houses remained scarce since the devastating earthquakes of 1783, so that it was difficult to find quarters for so many men. Ruffo kept them busy with marches and counter-marches, teaching them to move in column, suggesting how to deal with imaginary ambuscades. When some merchantmen were anchored off Gioia he pretended that the French had arrived, just to test their mettle. All were agog to attack the foe, and their disappointment was only assuaged by attacking the copious casks of wine they found instead. The incident ended in general intoxication.

All the republicans fled as the Cardinal approached with his fanatical army, and dozens of 'trees of liberty' were felled. He was anxious to establish his headquarters at Monteleone. This important city had an excellent strategic position on a commanding height between the two richest plains in the kingdom, at no great distance from the sea, and it was the seat of the provincial treasury. It had then some 200,000 inhabitants within a radius of thirty miles. While the Cardinal was at Mileto a deputation from Monteleone brought him 10,000 ducats and eleven superb horses, with a message of loyalty to the King on the city's behalf. He entered it on March 1, and this preliminary success helped to attract many other districts which had been wavering to the royal cause. Soon the whole of Calabria Ultra, except Catanzaro and Cotrone, was to follow the example of Monteleone, where the Cardinal did much to improve the silk industry, abolishing the duties which had begun to ruin it.

'I hear of all that Your Eminence is doing with so much courage, resolution and intelligence and I weep with remorse that we did not entrust Naples to you at the time of our departure,' wrote the Queen on February 16. The Cardinal had sent her the first glad tidings from the mainland. She followed his progress with imaginative enthusiasm, and she sent him frequent letters full of gratitude, encouragement and sensible suggestions. She proposed, for instance, that he should abolish the local customs for ten years, as well as other taxes at his discretion, and 'anticipate all those operations the French will perform to gain popular favour'. 'Truly it can be said that you work miracles,' she wrote. 'Creating out of nothing: this is what you have done with your small army.' She sent him the latest reports from Naples. 'Several passengers and a vast amount of infamous printed matter from Naples have come here. When all is carefully weighed and sifted, it seems that the government is in the hands of rabid but insignificant Jacobins; that the people are subjugated but suffer the yoke very unwillingly; that provisions are getting scarce, and that there is not the least enthusiasm for the new regime.' The King's letters reflect his own coarse humour and complacency. He showed a growing concern with the 'summary, military, exemplary punishment' of those who had been unfaithful to the Almighty and himself. He was afraid that the Cardinal would be too lenient. The Cardinal had sent Acton a damaging report about the incompetence of General Danero, the governor of Messina, which was the key of Sicily. This was remedied by the arrival of General Sir Charles Stuart with two English regiments from Minorca, who garrisoned the fort. Russian and Turkish squadrons had captured Corfu.

The prospect was improving in every direction. Yet no news arrived either from Gallo or the Queen's beloved daughter in Vienna. Maria Carolina was particularly aggrieved to be so cut off from her native land. Her letters became more and more importunate as she received never a word in reply. She attacked Thugut, she rebuked Gallo, and at last she poured forth her pent-up indignation with Mack. 'What is certain is that if Mack has not thrown himself at the Emperor's feet to ask him for 40,000 men to reconquer Naples, the only way to save his honour, he is the last of cowards and caitiffs. An army of fifty to sixty thousand men destroyed in fifteen days without even fighting a battle! It was he who wrote to the King urging him to enter Rome where the French were holding the Castle of Sant' Angelo. It was he—and his letters prove it—who advised him to escape first from Rome, and then from Naples. It was he who after swearing aloud and in writing that he would fight on in the mountains of Calabria, advised and imposed an armistice, and having snatched and pocketed, with his aide-de-camps, all the money the King could give them, he left with all his luggage and went to Championnet, supped and slept in his camp, and departed by land with the glory of having ruined the finest country in the world and plunged into desolation a family which had overwhelmed him with confidence and honours. A mere drum corporal could not have caused us greater misfortunes. It is too atrocious to believe that this was due to stupidity or ignorance. Time will unravel this mystery...' Turning to the subject of Thugut she exploded: 'Has hatred made him forget that I am the daughter of his benefactress who created him, of the immortal Maria Theresa?... He makes his young masters cut a sorry figure by preventing them from helping their parents, their allies who have struggled with and for them, and who have just been sacrificed by one of their own generals. Patience! But that not one letter, not one word of comfort or sign of interest or question about the existence of these parents, should arrive in Sicily when several ships bring mail here and to Messina, that you, our Minister, having received our letters and orders to assist us, should leave us without news since your letter from Barletta of January 6, all this produces a very bad impression, the worst of impressions. Everybody questions me. I dare not reply, and swallow my chagrin and humiliation in silence. They blame me for all the errors committed, even for the indifference of the Court of Vienna, where I was born and have a daughter on the Throne... The Sultan promises to provide us with 10,000 Albanians, and intervene so that we shall have peace with the Barbary pirates... Yesterday morning two English ships arrived with 1,300 fine troops, announcing the arrival of more with General Stuart. The troops were immediately directed by sea to Messina to defend the citadel... Cardinal Ruffo, braver than ever, works wonders. Almost without other means except enthusiasm he has subdued all the provinces of Calabria except two points where the cursed tree of liberty still stands.'

It was a cruel shock when the Parthenopean republicans were reminded that they had to pay the piper. Personally, Championnet was the most sympathetic of French generals; no doubt he was sincere in his desire to bring the blessings of liberty, as he understood them, to Naples. But he was a Frenchman first, and he knew what his government expected. He demanded an indemnity of two and a half million ducats from the capital and fifteen million from the provinces, to be paid within two months. (The value of the ducat was then equivalent to four French francs, so that fifteen million was equivalent to sixty million francs.) The provisional government raised a howl of protest. Its spokesman, Manthoné, made a speech which only the lenient Championnet could have tolerated: 'You have soon forgotten, Citizen General, that we are not, you the conqueror, we the vanquished; that you came here not through battles and victories, but through our assistance and agreement; that we gave you the castles; that we betrayed your enemies for holy love of our fatherland; that your feeble battalions were not sufficient to subdue this vast city; nor would they suffice to hold it if we were to part company. To prove this, go outside these walls, and return if you can...' Championnet said he would think it over, but the indemnity had to be paid just the same. Those who could not pay cash had to bring their jewels and silver to be valued by official agents, and many were imprisoned or penalized with the sequestration of their property for double the sum they owed. 'We tax opinions,' an agent remarked to a lady whose husband had followed the King to Sicily.

Opinions: the members of the provisional government had a plethora of these, but very little else. Lawyers, professors, doctors, masonic priests, they oozed professions of benevolence for their fellow-creatures, except for the tyrant and the scoundrels who had served him, whom they relegated to eternal damnation. Apart from their floods of oratory, what had these doctrinaires to offer in exchange for the 'tyranny' they believed they had destroyed? A pale imitation of the French Constitution and other French products, such as the introduction of the republican calendar, which caused general confusion and bother. They forgot that the cult of the saints was an important article of Neapolitan faith; often they seemed to forget that they were in Naples at all, that the tyrant was just across the water, and that the great majority were still his partisans. The law of primogeniture, ecclesiastical tithes, the whole feudal system were to be abolished. Commissioners were sent to the provinces to reorganize the communes, accompanied by 'democratizers' to lecture on the benefits of the new order: the rights of man, freedom of conscience, the crimes of royal despotism, etc. The masses were to be awakened, converted and educated, so as to feel the want of higher things and realize their recent degradation.

The naïve and self-assured dogmatizings of the middle-class intelligentsia who now came to the fore may be studied in the pages of their journal, the *Monitore Napoletano*, the first number of which appeared on February 2, edited and mainly composed by Eleonora de Fonseca Pimentel, the brightest and the best of them, an earnest idealist with little practical experience of mankind. Most of the 'civic allocutions', she pointed out, were far above the heads of the people, who spoke a different language. 'The populace still distrust the patriots, because they do not understand them.' Let civic missions be sent among them to preach in their own dialect! So Abate Cicconi published *La Reprubbeca spiegata co lo santo Evangelio*, a simple explanation of the republic and the Gospels combined; Abate Troysi composed a republican Mass; and others preached 'the religion of freedom and equality' under the various trees of liberty which had been set up. In spite of these efforts the people were not impressed: the abyss between the liberators and the liberated remained unfathomable.

Carlo De Nicola's diary is perhaps the most accurate barometer of non-partisan opinion throughout this period, and it is interesting to contrast his entries with the *Monitore Napoletano* of the same date. 'At last we are free, and even for us the day has dawned when we can pronounce the sacred names of liberty and equality and announce it to the Mother Republic as her worthy sons; to the free peoples of Italy and Europe, as their worthy brothers.' Thus the lyrical Eleonora on February 2, or 14 *piovoso*. On February 3 De Nicola writes: 'Our condition is progressively deteriorating. The people are in ferment and suffer the French ill, also because these have attempted to violate women, a thing most abhorrent to this population. It is true that the General tries to curb them, but it is impossible to prevent every disorder, and in the meantime we hear that more than a hundred Frenchmen have recently been murdered at night.' Though he tries to give the devil his due, he is bound to confess: 'The Government and the French do not know how to make the revolution popular, and they find means of constantly increasing the discontent. And the truth of the matter is that nobody in the Government has any experience of politics and good administration; there is a lack of prudence, conduct and religion. Among the French there is bad faith and a lust for plunder. The result will be as Voltaire said: "The French have always conquered Naples with ease, and lost it with the same ease." Oh, how many would gladly return to their former nullity!'

The members of the government have been loaded with haloes by Cuoco, Colletta and their devout followers. 'The souls of the men in power were strung too high by finding themselves destined to realize the ideal they had admired and suffered for so long. It had actually come at last, and they vied with one another as to which should be the most perfect republican.' In other words, they immediately started quarrelling and denouncing each other. The first president, Carlo Lauberg, a renegade monk, 'the first conspirator of the new Italian Risorgimento,' as Croce called him, was soon accused of extortion and peculation and left Naples under a cloud. His father had been French, and he, too, became a French citizen, earning some reputation as a chemist. He died in Paris in 1834, a member of the Royal Academy of Medicine. His fellow-conspirator Annibale Giordano, who became head of the accountants' department of the Marine and a member of the revolutionary council, was also to become a naturalized Frenchman under the name of Jourdan. He died in 1835, *'géomètre en chef du département de l'Aube'.* Giordano's first patron, Luigi de' Medici, had retired to his family feud of Ottaiano after his release from prison, but such was his ill repute among the populace that he was said to have been bribed by the French while Regent of the Vicaria to number all the houses of Jacobins in order to save them during the invasion, hence the destruction of these house numbers by the *lazzaroni* before Championnet entered the capital. When Medici saw that so many of his old cronies had been allotted high posts in the provisional government, he was impelled to return. His apologist, Signor Nicola Nicolini, attributes this to mere curiosity, and says that he returned not as an actor but as an impartial spectator. 'Curiosity killed the cat'—but the cat is proverbially credited with nine lives. Even so did it seem with Medici. His friend Lauberg was accused, amongst other things, of plotting to substitute an aristocratic for the ultra-republican government, and rumour again connected Medici with this. The only certainty is that he became a member of the republican civic guard. In March a number of placards posted in the streets called upon those citizens who had 'the heart of a Brutus' to come armed with daggers and 'witness the tragedy of the infamous Medici'. After Lauberg's flight, Medici was cashiered from the civic guard with the Princes of Sant' Angelo and Colubrano. A captain of the guard declared that whoever killed one of this trio deserved well of his country; as one Medici had destroyed the liberty of Florence, another would destroy that of Naples—if he were given the chance. In May the 'Patriotic Society' voted that he should never be allowed to serve the Republic in any capacity. But instead of retiring to Ottaiano he stayed on, consumed by curiosity—or was it invincible ambition? When the Republic was at its last gasp, Medici was accused of royalist sympathies and thrown into prison, which proved to be a blessing in disguise.

Vincenzio Russo was another of the conspirators of the 'Patriotic Society' who returned to Naples with the French army in the role of a medical officer. He had escaped in 1797 after denouncing his colleagues to the police, for which he atoned by a life of rigid austerity during his exile. The poverty and frugality which were forced upon him by circumstance became his ideals for the rest of humanity.

While practising medicine in Geneva and Berne, Russo decided to become the Italian Rousseau. His *Political Thoughts* were published: crude stuff in a similar vein to other eighteenth-century pipe-dreams. His 'system' was based on a peasant republic in which everybody possessed a plot of land for self-support. After death, this land was to revert to the republic for redistribution. Public offices held by these peasant citizens were to be without pay, except a reimbursement for the time otherwise spent in cultivating the land, for which slight deductions would be made from the quotas of other cultivators. Industry was to be domestic, limited to the strictly necessary; and trade reduced to the exchange of necessities. All luxury was banned; education was to be limited to republican ethics and the principles of agriculture. There was to be no religion and no clergy. No large cities, as nations were to consist of a series of small villages; no more wars, except to liberate oppressed nations or repel aggression. The united nations of the future would aspire to form a universal society.

In Rousseau-istic language he wrote that he would willingly drown the best ports in Italy, which were breeding-grounds of misery and corruption. He looked forward to the destruction of the world's splendid capitals, when their ruins would become the lairs of serpents, 'images of their former inhabitants'. 'Let us salute the country, the hermit silence of solitudes, the fresh breeze of dusky springs! Let us salute the refuge of peace, candour and innocence! What a contrast with the roar and wickedness of cities!' In this romantic mood he is rather endearing. Cuoco recorded that his eloquence was sublime, extraordinary. 'He thundered and fulminated: nobody could resist the power of his words.' He wielded considerable influence as supervisor of a 'hall of public instruction', where he inveighed against the luxurious furniture, banquets and uniforms of government employees and praised the Spartan virtues.

When he became a member of the legislative council, however, he made himself thoroughly unpopular. First he wanted to examine all the accounts of the provisional government, which were not above suspicion; then he submitted that the maximum pay of members was not to exceed fifty ducats; those who renounced their whole salary or part of it, according to their means, were to be registered in a Patriotic Album. He also suggested a system of progressive taxation for the formation of a national guard. But many objected to these proposals as a waste of time when dozens of more vital problems required solution. 'Do you imagine,' protested one, 'that three months of incomplete and unexpected revolution suffice to render us as virtuous as the Spartans during the first Persian war, or the Romans of the first Punic war? Would you have us return to our pristine acorns? Nay, first engulf our fields, cut down the olives and vines, destroy our industries, kill at least two-thirds of the population, and finally settle us on a hill-top, surrounded by lakes and protected by inaccessible mountains. There we shall be safe, since our poverty, more than the mountains, will keep the enemy far away; we shall let our hair and nails grow, and together with you, eating acorns and onions, we shall lead a delicious life!' No wonder Russo resigned after a week in office.

Remote from these academic discussions, the French agents and contractors who had squeezed Rome dry, arrived in Naples to repeat the process. While in Rome, Championnet in his innocence had complained of this evil to the Directory: 'The resources of the Roman Republic are already drained. A swarm of swindlers have swallowed everything. With greedy eyes they are watching to seize the little that is left. These leeches hide themselves under every form, but sure of being sanctioned by you, I shall not allow these unpunished despoilers to invade the army's substance. I shall get rid of these horrible harpies who devour the soil conquered by our sacrifices...' Apparently he failed to realize that the Directory approved of these activities. His threat was disregarded. The civil commissioner, Faypoult, was entirely out for plunder and confiscation. He imposed an additional war tax, and declared that all Crown property, including the antiquities of Pompeii and Herculaneum and the porcelain factory of Capodimonte, belonged to France; he sequestrated the property of banks, convents and absentee landlords, and even of foreigners whose countries were at peace with his own. And he published an edict that all taxes and other exactions were to be paid to him alone.

Seeing his authority thus brushed aside, Championnet yielded to popular clamour and expelled Faypoult and his whole gang from Neapolitan territory. The Directory considered this an act of insubordination, and recalled Championnet on February 27. As Barras wrote in his *Memoirs:* 'The loyal, generous and too candid victor was replaced by one of his lieutenants, Macdonald, who before and since the opening of the campaign had never stopped intriguing against his Commander-in-Chief.' General Macdonald, whom

Barras compared with Talleyrand, both physically and morally, had been lingering in Rome in anticipation of his new appointment, which adds a piquancy to his own version of the episode: 'One day I returned weary from an excursion in the neighbourhood and had taken a nap when a messenger woke me up. I perused the despatch and, to my intense surprise, found that I had been appointed Commander-in-Chief of the army in Naples as a substitute for General Championnet. The Directory, displeased with the tergiversations of the campaign, the armistice of Capua, and the depredations committed, had decided to recall him and make him account for his conduct. I must say in truth that this step was too severe, that most of the army was innocent of all these iniquities and regretted them, but that it deplored the weakness of its chief and had no confidence in him, so that with equal truth and without vanity or self-conceit I can say that it expressed great joy at my appointment, especially the troops who had served under me…'

Faypoult, who was on the best of terms with Macdonald, hurried back. A popular song thus summarized the situation:

> 'E venuto lo francese
> Co' 'no mazzo de carte immano,
> Liberté, Egalité, Fraternité,
> Tu rubbi a me, io rubbo a tte!'

Which may roughly be rendered:

> 'The Frenchman's come into our land
> With a mass of papers in his hand:
> Liberty, Equality, Fraternity,—
> Thou robbest me, and I rob thee!'

XIX

The King as a family tyrant—Nelson and the Hamiltons—Progress of Cardinal Ruffo's campaign—Corsican adventurers—Civil war—Troubridge in the Bay of Naples—Austria declares war on France—A Parthenopean deputation to Paris—Republican experiments in Naples—A royalist plot—The surreptitious withdrawal of General Macdonald.

'The King, God bless him, is a philosopher,' wrote Nelson, 'but the great Queen feels sensibly all that has happened.' To escape from his wife's sensibility, the philosopher moved into a comfortable villa by the sea, where he could amuse himself with hunting and fishing, as usual, among boon companions who avoided unpleasant subjects. 'Whether owing to religion, resignation, virtue or temperament, he is far more resigned to his fate than I,' wrote the Queen. 'Since the fixed assignment of the royal household has been reduced from 60,000 to 10,000 ducats a month to cover all expenses, it is he who makes us economize in everything and we are all very pinched, unable to order an extra mattress without special permission. He has a country-house and another, quite attractive, which he has furnished on the Marina, and he goes there often. Spending his evenings at the theatre, he is content. He has forgotten Naples and all his old habits, and I am convinced that he never wishes to see it again and is very satisfied here. But these unfortunate events have greatly embittered his temper, and he is far more despotically the master than he has ever been. Francis [the Prince Royal] has the same ideas; he pays far too much attention to his country-house, his animals and his dairy. But he does wish to return to Naples, and he is also much upset and irritated and prone to fits of violence though his health is good. My dear daughter-in-law [the Princess Royal, who was really suffering from consumption] has entirely recovered. She puts on flesh, has a good complexion and is evidently pregnant. She is much loved and esteemed in the country, for she is good and gentle. Her firm desire is to return to Naples, as nothing pleases her here and she does not conceal it in the least... Their daughter [the future Duchesse de Berry] is quite pretty but shows little vivacity. She is six months old, never smiles, understands nothing, and I have never seen such a backward child. Leopold is losing his beauty and amiability. He has reached the age when one wants to be more rational than one is, which embarrasses him and makes him less agreeable. Besides, he shares a room with his sisters and is dazed by the continual noise. Mimi is always the best and most virtuous soul alive. Amélie and Antoinette are also excellent children, and my keenest desire is to get them married.'

The Queen led a retired life in the gloomy Colli Palace. Once or twice a week she might visit a convent and chat with the nuns, but she seldom went to the theatre: 'I like neither to see nor to be seen. Circumstances are too painful.' Most of her time seems to have been devoted to her voluminous correspondence, the only outlet for her torrent of thoughts and emotions, and this outlet had been enlarged by Cardinal Ruffo's great enterprise. 'If I were to write to you every time I think of you,' she told him, 'I should be doing so the whole day long, because I make continual vows for your prosperity, and for Heaven to bless your activities...' She kept in constant touch with Nelson and the Hamiltons, thanks to whose presence she could feel secure. 'I see Acton very seldom to avoid his ill-humour,' she wrote, while Acton was avoiding her for the same reason.

In spite of heavy losses the Hamiltons had moved into the spacious Palazzo Palagonia and entertained on their former lavish scale. Nelson lived with them and shared their expenses, and the famous triangle was formed which led to so much gossip. The Sicilians took it for granted that Nelson was Lady Hamilton's *cicisbeo*. What could be more natural under the circumstances? The ambassador so old—'that walking piece of *verd-antique*,' as a lady called him—and the ambassadress so comparatively young! It suited the Queen that the Admiral's heart should be engaged in Palermo. There was little doubt as to his infatuation. However tired, 'almost blind and worn out', he was revived by 'good Sir William's wit and inexhaustible pleasantry and Lady Hamilton's affectionate care'.

Pryse Lockhart Gordon describes in his *Personal Memoirs* a visit to Sir William Hamilton and Lord Nelson at this time: 'Our introduction to the fascinating Emma, Lady Hamilton, was an affair of more ceremony, and got up with considerable stage effect. When we had sat a few minutes, and had given all our details of Naples... the *Cavaliere* retired, but shortly returned, entering by a *porte battante*, and on his arm or rather his shoulder was leaning the interesting Melpomene, her raven tresses floating round her expansive form and full bosom. What a model for a Roman matron! but alas! poor Emma was indisposed, "dying", she said, "of chagrin for the loss of her beloved Naples"; yet the roses on her cheek prevailed over the lilies and gave hopes that her grief would not prove mortal... She rehearsed in a subdued tone in a *mélange* of Lancashire and Italian, detailing the catalogue of her miseries, her hopes, and her fears, with lamentations about the dear queen, the loss of her own charming Palazzo and its precious contents, which had fallen into the hands of the vile republicans. But here we offered some consolation, by assuring her Ladyship that every article of the ambassador's property had been safely embarked in an English transport, and would be safely despatched in a few days. All this, we afterwards learned, she knew, as the vessel had actually arrived. During this interesting conversation the lady discovered that she was Lord Montgomery's *cousin*, and appealing to her husband said, "A'nt us, Sir William?"... and we were invited to dinner, her Ladyship regretting "that her small house could not accommodate him" (it was a palace of fifty rooms at least). The hero of the Nile now came forth from a corner where he had been writing, and cross-examined us about Naples, insinuating, we thought rather impertinently, that we had been guilty of high imprudence in remaining there so long. Lord Montgomery replied... that he would not have stirred till the French were at the gates,... lamenting only that so fine a city should have been left to its fate, and that patriotism there seemed to be extinct. These remarks did not seem at all to accord with the sentiments of the gallant admiral, and I observed some very significant glances pass between him and his fair friend.'

Subsequently when Lockhart Gordon dined with the ambassador: 'A stranger was announced, bearing a despatch from the Emperor Paul of Russia: the messenger was a Turk. Lady Hamilton, with her usual tact, recommended Lord Nelson, for whom the despatch was destined, to clothe himself in his pelisse and aigrette to receive the Turk: this was done in a moment. The party moved to a *salle de réception*. The folding doors were thrown open, and the Mussulman entered. The moment he caught a glance of his Lordship's costume, the slave was prostrate on the earth, making the grand salaam. This was the scene her Ladyship had anticipated, and it was got up with stage effect. The credentials being delivered were found to contain an autograph letter from Paul, complimenting the hero on the glories he had achieved; and in testimony of his Majesty's regard, the Emperor of all the Russias desired his acceptance of a gold snuff-box, on which was the imperial portrait. The letter [in French] was read to the assembly, and the present exhibited. It was superb, of chased gold; the portrait was set with large brilliants, a gift worthy of an Emperor. Lady Hamilton, by means of a Greek interpreter belonging to the embassy, flirted with the Turk, a coarse savage monster, and he was invited to dinner the following day to drink the health of the Emperor. It was considered strange that a Mahometan should have been charged with an embassy from a Christian prince, but the interpreter explained that the credentials had been sent to Corfu; but no Russian vessel being there, the governor had employed the captain of a frigate of a Turkish squadron in the bay, under orders to repair to Messina, to fulfil the Emperor's commands. The ship had been left at that port and the captain came overland to Palermo, as he had been directed.

'The only memorable event which occurred at the minister's entertainment, was this warrior getting drunk with rum, which does not come under the prohibition of the prophet. The monster, who had the post of honour at her Ladyship's side, entertained her through the interpretation of the Greek with an account of his exploits; among others, that of his having lately fallen in with a French transport, conveying invalids and wounded soldiers from Egypt, whom he had brought on board his frigate; but provisions and water having run short, he found it necessary to get rid of his prisoners, and amused himself by putting them to death. "With this weapon," said he, in his vile jargon, and drawing his shabola, "I cut off the heads of twenty French prisoners in one day! Look, there is their blood remaining on it!" The speech being translated, her Ladyship's eye beamed with delight, and she said, "Oh let me see the sword that did the glorious deed!" It was presented to her; she took it into her fair hand covered with rings, and looking at the encrusted Jacobin blood, kissed it and handed it to the hero of the Nile! Had I not been an eye-witness to this disgraceful act, I would not have ventured to relate it.

'Mrs Charles Lock, the beautiful and amiable wife of our consul-general, was sitting *vis-à-vis* to the Turk, and was so horrified at the scene (being near her accouchement) that she fainted and was taken out of the room. Her Ladyship said it was a piece of affectation, and made no efforts to assist her guest; the truth is, she was jealous of her beauty, and insinuated that, being a sister of the late Lord Edward Fitzgerald, she must necessarily be a Jacobin. N.B. She wore green ribbons. The toad-eaters applauded, but many groaned and cried "shame" loud enough to reach the ears of the admiral, who turned pale, hung his head, and seemed ashamed. Lord Montgomery got up and left the room and I speedily followed. Poor Nelson was to be pitied—never was man so mystified and deluded!'

Like the King and for better reason, Lady Hamilton believed in enjoying the present moment. As spring approached there were nightly banquets, followed by music and gambling for high stakes. Nelson was not accustomed to such late hours of revelry, but he enjoyed Lady Hamilton's enjoyment. The new English consul, Charles Lock and his wife, looked down their noses and sniffed, but Captain Ball called Lady Hamilton the Patroness of the Navy, and the respectable Lady Knight commended her daughter to the care of Sir William and his wife in the event of her own demise. 'I must say that there was certainly at that time no impropriety in living under Lady Hamilton's roof,' wrote Miss Knight. 'Her house was the resort of the best company of all nations, and the attentions paid to Lord Nelson appeared perfectly natural.'

As the air became warmer Palermo unfolded its glowing, fragrant petals: the valley of the Golden Shell—*Conca d'oro*—with its groves of acacias, palms and orange-trees, its citron-espaliers and walls of oleander, 'decked with thousands of red carnation-like blossoms', fully justified its name. The city had not changed since Goethe visited it in 1787, 'easy enough to survey, but difficult to know; easy, because a street a mile long, from the lower to the upper gate, from the sea to the mountain, intersects it, and is itself again crossed, nearly in its middle, by another. Whatever lies on these two great lines is easily found; but in the inner streets a stranger soon loses himself...' The mode of life of the higher ranks, imitated by the lower, differed little from that of the Neapolitans. They rose late, went out for a stroll, dined between three and four, drove or walked by the sea in the evening before going to the opera; then played cards, and retired to bed at daybreak. As their country houses, where they spent a few weeks in spring and autumn, were all in the neighbourhood, they lived there exactly as in town. They met their friends to play cards and eat ices rather than to indulge in serious conversation. A sleepy, sensuous, provincial existence, which was considerably shaken out of its rut by the coming of the Court from Naples.

'It was wonderful to see the improvement and resources which started up in Palermo after the arrival of so many strangers,' wrote Miss Knight. This is corroborated by that gossipy Sicilian Palmieri de Miccichè: 'From 1799 to 1814 Sicily flourished. During these years the almost continuous war of the whole of Europe against France on one side, on the other the Court of Naples... driven across the Straits, had caused the influx into Sicily not only of the diplomatic corps attached to this Court, and of wealthy families fond of travel or a change of air, Russian, German, English or Spanish (for whom this country was the sole outlet or escape, and the only foreign land they could visit), but also of the soldiers and statesmen of this Europe intriguing and plotting with Maria Carolina, the very heart of all conspiracies against France. The affluence of all these visitors had stimulated trade, created work, destroyed mendicity. The population increased, and everything began to prosper, especially in Palermo.'

But the Queen could not adapt herself to existence in her second capital; it was altogether too exotic and too remote from her beloved Vienna. With her habitual candour she told Gallo: 'Here I am completely miserable. Everything depresses me horribly. I cannot live here. The King likes it, and is becoming a despot in the family since he cannot be one as a sovereign. I dislike the country: the people, their customs and ideas, all are sixty years behind the times. I lack everything and live as at an inn. Either I shall recover Naples or depart. I cannot continue to live in a country for which I feel an insurmountable repugnance.' But apart from this personal aversion, and in spite of the worrying absence of news from Vienna, she had cause to be more cheerful: 'At this moment [March 19] everything contributes towards a happy solution of affairs. A slight effort would suffice to rouse Italy and drive out the French. The Russians promise us fifteen thousand troops; the Turks will send us as many and almost at once. The English fleet will help their disembarkation by throwing a few bombs. The public spirit is excellent but needs support. The moment is therefore entirely favourable. But the cruel and incomprehensible silence of Vienna spoils everything and destroys our hopes...' This was written for

Austrian consumption, but her hopes revived with the steady progress of the counter-revolution.

Thanks to Cardinal Ruffo, the last strongholds of the republicans in Calabria were falling, first Catanzaro, which had been considered impregnable, and then Cotrone, whose garrison had been reinforced by thirty-two French non-commissioned officers. There are several accounts of the pillage of these places, the horrors of which were an abiding memory. The Cardinal's troops marching to Cotrone were joined by all the armed men of the neighbourhood who scented an opportunity for plunder until, in Sacchinelli's words, 'they increased like a torrent in flood'. The Cardinal sent an officer to parley with the besieged, who court-martialled and condemned him to death as well as Baron Farina, Colonel Fogliar and other local royalists, the sentence to be carried out on the morrow. This did not dispose the besiegers to deal more kindly with the population when they burst into the city after a long night in the cold rain. The prisoners were set free, and Cotrone was delivered to a sack from which it never recovered. It was a Pyrrhic victory for the Cardinal as, loaded with the booty of two bloodthirsty days, the main bulk of his army deserted. The others mutinied, either because they had no share of the spoils, or because they had had a surfeit of hardships during that severe protracted winter. The regular militia and about a thousand irregulars were eventually coaxed to remain. The Cardinal renewed his appeal to the clergy to exert all their influence, as a result of which his army was soon increased to five thousand regular troops and over ten thousand irregulars. Moreover, he was greatly helped by the arrival of his brother Don Francesco Ruffo, who assumed the title of Inspector of his army.

The first of several attempts against the Cardinal's life was staged in Cotrone, when a priest requested a private interview with him. This was granted, but the man lost his nerve, stuttered, contradicted himself and behaved so suspiciously that he was put under arrest. An intercepted letter proved that he and two others had been commissioned by the republican government to assassinate the 'Monster Cardinal', who pardoned him nevertheless. Later on Ruffo had a lucky escape by riding a black horse instead of his usual white Arab. Another priest in his vanguard who happened to be mounted on a white horse was shot at from an ambush, but only the horse was killed. The assailants were caught; they too were found to be emissaries of the Republic. Many of his superstitious

Calabrians believed that Ruffo was invulnerable—*inciarmato*, or protected by enchantment. Sacchinelli traces this to an occasion when bullets were whistling over his head—on his white Arab the Cardinal was an obvious target—and he said joking to those around him: 'Spread out more, as the bullets do not hit me and I should be sorry if any of you were injured.'

Ruffo's campaign had been viewed with scepticism by the courtiers in Palermo. As soon as it seemed less arduous, many who had scoffed became eager to share his laurels. But the Cardinal was wary of these belated volunteers, even when the Queen recommended them. Having discovered that there was much espionage between Naples and Palermo, he was careful not to reveal his movements or the strength of his forces. He was even cautious in his commands to officers; he would suddenly change his route and swerve in an unexpected direction. The Christian army of the Holy Faith had much in common with Chinese Gordon's 'Ever Victorious Army', 'constantly on the verge of mutiny, supporting itself on plunder, and, at the slightest provocation, melting into thin air'. And Cardinal Ruffo himself had certain qualities in common with the eminent Victorian. He, too, as Lytton Strachey wrote of Gordon, 'by sheer force of character, established over this incoherent mass of ruffians an extraordinary ascendancy' and 'attained to an almost magical prestige'. But there the parallel ends. For the warrior prelate represented the aspirations of his people, rugged, fierce, even barbarous, but united inasmuch as they wanted neither the French nor a republic. They saw the King as chosen by Divine will: as did the majority in other provinces. The republicans were always a minority.

While Ruffo was recovering Calabria, other guerrilla leaders were recovering the rest of the kingdom: Sciarpa in the Cilento, Pronio in the Abruzzi, Salomone in Aquila, De Donatis in Teramo, Michele Pezza, better known as Fra Diavolo, and the notorious Mammone brothers, in Sora: soldiers of fortune who skilfully exploited royalist sentiment. To read of their adventures is to enter a world of picaresque fiction. Most fantastic of all, because it was fortuitous, was the contribution of some Corsican refugees. When the Parthenopean Republic was proclaimed seven Corsicans were stranded at Barletta. Afraid of being captured by the French, they left for Brindisi, hoping to embark for Trieste or Corfu. On their way they stopped at a village where an old woman gave them lodgings. Either as a joke or to obtain better service, they hinted that one of them was the heir to the throne. The old woman ran off and told the head man of the village, Girunda Bonafede, who promptly came and knelt before Corbara, the youngest of the party, with exuberant professions of loyalty. Fearing this might lead to trouble, the Corsicans slipped away before dawn. But the rumour soon spread, thanks to Girunda, who tried to follow them on horseback but took another road, asking everybody if they had seen the Prince Royal and his suite. On reaching Brindisi the Corsicans were acclaimed by a jubilant multitude, and deputations came to pay homage to the supposed Prince Royal. Corbara had to persevere in this assumed role, for in the state of public enthusiasm any alternative would have been his doom.

The two old aunts of Louis XVI, Mesdames Adélaide and Victoire, were in Brindisi at the same time, exhausted by their flight from Caserta in the depth of winter, waiting on an overcrowded ship for a Russian escort to take them to Trieste. These princesses were now persuaded to lend colour to the hoax, as it was all in the royal cause, by giving Corbara a private audience. According to one of their suite: 'He hastened to inform them that he was the Comte de Corbéra, a Corsican *émigré*, and very loyal to the King; that travelling on foot and ill equipped at that, he had never expected to be the object of so strange a mistake; that he had resisted it to the utmost, but always in vain... The Comte de Chastellux [majordomo to the princesses] asked him how he thought of terminating so dangerous and difficult a role. He replied that he had already persuaded the people to let him sail to Corfu, where he would apply to Admiral Ouschakoff for assistance. His gentleness, his noble disinterestedness, his prudent and sensible conduct in circumstances so critical and extraordinary, made him excusable and very interesting. It is certain that the populace would have massacred anyone who dared to deny that this foreigner was the Hereditary Prince.'

Subsequently Corbara and four of his companions embarked for Corfu, were captured by pirates and taken to Tunis, where they were rescued by the English consul. In the meantime De Cesari and Boccheciampe, the two Corsicans who had been left behind, had a spectacular success as leaders of royalist bands in Puglia. Here they posed as a brother of the King of Spain and a Prince of Saxony. Boccheciampe was captured by the French, but De Cesari continued to recruit more cavalry and infantry. Ruffo heard of his exploits and asked the Queen about his origin. 'As regards the so-called prince, we are entirely ignorant of his identity, and have no information about him,' she replied, 'but by a mere chance we suppose he may be Corsican, since one called Corbara has arrived here, who was taken for my son at Brindisi. The things this man relates about the fanaticism of the people for him are incredible; and as two of those anglican Corsicans were left, one of whom was blond, we think that must be the person. It is certain that all this pertains to the art of magic, and we cannot be sufficiently grateful to Divine Providence.' Eventually De Cesari joined forces with Ruffo, who made the pseudo-prince a general.

General Macdonald stated in his *Memoirs* that his military operations against the royalists were successful, but he had to admit that 'an insurrection crushed in one place cropped up in another'. Communications, especially with Rome, were interrupted most of the time, and unless travellers were heavily escorted, even with cannon, 'they became victims of bandits who perpetrated the most ferocious atrocities against them'. In fact, the Republic could do little to stem the counter-revolution. Their General Schipani, an ex-lieutenant in the royal army, was sent with a force to Calabria, but never got anywhere near his destination. He was utterly routed by Sciarpa at a village near Salerno. General Duhesme and Ettore Carafa, the ex-Count of Ruvo, had ephemeral successes in the provinces of Avellino, Salerno and Basilicata, but they left anarchy and ruin behind them. They burned as well as sacked the towns that tried to resist them, and in this they were more methodical than Ruffo. Carafa had joined the French in Milan after escaping from the Castle of Sant' Elmo; he combined military talent with a fanaticism as extreme as that of his most violent opponents. Being the only vigorous native leader on the republican side, he was viewed with suspicion by the doctrinaires in Naples, who thought him too ambitious. Besides, he was an aristocrat. The feuds of his family were all in Puglia as the Ruffo feuds were in Calabria. Duhesme was more interested in plunder: he levied enormous contributions on the cities he occupied, regardless as to whether they were royalist or republican. He extracted 40,000 ducats from Bari, 8,000 ducats from Conversano, and robbed the public post of 7,000 ducats. As Cuoco said, not a pair of silver buckles remained in the province of Bari after he left it. As soon as he was recalled, the royalists returned to power. The rich cities of Andria and Trani were royalist to the core, and General Broussier was sent to chastise them, aided by Carafa, whose father was Duke of Andria. For this very reason, perhaps, the inhabitants were more stubborn in their defence. Carafa was fired on when he came to parley with them, and it was he who led the assault. Every available weapon, from stones to boiling water, was employed against the Franco-Neapolitan invaders. The sack and massacre that followed were more ruthless than any perpetrated by Ruffo's Calabrians. 'The city,' as Carafa proudly reported, 'was all in flames, and the dead may be as many as four thousand.' The *Monitore*, to boost republican morale, announced that ten thousand 'remained the victims of their own crimes'. It is noteworthy that these glib idealists regarded the sacking and burning of 'rebel' cities—rebels against an odious foreign regime—as perfectly justifiable. 'The example of many places in the departments delivered to the flames will serve as a great lesson to the rebels,' wrote the high-souled Ignazio Ciaia to his brother. General Macdonald laid down the following laws:

'Every district or city in rebellion against the Republic shall be burnt and levelled with the ground;

'Cardinals, archbishops, bishops, abbots, parish priests, and all ministers of public worship shall be held responsible for rebellions in the places where they reside, and be punished with death;

'Every rebel shall be liable to pay the death penalty, and every accomplice, whether layman or clerical, shall be treated as a rebel.'

The death penalty also applied to priests in whose parishes a double peal of bells were rung, and to those who spread news adverse to France or the Parthenopean Republic; and the loss of life in these cases was to be accompanied by loss of property. Trani came next on the list for chastisement, then Ceglie and Carbonara, all sacked and reduced to rubble. Yet what outcries of righteous indignation were raised when Ruffo's Calabrians sacked a city! 'The ferocious Cardinal Ruffo' has become a traditional bogy owing to the fact that his most powerful enemies were lawyers whose forensic oratory deafened the small voices of unskilled, unprofessional witnesses. True, many joined his army in anticipation of plunder; this could not be remedied: it was diamond cut diamond on both sides. But Ruffo himself was strikingly moderate in a maelstrom of conflicting passions. He served a principle rather than a party, and he was always ready to forgive his enemies. He converted many a wobbling republican, and he was the first to preach an amnesty to the King and Queen, who could never agree with him on this point.

At the end of March Nelson sent a squadron under Commodore Troubridge to blockade the Bay of Naples, and by April 3 Procida and the neighbouring islands had hoisted the royal colours. Troubridge found the inhabitants on the verge of starvation. He immediately distributed flour among them and wrote to Sicily for provisions:

'Your Lordship never beheld such loyalty,' he told Nelson, 'the people are perfectly mad with joy and are asking for their beloved master.' They destroyed the trees of liberty, tore the tricoloured flags to shreds, and delivered all the republican officials they could seize to the English men-of-war. The local sailors and fishermen had evidently suffered, for they were thirsting for revenge. Troubridge also asked Nelson to apply to the Court for an honest judge to try the prisoners: 'The villains increase so fast on my hands and the people are calling for justice; eight or ten of them must be hung.' Nelson replied that a judge was on his way: 'Send me word some proper heads are taken off, this alone will comfort me.' For Nelson had no patience with treachery: speedy rewards and quick punishments were his simple recipe for good government. His piercing eye could only see black and white. Loyalty to King and country were the first of his canons, and he regarded the King's person as sacred, whatever defects and infirmities it might possess individually. Now, Commodore Caracciolo had not only turned tail, he had taken command of the republican marine and was publishing subversive proclamations. According to these, the perfidious English had been the chief cause of his country's calamities. Why had this man been allowed to leave Sicily? Weakness on the one hand, treachery on the other: Nelson began to doubt the motives of all these foreigners. He even had his doubts about Ruffo, whom he called 'a swelled-up priest'.

Troubridge also had misgivings. When the judge, Speciale, arrived from Palermo, he told Troubridge that he had been instructed to pass sentence in a summary manner, under his orders. Troubridge retorted that this must be a mistake, as the prisoners were not British subjects. Speciale then applied to him for a hangman and required an English man-of-war to send three disloyal priests to Palermo to be degraded by the bishop, and back to Procida for execution. He also proposed that Troubridge should ship about a hundred undesirables to some foreign port. Naturally

Troubridge refused. It struck him that the Sicilian Court intended to throw all the odium of these trials on the English.

One morning Troubridge was surprised to receive a man's head with a basket of fresh grapes. An explanatory note from a certain Vitella begged His Excellency to accept this little token of his attachment to the Crown. Troubridge ironically wrote 'A jolly fellow!' on the margin of this letter, and excused himself for not forwarding the head to Nelson, as the weather was too hot for such gifts.

The King's temper began to improve. His old jocularity transpired in his letters to Ruffo, though his itch for vengeance tended to give it a macabre twist. 'By the time you receive this there will be plenty of *caciocavalli*,' he wrote, alluding to the shape of the local cheeses which are hung up by the neck. He and Acton urged him to bear in mind that 'broomsticks and bread produce fine brats'; as soon as the dear little Russians turned up there would be celebrations and, with the help of Divine Providence, the accursed story would end. The better news that reached him daily had been such a tonic that his health, thank God, was perfect.

The Queen was relieved to hear that Austria had been forced to waken from its criminal inertia, as she put it, and to declare war on France on March 12. Thanks to the English squadron, her messengers came and went between Procida and the mainland, and she could correspond with her secret agents in and around Naples. She was therefore accurately informed about all that was happening, which gave her great satisfaction. She never missed an opportunity of sending Ruffo the latest news, interspersed with her comments, speculations and suggestions. Thus, according to the reports from Naples of April 12 'the poverty is great, but there is bread in abundance, all the neighbouring districts fearing to be despoiled by the French are hastening to sell their merchandise; there is a shortage of meat and salt, cash is extremely hard to find, taxes are enormous, and I see this from the newspapers. Evidently they regard Naples as a country to be stripped and left to its own devices. The people are all very loyal and make no secret of it, exclaiming: "Now we shall be free." The French (to our eternal shame) are very few, they are said to be barely two thousand four hundred or three thousand; the rest are Jacobins who try to shine by their excesses. There are frequent executions, but all among the populace... Everything proves that they feel insecure; they are sending away their womenfolk, and it is said that one of their battalions has gone to Capua, with the pretext of fighting the Emperor. They have forced everybody to take up arms. The violent, furious and bloodthirsty publications are innumerable, but I regard them as the cries of madmen. Yet I have been truly chagrined to find that our Caracciolo of the Marine is a scoundrel. We have copies of republican orders against us with his signature, including one of the most atrocious and rebellious proclamations describing the King as a vile tyrant, and swearing to destroy him and his family; it is altogether infamous, and I confess that I never expected such a thing of him. But it shows me how great and extensive is the corruption of the class which should be the least tainted. I am also sending Your Eminence a copy of a second scoundrelly pastoral letter from our stupid Archbishop, in which he insults the zeal of Your Eminence. I should not have mentioned this, as such things are beneath contempt, but since... he wished to blacken your pure intention by misrepresenting it as schismatic, I think it ought to be contradicted, but I leave the decision to you, whose mind is so far superior to ours...'

'Democracy and true liberty render people gentle, indulgent, generous and magnanimous,' wrote Eleonora Pimentel in the *Monitore* through her rose-coloured spectacles, while the same journal heaped opprobrious epithets on the King and Queen. Cardinal Ruffo was reported to have elected himself Pope Urban IX, and the old Cardinal Archbishop Zurlo was prevailed upon to denounce him. But Ruffo marched on towards Naples with enhanced prestige while the English were blockading the Bay. Profoundly dissatisfied, the Neapolitan people were only biding their time to strike a blow for the King. Considering all the factors against them, the optimism of the republicans was amazing. Championnet's disgrace should have warned them of the Directory's intentions. Macdonald was a very different type, a military careerist who intended to squeeze the utmost from a people he despised, sending part of the proceeds to Paris and dividing the rest with his political friends the commissioners.

Before his arrival the provisional government had sent a deputation to Paris to obtain formal recognition of the Parthenopean Republic and more generous treatment with regard to contributions. It consisted of the ex-Prince of Moliterno, the ex-Prince of Angri (one of the richest nobles to join the new order), Leonardo Panzini, who had been a secretary in the Foreign Office for many years, and Francescantonio Ciaja, younger brother of Ignazio, better known as a poet than as a president of the provisional government. Besides expressing the 'gratitude' of the Neapolitan people, they were to melt the hard hearts of the Directors by describing their present difficulties, for in Ciaja's words 'it would destroy every germ of future prosperity if an icy hand were to clamp down on us and sterilize us'. A solemn act recognizing the independence of the Republic would prove to the people that they were to be considered not as defeated slaves but as friends and free men, that their religion and property were to be guaranteed by the first Power in Europe; and that they would always preserve their territorial integrity. But ominous reports about Championnet's successor reached them on their way to Paris. He was said to be callous, avaricious and aristocratic; to favour the rich barons and accept money from them, while trying to discredit the government with the Directory by slandering its members.

The deputies announced their arrival on March 22 to Talleyrand, the Minister of Foreign Affairs, asking him to appoint a day for their reception. Talleyrand invited them to call on him next morning, and they were asked to return at three o'clock. The Directory's reply was distinctly chilling. The Directory thanked the Neapolitan Republic, but did not consider this the right moment to receive its deputation, as the Republic was not yet stable. It advised them to go home immediately, as their country needed them and held them in high esteem, which was proved by their present mission. It informed them, moreover, that it had a civil Commissioner in Naples to whom they could communicate their sentiments.

The astonished deputies wanted to send a courier to their government with this reply and requested a passport for him. But Talleyrand told them that this was unnecessary. All their passports had been issued, and they were expected to leave at once. Four days later the Minister of Police inquired why they had not left Paris, and each had to give his word of honour that he would leave within two days. Moliterno and Ciaja lingered on, however. The former obtained a medical certificate to the effect that he needed a cure, and sent in his resignation as General of the People; he had never been a convinced republican, and he hoped to reinstate himself under the royal banner.

The Directory was only interested in Naples as a source of revenue, for it had an unavowed deficit of 300,000,000 francs. Its strength had been derived from its military successes, but now the tide had turned. Jourdan was driven across the Rhine by the Archduke Charles; Schérer and Moreau were defeated again and again by the Austro-Russian armies in the north of Italy. After capturing Sérurier with 3,000 men on April 27, the Allies entered Milan. The Directory itself was scarcely more stable than the Parthenopean Republic, and Talleyrand was among those who were plotting its overthrow. Little of this was known to the Neapolitan deputies, but the pointed reference to the French Commissioner should have enlightened them about their own prospects.

Citizen Abrial, the official in question, arrived at the end of March with ample powers to reorganize the administration, divided by personal ambitions, petty quarrels and intrigues. He substituted a legislative and executive commission for the provisional government. He seems to have been well-intentioned and conciliating; both Macdonald and the Neapolitan 'patriots' thought well of him, but he had come too late. A letter addressed to the abortive deputation stated frankly the hopeless condition of their finances owing to the revolt of the provinces and the expense of maintaining a foreign army of 32,000 men and 10,000 horses, while the difficulty of transport redoubled the cost of provisions. The Republic was confined to the walls of Naples, which produced nothing. What could be expected from a people to whom liberty was preached with words, while in fact it was kept in odious servitude?

The days of the Republic were numbered, but the ruling doctrinaires enjoyed themselves hugely, at the expense of their fellow citizens, while it lasted. Apart from trying to force the dignity of man, the evils of despotism and the virtues of republicanism down the throats of incredulous, mocking *lazzaroni,* they devised fresh regulations every day. Many and varied were their expedients to promote democracy. Anybody so unlucky as to be called Ferdinand was bound to change his name, and as the traditional names of streets, from the Toledo to the blindest alleys, 'were only capable of instilling ideas of superstition and monarchical oppression', it was proposed that they be rechristened: Fortune, Success, Triumph, Victory, Hope, Fertility, Pleasure, Fecundity, Hilarity, Security, Felicity, Valour, Liberty, Glory, Tranquillity, Honour, Prudence, Faith, Concord, Modesty, Silence, Peace, Magnanimity, Vigilance, Grace, Love, Hospitality, Innocence, Frugality, Simplicity, etc.

Statues of monarchs, aristocratic coats-of-arms, and even historical inscriptions were to be removed from public buildings. What did it matter? exclaimed the worthy De Nicola in his diary. The people could not tell the difference between Philip V and Neptune; as for the inscriptions, they were seldom noticed. And it could not be denied that Naples had been a monarchy; history would certainly not forget that fact.

Eleonora Pimentel proposed that the popular puppet shows and *Rinaldi*, or public story-tellers, should choose republican themes and sing patriotic songs; and she protested, quite rightly, when a performance of horses was put on at the San Carlo. The theatre was regarded as purely educational: 'It should form one of the most jealous objects of the care and vigilance of the administration,' wrote the Minister of the Interior, Francesco Conforti, 'in order to prevent the people from being inspired by other sentiments save patriotism, virtue, and wholesome morality.' Alfieri's tragedies were laboriously cultivated. The doors of one theatre were walled up after the performance of Monti's *Aristodemo*, which was branded as anti-patriotic because it portrayed a dethroned monarch who recovered his crown.

A Pantheon was to be erected in honour of such political martyrs as De Deo, Vitaliani and Galiani. Manthoné proposed a law to assist the mothers of those who had fallen in battle, and when it was approved he exclaimed: 'Citizen legislators, I hope that my own mother will have a chance to ask fulfilment of your magnanimous promise!' All able-bodied men between the ages of sixteen and fifty had to serve in the civic or national army. Neither priests, monks nor government officials were exempt, and nobody could hold public office unless he had fulfilled this obligation. Those unable to serve had to pay a contribution. What a fine sort of liberty!—*che bella libertà!*—was De Nicola's comment. But he was soon able to add that medical certificates for exemption could be purchased from the four physicians 'distinguished for public spirit' who were appointed to examine special cases: 'Patents always degenerate into monopolies and thefts.' Taxes and customs duties continued to soar with the cost of living.

What a contrast with the wise policy of Cardinal Ruffo in Calabria! On March 3 he had written to Acton: 'I have an infinite deal to tell Your Excellency regarding the causes which induce me to do what I am doing, but at present I lack the leisure. I beg you to believe that circumstances of utility and necessity guide me, not the will to profit or dominate. I found that there were complaints about things you will find abolished or suspended in the edict I have published. I have made several exemptions from taxes, for instance half the hearth tax and tax on the industry of labourers and poorer classes of those districts which have proved the most faithful and enterprising in returning to their duty, always exploiting the jealousy between the people and the middle class and exonerating the poor, who are truly overburdened with charges, but not exempting them entirely.' He also reformed the land tax, 'as it was unjust and formed by a cabal of the wealthy'.

The appearance of the English squadron in the gulf unnerved the republicans. 'The people are exulting because they think there will soon be a change of government,' wrote De Nicola. Lightning rumours spread: the King was said to have landed at Procida, the Hereditary Prince in Calabria. It was even rumoured that the French had signed a treaty to restore Naples to the King. Royalist placards sprang up like mushrooms. The murders of French soldiers became more frequent; sentinels and patrols were suddenly attacked. On April 5 the French troops and civic guard were all on the alert; many respectable citizens were arrested, and houses were searched for hidden arms. Next day there were more arrests, and it was known that a serious plot had been frustrated. Its origins have never come to light, but novelists from Dumas Père to Vincent Sheean have made ample compensation, and Croce has told the tale with compelling pathos. For it contains all the elements of romance, owing to the woman who betrayed it, Luisa Sanfelice.

The conspirators were supposed to have an agreement with the English squadron, which was to make a feint attack while they slaughtered all the prominent republicans and seized Sant' Elmo. Certain tickets were secretly distributed among the loyal in advance, as passports to protect them in case of danger. One of these was given to Luisa Sanfelice, a well-born attractive young matron of easy virtue in difficult circumstances. No doubt the donor was in love with her. He was a young man called Gerardo Baccher, who had been a cavalry officer in the royal army. But Luisa had a republican lover too, Ferdinando Ferri, of whom she was evidently fonder than Gerardo, for she gave him her ticket with a word of warning. Ferri had been accused of serving as a royalist informer; anxious to clear himself from this taint he promptly reported the incident. Luisa was interrogated: it is said that she refused to divulge the source of her ticket, but the same night Vincenzo Baccher, a well-to-do merchant of English or German origin, his four sons and many other suspects were arrested. Vincenzo Cuoco, author of the famous *Saggio Storico Sulla Rivoluzione Napoletana del 1799*, played an important role either as a detective or as an adviser to Luisa, since he was singled out for equal praise in the *Monitore*. He is silent about this in his Essay; perhaps he felt ashamed, for both he and Ferri were to escape the penalty which fell on the frail woman. Thus in spite of herself, for she had no political creed, Luisa became a republican heroine. She was called the Saviour of the Republic, the Mother of her Country. Her reckless friend Gerardo Baccher lingered in prison with his father and three brothers: eventually two of them were shot. The full extent of the conspiracy was never discovered, but the arrests continued, a long list of distinguished names including the Prince of Canosa. The monastery of San Martino was suppressed, as the monks were suspected of being in the plot. Other conspiracies came to light; there were 'exemplary executions'; and the widening area of revolt and discontent proved that the despotism of Ferdinand and Maria Carolina seemed infinitely preferable to this despotism of 'liberty, equality, fraternity'.

On April 19 De Nicola noted in his diary that four thousand horses had been requisitioned by the French. Already it was rumoured that Macdonald and his army were withdrawing to Caserta. This was confirmed on the 24th, when Macdonald announced his departure after reviewing the civic guard. He pretended that the discipline of his troops had suffered from the effeminate life of the capital; besides, they were such a heavy burden on Neapolitan finances—a thought which had never troubled him till now. They were not going far, only to Caserta, Capua and Caiazzo. He would leave French garrisons in the Sant' Elmo and Ovo castles; the Carmine and Castel Nuovo would be consigned to the civic guard. At the first symptom of aggression he would return like a thunderbolt and exterminate the foe. In fact, he was preparing to evacuate Naples and Rome, foreseeing that he would be needed in the north. He wrote in his *Memoirs* that nobody had any inkling of his real purpose, which he did not even disclose to the French commissioner Abrial.

The government pretended to be sorry to lose their benefactors, but they were just as relieved as the royalists to see them go. The executive council issued a reassuring proclamation—what would now be termed a 'pep-talk'—winding up with the words: 'The Republic is established, and to her enemies nothing remains but jealousy, desperation, and death.' Somebody once remarked that sound is more than sense. Both the legislative and the executive councils seem to have been intoxicated by the sound of their own oratory.

XX

Revolt at Castellammare di Stabia—The imposition of a miracle—Republican rejoicings—Delusions about a Franco-Spanish armada—Exploits of Admiral Caracciolo—Cardinal Ruffo in Puglia—His capture of Altamura—Russian and Turkish auxiliaries—Twilight of the Parthenopean Republic—Cardinal Ruffo at the gates of the capital—Negotiations for peace.

Macdonald did not leave Naples without an appropriate flourish. While preparing to evacuate his army, he heard that Castellammare had been seized by royalists with the aid of two English ships, which had landed several hundred troops. The republicans were caught napping, the garrison mutinied and the town was sacked. There were similar risings elsewhere along the coast, but Castellammare was uncomfortably near. In this case Macdonald felt obliged to keep his word; its recovery was a matter of personal prestige.

'I did not lose an instant,' he wrote, 'and marched in person against Castellammare. Passing through Naples, I noticed many individuals already wearing red cockades in their hats. It was necessary to strike a decisive blow to prevent the insurrection from spreading and rising in Naples, where I only had a weak garrison, outside the forts. The latter were well equipped, especially Sant' Elmo, which always threatened to burn up the city with its guns: fear of this did much to keep the people quiet. The rebels from Calabria and Salerno had advanced towards Torre Annunziata and were stationed beside a stream. I attacked them; to overpower and put them to rout was a matter of a twinkling. While they were being pursued and cut down in all directions, those in the fort lost courage: some, after several volleys, seeing the English sail away, tried to save themselves by jumping into the sea; the others surrendered; the ringleaders and traitors were shot. But the united flags of England and Naples were still flying. I promised twenty-five louis to any one who took them, and they were brought to me half an hour later, not without casualties. Having recovered the tower, the guns of the defence were aimed at the ships and fugitives. At this point I must say that the brave and able Admiral Caracciolo contributed effectively to the success of this expedition... After setting things to rights, ordering the revolt to be quelled and the fugitives to be pursued beyond Salerno, I returned to Naples, preceded by the banners of the rebels, which were burnt next day on the royal square by the public executioner. The red cockades had vanished, and the excitement caused by this incident had entirely died out in the capital...'

Castellammare was sacked again; Gragnano, Lettere, Cava and Vietri were burnt as well as sacked, in accordance with Macdonald's invariable policy. After this sop to Cerberus, the Scottish-French general, in his own words, 'had the miracle of San Gennaro performed in our favour'. The saint's blood was wont to liquefy in the first week of May, and whatever his private opinion, Macdonald was aware of the importance of this tradition and wished it to gain a special significance on the eve of his departure. Should the miracle fail, the consequences to the Republic might be dire. As a precautionary measure he had marched his troops from Caserta to surround the city during the ceremony, but even these could not have saved him if the fanatical congregation ran amok.

On this occasion the atmosphere was peculiarly tense. The malcontent masses looked to their saint for a sign, and their raucous prayers assumed a menacing tone. According to General Thiébault, the President of the Republic walked up to the Cardinal Archbishop, showed him a pistol under his waistcoat and hissed in his ear: 'If the miracle does not happen immediately, you are a dead man.' Whereupon the quivering Cardinal handed the relic to his coadjutor, and the blood liquefied without delay. According to another contemporary, Nardini, the canons of the cathedral had been warned that their lives depended on the miracle's success. That some pressure was exerted seems certain, but no member of the administration was present officially. Eleonora Pimentel, the oracle of the *Monitore*, deplored the absence of the latter and the lack of propaganda. 'The next day [a Sunday] all the pulpits should have resounded with the miracle, and with the obvious decision of Heaven in favour of the Republic. This should have been linked with the other two facts prominent in the popular imagination, that in the beginning of winter, which is usually wet, the only fine days were those from the armistice of Capua to the peaceful entry of

Championnet; that it rained continually and was in every way adverse to Ferdinand's expedition against Rome, while it favoured the French during their march to Naples; and that Vesuvius, dormant since 1794, sent up a sympathetic flame on the night when the city was illuminated for the proclamation of the Republic.' But perhaps this was the only time in history when San Gennaro lost public prestige, for many booed him after the ceremony.

On May 7 Macdonald marched his army north to eventual defeat. Three hundred carts were requisitioned to move the baggage of troops who had come empty-handed, and five hundred cows 'to make a little broth along the journey for their sick'. Many Neapolitan friends accompanied them; not a few who were left behind felt exceedingly bitter, but these were the least vocal. They had been ruined and left to stew in their own juice, as the Queen had prophesied. In his last homily to the assembled government Macdonald told them that a state was not free when it depended on a foreign army for protection, and that they had no need of the French to fight the scattered bands of the Holy Faith. The irony of this was wasted on them. Colletta says that they were overjoyed, for 'being good and simple, it seemed to them impossible that men should dislike liberty'. But their experience of liberty under the Republic was to make the people sing:

> '*Signo', mpennimmo chi t'ha traduto,*
> *Priévete, muonace e cavaliere!*
> *Fatte cchiù, fatte cchiù llà,*
> *Cauce nfacce a la Libbertà!*'
> ('Lord, let us hang those who betrayed thee,
> Priests and monks and cavaliers!
> Make way here, make way there,
> Go kick Liberty everywhere!')

On May 10 the Provisional Government published a proclamation: 'Brave citizens, we are free. The Republic is already established on the most solid foundation. It is the fruit of that courage, virtue and love of fatherland which has ever been engraved in our hearts, and which the former Tyrants have only kindled blindly with their actions, to make us, without realizing it, complete the enterprise. If we have courageously driven tyranny from our pleasant land, it behoves us even now to destroy its very seed. Let us unite. The whole nation only presents one single will and an imposing mass of forces. Let us make the remnants of tyranny tremble for the brief span until their total destruction... etc., etc.'

Parades and celebrations followed; more royal banners and portraits of the King and Queen were committed to the public bonfire; some of the prisoners taken at Castellammare and condemned to death, were reprieved at the last moment with edifying speeches beside the tree of liberty in front of the old royal palace. The taxes on fish and flour were abolished. Even so the people sang such rhymes as:

'*S'è levata la gabella alla farina...
Evviva Ferdinando e Carolina!*'
('They have taken the tax off flour, that's fine...
So long live Ferdinand and Caroline!')

Devising ways and means to stimulate civic enthusiasm, Eleonora Pimentel persisted in pointing towards ancient Rome. Let generals distinguish the brave by crowning them with laurel before their comrades! To bolster flagging morale, Eleonora did not shrink from publishing blatant falsehoods; Republican defeats were transformed into victories. when Russian troops landed at Manfredonia she wrote that Cardinal Ruffo had dressed up a few hundred galley-slaves in Russian uniform. The hastily mustered legions which marched against the royalists were dispersed in all directions. One of them carried a black banner inscribed 'Conquer, Revenge, Die', which did not prevent the troops from deserting to the other side. As it became more apparent that there was little unity even in the government, and that the cornerstone of the Republic had been the French army, one piece of news assumed tremendous consequence. It was to exert a fatal influence on the course of events in Naples. A French fleet of nineteen sail-of-the-line had slipped out of Brest in a fog on April 26 and had been joined by five Spanish warships in the Mediterranean. To this Franco-Spanish armada the republicans pinned all their hopes. Its might was monstrously exaggerated by propaganda; it was said to be conveying an army of 30,000 troops. Whenever prospects looked bleak, that formidable mirage was conjured on the horizon.

Having summoned Troubridge, Nelson put to sea on May 19 acutely conscious that he was risking Sicily. Only the *Sea-horse* and the Neapolitan frigate *Minerva* under Count Thurn, together with a few smaller ships and gunboats, remained at Procida to keep up the blockade. This was Caracciolo's great opportunity. With a mixed flotilla of bomb-vessels, gunboats and galiots he attacked the English ships and damaged the *Minerva*, which he had formerly commanded. But the sea near Procida is apt to be treacherous, and when a wind sprang up the flotilla had to sail home. This action has been praised to the skies, but it failed to dislodge the foe. At any rate, there was no second expedition. Five of his crew were killed and four wounded, which created an uproar among the sailors of Santa Lucia. The government offered fifty ducats to the bereaved families, the same with a month's double pay to the wounded, and twenty-five ducats as a dowry to the daughters of those who had been killed. Their sons were adopted by the state, and a feast was given to all the crews under the tree of liberty in the palace square. But it was almost impossible to collect fresh recruits for the Marine.

After recovering the whole of Calabria, Cardinal Ruffo had marched into Puglia, the granary of Naples. Here the last and most obstinate republican fugitives had assembled at Altamura, a city of about 24,000 inhabitants on the border of Basilicata and Puglia, in a lofty position surrounded by high walls, hence its name. A General Mastrangelo had been sent with two cavalry regiments from Naples to organize its defence, and a 'democratizer' named Palomba to strengthen its will to resist. On April 17 Cardinal Ruffo had published an edict of general pardon 'for all who... after a short interval of time proportioned to local distances, shall return to the good cause, giving manifest signs that they have recanted from their error, into which they were seduced by disturbers of the public peace'. The King would not have approved of such leniency, but it was a sincere effort to check anarchy and curb vendettas. The edict was smuggled into Altamura, and the clergy tried to persuade the citizens to capitulate. But the democratizer had filled them with terror of Ruffo's brigands and promised French reinforcements. Besides, the city seemed impregnable.

While reconnoitring the neighbourhood two of Ruffo's engineers, Vinci and Olivieri, were captured. The Cardinal sent one of his officers, Raffaele Vecchioni, to parley with the republican general, offering good terms if the city surrendered and his engineers were released. When Vecchioni failed to return, the Cardinal decided to attack. In the meantime the republican general and his colleague fled to Gravina. The defenders exhausted their ammunition at the end of the first day's siege. The firing ceased, and Ruffo expected a truce. Suddenly a volley of shots rang out; then all was quiet. The Cardinal concentrated all his men on the Matera side of the city, leaving the Naples side free for the republicans to escape. As usual, he wished to avoid bloodshed if possible. All night long there was an uncanny silence. Noticing that the Matera gate was not defended, some of his soldiers burnt it down, but the Cardinal forbade them to proceed. Next morning they found the city deserted except for a few old people and invalids. Most of the inhabitants had escaped by the Naples gate and two breaches in the wall. A search was started for the missing messenger and engineers. At last they were traced to a cemetery beside the Church of San Francesco. Before retiring the republicans had shot forty-eight royalist prisoners, chained in couples, and pushed them, dead and dying, into a vault. The blood-stained slab was lifted; and among the corpses a few were still gasping for air when they were pulled out. Only three of those who had been buried recovered from their wounds; one was the messenger Vecchioni, who was still alive in 1820. It is incontestable that Ruffo's Calabrians were vindictive: their pugnacity made up for their lack of discipline. But in the course of his campaign it was the cruelties and excesses of the 'gentle patriots' that provoked reprisals, a fact overlooked by hostile historians. After this outrage the republicans could hardly expect to be let off lightly.

The Cardinal had intended to levy a fine and divide the proceeds among his army. All he could do now was to prevent his troops from deserting after the sack, as at Cotrone. He obliged them to pile up their loot on the square before the Matera gate; the other gates had been closed. In the meantime a certain Count Filo was hauled from his hiding-place before the Cardinal. While he was begging for mercy he was shot by a relative of the murdered Olivieri, and fell dead at the Cardinal's feet. The horrified prelate gave orders to stop the sack and divide the spoils immediately. 'Nobody was content with his share,' wrote Sacchinelli, 'each thought he had been defrauded; and I can truly affirm that it was the Cardinal's *genius* which prevented an outbreak of atrocities in that critical emergency.' During the next fortnight the population returned, and the women produced the same effect on the Christian army as those of Capua on Hannibal's. They became so attached to the place that when it was time to leave, their officers had to go from house to house to ferret them out. The spoil, except what was removed by the local peasants, remained in Altamura, as well as most of the soldiers' pay. Sacchinelli wrote as an eyewitness and his unvarnished account rings true. Neither Cuoco, Colletta nor Botta were on the spot, but they wrote with the advantage of literary style as fervent anti-Bourbonists, so that their fanciful descriptions have won credence.

At this period a French ship from Egypt arrived at Taranto, having been chased by Russians in the Ionian Sea. The passengers included three French generals, among them the father of Dumas Père, and the famous geologist Dolomieu, who wrote to Ruffo that they had been driven there by stormy weather, and being unarmed, requested a safe conduct to the Neapolitan frontier, or wherever the nearest French troops were stationed. The Cardinal replied that he could not give them an escort by land without compromising his authority and their lives, as the whole kingdom, and indeed the whole of Italy, had risen against the French; nor could he give them a passport by sea without British approval. They were sent to Messina, where the King had them imprisoned. After all, he was at war with France.

Micheroux had been negotiating for months with the Russian commander at Corfu, and the meagre result was that 450 Russians landed at Manfredonia under Captain Baillie, a soldier of Irish origin. Ruffo had expected at least two thousand, but the men were well trained and rumour would exaggerate their number. On his advance through upper Puglia, the Cardinal was greeted with frequent acclamations. His army was accompanied by a lively band playing bagpipes and other rural instruments, and there was much singing and folk-dancing along the road. The cheeses and wines of Puglia were an excellent restorative after strenuous marches. On May 29 they reached Melfi, where the saint's day of the King was celebrated. Here two Turkish officers from Corfu announced that Cadir Bey, the Commander of the Ottoman squadron, was ready to land several thousand troops in Puglia. The Cardinal was embarrassed. He had always stressed the Christian character of his army—the Holy Faith was his battle-cry—and the Crescent of the Infidel would not harmonize with the Cross on his banners. He replied tactfully that the Turks would be more valuable at Naples. Since the direct voyage from Corfu was easy at this season, he suggested that the commander co-operate with the British fleet. He then invited them to dinner with his officers, and supposing that they abstained from wine he offered them brandy. One of them said with a chuckle: 'Defend Christians, drink wine.'

The Christian army was becoming catholic in the broadest sense. Now Roccaromana, the former General of the People, offered to serve under the Cardinal as a simple private. He had retired in disgust to his family estate, repenting of his momentary folly. With his usual sagacity Ruffo congratulated him on his conversion and appointed him commander of all the armed squadrons in Terra di Lavoro, where Fra Diavolo had held sway, to blockade Capua and cut communications with the capital. Pronio, who had held the Abruzzi against the French, was to support him with half his forces and besiege Ruvo at Pescara with the rest. Before marching on Naples, Ruffo was anxious to co-ordinate all the bands which had been fighting independently for the royal cause. While he was at Ariano Scipione della Marra joined him with two companies of grenadiers and several cannon from Palermo; he also brought him a flag embroidered by the Queen and Princesses. On one side was the royal coat-of-arms with the inscription in gold letters 'To the brave Calabrians'; on the other the Cross with '*In hoc signo vinces*'. This was accompanied by a glowing letter signed by the august ladies. The banner was blessed by the Archbishop of Benevento and presented with suitable solemnity to the first Calabrian regiment.

Two men who pretended to be corn-brokers were arrested as spies near Ariano. They were conducted to the Cardinal while he was inspecting the Russian camp. One of them called Coscia had been the Cardinal's cook, and he confessed that they had been sent by the royalists to find out if the Russians had come, which the Jacobins denied. 'This is the vanguard,' said Ruffo, and, pointing towards Ariano, 'the army follows close behind. Return to Naples and tell what your eyes have seen.' He gave him some Russian coins to show as a proof and a note for his sister, the Princess of Campana. On the latter was written 'Malaga is always malaga'—a family code meaning that all was well and that they would soon meet again.

At Avellino the Cardinal received a letter from the King, informing him that the Prince Royal was sailing to Naples with a strong convoy of English and Portuguese ships, which he hoped would induce a peaceful surrender. The Cardinal was forbidden to attack it before the English squadron arrived. According to the increasing number of refugees and deserters, the Neapolitan population could hardly wait to be liberated. The republican forces consisted of disbanded veterans who remained loyal at heart, provincial fanatics and hot-headed students, as arrogant as they were insubordinate, and conscripted civilians who were anything but martial. General Wirtz, who had been a Swiss mercenary under the monarchy, was to defend the capital. General Federici, another renegade, was sent against Ruffo, but his regiment was dispersed by peasant hordes in Terra di Lavoro. The veterans joined the Christian army and the civilians evaporated. Federici and a minority of diehards crept back to Naples at night, leaving a trail of abandoned artillery. General Schipani marched on Salerno to clear the road to Calabria, but on hearing of Federici's repulse he entrenched himself between Torre Annunziata and Torre del Greco. The French garrison of Sant' Elmo played no part in these operations.

Had Ruffo marched straight to Naples at this juncture he would have occupied the city. But the King's letter restrained him. From Avellino he sent an adjutant, Giuseppe Mazza, to reconnoitre the outskirts of the capital and parley with the first republican commander he met, for which he was given credentials. He was authorized to offer good terms for a peaceful surrender. He went as far as the village of Casanova without detecting any hostile man or even troops. Cannon and other artillery littered the highway: the scene resembled the aftermath of defeat. Thinking he had adequately carried out his mission, and remembering, perhaps, the fate of previous messengers at Cotrone and Altamura, he hurried back to report that if the Republic intended to resist it must do so right under the city walls.

Naples was in a chronic state of alarm. Arrests and executions were intensified. The sentinels of the national guard became so 'trigger-happy' that their random shots killed a number of quiet citizens. The murderers of the Filomarino brothers were executed; and a panic was caused by a soldier dropping his rifle. Then a priest was shot for saying 'Long live the King!' His advocate pleaded that he had been drunk at the time, but the judges maintained that intoxication betrays a man's true sentiments: *in vino veritas*. Then three peasants of Mugnano were shot for starting an insurrection. More and more aristocrats were arrested, including Luigi de' Medici, who had served in the civic guard and done his best to pander to the new regime. He had even tried to form a party of his own, but in spite of powerful affiliations his past double-dealing was not forgotten and, luckily for him, it was thought advisable to keep him out of harm's way.

While Cardinal Ruffo was drawing nearer, the Legislative Council was still discussing the abolition of fiefs. On May 28 Mario Pagano introduced a law confiscating the property of those who had followed the Court to Palermo, now branded as public enemies. False news of French victories continued to be published, but it was difficult to conceal their own defeats. The spectacle of so many wounded soldiers lying at the Capuan gate and others dropping with fatigue who had lost all their equipment, was scarcely reassuring. The ultra-republican Duchesses of Cassano and Popoli went from house to house collecting funds for a new legion. The civic guard were warned to be prepared to fight the enemy, but many protested that they had only joined to keep order in the city and discarded their uniforms. One of their spokesmen remarked that Pagano and his friends ought to be sent instead of playing the fool in Naples.

A mere street-fight, a runaway horse, incidents that would normally pass unnoticed, sufficed to create alarm, wrote the diarist De Nicola, whose daily jottings are like the fever-chart of the Republic's galloping consumption. The current rhyme was scarcely exaggerated:

'Unica ed indivisa la Repubblica Napoletana:
Comincia a Posillipo e finisce a Porta Capuana'
('One and indivisible is the Republican state:
It begins at Posillipo and ends at the Capuan Gate.')

Even so the government was not downhearted. Alfieri's tragedy *Timoleone* was performed at the Patriotic Theatre with the following puff, a perfect sample of the brave new style: 'A great mirror of exemplariness, of moral and Republican virtues, was this historic upholder of the rights of man! His modesty, truly worthy of a philanthropic heart, even amid the lustre of his actions and of the acclamations of an entire people familiar with his sublime democratic sentiments, which led him (oh object of envy!) to stifle the tenderest voices of nature through heroism, deserves to be admired, to be followed, and to serve as a lesson to the whole regenerated World.

'Patriots of Naples, run hither in crowds to steel your hearts and revive your energies! In order to make the way easy for you the manager offers free entrance to all this evening (May 24), and those who wish to pay at the door will benefit their indigent brothers, among whom this sum will be distributed. Citizens zealous for your country, bring artists, relations, and friends! The action is worthy of you.'

Though many took advantage of the free seats, *Timoleone* had but a limited appeal. A few days later De Nicola noted in his diary: 'while the chief patriots display courage and energy, all their followers take to their heels at the slightest sound. Today the Patriotic Club held a meeting at Santa Lucia and the hall was emptied in a second when a cannon shot was heard. Everybody vanished: the chairman, Luigi Serio, was unable to persuade them to stay. Later it became known that the cannon was fired to call a small ship to order... as similar English vessels land here every day.'

In spite of *Timoleone*, Eleonora Pimentel, and the friars who were sent to preach liberty in the highways and byways, the people felt that the government was hypocritical. 'The licentiousness of the patriots is blatant, and the people hear and see it... As an instance of this, in one of the quarters of the civic guard four profligates combined to amuse themselves with practising pederasty, and it was not easy to make them desist. In the middle of the Toledo a lady was walking with her husband and a civic guard had the impudence to smack her posterior. The disorder that reigns in this street in broad daylight is visible to all wayfarers.' These seemed to the diarist sure symptoms of the Republic's decline.

At last even Eleonora Pimentel could not conceal the harsh facts. 'Exhausted in unequal combat,' she wrote in the *Monitore*, 'victims of rebel assassination, the very flower of Republican youth has perished... In spite of this unpleasant news, they did not fail to sing "The Victory of the French" at the National Theatre on Sunday evening; and there was a ball at the Fondo Theatre, for which the entrance fee was reduced to three *carlini* instead of five, to make it easier for the public to be present.' More fabulous French victories had been announced and the whole city was to be illuminated in their honour despite a shortage of oil. There is something splendid in such contempt for realities. 'Would you believe it!' exclaimed De Nicola, 'while these festivities are proclaimed and the city is illuminated, Naples is hemmed in by insurgents and on the brink of starvation.' And still the civic guard refused to move. Though threatened with ignominious degradation, many officers resigned. An expedition to Pozzuoli had to return, because it was raked by fire from English ships. On June 2 a *Te Deum* was sung in San Lorenzo for the victories of the French in Italy. 'It would be better to have prayers for our own safety,' wrote the diarist, noting more arrests from day to day: the ex-Marquis of Fuscaldo and his entire family, the ex-Duke of Calabritto, the ex-Duke of Miranda, the ex-Count della Cerra, the ex-Duke of Valentino, the Trajetto family, the ex-Duke of Atri, and others who had been royal officials, besides bevies of ladies. All those who went to visit them risked being arrested.

On June 5 a new law promised to reward those who denounced conspiracies; innkeepers and the owners of cafés were to report the conversations heard on their premises. A commission of five was to judge all political prisoners, conspirators and insurgents 'on the instant and by plurality of votes, and militarily without appeal or protest, and this was authorized to proceed without any form of trial, only having regard to the truth of the facts'. A few days later the Patriotic Club was in an uproar because this commission had not yet sentenced those who had been arrested for their political opinions. Gregorio Mancini made a rabid speech in favour of their prompt execution. Since some four thousand suspects were involved, this proposal seemed rather drastic. All Cardinal Ruffo's relations were among them, but these were segregated in the monastery of Monteoliveto, now the seat of the municipality.

On June 11 the Cardinal entered Nola, where he was joined by a small, fierce company of Turks. He had intended to make Portici his headquarters and wait for the Prince Royal to arrive with the British squadron, but he was swept forward by his own momentum. Acton had written him that if he could take Naples independently, so much the better, making it plain that he preferred not to become too indebted to any foreign ally. On June 13, the day of Saint Anthony of Padua, for whom the Cardinal had always cherished a special devotion, all the bells of San Giovanni a Teduccio were pealing and the parish priest was carrying the Holy Sacrament in a procession to meet the deliverer. The Cardinal dismounted and knelt to receive the benediction, and asked all the clergy to pray for victory.

On hearing of his approach the Executive Council ordered all civilians indoors as soon as the first volley was fired from Sant' Elmo. The members of the government and their families shut themselves up in Castel Nuovo. Early that morning the two brothers Gerardo, and Gennaro Baccher, together with three of their companions, Natale d'Angelo, Ferdinando and Giovanni La Rossa, were hastily condemned and shot in the courtyard of the same castle, 'all happy to die for so sacred a cause'. Eleven others, members of the 'small populace', were shot as well. The political prisoners, who expected the same fate, were kept as hostages. If the revolutionary tribunal had had more time, there would have been a holocaust. The shooting of these royalists, from whom they were never able to extract a single name, was an act of desperation at the eleventh hour. Already the army of Ruffo was at the gates.

As the civic troops rode through the market square, many shouted that it was high time the King returned. The cavalry mowed them down and shot about sixteen. Most of the fighting took place at the Maddalena bridge, where there was a well-equipped fort, but Caracciolo's gunboats and the sea-fort of Vigliena wrought greater havoc. When the latter was captured by Calabrian infantry and the banner of the Cross was raised, the forces under General Wirtz became demoralized and Caracciolo withdrew to the arsenal under the guns of Castel Nuovo. Wirtz fought gallantly, but his cavalry faltered. In vain he called '*Cavalleria, in avanti!*' He was fatally wounded, and 'that sufficed to discourage us all and to set the cavalry flying', as one of his followers wrote. Ruffo's cavalry pursued them as far as the Carmine castle. The remnants withdrew to the Nuovo and Ovo castles, to Pizzofalcone and the hill of San Martino, but the French garrison would not admit them to Sant' Elmo. That evening a tremendous explosion lit up the east coast. The sea-fort of Vigliena was blown up. As it is improbable that any of the temporary occupants survived, the tale of the wounded republican dragging himself to the gunpowder magazine and firing into it with a last loud cheer for Liberty, sounds like a posthumous legend. One of Ruffo's bravest officers and a hundred and fifty of his Calabrians perished in the accident. The main body of his infantry bivouacked with the Turks at the foot of the Maddalena bridge, and some of these arranged between them to capture the castle of the Carmine that night as a pleasant surprise for the Cardinal. The garrison was overpowered and massacred; the commandant, who protested that he was a foreigner and a royalist, was taken to Ruffo and released. This hastened the occupation of the capital, as Ruffo became master of the port and its batteries.

The half-starved populace, exasperated by the incessant bombardment from the castles, were like tigers released from a cage, regarding all Jacobins as their lawful prey. For those who would wallow in scenes of unbridled sadism, there is abundant literature on the subject. The victims were stripped and dismembered; their roasted flesh was devoured; their severed heads were borne in procession on pikes, or kicked about as footballs. Ladies who had shown republican sympathies were chased half-naked through the streets with every conceivable outrage; some were undressed to see if the tree of liberty had been tattooed on their limbs, or were made to pose as Liberty in the nude, pelted with filth amid obscene jeers. Their houses were systematically sacked. At first the mob dragged their victims to the Cardinal's quarters at the Maddalena bridge, but seeing that they were slaughtered in spite of his orders to release them, 'since war was only to be waged against the enemy still fighting in the castles', the Cardinal had them taken to the Granili, the huge granary nearby, which served as a provisional shelter as well as a prison. Here hundreds were cooped up in the stifling heat, with guards who robbed them of the little they retained, to endure every kind of torment for weeks together. 'The Neapolitan people,' wrote one of them, 'crucified us until the last moment of our imprisonment.'

Cardinal Ruffo was deeply chagrined by these excesses, which he could do nothing to stop. Ghastly as were the conditions inside the Granili, the prisoners were at least protected from the *lazzaroni*. Except the Carmine, the castles were in republican hands, and their resistance had been stiffened by a rumour that the Franco-Spanish armada was approaching. He had no spare troops to control the populace, and those he had were in full sympathy with them.

A long-delayed letter from the King now arrived, informing him that the Prince Royal had had to return to Palermo because the French fleet had entered the Mediterranean to join the Spanish squadron, a serious danger both to Naples and Sicily; that Nelson had gone to attack them but could not be certain of finding them; so that unless the Cardinal had conquered Naples and its forts, he was to withdraw to an impregnable position. Had this reached him a few days sooner, he would have had to obey. Ruffo replied that the republican army had been destroyed, and its remnants inside the castles were inconsiderable; that the French garrisons of Sant' Elmo, Capua and Gaeta were so closely besieged that they could not communicate with each other, and thus were reduced to impotence. So much time had elapsed without any glimpse of the Franco-Spanish fleet that he considered its coming an illusion; but whatever happened and wherever he retired, he could only expect help from Heaven and he thought he should expect that in the capital, where Divine Providence had led him almost by the hand, and where he could find better means of support than elsewhere. If he was not yet wholly master of the capital, he hoped to become so within a few days, as his army had been greatly reinforced with veterans, and looked forward to driving the French out of the kingdom. He deplored his inability to prevent the populace from slaughtering and sacking inside the capital, owing to his own critical situation, and his army's sympathy with the ideas of the people. Finally he begged His Majesty to end these calamities by returning to Naples, assuring him that he could not find greater safety than at the head of his army, nor affection more sincere than that of his subjects.

Ruffo had been relieved to hear that his own family were out of danger. They had been kept in a state of anguished suspense until their warders decided to abandon Monteoliveto in a hurry. Before the latter retired, Ruffo's niece, the Princess della Motta, had begged for some food and been told that this was superfluous as she would soon be shot. The poor lady was in the seventh month of pregnancy. But in spite of this consolation the Cardinal was more harassed in his moment of triumph than at any other time in his career, for the power he had called into existence was beyond his control. His Calabrians had always been undisciplined, and the popular anarchy was spreading like an epidemic. The republicans seemed determined to resist to the last gasp, blow up the castles and leave the capital in ruins. And perhaps, after all, the much-vaunted Franco-Spanish armada would sail into the bay. Hardened as he was to the horrors of war, pessimistic about mankind in general, he had become thoroughly weary of the monotonous round of violence, destruction and carnage, and he yearned for peace and order.

Much as he disliked Micheroux, the King's envoy to the Russian and Turkish commands, who had often exceeded his authority, on June 16 he sent him to negotiate with General Massa, the commandant of Castel Nuovo, warning him that further resistance was useless, since the castle was within short range of his batteries. Once the breach was made, the populace would not fail to massacre all the inmates. Massa asked for two days to deliberate; Ruffo said two hours must suffice. On receiving no reply, his batteries fired with redoubled vigour. Massa then hoisted the white flag and sent word that he would have to consult with Colonel Méjean, the French commandant of Sant' Elmo. Ruffo would not agree to this, so there was a deadlock. That night some republicans made a bold sortie from San Martino, wrecked the battery in the Villa Reale gardens and sacked two casinos and a coffee-house, while other republicans were dislodged from Pizzofalcone. Next day the walls of Castel Nuovo seemed about to collapse, and Ruffo ordered a quantity of ladders to be taken there. Again the white flag went up: Massa requested an armistice to discuss a capitulation which would include all the garrisons. This was granted, and Micheroux went to see Méjean, who demanded such exorbitant payment in cash that there was another deadlock. Convinced that the enemy were only playing for time, Ruffo threatened to end the armistice within twenty-four hours. But Micheroux, who was far more conciliating, persevered on his own initiative. On the 19th he wrote to Ruffo that Massa had applied for an escort to Sant' Elmo to ask Méjean's leave to surrender. The Russian commander had urged him to oppose this, but after a while he had agreed on condition that Massa gave his word of honour not to talk privately with the French commander; their conference was to be public. Consequently he had ordered all the batteries from the Carmine to the Chiaia to suspend hostilities till further notice. He wished to know, in the event of a capitulation, if there was to be a general pardon for those 'who had not committed positive crimes', and safe transportation to France for those who preferred to leave, with the option to sell or remove their goods within a definite period. The English seemed willing to guarantee this convention. Who was to sign the document? While awaiting the Cardinal's instructions, he informed him that the transaction might take four or five hours.

Ruffo's curt reply, scrawled on the back of this letter, betrays his irritation: Micheroux should never have allowed Massa to confer with the commandant of Sant' Elmo nor to gain so much time to repair the defences of Castel Nuovo. After taking such prejudicial steps, it was useless to ask his advice. If Massa wished to surrender, one or two hours would have been ample. Inside the castle they were putting everything to rights, and this was clearly their object. The pacts should be equivalent to those already proposed, since Massa was the first to yield, but he was sure it would end 'to our damage and detriment'.

The Cardinal knew even better than Micheroux that the terms were unacceptable to the King and Queen. The King had repeated Nelson's maxim about speedy rewards and quick punishments almost word for word: '*Rigore e castigo severo con chi ha mancato al suo dovere e premio per chi s'è ben condotto.*' The Queen had written him pages about the subject ever since he had set foot in Calabria. On April 5 for instance: 'Rebellious Naples and her ungrateful citizens shall make no conditions: order must be restored to that monstrous city with rewarding the faithful and chastising the wicked as an example.' And on April 14: 'No pity must be shown; and the weeds that poison the rest must be hunted down, destroyed, annihilated and deported.' 'Neither truce nor pardon nor treaty with our villains,' she also wrote to Gallo. 'Death for the ringleaders, deportation for the rest... Our country must be purged of this infection.' Lest there should be any misunderstanding, Acton had been even more explicit in laying down rules for his guidance. He had even rebuked him for his lack of severity. Finally, on June 14, in a letter which must have reached him in the midst of negotiations, the Queen said she longed to hear that Naples had been taken, 'but no treaty with our rebellious vassals'. The King might pardon them, but would never capitulate with criminal rebels who had been caught like mice in a trap...

All this harping on the theme of Nemesis must have revolted the Cardinal's Christianity. 'What is the use of punishing,' he had written to Acton; 'indeed, how is it possible to punish so many persons without an indelible imputation of cruelty?' But the King and Queen thought it necessary to be cruel in order to be kind. Now that Ruffo had reconquered all their lost kingdom except for a few fortresses, the success of his enterprise began to merge into a sanguinary sunset. In the tension of the climax he felt ready to risk the displeasure of his royal masters. His victory seemed dismally like defeat. And it was in a defeated spirit that he wrote to Acton on June 21: 'I am at the Maddalena bridge; and from all appearances the Ovo and Nuovo castles are about to surrender to the Russians and to Cavaliere Micheroux. I am so exhausted and worn out that I do not see how I shall be able to bear up if this goes on for another three days. Having to govern, or more precisely to curb, a vast population accustomed to the most resolute anarchy; having to control a score of uneducated and insubordinate leaders of light troops, all intent on pillage, slaughter and violence, is so terrible and complicated a business that it is utterly beyond my strength. By now they have brought me 1,300 Jacobins; not knowing where to shelter them I have sent them to the granaries near the bridge. They must have massacred or shot at least fifty in my presence without my being able to prevent it, and wounded at least two hundred, whom they even dragged here naked. Seeing me horrified at this spectacle, they console me by saying that the dead men were truly arch-villains, and that the wounded were out-and-out enemies of the human race, well known to the population. I hope it is true, and thus I set my mind at ease a little. By dint of precautions, edicts, patrols and preachings, the violence of the people has considerably abated, thank God. If we obtain the surrender of the two castles, I hope to restore calm there entirely, because I shall be able to employ my troops with this object. It is certain that we are in a cruel plight, having to make war while dreading the enemy's destruction. Add to this our numerous but irregular and unbridled troops, and it is enough to make one sweat in the depth of winter. The castles have been attacked so vigorously during the night that they are half demolished. The bombs have had the greatest effect against Castel Nuovo... The armistice has lasted a few hours, and we are waiting to see if the surrender of the two castles aforementioned will be completed by this evening. The English commander grumbles because the truce involves such a waste of time, and he would like to end it; but the immense danger to the city must not be forgotten, thundered upon incessantly from Sant' Elmo. Meanwhile the populace, and many outlaws who have come to fight for the King, besides eighty blasted Turks, are robbing and plundering without let or hindrance. All respectable folk are fleeing to the country. Our better soldiers are guarding the houses against pillage, but to little purpose. Often the pretext is Jacobinism: that is what they call it, but in fact it is plunder that often produces Jacobin proprietors. I found the same in small places. To the cry of "Long live the King!" they dare anything with impunity. It seems to me that this consideration should make us lenient with the rogues in the castles, and compassionate with the many guests locked up with them.

'I do not know what the conditions will be, but they will certainly be very clement for a thousand motives which need not be enumerated, and which may be inferred from their antecedents. I do not believe it possible to restore order to the country in a short time without any system, but it would be quite impossible with a new method...'

The rest of the letter described his reorganization of the government. It was not easy to find officials of unimpeachable integrity, but he had obeyed the King's orders in taking Marchese Simonetti as a counsellor, though he had a poor opinion of his talents. His own concern was with the restoration of peace, for he had 'supped full with horrors'.

XXI

The capitulation of June 19, 1799—Nelson returns to Naples with the Hamiltons—Their disagreement with Ruffo—The Queen's indignation: 'No truce with the rebels!'—The capitulation repudiated—Caracciolo sentenced to be hanged—The King on board the Foudroyant—*Méjean surrenders Sant' Elmo—Verdicts of the* Giunta di Stato.

The Republicans did not know what to think of the mild Micheroux, so pathetically anxious to come to terms with them. Perhaps their own situation was less critical than it seemed; perhaps the French had really won sweeping victories, and their formidable fleet was now on its way to relieve them; perhaps Ruffo's brigands had mutinied for more plunder. They had never taken the Cardinal seriously until the shock of his arrival. They were surprised by his peaceful overtures, and utterly distrustful. Manthoné urged his colleagues to struggle on to the bitter end, but the terms offered were so advantageous that Massa was in favour of accepting them. When asked his opinion of the defences, Massa replied that if he were in Ruffo's place Castelnuovo would fall within a couple of hours. Even so there was such dissension that the Republicans nearly had a free fight. Massa's opinion prevailed. He thought a few victims would be demanded, but the rest would be saved; he was prepared to sacrifice his own life for any of them.

On June 19 the articles of the treaty were signed by the commandants of the Nuovo and Ovo castles, and by Ruffo, Micheroux and the Russian and Turkish representatives; on the 21st they were approved by Méjean, the commandant of Sant' Elmo; on the 23rd they were signed with some hesitation by Captain Foote, who had been in charge of a small squadron since Troubridge's recall. Méjean made no terms for his garrison beyond the three weeks' armistice; he still hoped to drive a lucrative bargain if the Franco-Spanish armada failed to appear. The treaty provided that the Nuovo and Ovo castles were to be consigned to the allied troops, but the garrisons could choose between embarking for Toulon and remaining in Naples without interference. They were to hold the forts until their ships were ready to sail, and then march out with all the honours of war; their persons and property were to be respected and guaranteed. All the state prisoners were to be set free when the capitulation was signed, but the Archbishop of Salerno, General Micheroux (the negotiator's cousin), General Dillon and the Bishop of Avellino were to be sent as hostages to Sant' Elmo until the arrival of the Republicans at Toulon had been ascertained.

According to a British captain writing in the *United Service Journal* in 1845, our officers considered the gaining of such important posts, at a moment when the enemy's combined fleets might hourly be expected, to be an ingenious stroke of diplomacy. Charles Lock, the British consul in Palermo, also wrote (on June 30, 1799) that he considered the removal of the Republicans to Toulon 'a very wise measure... as it effectually sweeps the Kingdom of the disaffected who, when banished and their property alienated, may be considered as virtually dead'. But it was contrary to the King's and Queen's repeated instructions. On June 17 the King had sent the Cardinal his congratulations for having recovered the kingdom of Naples 'without those auxiliaries which our allies had promised us, and without which they did not think it could be accomplished'—referring to the 12,000 Russians whom he believed that Thugut, 'our sworn enemy', had diverted to the support of Austria. 'I am sure I need not repeat,' he added, 'what I wrote to you in my last two letters with regard to the method of treating both the good and the loyal and the infamous rebel Jacobins, especially the ringleaders. Nevertheless I recommend you fervently not to do anything derogatory to the dignity and decorum which it is so necessary to maintain, both for my honour and yours. As a Christian I pardon everybody, but as he whom God appointed, I must be a strict avenger of the offences committed against Him, and of the injury done to the state and so many poor unfortunates.' And again on the 20th: 'It is bruited abroad that in the surrender of the castles all the rebels shut inside them will be allowed to leave safe and sound, even Caracciolo and Manthoné, etc., and proceed to France. This I shall never believe, because God preserve us from them, to spare those savage vipers, and especially Caracciolo, who knows every inlet of our coastline, might inflict the greatest damage on us.'

To allow rebellious subjects to march out of the castles they had usurped with 'the honours of war' was pushing conciliation a trifle far. But the Cardinal believed in the rightness and wisdom of mercy, the folly and ultimate danger of persecution. He had in fact sent Caracciolo advice through his own niece the Duchess of Bagnara to escape by land, offering him a safe conduct through the invading army. But Caracciolo, who had left the arsenal on the 17th disguised as a peasant, preferred to hide in a village on his mother's estate near Naples.

While the ships were being prepared for those who wished to sail to Toulon, the Cardinal conferred with the Captain-General, Duke of Salandra, about the reorganization of the regular army, into which his Calabrian infantry and many of Mack's veterans were to be absorbed. 'The departure of the patriots is certain,' wrote De Nicola on the 24th, 'and during this night the Palace will be evacuated. Now they are solely occupied with selling their remaining property. A person who went to see how far he could approach the Palace described to me their lack of concern, as an instance of which he quoted the remark of one of Corleto's sons [Giuseppe Riario], who recognized him as a violin teacher and said: "We shall go and dance the *Ça-irà* elsewhere, while you stay on to enjoy this beautiful but infamous city."'

All seemed to be flowing towards a peaceful solution when Nelson arrived in the bay on the 24th with eighteen sail-of-the-line. He had stopped a few hours at Palermo on the 21st to confer with the Sovereigns and embark Sir William and Lady Hamilton with great secrecy. The Sovereigns could not have known about the signing of the capitulation, though a letter from the Queen to Lady Hamilton, dated the 18th, announced that the castles had been partly taken. It is easy to guess what was said at the conference, for the Queen had written in the same letter: 'What we need is a second first of August, another Aboukir.' The Sovereigns mistrusted the Cardinal's policy of toleration. He had been ominously silent of late. Nelson promised to enforce their wishes if need be. The Hamiltons were to assist him as advisers and interpreters. 'Milady', above all, was to keep him up to the mark, and the Queen had crammed her with minute instructions. The actress in her prevented her from being a mere spectator; and she revelled in her new role.

Nelson had been annoyed by his fruitless search for the Franco-Spanish fleet, and his truculence boiled over when he saw a flag of truce flying on H.M.S. *Sea-horse* and others on the castles. 'Haul down that flag of truce,' Lady Hamilton is said to have exclaimed on the quarterdeck of the *Foudroyant*, as the ship entered the bay, 'no truce with the rebels!' Sir William Hamilton had received a shattering blow: he had just heard that the ship *Colossus* had been wrecked with his entire collection of classical treasures, the cherished hoard of a long career devoted to their discovery and contemplation. Only that living work of art, Emma, still remained to him, but perhaps he had begun to perceive her flaws; perhaps, in comparison with those mute idealized statues now lost for ever, her irrepressible vivacity had begun to pall. Nelson's infatuation for her was a compliment to his taste rather than a cause for jealousy. Like many passionate collectors, he might have sacrificed his wife for his collection. A heartbroken old hedonist, he could not expect others to understand the quality of his despair. This personal calamity, for which he held the Jacobins responsible, made the polished ambassador as vindictive as the thwarted admiral, whose pugnacity had been stimulated by the Queen and the beauty he described as 'my faithful interpreter on all occasions'.

When Captain Foote of the *Sea-horse* came on board the *Foudroyant* with a copy of the capitulation, Nelson told him that he 'had been imposed upon by that worthless fellow, Cardinal Ruffo, who was endeavouring to form a party hostile to the interests of his Sovereign'. Foote respectfully observed that he had been placed in a most anxious situation; having had more reason, among many disagreeable and trying circumstances, to expect the enemy's fleet, rather than that under his Lordship's command, in Naples Bay; that he could not be supposed to know, or even imagine, that the Cardinal was acting contrary to his Sovereign's interests, when he saw him retained in his very high and confidential situation. His instructions had directed him to co-operate, to the utmost of his power, with the Royalists, at whose head Cardinal Ruffo was known to be placed, even before the squadron under Sir Thomas Troubridge had sailed from Palermo. Nelson gave him due credit for zeal, assiduity and good intentions, and sent him off to write a full report of his proceedings.

An hour later Sir William Hamilton wrote to inform the Cardinal that Lord Nelson disapproved of the capitulation and was determined not to remain neutral with the force at his command. Captains Troubridge and Ball would expound his Lordship's sentiments, hoping that His Eminence would act in concert with him next day at dawn. Their object could only be the same: to reduce the common foe and submit rebellious subjects to His Sicilian Majesty's clemency.

After annulling the armistice by signal, Nelson's fleet anchored in a close line of battle before the city. The Republicans, who had at first mistaken it for the Franco-Spanish armada, were plunged in despair. Cardinal Ruffo supposed that Nelson disapproved because he had not waited for him before attacking the city, and he decided to explain the circumstances himself. Next afternoon he visited the *Foudroyant*, and was saluted with thirteen guns. After the usual compliments, Nelson listened in frigid silence as the Cardinal gave him a résumé in French of all the events since June 13 leading up to the capitulation. One thought was uppermost in his mind as he listened impatiently to what he considered a contemptible rigmarole in frog-language and watched, with suspicion, the Cardinal's increasingly violent gesticulations, due to a guilty conscience, no doubt; why could not the fellow keep still? This thought was uttered by Hamilton, who was present with his wife. 'Kings do not capitulate with their rebellious subjects,' he snapped. 'Even if it were better not to capitulate,' said Ruffo, 'they are obliged to honour a treaty, after it has been made.' Not all the arguments of Nelson and the Hamiltons could convince him otherwise. Both sides were obstinate. The Cardinal said he would consult the other allies and withdrew.

In due course the Russian and Turkish commanders and Micheroux protested that the treaty of capitulation was 'useful, necessary, and honourable' to all concerned, as it ended the civil strife and expelled the common foe. They were determined to observe it religiously, and whoever dared to violate it 'would be responsible before God and the world.' Regardless of this, Nelson sent the Cardinal a declaration to be forwarded to the rebels, who were to surrender themselves to His Majesty's royal mercy. Ruffo refused point blank. If Nelson broke the armistice, he would withdraw his troops and leave the English to conquer with their own forces. Nothing daunted, he climbed again on board the *Foudroyant*, and there was another fruitless discussion lasting two hours, with the Hamiltons as hostile interpreters. Nelson decided that 'an Admiral is no match in talking with a Cardinal', and handed Ruffo his written opinion, that upon his arrival he had found a treaty entered into with the rebels, which he considered should not be carried into execution without the approbation of His Sicilian Majesty. Ruffo promptly warned General Massa that Nelson would not recognize the treaty, and advised the garrisons to seek sanctuary in Naples, since they could not sail under the nose of the British fleet. But the Republicans trusted Ruffo less than Nelson, and sent him a defiant reply. To give them another chance, Ruffo sent a herald before sunset to announce the surrender of the Nuovo and Ovo Castles, and warn the people not to molest those about to leave them, on pain of being shot.

Many high officials went to pay Nelson their respects, but few were admitted to his presence. The Hamiltons, however, were glad to see a *lazzarone* chief called Egidio Pallio, who promised the co-operation of ninety-thousand loyal subjects, but at present these lacked arms. Nothing loth, Emma consented to supply the deficiency on condition that he kept the city quiet until the King's arrival. The result of this little transaction was a renewal of the anarchy which Ruffo had tried to quell. Pallio's men proceeded to arrest whom they pleased and send their prisoners to Procida outside the Cardinal's jurisdiction. They tore down his edict forbidding the molestation of non-belligerent citizens, and even spread a rumour that the Cardinal was a Jacobin who had published this edict to protect his partisans. Inevitably they came to blows with Ruffo's troops.

When Nelson himself sent the castles his declaration, Ruffo withdrew his troops to their former positions. This caused a panic and a general flight, for it looked as if the city would be pulverized by the French from Sant' Elmo and the British from the sea. The most desperate of the Republicans in Castel Nuovo wished to explode the powder magazines, but Manthoné, firebrand though he was, mounted guard to prevent this. The hostages in Sant' Elmo trembled for their lives. Then, after so many fruitless arguments, delays and anxieties, the Cardinal suddenly received a letter from Hamilton, saying that Nelson was 'resolved to do nothing which could break the armistice', and Captains Troubridge and Ball handed him a written statement on behalf of Nelson that he would not oppose the embarkation of the rebels and garrisons of the Nuovo and Ovo castles. Heaving a sigh of relief, the Cardinal asked Micheroux to accompany the two captains to the forts for the final arrangements. All who wished to embark were taken to the transport ships; the others returned to their homes by night. Supposing his worst troubles to be over, the Cardinal ordered special prayers of thanksgiving in the Church of the Carmine, to which he repaired with full pomp as Prince of the Church and Vicar-General of the kingdom. He also wrote to thank Nelson and Hamilton for setting his mind at rest. Hamilton replied: 'We are all equally labouring for the true service of His Sicilian Majesty, and for the good cause. Different characters express themselves in different ways. Thank God, all goes well, and I can assure Your Eminence that Lord Nelson congratulates himself upon his decision not to interrupt the operations of Your Eminence, but to assist you with all his power to conclude the affair which Your Eminence has conducted so well hitherto in the very critical circumstances in which Your Eminence has been placed.'

While thirteen hundred marines took over the castles, Troubridge besieged Sant' Elmo with a mixed force of English and Portuguese, assisted by Russians and Neapolitans. On the 28th Nelson and the Hamiltons received letters from the Sovereigns and Acton. The gist of these was that they disavowed the capitulation; nothing but unconditional surrender was to be considered. The Queen returned the document with virulent unpunctuated comments in the margin, culminating with: 'This is such an infamous treaty that if by a miracle of Providence some event does not happen to break it or destroy it I count myself dishonoured and I believe that at the cost of dying of malaria of fatigue of a shot from the Rebels the King on one side and the Prince on the other ought immediately to arm the Provinces march against the rebel City and die under its ruins if they resist but not remain vile slaves of the Scoundrelly French and their infamous Mimics the Rebels. Such are my sentiments this infamous Capitulation if carried out afflicts me far more than the loss of the Kingdom and will have far worse consequences.'

To Lady Hamilton she wrote on June 25: 'I have received your dear letters from on board, undated, as well as those of Sir William to the General [Acton]. I am sending the same ship back at once, and I wish I could give it wings to reach you sooner. The General writes the King's wishes, and the King himself writes a note in his own hand for the dear Admiral. Conforming in all things to their will, I can do no less than tell you our own sentiment. From the 17th of this month until the 21st the Cardinal has not written to us. He has written very casually to the General, but not a single line to us. He says little of the negotiations, nothing of military operations and mentions very cursorily those he has appointed, many of whom are guilty, suspect and inadmissible. These are the foundations, according to the King and myself, which we submit to the excellent judgement, heart and mind of our dear Admiral Nelson. (1) The rebels can receive no more help from the French either by land or sea. Consequently they are lost and at the mercy of the King, offended, betrayed but clement. He offered them a first pardon, and instead of accepting it they defended themselves desperately. The commandant of the Ovo Castle replied verbally, and with the greatest insolence, to the written intimation of the English Captain [Foote] and drove away his vessel. During the armistice they made a sortie by night and captured our batteries. It is therefore impossible for me to deal tenderly with this rebellious rabble. The sight of the valiant English squadron forms my hope. The garrison of Sant' Elmo must retire, escorted to Marseilles or Toulon, without permission to remove anything. The rebels must lay down their arms and leave at the King's discretion. Then, to my way of thinking, we must make an example of the leading representatives, and the others will be deported... Note will be taken of these, and among them will be included the municipality, chiefs of brigades, members of clubs, and the most rabid scribblers. No soldier who has served them will be admitted into our army. Finally there must be an exact, prompt, just severity. The same should apply to the women who have distinguished themselves during the revolution, and that without pity...

'The Cardinal must not appoint any official without proposing him beforehand. The *sedili*, the source of all our ills, the first real assembly of rebels, who ruined the kingdom and dethroned the King, must be for ever abolished, also the privileges and jurisdiction of the barons, to deliver from bondage a faithful people who have restored the King to his throne, from which the treachery, felony, and criminal indifference of the nobles had driven him. This may not be popular, but it is absolutely necessary; without it the King would not govern six months in peace. After having done so much for him, the people will expect his justice to uplift them. Finally, dear Milady, I recommend Lord Nelson to treat Naples as if it were a rebellious city in Ireland which had behaved in such a manner. We must have no regard for numbers: several thousands of villains less will make France the poorer, and we shall be better off. They deserve to be dropped in Africa or the Crimea. To throw them into

France would be a charity. They ought to be branded so that nobody could be deceived by them. Thus I recommend to you, dear Milady, the greatest firmness, force, vigour and rigour. Our reputation and future tranquillity are concerned, and the loyal people desire it.'

That settled the matter. The transport ships were brought under the guns of the fleet and forbidden to sail. The passengers were like mice in a trap, to use the Queen's simile: the most notorious were imprisoned in the holds of British men-of-war, and those who had gone home were to 'submit to the King's clemency within twenty-four hours'. So Hamilton wrote to Ruffo informing him that the King entirely disapproved of the capitulation. So Ruffo also heard from the Republicans, who sent him a formal protest. The Cardinal deputed Micheroux to beg Nelson 'not to stain his glory' and endanger the lives of the hostages. But the latter were safe in Sant' Elmo, whose commandant Méjean was only interested in collecting a bonus before retiring. Prejudiced as he was, Nelson attributed the Cardinal's leniency to personal ambition, and probably believed the rumour that he wished to put his brother on the throne. The King's note authorized him to arrest his Vicar-General if necessary, and he was on the verge of doing so. On the 29th he wrote to Acton: 'The last placard of the Cardinal is that no one is to be arrested without his order, which is equivalent to wishing to save the rebels. In fact, yesterday there was a discussion as to whether the Cardinal ought to be arrested...' The placard referred to was an edict from the Regent of the Vicaria, or prefect of police, to stop arbitrary arrests or pillage under pain of death, since many harmless citizens had suffered from the rapacious *lazzaroni*.

Disgusted and mortified, Ruffo refused to take further part in the siege of Sant' Elmo. He who had done more than anybody to re-conquer the kingdom now tendered his resignation to his ungrateful Sovereigns. At the same time Nelson begged the King and Queen and Acton to return to the capital; he would endeavour to 'keep things tolerable' until their arrival.

The log of the *Foudroyant* mentions that on the 28th a boat was sent from each ship, manned and armed, to attend some vessels coming out of the mole, full of state prisoners. It then proceeds:

'*Saturday, 29th.*—Moderate and cloudy. Several of the principal prisoners of the rebels were put in confinement, in different ships. Launch watering A.M. Light winds. Washed below. Dried sails. At 9 a court-martial assembled on board, to try for rebellion Cavaliere Francesco Caracciolo. H.M. ships *Northumberland, Goliath, Alexander* and *San Sebastian* (a Portuguese ship), took the guard.

Sunday, 30th.—Moderate and cloudy. Employed occasionally. At 5 p.m. landed the remainder of the Marines from each ship. The sentence of the court-martial of yesterday [this was the log-term, for the sea-day began at noon] was put in execution, on board a Neapolitan frigate, on Cavaliere Francesco Caracciolo, who was hanged accordingly. A.M. Fresh breezes and cloudy. Mustered the ship's company at quarters. H.M. ships *Swiftsure, Vanguard, Powerful* and *Majestic* took the guard.'

Caracciolo's sentence had been decided in advance. The Queen had written to all her correspondents that she considered him the most noxious of all the rebels. When she heard that he was not among those in the castles she wrote: 'I am very sorry about the flight of Caracciolo, for I believe that such a pirate at large might imperil the sacred person of the King, and therefore I should wish this traitor to be put beyond the power of doing harm...'

For the last ten days the wretched admiral had fled from pillar to post until, since there was a price on his head, he was betrayed by one of his servants to the Queen's emissary Scipione La Marra, and hauled out of a well. Still in peasant disguise, he was dragged on board Nelson's flagship at nine in the morning, with his hands bound behind him. Captain Hardy ordered him to be unbound and led to a cabin guarded by a lieutenant and two marines. He refused to touch the food which was offered him. At ten o'clock Nelson ordered a court-martial to sit, consisting of five Neapolitan officers under the presidency of Count Thurn, an Austrian in the royal service, whose report to Ruffo was the only authentic account of this much-debated trial. At twelve o'clock Caracciolo was found guilty of high treason and condemned to an ignominious death. The sentence was then submitted to Nelson, who ordered Thurn to have it carried out at five o'clock the same day, by hanging him at the fore-yard arm till sunset, when the rope was to be cut, letting the body fall into the sea. This order was received at one o'clock; at half-past one Caracciolo was removed to his former ship, the *Minerva*, and he was hanged punctually at five. No witnesses had been examined in his defence. The proceedings, in accordance with Nelson's axiom of quick punishment, were as rapid as possible. The prisoner had asked in vain for another trial. He then begged Lieutenant Parkinson, under whose custody he had been placed, that he might be shot. 'I am an elderly man,' he said; 'I leave no family behind me, and therefore cannot be supposed to be very anxious about prolonging my life; but the disgrace of being hanged is dreadful to me.' When this was repeated to Nelson, he told the lieutenant, 'with much agitation', to go and attend to his duty. As a last resort, Parkinson went to plead with Lady Hamilton, but for once she was nowhere to be seen. It was said, however, that she was present at the execution, and that she was rowed round the frigate in a barge while the body was still dangling. This may have been an invention of her enemies, but it was quite in character. Charles Lock related that at dinner on the same day there was a roast pig at the bottom of the table, which was dissected by Nelson's secretary, and when the head was cut off, Lady Hamilton fainted. On recovering she said, sobbing, that it put her in mind of Caracciolo. 'Her ladyship, however, who was an amateur of this savoury dish, ate heartily of it—aye! and even of the brains.'

Caracciolo was generally described as an old man—Southey said he was nearly seventy. In fact, he was forty-seven years of age, but his recent adventures made him appear much older—'a short, thick-set man of apparent strength, but haggard with misery and want'. On the day of his execution Hamilton wrote to Acton: 'Here we have had the spectacle of Caracciolo, pale, with a long beard, half dead, and with downcast eyes, brought in handcuffs on board this vessel... I suppose justice will be immediately executed upon the most guilty. In truth it is a shocking thing, but I who know their ingratitude, and their crimes, have felt it less painful than the numerous other persons present at this spectacle. I believe it to be a good thing that we have the chief culprits on board our ships now that we are just going to attack St Elmo, because so we shall be able to cut off a head for every cannon ball that the French throw into the city of Naples.'

'Doubtless Nelson seemed to himself to be acting under a rigid sense of justice,' as Southey wrote. But there is also such a thing as humanity. True, Caracciolo had rebelled against his lawful sovereign and fired at his colours. Among the questions which arise, however, as Norman Douglas pointed out, are: 'When may an English warship be made the scene of a court-martial upon a foreign officer tried by foreign judges? Also this conundrum, which arises out of Ruffo's simultaneous existence as High Commissioner: Can Ferdinand of Naples, or any other human being, have more than one *alter ego* at the same time? And likewise this one: When is a treaty not a treaty?' But these questions did not trouble Nelson as they were to trouble his biographers, from whom we conclude that the morality of great men cannot be judged by ordinary standards, which would condemn his conduct in the bay of Naples. At bottom it is the old, old story: *cherchez la femme*; in this case, *deux femmes*—the revolution-haunted Queen and the gorgeous wanton who had become an ambassadress, with their different degrees of glamour. But it was thanks to his infatuation for the latter, in the first place, that these deplorable events occurred. The voluptuous propinquity of Emma filled him with a blind intoxication, so that he became 'genuinely convinced of the Deity's approval'. The flattering friendship of the Queen, the adoration of a celebrated hero, exalted Emma to the dizziest of heights. Both had left the humdrum earth for a fabulous Olympian sphere.

On July 2 the Queen announced the King's imminent departure in a letter to Lady Hamilton: 'I have received with infinite gratitude your dear and obliging letters, three of Saturday and one of the previous day, together with the list of the Jacobins arrested, who are some of the worst villains we have had. I have also noted the sad but merited end of the unfortunate, crazy Caracciolo. I am deeply conscious of all that your excellent heart must have suffered, and this increases my gratitude. I note all that you point out to me and am greatly obliged for it. From all that one sees and learns, the confusion is immense in that wretched and pitiful Naples. An effective land force to maintain order was needed, but finally, you, my good friends, have achieved prodigies, and I am thankfully aware of all your pains. This evening while I am writing to you, the Portuguese brig has arrived with letters of the 30th and that of the dear Admiral for the King. This has made the King decide to leave tomorrow evening. Already it costs me and will cost me copious tears, but the King did not think it expedient for me to go for the short period he intends to remain there... General Acton, Castelcicala and Ascoli will accompany him. Perhaps they will take a thousand infantry and six hundred cavalry under Acton [the Minister's brother Joseph] and Bourcard. The King wishes to embark on his frigate, accompanied by the English one and the Portuguese brig. I shall remain here very sadly, praying for everything to turn out for our glory and real welfare, but I am profoundly upset and calculate what I am worth and must become in future. It is definitely now, dear Milady, that I rely upon your friendship to write me everything, for all my correspondents will keep silence, seeing my impotence and fearing to compromise themselves. Although I am left behind in Palermo I hope my good friends will not forget me. This will mark an epoch for me. Do not imagine that I did not wish to go for no special reason or from caprice. I have many reasons: nobody wants me there; besides I fear to prejudice the love and enthusiasm which the King inspires, and which are not the same towards me. In short a thousand motives of prudence have made this a painful duty... I shall continue to profit from your friendship by addressing my various letters to you and telling others to bring you theirs for me. [Which meant that Lady Hamilton acted as a private post office for the Queen's correspondence.] I hope that affairs with the Cardinal will be arranged, but foresee many storms, when they will regret my absence. My heart is full and I have much to tell you...'

On the same day she replied to Cardinal Ruffo, who had asked to resign with the thinly veiled pretext of exhaustion: 'I have received and read Your Eminence's very wise and well-reasoned letter dated June 28. I note what you tell me, and your desire for repose: I think you are justified, but must spur your zeal, intelligence and heart to complete the task which you have undertaken and carried out so gloriously, by re-establishing order in Naples on a solid and sound foundation, so that from this dreadful calamity a better fortune and reorganization may result... The King leaves tomorrow evening with the troops he has been able to collect, and many things may be explained and settled by word of mouth. I am infinitely sorry not to be coming myself, but a thousand reflections have forced me to make this sacrifice. Among other things I shall pray all those who accompany the King to express my deep and sincere gratitude to Your Eminence, as well as my esteem for your quasi-miraculous operations. I am too sincere not to tell you that the capitulation with the rebels was extremely distasteful to me; that I was also pained to see many notorious rebels employed and protected, especially after the King's express orders. Consequently I refrained from writing, as my candour could not be silent; but now all is over, and matters will be explained at once *viva voce*. I hope that all will proceed in harmony, as there is so much to be done for the general welfare...'

The King and Acton had persuaded the Queen to stay in Palermo, and it is clear that she did so most reluctantly. This time the King chose to sail on a Neapolitan frigate, the *Sirena*, but it was a slow voyage owing to the lack of favourable winds. On July 10, he entered the bay of Naples, greeted by salvos from all the ships and cheers from the fleet of beflagged boats that rowed out to welcome him, while citizens thronged the shores. Troubridge's batteries were blazing against Sant' Elmo, which had hoisted the white flag, but lowered it to hoist the tricolour as soon as the King appeared. The condition of Naples, especially of the royal palace under the guns of the fort, did not encourage the King to land, but as Nelson wrote, 'the effusions of loyalty from the lower orders of the people to their Father—for by no other name do they address the King—were truly moving'. At four o'clock in the afternoon the King went on board the *Foudroyant*, and the Royal Standard fluttered from the mast-head. As he stood on the bridge gazing at Sant' Elmo through a telescope, a bomb shattered the French flagstaff and a flag of truce was raised for the second time that day. This auspicious event put the King in a rollicking humour. The *Foudroyant* became his headquarters for the next four weeks, during which he never once set foot on shore. Occasionally he amused himself with fishing and shooting sea-fowl. Cardinal Ruffo made a last eloquent bid for observing the capitulation, but he found the King in solid agreement with Nelson and the Hamiltons, who repeated all their former arguments.

Next day Sant' Elmo surrendered; and the treaty was signed by Colonel Méjean for the French, and by the Duke of Salandra, Captains Troubridge and Baillie for the Allies. At this juncture Ruffo kept aloof. Among the articles of the treaty, all subjects of His Sicilian Majesty were to be consigned to the Allies. That Méjean never raised a finger to save the Neapolitan 'patriots' who had helped him during the siege, and that he had haggled for money up to the last moment, must have been a bitter disillusion to those idealists who had put their trust in him and his country. When he had first raised the flag of truce, realizing that he could not hold out for long, he offered to capitulate for a million ducats; otherwise he threatened to destroy the city. Cardinal Ruffo replied that war was waged with arms, not with lucre, and that according to the rules of warfare he should concentrate his attack on his opponents, the batteries on the hillside; otherwise he and his garrison would be held responsible.

This firm retort produced its effect; and if a few bombs fell on the city afterwards, they fell from allied batteries wide of the mark. Troubridge had proposed to mine the fort and send both Frenchmen and hostages to the devil, as he said, but Ruffo resisted 'so barbarous a suggestion'.

When the French war minister Carnot asked Lomonaco, one of the surviving pillars of the Parthenopean Republic, to report on the causes of its collapse, he denounced Méjean, nicknamed *Méchant*, as the chief traitor 'who dug the grave of Neapolitan liberty'. What froze the Frenchman's ardour, he said, was the poverty of the Republic, which could not glut him with gold. He should have threatened to wipe Naples off the map unless the transports sailed within a stated period and every article of the capitulation were complied with. 'Sant' Elmo might have been to the city what Vesuvius is in eruption... Méjean could have hurled the lightning of national revenge from the summit of a fort which dominates Naples; and without any injury to himself, he might have reduced the area within range of his cannon to a heap of ashes.' Mercifully for Naples, he preferred his personal comfort. Lomonaco compared him to Nero fiddling while Rome burned. Though far from satisfied with the sum paid by Micheroux, a paltry 150,000 ducats (the Queen was furious when she heard about it), he haggled on, hoping for more.

When General Macdonald left Méjean in command of Sant' Elmo, he assured the Republicans that they would be safe under French protection; Commissioner Abrial had added that, in case of a reverse, the French would carry them away on their shoulders. 'These emphatic words had confirmed their conviction, that in the flood of calamity the ark of salvation had been entrusted to Méjean.' Alas for the power of mere words! The captain of the ark had another trick up his sleeve. Many of the Neapolitans in Sant' Elmo had hoped to march out with their allies, disguised in French uniforms. But Méjean picked them out, one by one, and consigned them to the royal police. Some were entitled to their uniforms, like Matera and Belpulsi who had served for a number of years in the French army.

Saluted by twenty-one guns, the Royal Standard was hoisted above Sant' Elmo, and Troubridge presented the keys of the castle and the banners of the garrison to the King, who sent the latter trophies to the Queen in Palermo. The recovery of the capital was now complete, but Nelson got more credit for it than Ruffo.

Charles Lock, the British consul, who had gone to Naples to obtain a house 'and to *accrocher* a little of the loads of furniture which the plunder of the wretched Jacobins has occasioned to be sold as cheap as dirt', was seething with resentment against the Hamiltons because he had not been invited to accompany them. 'If I am to be left Chargé d'Affaires' (as he had been led to expect), 'it was indispensably necessary for me previously to acquire some knowledge of the principal characters and progress of events in the Revolution, which the present occasion would so intimately have made me acquainted with. But for this I may thank that superficial, grasping and vulgar-minded woman whose wish to retain her husband in a situation his age and disinclination render him unfit for, has made her use every endeavour to keep me in the dark, and to make it difficult for Sir William to give up his employment at this moment...' On July 13 he wrote to his father: 'I rejoice that I was not of the party on board the flagship to Naples, which in my last to you from Palermo I regretted. But things have passed which should have been very repugnant to my feelings and have perhaps occasioned an irreparable breach between me and certain persons. You will hear with grief of the infraction of the articles convented with the Neapolitan Jacobins and of the stab our English honour has received in being employed to decoy these people, who relied upon our faith, into the most deplorable situation. I have no time to enlarge as Sylvester the messenger is going in a few hours, but the sentiment of abhorrence expressed by the whole fleet will I hope exonerate the nation from an imputation so disgraceful, and charge it where it should lie, upon the shoulders of one or two.

'The Castle of St Elmo surrendered yesterday. The garrison consisting of 11 or 12,000 men are embarked for Toulon... The reduction of Capua and Gaeta are to be undertaken successively. Eight hundred Marines are marched towards it and about 1,800 Portuguese, Russians and Swiss. It is already besieged by a numerous army of Calabrese under Roccaromana, who has till this month been a prominent Republican character. The air of the place is bad and I fear our troops will suffer. There are 15,000 Calabrese in Naples, who are as many robbers and murderers. They have committed great excesses. The regular troops lately quartered over the town have curbed them, but I suspect the departure of our fleet which cannot be distant will be a signal for the renewal of shocking scenes.' As Charles Lock was a cousin-by-marriage of Charles James

Fox, this letter was to have sensational repercussions, but it is only fair to add that the consul had little knowledge of the navy.

A few days later a gruesome incident occurred of which there are many romantic versions. A fisherman reported that Caracciolo had risen from the bottom of the sea and was swimming as fast as he could towards Naples. This sounded like a typical sailor's yarn, but soon enough the body was visibly approaching the *Foudroyant*. It was recognized as the corpse of Caracciolo, which had floated upright in the water, owing to the great weights attached to the legs—three double-headed shot weighing two hundred and fifty pounds. The King, always superstitious, was aghast. The Hamiltons and the royal chaplain hastened to assure him that Caracciolo had come to crave his pardon and a Christian burial. This allayed his horror, and he permitted the grisly corpse to be towed to Santa Lucia, where it was buried in the Church of Santa Maria la Catena.

Capua and Gaeta, the last bulwarks of the enemy, surrendered on July 28 and 31, and in each case Neapolitan subjects were consigned to the allies. At Capua one of them slipped away in the uniform of a Cisalpine captain, but just as he was about to embark for Toulon a French commissioner seized him by the collar and handed him over with curses to the allied commissioner. 'It is hard to say which hated the Neapolitan patriots most,' wrote Sacchinelli, 'the French republicans or the English constitutionalists.'

News of the final victory and mopping-up coincided with the anniversary of Aboukir, which was celebrated with due splendour on board the *Foudroyant*, as described by Nelson in a letter to his spouse: 'The King dined with me; and, when His Majesty drank my health, a Royal salute of 21 guns was fired from all his Sicilian Majesty's Ships of War, and from all the Castles. In the evening there was a general illumination. Amongst other representations, a large Vessel was fitted out like a Roman galley; on its oars were fixed lamps, and in the centre was erected a rostral column with my name; at the stern were elevated two angels supporting my picture. In short, my dear Fanny, the beauty of the whole is beyond my powers of description. More than 2,000 variegated lamps were suspended round the Vessel. An orchestra was fitted up, and filled with the very best musicians and singers. The piece of music was in a great measure to celebrate my praise, describing their previous distress. *But Nelson came, the invincible Nelson, and they were preserved and again made happy.* This must not make you think me vain; no, far, very far from it. I relate it more from gratitude than vanity.' No mention here of 'the swelled priest' Ruffo or of the woman who suffused him with so voluptuous a glow!

In sombre contrast with such scenes of festivity, enlivened by the King's boisterous laughter, was the dread of those waiting on the transport ships, not knowing whose turn would come next, as fresh prisoners were seized day by day and clamped in irons until they were taken for trial. But for Nelson, these might have sailed to France and been forgotten. Unwittingly he converted them into martyrs. Cardinal Ruffo, who knew his own people, had been right: forgiveness would have been a wiser policy.

The Cardinal had been silenced, the title of Vicar-General abolished; but in compensation he was appointed Lieutenant and Captain-General of the Realm. Many considered that he was wrong to accept such a post after the repudiation of the treaty he had signed, that he should have retired with his outraged dignity. But he was too attached to the monarchy to eclipse himself for personal motives when it stood in need of him. On board the *Foudroyant* the King and Acton had worked out a new form of government for the capital and provinces, a supreme committee (*Suprema Giunta*) under the presidency of Ruffo. The High Court of State (*Giunta di Stato*) was organized with judges who had a reputation for severity, such as Guidobaldi and Speciale, to try civilians, and a Court of Generals (*Giunta di Generali*) to try the military. According to General de Damas, more reliable than Colletta and the propagandists, 'the former was a tribunal of blood, but I must proclaim with my whole conscience that the second was one of justice'.

Acton was the King's mouthpiece, who deferred to Nelson, who was influenced by both Hamiltons and especially by Emma, the Queen's proxy. In spite of her absence, in spite of her waning ascendancy over the King, the Queen contrived to make herself heard through the medium of 'Miledy'. She sent her blacklists of offenders, interspersed with snippets of news and sighs over human ingratitude. 'Miledy' sent lists of prisoners in return. The Queen's letters were often full of self-contradictions. She visualized herself as a recluse; she declared that she would have no more to do with government. 'Finally, my dear Miledy,' she wrote on July 7, 'I have the misfortune thoroughly to know the nobility and all classes of Neapolitans, and I will always say the same, that only the bourgeois, artisans and populace are faithful and attached. The latter sometimes give way to excesses, but their sentiments are good. Owing to this conviction I have no commission to give you, for I am determined, on returning to Naples, to isolate myself entirely from the world. The experience of thirty-one years during which I have only lived and breathed to oblige other people and find myself deserted, has made an indelible impression on me. I am ready to return to Naples the moment the King wishes it... I conjure you to see that not a penny is paid to Méjean. After so obstinate a defence this would really make fools of us; I suppose the Cisalpine Generalissimo wanted to share the booty with Méjean. I beg you to spare us this weakness and disgrace as the brave Admiral has already saved us from the infamous armistice or capitulation with our rebels. In a word, I have so much to say on the subject that I shall never end... Every day we attend a *Te Deum*, and carry the Holy Sacrament in procession, to bless the sea and pray for the King and Naples. That is all I can do and I do it willingly, for I am useless otherwise. Farewell, dear Miledy, continue to send me your news, above all at this moment when it is becoming so engrossing. I rely upon your friendship not to fail me in this matter. I beg you to silence your benevolent heart and only consider the misfortunes they have sown and those they are still ready to reap. Poor Belmonte has heard of his brother's arrest; he is greatly afflicted, more on account of his guilt than all the rest. One sees only the unhappy, and that is very depressing...'

The guillotining of her sister and Louis XVI was still vivid in her memory. So she urged Lady Hamilton to harden her heart. But the ambassadress needed no urging. There was a pun alluding to her (assumed) maiden name: 'She might have been all Hart once, but she soon proved herself to be less artless than heartless.' Even if she had been as sensitive as the Queen's letter suggested, she could do nothing with Nelson in vengeful mood. She received sheaves of letters from old friends and acquaintances, imploring her to intercede for their relations, or applying to her for jobs and recommendations to the Queen. Among them was an anguished appeal from Domenico Cirillo, a cultured physician and philanthropist who maintained that he had been forced unwillingly into the Republican government. But he who rides a tiger cannot dismount, as the Chinese proverb says. He had been appointed president of the Legislative Council after Mario Pagano, and as such, despite his denials, had had to sign anti-monarchist proclamations. No doubt it was true that he was dragged into political prominence by the impetus of events. If Lady Hamilton tried to intercede for him, she failed. He might have been saved, wrote Nelson—'but that he chose to play the fool, and lie; denying that he had ever made any speeches against the government, and [saying] that he only took care of the poor in the hospitals'.

The King for all his lazy bonhomie was too primitive a character, too much of a *lazzarone*, to waste pity on those who had collaborated with the French; incapable of making distinctions, he lumped them all together. He was frightened into blind fury by the thought that he had known and trusted Caracciolo and Cirillo, and he could only see them as a menace to his divine right of sovereignty. He agreed with the Queen on this subject, if on no other. The High Court reflected their point of view and acted accordingly.

Many volumes have been devoted to the iniquities of this *Giunta di Stato* in order to prove the wickedness of the Bourbon dynasty. These have been compiled with dialectical skill and literary art. A famous Latin historian declared that he would have made Pompey win the battle of Pharsalia had the effective turn of the sentence required it. Colletta inherited this tendency to subordinate facts to phrases, with an added resolve consistently to blacken the Bourbons. All the official records of the state trials were destroyed in 1803 to set a seal on the King's amnesty, so that it has been easy for propagandists to invent 'authentic details' and weave silk purses out of the sows' ears of 'popular tradition'. A few facts may be gleaned from such documents as the records of the Bianchi Confraternity, who ministered to the condemned; a few anecdotes from contemporary diarists, especially De Nicola. The rest is hearsay, much bedizened by the rich Neapolitan imagination. Of 8,000 political prisoners 105 were condemned to death, six of whom were reprieved, 222 were condemned to life imprisonment, 322 to shorter terms, 288 to deportation, and 67 to exile, from which many returned: a total of 1,004. The others were set at liberty.

Nearly all intellectuals are rebels, and it is deplorable that most of the condemned were men of culture. The howls and execrations of the populace crowding to gloat upon their final agony added a poignant horror to their executions. 'I have always desired their welfare, and they are rejoicing at my death!' said Gennaro Serra before he was beheaded. And De Nicola wrote that when Eleonora Pimentel was hanged, 'the shouts of the populace rose to the very stars'. The masses to whom she and her colleagues had preached liberty, equality and fraternity, viewed these scenes with bloodthirsty gusto, to which the hangman and his clownish assistant, the *tirapiedi*, who clung to the prisoner's feet and swung with him into space, pandered with gruesome relish. But this royalist Reign of Terror, as it has been called, pales into a provincial side-show beside quite recent and far more systematic pogroms. Granted that the Court's policy of revenge was cruel and unintelligent, there is little to be said in favour of the rebels, whatever their individual talents. To quote Luigi Blanch, the most balanced of Neapolitan historians, 'they were an almost imperceptible minority seeking to establish, by means of conquest, a form of government not wanted by the country and in the same year so discredited in France that it ceased amid popular applause on 18 Brumaire [the *coup d'état* of November 9]. Their aims were opposed to liberal principles, based on national independence externally and on the consent of the majority internally. They were pleased by the disastrous campaign of 1798 and irritated by the vigorous resistance of the people... Had they triumphed they would have been all the more cruel as they were so few. Sacrificed, they inspired compassion for the individuals and sympathy for the cause. As executioners they would have inspired horror for both.'

Since then the technique by which a minority could seize power over the state against the will of the majority has been perfected, and most of us know where it leads. After a careful examination of the short-lived Parthenopean Republic one is driven to doubt whether it could have retained the power it had usurped with the aid of French troops and civil strife, except by subjecting the majority to violence and the constant threat of violence. This would have resulted in a police state far more inhuman than that of the Bourbons.

XXII

The King's happy return to Palermo—Rewards and celebrations—A tiff with some Turks—The Neapolitan occupation of Rome—The Queen's forebodings—Tactless behaviour of Mr Charles Lock—Bonaparte becomes First Consul.

Having done what he considered his duty during the four long weeks he had spent on the *Foudroyant*, the King was impatient to return to the tranquillity of Palermo. The discovery that he, so benevolent a *paterfamilias*, had violent enemies where he least expected them, after so many years of a reign in which he could detect no flaws, was a shock from which he was slow to recover. He conceived a prejudice against his old home. In Palermo he fancied himself popular; here nobody could spoil his innocent pastimes.

'My most Eminent [*Eminentissimo mio*],' he wrote on August 8 to Cardinal Ruffo, 'I will not delay a moment to inform you of my happy arrival in this capital after the happiest of journeys, since at eleven on Tuesday morning we were off the point of Posillipo and at two o'clock today we anchored in this port with a light breeze over the water, the sea as calm as a lake. I found my whole family in perfect health and have been welcomed in the manner you may imagine. Send me equally good news of your affairs.'

The King had sailed into Palermo with Nelson on the *Foudroyant* and received acclamations worthy of a hero. The Queen and her children dined on board in the glitter and noise of a flaming noon, and the whole party landed to the salutes of twenty-one guns on a special stage of gilded stucco where the senators in rich robes awaited them; then they drove in state to the cathedral for the solemn *Te Deum* amid thousands of cheering citizens. Palermo was drunk but not disorderly, as the Queen wrote to Ruffo. The fireworks, illuminations and festivities that followed merged into the celebrations in honour of the city's patron saint Rosalia, which were never more magnificent. Even less is known about this ascetic virgin than about San Gennaro, for since the age of sixteen she had lived alone in a cave of stalactites whose solidifying drops were to preserve her body from corruption; but her cult is equally fervid.

Splendid rewards were lavished on the loyal. When the Queen embraced Lady Hamilton, she clasped a diamond necklace and her portrait in miniature round her neck with the exergue: *Eterna gratitudine*. The King's portrait, set in jewels, was presented to Sir William. With her usual prodigality the Queen also sent 'Miledy' two gala coaches filled with fine dresses to replace those she had lost in her flight from Naples. Within a few days the Hamiltons received gifts reputed to have been worth £6,000. The King bestowed on Nelson the Sicilian duchy and domain of Bronte, whose annual revenue was calculated at £3,000. According to Southey, it was some days before Nelson could be persuaded to accept it. 'The argument which finally prevailed is said to have been suggested by the Queen, and urged, at her request, by Lady Hamilton upon her knees. "He considered his own honour too much," she said, "if he persisted in refusing what the King and Queen felt to be absolutely necessary to theirs." The King himself is said to have addressed him: "Lord Nelson, do you wish that your name alone should pass with honour to posterity and that I, Ferdinand Bourbon, should appear ungrateful?"' The King also presented him with a family heirloom, the diamond-hilted sword which Louis XIV had given his grandfather Philip V on his departure for Spain, and which he had received from his father on his accession to the throne. Jewelled snuff-boxes, watches and rings were distributed among Nelson's officers. Nobody was overlooked. Cardinal Ruffo and his brothers received considerable pensions and estates. Such guerrilla leaders as Pronio, Sciarpa, Fra Diavolo and Mammone were promoted and rewarded in various ways.

The climax of the festivities was a nocturnal *fête champêtre* in honour of Nelson and the Hamiltons, whose life-size effigies in wax were enshrined in a classical Temple of Fame, topped by a goddess blowing a trumpet. Fireworks represented the explosion of *L' Orient* at the Battle of the Nile. Pæans of praise were sung to the deliverer, and the nine-year-old Prince Leopold, his mother's darling, dressed as a midshipman, raised the laurel wreath from the waxen admiral's brow and placed it on that of the living one, thanking him for recovering the realm. Nelson's one arm hugged the little prince and his eye was wet as he thanked him on his knee. When the band struck up 'See the conquering hero', all the midshipmen of the *Foudroyant* were equally moved. Lieutenant Parsons, who left a sprightly account of the occasion, said that the fairy-scene surpassed Vauxhall on a gala night. His shipmates, in their excitement, could not resist charging the King's foot-guards with their dress-dirks, so that one brisk lad was shot through the thigh by an outraged guardsman and Nelson stopped their leave for six months. 'The day previous to the fête,' wrote the sour British consul, 'the Russian and Turkish fleets entered the bay of Palermo, the officers of which as well as the Russian and Imperial Ministers were invited to hear how much was due to Lord Nelson, Lady Hamilton and the English. The King addressed himself to the Austrian Minister: "Well," said he, "how do you like this? You see there is nothing forgotten." "No, Sire," replied the Minister, "no one but my Master is forgotten here".' To which the King might have retorted that his son-in-law had done nothing to be remembered.

Charles Lock had hoped to secure the privilege of victualling the British fleet in the Mediterranean, which would have enriched him by £4,000. Having failed, he spread rumours of scandalous abuses in this department, which led to friction with Nelson, fanned, as he supposed, by Lady Hamilton—'that infamous woman is at the bottom of all the mischief which has rendered my stay so uncomfortable for the last six months'. 'We have in Lady Hamilton the bitterest enemy you can imagine,' he wrote again. 'Her wish to engross the conduct of affairs entirely... prompted her to poison Sir William's mind against me; to this was joined a female vanity which could not bear that any English woman should be admitted by her countrymen except herself. She has prejudiced the Court in a most unjustifiable manner against us, and she has taken occasion to insinuate that my wife's principles are republican. As for myself, I am a poor creature led by my wife in everything! The Queen said our going out so little into the world was a proof of how we affected to despise whatever held to aristocracy. I have complained to Sir William and he has given me his word he will remove every impression of that kind on the first opportunity. He regretted the unfavourable impression the Courts had received of me as a Jacobin and in a friendly manner advised me to be on my guard. I observed to His Excellency that his kind intentions would avail me little while there was a person so able and so bent upon counteracting them... With all this malice, her Ladyship maintains every appearance of civility with expressions of goodwill to us both. Sir William's health is very much broken and his frame is so feeble that even a slight attack of bile, to severe fits of which he has lately been subject, may carry him off.' It is evident that Lock did little to modify the Court's adverse impression, in spite of Hamilton's advice.

Everybody suffered from the tropical heat of summer in Palermo, and tempers were frayed in consequence. Lock describes a bloody dispute between the inhabitants and some Turkish seamen: 'A little boy came up to a Turk who was bargaining at a stall and whipped his legs; the Turk was going to chastise him when he was prevented by a man who took the boy's part, on which the Turk drew a pistol out of his girdle and shot the man dead. The report was immediately spread that the Infidels were murdering the Christians, and they were attacked with sticks and stones wherever they were found; a hundred and twenty were killed, and eighty desperately wounded, amongst them the Turkish Admiral's nephew; fifteen of the Palermitans fell in this massacre and a number were wounded. It is owing to the cowardice of the officer on guard that the affair was not stopped at the outset. It was fortunate that it ended here, for the Turkish seamen turned to their guns and brought the ship's broadsides to bear upon the town. The great moderation and exertion of the Turkish Admiral prevented the execution of their intentions. However, he insisted upon some atonement from the government... A council was held, at which the Russian Minister Italinsky assisted. Italinsky proposed to execute upon the Marina in sight of the fleet, ten of the condemned Jacobins, who the Turks would believe were some of the murderers —a most sensible proposition, but it was rejected, from a prejudice one should have thought had not existed at the close of the 18th century, because it should not be said that a Christian's life had been sacrificed for that of a Turk. The Admiral with his fleet got under weigh next morning for Constantinople, in a great rage vowing he would sink the first Neapolitan vessel he met. An explanation has been sent to the Ottoman Court.'

'You may thank God that the Turkish squadron did not go straight to you,' wrote the King to Ruffo, 'since if what happened here last Sunday had happened in Naples, I doubt if the matter would have rested there, and it would have been much worse.'

Besides organizing festivities on a grand scale with depleted resources, the Queen never relaxed her political vigilance. If we compare her letters to Ruffo with the King's, it is hers that are incisive. In June, for instance, she had written to him proposing 'a clean sweep of the French and Jacobins in the Roman State'. She returned to the theme in July. Her only fear was that the Austrians would anticipate this move. The French defeat at Trebbia had filled her with elation. It was necessary to strike at once. Pope Pius VI died at Valence on August 29, leaving the Holy See vacant when the Coalition was victorious.

Accordingly a mixed army of Neapolitan regulars and irregulars under the command of General Bourcard invaded the Roman State, supported by a British naval squadron under Troubridge which sailed to Civitavecchia. Two rebellious French generals, Lahoz and Pino, were scouring the country with armed marauders; Fra Diavolo and his brigands had overrun the Alban hills, and Rome was in a fever of anarchy. General Garnier was obliged to surrender on September 27, and on the 30th the banner of Naples flew over the Castle of Sant' Angelo. Old General Naselli was appointed governor, and the King, without stirring from Palermo, was portrayed as a successor of the Cæsars. It was at this time that the colossal statue of Ferdinand in Roman disguise was ordered from Canova, a commission which the sculptor's devotees regarded as a blot on his otherwise blameless career. The marble monster did not reach Naples until 1819 and has suffered many vicissitudes.

The republicans had now been subdued, the King's authority re-established, and both the Queen and Nelson thought that he should return to Naples. But nothing would induce him to leave his safe little island. 'I am almost mad with the manner of going on here,' said Nelson. 'Plain common sense points out that the King should return to Naples, but nothing can move him... Unfortunately, the King and Her Majesty do not, at this moment, draw exactly the same way.'

The Queen's elation did not last long. What could be done with such a husband? While Nelson chafed at his lethargy, the Queen suffered from his new mania for petty economy at others' expense and from his despotic interference. 'Having no principle, no maxim, being very arbitrary, and angry with almost everybody, he does incredible things which nobody dare criticize. Moreover, the condition to which we have been reduced has made him excessively stingy. He supervises the royal household, the accounts. We are all kept so sparingly as to lack everything. The kingdom of Naples having been recovered, everybody asks and nobody obtains. He only pays me, my son and daughter-in-law half our pin-money. He pays no minister, no pension, nothing to anyone. It makes them yell, but it cannot be remedied. It is a true despotism and nobody can endure it... He will not hear of going to Naples, and says he wishes to die here and will not move from Sicily. This is in my opinion a real calamity... Acton speaks definitely of retiring, but I shall not believe this until it happens...' The King did not even pretend to care for her society: 'I think I am neither necessary nor agreeable to him.'

Count Roger de Damas said that if the Queen had been in a position to reign like Queen Elizabeth or Catherine the Great, she might have been a successful ruler, but that since she was married her power depended more or less on the King's taste for her—he did not use the word affection. Clever though she was, this dependence on the King's taste made it impossible to calculate how long her influence would last, as his fancy for another woman or partiality for a minister were always liable to distract him. When the King returned to her after one of his lapses, it was not only because he trusted her but because he got bored with government routine. Owing to this intermittent credit, as Damas called it, the Queen was not given enough time to develop a particular plan. She was forced to strike when the iron was hot without considering all the consequences, for fear of letting the opportunity slip. Many of her mistakes were due to this struggle with time and the King's caprices. As the King was notoriously susceptible to women's arms, especially when they were wearing long white gloves, the Queen often exploited this potent means of seduction. According to Damas: 'His brain becomes exalted when he sees a glove well stretched over a beautifully shaped arm. It is a mania he has always had and which has never varied. How many affairs of the greatest importance have I seen settled by the Queen's care to pull her gloves over her pretty arms while discussing the question which engrossed her! I have seen the King take notice of this, smile, and grant her wish... The Queen has spent her life leading the King and Acton by seduction, holding out her glove before one, her arm before the other, and always ending in doing what she wanted, but without being able to modify the effervescence of her character by reasoning... In one of her last letters she wrote to me: "I have always foreseen that as I grew older my power would diminish..."'

The Queen dramatized herself when she picked up a pen. However ill or depressed she might be, this outlet seems to have given her relief. Her passions had grown more violent in middle age. 'Ah, if I knew where to find the river Lethe,' she wrote, 'I would travel there on foot in order to drink its water, for I have great need of it. God knows I pardon everybody sincerely, but it is impossible to forget the wound in my heart and it will make me unhappy for the rest of my days.' She would sooner retire to Mount Gothard, she said, than to beautiful Naples, where she had been so mortified, maligned and insulted. She wished to punish those who had injured the state, but as for herself: 'I pardon all those who tear me to shreds, repeating humbly the words of my God: "Lord, forgive them, for they know not what they do!"'

Although she was easily swayed by pity for her enemies, her emotions were inextricably confused. As Luigi Blanch pointed out with acumen: 'While proscribing people *en masse*, she wished to save them individually. A sentiment of proud generosity made her want a personal enemy to be condemned in order to humiliate him by procuring his pardon. But it was difficult to inspire the King with the same feelings. She was in the strange position of not being able to mollify the man she had done so much to embitter.' She called Migliano a fool and his wife a viper, but she did her best to save them as well as Belmonte's republican brother, of whom she wrote to Gallo in Vienna: 'Belmonte's brother, Joseph Pignatelli, has been a municipalist and legislator, but never a soldier. In love with the Popoli, he absorbed her ideas and became convinced of the fortune of that Republic. He had gone into retirement before it fell. The English ordered him to report himself, and he was the only one to come forward and surrender. He has been in irons at the bottom of the hold, but since he trusted in the Admiral's word, by favour of my protection they have released him. He has written to express his gratitude. But like all the cursed Jacobins, thinking he has done nothing, he has gone to Trieste to see his brother and calls himself Copertino. I beg you to see that he comes to no harm... If he could remain unknown, all the better; if not, direct and save him... His sole desire is for a foreign commission.' She also promised Gallo to intercede for his republican nephew, Count della Rocca, and have his sentence reduced.

One of the Queen's oldest friends, the Marchesa di San Marco (Luigi de' Medici's sister), had not only refused to accompany her to Palermo, but had stayed on to curry favour with the new regime and spread scandal about her benefactress. Of course she was among the first to try to ingratiate herself with her as soon as the Republic collapsed. Still deeply hurt, the Queen wrote to Lady Hamilton: 'I will answer the San Marco one of these days. My heart, which never changes, prompts me to do so.' Not long after she wrote again:

'Should Mme San Marco be in need of money she can rely on me to help her during her lifetime, but all the ties of interest and friendship between us have been dissolved by her conduct.' However, the old favourite was soon forgiven. On August 16 the Queen wrote to Ruffo that the King, having made satisfactory inquiries about the San Marco, had granted her permission to come to Palermo. She hoped that the Cardinal would afford her the proper facilities.

The Queen's confidence in Cardinal Ruffo had been shaken by the capitulation. 'I believe he is tricking all parties in order to remain in despotic command on the King's departure,' she wrote to Lady Hamilton. In her environment suspicion was endemic, but there is no doubt that she appreciated Ruffo's courage and enterprise, unlike the King, who never cared for him. Nelson absorbed most of her hero-worship, but Ruffo had the residue, and in her letters to him, less intimate but quite as revealing as any she wrote to Gallo, she tended to posture accordingly. While the King was bursting with health and basking in the plaudits of his people, she portrayed herself as a tragic victim, broken in spirit and cruelly misunderstood.

Her enthusiasm for the Cardinal elicited an apologia which affords a rare insight into her character. 'I have duly received Your Eminence's letter of August 16,' she wrote. 'It is written with the hand and thought out of the brain of Your Eminence, which is to say that it is altogether profound, wise, beautifully reasoned, and persuasive, and my admiration for it continues to grow. It speaks with deep knowledge of the human heart, in the language of a great statesman; in fact it is perfect. Only one thing renders it useless and defective; the person to whom it is addressed, as if she were a person made to govern, florid, robust in health and heart. All these qualities I lack, my constitution is ruined, my strength and health are destroyed, and my heart is lacerated. I know and understand what should be done, felt and thought: I shall try to teach it to my children, but as for me, do not count on my physical or moral existence: my heart and soul are torn to shreds. With more energy, youth and health I would have (and this is a mere probability) a masculine virtue, a love of public welfare and glory, and I would forget the horrors that have been said, read, mocked, applauded, suggested, not by a few but by all, premeditated even while I lived in the midst of their homage and importunities, when they wanted to gain riches, honours, advantages and conveniences, and I only lived for them. Perhaps, I say, with more health I might have the strength and virtue to forget and go back to that unhappy existence, which has destroyed my iron constitution. But in my present state it is impossible: I have loved Naples and its inhabitants passionately, I have lived there thirty-one years, twenty-three of which were spent sadly and ill-advisedly in public affairs; I can say that I never thought of myself at all. I do not even own a country-house, a garden (a thing I have always desired), not a jewel, no capital, or anything. By now everyone has been able to ascertain the non-existence of my famous millions; I have not even been able to benefit those I wished to, having resolved not to depart from the strict rule of duty even in this respect. I have never accepted donations, either for my marriage or for the births of my children, the first heirs given to the nation; I have married three daughters without claiming a penny from the state. The public misfortunes which have weighed upon our heads, such as earthquakes whose like had not been known for centuries, revolutions, wars on land and at sea, several years of famine, threats of plague, devastating pests, these and similar misfortunes, and never anything personal, have made us resort to the painful obligation of demanding extraordinary subsidies, leaving the means, the how and the when to others. The distressing consequences of this to ourselves, I leave truthful and impartial pens to describe. If I have erred in proposing and supporting ministers not agreeable to the public, the honesty of my intention in choosing them is my excuse, and the deep conviction which I continue to hold, that nobody can establish order without years of energy, firmness and immutable decision, guided by the highest equity and justice. In fact I can only blame myself for being weak and having more heart than head, for feeling rather than reasoning. After this brief apologia to Your Eminence, whose opinion I esteem, an apologia which I could explain in detail year by year, dwelling more diffusely and at greater length on my public conduct, I swear that my heart reproaches me for nothing. Having done this, I must tell you sincerely that I have neither health nor will-power nor strength, and I have decided firmly and irrevocably to regard myself as dead in so far as the affairs of Naples are concerned. I know and feel the necessity of a prompt return, I believe it to be an absolute essential, if the King does not want to alienate entirely the souls attached to him; I shall not utter a word of contradiction, but as soon as the King announces his decision to go to Naples I shall be ready to leave within twenty-four hours, all the more so because I believe it would be really useful. But as I tell you this, I also assure you that I shall not utter a word to induce him to take this step; events are too uncertain for me to wish to compromise myself and bear all the reproaches besides the responsibility. I will go to Naples and lend my presence, I will do what little good I can as a Christian and with my limited faculties, but I shall not mix in any kind of public business, and in this I shall not change. I do not know the affairs of Naples, I have succeeded too ill in the past, I have not intervened, nor do I wish to, in the actual administration. I will show my sad face, I will let the public judge the effect which the horrors and epithets lavished on me have produced, reviving fresh memories and reflections. After drinking the bitter chalice of these recollections awhile, I shall ask for a few months' leave to distract my mind, restore my health and marry my daughters. I hope to obtain it; if not, I shall continue to be the Queen, strictly the King's wife, and nothing more; upon this my plan is settled, and I shall change it with difficulty. I speak to Your Eminence with complete sincerity; my mind is too disturbed, too prejudiced and ulcerated, to master that indifference which is needed in affairs; my scene is ended, mournfully it is true, but not so badly since my husband and children have recovered their states, and I shall spend the rest of my days, which will not be long, as the mother of a family and a Christian, trying to benefit my numerous and undeserved enemies. These are my firm intentions; I know they are not suited to the circumstances and the times, and they are not at all grand or heroic, but of this I am capable... I shall pray the Lord to enlighten and fortify the King and his ministers, but I shall reduce myself to this; my soul will forget the evil and will only remember the good it has received, in which the deeds of Your Eminence hold supremacy.'

Maria Carolina was never more true to herself than when she was inconsistent. The intentions so categorically affirmed in this apologia were contradicted in subsequent letters to the Cardinal; they were wholly at variance with her subsequent career.

The surface of Court life was gay, even frivolous, with concerts, balls and supper parties, enlivened by gambling for high stakes in which Lady Hamilton indulged freely, while Nelson nodded with fatigue beside her. His slavish attendance on the flamboyant ambassadress had become one of the curiosities of Palermo. The visiting Lady Elgin was shocked by so public a display of devotion, and Lord Elgin thought it was high time for old Sir William to go home. A Chinese fête was given in October, which Lady Elgin said surpassed anything she had ever seen in England: 'It really outdid the Arabian Nights.'

In November a force of fifteen hundred Russians arrived at Naples. 'The security they gave to that city is no doubt a considerable argument to determine the King to return thither,' wrote Lock. 'The Russian General Borosdine is come here to pay his respects to H.M. He is a gentle young man, he returns with us in the frigate. The King's eye was caught the moment he appeared by the sight of a pair of very large whiskers... He could not take his eye off them and betrayed evident marks of displeasure. The instant the General retired His Majesty complained and wanted to devise some method of obliging him to shave them. The people about His Majesty were under the necessity of telling him he could not interfere in the costume of a foreign power.'

The King considered whiskers a badge of Jacobinism. Courtiers could not be too careful about their costume. The imprudent Lock, who was fully aware of this and had been warned by Hamilton to be on his guard, got into a serious scrape because of a fancy dress he wore at a Court masquerade: 'The King expressed a wish that everyone should appear in character, and English ones, we heard, would be particularly acceptable to him. I was applied to by the Princess Castelcicala, whose husband is in great favour with His Majesty, to make a drawing of some English character in low life, a gipsy, haymaker, or peasant. I drew two haymakers, after which she dressed her daughters. My wife as a Peruvian went with three other ladies, representing the four quarters of the world. I might have gone in a Bahut (*bautta*, or black mantle with a hood) as numbers did, but to conform myself to the King's wishes, and to what I conceived his taste, for he spends half his life with the fishermen, I put on a masquerade dress I had made in England of a Thames fisherman, changing the red bonnet for a blue one for fear of giving offence, although it is very commonly worn by His Majesty's subjects. We rendezvoused at a house with ten or fifteen people belonging to the Court, who all approved my dress...

'*In fine* we went. I met Prince Castelcicala who having been Minister in England was used to the fashions there; he observed that I was *ben costumato*. Many more did for about a quarter of an hour after I entered the room. I had not presented myself to the King as the press was great. All at once Sir William Hamilton came up to me and whispered: "The King has taken great offence at your dress. He says it is indecent. You had better retire as soon as possible, put on a Bahut and return." I answered him: "I have only to observe to Your Excellency that I wore this identical dress at a masquerade when several of our Royal Family were present; it could therefore never enter my head that it would be offensive here. Since His Majesty has taken exception at it I will instantly withdraw, but I shall not return." I added: "It cannot be supposed that I have intended any disrespect to the Court by appearing in this dress which in character is economical, as I have spared no expense in that of my wife." Sir William Hamilton would not even allow me to apprise my wife of the cause of my sudden departure because she was at a small distance, but made me go out at the nearest door. I desired he would tell her, which he did not, and she remained an hour in the room, a situation doubtless indecent for her to be seen in after the public affront which had been put upon her husband. The King, who was standing upon a bench, followed me with his eye until I was out of the room. I heard afterwards that the Prince Leopold's little boy had first observed me, and remarked me to the Queen who was offended by the sight and said: "*Il n'était pas nécessaire que Monsieur Lock vint ici nous braver dans un costume sans culottes pour démontrer ses principes... ils sont déjà assez connus.*"

'It seems that the King, in a rage the instant he perceived me, called Sir William Hamilton. "Have you seen Mr Lock? Turn him out, turn him out at once, otherwise I will turn him out myself." Sir William answered he had not seen me, but he could not imagine it was my intention to offend His Majesty. The King reiterated the order. Sir William after having sent me out, returned to the King and said something in palliation, to which His Majesty replied, in Neapolitan dialect: "Say nothing more, for I know more than you do. He is a Jacobin." Had Sir William felt as an Englishman should upon this occasion, he would have realized the indignity to his Government which the application of such a term to one of its servants implied. He shrank into himself as a Neapolitan courtier before the wrath of his Sovereign, and said not a word. I next day waited upon him with the following memorial. It was not my intention to have delivered it had I found him in a disposition to pursue the affair as I conceived he ought. He only said it was very unfortunate that, immediately after every misconception and prejudice had been done away in their Majesties' minds I should have disgusted them so strongly. He said, "You are acquainted with Seratti" [the late Tuscan Minister, now one of His Majesty's], "try to interest him to speak to their Majesties, to endeavour to soften their displeasure." I was nettled at this attempt to throw me off his shoulders upon the hands of a stranger, and answered, I could not have much hope that Seratti would undertake my vindication, that I considered it was my duty to present His Excellency with the following memorial upon this affair, the clearing up of which rested with himself. Lady Hamilton came in at this moment; she said she had been with the Queen, that she had been two hours labouring to convince her Majesty that the affront was not premeditated... etc.; cursed nonsense it is needless to trouble you with.'

Lock's indignant memorial to Hamilton pressed for an investigation of the causes 'which have given rise to conclusions so detrimental to my Public and my Private character, and to vindicate the clearness of my conduct in the one and the other'. Conscious of his integrity, he demanded an explanation 'which will elucidate the truth and wipe out the stain of an aspersion concerning which should the slightest ambiguity remain, I will instantly resign my situation'.

The sequel of this undiplomatic incident continues: 'I heard that Sir John Acton expressed himself with great warmth against me. He said I might thank their Majesties' singular moderation that I had not been ordered out of the Kingdom in 24 hours, as my principles had long been known to the Government. It was said at his table that I had a *tournure Jacobine*, that my eye announced my republican temper, etc... It was observed that since the edict for shaving men's whiskers mine had increased in length, to demonstrate the contempt I entertained for Royal institutions. The truth is I had worn mine precisely as I had always done, that is on a line with my ear, which I since learnt was the line of demarcation they were not to exceed in the ordinance penned by His Majesty himself, his occupation at the opera being to observe those whiskers which trespassed upon the edict, to have their owners instantly seized, shaved and sometimes imprisoned. One night he had a Portuguese officer taken out of the pit to be shaved, who broke from his guards, joined a knot of brother officers who happened to be at the opera, and having informed them of the cause of his apprehension, they all rose towards His Majesty, pointed to their whiskers, burst into a horse laugh and sat down again. He has in the same manner fulminated against poor women's wigs. The penalty is three months' imprisonment. I shaved, you may be sure, immediately, as close and as high as I could. Lady Hamilton wrote the Queen a letter which I understand from numbers of people she showed it to, was written with the greatest earnestness in my favour, so well does this artful woman know how to create herself a merit, by this ostentation of what she termed doing *good for evil*... To be brief, the Queen consented to hear reason and to receive me. I went to Court with Sir William and Lady Hamilton and was very graciously received by Her Majesty. I had an audience of about a quarter of an hour. Her Majesty expressed her sorrow that so foolish a circumstance should have occasioned me any uneasiness, begged I would think no more of it, assured me she never should, and said: "*Je me charge de faire revenir l'esprit du Roi à ce sujet.*" I expressed my acknowledgments... She dismissed me by saying: "*Ah ça, n'en parlons plus, l'affaire, en vérité, n'en vaut pas la peine.*"... Coming from the Queen's closet we met Chevalier Acton. Sir William presented me. I had a short conversation with him, which passed very civilly; he said he would undertake the King and should be happy to see me whenever Sir William Hamilton would take me to him... My wife a day or two afterwards had an audience of the Queen which proved a singularly gracious one. Her Majesty desired her to inform me that the King would receive me *on any day*. Lady Hamilton was present. From that day to this I have not been able to get Sir William Hamilton to present me either to His Majesty or to Acton, although I have pressed him in the strongest manner...'

Since the King's policy, and especially the proceedings of the High Court of State, made havoc of Cardinal Ruffo's, the embittered prelate took advantage of the conclave which was summoned after the Pope's death, to retire from the scene with dignity. He was firmly resolved never to repeat his martial exploits. 'Certain follies are only committed once in a lifetime,' he declared. After his departure the Sicilian Prince of Cassaro was sent to replace him with all the honours of a viceroy. He was an honest if not a brilliant man, who soon came to the same conclusions as Ruffo, that the political persecutions had been carried too far, and that the King ought to proclaim a general amnesty. In the meantime De Nicola confided to his diary: 'The execution of the prisoners of state has become a matter of such indifference, that it no longer makes any impression: it does not serve as an example to the people, nor has the ignominy that used to belong to this punishment any part in the present executions. I wish this could be pointed out to the King, but by whom?' Cassaro did his best, but the King was mulishly obstinate. The amnesty was not proclaimed until the following May.

'General Acton's idea,' wrote Sir William Hamilton, 'still is to keep down the Nobility and favour the People as much as possible. Was he to be called upon for an opinion it would be that the King should return to Naples immediately, grant himself the General Pardon and put an end to the numerous Prosecutions on foot, and apply himself seriously to the formation of a better Government.' Hamilton still considered him 'the only man of business I have met with in this country, and although a slave to his office is reproached by the opposite party of undertaking everything, of excluding everybody else and not finishing anything himself'. He had begun to organize a new army for defence against another French invasion, and appointed two generals, the Chevalier de Saxe and Count de Damas, as inspectors of infantry and cavalry. 'They are worthy men,' said the Queen, 'but they are entering a quagmire, as all the military officers are infamous without exception.' They found the army in a hopeless muddle, complicated by the arbitrary promotions under Cardinal Ruffo, and it was not easy to be fair to all. Many had had to serve under the Republic to keep their families from starvation. 'To collect soldiers, horses, arms, clothing, equipment of every kind; to divide all these remnants into regiments without injustice to individuals from whom the King expected future service: such was our task,' wrote Damas. Eventually twelve regiments of infantry and six of cavalry were raised, the former consisting of a thousand men each, the latter of four hundred, 'all well equipped, tolerably trained and ready for a fresh campaign'.

The treasury had been depleted by the French occupation, the various tax exemptions and other immunities granted by Ruffo during his march through the provinces, and the expenses of the Court in Sicily; but Giuseppe Zurlo, the Minister of Finance, 'possessed the talent of finding money' despite these disadvantages. But the Queen's extravagance was to strain this talent to breaking-point. She was incapable of curbing her generosity, and Zurlo did his utmost to satisfy her frequent demands. The occupation of Rome proved an additional burden rather than a source of profit. The *coup d'état* of 18 Brumaire (November 9) had overthrown the French Directory; General Bonaparte became First Consul and dictator of the destiny of France. But at the end of 1799 Austria seemed to have triumphed in Italy. The only tricolour left flying was in Genoa. As Italy slithered more under Austrian control, Maria Carolina, in spite of her native sympathies, became alarmed. 'I think the Austrians have laid vast plans for Italy; I even think they have chosen a good moment to realize them. But I am worried, I must admit,' she confessed to Gallo. 'Appetite grows with eating. In the Tuscan *Presidi* they have already acted with an energy which strikes me as ominous. In all their proclamations in the Romagna they never mention the Pope, but speak of the legitimate sovereign. Their ministers declare publicly that "Italy must assume a different aspect."... I am not at all reassured.' She suspected Thugut's machinations. It looked as if he would cheat her of the reward which she felt was her due. Her imperial son-in-law maintained an inscrutable reserve. For this and for purely domestic reasons she hoped to revisit Vienna.

XXIII

1800—The Hamiltons' recall—Arthur Paget: 'a bad beginning'—Acton's marriage—The King's 'very proper sense of danger'—The new Order of Saint Ferdinand—Luisa Sanfelice—Election of Pope Pius VII—The Queen's departure for Vienna—A chequered voyage—The capitulation of Malta—Adieu to Nelson and the Hamiltons—Hohenlinden and Marengo—The treaty of Lunéville, 1801— The Queen's dejection.

The new year of the new century began with dismal tidings for Maria Carolina. Nelson's acting command in the Mediterranean had come to an end, and Sir William Hamilton, for thirty-six years British Envoy-Extraordinary and Plenipotentiary at the Court of Naples, had suddenly been recalled, and of course his wife would have to accompany him. Without this inseparable trio the Queen could not bear to face the stagnation of Palermo, and she was determined not to let them go without a struggle. Lady Hamilton was even more determined to prevent the curtain from falling on her husband's career.

Sir William had applied for leave in 1798 when his health had been at a low ebb, but since his request had not been answered he had come to regard himself as a fixture. Now he was informed that he was being relieved of his duties at his own request. He had made a hobby of studying the volcanoes near Naples, and in his published *Observations* on the subject he had written: 'The operations of Nature are slow; great eruptions do not frequently happen; each flatters himself it will not happen in his time, or, if it should, that his tutelar saints will turn away the destructive lava from his grounds; and indeed the great fertility in the neighbourhoods of Volcanoes tempts people to inhabit them.' He had not been prepared for this personal upheaval. The operations of Lord Grenville had been slow, and Sir William had flattered himself that he would not be recalled. Moreover, he had Emma to stand by him in lieu of a tutelar saint. He had long become denationalized, an *inglese italianizzato*, and he was tempted to linger in this volcanic neighbourhood until his dying day. At this Court he had taken root and become a flourishing institution. As for Lady Hamilton, she believed herself indispensable and irreplaceable. The Queen, 'half dead with grief', promised that her ambassador in London would solicit Sir William's reappointment. In the meantime she tried to persuade the King to write to England on his behalf. But the King, who enjoyed thwarting her, refused to interfere. All those who were in his wife's good graces he viewed with a jaundiced eye, and he had come to hate Lady Hamilton. This led to a storm which the Queen described in a letter to 'Miledy': 'Yesterday on your departure I endured a scene of frenzy—shouts and shrieks, threats to kill you, throw you out of the window, call your husband to complain that you turned your back... I am extremely unhappy, and with so many troubles I have only two alternatives, either to go away or die of sorrow... The accursed Paget is in Vienna. Everything distresses me and fills me with despair.'

Arthur Paget, the third son of Lord Uxbridge, had been appointed to succeed Sir William at the age of twenty-nine. When the post was offered to him he wrote to his father: 'They want to send me to Sicily, where everything is at sixes and sevens, and which at this moment is unquestionably a place of the highest importance to us; but it is not Sicily only, the Plan is I fancy to give me the *entire management of everything* in the Mediterranean, Adriatic, Archipelago, etc., etc.; in short nothing can be more flattering than the offer and manner in which it has been *pressed* upon me.' The post had previously been offered to Lord Wellesley: 'You may therefore judge of the Importance Ministers attach to it.' His instructions were to urge the King to return to his capital, and upon his arrival in Naples he reported that this was the universal wish among every class of Neapolitans. He arrived in March, and his first impressions were grim: law and justice were neither practised nor understood; the appearance of the troops was nearly as bad as their reputation, particularly the officers; and unless there was a radical change in the government, and that soon, new scenes of confusion and bloodshed were likely to happen. He was delayed for want of a ship to take him to Palermo, and he was unable to find a house. Sir William Hamilton would not surrender his own, as he meant to return next winter.

In spite of the importance attached to his new post in London, Paget had the coolest of receptions in Palermo. Instead of offering his successor every facility, Sir William put every obstacle in his way.

In a private and confidential letter to Lord Grenville of May 13 Paget wrote: 'Altho' I arrived here in the beginning of the second week in April, it was not in my power to present my Credential letters to their Sicilian Majesties till the 21st of the same Month. It is painful to me to state the reason of this to your Lordship, but I feel it my duty to do so. It seems that Sir William Hamilton was worked upon to consider his recall, and my almost immediate appearance after it at Palermo, as extremely abrupt... Finding at the end of two or three days that he said nothing about presenting his recredential letters, I mentioned the subject to him, and said that my only motive for doing so was (which I did in the most delicate way in my power) that I might be enabled to proceed upon the business with which I was charged. Sir William then said that he should keep his letters in his possession till it was convenient to him to present them, that he could not be guided by what I said *en l'air*, that he did not wish to remain here as a private Individual after so many years' service, and that without I showed him my Instructions and that they contained any thing which obliged him to present his letters of recall immediately, it was his Intention not to do so till the day before his departure, for which he was only waiting for the *Foudroyant* from Malta which was to convey him there. As to shewing Sir William my Instructions, it was a thing which I decided at once within myself not to do, for he certainly would have been obliged to communicate them to Lady Hamilton, who would have conveyed them the next moment to the Queen. I therefore without taking any further notice of the business remained quietly till the arrival of the *Foudroyant*, and the departure of Sir William, which was about ten days afterwards. But I must acquaint your Lordship that General Acton with the utmost readiness and civility received me as Minister during the whole of the Interval from the day Sir William presented me to him, which was about six days after my arrival at Palermo...

'It is not to be told the pains that were taken by Lady Hamilton to set the King and Queen and the whole Court against me, even before I arrived. I was represented as a Jacobin and coxcomb, a person sent to bully and to carry them *bon gré, mal gré* back to Naples, and it is enough to know the character of people here to be sure that all this Jargon had its effect. I must indeed except General Acton *in toto*. But her Ladyship's language in general has been extremely indiscreet, representing Sir William as an ill-used man, etc., etc. She has, however, persuaded herself and others that I am only sent here for an interval, and that Sir William will resume his situation at Naples next winter. On the other hand Sir William says that nothing shall induce him to accept it again unless a sort of second Minister is sent under him to do the business and represent.

'I am sorry to say that Lord Nelson has given more or less into all this nonsense. His Lordship's health is I fear sadly impaired, and I am assured that his fortune is fallen into the same state in consequence of great losses which both His Lordship and Lady Hamilton have sustained at Faro and other Games of Hazard...'

It is evident that Paget's host, the Consul Lock, was the source of this information. Lady Hamilton, he wrote, 'could not endure to remain at Palermo shorn of her rays in the capacity of a private individual'. According to Lock, Mr Paget was received with flattering distinction by the Queen, but Paget himself told a different story to Lord Grenville. 'After waiting near three quarters of an hour H.S.M. came into the room where I was, attended by Sir William and Lady Hamilton, Lord Nelson, etc., and where the whole court were, and spoke one or two sentences to me. I really, my Lord, should not mention this had it not happened that the Russian Minister who had taken the same step as myself was invited to a private Audience which lasted over an hour. This circumstance, coupled with the very disadvantageous manner in which Her Sicilian Majesty has on every occasion expressed herself of me made me imagine that she would do everything in her power to have me removed.'

The Queen wrote to Gallo: 'Paget, who replaces the kind, devoted Hamiltons, has made a bad beginning, advising us in a hard, abrupt manner, and almost enforcing the King's prompt return to Naples. The King was justly offended, as everybody wishes to be master in his own house. Evidently Paget wants to make us feel the full weight of his country's power.' This unwelcome envoy was the harbinger of a new type of English diplomatist. After thirty-six years of smooth intercourse with Hamilton, the Queen was filled with acute foreboding. That her instinct did not err is proved by a remark of Paget's to Grenville, after dwelling despondently upon the wretched state of the country and the corruption of the inhabitants—'so insensible to all principles of honour and morality,' he declares, 'I am of opinion that nothing useful or good can be effected but by the introduction and direct interference of Foreigners.' Almost the voice of Bentinck fourteen years hence! But the choice lay between the French devil and the deep blue sea of England, and she chose the latter regardless of floating sharks. After her flight from Naples she had written: 'The English have shown themselves most faithful, zealous and loyal. Without them we would already be pensioners or beheaded or imprisoned, for none of our ships would have sailed to Sicily... Within a fortnight Sicily would have followed the example of Naples and everything would have been lost... They have saved us personally, preserved Sicily, and will recover Naples. Whatever the motive, the service is real, and we cannot fail to be everlastingly obliged to them.' The growth of this sentiment had been fostered by Acton through the years; the Hamiltons and Nelson had justified it so abundantly that it survived her exasperation with her original mentor, who threatened to depart yet still clung on to power. She relieved herself of much bile on paper at his expense. Sometimes she longed for him to go, but who could replace him as mediator with less tractable envoys than the Hamiltons, such as the accursed Paget? Her outpourings on the subject are ironically humorous when we consider their former intimacy. 'Having nobody else to be jealous of,' she wrote, 'Acton has become furiously jealous of the King, since his recent mania to manage everything himself. Incredible things occur. Then both of them are jealous and envious of me... Acton talks of leaving, but will never do so.'

Most incredible was the news of Acton's marriage. For a bachelor of sixty-four, this really was surprising. Aghast, she wrote in February: 'Acton will marry a thirteen-year-old niece during the Carnival. He says he is certain to leave with his wife and family for England. It is desirable that this should be settled without delay... Since June, when we recovered Naples, nothing has been done but to increase the confusion. I suffer the impossible and it affects me physically, besides the mental anguish... Acton does nothing, consequently the King wishes to do everything. He does things, often badly, but convinced that all is perfect. He will hear and consult nobody. He writes, manages everything at Naples himself, but not at all under the best principles. He always answers: "*Lascia fare a me. Io ne devo rispondere. Io sono Re, Padrone.*" Acton has taken offence and consequently does nothing. It seems to me that the whole edifice is crumbling.' After this outburst, the Queen begged Gallo to burn this letter with his own hand and inform her when he had done so.

On March 3 she returned to the same theme: 'Acton has married his niece... He has the [King's] sole confidence and authority, and at bottom is far more null and idle than at Naples. Towards me he has displayed his real feelings, and the public is so well aware of it that whoever has expectations avoids mentioning or seeing me, lest it prove a hindrance. I must own that this is painful and humiliating, but it is true nevertheless.'

Paget, so sanguine before his arrival, began to lose heart. The King threatened to abdicate and swore he would never return to Naples with the Queen. The Queen wished to go to Vienna, and while the King was eager for her departure, Acton opposed it on account of the expense incurred, and from a fear that she would do more harm than good there, but in Paget's opinion, 'she will not venture to act contrary to General Acton's wishes, and I am almost sure that he will not consent to her doing any thing that would not be perfectly agreeable to England.'

Frustration was rife in Palermo: the King and Queen, Acton, the Hamiltons, Nelson, Paget, all were fretting for different reasons, and the Neapolitans were clamouring for their King's return. Paget unburdened himself to Sir Charles Whitworth: 'In my letter from Vienna I wrote you word that my instructions were positive about getting the K. of Naples back to that place, in consequence of which I have had a great deal of dirty work, and the worst of it is that I have not been quite so successful as one might have wished. I have exacted a promise that he will return, but I cannot get them to fix an early period; the truth is that H.S.M. *has a very proper sense of Danger*—in other words he is a sad Poltroon, and there are certainly a set of discontented people at Naples who are, as we should say, *up to anything*. The Queen has taken an aversion to me, and *op*poses everything I *pro*pose, but she has lost her Influence and Acton does every thing, and with him I am on the best terms, save that we quarrel and spar nearly as often as we meet... The Queen of Naples is certainly going to Vienna. These two Courts are always kicking and splashing at one another and she is going to endeavour to reconcile matters, but I have some idea that she might as well save herself the trouble, as I apprehend that M. de Thugut cannot bear her... She takes two or three daughters with her who will be sold to the best bidder.'

The King had founded a knightly Order of Saint Ferdinand, of which he was Grand Master, to honour royalists who had distinguished themselves in the civil war. The cross was of gold and silver with four lilies at each point, engraved with the saint's effigy and the motto *Fidei et Merito*, hanging on a blue ribbon bordered with red. On May 30 the King published an edict of amnesty, declaring that he hoped his subjects would be as children to him and as brothers between themselves, that he would therefore suspend and cancel political sentences, forbid accusations, denunciations and inquisitions by magistrates, and forgive, forget and annul crimes of lesemajesty. But as prudence set some limit to mercy, certain people were excluded from this pardon, such as fugitives, those previously condemned and those imprisoned for reasons of security. The gallows and the scaffold were removed from the market square which they had dominated for almost a year.

Conspicuous among the exceptions was Luisa Sanfelice, whom the republicans called the mother of her country for betraying the Baccher conspiracy. She had been condemned to death and reprieved in September 1799, but the King, egged on by the Baccher family, was inexorable. The sentence was postponed, however, because the Sanfelice pretended to be with child. Charitable physicians and midwives supported the pretence in their anxiety to save her. If she had erred, it was felt that she had paid the penalty during her long imprisonment with the constant threat of execution looming over her. That she was a woman who owed her misfortunes to love was enough to rouse popular sympathy in the warm-blooded south. The pretence was kept up long after her delivery was due; there was even an unfounded rumour that she had given birth to a daughter. As time went on, it was hoped that she would be forgotten.

The Baccher family had received substantial rewards for their loyalty, but the old father Vincenzo could not rest until his two sons were avenged. Blood called for blood. Seeing that the victim was about to escape, he took ship for Palermo to plead with the King. The simple-minded Ferdinand was deeply affected by his tears. But for this woman the royalist plot would have succeeded; she had betrayed him as well as those gallant boys. And now all Naples knew that he was being hoaxed. He promised Vincenzo that justice would not be bilked.

In July 1800, the Sanfelice was transferred to Palermo for another examination, and of course the pretence fell through. In August she was sent back to Naples to be executed. Only one thing could save her. On August 26 the Hereditary Princess gave birth to a son, whereupon she was entitled to ask three favours of the King. Instead of three she asked one: the Sanfelice's life. 'Anything but that!' he replied obdurately. There are several versions of this dramatic incident. According to Colletta, the petition was put in the infant's swaddling clothes; on hearing that it was for the Sanfelice, the King threw the baby back on its mother's pillow and left the room without another word.

The Sanfelice returned to Naples on the same ship that brought news of the Prince's birth and orders for public rejoicings, and the King's enemies did not fail to make capital out of his cruelty. But the craving for vengeance was a weakness which most of them shared. The Queen was in Vienna at the time, but it is unlikely that she could have softened the sentence. In the mass tension before the execution a soldier let off his gun by mistake when the Sanfelice was led to the scaffold. The executioner became flurried and dropped the axe on the victim's shoulders, so that amid the howls of the mob he had to sever her head with a knife.

Political propagandists made a martyr of this ill-starred light of love. Truth was so blended with fiction that fiction prevailed. Stendhal wrote about her in *Rome, Naples et Florence*, published in 1817, before Colletta and the others. Dumas Père's four-volume novel portrayed her as a romantic heroine. Other novelists and dramatists followed in his wake, and a popular painter depicted her in prison sewing clothes for the baby whose birth was to sign her death warrant. Rodinò rhapsodized: 'May the heroic name of the Sanfelice kindle in every woman's breast the sacred name of liberty which, imbibed by her children, shall never be extinguished!' Her dissolute husband vanished into a limbo of low life. According to Dumas and Mariano D'Ayala, her daughter was ashamed of her memory. Her reputed lovers, Ferdinando Ferri and Vincenzo Cuoco, who had shared her responsibility—and Cuoco had shared her laurels in the *Monitore*—were merely deported. They left her to her fate. Ferri eventually became a respectable Minister of Finance under Ferdinand II and died at the age of ninety, having passed a sponge over his republican youth. Cuoco settled for some years in Milan, where he published his famous essay on the events of 1799, the *Saggio Storico*, in 1801. He returned to Naples with the French in 1806 and became a Councillor of State, but lost his reason when Ferdinand was restored in 1815 and died insane.

Little did the King in Palermo dream that Luisa Sanfelice would be exalted as an angel and a martyr. After his shooting and fishing he slept without dreams. His days were much alike, his health was never better. If only the Queen would stop whining! Why should he ever leave this delightful island? Acton was there to deal with unpleasant matters. Whatever they said, he had no intention of moving. Let Acton give the British ambassador fair words. Consequently Paget reported that the King would probably return to Naples in August: 'The capital is perfectly quiet, and the provinces would be the same if he would go back, but if he does not I will answer for nothing. The discontents and jealousies between this Court and Vienna are at their highest pitch, and in truth the former having too much reason to feel uneasy, the Queen of Naples is going to Vienna immediately in the hopes of putting matters to rights, but she would act much wiser to keep out of the General's [Acton's] way, who cannot I understand bear her, and you are sufficiently acquainted with his character to know what is the consequence of his dislike.' Acton had spoken to Paget 'with most pointed asperity of Mr de Thugut and his projects of aggrandizement, of which he discovered a considerable degree of jealousy and uneasiness'.

Thugut's plan was to extend the Austrian frontier to Rome by getting the French conquests in Italy transferred to Austria and absorbing the remaining principalities. When Cardinal Chiaramonti was elected Pope Pius VII in Venice on March 14, three and a half months after the assembly of the Conclave, the Austrians would not let him be crowned in Saint Mark's though the Venetians offered to defray all the expenses of the ceremony. The Pope expressed his astonishment to Cardinal Hertzan and decided to be crowned in the Church of San Giorgio Maggiore, which took place amid so vast a throng that even the roof-tops were bristling with spectators. Hertzan then tried to persuade the Pope, on leaving Venice, to proceed to Vienna. When His Holiness declined, Thugut sent a special envoy, Marchese Ghislieri of Bologna, to obtain the voluntary cession of the three 'legations' of Bologna, Ferrara and Ravenna, at the same time offering the Emperor's congratulations. But Ghislieri could obtain nothing from the Pope's secretary, the future Cardinal Consalvi, and on addressing the Pope in person, was firmly but gently refused. Moreover, Pius VII made a formal claim for the return of the lost legations. The Emperor should beware, he said prophetically, of appropriating garments that did not belong to him, for not only would His Majesty be unable to use them, but they would communicate moths to his own apparel—meaning his hereditary states.

It would have been normal for the Pope to return to Rome by land. But then he would have to pass through territory which the Austrians wished to keep, and where popular ovations were inevitable, so the Austrian government made him travel by sea on a leaky old frigate. Owing to the incapacity of the crew, the uncomfortable voyage to Pesaro took twelve days. On landing he heard of the Austrian defeat at Marengo. His Holiness was met by Neapolitan troops ten miles from the capital, which he entered amid genuine rejoicings. General Naselli came to confirm the restitution of his domains and the Pope agreed with him that the Neapolitan troops were not to be withdrawn till the Austrians had evacuated his ports. Just after the battle of Marengo, Bonaparte deputed the Bishop of Vercelli to negotiate with Pius VII about the restoration of the Church in France. Though he realized that this would have to be purchased by concessions, the Pope was inclined to be more conciliatory as a result of the treatment he had suffered from Austria.

'My patience is at an end,' wrote the Queen to Gallo. She urged him to stay on in Vienna as a Councillor of State: 'In that case as soon as I arrive I shall send word that you are indispensable to me. We could live in calm and tranquillity, and you could really be very useful in helping me to arrange my quiet routine for the future... I have just been interrupted by one of those scenes which tempt me to flee from the world, but which it is impossible to explain except verbally. It is better to endure everything in silence and try to escape from it. I hope that my fate will be decided soon. Either I shall be able to lead a peaceful life for a few months or I shall go mad. If I do succeed in getting away, I shall adopt a different mode of existence on my return.' Accomplished courtier though he was, Gallo had other ambitions than to linger in Vienna at the Queen's beck and call. To her disappointment he arrived in Palermo on June 1, not long before her departure. Her second daughter, the Grand Duchess of Tuscany, had lost a six-year-old son, and begged her mother to visit her. This was an additional inducement to leave, but as Paget remarked, the journey to Vienna was a project as often departed from as agreed upon. By June she was finally prepared to travel with the Princesses Christine, Amélie and Antoinette and the young Prince Leopold. Nelson and the

Hamiltons had returned from a cruise to Malta, and there was a week of banqueting and official leave-taking and further hesitation, owing to the news that Bonaparte had crossed the Alps, before the Queen embarked on the *Foudroyant* on June 10.

The Queen's spirits revived as the ship sailed out of the bay. On the 15th she wrote to Gallo: 'The weather is so fine that the day before yesterday the ship *Alexander* drew near enough to enable us to speak for an hour with the passengers on board. My children practise with the speaking-trumpet and deafen me. The sea is so calm that you would think we were on our way to Posillipo, yet we see nothing but sky and water. We suffered a great deal the first two days and all of us had to lie down. But today is delicious, and I thank God for having given me the firmness to leave... I am no longer contradicted, tormented and threatened. This is a great boon, and I am happy and content.' But they were overtaken by a storm before reaching Leghorn on the 14th.

'Livorno! Livorno!' she exclaimed ecstatically as the ship dropped anchor, and she began to distribute parting gifts to Nelson, the Hamiltons and the officers of the *Foudroyant*. Lady Hamilton received another diamond necklace, designed with the initials of the Queen's children, who made efforts to write and thank Nelson in English. The Queen herself wrote: 'My dear and respectable Lord Nelson, To the numerous obligations, which all Europa and we particularly have to you, is to be added our gratitude for the care you have taken to transport me.' But she was detained another two days by bad weather before she could land.

The news was contradictory. General Melas announced that the Austrians had won a victory at Marengo on the 14th and public rejoicings were proclaimed in Leghorn. The Queen retired to rest brimming over with joy, and gave orders to be wakened whenever the next despatch arrived. After midnight she was roused by one of her ladies. Tearing open the despatch, she was said to have remarked: 'Let us read of the ruin of Bonaparte's presumptuous army!' But she read of a second battle, ending in a great French victory. Colletta, who sometimes forgot Tacitus to write like a novelist, described the Queen fainting into the arms of the lady who had brought her the bad news. The sudden shock of disappointment following her recent elation affected her physically. On the 28th she wrote to Gallo: 'I very nearly died. A congestion, an apoplectic fit, almost carried me off. A strong bleeding saved me, but a second attack nearly finished me. I recovered, but for several days I have been stupefied, my memory gone, my head quite empty. Even now I cannot eat or sleep and feel very ill... The fugitives of the Austrian army arrive here in a pitiful state. You see them dying in the streets, without clothes or shirts, and they no longer look human. The ill will of the generals and admirals is as incredible as their talk. They all want peace and repose. If all the Emperor's troops and generals are like those I see here, I advise him to make peace and never again think of war. Leghorn has a majestic appearance. I think there are certainly 500 ships, and everything abounds here... In my opinion the King's cause is lost. For I dare not flatter myself that Bonaparte is willing to leave a crown on his head, and his will is everything.'

For nearly a month she had to wait in uncertainty, longing to proceed to Vienna, but fearing that she might have to return to Palermo. Lord Keith, the naval Commander-in-Chief, who resented Nelson's conduct in Sicily, showed plainly that he regarded the Queen as a nuisance. 'It is no time for a Queen to be making visits and retarding public service,' he remarked. On the 20th he wrote to Paget: 'I must go to Leghorn... to be Bored by Lord Nelson for permission to take the Queen to Palermo, and Princes and Princesses to all parts of the Globe. To every request I have said my Duty to the Nation forbids it!' Alarmed by rumours of the approaching French army, the Queen asked for the *Foudroyant* to take her home, but Lord Keith sent the ship to Minorca for repairs. Lady Hamilton had had command of the fleet long enough, he retorted.

'I am truly and thoroughly desperate,' wrote the Queen on July 2. 'Since eighteen days I have been in Leghorn with my four children in the deepest dilemma. I await my sentence from Vienna, always with one foot on the ship, fearing every minute to see the enemy arrive and not have time to get away. Everything seems incomprehensible. Melas has been beaten, it is true, but that was no reason to conclude such an armistice and consent to hand over the fortresses to the French, who are already masters of the territory as far as Bologna, Imola and Faenza, so that I do not know which road to take... Melas has 65,000 men united under the walls of Mantua. All is not therefore lost, yet they make peace! Keith, whom I consider detestable, tells me laughing that we shall be included in the treaty... Keith, that is to say England, assumes a tone I did not know, and I am disgusted for ever with their words and behaviour.

I swear that once the peace is settled it will be an expert in cunning who can catch me again, except in the case of aggression against our country... The rest of Europe may be on fire, Thugut Emperor and Fox King of England, but even so I would not be drawn from a permanent system of neutrality or, to be more precise, of nullity. I only aspire to repose. I perceive too clearly that only force counts and that good faith only serves to make one a dupe. I am anxious to know what will become of me and my four children. If I cannot go to Vienna, I shall return, to my utter despair, to vegetate in Palermo and think only about my soul... Bonaparte threatens Naples, saying that he must bring us to reason. I do not understand the meaning of the word "allies" if the Emperor and the English, for whom we have sacrificed so much or rather everything, fail to remember us. It is a lesson I shall not forget.' On July 6 she continued: 'My situation is really critical. It is now four weeks since I left and three since I landed at Leghorn, where I am living at the Grand Duke's expense, of which I am deeply ashamed... I have studied all the routes, but none is free without a French safe-conduct which I cannot and will not demand. You cannot imagine how I have suffered at Leghorn. All are afraid that my presence will cause them embarrassment, even the Austrian generals, who have given me to understand that I should do well to leave... Keith's conduct towards me here is unworthy. He has 8,000 men and refuses to put them at my disposal: he will send them back rather than employ them for the King, to whom they could be so useful. We are made fools of everywhere.'

However, Nelson continued to feel responsible for what he called his sacred charge. 'Until I have got rid of my charge,' he said, 'nothing shall separate me from her. I should feel myself a beast, could I have a thought for anything but her comfort.' One night the Queen became so alarmed that she took refuge on board the *Alexander*, to which Nelson had removed his flag; the French were said to be within twenty-four miles and a howling mob had gathered outside the palace where she was staying, but as in Naples, she failed to realize that these were anti-French, and that in this case they were clamouring for Nelson to lead them against the common foe. Her first idea was to sail to Trieste by way of Messina, but she disembarked next day.

In spite of the risk, she decided to travel by way of Florence to Ancona, and sail from there to Trieste. Miss Cornelia Knight, who accompanied the party, left a record of the journey. 'The die is cast, and go we must,' she wrote. 'Lord Nelson is going on an expedition he disapproves and against his own convictions, because he has promised the Queen and that others advise her. I pity the Queen. Prince Belmonte directs the march, and Lady Hamilton, though she does not like him, seconds his proposals because she hates the sea and wishes to visit the different courts of Germany. Sir William says he shall die by the way, and he looks so ill that I should not be surprised if he did. I am astonished that the Queen, who is a sensible woman, should consent to run so great a risk.' At one point the coach containing Nelson and the Hamiltons overturned; the latter were hurt, but not dangerously. 'The wheel was repaired, but broke again at Arezzo—the Queen two days' journey before them and news of the French army advancing rapidly, it was therefore decided that they should proceed, and Mrs Cadogan and I remained with the broken carriage, as it was of less consequence we should be left behind than they... Just as we were going to set off, we received accounts of the French being very near the road where we had to pass, and of its being also infested with Neapolitan deserters; but at the same moment arrived a party of Austrians, and the officers gave us two soldiers as a guard. We travelled night and day; the roads were almost destroyed, and the misery of the inhabitants is beyond description. At length, however, we arrived at Ancona, and found that the Queen had given up the idea of going in the *Bellona*, an Austrian frigate, fitted up with silk hangings, carpets, and eighty beds for her reception, and now meant to go with a Russian squadron of three frigates and a brig. I believe she judged rightly, for there had been a mutiny on board the *Bellona*, and for the sake of accommodation she had reduced her guns to twenty-four, while the French, in possession of the coast, arm *trabaccoli* and other light vessels that could easily surround and take her...'

From Trieste she wrote on August 9: 'I told you we were become humble enough to rejoice at a Russian squadron conveying us across the Adriatic; but had we sailed as was first intended, in the imperial frigate, we should have been taken by eight *trabaccoli*, which the French armed on purpose at Pesaro. Sir William and Lady Hamilton and Lord Nelson give a miserable account of their sufferings on board the Commodore's ship (Count Voinovitch). He was ill in his cot, but his first lieutenant, a Neapolitan named Capaci, was, it seems, the most ignorant and insolent of beings.

Think what Lord Nelson must have felt! He says a gale of wind would have sunk the ship... I hope we shall be able to set off tomorrow night for Vienna. The Queen and thirty-four of her suite have had fevers; you can have no idea of the helplessness of the party. How we shall proceed on our long journey is to me a problem, but we shall certainly get on as fast as we can, for the very precarious state of Sir William's health has convinced everybody that it is necessary he should arrange his affairs...'

The Queen reached Vienna exhausted, but happy to see her eldest daughter after ten years and meet her numerous grandchildren. It was an intense relief to be far from her husband's tantrums, and from the hostile atmosphere of the Sicilian Court. Though the Prime Minister Thugut had tried to prevent her coming, she was welcomed with appropriate honours, and there was a family reunion on a large scale, for the Hapsburgs were nothing if not prolific: her brother Leopold had had sixteen children. The disaster of Marengo prevented any public festivity, but there were plenty of domestic amusements. Her son and daughters basked in the affection of their northern cousins, and the royal palaces overflowed with the merriment of bouncing little Archdukes and Archduchesses. Vienna seemed an ideal shelter from the storm, so comfortable and *gemütlich* after Palermo. But this interval of relief was ephemeral; inevitably politics regained tyrannical sway.

Malta capitulated to the British and Neapolitans in September, but Ferdinand, who had assisted the naval blockade and placed blind confidence in his ally, was entirely overlooked in the pact of surrender, as was Paul I of Russia, who considered the island his as Grand Master of the Knights of Saint John. While Sicily was thus delivered from a dangerous neighbour, the Neapolitan flag was not hoisted beside the Union Jack, and the Queen felt aggrieved. In this case the defeat of the French brought no balm to her wounded pride. It was undeniable that Naples alone could not defend Malta against attack. Lord Grenville wrote to Paget in October: 'The establishment either of Russia or France in that fortress might indeed give just cause of jealousy to His Sicilian Majesty, but no similar ground of apprehension could arise respecting Great Britain, which can have no views hostile to the security and independence of Naples.' But the Queen, who did not see it in this light, complained bitterly to Lady Hamilton: 'The French are driven out and that is all to the good, but the King and we were keenly mortified to have had no part in the capitulation, considering our troops, munitions, artillery and positive rights to the island... It is all the more painful to be so completely duped and receive so serious an injury from a friend. We are such fast friends of England that we are delighted that this great ally should keep a fortress which dominates Sicily, but her method of procedure, this contemptuous treatment, after all our care, cordiality, assistance and enormous expense—these are galling indeed. How often have I thought, if my friends [the Hamiltons] had been there this would never have happened.'

The Queen took final leave of Nelson and the Hamiltons who were returning to England, feted everywhere. Crowds gathered outside Nelson's lodgings and rose to applaud him at the theatre, and in fashionable drawing-rooms Lady Hamilton postured in her famous 'attitudes' and sang the 'Nelson Aria' to the accompaniment of Haydn. Sir William Hamilton had been a family mentor since the Queen's first arrival in Naples; Nelson had been an avenging arm, and Emma a soothing bosom. In her farewell letter to 'my dear Miledy', the Queen expressed her hope of seeing her soon in Naples: 'I repeat what I have always told you at all times, in all circumstances and places. Emma, dear Emma, will be my friend and sister and this sentiment will never change.' She thanked her again effusively for all she had done, and sent more messages of affection and gratitude to Sir William and thousands of thanks to the hero Nelson, whose memory was printed indelibly on her heart. In a postscript she added letters for 'the worthy Castelcicala', Circello, 'Miledy' Spencer and others. These evidently referred to Paget, who had written in July: 'I have just heard from authority I cannot doubt that His Majesty will be requested to recall me from this Court... I believe that Prince Castelcicala is charged with the commission... I understand... that this is an Act of the Queen's, brought about thro' the insinuations and Intrigues of Lady Hamilton who, before her departure, exacted a promise from His Sicilian Majesty thro' the Queen that he would ask to have Sir William Hamilton again appointed Minister, and that this is the first step towards it...' 'I dread much,' he wrote again, 'from the circumstances of Lady Hamilton being with Her Majesty, whose influence is great, and whose ends are wicked.' But Lady Hamilton had flaunted out of the Queen's life. They continued to correspond, but they never met again.

The Queen had hoped to influence her son-in-law, but he kept her at a tantalizing distance. Even Gallo, who had returned to Vienna, was so reserved that she complained of him to Acton and the King. 'In general I am led to think that Her Sicilian Majesty is not allowed to take any part whatever in affairs, a circumstance which cannot fail to mortify her, as she certainly left this country with very different expectations,' wrote the well-informed Paget. She had to watch her son-in-law's wavering with impotent rage. Bonaparte expected him to make peace after his heavy reverses in Germany and Italy, but he had recently signed a treaty with England, by which he received a subsidy of £2,500,000 and bound himself not to sign peace with France before February 1, 1801. He could only hope to gain time to reorganize his army. But after a careful survey of the military situation at the camp on the Inn where his forces were being mustered, the Emperor became so discouraged that he arranged with Bonaparte to prolong the armistice, though this involved the surrender of Philippsburg, Ulm and Ingolstadt. Thugut was replaced by Cobenzi, who had negotiated the treaty of Campo Formio; discussions with Paris were resumed, but the purpose of the Austrians was still to gain time and terms acceptable to England.

Bonaparte saw through these delaying tactics, and warned Austria that the armistice would end on November 5. He detected Maria Carolina's finger in this and bore her a deeper grudge. Although he was mistaken about her influence, she made no bones about her bellicose sentiments. Hostilities were renewed, culminating in a more complete French victory at Hohenlinden and another armistice on December 25. Appalled, the Queen wrote from Schönbrunn to Gallo: 'My situation is extremely painful. Abandoned by my own children, avoided and thrust aside by the rest of my family, who render me responsible for everything and make me bear the burden of everybody's hatred... I see that the Austrian monarchy runs singing and dancing, with giant strides, towards its own destruction... The Grand Duke [her son-in-law of Tuscany who had had to flee before the French invasion] urges me to go to Brunn or Buda. It is far away that I shall drain the chalice of offences, trouble and grief. I no longer have the courage and strength to bear the outrages with which I am charged before another nation. I shall speak to the whole world and it will give me its esteem. I am the daughter of Maria Theresa and will rouse other jealousies in those who, to my misfortune, have no heart.' Yet at the same time Austria had signed a convention with Naples, which the British ambassador, Lord Minto, considered 'as the strongest evidence that could be given, both of the zeal and judgment of the Marquis de Gallo, and of the fair and favourable intentions of Baron Thugut towards His Sicilian Majesty'. The Queen of Naples, he said, 'is strongly urged to return while there is leisure and tranquillity'. Already her son-in-law was anxious to get rid of her.

In Italy, where General de Bellegarde had succeeded Melas after his defeat at Marengo, another armistice was signed in January 1801. After his many successes Bonaparte became more exacting. Austria was compelled to accept his terms at the Treaty of Lunéville in February 1801, whereby France acquired Belgium and Luxembourg as well as the German districts left of the Rhine, occupied Piedmont, 'protected' the Cisalpine and Ligurian Republics, and controlled Tuscany, which with Parma, Modena and Lucca was to form the new kingdom of Etruria under a puppet Duke of Parma; the Papal States were to be respected pending a Concordat with the Pope, but Ancona was to be garrisoned. In spite of her repeated promises and the recent convention, Austria entirely abandoned Naples in the treaty. Gallo could do nothing; the Emperor's father-in-law and ally was only remembered when he could provide troops or divert the enemy from the Austrian front. Bonaparte was exasperated with 'the mad and implacable hostility' of the Bourbons of Naples, whose military operations could not have been more inopportune. Just when Austria was about to sign peace, General de Damas advanced with 8,000 Neapolitan troops into Tuscany. The French were driven from Siena where they were outnumbered, but they soon returned and drove the Neapolitans back to the Roman frontier. General Murat was ordered to march against Naples, but the order was revoked at the eleventh hour. When Bonaparte refused to receive Gallo or confirm General Brune's promise not to attack Naples, the Queen appealed to Paul I of Russia for assistance, trying to 'prod his self-love', as she said, since he had 'so openly declared himself to be our protector'. She appealed in the nick of time. The Tsar intervened in her favour at a moment when the First Consul wished to cultivate friendly relations with Russia.

After the peace of Lunéville, Vienna shook off its gloom and plunged into an unusually brilliant Carnival. The young princesses were able to enjoy the succession of balls, masquerades and varied entertainments. Despite differences of temper and climate, the Viennese vied with the Neapolitans in their taste for amusement and in their appreciation of pageantry. But the Queen was in no mood for any kind of enjoyment. 'Affairs in general, political and domestic, give me more desire to weep than to go to the theatre,' she wrote. 'I love the sovereigns, Vienna, its vicinity, this land where I was born, and the way of living here. But as for relying on them, never, never, never. I am certain, ultra-certain, of the collapse of this monarchy.'

XXIV

The Hereditary Prince and Princess return to Naples—The Treaty of Florence—Amnesty of February 17, 1801; the Giunta di Stato *abolished and all its records destroyed—Alquier as French ambassador—Death of the Hereditary Princess—A double marriage arranged—Treaty of Amiens—Murat visits Naples—Maria Carolina's prophecy—The King's return to Naples in June—The Queen's return in August—The Spanish nuptials of Princess Marie Antoinette—The Hereditary Prince and his child bride.*

Week after week Paget continued to badger Acton about the King's return to Naples. But obstinacy was one of Ferdinand's salient characteristics: he was quite content to remain in Sicily, and flew into a passion whenever the subject was broached. Moreover, he was surrounded by a set of men, whose advice Acton attributed to the most despicable and sordid motives. It was easy for these to play upon his fears and prejudices, by exaggerating the dangers he would risk by returning. With so much to contend against, Acton could not always keep his temper with the fretful Paget, though he agreed with him and promised to do his best. 'I am sorry to say that our last interview was by no means a pleasant one,' wrote Paget, 'having produced a good deal of warmth on the part of the General. Being informed by him that His Sicilian Majesty wished to remain here till after the lying-in of the Hereditary Princess, which is not to take place till July or August, I certainly remarked to him that I thought it rather a singular reason for desiring to postpone the execution of a measure wherein His Sicilian Majesty's Dignity as well as Interest were with reason thought to be so deeply concerned. To this the General rather hastily replied that His Sicilian Majesty was a perfect judge how to act in support of his own Dignity and Interest.'

Eventually Paget was able to report: 'The departure of the Hereditary Prince and Princess for Naples at length takes place this day [January 25, 1801]. H.R.H. will be accompanied by General Acton and has the most extensive power for the Government of that Country entrusted to him by His Sicilian Majesty. I must own... that I hope more good than I can augur from the presence of the

Hereditary Prince in that Country. The wish and the cry of the people always has been and continues to be for the return of the Sovereign. I therefore much doubt of their expectations being satisfied by the appearance of the Heir to the Crown.'

The royal squadron hove into sight on January 31, greeted by universal shouts of joy, salvos from all the ships and castles, and the ringing of all the bells. The delicate Princess looked radiant, and there were tears in the Prince's eyes. As soon as they reached the palace, the Princess appeared on the balcony and held up each of her children in turn, as if to present them to the people, while the Prince stood beside her saluting the crowd. The public gaiety was enhanced by illuminations, allegorical temples, trophies, obelisks, statues and arches, alluding to this happy event with Neapolitan fantasy. Hundreds of handkerchiefs waved from every window, hats were flung into the air, as the royal coach crawled at a snail's pace towards the cathedral, where the Prince and Princess brought their children to revere San Gennaro. 'Only the heartless could fail to be moved,' wrote the diarist De Nicola.

Honours and promotions were distributed at Court. With rare elation, Acton remarked to the senators and grandees assembled to welcome the Hereditary Prince: 'I have kept my word and restored the Prince to you. Soon I shall restore the King.' But the King's return was to be postponed as a result of Austria's desertion. He was to pay dearly for putting his troops at his son-in-law's disposal. Damas had valiantly supported the Austrian General de Bellegarde, who wrote to him after signing an armistice with the French at Treviso on January 16: 'I have just concluded an armistice from which you are excluded. I could only obtain a promise not to attack you, but you know how the people with whom we have to deal keep their engagements, so take your precautions.' Almost at the same time he received a placid letter from the Queen enclosing a copy of the Emperor's convention with Naples.

General Murat proposed an armistice which, after the exchange of many proposals and counter-proposals, led to the signature of peace on March 28. The terms originally demanded were the dismissal of Acton, the evacuation of the Papal States, the release of all French and political prisoners and, most important from Bonaparte's point of view, the closing of Neapolitan ports against English ships. Murat said no more about Acton's dismissal when Damas rejected this condition as offensive to the King's dignity, but he gained every other point except the embargo on British shipping. On this subject Acton wrote to Paget in his oddly un-English style: 'We shall certainly stand up the negative to such a strange demand as long as we can. As a determined partiality seems with Hatred and Vengeance to influence against me the Generals French and Russian I have prevented the King of it, and shall wait His Majesty's orders to retire myself entirely if a persistence continues from the French. Murat declares to Damas, that Gallo in Paris shall not receive any benefit from the Court of Vienna, but from the Russians alone. I hope then to have the pleasure to see you in Palermo on my way to Shropshire.' Finally it was arranged that the embargo was not to be mentioned in the treaty of peace, a concession obtained by paying Murat a million and a half francs.

Fearing to be made a scapegoat, Damas withdrew from the negotiations, and the final peace treaty was signed in Florence by the French minister Alquier and the Neapolitan Antonio Micheroux. The terms were severe, but Murat enforced them by threatening invasion. The King had to surrender the Tuscan Presidi, Porto Longone in Elba and Piombino, pay a war indemnity of 120,000 ducats within three months, allow political exiles to return and restore their property, publish an amnesty, and as a last straw, when these terms had been accepted, agree to the occupation of the Abruzzi from the Tronto to the Sangro, and of the province of Otranto, by 16,000 French troops who were to receive 120,000 ducats a month and all the necessary provisions, and hand over three frigates besides until peace was signed between France and England. The kingdom was thus reduced to a state of vassalage.

Paget, like Nelson before him, harped on 'the right of a Sovereign not to ratify a treaty He may be dissatisfied with', though he reminded Keith that the French, with an army of 40,000 men which they could easily detach against Naples, were not in a compliant mood. Forgetting the King's contribution to the recent campaign, but for which he would not have fallen into this predicament, Paget said that 'he might have made a very good fight', and blamed Acton's weakness and indecision. 'As long as General Acton remains at the head of affairs I despair of seeing any change for the better in them,' he wrote. 'He will listen to none but those who flatter him. At the same time there is not a Man in these kingdoms fit to hold his situation.' The British Cabinet took a more lenient view; so did Lord Minto, who wrote from Vienna: 'In two words let me say that having been made acquainted with the reasons which constrained General Acton to sanction the second Armistice and the subsequent Peace, I am in my own mind strongly inclined to admit the necessity under which he has acted. The intention of the Enemy, *it is clear*, is to conquer the Kingdom and probably dispose of it to the best bidder. They would have accomplished that object instantly by a rupture. They still intend to accomplish it; but the process must be somewhat slower, and some little time is gained to obtain such support, either political or military, as may by possibility interpose yet in time to save Naples and disappoint the enemy. ... It seems to me both agreeable to the character, and consonant to the practice, of our Government to show rather sympathy and indulgence than resentment to friends whose sincerity and fidelity have been so well proved in a moment of extreme necessity.'

'We have become a Gallo-Spanish province,' wailed the Queen. 'The whole treaty is infamous and Micheroux is a vile traitor to my mind... The kingdom of Naples is lost beyond a doubt. Let us save Sicily if possible, and humour allies who will help us to recover Naples at the general peace. Although but a stripped skeleton, at least let my children's patrimony be restored. Our ally can only be England. We must implore her to save and assist us and regard our weaknesses as committed with a pistol at our throat... The King has written to me very positively: "I conjure you by all that you hold dearest in the world and because I wish to die in your arms, not to take any premature step, not to move from where you are without writing me and waiting for my consent or a reply, which I will not send until conditions change. I beg this of you because nobody can be trusted." ...I had previously declared what I confirm again, that I should never be able to agree with the French on account of the implacable hatred I bear them, my principles which forbid me to condescend, and the attentions one has to show them now that they are masters in our house. Owing to this inability, I would be more injurious than useful to the King's service.'

The King's letter had been prompted by Acton's advice. Both dreaded the consequences of the Queen's hysteria. This was no time for gratuitous explosions. Even the swashbuckling Murat saw the need to play the diplomatist, and he did so with striking success. 'I am sorry that circumstances have deprived me of the pleasure of meeting you and repeating the assurance of all my esteem,' he wrote to Damas, the aristocratic expatriate. When his *aide-de-camp* Beaumont came to Naples in February, Acton gave orders that he was to be splendidly entertained and introduced to the nobility. He was noticed at the theatre in the same box with Damas, a Russian general and a one-armed English officer who had lost his other arm fighting the French. He was shown the royal museum at Portici, of which two rooms were empty since their treasures, as his guide explained, had been removed to Palermo. A very prudent precaution, Beaumont remarked. His guide said he hoped they would be replaced on the King's return. Now that everything had been settled, replied Beaumont, this hope would surely be fulfilled. But in spite of Acton's care, the Frenchman's visit did not pass without a hitch. At a private house where illicit gambling went on Beaumont noticed that the cockade had been removed from his hat and swore that the whole assembly would have to account for it, and the whole of France would take part in the affair. With this threat he left, after hinting that he suspected a Neapolitan officer who happened to be present. The dismayed host ordered all the doors to be closed so that whoever had taken the cockade could return it, and save everybody from a scandal. A guest proposed that the lights be dimmed so as not to see the culprit. Thanks to which the cockade was soon restored to its owner.

The new amnesty was proclaimed on February 17, the last day of the Carnival. The remaining republican prisoners were to be released, the exiles to be recalled, and the *Giunta di Stato*, or High Court of State for political trials, was to be abolished. The populace, who could neither forget nor forgive, threw mud at the proclamations in the market-place. On March 2 all the records of past political trials in Monteoliveto were ordered to be burnt in token of the King's promise, a fact which his enemies exploited to their own advantage. In April the French troops crossed the frontier. Murat told them to behave with moderation: 'Soldiers, you went forth to fight the Neapolitans. Your appearance sufficed to obtain what your valour was to conquer... You are about to enter peacefully the territory which you were to invade. You are going to occupy Neapolitan cities. Concord, confidence and friendship open their doors to you. You will preserve them in spite of all the wiles of the Cabinet of St James.'

A *Te Deum* was sung in the Duomo and the capital was illuminated for three nights, but a peace under such conditions could hardly be popular. It was rumoured that the Hereditary Prince wished to leave as soon as the French arrived, but he was warned that this would inevitably renew civil war, which would be followed by total occupation of the kingdom. De Nicola noted the resentment of the populace, since they had enjoyed their season of anarchy. In the neighbourhood of the market they prevented any sort of illumination, and threatened to burn any house that showed signs of festivity.

The new French ambassador, Alquier, presented his credentials in May. As a deputy in the Convention which had voted for the death of Louis XVI, he did not make a favourable impression. He had previously been ambassador to Madrid where he acquitted himself with skill, especially as a reporter of amusing tittle-tattle. His position, backed by an army in the country to enforce the treaty if need be, while shunned like a leper by Neapolitan society, was singular. This ultra-Republican was ready to champion the ultra-Aristocrats when it was a matter of France's prestige, as when a titled lady asked him to intercede for her husband who had not been released in spite of the amnesty. He and his colleagues had been condemned to various terms of imprisonment in the trial of the so-called 'City', for insubordination to the Vicar-General Pignatelli in 1799. Led by the royalist Prince of Canosa, the 'City' had contended that since the King's departure the government devolved upon the *Sedili* or *Seggi* of the feudal nobility, who represented the capital and consequently, in their own opinion, the entire nation. These *Sedili* had been abolished in 1800, which meant that the political power of the nobles as a body was destroyed. The Queen regarded them as rebels who had ruined the country and dethroned the King. The government did not consider them as included in the Treaty of Florence, since they were neither democratic nor pro-French, but had wished to form an aristocratic oligarchy. This thesis, as Blanch wrote, could be maintained legally, but Alquier would not miss a chance to butt in and earn the goodwill of many prominent families, although they were no partisans of his. He appealed to Acton, who replied that these were extraneous to the treaty. All the more reason, said Alquier, 'to prove that the government wished to heal the wounds of war with the balm of clemency: to make exceptions showed that they were only clement under compulsion'. Acton saw his point, and the 'Knights of the City' were given their freedom. Thus the quixotic Prince of Canosa returned to Naples, feeling that his adventures in symbolic guise resembled those of our

Redeemer, who 'experimented with the Peters, Pilates, Herods, and Judases to sustain the cause of Truth', and sublimated thereby, plunged into a long career of tilting, as his biographer Signor Maturi expressed it, against the windmills of his political fantasy.

Owing to the amnesty there were joyful family reunions, but so long as the King was absent society was dispersed, and taxation weighed heavily on all as a result of the French occupation. Apart from Alquier and the Russian minister, the rest of the diplomatic corps remained at Palermo, but several Courts, like Spain, were not represented.

A temporary reconciliation with Spain was soon arranged for dynastic reasons. The Hereditary Princess, who had always been consumptive, died in November at the age of twenty-five. She had had a sad life since her arrival in the midst of war, and had lost her only son in the previous July. A little daughter, the future Duchesse de Berry, survived her. Like the Queen, her aunt and mother-in-law, she was superior to her husband in intelligence and had endeavoured to raise him to a higher level. Cultured, modest, kind and dignified, she had won universal esteem. It was generally known that she had tried to save the Sanfelice and other political prisoners. De Nicola reflected public opinion when he wrote: 'She would have formed the happiness of the kingdom if with her principles and good heart she had been spared to govern us... We are under the lash of God, and even in this death I see a chastisement for us.' The weather changed suddenly, seemlng to weep for her, he added. Vast crowds went to gaze at her corpse, exposed in Santa Chiara, but since she had requested not to be embalmed many were overpowered by the terrible odour.

The Hereditary Prince, like his great-grandfather Philip V of Spain, for all his conjugal devotion, was incapable of enduring the ordeal of abstinence. Another wife had to be found for him immediately. A double marriage was soon arranged between the Prince of the Asturias and Princess Marie Antoinette, and between the young widower and the former's sister, the Infanta Maria Isabella. The Queen, who had not been consulted, was indignant at the prospect. Though anxious to find husbands for her daughters, she was deeply prejudiced against the Spanish Bourbons. She had hoped to marry all her children to respectable Austrians. 'You know my projects for my son [the Hereditary Prince],' she wrote to Gallo. 'Fate has willed otherwise. He wishes to marry his cousin, the

Infanta of Spain. I have seen it in his own handwriting to the General [Acton] only ten days after the death of his virtuous wife, saying that this long celibacy oppressed him. I blush that this is my son. But God wishes to humiliate and torment us. We must adore His decrees.'

Since the death of Tsar Paul I, Russia and Great Britain had drawn together. France appeared to be isolated when Bonaparte was busily organizing the French Republic and the governments of Italy, Holland, Germany, and Switzerland as well. To consolidate his new order Bonaparte wished to come to terms with England. After strenuous negotiations the preliminaries of peace were signed in London on October 1, 1801. The final treaty was not signed till the following March at Amiens. This was the first and only peace concluded between Great Britain and Bonaparte, and few people regarded it as more than a truce. 'I myself think that the mountain will deliver a mouse,' said Maria Carolina, who could only perceive the advantages that France would gain. 'I believe that Bonaparte will do everything everywhere that he wishes and decides, and that the whole of Europe will be content to watch him with stupefaction.' Among the provisions of the treaty Great Britain was to evacuate Malta within three months, while France was to evacuate the Roman States and the kingdom of Naples. Murat arrived with the rank of ambassador extraordinary to supervise the French evacuation. A guard of honour was stationed at the Palazzo Calabritto where he was staying, and he was received with dignified courtesy by Acton, but without any affectation of cordiality. The King sent him a fine sword with a diamond-studded hilt. At Caserta, where he was entertained with royal honours, he presented the Hereditary Prince with a brace of pistols manufactured at Versailles. Everybody was struck by his personal elegance and by the flashing brilliance of his staff, such a contrast with the republican austerity they had expected. All this pomp suggested a return to monarchical forms.

Once the French troops were evacuated there was no further excuse for the King to linger in Palermo, but Ferdinand continued to procrastinate. Paget, who had never ceased urging the King's return, was to leave Sicily disillusioned. 'His Sicilian Majesty is totally guided by General Acton, who has throughout shown himself to be a weak and undecided man,' he wrote bitterly, as if it were all Acton's fault; but the King's obstinacy was far more galling to his harassed minister. Paget could console himself with his new appointment as ambassador to Vienna. The Queen wrote in February: 'Acton has gone to Palermo for a fortnight, without his family, having promised to bring the King back to Naples... If he fails I foresee that he will leave, all the more so since he has inherited 90,000 ducats from his cousin Langdale, and his family between £6,000 and £7,000 sterling, besides country-houses, furniture, etc... There will be a crisis, especially if the King does not yield in returning to Naples, in which Acton's honour is involved. He has been much flattered and caressed on this account.' But Acton had another reason for this journey which the Queen did not mention, perhaps because she was unaware of it. According to Giuseppe Torelli's *Memorie Segrete* (attributed by Helfert mistakenly to Baron Cresceri): 'In January 1801, General Acton left suddenly for Palermo after assuring everyone that he would return to Naples, and there it was observed that for several days he never left the King's side even at the theatre, which he was not accustomed to frequent. This time he did not urge him to return, but performed an act of gratitude towards his benefactress. She had drawn a bill of exchange for 60,000 ducats in Vienna and the King, saying that her allowance had been paid, wanted to protest it. Acton never left him until he had given his word to redeem it, and then returned to Naples... If the King had not consented, Don Gennaro Russo, a Neapolitan merchant, had offered to redeem it himself lest it be said abroad that the Neapolitans had suffered the shame of seeing their sovereign's bill of exchange dishonoured.'

As for herself, the Queen would not return until she was called: 'I am waiting for the King to express in writing his desire to see me again, so as not to hear him tell me the next day: "*Chi ti ha chiamato*"—depressing to one who returns with intense repugnance.' But in Vienna she was made to feel that she had outstayed her welcome. Her old protégée the Duchessa Giovane, who had penned so many edifying tracts, such as 'What are the durable means for leading men towards good without external violence?' and 'Ideas upon rendering young men's travels useful to their own culture, and beneficial to society', had turned against her after wheedling her out of large sums of money. She had made trouble between the Queen and her daughter the Empress, who had given her the post of *Oberhofmeisterin* to the little Archduchess Marie Louise, Napoleon's future wife; and she had slandered both the Queen and the Empress in scurrilous letters to Acton and the King. Her treachery was unveiled too late, the mischief had been done. 'I am revolted by the whole of humanity,' exclaimed the Queen. 'My daughter [the Empress] shows her desire for my departure; surely this will force me to leave, even if I die of it... She hates us all, her sisters as well as me, and stirs up her husband against us... I regard her as dead, and all is finished between us.'

Wanted neither in Naples nor in Vienna, and suffering from a painful disease, the Queen wrote on and on, thinking less of her correspondent than of herself. She was hypnotized by Bonaparte. What would he do next? The horror and fascination he exerted on her, the problem of his future, became an obsession: it must have done much to distract her from physical pain. She had fitful gleams of political vision. In March she wrote: 'Either Bonaparte will put a king on the throne of France and will crown himself king of Italy, or his ambition will urge him to control everything. He will not be satisfied before then... He will need to become master of our two kingdoms or at least of Naples which is on the continent. For the present he is satisfied to hold it tributary, but he will raise demands and extravagant claims: a moment of ill-temper, a refusal on our part, may happen when... one is reduced to being the mere agent of a Murat or a Melzi, and then one is lost. That is the depressing, and to my mind definite, prospect I can foresee. England has advised us only to think of saving Sicily... unless the Spanish marriages can save us. They [the Spaniards] are powerless themselves and will be very lucky if they are not the first to be invaded.' After a sermon on prudence and moderation, which proved that she could not practise what she preached, she declared: 'The government should await events in silence... and remain neutral everywhere. That is what we fail to do. We wish to cut a figure, are English in our hearts and affections and French out of fear and discretion, and, despised by both, we shall certainly lose our States.' As this was addressed to Gallo, who had been appointed ambassador to France at Bonaparte's request, it must be taken with a grain of salt; the Queen was something of a chameleon in her correspondence.

Gallo did much to improve relations with Bonaparte, and the double marriage arranged with Spain seemed to denote a change of policy. Bonaparte's aim was to drive the Hapsburgs from Italy and substitute the Spanish Bourbons, whom he had less cause to fear. Drummond, who succeeded Paget as British ambassador, was convinced that the Spanish marriages had been arranged by Alquier, who had formerly been in Madrid. The friendship of Spain was very suspicious, he wrote. The Queen of Spain had written to the Queen of Naples that all branches of the House of Bourbon should be united and, with the assistance of Austria and England, should endeavour to restrain the ambition of France. Godoy had written in the same style. Drummond suspected that this language had not only been permitted but recommended by Lucien Bonaparte: 'I am the more confirmed in this, that an invitation has been sent to their Sicilian Majesties requesting them to go to Spain, and making it a point that the Hereditary Prince should go and reside there until the Infanta, his intended bride, shall be marriageable. You will easily see that this is a manoeuvre to get the Prince into proper training, in case it shall be his fate to ascend the throne.' At the same time he was able to announce, on March 3: 'The Sicilian Parliament is to be assembled on the 8th of this month... as soon as it breaks up the King is to return hither. I am glad that he has been at last persuaded to take this measure, though I much fear he has delayed it too long.'

Alquier was more optimistic: he thought the King's return would improve conditions and stabilize the country. The evacuation of the French troops would relieve the treasury of a heavy burden: already they had cost some twenty-six million francs; the Court of Palermo and the Queen in Vienna had also incurred abnormal expenses. After three years' absence the King rode into the capital on horseback from Portici on June 27. The population, roughly computed at 450,000, was increased by more than 200,000 who had flocked in from the provinces for the occasion. Alquier described the scene with faint irony: 'Fixed stations had been assigned to various groups of officials, where appropriate speeches were to be addressed to the King. But this solemn homage was drowned by the tumultuous acclamations of the mob, who cherish a love for Ferdinand IV of which assuredly this monarch is well worthy. The pomp of his triumphal march was interrupted to such an extent that the King took more than four hours to traverse a distance that usually takes little over half an hour, and the *lazzaroni* would have thrown him from his horse if the transports of their excitement had not been subdued by clubbings. [De Nicola says that the King struck a soldier who tried to drive off a *lazzaro* with the point of his gun.] The diplomatic corps were waiting at the palace, where I was presented by Chevalier Acton. The King's passage was adorned with temples, porticos and triumphal arches, whose inscriptions recalled the wonders of his reign, and everywhere the titles of invincible and peacemaker were attached to his name... I thought I should demand a special audience with the King, to whom I had been presented at a moment when it was impossible to speak to him. It was granted me forthwith. I told him that the First Consul would be very interested to hear of his return to the capital. The King replied: "Much obliged to your Consul." The audience, which lasted nearly half an hour, was devoted to such topics as the heat of the day, the geniality of the *lazzaroni*, and a bath which the King had taken that morning. One is assured that Ferdinand was born with talents which were stifled by a bad education. I left him convinced that his tutors had been grossly remiss.'

The Queen was detained in Vienna by an excruciating operation for hæmorrhoids which she bore stoically. She sent a medical report with what she described as 'two very indecent drawings' to Gallo, adding: 'Only your interest in my health can excuse my sending these to you.' She dreaded returning to Naples, but foresaw that the King would recover from his aversion: 'He will soon be cheerful and contented, brother and comrade with everybody, while I shall suffer more every day.' In one respect, she said, she thought herself superior to the great Bonaparte: she had no fear of death. She would rather live in a suburb of Vienna than in her own beautiful capital. 'But it is a question of fulfilling one's duty.' She would accompany her son and daughter to Barcelona if necessary. While it was gratifying to hear of the King's fervid welcome, she had no desire to share it: 'I should like to arrive in Naples very quietly. Hosannas do not thrill me; they even give me melancholy thoughts; and I have no illusion about deserving triumphal arches.' As the moment of her departure drew near her sighs fell thick and fast. 'I leave as one condemned to death and certainly to torment for the rest of my life... I shall attend the Council; I shall deliver my opinion; but my door will be closed to every class and rank, as I do not wish to be accused of dealing with spies.' From Trieste she wrote of her despair on leaving placid Vienna for the uproar of Italy. 'Already I have a foretaste of it at Trieste, which displeases me chiefly because of its resemblance to Italy, but one must endure one's fate. Unless I had children to marry, no force human or divine would have brought me back.'

There were no manifestations of joy when the Queen returned

on August 17. The contrast between her silent reception and the deafening ovation that had greeted Ferdinand showed that she, the foreigner, was blamed for past calamities. Those who had returned since the amnesty bore her a lasting grudge, and the slanders they spread about her were widely believed. De Nicola noted that in the royal box at the San Carlo she never turned her face to the audience; she did not even come to the front as she used to, 'which greatly disgusted the public'. Inwardly she was hurt, but she was too proud to show it. What would the King have achieved without her? Had she not averted a French conquest? But those who had been amnestied would have preferred the latter.

Since the general peace and the return of the royal family, it was hoped that a period of reconstruction and reconciliation would restore prosperity. Three years' absence had weakened the Queen's influence; ill-health and worry had aged her prematurely, whereas the King was as boisterous as ever. But beneath his rusticity there was a core of shrewdness and common sense. Acton had never tried to be popular with any class, but nobody could deny his practical intelligence. In this respect his enemy Alquier thought more highly of him than his compatriot Paget. 'It is a long time since Chevalier Acton has had no cause to fear the Queen's influence,' he wrote. 'This Minister has doubtless made great mistakes during his long domination, but it is none the less an established fact that today he is the only man capable of controlling the turbulent and repairing the evils caused by a war so foolishly embarked on... I am convinced that it is important to the preservation of this state that Chevalier Acton should continue to wield authority. As absolute ruler of the King's wishes, he does not need to ingratiate himself with or oppose the Heir Presumptive, whose profound nullity saves him from trouble in this connexion.'

But 1799 had left scars which not even time could heal. To illustrate this, Blanch tells of an official party given for the royal family in the Palazzo degli Studii, now the National Museum. 'Everybody had been invited, and nobody failed to attend for fear of being marked as a political suspect. Our impression of that gathering is still fresh. The habitual visitor of a prominent man in time of prosperity who had timorously deserted him in adversity met him and his family again, and there was embarrassment on both sides; but neither could betray their feelings. Those who had been condemned to death and who had returned from island fortresses met the members of the terrible High Court of State, and both felt frustrated because neither had been able to accomplish their aims. The former were still alive and had returned to society; the latter were still powerful and secure. The King looked sad and solemn; he showed clearly that he would not change his direction. Those who had been involved in persecutions or whose families had been implicated had already been excluded from Court; and the conduct of public officials during that period was still under scrutiny. The Queen's manner with the unfortunate was amiable, mingled with an irony often more cutting than silence, while she was effusive with those who had helped to recover the kingdom; and the class to which the latter belonged, even though it was the lowest, did not deprive them of this honour but rather enhanced it. General Acton was cold, hard and polite. The Hereditary Prince aroused such little interest that nobody noticed his attitude. The Princesses were young, and their inclinations were generally known, but owing to their special position they could only show this by their facial expressions, which were sweet and friendly. This party was a mutual reconnaissance, the result of which was that there was nothing to hope for, that everything, inwardly if not outwardly, remained as it had been. Next day the pessimists triumphed over the optimists. What mattered was the Queen's future attitude towards General Acton at the Council, and what the King would do, if these two directors of his policy were to part ways.'

The marriages of the Hereditary Prince and his youngest sister Marie Antoinette were celebrated by proxy soon after the Queen's arrival. The Cardinal Archbishop Ruffo Scilla officiated at the ceremony in the Royal Chapel, where the Hereditary Prince stood proxy for the Prince of Asturias, as the latter had done for his marriage to Maria Isabella in Spain. The public festivities were the same as for the King's return: in front of the amphitheatre on Largo del Castello, modelled on that of Pompeii and packed with spectators in Roman costume, a plaster statue of Discord collapsed and another of Harmony rose in its stead. The Marquis de Mos had been sent as Spanish envoy for the occasion. Alquier described him as worse than mediocre: 'This ambassador, devoid of all dignity and sense of proportion, is already at Chevalier Acton's feet. With such a man the opportunity of recovering Spanish influence at the Court of Naples must be regarded as wasted. It seems to me very probable that Acton will dominate both cabinets in an emergency. This minister, so fertile in ruses and intrigues, will know how to profit from the brotherly effusions in which these two Courts have been wallowing so ludicrously. As for him, he has achieved his purpose: his reconciliation is complete, and he has averted... the only risk his authority had reason to fear during the King's lifetime. Spain overwhelms him with eulogies and caresses, and Charles IV has just bestowed on him the Order of the Golden Fleece.'

Although the Queen had written tactfully to Maria Luisa, her sister-in-law, even condescending to flatter her gross favourite Godoy, now promoted Prince of the Peace, it was impossible for either of these ladies to forget the insults they had formerly exchanged. Maria Carolina never approved of these marriages, and had a premonition that she would not see her beloved Antoinette again. The King had at first been tempted to visit his brother Charles, from whom he had been parted since childhood, but the moment was not propitious for such a journey. Alquier, an accomplished eavesdropper, reported: 'The letters from Aranjuez merely announced great preparations for hunting and fishing and, from all appearances, this solemn reunion would have been more formidable to the wild animals of Spain than to politics. But however insignificant, it would not suit Chevalier Acton. It was inevitable that old quarrels would be explained, and that consequently both monarchs would be enlightened about many facts they had only known dimly before, in which both Queens and Chevalier Acton were so deeply involved that all three are anxious to keep them dark. The minister has therefore clearly demonstrated to the King that the welfare of the state would suffer from his absence. Ferdinand, who is the one person in his kingdom least acquainted with affairs, has yielded to the force of this argument, but to soothe his brother's impatience and regret, he has promised to go to Madrid for his daughter's first lying-in.'

Princess Marie Antoinette, who was ambitious and intelligent and had a natural desire to be married, left Naples without reluctance. Her mother was filled with tragic forebodings. 'I thought the grief would kill me,' she wrote, 'embracing her for the last time in my life... Breakfast, dinner, supper, all made my tears flow. I missed this dear child everywhere and was all the more worried because the weather at sea was bad... I live in retirement at Portici, seeing nobody, reading, drawing, writing, embroidering and playing the harpsichord with my two daughters who share my solitude.' The death of her second daughter, the Grand Duchess of Tuscany, was an additional sorrow. All too soon her suspicions about Antoinette's marriage were confirmed:

'Antoinette is in despair. She left with the most sanguine expectations, but that is all over. Her husband has a hideous face, a frightening voice, and is an utter simpleton. The life there is abominable, like that of five centuries ago.' The Neapolitan ambassador, San Teodoro, who had helped to make this match, ordered the Princess to submit all her letters to her mother-in-law for examination: she was to write home that everything delighted her, everything was perfect; otherwise he would intercept her correspondence. Besides, he summoned all her suite and warned them that they would be dismissed if they told any tales. The poor Princess wrote that she would have preferred a convent: 'I know I shall die of it, but pray God that while this Hell lasts I may resign myself to it in order to reach Heaven.'

Everybody gasped when the Hereditary Prince returned with his child bride, who looked even younger than her fourteen years. The King himself, no stickler for intellectual ability, was amazed by this apparition, 'little, and as round as a ball'; the Queen was startled out of her dejection. There was no satisfaction in repeating: 'I told you so!'—but there was some relief in confiding her impressions to Gallo. 'A fine, fresh, healthy face, not Bourbon in the least, but white and red, with black eyes. She is very stout and sturdy, yet her legs are very short. So much for her exterior. The rest cannot be described because I myself cannot understand it. She is null in every respect, knowledge, ideas, curiosity. Nothing, absolutely nothing. She speaks a little Spanish but neither Italian nor French, and only monosyllables, Yes or No, indiscriminately. She smiles all the time, whether she is pleased or not... Francis's child aged four has far more intelligence. It is incredible. Francis has engaged masters to teach her Italian and the rudiments of geography and arithmetic. She knows nothing except a little piano. I have tried to praise and enliven her. She feels nothing; she merely laughs. It is an automaton which might acquire certain attitudes but never real maturity. Were I the ambitious, intriguing woman I am said to be, I should be enchanted to have such a daughter-in-law who will never become anything, but I am too conscientious for that. I try every means to mould her as a companion for her husband, even if this may turn her against myself. Believe me this child is a tough present, for she will neither ennoble nor improve our race. All the numerous Spanish clique, all their projects and schemes, have received a knock-out blow by the arrival of this Princess and her perfect nullity... My son behaves very well and treats her kindly, but he is revolted, bored and disgusted to the last degree by the Court of Spain, by all he has seen and heard there of crime, triumphant vice, magnificence in appearance but emptiness in reality. What they thought would allure him has alienated him for ever, and the impression will never change as long as he lives. It is to this infamous brothel that I have had the misfortune to sacrifice my daughter, my darling Antoinette. The Prince of Asturias has an ugly face, a tubby figure, round knees and legs, a piping delicate voice, and is utterly stupid. Though he is physically amorous, they are not yet husband and wife after sleeping together a week. He is disagreeable, dull, as lazy as his sister, and he never leaves his wife a single moment. He has no education, an unpleasant continuous giggle; and their existence is cramped, without comforts or amenities, and subjected to scandalous espionage. Poor Antoinette sends letters that make me weep. She writes: "Mother, you have been deceived. For you are too good a mother to have sacrificed me like this if you had known." She says again: "I shall not live, but I wish to behave well and deserve eternal life." The day her brother left, she begged him sobbing: "I beseech you to take me away or kill me." I cannot have a moment's peace knowing my dear child to be so miserable, and I think it monstrous that San Teodoro should have dared to deceive us so. He has been extremely impertinent to my daughter, demanding her obedience and correcting her most impudently. In fact his whole tone, as my son assures me, is enough to make one throw oneself out of the window... I must thank God that I did not go to Barcelona, for I should have brought my children back without concluding the marriages, unable to sacrifice them thus, and all Europe would have cast stones at me.'

If the Queen of the Two Sicilies was shocked by her Spanish daughter-in-law whom she openly called a bastard, since Godoy was reputed to be her father, the Queen of Spain loathed the clever Princess who had married her eldest son. For Marie Antoinette soon gained an ascendancy over her husband. This young couple, both eighteen years of age, were bound together by their hatred of the insatiable Maria Luisa and her arrogant favourite. 'The attachment of these unfortunate young people was the only alleviation they found in a life of constant troubles and vexations,' wrote the Duchesse d'Abrantès, who observed that 'always, when they were together, the Prince followed with his eyes those of the Princess, that he might be guided in what he was to do.' The same French lady went so far as to compare the Princess's personal magnetism with that of Napoleon: 'Hers was the same expression, first grave, then softening, then altogether charming. The Princess was not pretty; some even considered her plain; it is possible. I did not trouble myself about it; to me she appeared pretty and graceful, and I found her so because she desired it.' But the Queen of Spain referred to her daughter-in-law as 'that offscouring of her mother, that poisonous viper, that animal bursting with spleen and venom instead of blood, that diabolical serpent'. And when the Princess died at the age of twenty-three, it was generally believed that she had been poisoned.

XXV

An exchange of courtesies: 'A single branch of olive'—Alquier's missed opportunities—Conversational indiscretions—A pen-portrait of the Queen—The new favourite Saint-Clair—The fall of Zurlo—The French occupation of Puglia—The Queen pleads with Bonaparte—The rise of Medici—Hugh Elliot—'Between Scylla and Charybdis'—The cabal against Acton—The tribulations of Gallo.

Convinced that 'a loyal and genuine understanding' with the First Consul was the best policy for Naples, Gallo recommended that special acts of courtesy, preferably in tangible form, would work wonders. Talleyrand was even more susceptible to such personal attentions. 'Bonaparte sees things on a large scale and makes the decisions,' wrote Gallo, 'but Talleyrand directs him...'

Knowing that the First Consul was partial to rare antiques, Alquier suggested sending him a judicious selection when the three Neapolitan frigates were returned. Forwarding a list of these articles, he wrote: 'I hope the First Consul will be pleased with the choice, and with the care that has been taken to collect for him some of the most valuable pieces found at Herculaneum and Pompeii. Some adorned apartments, others served for war, apparel, sacrifices, and baths; to these have been added various utensils employed by the ancients inside their houses and for daily use. After seeing the arrangement of mosaic pavements and antique frescoes at Portici and Caserta I asked for some examples to be despatched to the First Consul. Those on their way to Paris... would furnish a delightful decoration. The Etruscan vases have been chosen from the finest in the King's possession, but the manuscripts from Herculaneum are certainly the most precious things they could have offered. The King has emphasized their great value by telling me that he had refused to oblige several European sovereigns who had begged him for them, but it is quite simple, he added, to offer such rarities to the First Consul, since he seemed to fancy them. I assured the King that under the auspices of the First Consul we should endeavour to decipher these manuscripts in France, and that if we made some useful discovery we should hasten to communicate it to His Majesty, so that he might avail himself of it to unravel the infinite number of papyri in the Portici museum... I thought I should ask Chevalier Acton what products of French industry would give the King most pleasure. He replied that, in anticipation of this question, he had already consulted the King, who had expressed the keenest desire for rifles and fowling-pieces. The King confirmed this the last time I had the honour of seeing him. He even bade me observe to the First Consul that he always shot with simple guns, and that double-barrelled ones would not serve his purpose. He added: "It was I who chose all the bronzes; the golden toilet articles were chosen by the Queen..." He wants reliable, well-made firearms rather than unique specimens. I beg you to hasten their despatch. Would it not be as well to send the Queen some porcelain? She would appreciate it all the more since that which she formerly received from France was stolen or smashed by the *lazzaroni* when the palace was sacked.'

When the Queen was asked what Bonaparte could send her, she replied: 'A single small branch of olive in token of peace and harmony would be acceptable, but nothing else.' The retort is exquisitely characteristic. Even if it were lost, the delicate irony gave her a glow of satisfaction. In spite of her sorrows her spirit was far from crushed. Since taking leave of the Hamiltons her enthusiasm for England had waned. She resented the high-handed occupation of Malta; above all, she resented Acton's challenge to her authority. During her absence his power had become supreme. 'Acton is the only person who enjoys the King's confidence,' she confessed to Gallo. It was galling to be frustrated by a man whom she had launched on his career, but she had to tread with caution.

Alquier was well informed about the situation. 'The King lives on the worst of terms with the Queen,' he wrote. 'Scarcely had she returned from Vienna when he left alone for Caserta. The sole purpose of his frequent excursions to Portici and other pleasances, is to escape from a woman whose ill-humour has become unbearable to him, and whom age has deprived of all the charms that formerly bound him to her. Their disagreement shows in the coldness and constraint which they do not conceal, even in public. It is certain that the Queen has no influence, and that she is a stranger to all affairs. Her turbulent activity is reduced to miserable intrigues and to directing a very extensive espionage, which has always been her most cherished occupation.'

Was this not an excellent chance for Alquier to try to convert her? From her father, the Duke of Lorraine, she had inherited a few French tastes which even the Revolution had not quenched; especially for French wit and politeness. From Alquier's point of view she was surrounded by the wrong sort of Frenchmen, bickering and scheming *émigrés*, but most of these were venal. At times her admiration for Bonaparte's genius overruled her abhorrence of his other qualities. A subtle psychologist might have exploited her discontent, but Alquier lacked the patience of an inspired ambassador.

Alquier soon changed his mind about Acton. He had been misled by his outward urbanity and French veneer. The Prime Minister was extremely cautious, and he was eager to preserve neutrality. But after several discussions it was plain where his sympathies lay. Malta was a sore point. When Alquier complained of the provisions being sent there, Acton would deny the facts or belittle them. As for the evacuation of that island, it did not seem to interest him. If he conceded that England was wrong, 'it was with all the indulgence of the liveliest affection, or in a tone such as one admits the errors of a friend'. According to De Nicola, when Alquier protested about the murder of a French officer by brigands, Acton replied that this was one of the effects of that liberty which the French had tried to disseminate. Alquier was forced to conclude that as long as the Prime Minister's viziership lasted, and it might last long, Naples would never become attached to France: 'You may depend upon it that in the Sicilian Cabinet Chevalier Acton is only a member of the British Cabinet.' 'What can we expect from the Court of Naples,' he exclaimed, 'when it is directed by a British subject? Everything about Chevalier Acton is English: titles, hopes, speeches and material fortune. His wife has no other title but Milady; he has just put his nephew in the British navy; when he speaks of the British he says *we*; and when, a fortnight since, the King and Queen christened his child in the royal chapel, the British minister and his distinguished compatriots in Naples were the only guests.'

In spite of the Peace of Amiens, Alquier had a fixed obsession from now on: to eliminate Acton. The Queen was itching to get rid of him, too, but for a different motive. If he went, only she could replace him. The King, however reluctantly, would have to turn to her.

With more tact Alquier might have won the Queen's support at this crucial moment. He, the regicide, was astonished by her graciousness. How different from the haughty virago he had dreaded! What a pleasant contrast with the Queen of Spain! She had put herself out to charm him, and she nearly succeeded. He was disconcerted by her candour, her wit, her spontaneity. Though she might be excused for not loving the First Consul, she told him, she would gladly travel hundreds of miles to see him. At least she had one sentiment in common with him—a love of glory. But he had pursued his object on a universal scale and obtained it, whereas she had sought it among the bushes and had only succeeded in pricking her finger-tips. In sending the First Consul her compliments, she wished him to know that she had a boundless admiration for his triumphs when, since the death of Catherine and Frederick the Great, there were only contemptible men on the thrones of Europe.

From Alquier's minute accounts of his discussions with the Queen it is evident that both enjoyed them. The Queen was an avid collector of news; apart from her insatiable curiosity, she was proud of her extensive correspondence. To encourage Alquier she was disarmingly indiscreet. The regicide was undoubtedly flattered by these bursts of royal confidence; he would have been more so, he remarked, if he had not reminded himself that he shared this honour with the chamber-women of the palace. 'I see the Queen often,' he wrote. 'It is in the morning, always *tête-à-tête* in her room, that she grants me these interviews. I never leave without marvelling at all that this extraordinary woman can say in the course of an hour, things agreeable and strange, ingenious and absurd, surprising in their wisdom or their folly.'

In a rambling conversation about Spain, for instance, the Queen told the ambassador that the Hereditary Princess was the daughter of Godoy, whom she resembled in every feature: 'The Queen discussed the Prince of the Peace, whom she calls "the man of vice", after speaking of the King of Spain's blindness, with an affectation all the more singular considering her own experience. "Has this man," she asked, "enough talent to justify the credit he enjoys with his masters?" I replied that I had not stayed long enough in Spain to discover if he deserved the confidence of the King, but that it sufficed me to have seen him to decide he had claims to the kindness of the Queen. Her remarks confirmed the fears of this Court about the plan attributed to the Prince of the

Peace to prevent the heir from succeeding to the throne. "We have been assured," said the Queen, "that he intends the Crown to pass to the youngest Infante, which would be doubly dreadful, for I need not tell you the history of that child. But what do you think should be done, if the King died and that dare-devil carried out his plan?" Much embarrassed, I protested that it seemed to me too criminal and absurd to be credible. But the Queen repeated her question with a persistence which did not allow further evasion. "If they attempted such an act of violence or folly," I said, "I have no doubt that the young King would find all the means at his disposal to frustrate it." "But you are well aware of his incapacity; it would be impossible to get him to take a single step." "In that case, Madam, the young Queen, to whom you have taught history so well, and that of your family in particular, would remember that Queens occasionally mount a horse. She would find examples of firmness and courage in the life of your august mother, which it would then be both glorious and useful for her to imitate." While finishing this conversation, which had gone much further than I had intended it should, I was thanked for what she called my frankness and good advice, and I left firmly convinced that all we had been saying would be repeated, distorted and exaggerated, as usual.'

In January 1803, Alquier prophesied that the Queen would probably recover her former influence. Still he did not attempt to convert her. War seemed to him inevitable, and he was in favour of strong methods. Acton should be removed, and French troops should be marched back into the kingdom. He wrote in March: 'The government would be more compliant, if French troops occupied the capital. It would show lamentable ignorance to rely on the good faith of Neapolitans in any engagement whatever.' At the same time the King and Queen were trying to humour Bonaparte, and Acton took pains to prove his impartiality. Besides the treasures from Pompeii and Herculaneum, the King had sent his favourite musician Paisiello at the First Consul's request. Such an ambassador as Alquier, an embittered Jacobin at heart, was bound to make mischief. He thrived on meddling, and in this respect he had much in common with the Queen. Each pumped the other for information; each had spies among the French *émigrés*; and they were bound to find each other out. Thus of all the pen-portraits of the Queen, Alquier's is perhaps the most incisive: 'The Queen is neither good nor bad. Born with a great deal of intelligence and natural grace, and, thanks to her education, endowed with more knowledge than women usually possess, she had a fair claim to govern, when she came to Naples and found a man on the throne incapable of governing. A relish for pleasure was mingled with a passion to dominate, hence the double intrigues in politics and gallantry; hence also the infinite contradictions which have irritated the most irritable mind that ever was. The Queen's life is a prolonged crisis of vapours, and it is owing to this restless constitution that she has been successively a tender friend or an implacable foe, lenient or vindictive, pious or frivolous, a mistress without restraint and excessively jealous; and that on the same day she is busy intriguing with Vienna, London and Petersburg and prying into the domestic affairs of a Neapolitan burgess. She would have been a perfect Queen if she had limited herself to being a wife and parent, but nature ordained it otherwise... Like her mother, she has brought up her daughters well and lives with them in gentle and touching familiarity. She despises her eldest son, who since childhood has disappointed her with an absolute lack of character, and who humiliates her by his ignoble and puerile tastes. Her generosity has been praised: she is in fact munificent without discretion or measure, and this prodigality has contributed not a little to the ruin of the state. Above all, the wide scope and force of her mind have been commended, and that is an error. Her mind, displaced from the feminine sphere and tormented by an ambition to direct policy, has degenerated into a habit of mischief-making which has always been disastrous to the Queen and the kingdom and sometimes, perhaps, to Europe. The Queen hates us assuredly; how can she fail to hate us? Does not the legitimacy of her resentment justify the animosity she bears us? The necessity to intrigue and interfere worries her still, and will never be extinguished. She spends her days in her study and at her desk, and no minister writes so many letters as the Queen of Naples. But the distance from affairs to which Chevalier Acton has driven her has greatly diminished the importance of this activity, and since she cannot correspond with Cabinets she is busy with café spying. Another taste which has been conspicuous in her life, that of pleasure, has not abandoned her. Commander Ruffo, whom you have met as ambassador in Paris, is obliged to purvey this, and pander to this famous wreck of bygone graces and gallantries... In a private condition she would have produced the same results:

she would have been the delight of a few men, but she would have been the torment of her husband and the terror of the neighbourhood.'

Another source of information Alquier owed to the Queen's recent craze for a French *émigré*, the Marquis de Saint-Clair. According to Comte Roger de Damas, one of the very few friends who were fair to her memory, the Queen had had lovers ever since her marriage, but none had obtained the ultimate favours or won her complete confidence. 'This may sound incredible,' he added, 'but *I am convinced of it.*' It sounds less incredible to modern ears. Considering the Queen's domestic and political anxieties and indifferent health, it is hard to conceive that her passions were more than sentimental. Saint-Clair's cousin Hippolyte d'Espinchal described him in 1800 as a charming young man of twenty-three with perfect manners. A captain of the royal bodyguard and a tutor to Prince Leopold, he was almost half the Queen's age. Damas described him as *un très honnête homme*. Alquier, who could not resist being malicious at the Queen's expense, wrote: 'She is entirely engrossed in her amorous liaison, to which she abandons herself without decency or restraint, and with a delirium that would compromise a giddy girl of twenty. Saint-Clair, the new favourite, excessively preoccupied with his duties, is less than mediocre without ambition or talent. He has not even enough talent to reply to the twenty notes which the Queen scribbles to him every day, unless the Abbé de Saint-Cernin, formerly Grand Vicar of Cahors, takes the trouble to dictate them to him. This abbé is certainly the busiest body in the Two Sicilies. Acting as the confidant of the Queen's favourite and of the King's mistress at the same time, he is the Queen's spy with me, and renders me the same sort of service with her.' Thanks to this abbé, the ambassador got wind of a plot to overthrow Acton in March. 'The whole intrigue is known to me, and too many are mixed up in it to count on its secrecy and success. Nearly all of them are Frenchmen living in Naples under the Queen's protection since the Revolution. I have one of these at my command by sure methods. He has already told me much, and will tell me more... It is imperative that M. de Gallo should have no inkling of this. If he knew one word of it he would write a hundred, and thus ruin two or three worthy people resolved to take a foolish risk which we must wink at, as it might prove helpful to us.' But the plot miscarried, as Alquier foresaw.

In the meantime another minister fell who was difficult to replace. Considering the chaos of the national economy, Giuseppe Zurlo had done uncommonly well as head of the financial administration. 'Zurlo would be a genius anywhere,' said the Queen. 'Here he is a constellation, an eagle without a peer.' And indeed she had cause to be grateful, for he had always found money for her wants. The mere cost of the French occupation had exceeded four million ducats a year, and there had been no retrenchment at Court: the Queen's travels and illness had incurred vast expense, and the royal marriages had helped to deplete the treasury. A bad harvest made matters worse: corn had to be imported from abroad for provincial distribution, and the provisioning of the capital had to be subsidized. The salt tax was increased, the tax on fish restored, salaries and wages were months in arrears; and there was such a general outcry against Zurlo that he hardly dared to venture in public. But he had weathered so many storms in the last three years that in spite of the King's prohibition, he could not resist borrowing in secret from the banks. After a few months he intended to repay the loan as furtively as he had borrowed it, by which time he expected the finances to recover sufficiently to enable him to start reforms. Success depended on secrecy, but with so many enemies a leakage was inevitable.

On March 5, 1803, a royal despatch forbade all secretariats to indulge in further expenditure without the King's permission. This was followed by a frantic run on the banks to withdraw deposits. The banks closed on March 10, and it was rumoured that Zurlo had fallen. He failed to attend the Council of Ministers on the 15th, on the plea of illness. Next day a royal despatch announced his resignation, adding that the Council of Finance, abolished in 1799, would be re-established. Another despatch expressed the King's surprise and regret that without his approval or knowledge there had been arbitrary proceedings in the administration of banks; however he had taken measures to protect them in future against 'the arbitrary orders of any minister'. De Nicola reported that the King was so furious that he wished to have Zurlo whipped through the streets of Naples. 'The Queen, the Princess, and Acton had to calm him, and I was told that he turned upon Acton and said: "You have betrayed me."' While most historians blame Acton and the Queen for sacrificing a scapegoat whose chief fault had been his eagerness to oblige them, De Nicola, who had no axe to grind, makes it plain that Acton tried to shield him from the King's fury. Zurlo had been allowed to move quietly to the country, but the King insisted on his arrest. For the next sixteen months, without any trial, he lingered in the Castello dell' Ovo, until he was released without a stain on his character. The Florentine Francesco Seratti, who was appointed to succeed him, was quite unequal to the situation. He had been Minister of the Royal Household and had little experience of finance. He could only inveigh against the methods of his predecessor, who had had to close an eye to the time-hallowed bribery and corruption that was rife in his department. After three months he resigned in disgust, and for twenty-two days his post was vacant. Neither troops nor government officials were paid, and the banks remained short of currency. At this juncture Bonaparte announced that he was sending French troops to occupy their former garrisons in the kingdom, and that they were to be fed and paid by the Neapolitan government.

Since the Treaty of Amiens, Bonaparte's annexation of Piedmont and Elba, his refusal to evacuate Flushing and Utrecht, and his occupation of Switzerland in defiance of the Treaty of Lunéville, had increased British fears about his future ambitions. Besides other provocations, Colonel Sebastiani's report on Egypt in the *Moniteur*, stating that 6,000 French soldiers would suffice to reconquer that country, induced the British government to declare that they would not evacuate Malta. This led to Bonaparte's historical hysterics with the British ambassador Lord Whitworth and the outbreak of war in May. In a last effort to save the peace the British government undertook to evacuate Malta when the French withdrew from Holland, but Bonaparte would not hear of such terms. On May 31 he notified the Neapolitan government that he would garrison the Puglie, since Great Britain refused to give up Malta. Two weeks later the first French troops marched into the kingdom under the command of General Gouvion Saint-Cyr, and Alquier wrote to Acton: 'Your Excellency knows better than I do, Monsieur le Chevalier, how important it is to the discipline of an army and to public tranquillity in the provinces that wise arrangements be made without delay to ensure the payment, provisions and clothing of the troops, and I flatter myself that Your Excellency will let me know what measures have been determined, so that I may inform Lieutenant-General Saint-Cyr.'

The first measures were letters to Bonaparte from the King and Queen. 'General First Consul,' wrote the Queen, 'it is as a wife, as a fond mother of my children and well-beloved subjects that I write you this letter. I rely on your greatness of character to grant the request of the King, my dear husband. The entry of the French troops in our kingdom, which is at peace with France and follows the rules of the most exact neutrality, ruins us above all with the enormous and unexpected burden of defraying their cost. Our country has suffered too much from war, the subsequent anarchy and the formidable price of peace, and from several years of bad harvest besides, to bear this additional burden. I leave apart all discussion of justice and right, as I have too high an opinion of your intellect not to be certain that you would realize the force of my arguments. I speak as the mother of my children and my people. I ask you to relieve us of this burden of troops in a neutral country, and of the appalling expense of supporting them.' She wound up with a repeated assurance of strict neutrality.

Bonaparte wanted more than neutrality: those who were not for him were against him. He had violated the treaty of Florence, and he expected Naples to be humbly grateful; were not his troops an earnest of friendly protection? And General Saint-Cyr, as Gallo had written, was one of the most honest and upright of French generals, altogether a fortunate choice. As a special favour Bonaparte condescended to pay his troops, except their victuals, forage, quartering and other expenses. At the same time he warned the King to 'distrust everything connected with a nation which has borne so pronounced a hatred against his family through the centuries, and which only regards the Continent as an instrument of odium against France.' Alquier's diatribes against Acton were beginning to bear fruit. Bonaparte's answer to the Queen was more outspoken. 'I beg to convince Your Majesty that after having done you great injury I am now desirous to be agreeable to you. It is the internal policy of France to consolidate peace among all her neighbours; it is her external policy to assist a weaker state, the welfare of which is important to French commerce. But I wish to answer Your Majesty confidentially and without reserve.

'What must I think of the kingdom of Naples in its geographical and political relations, when I see at the head of its entire administration a man who is alien to the country, and who has concentrated in England his wealth and all his affections? In the meantime the kingdom is governed less by the will and principles of its Sovereign than by those of this minister. I have therefore decided as a wise precaution to consider Naples as a country ruled by an English minister. I am loath to meddle in the internal affairs of other states: only sincerity prompts me to tell Your Majesty the true reason which justifies my measures towards Naples, of which you might complain. Yet I wish to convince Your Majesty of the great value I attach to all that tends to restore order and tranquillity to the Continent, and contribute to its happiness.'

Before receiving this reply the Queen filled Europe with her protests. 'It is as if we were assaulted on the public highway,' she wrote to her daughter the Empress. 'This measure is worthy of Robespierre,' she wrote to Gallo. 'I hope that the British will be generous enough not to seize the Sicilian ports. I hope so as Queen of Naples, but in their position I should already take this precaution, and the Corsican despot would complete our ruin... The King is in a furious temper, and I fear for his health and mind and what he will do next. He talks of abdication, flight to Palermo, concealment, war, in rapid succession... Just when we were setting out in grand gala for San Lorenzo to thank God on this anniversary of the kingdom's liberation by the gallant Cardinal, we received despairing news from the Abruzzi announcing the arrival of the French at Pescara, and talking of penury, famine and the impossibility of supplying the French with provisions.' On June 19 she continued: 'The King is overwhelmed by fits of weakness, fear and fury. He has shut himself up at the Belvedere from which he will not move, or decide to do anything. This causes cruel confusion in our affairs.'

The prolonged financial crisis brought Luigi de' Medici out of his temporary shell. His imprisonment during the last days of the Republic had been a windfall. The wags said that he had paid large sums to get himself arrested: the upshot of it was that he came out with what Signor Nicolini has called 'a political virginity'. His sister, the Marchesa di San Marco, wormed her way back into the Queen's good graces, and Zurlo, at the height of his renown, befriended him and initiated him into the mysteries of Neapolitan finance. But his past was hard to kill. That snake in the grass, Annibale Giordano, held another trick in reserve. He and his French colleague Basset, who had both been condemned to death, trumped up a new charge against the ex-Regent of the Vicaria. Having obtained pardons in exchange for revelations, they accused Medici of plotting to gain power under the Republic. Thanks to their whilom intimacy, Giordano embellished the story with details of such deceptive realism that Medici was arrested for the third time and tried by the third *Giunta di Stato*. After a minute inquiry, the alleged plot was proved to be a fabrication. Medici should have been released and his prosecutors punished; but the former was exiled and the latter saved their necks. Of course the vindictive Acton was said to have influenced this verdict; considering the sanguinary reputation of the *Giunta di Stato*, it was mild.

The amnesty of May 30, 1800, enabled Medici to return, a broken and embittered man, according to some, but his ambition burned as brightly as ever. Zurlo's disgrace and Seratti's failure provided him with another chance. He had learned much from Zurlo, and he was always receptive to new ideas. According to Luigi Blanch, he wrote a memorial on the financial situation, proposing various remedies and expedients; its whole tone was refreshingly constructive. His sister handed it to the Queen, who was favourably impressed. The King had told her: 'Do as you please, I do not wish to be driven crazy by these scoundrels.' Knowing his stubborn prejudice against Medici, she had recourse to a feminine ruse. She submitted the unsigned memorial to Acton, feigning ignorance of its origin. Acton was even more impressed; seeing a way out of the wood he exclaimed that its author deserved the vacant ministry. Blanch says that as Acton's yoke weighed heavily on the Queen, she was delighted to divulge that Medici had written it. Acton was thus faced with the alternative of retracting his words or promoting a personal enemy. Without hesitation he adopted the latter course. As often before, the King could not resist the arguments of Acton and the Queen combined, much as he disliked recalling a man he had never trusted, and who had only returned thanks to an amnesty foisted upon him by the French. He refused to grant him the title and rank of minister, so Medici was appointed vice-president of the Council of Finance under the presidency of the Prince of Luzzi. The relative speed with which he restored order to the national economy showed that Zurlo's optimism had some foundation. In the opinion of Piero Pieri, Zurlo had fallen through sheer bad luck when he was about to tide over his worst difficulties. Where he had sown with hard labour, Medici was to reap with ease. His appointment was popular, though De Nicola described it as 'stupendous and almost unexampled' after all he had been through.

Medici's old post of Regent of the Vicaria had been abolished and a superintendent of police was created instead. The choice of the Duke of Ascoli was equally surprising, but it was justified by events. A boon companion of the King, he had spent most of his life in social and sporting pursuits. Yet he proved to be efficient as well as shrewd, and remained on good terms with officials who loathed each other. He was even on good terms with the Queen, who hoped he would subdue Acton's influence on the King. Though he considered this appointment as a harmless royal caprice, Acton treated him with special consideration. Ascoli did much to restore public confidence by letting bygones be bygones. He imposed penalties against the abuse of the term Jacobin, for instance, and those intractable *lazzaroni* who had had their own way since 1799 were curbed by the threat of corporal punishment. His sincerity, fair dealing and genial manners won general praise.

The new British ambassador, Hugh Elliot, arrived on June 18, having sailed with Nelson from Portsmouth to Gibraltar on the *Amphion*, and then transferred to the *Maidstone* with Gaetano Spedilo, who had been Sir William Hamilton's valet for thirty years. Provided with letters from the hero of Aboukir, who was now appointed to the Mediterranean Command, Elliot was welcomed at Court just when the French troops were entering the kingdom. The King shook off his apathy and came from Caserta to give him an audience, repeating with fervour how delighted he was to see Nelson back in the Mediterranean. Then he hurried back to Caserta to avoid meeting General Saint-Cyr. The Queen and the Hereditary Prince entertained Saint-Cyr and his wife at Portici in the King's absence, and Alquier congratulated himself on their flattering reception. 'I had taken great pains to obtain these attentions,' he wrote to Talleyrand, 'to which the Queen was little disposed, amid the vexations of every kind created by the arrival of our troops. But I managed to persuade the Queen how important it was for her to assume all the semblance of goodwill; she promised this, and indeed her behaviour was perfect.' Saint-Cyr did not return these courtesies. At first the conduct of his troops was orderly, but they soon behaved as if they were on conquered territory.

Elliot was more than a match for Alquier, and he promptly took measures to protect Sicily against a French invasion, for as Nelson had written to Acton, if Naples were lost Sicily might still be saved, but if Sicily were lost Naples would suffer the same fate. Acton, who had been resigned, under protest, to the reoccupation of Pescara, Otranto and Taranto, was better able to resist further demands with Elliot's support. He pointed out that the British would occupy Messina if the ports were closed to their ships. But as England was in no position to defend Naples if Saint-Cyr's 13,000 men marched on the capital, Acton urged Nelson not to compromise the government by any abrupt manoeuvre. H.M.S. *Gibraltar* was left in Neapolitan waters to protect Elliot and the royal family in case of emergency. Thus if the French approached Reggio, the British would garrison Messina; conversely, the French would occupy Naples.

'We are steering between Scylla and Charybdis,' Elliot wrote, 'it is as dangerous to do too much as too little.' He made a secret agreement with Acton: the Neapolitan garrison in Malta was to be sent to Sicily; advance information of French movements was to be forwarded speedily to Naples, Malta and Messina by special agents; Calabria was to be rearmed and Sicily put in the best state of defence; gunboats and other small vessels were to be assembled at Messina to prevent a French landing. His rival Alquier proposed an offensive and defensive alliance with France, offering a chunk of the Papal States as a bait. Bonaparte had no money to spare, but he could always be generous with others' possessions. Gallo was tempted to accept this proposal, but he had to walk warily beside Acton. The King made no bones about his opinion. He wrote off to Acton: 'Dear friend, on awakening this morning I received your letter with that from Paris which I send you. The system adopted by us from the beginning [viz. neutrality] has often been explained, here to the French ambassador and there to Gallo. So the French hope to see me join them against the English! I would perish before uttering such a blasphemy. The opposite rather, whatever it may cost us. Truly, we have a fine motive to become the friends and allies of one who declares: You are right, we realize that our course of action is unjust and injurious to you, but it must be so because we wish it. What glory and honour would it be for us to join those who have done us every possible injury against the English who have saved us, and with whose aid we recovered our lost kingdom?' The Queen told Elliot the same: 'I am not English; I am what I should be, Neapolitan. But I recognize too clearly the services rendered to this country by His Britannic Majesty and am too keenly aware of the misfortunes we owe to the French to hesitate a second about the side we should embrace.' And she added that the Hereditary Prince agreed with her. 'As for Gallo, he may be considered simply as one of Bonaparte's conquests,' wrote Elliot, 'but he is too well known here to do us much harm.'

Elliot also parried Bonaparte's blow at Acton. It was an open secret that the Queen had been intriguing against the old minister, whose removal, irrespective of France, would have been a personal triumph. She was looking for a substitute acceptable to England. After receiving Bonaparte's letters she tried to probe Elliot on the subject. He found her more excitable than usual. Whenever Bonaparte's name was mentioned she accompanied it with 'some appropriate epithet'. The British ambassador expressed surprise that Her Majesty should be so angry with the First Consul when he had graciously agreed to bear part of the expenses of his troops in the kingdom. The Queen showed him Bonaparte's letters, which had not been shown to Acton, and asked him point blank what he thought about Acton's removal. 'Who should be put in his place?' she asked, 'Gallo, Castelcicala, Commander Ruffo? For I am much afraid that if General Acton were to see the First Consul's letter he would ask to resign at once.' Elliot required time to consider a question fraught with such serious consequences, and the Queen expatiated on the insolence, perfidy, ambition and other qualities of Bonaparte with incredible heat. She said the King had never been so indignant in his life.

Bonaparte's letters were then shown to Acton, who offered to resign, but the King said he would abdicate rather than part with so devoted a servant. Elliot was far from convinced that Bonaparte's demand was unpalatable to the Queen, who was surrounded by scheming *émigrés*, a title which, as he said, 'no longer denotes any real degree of hostility towards the government of Bonaparte. I must confess that the First Consul cannot make use of any better channel to forward his own purposes than that of French emigrants at foreign courts.' The Queen, he told Lord Hawkesbury, had many talents, an energy and degree of courage above her sex, and qualities which might help her to struggle against difficulties under whose load weaker minds would sink. But in all cases requiring discretion, prudence and composure she needed guidance and control. For her guidance he wrote a long reasoned epistle pointing out how greatly the situation had improved in the last two months, owing to

Acton's foresight and to British support, with Nelson guarding the Mediterranean and a strong force at Malta ready to protect Messina. But the cost of defending Sicily adequately was considerable, and he would have to apply to his government for a subsidy. Appealing to the Queen's common sense, he asked: 'Would I be justified in demanding this aid if General Acton resigned his post to one who succeeded him by Bonaparte's command and whose only aim would be to support French policy?' As an honest man and as a conscientious ambassador, he would not take another step without receiving positive assurance that Bonaparte's insolence would effect no change in Acton's position. 'Only General Acton possesses his Master's confidence. Only he recognizes the sentiments of justice, grandeur and virtue which inspire the counsels of my Sovereign.'

Acton remained high in the saddle, looking down imperturbably at those who strained at the leash. He had seen so many French ambassadors come and go. Alquier would go the way of Mackau and the rest. But this time there was also Saint-Cyr to reckon with. Alquier and Saint-Cyr combined to poison the atmosphere with endless protests, complaints and suspicions. Saint-Cyr broke the customs and health regulations, billeted troops wherever he thought fit, even in hospitals and convents which had been exempted by royal decree, and tolerated all sorts of abuses. Since the Neapolitan fleet had been destroyed and the army reduced to a shadow, it was more difficult than ever to guard against African pirates. Licata in Sicily had been attacked by a Tunisian flotilla. Though the inhabitants had driven the pirates back into the sea, the incident might be repeated elsewhere with impunity. But as soon as Saint-Cyr and Alquier heard of rearmament in Sicily and Calabria they raised such a hue and cry that Bonaparte took notice. He sent word that the Calabrians were to be disarmed before November 20. The King bestirred himself to write to Gallo that the Calabrians had only been ordered to rearm against the pirates—'but if the French think themselves included in that class, they are quite right'. In the province of Lecce 164 people had been kidnapped from their homes by the corsairs; something had to be done against them. If Bonaparte thought him as soft as his brother the King of Spain, he was roundly mistaken: he would not allow anyone to kick him in the face. Let the French mind their own business and leave him in peace. But Bonaparte was adamant: any sort of military activity had to stop.

The Queen also vented her spleen to Gallo: 'The First Consul is mistaken when he always speaks of an English minister. Only the sovereigns are responsible, not the minister, and our sentiment is the result of the good which one nation has done us and the evil wrought by another, an evil which makes us detest it and ensures our sympathies and preferences for the other. Lately, however, the King has tolerated everything for the sake of peace and tranquillity. Indeed, he has shown himself more French than English at heart... It is his sentiments, not the minister, which have inspired his decisions.'

Gallo had become the Aunt Sally of both governments, and he writhed under the battery of complaints which he could never satisfy. He was alone in his wish to appease the First Consul. 'I am the unhappiest of men,' he exclaimed, 'and now this unhappiness has reached a climax, because it has oppressed my mind and health.' Paris was full of exiled Neapolitan 'patriots' plotting against the monarchy. Some of these were also conspiring against the French, but it was difficult to sort them out. Perhaps they were none too clear about their aims, which were confused and often contradictory. Gallo had to keep an eye on them, for if they did not succeed once they would always try again.

The worst thorns in his flesh were the Prince of Moliterno and the widowed Princess of Belmonte. The former was unable to return to Naples after the Treaty of Florence as he had been excluded from the amnesty. A French army colonel on half-pay, he had settled in Paris and gone through a form of civil marriage with an Irishwoman, a Mrs Newman, who had not been able to divorce her husband in England. Mrs Newman helped him financially and introduced him to a set of Irish exiles. The Princess of Belmonte, formerly a monarchist but now a rabid republican in her sixties, had numerous friends in the Ministry of Foreign Affairs and presided over a *salon* of disgruntled Neapolitans. Thanks to those who were playing a double game, Gallo knew that Moliterno was plotting to revive a republican regime in Naples, and that many of the conspirators of 1794-5 were involved, including Melchiorre Delfico and Cesare Paribelli. Moliterno's plan was to start an insurrection with British support and drive out the Bourbons, but he and Mrs Newman, travelling to England under assumed names, were arrested at Calais on their way, taken back to Paris and imprisoned in the Temple. Here they were soon joined by their chief collaborators, the lawyer Fiore and the veteran conspirator Belpulsi, who had served as an officer in the French army for ten years. Some of their agents had also been seized at Calais with compromising papers. But in spite of all his efforts Gallo could never catch a glimpse of these interesting documents: the French police would not co-operate with him, and the trial dragged on for months without result. Moliterno plagued Gallo with appeals to be sent back to Naples for trial as a baron of the realm. Gallo's other torment, the Princess of Belmonte, had retired to Spa. At the end of August 1803, he was amazed to hear that Moliterno and Fiore had been released. The Minister of Justice told him that after a year in prison it was thought humane to send them outside Paris, still under police supervision. This did not satisfy Gallo, who thought his sovereign entitled to greater consideration, since the conspiracy against him had been serious, but Bonaparte regarded it as a joke. Gallo was even more surprised to receive a visit from Moliterno, who still wanted to go home for a fair trial. He said he had been conspiring, not against the King but against the French, to drive them out of Italy with English support. Boasting of his influential connexions, he offered to persevere in this with the King's permission. Gallo tried to extract a written statement from him, but Moliterno refused to fall into the trap.

When Gallo heard of the Lechi conspiracy he suspected it had some connexion with Moliterno. General Lechi, who commanded the Italian division of the French army of occupation, was said to have made overtures to the Neapolitan government for a general rising against the French in Italy. But Acton's readiness to report this made Alquier sceptical. He thought it unlikely that Lechi would take such a risk, even if he was on bad terms with Saint-Cyr. Probably an intrigue had been started by his underlings with or without his knowledge, and Acton wished to exploit this to sow discord in the French army and distract attention from the arming of Calabria. In any case the conspiracy was aired and its agents were watched; Saint-Cyr thought it prudent to shift his Italian troops to Lecce and Otranto. Bonaparte affected to laugh the matter off as 'a miserable Neapolitan intrigue'. Remembering Cardinal Ruffo, however, he threatened to swoop down on Naples if he heard anything more about the arming of Calabrian peasants.

The Queen refused to be daunted. She told Alquier: 'France sees in Naples the Emperor's father-in-law, the brother and the son-in-law of the King of Spain, and the ally of Russia. The First Consul, who has prodigious intelligence and tact, would not care to antagonize so many people in order to crush a paltry power like us.' To Gallo she wrote: 'To reduce Naples to a Parthenopean Republic is to believe in the philosopher's stone. Naples has none of the requisites for a revolutionary republic. Fire and blood and, above all, pillage, yes; but a son never obeys his father or a younger brother his elder; they all hate and envy each other, and are ready to tear each other apart. In my opinion the co-existence of Naples and a Republic is utterly impossible. Hence the distance separating us from France and the fact that they do not know what to do with Naples saves us. For I do not think they will give Naples as a dowry to Madam Pauline and Prince Borghese. We shall be exposed to vexations and threats to extort money from us. I see clearly that you have not repeated half the insults which the Corsican cur permitted himself to utter against Acton... He is mistaken! It is not Acton, but the King, his son, myself—we all detest him and indeed are well paid for doing so; the wretched life he leads us keeps our hatred alive... They are installing the Italian troops at Taranto and Lecce and the French at Barletta, Trani, Bari, to sever communications between the Italians and Italy. Before leaving they remove all the millstones and empty the granaries to deprive us of grain and oil and cause us as much damage as expense.'

XXVI

The Queen's mounting exasperation—Execution of the Duke of Enghien—Alquier's rupture with Acton—Bonaparte becomes Emperor— 'Gloria in Excelsis Demonio'—'The Emperor, your master!'—Elliot's interview with the King—The pinpricks of foreign occupation—Risk rather than self-abasement—Count Roger de Damas—'Dunque la guerra!'—The Queen appeals to Bonaparte.

While the Queen chafed more and more stridently against 'the intolerable burden' of the French occupation, the King went blithely off to the hunt. Onorato, his master of hounds, took infinite pains to keep him amused, and four gentlemen of Palermo, who were excellent shots as well as boon companions, came over to join his expeditions by request. 'Amid heavy taxation and financial distress,' wrote Alquier, 'all is being prepared for the great hunts at Persano, which absorb from three to four hundred thousand francs.' At Persano the King recovered his ebullient youth. 'He forgets everything,' said the Queen, 'and only on his return from there will he grow irritable and desperate again, making others desperate too.' As soon as he stopped hunting he repeated his old refrain: 'I want to go back to Sicily.'

Alquier was more anxious than ever to get rid of Acton. He gloomily reminded Talleyrand: 'I had already warned Your Excellency that the First Consul's letters [to the King and Queen] would produce no effect. The King, delighted to hear that he will not have to pay our troops, has taken little notice of the First Consul's advice. As a mere formality, Chevalier Acton has offered his resignation, which has been refused, and the King will keep him from habit even more than from obstinacy. His confidence is strengthened by the fears this minister has injected in him about the malcontents in the interior and the supposed French plans of invasion, but affection has no part in it. The King loves nobody, not even his own children, as the Queen said to me. This Princess hates Chevalier Acton, who has outraged and defied her, but she has derived no advantage from the First Consul's letter, and she would only raise her voice if France should formally demand the minister's dismissal... If a happy event should overthrow the implacable Acton, the Marquis of Gallo would not replace him: such as you know him he is, to the shame of his country, one of the strongest in the land. But the Queen dislikes and despises him. She cannot forgive his former liaisons and habitual correspondence with one of her women called Bartelli, who informs Acton of her domestic details and whom she dare not dismiss.'

To wear Acton down, Alquier complained to him about trifling incidents. The arrival of a French *émigré*, the reception of an Englishman at Court, a casual remark of the Queen's, the removal of guns to the coast, an order to a provincial garrison or the repair of an old frigate. Two days after Christmas he wrote to Talleyrand: 'The officers of the *Gibraltar*, still in the roads, have just given a ball on board to Milady Acton. The party was very brilliant, very gay, and above all very anti-French. All the *émigrés* in Naples were invited and one of these, the former Comte de Chastellux, was the first to sing "God save the King".' But Acton, he said ruefully, had as great an affection for office as for the English; he was more cautious, more seemingly impartial as a result. He did his utmost to soothe French wrath with gentle answers. What had the First Consul to fear from the Neapolitan army, which barely consisted of eight thousand ill-equipped troops? Naples could not afford more recruits. The marine was pitifully reduced. More ships were needed for trading purposes; and African pirates were a constant menace. The French army monopolized the granary of the kingdom, only a few days' marching distance from the capital; nothing could stop Saint-Cyr if he intended to march. Yet Alquier believed that the Queen and Acton, united in this respect, were impatient to join the coalition against France for a third time: 'It is difficult to conceive that a Power which can hardly be seen on the map of Europe should dare to dream of attacking France. But this improbability is explained by the furious English animosity of Chevalier Acton and the madness of the Queen.' The more levelheaded Saint-Cyr wrote to the French Minister of War: 'I persist in assuring you that you must beware of the Court of Naples. It will throw itself into the arms of the first powerful enemy which declares itself against the Republic, as it is entirely under British influence.'

At the same time the preparations of the French fleet at Toulon dismayed the Queen, who dreaded an attack on Sicily, while Saint-

Cyr's activities seemed to presage an attack on the capital. In February 1804, she wrote to Gallo: 'Despair gives me courage, for I feel that whatever may happen, even death, is preferable to my present life... Our people only need a little *Fiat* from us to massacre all the French... The French treat us, with a few modifications, as a real province, criticizing, asking for an account of every transaction, behaving as a sovereign who still deigns to permit the little vassal to move, but not to set its house in order or do anything constructive.' Encouraged by the news of Russian reinforcements at Corfu, she expressed her impatience with less restraint. She even rallied rhetorically to Acton: 'We must put ourselves in a state of defence and not wait to be devoured... If the First Consul in his plans (whose execution, however, depends on the Supreme Being who directs all things) has decided to annex and subject us like the Cisalpine, Etruria and Rome—I do not mention other Powers and confine myself to Italy—he is mistaken. Ferdinand IV, the oldest of ruling sovereigns, who has reigned for forty-five years, will never, never, never descend to being either a tributary or a prefect of the kingdom of Naples. He will endeavour to avoid this misfortune by every means of peaceful negotiation... I shall write to Russia, Vienna, Spain, everywhere in the same tone, so that the whole of Europe may know our way of thinking... To speak of three frigates and seven thousand troops as armaments, hostilities, threats; to deprive us of our revenue and the control of our provinces; to propose removing our minister, a man of honour whose principles have never varied; in fact, to treat us as the Sultan of Turkey does the Bey of Tunis or Tripoli: I refuse to submit to this... As for the minister they cannot trust, this is a ridiculous pretext. You, Gallo, might be this minister tomorrow, and you would be called more English than Acton. For you would have to obey the wishes of your masters and could oppose them even less than Acton, for whom the King has immense affection, confidence and friendship. If this old minister has failings, it is due to too much pliability. What need was there to excuse ourselves for enlisting necessary recruits, and to render an account of our every transaction at home?... It is for this weakness of Acton's, owing to his fear of compromising us, that I reproach him, but since it springs from an honest principle I can only praise him for it... To be neutral we wish our kingdom to be free from foreign troops.'

Gallo replied on March 19, imploring the Queen to be more

discreet in her letters, many of which had been intercepted. Vast sums were being spent on espionage, and all the *émigrés* with whom she consorted were closely watched: 'Everything arouses suspicion, everything is taken in the most sinister sense... I feel utterly discouraged and desperate because, doing and suffering all that is humanly possible in the royal service, I see that it is a waste of time, trouble and devotion. I can obtain nothing on one side; on the other I must always be the harbinger of bitterness, hardness and injustice. Consequently I must always be disagreeable and unhappy... Ill-humour and distrust are evident here on every occasion. As soon as one difficulty is overcome, another crops up... They always think they divine our *hidden views*. Besides, I cannot find facts, arguments and reasons enough to defeat their first impressions. Much time, care and method has to be employed to calm their minds... I cannot sufficiently beg Your Majesty to be infinitely reserved in your correspondence... I have definite information of reports coming here that Your Majesty has been treating with several Courts, writing letters and making proposals in your name to excite the Coalition and war on the Continent against France.' Did Gallo realize that Alquier contrived to see most of his correspondence? In any case, he did not have to worry: from the French point of view it was innocuous. Self-pity was its keynote.

Sometimes Alquier thought it desirable for the Queen to recover her influence. Even a hysterical and capricious virago would be easier to cope with than the crusty old Englishman. Much as she detested the Revolution, she held no brief for the French Bourbons.

Time and her natural inconstancy might weaken her private and political grudges; she might even detach herself from the English. The attraction of Saint-Clair, Damas, and other *émigrés* suggested that she was drawn to the French by temperament. But again Alquier changed his mind: it seemed impossible to convert her 'in her country's interest, to a system whose necessity had been demonstrated a thousand times, and always in vain'. So far as decorum allowed, he tried to steer conversation towards special topics, when it had a certain charm. Her anecdotes, for instance, were often worth retaining. Discussing the Court of Vienna, the Queen told him: 'The First Consul probably does not realize to what an extent his fame has subjected the Emperor. You may judge this from an incident during my last visit to Germany. We were having a family dinner at Schönbrunn, the Emperor, the Empress, my three other daughters and I. They had much to say about the Consul and I did not agree with the majority. Francis replied: "Whatever you may say, Mother, if Bonaparte asked to marry my daughter, I would give her to him." "What, you would do that?" "Certainly," he said in the most affirmative tone, "and if he offered me this proposal tomorrow I would undoubtedly accept it."' The Queen must have known that this would instantly be repeated to Bonaparte. The date of Alquier's letter to Talleyrand is worth noting—March 27, 1804. Neither he nor the Queen could have attached much significance to the Emperor's remark. Evidently the First Consul did. The anecdote must have sunk into his mind like a pebble in a pool whose ripples continued to widen. The sequel is all the more curious considering the Queen's avowed horror of the 'Corsican brigand'. Six years later he was to marry her granddaughter, the Archduchess Marie Louise.

On March 21 the Duc d'Enghien was shot. Alquier wrote to Talleyrand: 'The judgment and death of the Duc d'Enghien have made a profound impression on this Court, but this salutary example has excited more astonishment than sorrow... I am sure that the Queen remarked: "I used to know the poor devil. He was the only one of the French Princes who had courage and a superior mind. All the rest are cowards. However, I find some consolation in the hope that this will injure the Consul."' What the Queen actually said to Gallo was: 'The Enghien affair is a dark stain on the First Consul's glory. He has violated the law he had sworn to... he has violated human rights. Once that is done, appetite grows with eating, and he will do it more often... But at present who can be called safe? Nobody.'

In Paris, Talleyrand continued to tilt at Gallo about the grave disadvantage of a man devoted to England presiding over the councils of Naples; in Naples, Alquier continued to fire volleys at the Queen and at the minister himself. To Acton he read aloud the animadversions of Talleyrand: 'He listened with concentrated rage, and replied with a dignity which it cost him a great effort to assume and preserve: "Very well, sir; it is clear that Acton is the object of all your distrust and that he must resign: he will do so." I retorted that he knew as well as I did what the King's interest and that of the state required. His resignation was offered next day and, as might have been expected, it was rejected by the King, with the hysterical outbursts of violence to which he gives way at the slightest contradiction. He ended this scene by declaring that he would abdicate rather than accept his resignation or demand it. Next day I saw Chevalier Acton who, reassured by the invincible obstinacy of his master, seemed perfectly calm and as little determined as ever to withdraw from affairs.

'The Queen, to whom I presented myself a few days later, spoke with affected indifference of Acton's resignation and the King's resistance. But her usual rashness and impropriety returned when the Marquis of Gallo was mentioned: "If Chevalier Acton's resignation were finally accepted, Gallo would be summoned and it is with him that you would have to deal. I hate and despise him more than you could believe. Under his grand airs he covers the petty intrigues and wretched ruses which are habitual with him. Fundamentally he is slippery, grovelling and vile, like any Neapolitan. A charming Minister of Foreign Affairs for bowing and scraping, but careless and vacant in matters of consequence. If he returns I shall have the pleasure of seeing him behave like a valet as usual. A man of honour would have fallen dead under the table, after what I have heard the King say to him twenty times at the Council. But he dared to laugh about it when the session was over and went off gaily to spend the rest of the evening at the theatre. In spite of my opinion of him, he would probably be a convenient minister if I wished to exert my influence on affairs. Realizing that he would need my support with the King, who loathes and distrusts him and never mentions him without the appellations of *Birbone, Birbante, Infame*, he will do whatever I wish, and lick the dust of my antechambers..."' 'The Queen is surely the only sovereign in Europe capable of so disparaging a man she may have to put at the head of the government tomorrow. But this was not all she had to tell me: I had to listen to six mortal pages of her extravagant reply to Gallo, who had informed her that the First Consul was aware of her correspondence with various Courts and Ministries...' This led her to protest that the whole affair had been absurdly exaggerated. Doubtless the Austrian foreign minister Cobenzl had been making mischief at her expense: he could not forgive her contempt. But Alquier contradicted her brazenly, quoting chapter and verse. Such interviews were deeply mortifying to the daughter of Maria Theresa. When the ambassador told Talleyrand that 'her aversion to us amounts to frenzy', one is scarcely surprised.

The atmosphere was overcharged with electricity. It was evident, as the Queen said, that Alquier had an order in his pocket to provoke a final rupture with Acton. In his effort to maintain a precarious balance the old minister's temper was badly frayed by the Queen's intrigues on the one hand and Alquier's accusations on the other. His discussions with the French ambassador became more violent. 'What are the English ships doing here?' asked Alquier. 'What are the French troops doing? This is an obvious aggression,' Acton replied. Alquier then protested against the English capture of a French ship in Neapolitan waters. 'That is no concern of ours,' Acton answered. He knew that Alquier was prone to exceed his instructions. Now he was accused of allowing British agents to recruit Neapolitan soldiers for Malta. To satisfy Alquier, he promised to complain about this to London and investigate the local agents. The ambassador remarked that these measures seemed infinitely mild, and that they would have been more prompt and severe if a Frenchman were caught enlisting a single Neapolitan. No doubt his account of the final explosion was prejudiced, but on this occasion he had the advantage of keeping his temper when he had purposely goaded Acton to exasperation. 'The Minister retorted with extreme vehemence that he was doing what he had to do; that all this was no concern of France but of the Court of Naples; that the ambassador had no right to interfere; that it was true that the English had taken several of the King's subjects but it was false that they were recruited; that he knew nothing about their having formed regiments of deserters at Malta and did not believe it; nevertheless, he added, you will take it, Mr Ambassador, as you please. To these inconceivable arguments and to the improper remark I have just quoted, I rejoined with the utmost moderation that I was greatly shocked that the King's Minister should permit himself such language with the French Ambassador... Acton repeated part of what he had said previously, with a violence almost amounting to mental aberration, and with so intolerable an indecency of tone and phraseology that to end this scandalous scene I declared in the most positive manner that I would cease to deal with him.' According to the Queen, Acton's last word was that this was just what he wished. She wished it herself, but though she had long been prepared for it, she was stunned by the event.

Acton resigned again; again the infuriated King threatened to leave for Sicily or abdicate, and with great difficulty the Queen persuaded him to accept a compromise—since Bonaparte threatened to declare war unless Acton left the capital before his special messenger arrived. Antonio Micheroux, the unfortunate negotiator of the Treaty of Florence, would be appointed provisional Minister of Foreign Affairs with the Prince of Luzzi as his counsellor. Acton would retire to Palermo with an annual pension of about £6,000 and the valuable fief of Modica near Syracuse. But all reports on important matters of policy would continue to be sent to him, so that in fact Luzzi and Micheroux were no more than his under-secretaries. The King hoped that 'his best friend' would return in the autumn. But as Talleyrand remarked, it would be difficult for Acton to retain the same influence in Sicily: time and distance would make him seem less necessary. Elliot regarded his presence as the best safeguard of British interests, and said that his departure was irreparable from that point of view.

The Queen wrote to Gallo on May 27 with ill-concealed relief: 'The King's ministry is composed of conciliators, people devoted to France. Let this consequently be the moment to recall her entire army and leave us to enjoy our neutrality... You will have heard that the King has yielded to the repeated requests of the upright and worthy General Acton to retire and look after his health. I cannot deny that his departure was extremely painful to me, but it was necessary. He took away his wife and children, and as he left on the evening of May 24, I hope he has safely arrived. The loyal and honest party, the great majority, regret him for his impartiality and justice.' In a sort of obituary notice to Talleyrand, Alquier observed that the Queen had gone several times to Acton's residence during the two days before he sailed. 'The public supposed this to be a tribute of respect and affection, but the fact is that the Queen wished to recover from her old favourite the private letters she had written him, which he only surrendered with the greatest difficulty.'

While gloating over his partial victory, the ambassador could not predict any change of policy. His rupture with Acton had severed most of his social ties, and he found himself cold-shouldered. For twenty-five years Acton had held all the reins, and his omnipotence at Naples had become proverbial. Though never popular, he was feared and respected. 'Always a minister and never a man,' as Blanch put it, 'he lived aloof, and never climbed any stair but that of the royal palace.' It was felt that he might suddenly return and climb that stair again. Alquier considered Micheroux as even less than a subordinate clerk of Acton's. He was to find that Acton had exerted a moderating influence on both the sovereigns. The Queen presided over the Council during the King's frequent absence. At first she had held back with calculated modesty. But she had to yield to his almost unanswerable argument: 'You know very well that I have not time enough.' So the Secretaries of State made their reports to the Queen, who agreed to have half an hour's session with the King every Monday wherever he happened to be. Often this wearisome formality entailed long journeys to distant hunting lodges. Without Acton to restrain her, the Queen followed a hectic zig-zag between Alquier and Elliot, while the King let things slide. Micheroux had to admit to Acton: 'The machine does not run in your absence.'

When Bonaparte became Emperor of the French on May 20 the substitution of a monarchy for a republic seemed a possible improvement. Micheroux sent Gallo his new credentials, and the King was induced to send the new Emperor a letter of congratulation. But while Napoleon replied with empty compliments, he did nothing to withdraw the ruinous army of occupation. Gallo wrote in his usual gloomy strain though he must have been comforted by Acton's retirement: 'I have no longer the strength to believe in affairs. Morally I am too sensitive, physically too delicate. I count twenty-six years of toil and trouble, and the latter six or seven would have sufficed to exhaust and disgust any man. The last would have killed an ox... At present the First Consul wishes the Pope to consecrate and crown him. It is rather extraordinary, rather difficult, but if he really wishes it the Pope will come. If he wishes all Europe to come and hold the stirrup and bridle of his horse, all will obey. What a singular epoch we are living in!'

Utterly disregarding Gallo's pleas for discretion, the Queen sent him a long philippic against the upstart on June 6 from Portici: 'It was not worth the trouble to condemn and slaughter the best of kings, dishonour and revile a woman, a daughter of Maria Theresa, a holy princess, to wallow in massacres, shootings, drownings, and kill six hundred prelates in a church, perpetrating horrors of the most barbarous ages at home and abroad, writing whole libraries on liberty, happiness, etc., and at the end of fourteen years become the abject slaves of a little Corsican whom an incredible fortune enabled to exploit all means to succeed, marrying without honour or decency the cast-off strumpet of whom the murderer Barras was surfeited, Turkish or Mohammedan in Egypt, atheist at the start, dragging the Pope after him and letting him die in prison, a devout

Catholic after that, practising every deceit, shortening the lives and normal careers of sovereigns who might assert themselves, only allowing the dummies to vegetate, then atrociously, without a shadow of justice, assassinating the Duc d'Enghien, plotting himself (and he did not blush to admit it, so blinded is he by passion) a conspiracy to victimize the rulers he still feared, and on top of all these abominations he is acclaimed as Emperor: he and his race of Corsican bastards are to dominate almost half Europe, yet every thinking person is not revolted. Far from it, their egoism and weakness are such that they study how low they can prostrate themselves before the new idol... Send me word of the august Emperor's intentions regarding Italy: whether he will deign to accept us as his slaves or will leave us in our obscurity... Tell me what the other Powers are saying. I imagine a *Gloria in Excelsis Demonio* will be the general refrain...

'We do not belong to any Coalition and have no desire to belong. Besides, we lack the means and even more the will. But little as we wish to enter a Coalition, we will not tolerate being wholly subjugated and provincialized... Our two kingdoms have so many resources and natural riches, that well-administered they could be self-sufficient. My sole aim and desire is to leave our children their patrimony, and our son the kingdoms as we received them.

'The King is always at Belvedere. He comes here occasionally for a few minutes. At other times I go there, which is very trying in the awful heat and dust. We are entirely separated and have to write each other everything... The King has not, and cannot have, the slightest confidence in Micheroux. I have none at all, and for several reasons: stupidity and lack of principles. For me this is an added torment. I did not oppose his appointment, still believing that Acton would remain at the head of affairs. But without Acton, Micheroux cannot have our confidence, and the good Luzzi is a paste which can assume every shape... The Prince attends Councils in his father's absence, and I only attend them on the King's account... The King dislikes the city and Portici, which bore him, and longs for solitude, as he cannot adapt or subject himself to the supremacy of the French, and be ordered about by them or Bonaparte. He only sighs for Sicily, which he prefers, as he has never been offended and insulted there. In fact he is in a state of fury which depresses me. He is very determined not to receive Alquier's credentials but to let his son represent him... because he declares he would have convulsions or a stroke, which would kill him. In fact it is beyond belief, the rage consuming him and the effort required to procure his consent to General Acton's retirement. I hope they will finally be pacified on this subject without demanding his expulsion from Sicily, for I assure you that the King would never agree to it... We have heard that General Acton arrived at Palermo on the 31st [May]. He received an ovation, and the Sicilians say: "A man persecuted by France must be incorruptible."'

Eventually the King was persuaded to grant Alquier an audience. But the Queen was embarrassed by the insertion of the words 'Ally and Confederate' in Napoleon's letter, beside the conventional titles of brother and beloved cousin. 'This is an honour which we do not deserve and cannot explain,' said the Queen to Gallo. 'It would be more correct to use the word *oppressed*. For the troops unjustly quartered on us, who are billeted at our expense and are ruining us, would not have been sent by an *ally* or a *confederate*... I hope this is not a pretext to pick a quarrel with us. For the title will certainly not be returned.'

The Queen's embarrassment was nothing beside that of the ardent republican who had voted for his King's execution, when he had to present his credentials as an Emperor's ambassador. Maria Carolina took advantage of this to taunt him by repeating several times with ironical emphasis 'The Emperor, *your master*,' in her reply to his speech. The King's reply was concise but ambiguous. He merely said: 'You will assure the Emperor of the French that my sentiments towards him will never change.'

Elliot was far from pleased by the undignified haste of this recognition. He wished to know where he stood in Acton's absence. Acton wrote from Palermo that he still directed every department of the administration, but the Queen maintained that his position was honorary: at his advanced age he was incapable of sustained effort; he was losing his memory and grip of affairs. Most of the Queen's French friends were hostile to England as well as to Acton, if not spies in the pay of the French ambassador. Though the Queen assured Elliot that her attitude towards England was the same, he wished to guard against unpleasant surprises. Brushing precedent aside, he approached the King directly, and he was dazzled by the result. The King appeared in a new light altogether—or had he been hiding the old light under a bushel? Elliot was impressed by what he called 'a masterly *exposé*' of the motives dictating the King's conduct since the French occupation. He declared that he had never heard more moving eloquence than this recital of the circumstances, alas too frequent, in which the King had been forced to sacrifice his most ardent sentiments to the welfare of his people. As a King, a Bourbon, a Christian and a man of honour, he abhorred French ideas and the murderers of his cousin, especially the impious usurper of his throne. But as the protector of the lives and fortunes of his subjects, he could sacrifice neither in an unequal struggle if this could be avoided by prudence and foresight. Hence his reluctant consent to Acton's departure. Bonaparte had skilfully selected this bone of contention because he knew that the King would be blamed by his subjects if they were driven into war on the minister's account. Rather than wait for an ultimatum, he preferred to let his minister retire with dignity, but to prove that his policy was unchanged, he sent Acton all the despatches from England and Russia by special messenger, instructing him to answer them. 'I should be very grieved,' he said, 'if I thought the British government required a safer guarantee of good faith than Ferdinand's word of honour. Rest assured that, however negligent I may be in other respects, I shall always preside in person over the distribution of the subsidies furnished to a friend by your brave and generous nation.' If a crisis compelled him to mobilize, however, he would have to ask for an increased subsidy, to defend his dominions and co-operate effectively with the Great Powers. In all secret and confidential matters he urged Elliot to address himself solely to the Queen, as the only person in Naples he could trust. Thus ended what Elliot described as the most remarkable conference he had ever taken part in; he said he was overcome with surprise and admiration by this unexpected display of the King's character and consummate ability. But it was a flash in a pan. The King returned to his open-air pastimes, leaving the Queen to wrestle with airless politics. Although she groaned, this was really what she enjoyed.

Assiduous at the Council board, she was anxious to hear and know everything, and she tried to do much too much at the same time. It was doubtless a mistake for her to deal personally with foreign ambassadors. But the Queen could not resist the temptation to pull the strings herself. She needed an outlet for her flights of fancy and, as Blanch remarked, she wished to impress even her enemies as a person of exceptional spirit who was not to be confused with the common run of rulers. Thus while many pitied her for having to be polite to the regicide ambassador, she seemed to take a perverse pleasure in his company and often saw him of her own free will. On these occasions, as Alquier reported, she was apt to broach intimate topics in a most unconventional manner. She would have avoided many a slip by seeing less of Alquier and Elliot, each of whom goaded her against the other. Alquier was the more aggressive; nothing could be done to increase the army or improve its conditions without rousing his strenuous opposition, backed by Saint-Cyr and threats from Bonaparte.

The French troops in Puglia were a heavy drain on finances, and Medici just managed to keep his head above water. Reforms were out of the question: all the government could do was to prevent things from deteriorating. This was not easy when Saint-Cyr seized Austrian and Spanish ships laden with corn to relieve the famine in Sicily and cheated the Customs of its import and export dues so that there was an enormous monthly deficit. To aggravate such pin pricks, a Neapolitan called Giuseppe Di Paolo was accused of inciting Cisalpine soldiers to desert. After a summary court-martial he was sentenced on the strength of a single witness of doubtful integrity, since he was probably a deserter himself. General Saint-Cyr ordered him to be shot, in spite of the intervention of Marchese di Rodio, the Royal Commissioner, who begged him to postpone the execution. After a minute investigation, a royal despatch was sent to Gallo, demanding satisfaction for this 'monstrous abuse of authority'. Far from respecting the neutrality of Naples, France had 'violated her treaties and trampled on all principles of justice'. But Gallo could not even obtain a mild moral satisfaction.

As an extra twist of the knife 8,000 more troops were sent to increase the French garrison at Taranto. These should be welcomed as precious auxiliaries, said Napoleon. The Queen wrote to Gallo: 'I give you my word of honour, my sacred word, that we would remain thoroughly neutral, would admit neither the Russians nor the British, and even, if necessary albeit with regret, would purchase our peace: but on condition that we are delivered from these troops.' In October she offered to pay an indemnity of 100,000 ducats a month until the end of the war if France evacuated the kingdom. In November she offered to close the ports to all belligerent powers and sign a treaty like Portugal, which had purchased her neutrality from France in 1803. But nothing less than a declaration of war against England would satisfy Napoleon, and he refused.

Thanks to Serracapriola, the Neapolitan ambassador in St Petersburg, the Russians had sent considerable reinforcements to Corfu. When Alquier inquired about their destination, the Queen said she did not know: her position *vis-à-vis* the Russians was the same as *vis-à-vis* the French. But it was obvious where her preference lay, for the Russian envoy de Karpoff was a general favourite at Court.

If Bonaparte would not allow her to be neutral, why should she not join England and Russia? The Queen preferred dangerous risk to self-abasement; the King preferred Sicily. 'One does not let oneself be crushed without a murmur,' she wrote to Gallo. 'The King had decided to leave immediately after the Princess's delivery, but my tears and entreaties have made him renounce this plan. Nevertheless, he is prepared to leave at the first move of this scum to avoid falling into their clutches... I admit that things look much blacker to me than in 1798. They intend to grab Gaeta and Naples, but they will not succeed without copious bloodshed. We are firmly resolved. Abandoned by all, betrayed as we are, we shall fall gloriously, adding fresh victims to the long list of those sacrificed to Bonaparte's ambition. We shall arm the people, rouse the masses, and do all that can be done... My dear children make my heart bleed. But when I think that they might become exiles, beggars and outlaws, I tell myself: Better to fall with honour for their sakes...' 'Never believe,' she wrote again, 'that we shall become France's ally ...We shall employ all our tact to win Alquier with words and money, to which he is not inaccessible, to gain time and avoid a rupture. But we shall never declare war on the English, our one and only resource against French violence.' She even proposed that Gallo should bribe Talleyrand, having heard that he was very susceptible to bribes.

General de Damas was standing in the background, waiting to be summoned. He had been absent three years, and in the previous December the Queen had asked Alquier if he would mind his recall. Alquier replied that France would attach little importance to the arrival of Damas, but he left it to Her Majesty 'to consider if it were not wise to avoid all measures suggestive of rearmament'. Acton had never liked Damas, but in his last conversation with the

Queen he had recommended him as the best person to reorganize the army. She summoned him now, and the King appointed him Inspector-General of his forces. Alquier still raised no objection, but he demanded a written assurance that there would be no recruiting or replacing of troops.

An epidemic which had broken out at Leghorn gave Damas a chance to mobilize on the sly by ordering a sanitary cordon to guard the frontier. Alquier's suspicions were soon rattled. He declared that he preferred the plague to the precautions against it, and would leave the country unless the cordon were disbanded. The Court prevaricated; the health of the population was said to be in danger, etc., but Saint-Cyr also began to clamour for Damas's dismissal. Alquier could feel safe from the plague as everybody shunned him, said Damas. His objection to the sanitary cordon was insurmountable, so it had to be dissolved. At the same time, however, the King sent a secret proclamation to all the provincial governors to mobilize the masses if the French crossed their boundary line. Though the secret was kept, nothing could lull the ambassador's suspicions. As he lived opposite the Villa Reale gardens, part of which was used as a drill-ground, he was constantly nettled by the sight of soldiers and the noise of their firing practice. He became neurotic about the subject.

The Tsar looked upon the occupation of Taranto as a step towards the annexation of southern Italy and more ambitious designs on Turkey and the Far East. His chargé d'affaires in Paris had protested against this occupation. Since Talleyrand turned a deaf ear, an Austro-Russian treaty was signed in November agreeing to help Naples if she were attacked by France. This emboldened the Queen to resist Alquier' s demands. Their meetings grew more tempestuous. The ambassador reported on November 23: 'I was informed some time ago that the Queen, who required me to arrange in advance the day and hour to visit her, in accordance with Court regulations, had granted the British minister the right to see her without any preliminaries. Since then I decided to break off relations with her. On being told the reason of my estrangement, the Queen bade the Prince of Luzzi write that I was free to go to her apartments whenever I wished, and that she even dispensed me from appearing in Court uniform. I did not think fit to profit from so tardy a return for the lack of respect I had suffered... A ruse which I could not anticipate obliged me to see the Queen a few days ago, to my deep regret. I went to Portici to confer with the Prince of Luzzi, when an usher at the door of the Secretariat announced that the Prince was expecting me in his apartment. A man in the King's livery offered to guide me through the corridors of the palace, but instead of taking me to the Prince of Luzzi he led me to a chamber where I met the Queen. She spoke of the offences she had given me, but soon realizing how little I thought of this justification she went on to speak of my discussions with her minister about the infringement of neutrality, and declared that the King had authorized her to hear me on the subject in the presence of the Hereditary Prince and Luzzi. Both were summoned and I repeated what I had said at previous interviews. The Hereditary Prince made sensible comments in a very proper tone, but it is impossible to recount all the Queen's absurdities and improprieties. From this flood of inconceivable folly I shall only quote one remark as worthy of record. "You will not prevent us from hoping," she said, "that Russia will continue to press France to rid us of her troops." I replied that perhaps this hope was too lightly conceived, that His Imperial Majesty was disposed to do everything for the King but would never concede anything to a Power which tried to use pressure, and that Her Majesty would be wiser to renounce all mediation on the subject. "You assure me then that he will not defer to the very serious demands of Russia?" she continued. "Ah, so much the better! You make me happy, you enchant me!" Then turning to her son, she cheerfully exclaimed: "*Dunque la guerra!*" ("Then it is to be war!"). I was the first to break off this conversation and remarked to Luzzi as he was showing me out: "I beg you tell the Queen, sir, that it is merely owing to my respect for the Prince Royal that I did not give her the retort she deserved. Furthermore, that I shall never visit her again as long as I live, unless I am commanded to do so by my Court.'"

Besides the dismissal of Damas, Alquier now insisted on the banishment of Elliot and the reduction of the army to 10,000 men. To banish Elliot would be to declare war on Great Britain, which was out of the question. The Queen was determined not to lose Damas without a struggle. She took up the cudgels with passionate intensity. Alquier had shed the last vestiges of diplomatic urbanity; he had become 'a furious viper, poisoning everything, thinking that this would lead to his advancement'. 'Alquier is a tiger,' wrote the Queen in December, 'everything provokes him... He has even said that he regretted Acton, which I had foreseen. For he had expected to domineer, and he has found out his great mistake... The King's repugnance to living in Naples makes anything seem less bad which will carry him to Sicily. Francis is a worthy man but thoroughly disgusted, prematurely aged, and dreading the prospect of inheriting the crown, having seen too clearly the trials in store for him... In this century it is unfortunate to have been born with a heart and soul.'

The ambassador's resolve not to see the Queen was soon broken, though their encounters had ceased to give either the faintest pleasure. Besides Damas, Alquier wished to exclude all foreigners from the Neapolitan service. Only natives were to be employed or, as the Queen said, 'those whose corruption, cowardice and vile inertia have been proved'. He went so far as to mock the King's alarms: 'He said in the most outrageous manner that he was surprised that the King had not yet run away. I said that the King had no thought of it but it was excusable to feel some alarm. He has suffered too much and his memories are too bitter. Besides, it is not for the ambassador of one sovereign to disparage other sovereigns. He said France would take the country the moment she desired to, that we are only here on sufferance and would be driven out as soon as we gave annoyance. You must grant that however true these are not agreeable things to listen to.'

On the other hand, Alquier wrote to Talleyrand: 'The Queen, more wild than ever, is incapable of listening to reason. Her madness is at its height since she is no longer restrained by the imperious authority of Chevalier Acton. She will not even hear her ministers: their wise resolutions and Gallo's conciliating advice are opposed by the strange orders emanating from the Queen's cabinet.' He attributed this to Elliot's incessant warnings of invasion and Damas' rodomontades, as well as to the ruffianly guerilla leaders admitted to confer with her in private. 'This Court is the dregs of Europe,' he exclaimed, 'what a torment is my life here!'

Despairing of any satisfacton from the French ambassador, the Queen appealed to Bonaparte directly. She also sent the suave Prince of Cardito to placate Saint-Cyr about 'the so-called armaments which the malice of Alquier has exaggerated'. Saint-Cyr was polite and reasonable; all depended on Napoleon's reply.

XXVII

Napoleon's reply and the Queen's vindication—The Damas controversy; Damas obliged to leave—Mme de Staël visits the Queen—Napoleon King of Italy—A calculated explosion—Delayed credentials—Two Russian generals arrive in Naples—Alquier apes his master—Spanish intrigues—An earthquake—The expulsion of Prince Scherbatoff—A secret treaty with Russia—Gallo's treaty of neutrality with France—French evacuation of Puglia—Ulm—Trafalgar—The return of Damas—The departure of Alquier and landing of the Anglo-Russians.

Napoleon replied to the Queen on January 2, 1805: 'Madam, Your Majesty's letter has been delivered to me by the Marquis of Gallo. It is difficult for me to reconcile the sentiments it contains with the hostile projects which appear to be nourished at Naples. I have in my possession several of Your Majesty's letters, which leave no doubt as to your real secret intentions. However great Your Majesty's hatred of France, how is it possible, after all your experiences, that the love of your husband, children, family and subjects does not counsel a little more prudence and a policy more compatible with your interests? Cannot Your Majesty, whose mind is so distinguished among women, cast off the prejudices of your sex? Must you treat affairs of state like affairs of the heart? You have already lost your kingdom once: twice you have caused a war which has nearly ruined your father's family. Do you wish to cause a third? At the request of your ambassador at St Petersburg, ten thousand Russians have already been sent to Corfu. What! Is your hatred so fresh and your love of England so exalted, that you wish, although certain to be the first victim, to set the whole Continent ablaze and thus procure a diversion in favour of England? I confess that passions so powerful would earn some portion of my esteem if plain reason did not show their frivolity and impotence. Your nephew, the Emperor of Austria, does not share your sentiments and has no desire to renew the conflict, which would produce results detrimental to his empire. Russia herself, whom your ambassador has induced to send ten thousand men to Corfu, is well aware that this is no way to make war on France, and the temperament of Alexander is not warlike. But supposing that the calamities of your family and the collapse of your throne should cause Russia and Austria to arm, how can Your Majesty, since you have so good an opinion of me, think that I would remain so torpid as to submit to my neighbours? May Your Majesty listen to this prophecy, and hear it without impatience: the moment you cause war to break out you and your family will cease to reign, and your children will wander all over Europe begging assistance from their relations. By such inexplicable conduct Your Majesty will have ruined your family, whereas Providence and my moderation would have preserved you. Can you thus renounce one of the most beautiful kingdoms in the world? I should be sorry, however, if Your Majesty mistook my frankness for a threat. No, if I had planned to wage war on the King of Naples I should have done so on the first appearance of the Russians in Corfu. A cautious policy might have required this, but I wish for peace with Naples, with all Europe, even with England, and I fear war with nobody. I am ready to wage it against whoever provokes me, and to punish the Court of Naples, without fearing the resentment of anyone. Let Your Majesty take this advice from a kind brother: recall the leaders of your militia, abstain from any kind of mobilization, banish the Frenchmen who excite your anger against their country, recall from St Petersburg a minister whose every step is calculated to injure the affairs of Naples and lead her into imminent danger, expel Mr Elliot, who only frames plots for assassination and encourages the subversive element in Naples. Let Your Majesty confide in the head of your family and, I venture to say, in myself; and avoid doing yourself such harm as to lose a kingdom which you have preserved amid so mighty an upheaval, in which so many states have perished. I do not pay court to Your Majesty in this letter: it will not be agreeable to read. May you perceive in it, however, a proof of my esteem. It is only to a person of strong and superior mind that I should take the trouble to write with so much frankness.'

Fortunately the Queen did not read this in Alquier's presence. She crumpled the letter in her hand, threw it on the floor, and paced the room like a caged lioness in hysterics. Finally she retired to bed for twenty-four hours with a burning fever.

When she forwarded the letter to Elliot, lamenting that she had ever made overtures to Bonaparte, he replied: 'The first feeling of a gentleman on reading such a letter, addressed to a princess, wife of a sovereign, daughter of Maria Theresa, must be a strong desire to inflict personal chastisement on the writer. The arm and not the pen would give the fittest answer.'

Damas endeavoured to placate her. He pointed out that just as Bonaparte's power was due to his military strength, his epistolary style was due to his education; she should forget it until she could retaliate. He persuaded her to conceal her indignation from Alquier. Her own letter to Bonaparte had been courteous and dignified; how could cordial relations be maintained when he dictated what ministers and generals she ought to employ? But Talleyrand wrote to the ambassador: 'The Neapolitan government's persistence in protecting M. de Damas is a veritable offence.' And Talleyrand was Damas's cousin.

Alquier continued to heap coals on the fire. He sent another note demanding the dismissal of Damas as an enemy of France who, by his past and present behaviour, betrayed his wish to renew the conflict. The Queen expostulated that Damas had left France three years before the outbreak of revolution and that he had entered the King's service from the Russian, so these objections did not apply to him. Regarding Alquier as the arch mischief-maker, she proposed to negotiate with Bonaparte directly in future. Without letting her pen run away with her, she replied to Bonaparte point by point, explaining everything but yielding nothing.

First she let off steam to Gallo: 'You will never imagine the rage and despair which the extremely insolent screed of the scoundrelly but too lucky Corsican has caused me. I wished to leave everything on the spur of the moment, to retire, and being a woman, unable to avenge myself on the villain, renounce the world and government for ever. My few old friends and my children all wept and beseeched me not to let myself be offended by so infamous a creature. In fact they said so much, and in so many ways, that with the aid of religion they calmed me and induced me to write this letter which cost me infinite strain. But one must appease the lion to pare his claws... This stubborn persecution of Damas is assuredly his greatest certificate of honour... It proves his talents and above all his incorruptibility. In brief I have never had so high an opinion of General Damas as on this occasion.' On the same date, January 25, 1805, she addressed Napoleon as follows: 'Your Imperial Majesty's letter was delivered to me by Mr Ambassador Alquier. The frankness with which you express yourself regarding the grievances you attribute to me inspires me to reply with equal frankness.... Your

Majesty alleges that you hold proofs of my hatred against France. I do not remember having written anything to substantiate this. If Your Majesty would entrust these papers to your ambassador, and they are authentic, I could explain the phrases which might be misinterpreted. Your Majesty must not ascribe to a monarchical government in France the hatred I might have expressed and have never concealed for the republican government, whose atrocities, spoliations, instability, weak foundations and devastating principles were only an object of fear and constant mistrust to all Powers within reach. Your Majesty cannot take this ill, since you were the first to recognize its numerous disadvantages, and replace the defective government by one better adapted to France. The King, my husband, requested the Court of St Petersburg to intercede with that of Paris through our ambassador, in order to be delivered from the painful burden of French troops in our states, since we are neutral by every treaty and absolute strangers to the discussions between France and England. Consequently, in all justice, we do not deserve to be victims of the disputes between these two Powers.

'Your Majesty must have received evidence from M. de Gallo that the troops at Corfu did not come on our account... I am too attached to my duties as a wife, queen and mother to wish to start a war whose futility I have long recognized, and which I should regard as the greatest calamity to our subjects and children.

'Your Majesty is perhaps not prepossessed in my favour, but I like to flatter myself that you respect me. This would not be the case if callously, and without resentment, I had looked on at the misfortunes of a revolution which has touched me so closely even in my next of kin. My heart was broken by this revolution, but I have long felt that it was my duty as a Queen to stifle too cruel memories and if a few linger, I dare tell Your Majesty that it is for you to help me forget them by your justice and moderation.

'Let not Your Majesty construe as exalted attachment my desire to remain on good terms with England. This Power has never given us cause for complaint; on the contrary, she has always respected our neutrality, even when the return of the French troops might have given her a plausible pretext to violate it... Is it not essential to our welfare to maintain this harmony, since our extensive coasts, fisheries, transport of provisions from the provinces, on which the capital depends, would otherwise be lost?

'Your Majesty has been misinformed about our so-called mustering of troops, which only consisted of a few militia, whose sole purpose was to stop the contagion from Leghorn... As soon as the epidemic subsided we gave orders to raise the sanitary cordon.

'Your Majesty speaks of Frenchmen who inflame me against their country. Perhaps you refer to M. de Damas; the notes of M. de Talleyrand and M. Alquier support this conjecture. I must assure Your Majesty that you have false reports about this officer, whose loyalty and moderation deserve your esteem. This general left France long before the horrors of the Revolution and served in Russia, from which he passed into our service before the war. Appreciating his honesty and loyalty, the King, my husband, has newly appointed him Inspector General... to reorganize the few insufficient troops he still retains, which were about to melt away for lack of an efficient and reliable commander. After this candid explanation I hope Your Majesty will not insist on a demand so very distressing. As to Mr Elliot, we shall have to negotiate with England on the subject, under the law of nations, as a public man accredited to us.

'I think I have replied in detail to all the questions raised in Your Majesty's letter. I should like you to believe the assurances I have pleasure in renewing, that I only wish to be at peace with France... Let Your Majesty be persuaded, therefore, that you will ever find the King my husband and me both frank and faithful, as we ever hope to find you; and for this reason I propose to correspond with you directly on all major affairs, if it could be arranged, avoiding the delays and misunderstandings which are often caused by the mistakes of ministers.

'I shall not speak to Your Majesty about the continued occupation of our states by the troops, and of the latter's increase, relying on your sense of justice and professions of friendship for the King my husband.'

The Prince of Cardito was sent to Saint-Cyr with a friendly letter from the Queen repeating the same arguments. 'I hope,' she added, 'that the false, insidious and exaggerated reports of the ambassador Alquier will not disturb our peace and harmony.' By negotiating with the general instead of the ambassador she hoped to widen the breach between them. Saint-Cyr wished to avoid hostilities at the heel of the peninsula when France was about to fight a formidable coalition. Again he received Cardito politely, and said he would wait for the Emperor's decision.

Napoleon's second reply to the Queen was less violent but

equally firm. 'Is it so difficult to keep quiet?' he exclaimed, like a spider to a fly struggling to escape from its web. Damas must go: otherwise Saint-Cyr was to march on Naples. At the same time Napoleon warned Saint-Cyr not to trust the Queen. 'I possess letters from this woman,' he wrote, 'in which she says she would have the 15,000 French troops massacred, but for fear of those who might follow.'

The Queen was giving a concert for the Electoral Prince of Bavaria when Saint-Cyr's ultimatum arrived. Unless Damas were gone within three days and Elliot prepared to leave, Saint-Cyr would advance on the capital. Upon hearing this from Micheroux, the Queen turned pale and said to the Hereditary Prince: 'The French are marching.' The Prince whispered the news to his sisters, and all were dismayed by the worried expressions of the royal family. Soon the concert broke up. The Queen told Damas to mobilize secretly the same night. Damas went home and summoned the colonels of the garrison, who were given verbal instructions; orders that might create alarm at that hour were postponed till the morrow. He visited the Queen at daybreak and found her determined to defend Naples. The small and inadequate Neapolitan army was mobilized on the second day. But the majority in the State Council did not consider it worth while to plunge the country into war for the sake of Damas. The Queen appealed to their honour: would not the whole population unite against the invader? But Micheroux had previously promised Alquier that Damas would go, and after a stormy debate the King and Queen were persuaded to yield. Nothing could be done about Elliot, for that would mean war with England. The same day Damas had a long coversation with the King at a ball given for Prince Leopold. The King spoke with great bitterness of his humiliating position and told Damas that he could still serve him usefully in Messina, to co-ordinate with the Russians for his eventual liberation. Before sailing on March 12, Damas was loaded with gifts and honours, whose incredible prodigality, wrote Alquier, could only be explained by the Queen's desire to distinguish a man objectionable to France. Besides a stipend of 60,000 francs, the Grand Order of Saint Ferdinand was bestowed on him, which gave him the privileges of a grandee of Spain of the first class, so that he could remain covered in the King's presence. The Queen announced his departure to Napoleon in a letter throbbing with wounded dignity: 'I admit that we were deeply pained to have to lose this officer.' Alquier wrote to Talleyrand: 'I hope that the most important business that His Imperial Majesty may charge me to negotiate will never give me as much difficulty and disgust as this one.'

When the Damas controversy was at its height another enemy of Napoleon, the bold and brilliant Madame de Staël, appeared at Naples. Although he had banished her from France, Napoleon had recommended her to official circles in Italy as a celebrity worthy of attention. To his brother Joseph he wrote jestingly that if the Queen of Naples clapped her in prison he was to lead 20,000 troops to her rescue. But the Queen was curious to meet this newest of new women in spite of political differences. The two ladies were temperamentally akin: they had the same sort of exuberance, the same volubility and passion for intrigue. Napoleon described Madame de Staël as 'a restless intriguer with a mania for writing *about* everything and *of* nothing'; the Queen also shared this mania. They seemed predestined to meet, but it was Alquier, oddly enough, who acted as go between. Considering the tension between him and the Court, the ambassador behaved in this case with striking impartiality. Moreover, Madame de Staël was on friendly terms with his adversary Elliot, and introduced one of his adventures into *Corinne*. Oswald, the hero, sees a man struggling in the waves of a stormy sea, and after vain attempts to induce any of the *lazzaroni* bystanders to go to his assistance, plunges into the sea himself and succeeds in swimming ashore with the drowning man; but not until his own strength was so exhausted that he was at first believed to be dying. Madame de Staël adds in a footnote that this feat was performed by Elliot. The Queen sent for him at the time to express her admiration for this humane action, and a number of sonnets were composed to commemorate it.

According to Luigi Blanch, when Alquier told Madame de Staël that the Queen was eager to receive her, she said she would rather not meet the woman who had instigated the persecutions of 1799. But Alquier assured her that she would find the Queen's conversation both interesting and agreeable, and would certainly change her mind about her. Alquier judged correctly, for the Queen was most amiable and Madame de Staël amused her with spicy anecdotes about the Corsican despot. No doubt both ladies dramatized themselves. The Queen spoke fatalistically about recent events: she and her reputation had been the sport of circumstance; if she had erred, it had not been with malice prepense. 'The damage is done,' she said, 'and is irreparable. Between ourselves and the country, we have done each other such mutual harm that confidence has vanished. Whichever tried to propitiate the other would not be believed. On the contrary, each would suspect hidden treachery under a benevolent appearance.' The impulsive author of *Corinne*—she who had said, 'I understand everything which deserves to be understood: what I do not understand is nothing,'—was able to understand and even sympathize with the Queen's predicament.

A very different author, Augustus von Kotzebue, now more famous for his murder than for his writings, says that he arrived at Naples with strong prejudices against the Queen, but that he left it 'convinced of her amiable manners and disposition'. After seeing her at this time he wrote: 'I am certain that the Queen always acted for the best... The Queen is a most tender and affectionate mother to her children: this maternal heart is also a royal heart; nothing but the worst usage is capable of hardening it against the people, or of blunting its sensibility. "To make the people happy," said she to me, "we are often obliged, though against our inclinations, to act the despot; and if we do, we are not beloved." I expressed my opinion that this was not always the case, and as an example I mentioned Maria Theresa. "Oh!" replied she, "my mother was nevertheless unhappy towards the conclusion of her life; for the ungrateful people universally wished her death. And why? On account of a paltry impost." Of the illusions of royalty she speaks with an amiable candour and sincerity, which excite irresistible prepossessions in her favour. She longs for the period when general tranquillity shall allow her to resign the burthen of public affairs, and to withdraw, with her husband, into solitude. "Then," said she, "then it will be seen who was attached to Maria Carolina, and who merely paid their court to the Queen." Assuredly those who have the happiness to be near her, and to hear her often speak in this manner, must be attached to her. "The highest felicity on earth is the happiness of being a mother," said she to my wife, who expected shortly to enjoy it. "I have had seventeen living children; they were my only joy. Nature made me a mother; the queen is only a gala-dress, which I put off and on." At these words she took her dress between two fingers, and loosed it again almost with an air of contempt. "He who possesses an independence," said she, with an emphasis that was not affected, "is far more happy than the prince on his throne." It would be improper to repeat all that she said concerning the present times, the Jesuits, etc. All, however, manifested an enlightened mind; and a heart, filled, indeed, with acrimony, but excellent at the bottom. She is accused of falsehood and artifice; but I really doubt whether it is possible so grossly to deceive one whose principal employment has for thirty years been the observation of mankind. What she said to me, she both thought and felt; nobody shall ever persuade me of the contrary.

'... The reciprocal behaviour of the children to the mother, and the mother to the children, which I had an opportunity of observing, is so tender, so unaffected, as to inspire the bosom of the stranger with the most agreeable sentiments. It is likewise a commendable trait in the character of the Queen, that she is still so strongly attached to her native land. On entering her ante-chamber you hear nothing but German, and honest German faces everywhere smile upon you. The Queen receives every week from Vienna a written account of all occurrences remarkable or not in that city. She calls it her chronicle of lies, but has suffered it to be sent for thirty years without countermanding it.'

The sovereigns were still smarting from Damas's expulsion when they heard that Napoleon had decided to crown himself King of Italy. The threat inherent in this title was direct, whatever Talleyrand might say. In spite of their weakness, the King and Queen demanded an explanation. Napoleon was infuriated by their audacity. He had gone so far as to tell Gallo that he would withdraw some of the troops from Puglia as soon as he felt he could rely on the Court's 'friendship and sincerity'. He had recalled the odious General Lechi. And instead of giving Gallo his new credentials the Court sent him a note expressing the King's surprise and alarm at 'the vague generic title of King of Italy assumed by the Emperor'. Gallo had preceded Napoleon to Milan; he was now ordered to leave unless he was provided with a written explanation. A few days later he was ordered to stay on and delay recognition until Austria had made a decision; he might try in the meantime to obtain permission to bring the Neapolitan army up to full strength and thus safeguard the kingdom's neutrality. But as Gallo was too Francophile for the Queen, she thought of sending the Prince of Cardito as an extraordinary envoy, which only complicated matters.

Napoleon continued to ask why the ambassador's credentials

had failed to arrive, and this drop of gall in the ocean of his triumph enraged him more and more. Besides, the Queen had snubbed him. 'I must come to terms with that woman,' he had told a confidant before leaving Paris; and the remark had been intended for repetition. He also made pointed inquiries about the Queen's daughters and said he had heard a flattering account of Princess Amélie, since he wished to find a suitable wife for his stepson Eugène Beauharnais, whom he had chosen as his viceroy. Seizing what seemed to him a fine opportunity to save the Two Sicilies, Gallo wrote to the Queen about it. So deeply had he fallen under Napoleon's spell that he supposed she would be gratified by such a connexion. The Queen answered with a sarcastic diatribe on the family and pretensions of the Corsican parvenu. From Gallo's awkward silence Napoleon inferred that his suggestion had been scorned, and he was visibly embarrassed. Gallo was even more so. Yet he stood his ground, pleading for new instructions from his Court on the one hand and for an elucidation of Napoleon's new title on the other. Talleyrand said curtly that the assurances he had already given him were sufficient; where were his new credentials? Napoleon's temper was not improved by news of Russian reinforcements at Corfu and British at Malta. Their Majesties of Naples still demurred to his new title unless he evacuated their kingdom, so that Gallo was relieved when the Prince of Cardito came to take over his mission: he himself would attend the coronation in a private capacity.

Cardito was informed that Napoleon would only see him on the first day of public audience. When he remarked that his King still wanted the assurances previously applied for, Talleyrand said it was doubtful whether the Emperor would accept his credentials. Both Gallo and Cardito attended the grand ceremony in Milan Cathedral on May 26, when Napoleon placed the iron crown of Lombardy on his own head. On June 2 Cardito was at last received with all the other ambassadors. After a few gracious words to Gallo, Napoleon treated Cardito to a contemptuous harangue. He had intended to produce one of the Queen's intercepted letters and read it aloud, but as this had been mislaid he repeated its contents in Italian, making several slips which sounded ambiguous and roused much laughter in the Italians present. Cardito nearly fainted. The British ship at anchor in the bay would not prevent the Queen from being dethroned, said Napoleon, adding a volley of crude epithets which were expurgated in the official reports. Apparently he called her a Lesbian as well as the worst Messalina of the age. Pointing at the Duke of Monteleone, who had been exiled for political reasons, he said it was a rotten government which compelled such distinguished men to live abroad. When General Pino introduced his Italian staff, Napoleon declared: 'I count upon these gentlemen for the expedition to Naples.'

But Cardito had not yet drained the cup of humiliation. Next day Talleyrand repeated the substance of Napoleon's speech, criticizing the pro-English and Russian trend of Neapolitan policy and their strange lack of consideration in sending a new envoy without credentials. Within a fortnight the Emperor would be in Bologna; unless the credentials were presented to him there he would sever relations with Naples. Cardito went to Florence to await further instructions while Gallo remained in Milan to patch things up. Owing to the pitiful failure of Cardito's mission, Gallo was left to cope with the angry despot. As Micheroux was dying the Prince of Luzzi replaced him as provisional Minister for Foreign Affairs, while Marchese di Circello was recalled from London to succeed him. Luzzi was a muffled echo of the Queen, and his bewildering orders and counter-orders reflected her changes of mind. When the new credentials were despatched to Gallo after further procrastination, he was told to present them as late as possible and obtain beforehand a written assurance about the title and the evacuation of Puglia. He presented them on June 23, almost a month after the coronation, and had to listen to another tirade and more threats which he was enjoined to repeat to his sovereigns. Cardito's return to Naples with a verbal account of his reception gave the Queen another attack of fever. 'Cardito has returned exactly in the state of mind you predicted,' she wrote to Elliot, 'dazzled by the strength, the greatness of Bonaparte, finding him detestable, but finding no remedy, no means of conquering him. In short, he has returned more Neapolitan than he set out. Poor people! They must be saved in spite of themselves.' She could not resist a sarcastic comment on Napoleon's new order of the Iron Crown: 'Josephine has also created an order—a star which is worn on the bosom. I give her this motto for it. "Evil be to him who does *not* think evil of it."'

The Queen was convinced that Napoleon would attack Naples at the first favourable opportunity. England and Russia had agreed to defend the kingdom, and two Russian generals, Lacy and Oppermann, had arrived in May to study the military situation on the spot. Besides consulting Austria, the Queen had asked General Lacy if she could count on Russian co-operation in case Napoleon started hostilities. The General replied that he could do nothing yet; Malta was still waiting for reinforcements and the number of English ships available was limited; he advised her not to be too precipitate. This explains the delay over Gallo's credentials. After Napoleon's public outburst to Cardito she wrote to Gallo: 'The scene would have been indecent if a genuine sovereign had made it. From Napoleon Bonaparte it does not cause astonishment, scandal or offence... Cardito was so appalled that he said he would infinitely rather go to prison than accept another mission to the French, especially to Napoleon.'

Alquier returned to Naples on July 6, and modelled his behaviour on that of his master. Having heard of the Russian generals and rumours of rearmament, he threatened an immediate invasion. During his first interview with the Queen, he used such coarse language that, as Damas said, it was impossible to doubt that he had received orders to insult her. 'The Queen was so taken aback that she did not know what to answer; she could only burst into tears and repeat with convulsive gestures: "And who sends me such dreadful messages? A Bonaparte! Who does he choose for his mouthpiece? An Alquier, an Alquier!" The monster himself was alarmed by the Queen's condition...' When the King heard about it, he wished to throw the ambassador into the sea, renounce everything and sail to Sicily.

The Queen, having borne the full brunt of Alquier's attack, now had to pacify her raving husband. She made an effort to save appearances for fear of immediate reprisals. As usual she unburdened herself to Gallo about 'the last infamous interview with Alquier who, with his eye to the Senate, treated me as the last of beings, shouting arrogantly like a mad desperado the same compliments as you and Cardito were regaled with by Napoleon. The regicide Alquier shouted these in my cabinet, to the daughter of Maria Theresa! Having promised the King and all the ministers that I would be patient and conciliatory, I had to bear with this insolence for three hours without uttering a single sarcasm, or replying as I could have done. In a word, having suffered, repressed myself and submitted to all this, I felt so humiliated that after shedding torrents of tears I spat blood and had six days of bilious fever, two with attacks of giddiness, so that I can hardly drag myself about.

Also I have decided, not to please your Corsican but to please myself, to prolong my life by leaving this dog of a trade... At the end of the month I shall go to the country with my three children, and will write no more business letters or talk to any foreign minister. The King will do what he can and as he wishes, as if I were dead, which I soon will be, unless I make this decision.'

Micheroux died, and Acton's absence was regretted more and more. Blanch, who held no brief for him, wrote: 'His withdrawal from affairs at this time was as fatal as his presence had been formerly.' Alquier himself told Blanch: 'I worked hard to get rid of General Acton, and the Queen encouraged me. I was the first to repent it. I did not think he had great talents but he had great strength of character, and having convinced everybody of this he was obeyed. Even though he was an enemy of France, when he had agreed to anything one was sure that it would be done. When he left, a regulator was missing: each pulled the cord in a different direction and the cart was overturned.'

Circello had become Foreign Minister in spite of French objections to his supposed pro-English leanings; a courteous old gentleman, he always agreed with the Queen. The unpopular Castelcicala remained ambassador in London. The Duke of San Teodoro (the name is also given as Santa Teodora) returned from Spain as a result of a Court intrigue which froze relations between the two countries. Godoy, having failed to ingratiate himself with the Princess of the Asturias, devised a plot to discredit her, abetted by his doting mistress the Queen. He circulated a rumour that she was having a love affair with a young Neapolitan bodyguard, and that her loss of health was due to an adulterous pregnancy. The Neapolitan ambassadress and her ladies-in-waiting were accused of complicity and expelled from Spain, as well as the bodyguard, who was so ill that he was suspected of having been poisoned. The Queen and Godoy exploited the foolish King's credulity and his son's jealousy, but the latter was untouched by the scandal. The Princess, already consumptive, was also said to have been poisoned; at any rate, her health deteriorated as a result of this persecution. Her mother, who had hated this marriage, was deeply upset, since there was nothing she could do to help her. She could only try to console the other victims of the plot, upon whom she lavished kindnesses.

The Queen was still in Naples on July 26, when a violent earthquake shook the city. The day had been oppressively hot and overcast, followed by a gale after sunset. The first shock, accompanied by a loud rumbling, threw the Queen off a sofa. Prince Leopold and his sisters ran into her room half dressed, and all waited under an arch while the walls seemed about to collapse. When the shocks subsided they spent the night in a carriage outside the palace. Everybody escaped into the open air, so that casualties in Naples were few though many buildings were damaged. The worst havoc was caused at Molise, where some forty villages were destroyed and six thousand people were killed. 'With all the evils overwhelming us,' wrote the Queen, 'I did not count on an earthquake... One comfort in this misfortune was the good order that reigned at a moment when 500,000 inhabitants were stricken with terror and bewilderment. There was no robbery or violence or the slightest misdemeanour, and this does credit to the vigilance of the Duke of Ascoli.'

While the King was hunting, the Queen had to stay on in Naples during the torrid summer. Exhausted by so many trials and tribulations, she went to Castellammare to recuperate, but she was incapable of relaxing. She wrote to Damas twice a week, often in cipher, consulting him about every question raised by the Russian generals, who were very fussy and exacting. Serracapriola had painted too rosy a picture of the Neapolitan army; they had expected to find 24,000 troops of the line, whereas they barely found 12,000. They were satisfied with the cavalry and artillery, however, and had a favourable impression of the garrison at Capua whose manoeuvres they had watched. This had been used as a training centre by Damas. The first Russian plan had been to allot 30,000 troops to the defence of the kingdom without any British support, but it was eventually arranged that the British forces at Malta were to join the Russians under the supreme command of General Lacy. All this was kept secret in spite of Alquier's spies and Elliot's indiscretion. Damas, who suspected British designs on Sicily, relates in his *Memoirs* that Elliot was none too pleased with this secrecy. 'Lacy being of Irish origin, was flattered to be treated as a compatriot of the British minister and allowed himself to be influenced by him in many ways, but he never divulged his mission, however much Elliot tried to coax him. Both generals visited him, but they asked him not to mention their rank. Elliot paid no attention to this and one day when he was holding a large reception he introduced Oppermann to the whole party as General Oppermann, to the great surprise of his guests. The Russian was shocked and kept Elliot at a distance in future.'

There were several rifts in the allies' lute. Elliot had little confidence in Damas and tried to have the Prince of Hesse-Philippsthal, whose sister had married Acton's brother Joseph, the Marshal, or General Bourcard, appointed to command the Neapolitan forces, but Lacy refused to do anything unless Damas were given the command, and the King agreed with him. A more serious rift was caused by the Queen when she was on the worst of terms with the French. This was typical of her impetuous temper. Prince Scherbatoff, who had killed the Chevalier de Saxe in a duel two years before, arrived in Naples under an assumed name. As the Chevalier had been related to the King and was a great favourite with the Queen, it was tactless of Scherbatoff to come. On hearing of his arrival the Queen sent him word that his visit was unwelcome, but he stayed on. As a result he was suddenly arrested in his bedroom at night and escorted across the frontier. The Russian chargé d'affaires, Karpoff, protested vigorously. Receiving no reply, he broke off diplomatic relations. Elliot championed him and blamed the mischievous suggestions of designing French *émigrés* working on 'the Queen's unhappy sensibility'. Medici exploited the incident to prove the Queen's impartiality. The King knew nothing about it until some time after it had taken place. As Alquier was in Milan at the time, the Queen remarked humorously to Lefebvre, his chargé d'affaires: 'Nobody will believe this in Milan, where they suppose we are on our knees before the English and Russians.' To complicate matters, an English man-of-war, the *Excellent*, which was stationed at Naples, had sailed to Baia to exercise her crew, and the Queen supposed this was to give a Russian ship of the line, also anchored off Naples, a chance to seize the Neapolitan frigate *Archimede*, as an act of retaliation. She sent orders to all Neapolitan ships to be on guard, and the *Archimede* was prepared for action, supported by another frigate. Elliot hastened to reassure the Queen, whom he found 'in a state of unnatural excitement' which culminated in a violent attack of fever. The rift with Russia continued until the new minister Tatistcheff arrived in mid-July and harmony was restored. Negotiations were immediately started to renew the treaty of alliance of 1798. In the meantime Gallo continued to promise the strictest neutrality if the French would withdraw their army of occupation. Napoleon seemed inclined to listen to him, as the troops would be more useful in the north. The Queen interpreted this as a hint of imminent invasion, so she hastened to sign a secret treaty with Tatistcheff on September 10, which was chiefly to Russia's advantage. The King was to oppose any extension or reinforcement of the French occupation: if this led to hostilities the Tsar would send a force sufficiently large to liberate the kingdom, supported by 6000 British troops. The Russian general was to choose the time and place of landing, and all the Neapolitan forces were to be under his command. Naples was to furnish the Allies with horses and mules and submit to other necessary requisitions, pay and maintain the Russian troops as well as the legion replacing them in the Ionian Isles, and provision the Russian fleet. The Tsar was only bound to uphold the kingdom's integrity at the final peace.

Damas was recalled with great secrecy from Messina, and remained hidden for six weeks in a small villa at Portici, where he had daily conferences with the Russian generals and Neapolitan ministers, except the Minister of War, who was not told of his arrival. All military arrangements were made in the Queen's name, and she sent the Minister of War his instructions. Damas was appalled at the implications of the Russian treaty, 'signed by a fool [Circello] and approved by the Queen, who was blinded by rage and tired of a dependence from which any change would have been a consolation and a release'. Naples had thrown herself into the arms of an ally a thousand leagues away, and would therefore be at the mercy of the Russian minister and generals. The reciprocal advantages had certainly not been balanced. The effect of this was soon apparent: the Russian generals were more disposed to dictate than to discuss. Damas saw this as a change of yoke but not of situation. In case of a military reverse, the King risked losing everything while his Allies would lose comparatively little.

The new treaty with Russia was scarcely signed when Gallo sent a jubilant message that he had obtained the longed-for evacuation 'in the happiest manner he could have desired'. On September 22 he had signed a treaty of neutrality with France on seemingly easy terms. The French troops were to evacuate the kingdom one month after its ratification. The King was to resist any attempt against his neutrality, and forbid the ships of belligerent nations to enter his ports; he was not to appoint any French *émigré* or subject of any Power hostile to France to any military command. Acton was to be banished entirely. Privately Napoleon had already ordered Saint-Cyr to march on Naples as soon as he crossed the Rhine. For the time being the treaty suited him, though he had no intention to abide by it. As he wished to concentrate his forces in Lombardy, Saint-Cyr was to withdraw as soon as it was ratified. The double-dealing was not all on the Queen's side.

The text reached Naples on October 4. Alquier allowed the Court forty-eight hours to ratify it, threatening to treat any further delay as a refusal, whereupon Saint-Cyr would invade the capital. The Queen tried hard to temporize, but on October 7 Alquier asked abruptly for his passports. Next day when war seemed imminent the King ratified the treaty against his will, but at the same time he sent the Russian minister a declaration which annulled its validity since it had been extorted by force. 'A remarkable peculiarity,' wrote Alquier to Talleyrand, 'in the midst of a discussion the result of which would either bring peace to Naples or deprive the King of his crown, was that this prince happened to be exclusively preoccupied with the affairs of his vintage at the time, and it was in a vineyard among his grape-gatherers that he appended his signature.' Again he repeated: 'This Power will not keep its engagements.' The French started to evacuate Taranto on the 14th.

The Queen said nothing to Gallo about the declaration to Russia which annulled the treaty with France. On October 9 she wrote to him: 'The French came here without any treaty, by means of force. Why do they need a treaty in order to leave? They have always said: "We must be there for military purposes, notably on account of the Russians at Corfu and the British at Malta."... As for General Acton, confidence cannot be commanded, and if the King has confidence in this old servant, he will consult him even if he is in America. Besides, I think the Emperor attaches far more importance to General Acton than we do, and this does the General much honour and confers great distinction on him, proving that he is above seduction... and I sincerely congratulate him on it.' On October 15 she wrote to Gallo in cipher: 'I am too interested in your welfare not to tell you to find a pretext to be outside the French frontier and beyond their claws during the whole month of November. I fear their well-known villainy and shall duly inform the King that I have sent you warning... Soon we shall be forced to join the Coalition and I fear their vengeance. Keep this entirely secret and recognize my true friendship for you. Think of yourself.

Adieu. Consider your own safety.'

As soon as the Queen heard of the French evacuation she began to hear of French victories in Germany. Alquier informed her of the capitulation of Ulm on October 19, congratulating her that the Austrian army had suffered a far worse defeat under Mack than the Neapolitan, and absolving the latter ironically from blame. On this occasion the French took some 50,000 prisoners. True, this sensational victory was followed by the crushing naval defeat at Trafalgar on October 21, but Nelson was dead. 'I shall regret him all my life,' wrote the Queen with genuine feeling. 'Twenty vessels may increase his glory, but nothing can console for his loss. So much courage, virtue and modesty—all united in one individual, is not to be found again. For him it is happiness, for us a heavy misfortune.'

Acton wrote that it would be reckless to compromise Naples further after Ulm, and for a moment the Queen was tempted to recoil. But she did not know what to believe. She had also heard of Austrian victories and that Murat had been captured while pursuing the Archduke Ferdinand. Alquier wrote on November 1: 'Count Kaunitz [the Austrian ambassador] without ascertaining if this news was correct, has ordered all Austrian ships in the bay of Naples to be decked with flags, and he is to hold a celebration at which the King and royal family will be present. It is impossible that in Vienna, Petersburg or London itself there should be livelier transports of joy than those of the Neapolitan Court, with so revolting a lack of propriety, two weeks after signing the treaty of neutrality.' On November 6 the Queen wrote to Damas: 'All has been changed and upset since our Convention... I do not refer to the French treaty which I was forced to sign with a pistol at my throat, even less to the departure of the French troops: I have not the slightest trust in their good faith and am sure that, just as it suited their convenience to leave, as soon as it suits them to return they will do so... I do not share the egotistical delirium of the country, which believes itself safe since the French are outside the frontiers. No; but I do feel concerned about the awful events of the war of which I get only confused and alarming information. Another advantage secured by Bonaparte, he is at the gates of Vienna: a truce, a congress, a conference and a suspension of hostilities will be the result. If the victor, stung by our broken neutrality, adds this new grievance to all those he harbours against me and declares that owing to our betrayal, our bad faith, he will not include us in this armistice and peace, the Emperor of Austria, who has no more means, will certainly not continue the war to save us, and all the French might will fall on us and crush us.' Consequently she proposed to Tatistscheff that the allied troops should remain at Corfu and Malta and await developments instead of coming directly to Naples. The astute Russian agreed on condition he was paid 500,000 ducats immediately, and 276,100 ducats every two months in advance for military provisions and forage. This proposal, which some regarded as a sheet-anchor, was rejected by the State Council.

Again the Queen had changed her mind: in her heart she wanted war. The tremulous Council had been swayed by her personal magnetism. Damas returned to Naples, and in accordance with etiquette announced this to all the diplomatic corps, including Alquier, who was furious. On November 19 the first Russian convoy sailed into the bay. The Queen wrote at once to Elliot: 'Bound ever and openly at this moment to the good cause, I feel all the enormous weight of a responsibility in so many varied difficulties; but certain of the principles, pure and honourable and disinterested, which guide my actions, I allow myself to be blamed, to be torn in pieces, to be criticized, provided I have the happiness of saving their patrimony to my husband and our children by means of the assistance of our brave allies. I entreat you to place entire confidence in us. My character will always deserve it.' Alquier lowered his arms and demanded his passports, which were sent to him with a velleity of regret, as if to show that Naples was still at peace with France and had only yielded to an act of aggression, as when Saint-Cyr had marched into the country. On November 21 Alquier left for Rome. The fat was now in the fire. Seven thousand English troops landed at Castellammare, thirteen thousand Russians and Albanians at Naples. In contrast with the gloom of the general public, wrote Blanch, the Queen could not conceal her elation.

XXVIII

Defensive preparations—The King's cynicism—Austerlitz: 'The dynasty of Naples has ceased to reign'—Old General Lacy's Council of War—The Queen's attempts to ward off catastrophe—A last appeal to Napoleon—Evacuation of the Anglo-Russians—The Queen's effort to organize resistance—Her last letter to Gallo—The failure of every mission—'I fear we shall never see Naples again'—A foothold in Calabria.

While the Queen was exhilarated by the landing of the Russians, her numerous enemies, who believed that Napoleon was invincible, regarded this as a prelude to her downfall. The King showed plainly that he had no illusions; he remained a cheerful pessimist. Now and then he returned to the capital from his hunting excursions to pour cold water on his wife's enthusiasm. He teased her maliciously about Mack and the rout of the Austrian army. She had always stood up for Mack and blamed Neapolitan cowardice for the catastrophe of 1798. The King enjoyed rubbing this awkward fact in. He thought no better of the Russian Generals Lacy and Oppermann. Having first appeared in civilian clothes like seedy commercial travellers, these generals now strutted about in full panoply with stars and spangles that struck him as equally comic. 'The public sees these Russians with pleasure,' wrote the Queen to Gallo on November 23, 'their exact discipline causes no inconvenience and their martial aspect seems a promise of defence. But I do not share this feeling, as their number is so restricted.' She asked Gallo to leave a door open for reconciliation, since the government had not declared war against France, and Alquier had packed in spite of assurances that it would remain neutral. It was Alquier who had slammed the door, not the Queen.

Damas, who had served in their army, was on friendly terms with the Russians, but he was taken aback by their extravagant demands. General Lacy had distinguished himself in Poland many years before, and he should have been left in comfortable retirement to reminisce about bygone derring-do. Sir Henry Bunbury described him as a simple, kind-hearted old gentleman, and to use his own phrase, 'always for fighting'. Irish by birth and English at heart, he could not express himself easily in any language except Russian, and spoke English with a strong brogue. He had landed more dead than alive after a rough sea voyage, and had had to travel from the coast by litter. Old, ailing and querulous, he relied increasingly on his Quartermaster-General Oppermann to make decisions for him. He used to bring his nightcap in his pocket, put it on and go to sleep while others discussed business at the councils of war. Oppermann was an Alsatian *émigré* who found fault with everything. Damas considered him a 'bundle of thorns', grim, uncouth and hopelessly mediocre; 'he had none of the requisite qualities even to blind one to his lack of talent'. Lacy and Oppermann were both handsomely lodged at the Angri Palace, where all their expenses were defrayed by the King. Not satisfied with this, they asked to use the Hereditary Prince's casino, where he went to relax in domestic privacy, and were offended when it was refused. The English general, Sir James Craig, was very moderate in comparison and insisted on paying for everything; he was scathing about the sordid avarice of the Russians.

Horses for the allies were requisitioned in the capital. The English paid exorbitant prices for theirs to mount three hundred dragoons. Owing to the restrictions enforced by the French, the Neapolitan army had been sadly neglected, recruiting had been stopped, and funds were insufficient. Damas hoped to raise and train a new army of conscripts. A levy of 30,000 troops in the kingdom was decreed, excluding Sicily, but Damas did not expect to raise more than 18,000. Military service was generally dreaded, and many mutilated themselves to avoid it. One of these was branded with the letter I (Infamous) for cutting off a finger. The Neapolitan army consisted of ten infantry and four light-infantry battalions, eighteen companies of grenadiers and eight small squadrons of cavalry, altogether between nine and ten thousand men. According to Damas, the Russians had eleven thousand men including two thousand Albanian savages: General Lacy said he was expecting a reinforcement of twelve thousand, including a Cossack regiment, within in a week, but this never arrived. Damas gives the British total as six thousand. These troops might have been effective had they been used offensively, but all Lacy's preparations were strictly defensive. He kept as close as possible to the Tyrrhene Sea, as if to embark with greater facility, and sent the Neapolitan troops towards the

Adriatic. He chose Teano for his headquarters. The English guarded the line of the Garigliano on the left, the Russians chiefly the narrow pass of Mignano in the centre and the Neapolitans the Abruzzi boundary on the right. It seemed strange, as Blanch remarked, to send so many foreign troops to defend a country which could only be threatened when the war was over and the Coalition had collapsed, but Napoleon 'affected the brains, the courage and even the hatred of his enemies like the head of Medusa'. If these were not paralysed, they committed incredible blunders.

The King remained a cynical onlooker. He was more glum than usual when the Russian and English generals were introduced to him at Portici: he stood beside the Queen like a silent reproach while she tried to make her guests feel welcome. When conversation flagged the Queen, thus handicapped by her husband, had a sudden inspiration. Having noticed a precious diamond in Lacy's sword-hilt, she asked him if it were a token of some glorious feat of arms. Lacy replied that it was a gift from the Empress Catherine for his capture of a city in the last Polish war, adding that he would be happy to bare his sword in defence of Their Majesties, and he would not sheath it again until he had exterminated their foes. The Queen, who loved heroics, became eloquent and tried to rouse the King from his apathy. But the King only remembered Mack, and muttered the Neapolitan word for 'Donkey', loud enough to make some of the courtiers laugh. Then he said: 'It is time for dinner', and dismissed the generals, who had not understood his comment. The incident was soon repeated in the capital where it added to the King's popularity.

The King did not allow the military preparations to interfere with his sport. Blanch relates that the colonel of an Albanian regiment, provisionally commanding a brigade which he was marching into Abruzzo at the end of November, happened to meet the King returning from the hunt of Mondragone and paraded the men in his honour. The King called for the colonel and asked him where he was going. 'To Abruzzo,' he replied. 'What for?' inquired the King. The colonel answered in some amazement: 'To enter the campaign.' 'Against whom?' the King continued. Even more amazed, the colonel said: 'The French, Your Majesty.' 'God help you,' muttered the King. While the Queen and Damas were trying to appeal to public patriotism the King's whole attitude undermined their efforts. He made it obvious that he disapproved of the Queen's policy. Besides, there was scant sympathy between the English and the Russians, and both distrusted the Neapolitans, who regarded them more as dangerous *agents provocateurs* than as allies. When we consider the conflicting characters of the protagonists the vicious circle is complete. Ever and anon came fresh reports of Napoleon's triumphs.

News of Napoleon's overwhelming victory at Austerlitz (December 2) reached Naples about a fortnight later; that of the armistice between the Emperor Francis and Napoleon and of the peaceful Russian withdrawal from Austria was known unofficially on December 20; it was not announced officially until January 10. Napoleon had heard of the Anglo-Russian landing at Naples while he was at Austerlitz. He was not surprised; perhaps he was even pleased, for this time the Queen was hoist with her own petard. Peace negotiations between France and Austria were completed at Pressburg on December 26. Napoleon refused to admit any stipulations on behalf of the Bourbons of Naples. After the treaty was signed he launched his famous proclamation to the French army: 'Soldiers, for ten years I have done everything to save the King of Naples, and he has done everything for his ruin. After the battles of Dego, Mondovi and Lodi, he could have only offered the feeblest resistance; I trusted this Prince's word, and treated him generously.

'When the second Coalition against France was dissolved at Marengo the King of Naples, who had been the first to wage this unjust war, abandoned by his allies at Lunéville, remained alone and defenceless. He pleaded with me, and I forgave him a second time.

'A few months ago you were at the gates of Naples. I had good enough reasons to suspect the treachery that was being hatched and to avenge the outrages he had committed against me, but I was generous, I recognized the neutrality of Naples. I ordered you to evacuate this kingdom and for the third time the House of Bourbon was established on the throne and saved.

'Shall we pardon for a fourth time? Shall we trust again a Court without loyalty, without honour, without sense? No, no! The dynasty of Naples has ceased to reign: its existence is incompatible with the peace of Europe and the honour of my crown.

'Soldiers, march! Drown—if they should wait for you—those weak battalions of the tyrants of the seas. Let the world see how we punish perjurers. Hasten to show me that the whole of Italy is subject to my laws and to those of my allies; that the most beautiful land on earth is finally free from the yoke of the most perfidious of men; that the sanctity of treaties is avenged and that the spirits of my brave soldiers murdered in the ports of Sicily on their return from Egypt, after escaping the perils of shipwreck, of the desert, and of battle, are at last appeased. Soldiers, my brother will lead you: he knows my plans; he bears my authority and has my full confidence: encircle him with yours!'

On hearing of the battle of Austerlitz, General Lacy summoned a miscalled Council of War at Teano without including a single Neapolitan officer. Regardless of the treaty of September 10, the Russian and English generals decided to limit the defence of the kingdom to Calabria alone. Lacy wrote to Damas on January 4 sending him a copy of the protocol agreed upon in his absence. This stated untruthfully that the Russian and English troops had been called while Saint-Cyr was still in the kingdom, but that the hazards of the sea voyage prevented them from arriving until the French had left. Lacy had, in fact, ordered the convoy to wait in Sicily until the French withdrew. The Russian treaty with Naples was wholly concerned with the defence and security of the kingdom; the term military diversion had never been mentioned, but now the cat was out of the bag to stare brazenly in the Queen's face. The protocol continued: 'Shortly after the landing of the allied troops the reverses of the war in Germany became known, as well as the total retreat of the army of the Archduke Charles to the frontiers of Hungary. Since then the Generals of the Anglo-Russian forces were convinced, to their deep regret, that their purpose in coming to Naples, which was to create a diversion in favour of the operations in North Italy, could no longer be fulfilled. The French might easily take advantage of the period of rest necessary to the Austrian troops to send a considerable force to Naples... The Generals had received positive news that between thirty-five and thirty-eight thousand French troops were already on the march... The opinion of the plurality was to retire to Calabria.' This was signed by Generals Lacy, Anrep (his second-in-command), Stuart (Craig's second-in-command), Oppermann, and Lieutenant-Colonel Bunbury. General Craig added a postscript stating that he disagreed with the majority. He considered it useless to go to Calabria. 'My opinion is that we should embark and preserve our troops for occasions when we may render greater service to our sovereigns.'

Brigadier Campbell agreed with him.

Damas says that his blood froze when he read these documents. Lacy had often repeated that 'if 80,000 men were to march against us we should all succumb together, but if he only had to deal with 40,000 he would confidently take up the challenge'. How could the advance of 35,000 necessitate so disastrous a retreat, exclaimed Damas, 'when we had as many in impregnable positions, without counting the militia, the masses, the resources of strongholds and of a numerous population, already prepared for defence?' He decided to go to Naples at once. On his way there he received a letter from the Queen: 'The King wishes to speak to you: try to reach Belvedere before nightfall. He wishes to discuss what is to be done, and will try to move his army into Calabria and from there, if further resistance becomes impossible, to Sicily... I do not know what the Russians have decided, and do not even understand, after their orders, how they can remain. Cardinal Ruffo has left to negotiate [he left for Rome on January 7]; may God grant him success. Our position is very distressing, and this is no longer a century for honourable people to live in.'

The Tsar's orders to embark for Corfu were taken too literally by Lacy and Oppermann. They were only to retire 'if the enemy had not arrived [*en présence*], not compromising the dignity and honour of the Emperor's arms, and restoring neutrality to the Court of Naples'. The Russian ambassador and Colonel Pozzo di Borgo, the Corsican diplomatist who was attached to the Russian army, were opposed to their withdrawal, as were the second generals in command, Anrep and Stuart. Damas decided to plead with Lacy to defend the Volturno while negotiations with the French were in progress. Tatistscheff accompanied him, and Anrep, who was mortified at the prospect of leaving Naples in the lurch, escorted them to their carriage with tears in his eyes. 'It is a question of the common welfare, of our own interest, and the honour of our uniform,' he said. 'We should support you all the more since we have sent your army corps to the remotest corner of the kingdom in vain and have sapped your vital resources.' Damas embraced him effusively.

Lacy was fast asleep when Damas and the ambassador called, so they saw Oppermann in the meantime. He agreed with all they had to say but pretended to fear English opposition. 'It is a sacred duty, however,' he remarked. From his expression it was evident that he had no desire for a change, but was anxious that the decision should not be imputed to himself. 'This man had never known honourable sentiments, but his words remained, and I counted on making use of them with the old man who only thought through him. Tatistscheff and I saw Lacy when he woke up at three in the morning, and I spoke as to a hero who could not tarnish the end of his career... "What you tell me I consider as a duty," he replied, "we shall do it, yes I tell you, we shall do it. Why not? Yes, we shall do it." "Can I count on this?" I asked (not counting at all). "Why not? We shall do it." "Can I assure the King that this is so?" "Why not? We shall do it." One could hope for no more eloquent guarantee... I returned with this promise, such as it was, to the King and Queen... The Queen spoke to Elliot about it, who said that Craig demanded nothing better than that the Russian generals would abide by their original decision.' Damas was convinced that Elliot was intriguing obstructively behind the scenes—'with Sicily so near his grasp why should he let it escape him?'

The Queen seldom rose from her writing-table except to plead with Tatistscheff and Elliot. Her letters prove it. On learning the decision of the Council of War she gave full vent to her indignation and 'said far more to Elliot than she had ever said to Alquier'. To deliver the kingdom to the French without striking a blow was an infamy for which she failed to find a name. The King's first impulse was to forbid any foreign troops to enter Calabria or Sicily. He even gave orders to fire on those who attempted to land in any Sicilian port without his written permission. In a desperate letter to Damas on January 4 the Queen wrote: 'Craig continues to push and shout that he wants to leave. Lacy, too, is afraid of being outflanked; in fact, they are a compound of cowardice and baseness which make them utterly contemptible; and I am determined to try to negotiate and prevent the French invasion, cost what it may... It is reported that Saint-Cyr's column, which is said to be twenty-eight thousand strong—others say it only consists of ten thousand—is marching towards Jesi and Foligno, to be stationed at Civita Castellana. This is not so very alarming, but the smell of gunpowder sickens the feeble organs of General Craig, who therefore wishes to avoid the chance of getting a mere whiff. I hope he will go and become a monk, after having dishonoured his country and made it lose all influence in the commerce of the Mediterranean, the Levant and Egypt; they will feel the effect of this step for a long time to come, for I am entirely disanglomanized.'

'We live in an abominable age, when honest people are victims,' she wrote again two days later; 'Oppermann only deserves the profoundest contempt; he dared not say anything to me against our troops, but everything in the world to discourage me and have his decision approved. I had a scene with him which lasted two hours, and I told him what he deserved in Tatistscheff's presence; the result is that they will stay, convinced they are being sacrificed because they cannot embark: a shameful, panic terror has seized their souls and they cannot be relied on... This morning we received the terrible news from Rome of the peace signed by the Emperor of Austria and Napoleon on December 29... It seems that Russia is not included; actually we must hope for direct messages and couriers, and it would be desirable for Bonaparte to forget Naples as completely as my relatives, children and ministers have done, but unfortunately he has not forgotten it in the least.' The same evening she added that a so-called *aide-de-camp* of the Tsar had arrived with orders for the prompt departure of the Russians, 'for the noble reason that, since a large number of Frenchmen may fall on top of us, he is anxious not to expose them; he does not mention any peace, or armistice, or obligation contracted, and very dearly bought, to include us... What times, what horrors! No treaty, no word is sacred; everything is violated. The Russian Emperor is also withdrawing his troops from Holland: this delivers us, bound hand and foot, to the French whom they enticed here; and I see that our ruin is certain beyond repair... It must be admitted that we have been thoroughly duped.' And more in the same strain.

To Gallo she wrote simultaneously: 'The fatal troops who wished to land here and liberate us in spite of our entreaties (for they gave us more trouble than the French) have suddenly taken panic and talk of leaving.' Still unaware of Napoleon's verdict, she discussed the possible and impossible conditions of a peace treaty. The impossible conditions were: 'To cede the kingdom to our son by stipulation. To put only French troops in our fortresses and ports, which would be to lose the crown systematically. Any marriage with the Bonaparte family is utterly impossible; all humiliation and baseness are to be avoided. A profitable treaty of commerce might be mooted. In case of absolute necessity, let them take up their positions in Puglia until the general peace. I should consent to the exclusion of the English from all our ports, but I fear and am even certain that in this case they would invade Sicily. We must also avoid having to banish honest men like Acton and Damas, who cannot seem important in the eyes of the great Bonaparte. We would form a ministry acceptable to France. Finally, to prove that the King thinks no more of the English, he would cede his right of sovereignty to Malta. Conduct yourself with your usual prudence and wisdom. This will render you the arbiter of our fate... I trust in you... In the last resort, offer also an offensive and defensive alliance.'

The Queen would stop at nothing now to ward off catastrophe. On January 7 she wrote to Napoleon: 'Victims of the most selfish and perfidious politics, dragged forcibly and then abandoned in the abyss by so-called friends and allies, the bandage with which they have long blinded us, myself in particular, has at last and for ever been torn off.

'Your Imperial and Royal Majesty has just crowned his reputation and military glory. He may still cover himself with a new glory by giving to the sovereigns he has so easily vanquished the example of generosity, especially after victory, by forgetting all resentment...

'It is in ceasing to be an enemy of Your Imperial and Royal Majesty that I appeal to your generosity and rely upon it. It is as a wife, doubly as the mother of my children and my subjects, victims as I am of blind confidence in selfish allies and friends, not attempting to disguise the truth but admitting the faults that produced this blindness, faults into which I was drawn by the love of good and intention to do it, but which I desire to correct; it is on so many grounds, I say, that I do not blush but glorify in begging Your Imperial and Royal Highness to forget the past and lay the foundation of a sincere and lasting union which must finally replace the mutual enmity that has existed too long between us, a foundation which will be sacred to me since it will be based on the gratitude and admiration with which I have the honour to be, with the deepest consideration, etc.'

Only the Queen's anguish can excuse this abject letter. Having announced his intention to 'hurl from the throne that criminal woman who has so shamelessly violated everything that is sacred among men', His Imperial and Royal Majesty did not deign to reply. On December 31 he had written to his brother Joseph:

'My intention is to seize the kingdom of Naples... I have appointed you my Lieutenant Commander-in-Chief of the army of Naples. Leave for Rome forty hours after receiving this, and may your first despatch inform me of your entry into Naples, that you have driven out a perfidious Court and subjected this part of Italy to our laws... If my presence were not necessary in Paris, I would have marched to Naples in person, but with the generals you have and the instructions I shall give you, you will do what I could have done. Do not reveal your destination...'

On January 10 the allied generals decided to evacuate without even attempting to defend Calabria. In their hasty withdrawal the English destroyed the pontoon bridge over the Garigliano and killed the horses they had bought so dearly. 'I happened to be with Lacy,' wrote Damas, 'when he received Craig's report of this prudent expedition. He and Oppermann were much embarrassed, as Lacy must have given orders or at least his consent for such a measure. "Now that the Neapolitans," I said, "must attempt alone what they were planned to do in conjunction with famous warriors, this is an unfortunate lesson for them." I only referred to the British, but next day we learned that the Russian regiment retiring from the Abruzzi, having heard of the flight of the British without knowing the real reason, sank the ferry-boats on the Volturno after using them.' The embarkation of the British from Castellammare was enough for Lacy to discard his promise; he pretended that his presence would only hinder negotiations with the French. Cardinal Ruffo urged the Court to delay the allies' departure, if only to support his negotiations and enable him to obtain some compromise. He had been authorized to make the most ample concessions. The French in Rome were not yet sufficiently organized to invade Naples while the allies were still there. On the 17th Circello sent Lacy a final protest, saying that the Tsar could not have realized the plight of the kingdom when his letter arrived; had he done so, he would have been the first to ask Lacy to 'remain faithful to the laws of honour'.

Until the very last moment the allied generals continued to claim the fullest co-operation from the Neapolitans they were deserting in the hour of need. 'I wish General Craig a good voyage,' wrote the Queen to Elliot, 'and that no tempest may increase his fears. Never, so long as I live shall I forget his visit.'

Before leaving, the Russians wished to occupy the forts of Capua, Baia and Pozzuoli. As the last two had no connexion with their fictitious line of defence, it was evident that they hoped to be protected by these forts while preparing to embark, since they were afraid of hostile demonstrations. The King and Queen saw through this and refused to oblige them. However, they tried to seize the fort of Gaeta, but were repulsed by its irate governor, the Prince of Hesse-Philippsthal, who threatened to fire on them. Without entering Naples they embarked from Baia between January 16 and 18, protected by the police against the insults of the populace, taking with them, as Damas wrote, the Crown they had come to support. This scampering off a month before the kingdom was attacked was a joke in questionable taste. Even as a military diversion, the whole business had been futile.

Few suffered more than the Queen, who now found herself alone, confronting the colossus before whom the other Powers were falling like ninepins. To Elliot she wrote: 'Degradation and injury will be the price we shall have to pay for the short and expensive Anglo-Russian visit. We are sick at heart: nothing could have surpassed our good faith and dignity.' She continued to repeat: 'I have nothing to reproach myself with.' This time Acton had no share whatever of the responsibility. His prudent advice had been disregarded, and his absence was generally deplored. Gallo had submitted his resignation in December, saying that he felt his honour as a gentleman had been compromised rather than his character as an ambassador. The Queen appealed to him in her agony: 'Torture your wits, your talents, your knowledge of affairs to succeed. Neglect no means whatever, self-love, generosity, grandeur of soul, nobility, try every expedient to save us... Each moment is vital. I am truly in despair. My gratitude, if you save us, will be boundless.' She was writing to herself rather than to Gallo. It was she who tortured her wits, who attempted all means to stop the French advance. Gallo had given up hope.

Neither Cardinal Fesch, nor Alquier, nor General Masséna would listen to Cardinal Ruffo, who decided to go to Paris in spite of every obstacle to plead his sovereign's cause. Under the circumstances it is hardly surprising that he was less successful as a diplomat than as a *condottiere*. He was stopped on the journey and told to turn back; Talleyrand sent him word that 'the fate of Naples was settled irretrievably'. The Duke of San Teodoro, who had followed in his wake, fared no better. The King wished to leave as soon as his allies deserted him, and the Queen used every argument to postpone his departure. But whenever she spoke to him he overwhelmed her with bitter words. The Duke of Ascoli and Prince of

Jaci, who still had a certain influence, persuaded him to stay while the French were beyond the frontier. He decided to go to Mondragone and make a holocaust of all the game there. At least he had the satisfaction of boasting that he had not left a single wild boar for the French. The Empress of Austria wrote her mother a letter which was a covert condemnation of her policy. But for the moderation of the victor, she said that the peace treaty might have been much worse. Considering the exclusion of Naples, the Queen was enraged and trampled the letter underfoot. Her other daughters reproached her too. The Hereditary Prince led the life of a recruiting officer: he spent six hours a day at the Granili counting and distributing the new recruits. 'Many thought that the Queen had allotted him this task to make him unpopular,' wrote Blanch, 'but this was needless. The Prince might have exercised it with greater dignity and usefulness, but he liked details and it seemed that the consequences of events had little influence on his future.' The Princess was almost seven months with child; her firstborn had just been weaned. 'Fortunately,' as the Queen said, 'she is so apathetic that she feels nothing keenly, which is good for her health.'

The Queen still had a ray of hope: to rouse the masses in defence of their King and Country. Damas encouraged her. Though he saw little chance of saving the kingdom, at least he would put up a good fight in Calabria. When the Queen spoke of her vain regrets, he asked her: 'To remedy this grievous situation, are you capable of everything? Would you take it upon yourself to make a personal appeal to the people?' 'I then recognized all the ardour of her character, all the energy of her soul; but these did not leave her cabinet, for her imagination travels a vast distance in the twinkling of an eye without her mind being able to concentrate on the same object.' The Queen did show herself to the people again and again, but she had never shared her husband's popularity. Her woebegone appearance inspired less sympathy than Ferdinand's beaming nose. Memories of 1799 dulled enthusiasm in the capital; the propertied classes feared a repetition of chaos, pillage, bloodshed and reprisals. The King might have galvanized them, but he thought it absurd to oppose an army which had defeated the Austrian Empire. As for the guerrilla leaders who had fought under Ruffo, most of them lost their nerve without him. All the rumours of armaments which had disturbed Alquier and Saint-Cyr were proved to be dismally hollow. The Queen's energy was whetted by misfortune, but the King had

had enough of it. He sailed for Sicily on January 23, leaving the Hereditary Prince to govern 'with the most ample and extensive faculties', which were shared by the Queen.

Maria Carolina remembered her mother's role in Hungary; she would stay in Naples to organize the resistance. Her indomitable spirit shines through her last letter to Gallo, dated January 26, 1806: 'The King sailed for Palermo on the evening of the 23rd, only taking with him Seratti, Trabia, Tanucci-Rossi [his first equerry] and Jaci, leaving all authority to his heir and leaving me to look after the family... Perhaps, my dear Gallo, this will be the last letter I shall write to you for a long time. God knows where we shall meet again and how we shall be able to communicate. In any case, I recommend my beloved family to you. Take care of them, serve them, help them. I am sick at heart, of the most poignant chagrin, but without remorse in my soul, and this gives me courage and resignation. Perhaps I have erred in my calculations, but the purest and most upright motives guided me. In fine I am the victim of my sentiments, and I dare say I deserve a better fate. God ordained it so. His holy will be done! I am prepared for everything; I fear nothing. I shall expose my two sons to every danger. My heart bleeds, but it is a cruel expiation to duty and honour. I shall become a wanderer, in poverty, never having thought of myself but of others... (In cipher.) The King is in Sicily, desperate. How can we save him, either from the shame of having to abdicate and be driven out, or from the danger of being captured? I have been consistent with all the rest of my life in sacrificing myself to ensure his safety and he has willingly accepted it. In God's name try to save us, and may the greatness of our atonement in abdicating suffice without further exactions and without violence to our unhappy country and the new reign of a young man who, if he is well treated, will remain grateful and loyal, whereas brute force revolts his character... It is an additional piece of knavery for Bonaparte to drive us out without any declaration of war. Do not believe, however, that I am his dupe. His intention to take the whole of Italy has long been a foregone conclusion. Even if the Anglo-Russians had not come, he would have found another pretext. For it was already decided: the House of Austria laid low, we became the next victims... I speak as a blind person does of colour, for I do not know what the master of the world will decide about our fate. The Emperor Francis and my daughter write in trepidation, imploring me to consider my safety.

What is one to think of that? Will he make me a pendant to the Duke of Enghien? It would honour me, but it would not be the greatest of his triumphs.'

A few days later, on January 31, Napoleon wrote to his brother Joseph: 'The Marquis of Gallo has left the service of Naples. He is going over to serve you with all his abilities. He will be the first Neapolitan to swear allegiance to you. It is supposed that the Prince Royal has remained in Naples: if this be true, have him arrested and sent to France under good escort... No half-measures, no weakness. I wish my blood to reign in Naples as long as in France. The kingdom of Naples is necessary to me.' When the Queen heard of Gallo again, he was Joseph Bonaparte's Minister of Foreign Affairs. She had scolded him and frequently complained of him, but she had continued to confide in him for twenty years; with all his faults she had never doubted his basic loyalty. Her 1,400 letters, which he carefully preserved despite her injunctions to burn them, prove that she trusted him in essentials. He owed his career to her. She had constantly supported him against the King's and Acton's opposition, even against her own recurrent suspicions; though a hard taskmistress, she had overwhelmed him with favours and honours. And at last, when the Anglo-Russians landed, she had warned him to seek safety across the French frontier. His *volte-face* added to her bitterness.

Joseph Bonaparte, whom his brother had chosen for the throne of Naples, was shrewd enough not to discourage negotiations entirely; he even told the Duke of San Teodoro that having refused the crown of Italy he would not accept that of Naples. San Teodoro seemed to cherish the illusion that the Hereditary Prince would be suffered to remain. He was kept running to and fro with alternative proposals. On January 31 Joseph Bonaparte proposed an eight days' armistice in exchange for Capua and Gaeta; on February 4 San Teodoro returned to the French headquarters with an agreement to surrender these forts if the armistice were prolonged to thirty-five days. But the French rejected this; on the 8th they had reached the frontier. As San Teodoro was Gallo's nephew, the Queen began to suspect that he had agreed with his uncle to betray her.

When the French were marching to Terracina, Damas urged the Hereditary Prince 'not to delay the last and strongest expedient, the immediate mustering of the masses'. But the Prince's advisers dissuaded him and frightened the different leaders, whom Damas considered poltroons, so that they said that they could only muster a few hundred. Some required two weeks, others a month, and time was running short. Damas said bluntly that he could not defend Naples without the help of the population. Calabria was the last resort. On February 6 the Hereditary Prince announced his departure for Calabria 'to co-ordinate all possible measures, and leave nothing undone for your recovery... Remember that the legitimate sovereigns whom God has given you, wherever they may be, will ever turn their eyes towards you and will make every effort to return to you. Implore the Almighty to appease His anger for our sins, that He may remove these scourges from us and grant our country a stable peace, and lead us back to you, our well-beloved subjects, who will always be the object of our paternal care and my delight.'

Dressed in mourning, the Queen visited many popular shrines with votive offerings, and the nobility of her attitude and expression compelled admiration. Her anxiety to stay on and defend the capital when the outlook was infinitely blacker than in 1798 suggests that she hoped for a miraculous intervention. But when her eldest son decided to join the army in Calabria and San Teodoro's last mission had failed, she realized she could do no more in Naples. After hearing that two French columns had crossed the frontier she reluctantly decided to embark. She went once more with her daughters to visit the small chapel of Saint Anne on the Chiaia. 'We are leaving,' she told the crowd of bystanders; but they only replied that they would pray for her happy journey. She had expected a more chivalrous answer, at least some promise of defence. The Hereditary Prince had delegated his power to a regency, consisting of General Naselli as president, the old Prince of Canosa and the magistrate Cianciulli as counsellors; these were determined to avoid the anarchy of 1799, and the Duke of Ascoli supported them as chief of police. Several thousand respectable citizens volunteered to form a civic guard to keep order. Although there was general consternation, the *lazzaroni* were singularly quiet.

On February 11 De Nicola wrote in his diary: 'It is impossible to describe the atmosphere of the royal palace this morning. It was certainly a moving spectacle; the impression it made on me was such that I felt inclined to leave Naples myself. All the area in front of the palace was swarming with people, and every shade of passion was depicted on their faces as they talked and gazed at the balconies and the traffic of transportation, of Court carriages on their way to the royal chapel, and others coming and going. All the ample square was thronged with carriages, carts and baggage being loaded and taken off. The royal chapel with the Blessed Sacrament exposed was prepared for the benediction of the royal family, as if it were the last function that they would attend there. Everything in fact caused sorrow and alarm, and mine was increased by those who shouted "Long live the King!"—since the same voices were so terrible in 1799 and evoked such memories that at certain moments I thought I saw the people in revolt. All the rest of the city was in a perpetual turmoil of removal; you knew not whence they came or where they went, but there was a continuous departure. After benediction in the chapel the Court returned to dine in the palace, and it was said that the Queen showed the keenest sorrow and despair upon having to flee and abandon the kingdom in this manner... Finally at four o'clock in the afternoon they all embarked, but it is said that the Hereditary Prince and Prince Leopold will go to Calabria. This is the second time in the course of eight years that Carolina of Austria and Ferdinand of Bourbon have fled: may God help them to return and recover the kingdom as they did before, but without so much terror and bloodshed.'

The Queen's two unmarried daughters, her daughter-in-law the Hereditary Princess, her two granddaughters and eleven ladies- and gentlemen-in-waiting embarked with her on the Neapolitan frigate *Archimede*, escorted by a large convoy of ships full of fugitives and what valuables they had been able to remove, together with much furniture and equipment naval and military. Though she had aged considerably since her last exile, the Queen never complained of the husband who had left her to shift for herself. As a daughter of Maria Theresa, she stiffened herself against the blows of fate, 'more determined than ever to defend the meagre patrimony of her children; never to bow before the colossus she admired as much as she detested'. But she had a strong premonition that she would not see Naples again. Before sailing she wrote to her eldest daughter, the Empress of Austria: 'I am going to a poor country, a land without resources, the air of which does not agree with me... The sacrifice is fulfilled; we are on board, and I fear we shall never see Naples again. This thought overwhelms me; it is a dreadful misfortune, a crying injustice, for which I hope God will give us compensation.'

The blows of fate fell thick and fast. The convoy was scattered by a violent storm. Twenty-six of the transport ships were driven off Baia and Castellammare, where several were captured by the French and the rest surrendered. This meant that most of the movable property of the fugitives as well as the archives of the Foreign Office fell into the hands of the enemy. It took the *Archimede* five days to reach Palermo.

'There is a great difference between the present loss of the kingdom and that of 1799,' wrote Damas a few months later, 'the feeble, the discontented, the indifferent, and the timid look upon Joseph Bonaparte as a king, and a people grows more readily accustomed to a change of dynasty than to a republican constitution. Fools will see a Court; vain idlers will get appointments; the military will have the delusion of ceasing to wage war... the women will have French lovers; perhaps the people will pay fewer taxes and Acton cannot return: these are good enough reasons to reconcile the country to its new situation. If habit is a second nature, that will be the only thing to make the people desire their former masters.'

Loathing Acton as he did, for the old minister had never spared his tender feelings, Damas portrayed him as Ferdinand's evil genius, who had delivered Sicily to the British and reduced the King to the status of an Indian nabob. 'How does he succeed in blinding the King to his rash policy?' he asked. 'The Queen could enlighten the King; the Hereditary Prince might try to win his confidence and discuss future policy with him; but Acton sets the King at variance with his wife and son and makes him distrust both; finally he dominates by destroying all domestic intimacy, all legitimate authority, in order to display his own.' But this is too simple an explanation, even if it contains a modicum of truth. More dispassionate writers, such as Blanch and R. M. Johnston, agree that while the Queen had been thirsting for revenge and triumph over her enemies, Acton had tried to make her steer a more prudent course. Absence from Naples had been his disadvantage, as Talleyrand had foreseen when he had insisted on his removal. He had been opposed to the Anglo-Russian landing, as he considered that everything depended on developments in Central Europe and that this was a mere sideshow. English at heart, his policy had never been English enough for his compatriots. But when the continental portion of the Two Sicilies was lost, British protection of the island seemed the only favourable solution.

What would have happened if Naples had stayed neutral? Damas has answered this question more sensibly than the Queen's detractors. It might have been possible, he says, for the King to continue reigning, if it could be called reigning to depend in every minute detail on the will of a foreign government. But after forty years of absolute monarchy, Ferdinand could never become reconciled to sharing his throne with the French. Even if the allied landing had not occurred, Napoleon would certainly have reoccupied Puglia. His next step would have been to point out that Naples was not strong enough to guarantee Sicily against British influence or occupation, and that he would therefore be compelled to garrison Messina. Powerless to object, Ferdinand would have lost both his kingdoms within three months. As for the Queen, she would have been even more miserable. To have been a victim of bad faith was less agonizing than the shame of submitting to the French yoke. She would have been consumed by remorse, and would have heaped it on those who had advised her to yield. Sicily she regarded as 'a poor thing but mine own'. She was determined to preserve what was left of her sovereign rights, still hoping to retain a foothold in Calabria.

XXIX

Joseph Bonaparte enters Naples—Acton regains power in Sicily—Damas's defeat and retirement to Vienna— The Calabrian campaign continues— The Queen's party—Arrival of Sir Sidney Smith; his capture of Capri and Ponza—Rodio's execution—The Prince of Hesse-Philippsthal resists at Gaeta—Battle of Maida—Surrender of Gaeta—Courier's letters from Calabria—The young Prince of Canosa—Acton resigns and the Queen recovers power.

After crossing the Neapolitan frontier on February 8, Joseph Bonaparte issued a soothing proclamation to the people, whom he dissociated from the government he had come to chastise: 'Your altars, the ministers of your religion are the same as ours; your laws, your property will be preserved: the French soldiers will be your brothers.' He encountered no serious resistance except at Gaeta, which was to hold out six months under the gallant Prince of Hesse-Philippsthal. The dazed and doddering regency was chiefly concerned with preventing an outbreak of disorder. Two envoys, the Duke of Campochiaro and Marchese Malaspina, were sent to the French headquarters to announce the royal family's departure and propose a twelve days' armistice. 'Not five minutes,' Marshal Masséna retorted. After some show of hesitation they subscribed to the conditions dictated. Having been instructed not to cede the fortresses, they ceded them all, including the islands of Ischia and Procida, so anxious were they for an assurance that the French troops would enter peacefully, which was given in exchange for the promise of a friendly reception. One of the French generals, Duhesme, could remember the three days of carnage before his last entry with Championnet, and Alquier had warned Joseph to beware of poison; the Queen had many followers and was 'capable of every crime'. The French troops were forbidden to touch food that had not been tested. But this time the *lazzaroni* were passive and indifferent.

On February 14 a division under General Partouneaux marched into the capital under a heavy downpour of rain, ragged, sopping and down at heel, with bread fixed on their bayonets. They were followed by a herd of cattle and an assortment of bedraggled women, some in carriages, others on horseback, many of them armed with pistols. Next day Joseph Bonaparte made his formal entry to the sound of cannon, church bells and military bands, and took up residence in the deserted royal palace. Gallo had set an example; all those who had been left to negotiate with the French, except Canosa and Naselli, submitted to the new regime. Joseph evinced his appreciation by presenting a collar of diamonds to San Gennaro.

'Naples captured, everything will fall,' wrote Napoleon to his brother, who was to help him dominate the Mediterranean; 'the principal and constant aim of my policy.' But he under-estimated the force necessary to conquer Sicily. At the end of February General Reynier marched with 10,000 troops into Calabria, where Damas hoped to make a last stand with some 14,000 men, of whom only half were regulars. Damas was a brave soldier but a poor tactician. Medici, the Minister of Finance who had accompanied the Hereditary Prince and Prince Leopold, knew nothing about military matters. He had brought enough money to pay for provisions, but he had made no preparations for their supply or transport in a country where mule tracks were the chief arteries of communication. In many places the inhabitants armed themselves and declared that unless the troops vanished before the French arrived, they would join the latter—'not because they were against the royal government,' says Blanch, 'but because this was powerless to protect them and they wished to save their property.' 'I had to guard myself as much against the people as against the enemy,' wrote Damas. 'If I had had more vanity than zeal for the good cause and more judgment than disinterestedness, would I have undertaken to oppose a French army when I was lacking in resources of every kind, as feeble in numbers as I was, and embarrassed by the presence of the two Princes?' Damas was the Queen's champion; like the Queen, he was a romantic; as a foreigner, he never got to know the country or the people.

The Queen's letters to him are pathetic and illuminating. Amid the cold and discomfort of Palermo she shut herself up in the bleak bare palace, and while the King went shooting and her daughters visited convents and busied themselves with local charities, she wrote until she suffered from eye-strain. As in her letters to Cardinal Ruffo in 1799, she was trying to encourage herself as well as her correspondent, but she felt a deeper sympathy for Damas and was more ready to excuse his failure. Countess Razoumovski had become an inseparable companion, as Lady Hamilton had been before, and this 'perfect, unique friend', an ultra-sensitive *femme de cœur*, was devotedly attached to Damas. Alquier had blamed her and Countess Zichy, the wife of the Austrian Minister of Finance who had also accompanied the Queen from Vienna, for stirring up the Queen's hatred of France. 'Three men equally without wit, talent or means figure in this strange coterie,' he wrote with his usual malice before leaving Naples, 'Damas coupled with Mme de Razoumovski, Saint-Clair with the Queen, and Roth, a Hessian officer, with Mme de Zichy; and the kingdom is ruled by this infamous brothel! Unless one has been an eye-witness, it is hard to believe that the loves of three ladies whose ages add to a total of one hundred and fifty-eight years could have brought about the recent crisis, and that this shameful cabal has even exerted a direct influence on the Court of Vienna... Never have such great events had a more ignoble cause.'

Acton had regained his previous authority, to the Queen's intense vexation. Their meeting was 'a scene of violent recrimination and tears'. He was less interested in recovering Naples than in saving Sicily. General Craig had been waiting patiently with all his troops on board transports at Messina, and it was Acton who persuaded the King to let them land and occupy the forts. He also wrote to Admiral Collingwood begging him to send a fleet to defend the island. 'Acton and Elliot,' wrote Damas, 'cursed the Hereditary Prince's sojourn in Calabria and all our efforts to maintain ourselves there; they awaited a reverse which would drive us out with the same ardour as the King and Queen awaited news of a victory.' Acton thought that Damas should have withdrawn to Sicily and held his army in reserve for a more promising occasion. He regarded the Calabrian campaign as a waste of men and money. His view happened to be correct, but that did not endear him further to the Queen, who had set her heart on the Calabrian venture. That she had qualms, however, is clear from her letters to Damas. Already on March 2 she wrote to him: 'My dear and worthy friend, whom I esteem infinitely and for causing whose misfortune I reproach myself keenly, allow me to speak to you as a true, attached, eternal and sincere friend. Do in Calabria all that your zeal, courage, energy, goodwill and knowledge dictate, but if the misfortune which pursues us so doggedly should oblige the army and my sons to leave Calabria and come to Sicily, accept the sincere advice of a grateful, devoted friend for your glory and welfare. Write two fine letters, one to the King, the other to Acton, relating minutely the steps which compelled this retreat; resign the command of the army to the King, begging him to choose another commander, saying that you are unfamiliar with Sicily, but that wishing to prove your devotion and to sacrifice your blood for him, you ask to serve his person or his son as a volunteer. Otherwise... you will apply for permission to retire to Germany, grieved that unhappy circumstances did not allow you to serve him as usefully as your heart desired, and ready at his slightest whim to serve him again. It is with pain that I tell you all this, but I am on the spot and see everything that malevolence can do, and we must baffle and confound the rascals... Once we have lost foothold in Calabria, I consider the kingdom of Naples as lost, our fate very wretched, and as for me, I am firmly resolved not to remain in Sicily, but to find myself a little retreat to end my days in peace and tranquillity.' In a postscript she added that as there was said to be a shortage of funds her daughters had gladly given up their dowries, all the property they had left, which she was sending him by the same boat. '*Je donerois mon sang pour aider à la chose.*'

On March 6 the French had a preliminary skirmish with Damas's rearguard at Lagonegro and captured three hundred men, three flags, four cannon and a mass of equipment. This set the pace for the next few days. Damas' main force occupied a mountain plateau near Campotenese which was excellent for defence but had only a narrow outlet for retreat. The French attacked this position in melting snow and heavy fog on the 9th. Besides the snow and fog the mud was knee deep, disadvantages less serious to the assailants who knew their objective. 'Reynier sent his light infantry up the mountain flank on his left, and placed his most dashing brigadier, General Compère, in charge of a column intended to advance on the Sicilian centre with the bayonet. The light infantry, with wonderful agility, wormed their way along the snow-beaten cliffs, turned a difficult passage in single file, and finally came out on Damas's right flank and rear. They immediately advanced in skirmishing order and opened fire; the royal troops attempted to manoeuvre so as to face this unexpected attack, and in doing so fell into confusion. At this moment Compère, who had gradually edged up nearer and nearer, rushed his column forward; one or two volleys were fired, and then in a moment the Sicilian line broke and Damas was defeated. A crowd of fugitives rushed down the pass only to find the narrow egress blocked by the firstcomers, and the active French troops were able to capture not only all the artillery of the defeated army but 2,000 prisoners, including two generals and many officers of rank.' [1]

The same night General Reynier slept at Morano and Paul-Louis Courier, who was on his staff, described his impressions in one of his most vivid letters, while the general, oblivious of the pangs of hunger, sat down in an empty house to write his report, and the troops were plundering and massacring in the town: 'I would plunder too, by Jove, if I knew where to find something to eat. I always return to that theme, but without the faintest hope. The writing continues, they will never finish... We are in a pillaged house, two naked corpses at the door; on the staircase there is something rather like a dead man. In the same room with us a woman who screams that she has been raped, but who will not die of it, and this is General Reynier's office; the neighbouring house on fire, no furniture in this one, not a morsel of bread. What will we eat? This idea worries me.'

Damas had been led to suppose that the Calabrians would shed their last drop of blood for the King; now they concealed their provisions from the remnants of his famished army. Within thirty hours he lost through desertion almost five battalions and a cavalry regiment, together with three-quarters of their officers. At Cosenza the leading citizens threatened to join the French if he offered any resistance outside their walls. This threat was carried out as soon as he left the city. One week later Damas and the royal Princes crossed over to Messina. According to Damas some 4,000 Neapolitan troops were ferried over; according to Reynier about 2,500. During his retreat the Hereditary Prince had scattered proclamations urging the villages to form *corpi volanti* or flying corps to harry the invaders. Many of those who had been left behind were to fight far more effectively as guerillas. The Calabrian campaign dragged on for another four years, 'a war of ambuscades and skirmishes, of midnight assassinations and the firing of villages'. The desperate Queen was the spirit who kept it going.

[1] R. M. Johnston, *The Napoleonic Empire in Southern Italy*, p. 90

Gaeta still held out against the invaders. 'This royal banner flying above its walls seems to me rather a prolongation of regret than of hope,' wrote Damas disconsolately; 'may Heaven make its perseverance profitable! Without a war in the north, I do not think it possible.'

The Queen felt as sorry for Damas as for his defeat, and sent a letter of affectionate condolence: 'Think of what has happened to everybody, to the armies of Austria and Russia, and we had mere recruits... Such is the cruel hazard of war, my heart bleeds for it; these are victims of the cursed Corsican's boundless ambition... I have been interrupted by the King's sudden return after a week's absence; he is grieved, but not at all angry or surprised by what has happened, saying that his knowledge of the army was the reason why he did not want to join it. This proves that he pities you and does not blame you. Calm yourself, therefore, sure of your own good conscience.'

Acton, however, regarded him as responsible for the disaster, which he had aggravated by deluding the Queen with false expectations. Sooner than struggle against his antagonism, Damas retired to Vienna with the ailing Countess Razoumovski, who died in December. The Queen continued to write to him as long as she lived. She begged him to keep her informed of happenings in Vienna, since the Neapolitan ambassador, Alvaro Ruffo, was a lazy and erratic correspondent. 'I like to flatter myself that you are only on leave,' she told him, 'and that we shall meet again in better times.' Damas seems to have appealed to the gentlest side of her nature. When he compared her to a precious stone lost in a swamp which her true friends would always be able to find, she replied: 'I have ceased to be anything; misfortunes and sorrows have destroyed me, but I have a grateful heart which appreciates real merit.' The soldier's compliment was not inept. Maria Carolina had the hardness of a precious stone: she also had its glow, which sympathy could kindle. How brightly she would have shone in a favourable setting! Even if she was not lost in a swamp, her fine facets were rubbed and dulled until only the hardness remained. Less than at Naples was she in harmony with herself and her surroundings. Still she sought to live intensely, so that she welcomed anybody who promised to feed her inner flame. More and more she lived by her emotions and for them, and these revolved round one theme: the recovery of Naples, the patrimony of her children.

Acton's return to power frustrated her plans, as his policy was entirely based on British support. He accompanied the King on a visit to Messina to discuss the best mode of defence with the British generals. The King was gratified and impressed by the discipline of the troops, who seemed well prepared to meet the threatened invasion. Sir John Stuart succeeded Craig as their commander; he had been opposed to the Anglo-Russian evacuation, and although Sir Henry Bunbury described him as flighty and superficial, he was more agreeable for this reason than his hide-bound predecessor. Bunbury relates that while the King was at Messina 'he happened to be on a battery, just as some large boats in the French service, laden with ordnance and stores, were trying to steal along the Calabrian coast to Reggio. Some of the Sicilian gun-boats were firing at them, and the enemy, running field-pieces along the shore, were endeavouring by a return of shots to protect their vessels. I chanced to be standing beside His Majesty: he was watching the skirmish on the opposite coast with childish eagerness; at every shot he laughed aloud, threw out his long bony limbs in strange gesticulations, and poured forth vollies of buffoonery in the *lazzarone* dialect. It never seemed to occur to him that the people in the boats on both sides were his subjects; and that the shots might strike off their heads or legs. No, it was a sight he had never witnessed before and he was himself in perfect safety.'

On April 12 Acton sent Elliot an official note entrusting Messina and its neighbourhood to British protection, and placing 6,500 Sicilian auxiliaries under Stuart's orders. The latter failed to materialize, and the garrison remained predominantly British. The Queen looked askance at these proceedings. No doubt the British were indispensable, but she preferred them at sea; on land she was afraid of their encroachments. She felt that Calabria was the proper place for them; they should be helping her to reconquer Naples; not a moment should be lost! She resented and mistrusted Stuart's unwillingness to embark on offensive operations. 'God forfend,' she wrote bitterly of Acton, 'that he will ruin the Master who shows such a weakness for him, and that he will put him in chains at Messina and then drag him to Malta: this is the general fear in Palermo which I share. As for me, I am resolved to do anything rather than go to Malta.'

Although overshadowed and thwarted by Acton, the Queen's party was exceedingly active. Besides her favourite Saint-Clair and the scheming cabal of French and Corsican *émigrés*, the most prominent members of this party were Circello, Medici, the Tuscan Seratti, the Sicilian Artale, the quixotic Prince of Moliterno, who had returned from exile and won her pardon, and the fanatical young Prince of Canosa. And as all was grist that came to her mill she patronized a squadron of secret agents, many of dubious loyalty, a few little better than brigands. Their chief was Colonel Castrone, shifty and almost illiterate but an accomplished intriguer, who was put in charge of the police at Palermo.

The Queen now spoke of Acton as the most evil and ungrateful of men, 'whose wickedness has altogether surpassed what I could have imagined, and I admit that this black ingratitude is deeply distressing to me and disgusts me more and more with this world'. She was equally indignant with the Duke of Ascoli, whose influence over the King was even greater than Acton's. He was called the Sejanus of Sicily, as he kept the King amused and distracted him from more serious pursuits. While the Queen would have sacrificed all the resources of Sicily to the recovery of Naples, the King had no wish to alienate his only remaining subjects. Let the Queen spend her money on the defence of Gaeta if she chose, he thought it thrown away. The Queen's indignation is comprehensible. But the defence of Gaeta would have been impossible had not England controlled the sea. Lord Collingwood, the British Commander-in-Chief, had other worries: his chief anxiety was to prevent the French Atlantic fleets from entering the Mediterranean. When Admiral Sir Sidney Smith was sent out to co-operate with the land force in Sicily, Lord Collingwood wrote to him (March 21, 1806): that the chief object of the British forces was to prevent the French from obtaining possession of Sicily, and that his ships were to be disposed accordingly; should the Sicilian Court come to terms with France, his instructions were still to hold good, 'notwithstanding any remonstrance which the King of Naples may make on the subject'.

Sir Sidney Smith arrived with the prestige of many gallant exploits at the siege of Acre. 'All he wants is to make a noise,' wrote Napoleon, who called him a fire-ship captain and asked his brother to mention him as seldom as possible. Fantastic and exuberant, he never failed to blow his own trumpet, but he was also chivalrous and brave, cut out to be the champion of a Queen in distress and the bugbear of stodgy martinets. His breezy advent soon shattered the Sicilian doldrums. The Queen thought she had found another

Nelson. Here was an Englishman she could admire and understand. Their mutual sympathy was immediate. 'Schmidt', as the Queen persisted in calling him, listened eagerly to her projects to rouse Naples against the usurper and promised his best support. He was as good as his word. On May 11, when Joseph Bonaparte made his first entry into Naples as King, Sir Sidney sailed into the bay to spoil his triumph. He was too civil to bombard the city, but he captured the island of Capri. After shipping the French garrison to Pozzuoli he proceeded to seize Ponza. Capri was a visible reminder to Joseph that he was by no means monarch of all he surveyed; Ponza became the headquarters of the young Prince of Canosa and a hotbed of royalist conspiracy. The capture of these two bases helped to console the Queen for the loss of a prominent henchman, Marchese Rodio.

Napoleon constantly urged his brother to indulge in some salutary terrorism, and Rodio was among the first of his Neapolitan victims. He had been governor of Matera and 'director-general of the flying battalions' when he was cornered and forced to surrender on March 15. On April 25 he was tried by a military commission on the charges of rebellion and incitement to insurrection. The day after being acquitted he was tried by a second commission and condemned to be shot. This judicial murder was commonly attributed to Saliceti, Joseph's ruthless Minister of Police, but the gentle Joseph himself wrote to Masséna on April 21 expressing concern that Rodio had not yet been condemned: 'I would not know what to think of the commission unless he was judged before my return to Naples. Prompt justice must be done.' Rodio's eloquent self-defence made him a martyr to his sovereigns' cause. As one of Cardinal Ruffo's most efficient leaders in 1799 he had incurred hostility among the liberals, but Paul-Louis Courier reflected the opinions of many French officers when he wrote: 'His death is looked upon here as a murder and as a mean revenge... Everyone is horrified, perhaps the French even more than the Neapolitans. He was shot from behind like a traitor, a felon, a rebel to his *legitimate* sovereign... Assuredly, sir, this does not belong to the time and century in which we are living: all this has happened in some part of Japan or Timbuctoo, in the time of Cambyses. I agree with you that manners have softened; Nero would not reign today. However, when one wishes to be master... the means must fit the end. Master and good, master and bad, are these words consistent? Grammatically yes, like honest thief or equitable brigand. I knew Rodio: he was a pretty man, with little wit or intelligence, incredibly fatuous, in brief, good enough for a Queen.'

The liquidation of Rodio was a great relief to King Joseph; the Prince of Hesse-Philippsthal was less easy to remove. His defence of Gaeta was a constant challenge. And Napoleon kept harping on Sicily; 'I would rather a ten years' war,' he wrote, 'than leave your kingdom incomplete and Sicily an unsettled question'. Having reached the Straits of Messina, General Reynier had to stop short. He did not feel strong enough yet to control Calabria and embark on the invasion as well. The siege of Gaeta neutralized an increasing number of French troops.

As long as this fortress held out the new regime was kept on tenterhooks. Its position on a rocky peninsula invited comparison with Gibraltar. Its governor, the Prince of Hesse-Philippsthal, was a son of the Landgrave William II whose states were to be absorbed in the kingdom of Westphalia, and his elder brother had been killed by the French in Holland. In spite of his long array of lofty titles, he had led a dreary life as a soldier of fortune. A dumpy little man with an aquiline nose and a moustache, whose rubicund face showed that he was as valiant at the trencher as in the trench, he had suffered in matrimony. His Princess was a fine-looking woman but far too flighty. Damas had been wounded by the Chevalier de Saxe on her account, and her reputation was such that Charles Lock, on his brief return to Naples in 1804, rebuked his wife for sending her a present. 'I wish you had consulted me before you took this step,' he wrote. 'I could have told you what I knew before I left England: that the profligacy of her conduct has been so scandalous, even in this dissolute country, that the Queen was under the necessity of ordering her away nine months ago. For God's sake never more allow that woman's name to pass your lips.' The Prince sought consolation from Bacchus. If he could not control his wife, he controlled an unruly garrison of some 6,000 men, of whom a large proportion were jail birds. According to Sir Henry Bunbury, who knew him, 'his familiar buffoonery and his daring example mastered their fears, their affection and their admiration'. When the French were under the walls he shouted at them through a speaking-trumpet: 'Gaeta is not Ulm! Hesse is not Mack!' And in a spirit of sublime self-denial he handed the key of his wine cellar to the Bishop of Gaeta with the stipulation that he would allow him a single bottle a day.

Though the Queen had sent him supplies at her own expense, he was often at a low ebb until Sir Sidney Smith appeared. Besides dropping guerrilla leaders at key points on the Calabrian coast with proclamations inciting the people to revolt, he sent badly needed provisions to Gaeta, as well as four heavy guns, some English gunners, and Colonel Michele Pezza, better known as Fra Diavolo. Furthermore, he sent a small squadron of gun vessels under Captain Richardson to blockade a French flotilla in the Garigliano. After harrying the French lines with his band of cut throats, Fra Diavolo became bored by the monotony of routine in the fortress. Hesse discovered that he was negotiating with the French and sent him back to Palermo under arrest, but he was too plausible a rogue not to exculpate himself, and his services were soon called for again. Thanks to Smith, the Prince was enabled to repel attacks with fresh vigour. After dinner he usually treated the French to a warm cannonade. One of their best engineers, General Vallongue, was killed while directing the siege artillery. Reinforcements continued to arrive until there were at least 10,000 besiegers, including fourteen generals, under the supreme command of Masséna.

While Gaeta was thus hard pressed, Sir Sidney Smith induced Sir John Stuart to strike a blow at the French in Calabria before they became strong enough to invade Sicily. The blow succeeded beyond expectation. On July 1 Stuart's expedition, consisting of 4,795 infantry with sixteen guns, disembarked near the village of Santa Eufemia on the gulf of the same name. On July 4 Reynier's force of 5,150 men suffered a lightning defeat at Maida. The victory has been called useless, but it served its purpose. The invasion of Sicily was indefinitely postponed, and the whole of Calabria was set ablaze with insurrection. Some considered that if Stuart had promptly marched northwards 'nothing could have stopped the British short of Naples'; but his force was small, exhausted by the heat and riddled with malaria. If the Calabrian guerrillas were as effective as the Queen believed—they were certainly strong in numbers—they could do the rest. The surrender of Gaeta on July 18 made it necessary for the British to return to Sicily. Hesse was seriously wounded on the 10th, and he had been the very soul of the resistance. Colonel Hoz, his second in command, could have held out longer, but he lacked Hesse's magnetism and initiative. Masséna, who was extremely short of ammunition, granted the defenders very lenient terms. Over a thousand of them, including thirty officers, went over to the enemy. The others were allowed to sail for Sicily on parole.

After the fall of Gaeta and Stuart's return to Messina, the Queen's chief weapon against the usurper was insurrection. A royal edict of June 28 invested Smith with supreme authority over all the King's forces on land and sea, and in formally accepting it he promised the Queen that he would now 'dare to do more than Bonaparte would venture to imagine'. Sir John Stuart was told nothing about this extraordinary commission and only Elliot's tact prevented a rupture between Smith and the General. The Admiral disembarked more bands of irregulars with arms and ammunition and strenuously patrolled the coasts from Scilla to Naples, while his military compatriots looked on with disapproval. The insurrection in Calabria did not interest them; to co-operate with cut throats was *infra dig*. Hudson Lowe, the governor of Capri, was an exception, but even he cooled when it came to collaborating with the Prince of Canosa. Stuart might have continued an offensive in the flush of victory, but his staff were all against it. On his return he was superseded by the Prime Minister's brother, General Henry Fox, who was also to represent his government at Palermo. Elliot was recalled. Fox was wax in the hands of Sir John Moore, his second in command. Sidney Smith told Moore that only lack of arms and money had prevented him from driving the French out of southern Italy and restoring King Ferdinand to his throne. Moore did not sympathize. In a despatch to General Fox he wrote (August 24, 1806): 'His interference in Calabria, where in his imagination he is directing the operations of armies, but where in reality he is only encouraging murder and rapine, and keeping up amongst that unhappy people, whom we have no intention to support, a spirit of revolt which will bring upon them the more severe vengeance of the French government. As long as Sir Sidney had money, he distributed it profusely; and now, with as little judgment, he is distributing arms, ammunition, and provisions...'

The guerrilla leaders kept clamouring for more assistance. Smith did what he could for them: he landed Fra Diavolo at Amantea, north of Maida; he captured Fort Licosa on August 14. But he was not supported by the prudent Fox, and the Queen protested in vain against this desertion of her dearest cause. Stuart had announced himself at Santa Eufemia as a friend and liberator, and his victory had been the signal for revolt. Church bells rang and bonfires blazed on the hills, spreading the news from village to village.

Courier's letters revive the horrors and humours of this diabolical campaign. For instance: 'After having sacked without knowing why the pretty town of Corigliano, we came (not I, for I was with Verdier, but I arrived three days later); our men climbed towards Cassano, beside a small river or torrent which is still called the *Sibari*, though it has ceased to flow through Sybaris... The Swiss battalion was leading, all in tatters like the rest, commanded by Muller, since Clavel had been killed at Santa Eufemia. Seeing this red company, the inhabitants of Cassano mistook us for the English: this has often happened. They come out to meet us, embrace us and congratulate us on having given those rascally Frenchmen, those excommunicated robbers, a thorough trouncing. They did not flatter us, to be sure, on this occasion. They told us of our follies and said even worse of us than we deserved. Each cursed the soldiers of *Maestro Peppe* (Master Joe); each boasted of having killed a few. With their pantomime, joining the gesture to the word: "I stabbed six of them; I shot ten." One said he had killed Verdier; another had killed myself. This is really curious. Lieutenant Portier, whom you may know, saw one of them holding his own pistols, which he had lent to me, and which I lost when I was plundered. He jumped on him: "Whose pistols are those?" The fellow replied-you know their style: "Sir, they are yours." Little did he suppose he was telling the absolute truth. "But where did you get them?" "From a French officer I killed." Then Verdier and I were believed to be dead; and when we arrived three days later, we were already on the verge of being forgotten.

'You see how they recommended themselves and settled their affairs. Thus we received all their confidences, and they only recognized us when we fired at them point-blank. Many of them were killed. Fifty-two were taken and shot that evening on the square of Cassano. But a feature of party rage worth noting is that they were despatched by their compatriots, by the Calabrians our friends, the good Calabrians of Joseph, who asked as a favour to be employed in this butchery. They had no difficulty in obtaining this boon, for we were tired of the massacre at Corigliano. Such are the feasts of Sybaris; you may guarantee the strict accuracy of this account. The famous miracle was that a few days later, in a neighbouring village, they slaughtered fifty-two of our men, neither more nor less, who were pillaging without any thought of evil. The Madonna, as you may believe, took part in this good business, the accounts of which were embellished and propagated to the glory of the Holy Faith.

'The scene at Marcellinara was of the same kind. We were mistaken for Englishmen, and as such welcomed in the town. When we reached the square, a crowd surrounded us. A man with whom Reynier had lodged recognized him and tried to escape. Reynier made signs to arrest him, but he was killed. The whole company fired at the same time; in two minutes the square was covered with corpses. We found six of our gunners in a cell there, stark naked and half dead of hunger. They were being kept for a little *auto-da-fé* which was to be held on the morrow... Scarcely a fortnight ago we took down one of our men who had been hanged and stabbed, in both cases clumsily, and now he can eat and drink as you do. They kill so many, and in such a hurry, that things are only half done... People who do not reflect, at whose head you can put myself, may still find agreeable moments here: they eat and drink amid all this devilry; they make love as elsewhere and even better, for they do little else. The country provides in abundance the wherewithal to satisfy every appetite, hair and feather, meat and fish; more wine than one can drink, and what wine! more women than one can want. They are dark in the plains, fair in the mountains, amorous everywhere.'

All the chroniclers of this campaign were haunted by the atrocities perpetrated on both sides. The Calabrians were defending their King, their religion, their homes, their country, against invaders they had no reason to love and compatriots they regarded as traitors and oppressors. They were primitive, credulous, impressionable, passionate and correspondingly cruel. Under the Bourbons the government had hardly been visible in the remoter provinces; these had scarcely known the blessings of officialdom, the amenities of garrisons. Their pastors were their spiritual masters, and they turned to these for guidance. The new government was only too painfully present: it had brought them war and devastation, requisitions, extortions, and the excesses of a frightened enemy. They might be excused for failing to appreciate its benefits. The Pope's refusal to recognize Joseph Bonaparte as King of Naples, and the latter's wholesale suppression of convents and monasteries had set the priests against it. This rugged country of mountains and impenetrable forests, where many towns and villages were perched like eagles' nests over precipitous ravines, seemed an ideal stronghold to the men of spirit who had been born and bred there.

Napoleon had warned Joseph: 'A fortnight sooner or later you will have an insurrection. It is an event which happens constantly in conquered territory.' It would have happened in spite of the Queen. But the Queen was the driving power behind it. Her sorrows and disappointments, combined with her hatred of the usurper and her mistrust of her only ally, made her a glowing centre of resistance. The increasing doses of opium to calm her jangling nerves and the shooting pains of neuralgia never dulled her determination; perhaps they intensified it. One characteristic she shared with the Calabrians across the straits: fierceness. She had come to believe that she was waging a holy war. It had its compensations, in excitement, in the intrigue that beguiled her imagination, in the atmosphere of mystery that appealed to her temperament. It brought her in contact with heroes, villains and eccentrics, whom she would not have met under ordinary circumstances. At least they possessed the virtue of being warm-blooded.

Before leaving Naples, Medici had had an inspiration: he had introduced the Queen to a kindred spirit. The young Prince of Canosa was a fanatical aristocrat who had been persecuted for his opinions as if he had been a Jacobin. He attributed the kingdom's calamities to a policy which had alienated the nobles. But his attachment to the Crown had never wavered; and he did not hesitate to leave his wife, children and property to follow the royal Princes to Calabria. The Queen had invoked him at a crowded audience: 'Come here, my son. Oh how treacherously the King has been deceived about those who are truly faithful to him!' From that moment he became the Queen's devoted slave. It was Canosa who organized conspiracy and espionage on the islands of Ponza and Ventotene. Castrone chose the instruments, but he directed them. Through an elaborate network of correspondence, by distributing money, manifestoes, leaflets and posters, which were more widely diffused at Naples than those of Joseph's government, by spreading alarming reports and false rumours, he did much to undermine confidence in the new regime. Even Saliceti was baffled by his versatile technique. Canosa saw himself 'as a single man planted on the rocks of Ponza who fearlessly defied Napoleon'. Like the Queen, he was a prolific writer; like her, he believed that 'we should do everything in our power to reconquer the kingdom with our own forces'. To wait for the allies to reconquer it, 'like the Hebrews awaiting manna in the desert', would cause a fatal delay during which the enemy would drain the best resources of the kingdom. In the meantime, thinking themselves abandoned, the royalists would join the usurper in despair, so that when the country was liberated at last it would be difficult to know whom to trust, for the whole of society would be corrupted.

The Queen tried to persuade General Fox to embark on a new plan of invasion, but Sir John Moore pointed out that it was 'chimerical and absurd', which did not deter the Queen from persevering. By dint of protestations and cajolery and pulling wires in London, she hoped to force Fox into aggressive action, but all the English generals were prejudiced against her. Sir Sidney Smith was her only English sympathizer. 'The loyal Schmid,' as she wrote, 'is quibbled with, pestered, prevented and paralysed by his selfish and wicked compatriots, who are bent upon his ruin.' Very well, she would prepare an expedition without their help. As soon as the Prince of Hesse recovered from his wounds he should lead it.

Such tireless energy was bound to prevail over the King's party, of which Acton was the worn-out corner-stone. The King soon returned to his sporting pursuits and spent little time in Palermo. 'His style of living is certainly not very royal,' remarked Drummond, 'and there are few country gentlemen of two thousand a year in England who do not keep a better table. But he amuses himself with hunting and farming and seems happy enough.' The Hereditary Prince took after his father, and his dairy farm was a model of its kind. According to Torelli's *Memorie Segrete*, 'his gravest occupation was to milk the cows at Boccadifalco, his country estate, to sell his butter and investigate the backsides of hens in order to separate those which had eggs. One day the nuns of Cancelliere, who were not in *clausura*, were walking in his dairy. On meeting them he courteously invited them to taste his butter. Surprised by such an honour they respectfully declined, but he repeated the invitation and, ordering his steward to serve them, he left them, saying: "Taste it, it is excellent." Obliged to breakfast by his insistence, they went to thank him. "Did I not tell you it was excellent?" he remarked. Calling his steward aside, he asked if they had paid, and hearing that they had not, because he had supposed that His Highness wished to give them a present, he said: "For shame, make them pay. It is an expensive item." The steward blushed to have to play this role, and the poor nuns collected three *onze* from their slender purses with the assistance of their chaplain.'

Acton felt too old to contend with the apathy of the King and the Hereditary Prince on the one hand, and with the caprices of the Queen and her adherents on the other. His Tuscan protégé, Seratti, having failed to satisfy his ambitions, now turned against him. Knowing this, the Queen used Seratti to undermine Acton's influence. Age, ill-health and misanthropy did the rest. He resigned at the end of August, and the King once more allowed his wife to rule. Her partisans filled the ministries: Circello, that of Foreign Affairs combined with War and the Marine; Medici, Finance; Seratti, Justice. As Minister of Foreign Affairs nobody was more foreign to affairs than Circello, said Elliot's successor Drummond. Seratti, having served the Queen's purpose in helping to oust Acton, resigned on the plea of infirmity. Medici was the most intelligent of these, but he made the mistake of treating Sicily like Naples. The fall of Acton satisfied a seven years' grudge. To Damas, another of his enemies, the Queen wrote in December: 'Acton does nothing, and is not even consulted; the King sees him very seldom and pays no more attention to him. Since he has been dismissed and forgotten, I see him occasionally, letting bygones be bygones, only remembering that I used to be his friend.'

XXX

Failure of Hesse's expedition and of royalist plots at Naples—Saliceti versus Canosa—Paget on dissensions at Palermo—Tilsit—The Empress of Austria's death and the Emperor's remarriage—Canosa's difficulties—The Saliceti explosion—Napoleon's advice to his brother Joseph— Treaty between England and Sicily, March 30, 1808—Insurrection in Spain—Arrival of the Duke of Orléans—His engagement to Maria Amalia—Fruitless mission to Spain—Murat enters Naples as King, September, 1808—His capture of Capri—Stuart's lukewarm expedition—Marriage of Maria Amalia.

The recall of Sir Sidney Smith, in January 1807, deprived the Queen of her last English champion. The other English military and civil officials in Sicily became increasingly hostile. Since Napoleon had seduced Turkey, a British fleet was sent to bombard Constantinople and 5,000 troops from Messina were sent to Alexandria, but both expeditions failed. There was also an insurrection at Malta to be suppressed. The moment was not propitious for an excursion to Naples, but the Queen refused to allow this. As Elliot had written: 'Her Sicilian Majesty... with great susceptibility of temper, of a lively, imaginative and active enterprising spirit, does not, or perhaps does not choose to, see the difficulties which oppose the attainment of any favourite object.' Obsessed with the recovery of Naples, the Queen tried to force Moore to co-operate. Drummond supported her, but Moore remained impervious to his arguments. Though the Queen was afflicted by the death of her daughter, the Empress of Austria, on April 13, 1807, she did not lose heart in advocating prompt military action. 'As there is no way to make the English move in spite of our prayers and persuasions,' she wrote to Damas on May 10, 1807, 'the King has finally decided to do everything to tempt fortune, and four thousand men have gone to Reggio under the Prince of Hesse's command... The vexations inflicted on the people [by the French], the spoliations, depredations, and the forced levy to send them into Lombardy has disgusted everybody. There is sporadic fighting everywhere and they appeal to us: consequently we should risk everything to succour our faithful and oppressed subjects. The conduct of the English is not only strange but infamous, and I suffer every kind of pain, sorrow and chagrin.'

The King announced the expedition in a proclamation to his faithful Calabrians, promising to abolish many taxes and exempt from others those cities which had been sacked and burned by the usurper, besides granting rewards to subjects who had been penalized for their loyalty. The Prince of Hesse also published a stirring proclamation as 'the harbinger of victory'. But his enterprise proved a fiasco. In a brief action at Mileto on May 28 he lost 1,633 men and six guns. The guerrillas who should have helped him fired on his retreating columns and plundered their baggage-train. 'How my enemies in Palermo will laugh!' he exclaimed as he watched the rout. Only Colonel Nunziante's regiment was able to hold the French at bay. Moore's reluctance to co-operate was grimly justified. This put an end to regular warfare in Calabria, but brigandage continued on a formidable scale.

Hesse's expedition had been co-ordinated with an insurrection at Naples, but this was nipped in the bud. A certain Iovane, pretending to take part in the conspiracy, showed all his correspondence with Salvatore Bruno, who commanded the Capri flotilla, to Saliceti, Joseph Bonaparte's Minister of Police. The leading conspirators were arrested on the night of May 22, and a dozen were hanged, including two distinguished ex-colonels of the royal army, Marchese Palmieri and the young Duke Tommaso Frammarino. A reign of terror ensued. On June 2, when Palmieri was executed, one of those scenes of mass hysteria ever latent on such occasions broke out like a tidal wave. Nobody knew how it started: there was a panic helter-skelter flight in all directions and the troops not only fired on the running crowd but charged it with swords and bayonets. About eight were killed and forty were seriously wounded. The soldiers pursued stragglers as far as the Toledo, where carriages were stopped and harmless passengers were molested. Palmieri nearly escaped in the pandemonium, but he was captured and strung to the gallows. About ten days later Agostino Mosca, a colonel of royalist guerrillas, was arrested near Castellammare where Joseph Bonaparte was due to pass. So corrupt were Saliceti's police and so eager to crush all semblance of revolt, that the evidence against him was probably forged. A bracelet of hair, said to be the Queen's, besides several letters urging him to murder Joseph, including one from Maria Carolina herself, were alleged to have been found on him. He was condemned to proceed in penitential garb with a lighted torch as far as the square of Gesù Nuovo, where one arm was to be cut off, after which he was to walk on with the torch in his remaining hand to the stake where he was to be burnt alive. But the Bianchi confraternity, who always ministered to the condemned, protested so vigorously against this sentence that the torch was fastened to one arm and he was hanged in his red Sicilian uniform, fortunately quite drunk, after which his corpse was consigned to the flames. Pasquale Viscardi, who was to have kidnapped Saliceti, escaped. Subsequently four others were executed for plotting against Joseph's life, including a wealthy merchant called Talamo. As if to advertise the unpopularity of the Bonapartist regime Saliceti published a long report in July 1807, accusing Canosa of instigating Joseph's murder. Canosa reprinted this with his own comments, accusing Saliceti of inventing plots to make himself indispensable and of extorting confessions by unlawful means. But Canosa had to confess himself beaten by the Corsican's terroristic methods, for the Neapolitan loyalists were sadly demoralized.

In July, Sir Arthur Paget passed through Palermo on his way to the Dardanelles. He went to call on Drummond, and on returning to his ship found Circello waiting for him. 'He told me that he had been sent by the Queen, who insisted upon seeing me, and that his orders were "to bring me ashore, even if I were in my *robe de chambre*". I, however, resisted, and having satisfied him that every moment was most precious to me, he proceeded to lay before me a string of complaints against our generals in Sicily, and implored my interference, either in persuading them to adopt a different line of conduct towards the Court or to represent it to my government. After a very long conversation he took his leave. It was then, as it had been the whole morning, a complete calm. Finding that we could make no way, and knowing that the ship was seen from the palace, and possibly therefore that my refusal to obey the Queen's summons might under such circumstances be attributed to *mauvaise volonté* on my part, I decided to go ashore. I got to the palace about half-past ten at night, and remained with Her Majesty nearly two hours, in the course of which she went over the same ground that her minister had in the morning, only in more forcible and pointed terms. Her complaints were principally directed against Sir John Moore, as she considered General Fox to be completely under his control. Such, she said, was their conduct towards the King and herself, such their general treatment of her subjects, that she should consider Sicily as a conquered country were she not persuaded of a contrary disposition existing on the part of the English government.

'Those generals accuse the Sicilian government of not recruiting the army. "How," she said, "can we recruit our army when they suborn our subjects? They pay them better than we can afford to do. But with respect to our army we have five or six thousand men ready for any service, and to be embarked tomorrow. The transports are in the harbour, the artillery and stores the same, the cavalry can be embarked in two days, and when we inform the generals of this and present to them a plan, as we have done, for an expedition against Naples, instead of concerting with us our proposals are rejected with contempt. They insinuate as their justification that we are betrayed; nay more, they have said that to spill British blood to set such a tyrant upon the throne of Naples and such a family, was paying too high a price. They who accuse us of betraying them are themselves the tools of a *tas de mécontents et de factieux* who surround them at Messina." All this and a great deal more of the like were not very pleasant or edifying to listen to. The Queen, as did Circello in the morning, finished by assuring me that I could be of the greatest use to her, and by beseeching me to exert all my influence with the generals to bring about another order of things...

'I did everything in my power to set matters right, for after all, as it is not the intention to dispossess those sovereigns of their remaining kingdom, and as (if even it were an object) it would be very difficult, if not impossible, to get rid of the Queen in any other way, it is certainly most desirable that harmony and confidence should if possible take the place of strife and mistrust between the Sicilian government and our generals in that island, and I flatter myself that my efforts to that effect were not altogether unsuccessful... These dissensions are not confined to the above persons. On the contrary, they exist to perhaps a greater degree between the Queen and Mr Drummond, and also between Mr Drummond and the generals, so that in point of fact the three parties are at open war without any of the two being of the same side. Mr Drummond inveighs with equal vehemence against both, and by what he says of the generals one would imagine that the Queen and he *s'étaient donné le mot pour les dénigrer*. But then he is not less violent in his language against her. He appears to have attached himself to the King, and is of opinion that His Majesty really applies himself to business and will in time take the government into his own hands, and that then affairs will be conducted much better. Upon the whole, next to possessing the island Bonaparte himself could hardly wish the situation of affairs in it to be different... I really do not think it necessary for me to enter into any detail of the defence made, and the recriminations which burst forth at headquarters against the Court of Palermo. I will briefly state that it appeared to be the decided opinion of both Generals Fox and Moore that no faith whatever is to be placed in the Sicilian government, administered as it now is, and so long as the Queen directs its Councils, and that the Sicilian army, if it is so to be called, is in so wretched a state, that no useful co-operation is under the present circumstances reasonably to be expected from it... As to bringing about a proper understanding between Sir John Moore and Mr Drummond, that is what I thought fruitless to attempt... but it is lamentable that persons in their situation should not possess each other's esteem and confidence.'

The failure of Hesse's expedition had not damped the Queen's ardour. But she was seriously alarmed by the treaty of Tilsit between Napoleon and Alexander I of Russia. 'I await my death warrant,' she wrote to Damas, 'I cannot tell you how shocked, disgusted and revolted I have been by the infamous peace concluded by the puny Alexander... If Moscow and Petersburg were in the power of his enemies he could not have committed a more despicable action. The peace of Austerlitz is a masterpiece compared with this; at least the Emperor of Austria only injured himself and not his allies, nor did he demean himself by rigging himself out in the livery of the man who dubbed him a parricide and printed it in all the public papers.' And page after page in the same strain. 'But as long as I have any breath I hope to be of use to my family and fulfil my very difficult duties...' The Tsar, her former ally, who now recognized Joseph Bonaparte as King of Naples, she described as 'the most handsome but certainly the most worthless of men'. At this juncture Saliceti made overtures to Canosa through the latter's sister-in-law, whom he had set at liberty, saying that the French wished to come to an agreement with the Bourbons of Sicily and offer them compensations. What sort of compensations? Canosa was tempted to take the bull by the horns, but the Queen ordered him to let the matter drop.

The death of her eldest daughter had severed Maria Carolina's closest tie with her native land. 'God has chosen to bereave me of her upon whom I depended to take my place with my dear children,' she wrote to the Emperor. 'His holy will be done; but I rely confidently upon your goodness and friendship to help and protect my dear children after my death.' That confidence was soon shaken by the news of his engagement to the young Princess of Modena. Like her own Francis, the Emperor could hardly wait to marry again. The Queen's next letter to him began: 'My very dear Son—Pardon me if for the last time I make use of a name which was so close to my heart.' Henceforth she addressed him simply as 'Your Majesty'. He, too, was to recognize the usurper as King of Naples.

Of the Queen's two daughters in Palermo, the virtuous Maria Cristina married the equally virtuous Duke Carlo Felice, brother and heir of the King of Sardinia, and this well-matched couple spent more time on their knees in chapels and churches than in the bridal chamber. They departed for Sardinia in September 1807, and Maria Amalia remained alone with her mother, profoundly depressed. The Hereditary Princess, more animal than human, was no companion to either of them. The Hereditary Prince was busy farming; the King was either fishing at Solanto or shooting at Colli, Ficuzza and Bagheria; he only came to Palermo when his presence seemed indispensable. At least the Queen had plenty of political excitement to distract her. Princess Maria Amalia was approaching twenty-five, yet no eligible partner appeared on the horizon. To her diary she confided: 'Sicily is under the heavy yoke of the English. Our affairs are confused and chaotic, with an extreme slowness in execution. Finally, unless God puts forth His almighty hand our total ruin is to be feared, and it will be a miracle of divine mercy if we preserve the rest of our magnificent patrimony. Torn by all the keenest sentiments of filial love, love of my country, compassion, justice, equity and honour, my heart is floating in a sea of anguish. At every gesture that escapes me, at every word I dare to utter, I am afraid I might have committed an indiscretion... I wake up at night, I rise in the morning with this thought: what will happen to me today? what bitterness must I experience? I raise my eyes to heaven and find consolation in our holy religion, reflecting that we are exiled in this world, and that there is a better world to come.'

The Queen still presided over the Council of Ministers; every moment was taken up with her vast correspondence, audiences and private interviews with messengers and secret agents, Neapolitan refugees who had sacrificed their possessions to follow the Court, and parasites who took advantage of her mania for intrigue, of whom the most pernicious was Castrone the chief of police in Palermo, who handled her dealings with agents on the mainland far more to his own profit than to hers; while Colonel Carbone sent her frequent reports from Messina. Any other woman would have sunk with nervous prostration under such a weight of correspondence and such an endless succession of audiences, apart from her constant anxiety and domestic losses. But she regarded all this as the normal routine of government, a duty she was determined to fulfil. Her reckless generosity prevented her from getting rid of many a useless hanger-on. Yet even after Tilsit she continued to inveigh against the English in general and Sir John Moore in particular, whom she openly called a traitor.

Canosa tried in vain to make her realize the absurdity of this attitude, which was bound to estrange her sole remaining ally. 'I was greatly astonished to hear that Moore is a traitor,' he wrote to her. 'That is a thing I shall never believe. An English general who is a traitor would be the same as a French general who is honest; these seem to me two stoical paradoxes which fail to carry conviction, though I am so appalled by the corruption of this century that I sometimes fear that even I shall become a villain by contagion.' For the present he had given up the idea of an insurrection: his latest projects were either to seize the islands of Ischia and Procida or swoop on the port of Anzio and capture some forty French and Genoese ships full of merchandise; but his naval advisers raised technical objections. Colonel Hudson Lowe, who tampered with his ships and agents at Capri, was a thorn in his flesh, but he suspected that Lowe had been set against him by a jealous rival. 'Such conduct is absolutely insane and paralyses all my operations,' he complained. 'Stuart should order that madman to mend his manners, and not to molest my ships, or the persons sent by me on affairs of state.'

The loyalist agents at least contrived to give the enemy a nasty shock. Saliceti had come home at one o'clock in the morning of January 31, 1808, when he was thrown down by a violent explosion. 'He rushed to his daughter's room,' wrote the French minister Miot, 'but already the three stories of the wing she inhabited had collapsed. He heard her voice, and in hurrying to rescue her his head and legs were badly bruised. With the aid of his servants, he managed to extricate her from five or six feet of wreckage under which she had been buried for more than fifteen minutes. By a strange piece of luck her husband, who had been sleeping near her, had not been dragged down with the falling masonry, and found himself in the middle of the courtyard without any injury.' One servant was killed, three others were seriously wounded, and twenty-two rooms of the house, Palazzo Serracapriola on the Riviera di Chiaia, were demolished. Saliceti was so unnerved that he did not appear in public for two months.

It was soon proved that the explosion had been caused by an 'infernal machine', and seventeen suspects were arrested. The trial dragged on until June 10: 138 witnesses were called and twelve volumes of evidence were compiled. Pietro Colletta, the future historian, was one of the fiercest of the judges who condemned six of the seventeen accused to death. Onofrio Viscardi, an apothecary whose shop was on the ground floor of the Serracapriola Palace, was tortured until he declared that his three sons were guilty, instigated by the Queen and the Prince of Canosa. As he was seventy-six years old he probably said whatever the police prompted him to say. The Queen and Canosa were branded as authors of the outrage in the official report published by Saliceti. Canosa rebutted this by accusing Saliceti of extorting a denunciation of innocent persons from the senile apothecary, which was later confirmed by Pasquale Borrelli, secretary-general of the prefecture of police. Tit for tat, Canosa also charged Saliceti with hiring two assassins to murder himself. These were arrested and sent to Palermo after confession. Signor Maturi, Canosa's biographer, has exculpated him and the Queen.

Saliceti's police became more ruthless and despotic. In the meantime Napoleon scolded his brother Joseph for his excessive mildness and kept on firing at him such orders as these: 'Pile on the taxes, show severity, make examples!... In a conquered country it is not good to be humane... Never trust the Neapolitans—keep an eye on your kitchen: only employ French cooks and carvers... shoot down at least a hundred rebels... Sack five or six large villages... Rob without reservation, nothing is sacred after a conquest... Your courtiers tell you that you are loved for your kindness. Mere folly! Lose a battle on the Isonzo, and you will see how to test your popularity and Carolina's unpopularity... You exaggerate the hatred which the Queen has left behind her. You do not know men. There are not twenty people who hate her as you think, or twenty who would not yield to one of her smiles or graces... Do not even consider forming a Neapolitan army: it would desert you at the first sign of danger.' The kingdom was to defray all the cost of occupation, apart from which Napoleon claimed an annual tribute of a million francs; the revenues of large fiefs were assigned to his generals and ministers—Fouché Duke of Otranto, Godin Duke of Gaeta, Macdonald Duke of Taranto, Oudinot Duke of Reggio, Talleyrand Prince of Benevento, etc. A horde of rapacious Frenchmen arrived to exploit the conquest.

The maze of plots and counter-plots thickened in Sicily as well as in Naples. General Stuart was alarmed by the discovery that some Sicilians were corresponding with the French in Calabria; fearing a conspiracy, he had them arrested. The King claimed the prisoners and sent Marchese Artale to Messina to try them. Many prominent Sicilians objected to this choice and blackened his character to Stuart—on account of his incorruptibility, said the Queen's party. One of the prisoners committed suicide, and Stuart was told this was due to torture. As the odium was made to fall on the English, Stuart became indignant and insisted on Artale's removal, though Circello assured him that he was famous for his integrity and that it was a mistake to judge him by English standards: the Sicilian code was different. However, Stuart went so far as to demand a pardon for the accused, which was obtained from the King in spite of the Queen's opposition. This caused one of the first open rifts between the Queen and her allies, which was to widen into a yawning chasm. Yet a treaty between England and Sicily was signed on March 30, 1808, whereby England was to maintain 10,000 troops on the island, to be increased if necessary, and to pay an annual subsidy of £300,000 sterling; an additional treaty was signed in May 1809, increasing the subsidy to £400,000. So substantial a grant of money entitled the English to a voice in the affairs of the island they were defending, but the Queen objected to the increasing loudness of that voice. An observant Scottish traveller, John Galt, remarked: 'Considering how much the Government of Sicily is indebted to Great Britain, we ought to possess a greater influence in the direction of its public measures than we have yet obtained. That the Queen has hitherto resisted all interference of this kind is not surprising, when we consider the character of the persons to whom the management of our affairs in Sicily has been entrusted. However respectable as private individuals, none of them have been men likely to carry that authority, as statesmen, which was necessary to overawe the intriguing spirit of the Neapolitan Court... None of the Sicilian statesmen, during the first time that I was in the island [1809], were spoken of as persons of much capacity, nor did I find that they had improved in reputation when I returned the second time [1810]. The talents of the Queen kept them in a state of inferiority, from which they had not energy enough to rise. They were allowed, however, to possess a kind of prudence, which tempered the impassioned conduct of the Queen; but it was alleged to have in it more cunning than wisdom.' These remarks are pregnant in the light of future developments.

Thanks to Godoy, Spain had been Napoleon's passive ally, but he could not resist an opportunity to depose its King in order to give his brother Joseph a more important throne. Charles IV, who had abdicated in March, was allowed to retire with his wife and her paramour to the château of Compiègne, while Ferdinand VII was interned at Valençay. The tragi-comedy is extremely complex. It was one of Napoleon's most iniquitous ruses; it was also one of his grossest blunders. After the famous *Dos Mayo*, when the people of Madrid rose in patriotic frenzy to prevent the French from removing the last remnants of the royal family—scenes perpetuated by the art of Goya—Murat announced to the 'Junta of Regency' that Napoleon wished them to choose another King. Not knowing the Emperor's decision he had hoped to be chosen himself. It was an acute disappointment when Napoleon informed him: 'I intend that the King of Naples shall reign at Madrid. I will give you the kingdom of Naples or Portugal. Reply to me at once what you think, for this must be arranged in one day.' He was forced to propose Joseph Bonaparte to the Junta. For himself he chose Naples. The obsequious Junta sent a deputation to Napoleon in June offering the crown to his brother, while their whole country flared up against the treacherous Corsican. The news of this spontaneous insurrection was heartening to Maria Carolina, who expected Naples to follow the Spanish example. As the imprisoned monarch was his close relative, Ferdinand of the Two Sicilies considered himself the presumptive Regent of Spain and thought of delegating his younger son Leopold to represent him in this capacity.

In June the Duke of Orléans arrived in Messina, and it was an open secret that he had come to ask for the hand of Princess Maria Amalia. He was thirty-five, and after a stormy career in which he had contrived miraculously to keep his head, he was anxious to reinstate himself with the Bourbons, to blot out the memory of

Egalité and his connexions with the tricolour. Though the Queen dreaded meeting him, she was resolved to be tolerant when the King invited him to Camastra, his country house near Palermo. The Duke had been toughened by experience, and he was perfectly self-sufficient. When he became King of France he told M. de Bacourt: 'I had great difficulty in getting to Sicily when I wanted to go there to marry the Queen. The British government would not allow me to make this voyage... Eventually they relaxed this severity, and when I reached Spain Admiral Collingwood agreed to send me to Sicily, but he was careful to warn me: "If you go to Palermo, God preserve you from Queen Caroline! She is certainly the wickedest woman He has ever created." It is true that she was no angel, but personally I was well pleased with her and I ought to be doubly grateful to her, as I became her son-in-law. As soon as my arrival was announced, she waited for me on the palace steps, and when I introduced myself to her she took my hand and, without a word, led me to her apartment. There, in a window embrasure, she held my head between her hands and gazed at me awhile without speaking. "I ought to hate you," she said at last, "as you have fought against us: in spite of that I have a liking for you. You came here to marry my daughter; well, I shall not hinder you, but tell me frankly what part you took in the French Revolution. I forgive you everything in advance, on condition I know everything."' The Duke said he made a complete confession; in any case he received absolution. On June 22, 1808, Princess Maria Amalia recorded laconically in her diary: 'Mamma sent for Isabella and me, and presented the Duke of Orléans to us. He is of average height, rather stout, in appearance neither handsome nor ugly. He has the Bourbon features, and his manner is very polite and well-educated.' Yet this was something deeper than love at first sight: it was the beginning of a lifelong devotion.

Since the Junta of Seville seemed to favour the King's claim to the Spanish Regency, he decided to send Leopold to Cadiz as his substitute, though the Prince was only eighteen. Seizing a chance to win his spurs in the royalist cause, the Duke of Orléans offered to accompany him. The King and Queen consented, but not without hesitation, as the Prince's other escorts, the Prince of Cassaro and Marquis of Saint-Clair, were deeply prejudiced against him. It was rumoured that the Queen was sending Saint-Clair with Leopold to make way for a new favourite, a young Neapolitan officer called

Afflitto. According to Mellish, a secretary in the British Legation, 'Circello did all he could to engage the King to prevent Saint-Clair from going with the Prince... and obtained no other advantage than being called all the names which a furious woman with a rapid utterance could articulate in the course of half an hour'. Having lost so many of her children, Maria Carolina grew suddenly nervous about letting Leopold go, though Drummond had procured an English ship, the *Thunderer*, to take him to Gibraltar. Acton, with his usual foresight, was against the whole enterprise. Drummond wrote to Canning: 'The Queen changes her mind about it twenty times a day, and General Acton, all falling to pieces as he is, goes tottering to her apartment, to warn her against adopting any advice which is given by me.' Motherly ambition, fanned by the Duke's enthusiasm, overcame her qualms. At a farewell dinner the King became so exhilarated that he promised the Duke his daughter's hand if his mission was successful. According to a memoir which was attributed to the Queen by R. M. Johnston but which was probably composed by one of her close confidants, the delighted Duke rushed to bring his future mother-in-law the news. 'Her Majesty received it not only with surprise but with such obvious signs of disapproval that they could not escape the Duke's notice.' According to another, before he left she embraced him saying: 'You see that I regard you already as a son.' The Princess certainly regarded herself as betrothed. 'I recommend my brother to you,' she said. 'I can assure you that it is a consolation to know that you are accompanying him.' 'If you only knew how very dear you are to me!' replied the Duke. 'Continue to cherish your dear friendship for me at all times.' 'Depend upon it; my feelings are unchangeable.'

The expedition was fruitless. The British were engrossed in the primary task of defeating Napoleon, and had no wish to be bothered with side-shows. They had no objection to Prince Leopold, but they mistrusted the Duke of Orléans and were even more suspicious of Saint-Clair. The Prince was barely allowed to land at Gibraltar. Drummond had been too precipitate. Canning wrote to him that even if the Junta of Seville demanded the Neapolitan Prince as Regent, the British government would oppose it and Admiral Collingwood had instructions to this effect. 'To proceed in a British ship to a British fortress, under the apparent protection and with the implied approbation of His Majesty, was to put His Majesty under the necessity of either forwarding an enterprise which he had not authorized, at the certainty of one species of inconvenience, or of disavowing it at the risk of another.' Prince Leopold sailed back to Sicily in November, while the Duke of Orléans went to England to plead his cause. Drummond was recalled, and Lord Amherst was sent to Palermo to replace him.

Murat was in no hurry to occupy his throne. The crowns of Westphalia, of Poland, of a kingdom to be carved out of Switzerland, and then of Spain and the Indies, had shimmered like the *fata morgana* before his tantalized vision. Naples seemed small beer after these. His wife Caroline remarked that its crown was too small for her head; this was out of proportion to her figure, hence Talleyrand's quip that she had the head of a Machiavelli on the body of a pretty woman. Murat went to Barèges in the Pyrenees to recuperate from an illness mainly due to disappointment before entering his new capital as 'Joachim Napoleon, by the grace of God and by the Constitution of the State, King of the Two Sicilies, Grand Admiral of the Empire', on September 6, 1808. Joseph Bonaparte had left Naples secretly on May 23, entrusting the government to Saliceti and Marshal Jourdan; in June he had announced his accession to the Spanish throne and issued a constitution to his former subjects as a parting gift, providing for a 'national government' which never materialized and caused little more than fleeting embarrassment to his successor, who guaranteed it with smiling *bonhomie*.

Everything about Murat's person was calculated to appeal to the Neapolitan foible for the picturesque, the novel, the overemphatic from the moment he rode into the city with a single aide-de-camp to show his confidence in his new subjects. Here was a figure straight from the *Orlando Furioso*. His wife, an accomplished charmer, made an equally pleasing impression in spite of the unfortunate homonym. She had one thing in common with her older namesake in Sicily: a determination to rule. There was a strong element of burlesque about the Murat Court, as if the kingdom of Naples were some heroi-comic Ruritania. The gallant soldier plunged into his new role with Gascon gusto. Not only was he brave, he was bountiful and brimming with good intentions. His regrets evaporated in the sunlight of this entrancing Eden.

There was only one blot on the horizon before Murat's window. The island of Capri, at the entrance of the bay, was still in

Bourbon possession. Considering it another Gibraltar, Hudson Lowe, the commander of the garrison, ordered himself 'four dozen champagne; three dozen burgundy of three years old; three dozen burgundy of four years old; six dozen of the best wines, such as Frontignan, and any others which may be held in good estimation', and sat back licking his lips in anticipation. He had received several warnings of an impending attack. On October 4 the French expedition, commanded by Generals Lamarque and Pignatelli Strongoli, left Naples and Salerno on requisitioned transports, escorted by one frigate, one corvette and twenty-six gunboats, while Murat watched operations from Punta di Campanella. The British fleet was nowhere visible. 'And where,' asked Sir Henry Bunbury, 'was His Britannic Majesty's frigate the *Ambuscade*? Instead of dashing on the enemy or hanging on their skirts... Captain D'Urban sailed away for Ponza, to apprise the Neapolitan squadron on that station, and any English ships he might meet, of the attack on Capri.' Hudson Lowe's attention had been diverted from the French landing at a rocky point of Anacapri by two feint attacks on the north and south harbours of the island. The French scaled the rocks like veteran mountaineers, while the Maltese riflemen above them were either stupefied or could find no mark to hit. Next morning they controlled the west of the island. The garrison of Lower Capri held out against them for two weeks, while winds and storms prevented ships from coming to the rescue. Lowe capitulated on October 16 for want of provisions; considering the vaunted impregnability of his position he made some sorry blunders. But islands were ever his doom, for he has gone down to history as Napoleon's gaoler.

This bold feat so soon after his arrival added immensely to Murat's prestige, and a fine medal was struck to commemorate the victory. In his elation he issued a series of decrees recalling political exiles, restoring the property of those who had followed the King to Sicily, reprieving political prisoners, pardoning deserters and abolishing restrictions on fisheries. He even drove in state to pay homage to San Gennaro. Napoleon criticized these measures as if he were merely a French governor. 'Why recall the exiles and restore property to men who are still armed and conspiring against me?' he asked. 'You are making sacrifices to a false popularity. It is absurd to cancel the sequestration of this property and so provide support for those who are in Sicily. You really must have lost your head!' As for the patron saint of Naples—'I was pained to hear of your playing monkey tricks for San Gennaro.' Though Napoleon might scold, King Murat had won many converts. The news of his amnesty caused a mutiny at Ponza, where many felt that it was thankless and unprofitable to remain in the service of the Bourbons.

Maria Carolina was despondently aware of the vast difference between Joseph Bonaparte and Joachim Murat, whose political shrewdness seemed even more dangerous than his military prowess. The loss of Capri provoked her even more against the English. Yet she still believed that the Neapolitans were ready for an insurrection. Surrounded by fanatics such as the one-eyed Moliterno, who competed with Canosa in concocting quixotic schemes, she lived upon opium and hot air. Those English had to be jolted into action. It was rumoured that Moliterno himself would lead the next expedition, though he had applied secretly to Murat for permission to return to Naples and his application had been rejected. He strutted about like a peacock, boasting so loud of his plans that Stuart demanded an explanation. Circello denied that the King had entrusted Moliterno with such a mission, and he was evidently told to keep quiet. Negotiations with Stuart were difficult enough without gratuitous histrionics. Stuart thought his troops would be more useful in Spain, where Sir John Moore had been mortally wounded in the battle of Corunna (January 16, 1809), having wrecked Napoleon's plan for the conquest of the peninsula. Canosa continued to send exaggerated reports of discontent in Naples, and in March Count de la Tour arrived as a special envoy from Vienna to urge another expedition. 'From all that I see, read and presume, the struggle with the Corsican monster will at last begin again,' wrote the Queen to Damas on March 5, 1809. 'Here we are only waiting to know that the Emperor has started hostilities to march upon Naples. General Stuart, he of Maida, will command everything: Hesse has no head, Bourcard is or pretends to be ill, not wishing to leave his dear command in Sicily; you know the rest; thus there is nobody to give the command to and Stuart will lead our troops together with the English.' 'I do not think the recovery of Naples will be difficult,' she wrote in April, convinced that 'the whole of Italy was ready to unite to expel the oppressors.' Her son Leopold had grown very big and strong, and was yearning to distinguish himself in the conflict.

While England was concerned with the safety of Sicily, Austria required a diversion to paralyse the French in Italy, and the Bourbons were intent on recovering their lost kingdom. Stuart was lukewarm even when he decided to take part in the expedition. Precious time was wasted as a result of his excessive caution. His orders and counter-orders depended on the news he received from Austria, Bavaria and the north of Italy. The Archduke Charles had been defeated in Bavaria; and Napoleon was back in Vienna on May 12. The Sicilian troops under General Nunziante had embarked and disembarked and been blessed twice over in church; Prince Leopold had been given his father's blessing; and the Queen had wept with emotion at two solemn parades, before they received final orders to sail from Milazzo on June 11. Much against Stuart's will, small parties were landed along the Calabrian coast, but the Calabrians failed to support them owing to General Partouneaux's ruthless measures. The Anglo-Sicilian fleet appeared in the bay of Naples on June 26, but there was no flicker of an insurrection. On the contrary, Napoleon's sister was greeted with loud cheers when she drove along the Chiaia to watch the cannonade in the distance. Though he captured the islands of Ischia and Procida, Stuart would not attack the capital. The British frigate *Cyane* was worsted in a fight with Murat's only frigate, the *Cerere*, under the command of Giovanni Bausan, who became a national hero in consequence. News of Napoleon's decisive victory of Wagram and a critical despatch from Lord Collingwood sealed the fate of this bungled enterprise. Ischia and Procida were abandoned on July 22 and the whole expedition sailed back to Sicily. Chaos and anarchy were revived in Calabria: the troops that had landed there were joined by insurgents who waged a devastating war of brigandage against the French. Apart from this negative repercussion, the only result was further to embitter relations between the two allies when England alone was left to fight Napoleon. 'Stuart can only evacuate,' wrote the Queen, 'he has no other tactics.' Canosa wrote a lengthy analysis of his cumulative demoralization: to capture Naples 'only the will had been lacking'; 'our whole party will be discouraged and dispersed'; after the last four years of vain expectations the most loyal would lose heart... Then, as if evacuation had become an epidemic, Canosa senselessly abandoned the islands of Ponza and Ventotene.

This succession of disasters affected the Queen's mind as well as her health, and she resorted more frequently to opium to calm her nerves. She was fifty-seven, but she felt infinitely older. She talked of the duty and virtue of resignation, but she was utterly incapable of practising it. 'It is terrible to say and think this, however true,' she wrote to Damas on October 24, 'we are in the most deplorable of all situations, dominated, degraded, and maltreated by the English, who are the only ones to guarantee us from being invaded by the French. At a distance it is easy to choose the better of these alternatives, but one must experience what we suffer to understand how painful this bondage is, and how cruelly they make us feel it.'

When the Duke of Orléans returned to Palermo the King had changed his mind about his marriage. All the French *émigrés* were against him, and Castelcicala reflected their views when he wrote from London: 'The Duke of Orléans is a man of boundless ambition: his sovereign's enemy, he has only gone to Sicily in these troubled times to make a revolution with the English and profit by it.' Circello agreed with him and advised the King to procrastinate. The Duke's past was no recommendation, and what had he to offer in future? His mission to Spain had failed. Surely a more eligible prince would turn up. So the King said that his finances were too low for him to afford a proper dowry. The Duke, however, was willing to renounce the dowry; as for the Princess, she was determined to marry him. If she were prevented from doing so, she threatened to take the veil. Much upset, the King embraced her and begged her to confide in him. 'I have always wanted a modest settlement which would allow me to live near my beloved parents, rather than a throne which would remove me from them,' she tactfully replied. 'The more I see of the Duke the more I esteem him, and I sincerely admit that I should be very happy to marry him.' This put an end to her father's objections.

The Queen wrote to Damas on October 29: 'To add to all my sorrows, my daughter who is twenty-eight years old and despairs of not getting married, has become engaged to the Duke of Orléans (dreadful name!). The King approves of it and I can only sigh and submit. He is a man of considerable intelligence, resource and great ability... I must put a good face on a matter that pains and humiliates me to excess, but my daughter is twenty-eight, knows everything and regards him as a hero, a god.' He seemed to be the only member of the Bourbon family capable of embarrassing Bonaparte, she added. The King had fallen on a staircase and hurt his leg so that he was bedridden; an evil omen, said the superstitious. Owing to this accident the couple were married in the King's bedroom where an altar had been set up. A more pompous ceremony followed amid the Byzantine mosaics of the Palatine Chapel. Neither bride nor groom were in their first youth. The Duke was thirty-six: his stoutness could be described as imposing, his physique preponderantly Bourbon, a solid bulwark to the slim ecstatic Princess in her silver gown of Sicilian embroidery. 'My legs trembled,' the bride wrote in her diary, 'knowing the sanctity and force of the promise I was making, but the Duke pronounced "Yes" in so resolute a voice that it fortified my heart.'

'Naughty Amélie has married the Duke of Orléans; they have nothing to live on, are poor but happy, and love each other infinitely,' wrote the Queen. This conjugal happiness, which lasted forty years, contrasted strangely with her own chronic gloom. The King might have been content, for he was capable of resignation, had the Queen not prodded and taunted him. The traveller John Galt, like everybody else, regarded his enduring good nature as his chief merit. 'He is, I think, very popular among the Sicilians; who, in no small degree, manifest the same characteristic as their sovereign. Not taking any active part in the proceedings of the government, he escapes the odium of its measures; and he has, occasionally, interfered in cases of particular grievance, in a way that has obtained the applause of his people; so that, in those acts where he has appeared at all as the monarch, he has been always seen to advantage. I have been told that he is partial to our national character... An anecdote, which I have heard, serves to illustrate both this part of his character and his constitutional good humour. A party of English officers and gentlemen were dining together in a house situated over a gateway through which carriages pass in going to one of the theatres. It was in the winter-time, and they had a wood fire. Just at the moment when the royal carriages were approaching, one of the company, in frolic, happened to fling a burning stick at another, who, in warding it off, threw it out of the window, and it fell on the King's coach. In an instant the house was filled with guards. The simple fact of the accident was told to the officer, who immediately reported it to the King. "Oh very well," said Ferdinand, "let them alone; they are only drunk;" and accordingly no further notice was taken of the affair.

'The Hereditary Prince is seldom the subject of conversation, being known merely as a man of quiet manners and domestic habits.'

But the Queen loomed over them like Mount Etna, always ready to erupt.

XXXI

Opposition in the Sicilian Parliament—The Peace of Schönbrunn—Napoleon's marriage to Marie Louise complicates the situation—English suspicions against the Queen—The Duke of Orléans invited to Spain—A forged letter from Napoleon—Murat's invasion of Sicily—Appeal of the Sicilian barons to Lord Amherst— The one per cent tax—Arrest of the five factious barons—Arrival of Lord William Bentinck— The Queen's stroke—Death of Acton—Compromising letters—Bentinck's duel with the Queen—The Hereditary Prince appointed Vicar General, January 16, 1812.

Sicily was poor but proud; and a growing body of Sicilians resented their sovereigns' preference for Neapolitans and their own exclusion from the government. The Queen's eye was fixed on Naples: Sicily was no more to her than a tedious caravanserai. She had not changed her attitude since her former exile when she wrote to her daughter in Austria: 'This is a different country; people are constitutional; the King has not a penny without the consent of Parliament; everything, including justice, is under dissimilar regulations and stands on a totally different footing; but we must put up with it.' Unfortunately it was not in the Queen's nature to put up with it.

The Sicilian Parliament was a creaking old feudal institution which exerted a certain control over taxation, but little else. In his history of the Sicilian Constitution, Niccolò Palmieri wrote: 'The Parliament had long been regarded as a pompous pageant to which scant importance was attached, and if the barons had not had a personal interest in preserving the national prerogatives, the people would have let themselves be divested of it some time ago. Such was the preponderance of the barons in that assembly, and such the spirit of selfish interest they had usually shown, that the people might even have welcomed its dissolution.' It consisted of three chambers which met and voted separately: barons, clergy and tenants of the Crown, the last corresponding with the English Commons; and it had the right to assemble at least once every four years.

Money, more money, was needed to finance the reconquest of Naples and satisfy the incessant demands of the Queen's courtiers and secret agents, in spite of the increased British subsidy. If Mount

Etna were made of gold, said Lord Collingwood, the Court would still be poor. The Finance Minister Medici hoped to raise an extraordinary subsidy of 360,000 ounces (the ounce was equal to 13*s.* 4*d.*) in addition to the usual donatives, and he had canvassed busily among the members of all three chambers. Finding the barons in opposition, he tried to win over the clergy and tenants of the Crown by telling them that all the burden of the new taxes would fall on the barons. But the latter had checkmated him by promising to relieve the clergy of some of their land taxes. When the Parliament met again on January 25, 1810, the majority of barons, supported by the clergy, would only agree to a subsidy of 150,000 ounces for four years and a gift of 100,000 to the Hereditary Prince on the birth of his son. They abolished other taxes and imposed a five per cent duty on personal property. The victorious Opposition, led by Carlo Cottone, Prince of Castelnuovo, and his nephew Giuseppe Ventimiglia, Prince of Belmonte, were given a public ovation. From now on the people began to take an interest in their Parliament. As Palmieri wrote: 'In 1810 it sufficed a few honest and courageous men to rouse the nation and communicate their energy to others.'

The Queen regarded the Opposition as Jacobins and was all the more indignant when the Duke of Orléans gently urged her to compromise. She proposed to find money without the aid of Parliament, just as she had sent Hesse's expedition without the English. To gain time the King hesitated to sanction the Parliament's last acts, which were submitted to a select committee of magistrates. These were to examine whether the King was legally entitled to accept some of them and modify the rest. All except one concluded that the King was authorized to change any Act of Parliament at will. However, the Duke of Orléans persuaded the Queen to accept the donatives voted and include a few Sicilians in the ministry. One of the wealthiest barons, the Prince of Trabia, succeeded Medici as Minister of Finance; the Princes of Butera and Cassaro and Emmanuele Parisi were also given posts. But as these were all devoted to the Queen, the Opposition were not satisfied. Belmonte, who had expected an appointment, was aggrieved and defiant. The struggle had only begun, but it was to become an essential part of her struggle with the English.

The Queen's overriding desires were to be undisputed mistress at home and to recover her lost possessions. Whoever thwarted these became her foe. The British were less interested in the Neapolitan Bourbons than in preserving the independence of Sicily. So far they had not interfered in the civil administration, but since they had given up all attempt to reconquer Naples she suspected their designs on the island. When Stuart wished to occupy Trapani in addition to the other Sicilian forts, she protested to her son against what she called 'this usurpation and the others which are being planned'. It would mean, she wrote, 'an increase of oppression and slavery'. To allow a foreign general to enlist recruits in the kingdom was equal to ceding a right of sovereignty. 'My opinion, proved by example, is that the more we yield the more we shall lose.'

The Hereditary Prince, who had a keener sense of realities, replied: 'Not having the strength to oppose them we might throw ourselves into the arms of the French, who would wrest this last refuge from us at the first opportunity. Whereas now we exist and keep our throne, waiting for a change of circumstances which will end this state of subjection and degradation. But in order to exist with honour we should be straightforward, sincere and loyal with the English, while preserving our own authority and dignity to make them respect us.' This was calm common sense, but the Queen regarded it as pusillanimous. She would defend her sovereign rights against friend and foe, and she had begun to feel that there was little to choose between the former and the latter. The Peace of Schönbrunn (October 15, 1809) had struck her as a crowning infamy. 'It has destroyed the House of Austria... Truly, only the Spaniards still have spirit and a sense of honour. We run the double risk of being conquered by Bonaparte or subjugated by the English; in either case we shall be ruined.'

Since France was again at peace with Austria, Murat, who had styled himself 'King of the Two Sicilies', began to organize an expedition for the conquest of the island. But his relations with Napoleon were far from smooth, as he was constantly being reminded of his subordinate position. Napoleon's marriage to Maria Carolina's eldest granddaughter, the Archduchess Marie Louise, in March 1810, had complicated the whole situation. Murat had opposed this marriage as impolitic, reviving unpleasant memories of that other Austrian, Marie Antoinette, but in fact he feared it might hinder his invasion of Sicily. On his return journey to Naples after the ceremony he heard that Maria Carolina was already negotiating with Napoleon through her granddaughter, and on April 22 he wrote to his Emperor with evident anxiety: 'News from Palermo tells of serious misunderstandings between the Court and the English, who, since the marriage of Your Majesty and the preparations directed against Sicily, believe that Maria Carolina has an understanding with Your Majesty with a view to expelling them from Sicily and keeping it for herself. These reports are quite positive on the point.' Napoleon did not answer. He kept Murat on tenterhooks while he continued to prepare for the invasion.

That the Queen was less alarmed by Murat's activities than by those of her ally is apparent from her letters to Damas. 'We are between the French and the English,' she wrote on March 16, 1810, 'the former desire, but moderately [sic], to wrest Sicily from the English... but since they have no navy they realize that it will not be easy either to capture or to keep it; thus they carry on their usual manoeuvres, corruption, dissension, seduction, and await the effect of these, from which they will profit. The English are more consistent: with their money, principles and form of government, all classes are cajoled, excited and seduced with the hope of becoming members of the government; the troops better paid, commerce more free, stable incomes assured, all this is presented under every aspect to different classes and produces an effect. I believe we shall lose Sicily by this side far more than by the other, which has no navy. The atrocity of doing this as an ally and protector is their only restraint. They see that I am watchful and that they cannot seduce me, hence the calumny, clamour and immorality of every kind perpetrated against me, as a person inconvenient to their projects. I am convinced that our lot is decided, and that without a successful general war including Russia, Austria and Prussia, in fact a great upheaval, we shall certainly be the victims sacrificed: the choice is between sharing the Duke of Enghien's fate or shamefully begging a pension. I confess I prefer the former, and am firmly resolved to risk everything.'

At first the Queen expressed horror at her granddaughter's marriage. 'I have said goodbye for ever to my native land which I have loved so deeply. Amid all the sinister events threatening me I had hoped to find a haven there to die in peace, but that is ended... If the tyrant and his concubine (for she is only that) meet with the fate of tyrants, what will be left for the Emperor's other children but the infamy of this alliance?' Not having heard from Ruffo, her minister in Vienna, she supposed that the English had intercepted his messengers, 'for they keep us blockaded much better than the enemy, so that no news can reach us'. On May 10 she wrote: 'I cannot believe, after all the abomination of what has happened, that Ruffo has not sent me a messenger, and that he is waiting for the first offspring of this monstrous union to announce it to us... What you will find hard to believe... is that after a mortal illness, from which I have not yet fully recovered, owing to this degrading marriage which overwhelms me with grief and chagrin, the English suspect me of having caused it so as to further my own ends. I am too familiar with the illustrious contracting parties not to know what I may expect or fear from them... I confess I am not at all easy about our future, between a ferocious active enemy with such ample means and a treacherous so-called friend, who wants to oppress us and make us appear traitors as a low pretext for hiding his own villainy.'

The Queen's past conversations with Alquier prove that she could not have been wholly surprised by Napoleon's marriage, and there is no doubt that many Neapolitan and French *émigrés* in her circle were hoping that it would lead to some friendly arrangement. Stuart wrote to Lord Liverpool on May 1: 'I do not, nor can I, believe that a great female personage among all her real or imputed misconceptions can have any interests in common with the invader of her continental dominions, or could figure any probable benefit to herself or family from his acquirement of a footing in these. But Her Majesty does not at all times act or think for herself, and she is surrounded and influenced by many whose principles are certainly to be doubted.' And Mellish wrote to Lord Wellesley on May 14: 'The Queen... has for many months carried on a correspondence with Austria through Fiume... and it is strongly suspected that she has through this channel made overtures to Bonaparte.' These suspicions were cunningly fostered by Murat, who shared them.

On May 5 the Duke of Orléans was invited by the Spanish Regency to command the army of Catalonia. With soaring hopes he accepted. 'He leaves in a week's time,' wrote the Queen, 'and you may picture the despair of his wife, six months with child, who imagines every possible danger to which he will be exposed, and is full of anguish in consequence. His role will certainly be difficult, but with God's blessing it might become very brilliant and useful.

It would be a strange but splendid spectacle, and would further show the inexplicable decrees of God's omnipotence, if one of my sons-in-law with copious resources has so degraded himself as to sacrifice his daughter to this monster for his own tranquillity, and another son-in-law with nothing else but his sword and his heart were to dethrone the same monster... That would be very consoling, but I dare not hope, I can only wish for it.'

On landing at Tarragona the Duke did not receive the welcome he had expected, for the Spanish Regency had changed its mind. Having invested themselves with sovereignty, the *Cortes* feared a rival power; Louis XVIII had begun to distrust his ambitious cousin again; and Lord Wellesley, the British representative with the Junta, declared that the British forces would be withdrawn if the Duke were given an appointment. The Duke still had influential partisans; he protested and pulled every wire until he was asked to leave the country. Frustrated at every turn, he embarked for Palermo on October 5, yet he was too sagacious to bear the British a grudge.

The British in Messina were watching and waiting for Murat's expedition to venture across the straits. As the summer wore on dissensions arose in the French camp: Murat had been so disgusted by the arrival of Colonel Leclerc from the French War Office to keep an eye on him that he was tempted to drop the enterprise, but his confidence soon returned; the senior French officers, including General Lamarque, believed the whole thing was a feint; not without reason, since Napoleon's attitude was ambiguous. A diversion from Spain was more useful to Napoleon than the conquest of Sicily; he was content to keep the British forces immobilized, and probably feared that the expedition might be cut off by the British fleet. General Grenier, Murat's chief of staff, was said to have had orders from Paris not to let the French troops cross the straits. There was also considerable jealousy and ill-feeling between the French and Neapolitan officers. And Queen Maria Carolina was as great a source of worry to Murat as to the British, for his chief of police, Maghella, Saliceti's successor, had sent him an intercepted letter proving that the Queen was corresponding with Marie Louise. Murat turned this to account by proclaiming to his troops that the Sicilians were ready to join them and expel the British. This proclamation reached Palermo, and Lord Amherst demanded an official contradiction. He wrote to Lord Wellesley on June 19: 'His Majesty's troops will have enough to do to oppose the enemy that attacks them in front without being obliged to guard against the possibility of defection in their rear... It is therefore surely become necessary that this weak and corrupt government should no longer be allowed to alienate the affections of its own subjects and bring into danger the brave troops of its ally.' Like Sir John Moore, he thought it absolutely necessary 'that the Queen should cease to take the lead in public affairs'. His alarms had been increased by the publication of a so-called intercepted letter in a Cadiz newspaper which was given wide publicity. This purported to have been addressed by Napoleon to the Queen, alluding to an agreement to drive out the British. The Queen did not see it until July, when she summoned Amherst and vehemently protested her loyalty. The letter was a forgery, but it did not help to clear the air.

Murat's invasion had been postponed so often for one reason or another that the Queen was frankly sceptical. On June 6 he had written to Napoleon: 'Sicily will be conquered and the English beaten, or you will have lost your best friend.' The attempt was finally made on September 18. One division of 3,000 Neapolitans and Corsicans under General Cavaignac landed south of Messina, but the two French divisions never left Calabria. Apparently General Grenier had received orders from Paris: he refused to move. Attacked by a superior force, Cavaignac hastened to re-embark before the English squadron cut off his retreat. A battalion of 800 Corsicans was captured; their regimental banner was sent to the King as a trophy, and as a proof of British zeal in defending the island. But that zeal was not appreciated by the Queen. Murat tried to mask his failure, and Napoleon rebuked him for rashness and inefficiency; relations between the two brothers-in-law were so strained that it is a wonder they did not break sooner. Caroline Murat took her brother's side and flaunted her conjugal infidelities; from every point of view poor Joachim was to be pitied. His crown was his only solace; whatever happened, he was determined to be an independent monarch.

As the threat of invasion dwindled, the Queen's conflict with the Sicilian barons became acute. Prince Belmonte appealed to Lord Amherst, who wrote to Lord Wellesley on July 28, 1810: 'I have been invited to address myself to the principal Sicilian barons, urging them to insist on certain concessions from their sovereign, and promising them the protection of the King whom I represent under any circumstances which may arise from the more than usual freedom of their demands... The professed object of the persons to whom I have alluded is to obtain for Sicily a constitution as nearly similar as possible to that of Great Britain. They declare, indeed, that their own form of constitution, if duly adhered to, would insure to them all the advantages derived from that under which the English have the happiness to live—but they complain that the King has already been guilty of gross violations of the institutions under which he holds his crown, and that they have no security against a tyranny wholly repugnant to the original freedom enjoyed by the inhabitants of Sicily. They announce their intention of urging their demands to the King by the legal organ of his Parliament; but they foresee an opposition on the part of their sovereign which nothing will overcome but the interposition of England; and which, if England refuses to interfere, will drive them into rebellion, and perhaps ultimately into the arms of France.'

Amherst replied that as ambassador he was forbidden to interfere in the internal concerns of Sicily, but he could not conceal his sympathy, especially when he was told that their first demands would be 'an unity of military command under the British general, and an administration composed entirely of Sicilians'. He admitted that it was not fair to blame the present government for all their grievances. 'A great many arise from the defects of the constitution and from the unjust and impolitic privileges heretofore conceded, and still retained by certain descriptions of persons.' But these persons seemed willing to sacrifice privileges which 'would clearly stand in the way of the establishment of that free and enlightened form of government under which they wish to live.'

Amherst was an advocate of interference. 'One party calls out for it; the other, I am sure, stands in need of its application. The affairs of this government must be directed by other hands than those to which they are now committed. The King withdraws himself from public business. The Queen regulates her conduct by the reports of spies perpetually at variance with each other. No ministers will be able to stand, unless supported by Great Britain, against the pernicious influence of the Queen, and the nation is clamorous for British interference, by which it knows that its independence will be maintained and its prosperity secured.

'I take the liberty, therefore, of recommending to your lordship that my successor should find himself empowered to control the influence of the Queen, to demand for the British general the command of the army, and to require that the government should be administered by Sicilians. All these points I conceive to be of the first necessity. Their accomplishment would be equally beneficial to our allies and ourselves...'

Determined to find money in spite of the refractory Parliament, in February 1811 the Queen levied a one per cent tax on all payments, and put up monastic lands for auction by means of lottery tickets. The King, who was going through a religious phase, had scruples about the sale of ecclesiastical property. He was living in retirement at Villa La Favorita with two Jesuit preachers to promote his spiritual exercises. One of these Jesuits, Father Strassoldi, was said to have cultivated his scruples. When he died suddenly of a violent colic, it was rumoured that he had been poisoned by one of the Queen's agents.

Most people dodged the tax, and the lottery was a failure. Princes Belmonte and Castelnuovo drew up a protest against these arbitrary measures which was signed by forty-six barons. Copies of this were sent to London and published in the English press. The Duke of Orléans remonstrated with the Queen and implored her to be more moderate; the Duchess, who had been converted to his liberal views, also pleaded with her mother. It was a rehearsal for the role which Louis Philippe was to play later in France. The Queen told her daughter: 'Since I have committed the folly of taking him for a son-in-law, I must put up with him as your husband and the father of your child. [The Duchess had given birth to the Duke of Chartres on December 3, 1810.] But he should realize that legitimate authority always wins.' She persisted in regarding the barons as Jacobins.

On the night of July 19 five of the leading barons, Belmonte, Castelnuovo, Aci, d'Angiò and Villafranca, were arrested and taken to a ship in the bay for deportation to various islands. Next day their arrest—'for giving abundant proofs of a factious spirit and preparing to disturb the public peace'—was announced in a royal proclamation. While the ship was delayed by lack of wind, the Queen drove through the streets with a jubilant air. The Duke of Orléans was summoned to the palace, but he refused to go for fear of being arrested. His horse was saddled to take him off to a hiding-place in the country. But his alarm was groundless.

The Queen's triumph was ephemeral. Lord Amherst had asked to be relieved of his post, and the Queen was glad to be rid of him.

The King bade him a gracious farewell: '*Se ho detto o scritto qualche cosa da offendervi vi domando perdono. Bisogna che Ferdinando Borbone e Lord Amherst siano amici* ('If I have said or written anything to offend you, I beg your pardon. Ferdinand Bourbon and Lord Amherst must remain friends'). But Lord Amherst had paved the way for a militant successor. It was owing to his advice that Lord William Bentinck was sent out as Commander-in-Chief of the British Forces in Sicily and Plenipotentiary and Envoy Extraordinary. He arrived in Palermo on July 23, soon after the arrest of the barons. The Queen is said to have exclaimed: 'They are sending us a viceroy, not an ambassador!' And the King to have retorted: 'What difference does it make to me and my subjects? We shall only have a master instead of a mistress to manage us.'

Bentinck had already had an unusually varied and hectic career for a man under thirty-seven years of age. The second son of the third Duke of Portland, he was born in 1774, and at seventeen he had entered the Coldstream Guards, since when he had acquired experience of war on a large scale, serving as British military representative to Suvóroff (also spelt Suwarrow among other variants) during his great campaign in Northern Italy and Switzerland, then witnessing the battles of Marengo, Trebbio and Novi. A staunch Whig, he had also acquired some practical knowledge of the political conditions of Northern Italy. In 1803 he had been appointed Governor of Madras, where his 'firm attitude' in upholding an absurd army regulation, forbidding the Sepoys to wear their caste marks and ear-rings when in uniform and imposing an objectionable new turban, led to a bloodthirsty mutiny at Vellore. Recalled by the directors of the East India Company in 1807, his injured feelings were salved by a bout of military activity in Spain, where he commanded a brigade at the battle of Corunna, was promoted to the rank of Lieutenant-General, and served under Sir Arthur Wellesley in Portugal until he was sent to Germany to raise a foreign legion while Napoleon was master of Central Europe. His ambition when he landed in Sicily was to organize a strong Anglo-Sicilian expedition to support the Duke of Wellington in Spain. Unfortunately he had to deal first with a complicated political crisis. And he was every inch a soldier: no diplomatic nonsense.

His instructions were: 'You will particularly study the political views and inclinations of their Sicilian Majesties, and endeavour to make yourself as agreeable to them as possible... Your Lordship therefore will direct your earliest attention to a full and distinct explanation of the views of the British Government... You will assure the Court of Palermo that no design was ever countenanced by His Majesty... to sacrifice the legitimate rights and interests of His Sicilian Majesty... Your Lordship will assure the Court of Palermo in the most unqualified terms that this Government has never entertained or countenanced a design of interfering in the internal government of Sicily...' So far so good; clear if not too concise. Considering the political views and inclinations of their Sicilian Majesties, the rest of his instructions contradicted this preamble. 'It cannot be expected that the discontent now prevailing in Sicily will be allayed, unless a due share of influence in the councils of the Court of Palermo be given to native Sicilians, and unless a due attention be paid to the advice and wishes of the Parliament... You will declare that you are commanded to signify to the Court of Palermo that if a perseverance in these ill-advised measures should produce the consequences which you apprehend, neither the terms nor spirit of the alliance would require that the British arms should be employed to assist that Court in enforcing such a system of Government against the resistance of the people of Sicily.'

Bentinck repeated all this in an official note to Circello, and went off to inspect the garrisons of Messina and Milazzo. Circello's reply pointed out that Bentinck had an erroneous conception of the Sicilian Parliament, whose every act depended on the royal sanction, and which offered petitions but not advice. The King had a perfect right to reject petitions, and the document signed by forty-six barons infringed his sovereign authority; in any case, the Parliament was not a permanent assembly and could not be represented outside its legitimate sessions. As for Bentinck, he was to mind his own business, which was restricted to the defence of the island.

Realizing that the Queen had inspired this retort, the soldier did not attempt to disguise himself as a diplomat when he went to see her. Instead of tact and patience, he mingled threats with accusations. Far from endeavouring to make himself as agreeable as possible, he was John Bull charging full tilt into a china shop. The Queen subsequently described him as 'a boorish corporal'; some say that she even called him one to his face. Not even Alquier had made her so indignant. She was more determined than ever to resist his demands.

'The determination of the Court to refuse all my demands, as they were called, had been publicly known,' wrote Bentinck to Wellesley. 'The refusal was a matter of exultation on the part of the Queen.' Bentinck's own opinions were formed: Sicily required a new constitution and he would see that she got it. The Queen was solely concerned with Naples: 'Naples is the pivot round which everything turns, to which everything, honour, character, alliance will be willingly sacrificed, and without a direct reference to the recovery of which no measure of a conciliatory nature can have the least effect.' Before Bentinck had spent a month in Sicily he decided to return to England for wider powers to enforce the measures he considered necessary. On August 14 he announced his departure to Circello, whose 'surprise was great and the impression of alarm was so strongly marked, that for the first time I saw some glimmering of hope'. This faint light was blown out by the Queen. Bentinck sailed in the frigate *Cephalus* on September 4.

The Queen wrote at once to Butera that this was the moment to forestall Bentinck's perfidious aims. It is probable that she contemplated overtures to Napoleon in her blind exasperation. General Manhès, the French governor of Calabria, had already been plotting an insurrection against the British in Messina, and the Queen had only to say the word for Trabia to act, since he commanded the Sicilian militia there. But the Queen hesitated, and on September 16 she was prostrated by an apoplectic stroke. She had taken an emetic against the advice of her physicians, and, experiencing no relief, had drunk twenty-four glasses of water and fallen senseless while conversing with the minister Tommasi. For the next twenty-four hours she remained unconscious, then gradually she recovered. Any other woman of her age would have retired to convalesce; not Maria Carolina, who as soon as she could move plunged back into the whirlpool of public business. Neither her recent shock, nor the pangs of neuralgia, nor the opium she took to relieve them, could prevent her from fighting on against Bentinck and the barons. She was often swept by hurricanes of fury akin to madness. However misguided—and who was left to guide her?—the Queen's spirit was indomitable. Acton, whom she had often regretted since his retirement, had died on August 12. The author of the *Mémoire* attributed to the Queen by R. M. Johnston shared this regret: 'In spite of his great faults his successors raised a monument to him, as it were, and if he had remained at the head of affairs, things would have gone better.' Maria Carolina had railed at him in her revulsion against the English, but she paid him tribute in her private diary: 'Learned with deep sorrow of the death of worthy General Acton, whom I have known intimately for 36 years, for 32 years the master—honest, talented and devoted, with inflexible principles—I wept much over his irreparable loss.' Sir John Acton left two sons and a daughter. The eldest son, who died young, was the father of Lord Acton the historian; the younger son became a saintly Cardinal. In spite of the close relationship between this bulwark of the Bourbons and Gladstone's friend, the apostle of liberty, it is doubtful whether they would have approved of each other, for Sir John was a firm believer in absolute power, untroubled by thoughts of corruption.

On October 12 an officer called Cassetti was arrested with compromising letters to the Queen, the Duke of Ascoli, and Castrone, the chief of police. The letters were hastily burnt by an accomplice, but their contents were known and Cassetti was very communicative. The trial was complicated by the discovery of other missives, one from Manhès to the Queen, dated November 2. Murat's police might have arranged for these to fall into English hands, and Castrone employed agents who often played a double game. Not one letter from the Queen was found among this correspondence, which dealt with a plot to drive the English out of Sicily; and the Queen could not be held responsible for the letters addressed to her. Yet in her actual state of frenzy it is possible that she gave the conspirators her blessing. According to the French General Goldemar, the French had been on the verge of seizing Sicily during Bentinck's absence, but the Queen's 'Machiavellism' and excessive intrigues had balked them.

Bentinck returned like a whirlwind on December 7. The unequal duel between two stubborn wills began again. Bentinck was in the prime of life with power to carry out his threats. The Queen, prematurely old and broken in health, was comparatively defenceless; Bentinck himself wrote: 'Her mind enfeebled by age and by the vast quantities of opium and the operation of violent passions, has reached a state little short of actual insanity.' Bentinck's first move was to suspend the British subsidy until his demands were satisfied. These were: the supreme command of the army, the exile of Ascoli, Medici and Castrone, the removal of refugees from public office, and the recall of the five barons. Cassaro was to form a new ministry, and the King (a mere euphemism for the Queen) was to take no part in the administration.

In a long despatch to Wellesley (December 26, 1811), Bentinck reported the first stage of the duel: 'On the 13th I was introduced to the Queen. I began by stating that... I judged it a becoming mark of respect to open first to Her Majesty the communications I had to make... I thought it right to preface that the Prince Regent [George IV] was actuated solely by motives of friendship and regard, and had never any other objects in view but the honour and independence of His Sicilian Majesty and his family. Here the Queen stopped me and asked if I was an honest man and could make such a remark... The Queen repeated what she had said in her former conversation that for six years it had been our settled plan to take the country. That *spirituel* Fox had said so; Moore who was a Jacobin *enragé* did not deny it. Drummond, *qui parlait comme un fou*, Stuart and myself were all working to the same end. That she always said so to her ministers who thought she was *folle*, and that she did not see things in their right point of view—now they saw the truth of her opinions. I asked Her Majesty if the having refrained for six years from having done that which was always easy to us was not a proof of the injustice of that accusation? She answered: "No, that would have been too like Bonaparte—your object has been to do this under the cover of forms, to save your reputation if possible..." When I mentioned to the Queen that the object of the alliance could not be attained unless a greater influence in the Councils were given to the Sicilians, she began by enumerating the present members... Circello, *qui est une bête*, Medici, who was an able man, Arriola, Minister of War, *pour celui-là c'est une bête, vous pouvez le faire bouillir, cuire et rotir si vous voulez* [he is a fool, and you can boil, cook and roast him if you wish to]... "Who then would you propose for this Council?"... "Cassaro, a very honest man," adding ironically, "*un grand esprit, il a une sublime idée de la géographie, il le trouverait fort naturel, si vous lui disiez que l'escadre anglaise avait mouillé dans le port de Vienne* [a great intellect, he has a sublime idea of geography, and would think it quite natural if you told him that the English squadron had anchored in the port of Vienna]..." She mentioned other names in terms of equal praise... Respecting the army, the Queen said that the command never could be given to me. She declared it also to be impossible to bring back the Barons... Upon both these points she was very violent and would listen to no reasoning upon the subject... She expressed her determination to leave the country, not to beg her bread in England or in Italy, but to go to Germany, and hoped a frigate would not be refused her to take her to Durazzo or Constantinople. The King might do as he pleased... The impression created by the two conversations I have had with Her Majesty is that with exceeding good abilities she probably never had any common sense.'

To Robert Fagan, the British consul, with whom she had been on friendly terms, the Queen had delivered another tirade: ' "What do you think, Fagan, of their depriving me of the subsidy, and reducing all my pensioners to absolute want?... By this vile step England will acquire great honour in the face of Europe... Sooner than submit I am determined to live on bread and water... Good God! only think of their wishing to deprive my husband of his power and authority in the decline of life, after he had reigned fifty-four years! Believe me, he is so disgusted with their infamous conduct that he will not come to town again; he is determined to answer no letter and says, let King Bentinck do as he pleases, I am no longer King... Do you think me a child that I do not recollect the advice given by General Moore to dethrone me?... and at present you have your ships before Palermo with 3,000 men hid on board;[1] so I presume the generous English nation mean to force me either to accept the bonds they choose to impose on me, or I am to abdicate the throne; but if they take such measures I declare that I will place myself at the head of the army and make every possible effort of resistance..." I [Fagan] here attempted to tranquillize her, but it was impossible... "Tell Bentinck that if only fifty armed troops are landed from the vessels it will be a most fatal day, and that blood will probably flow in torrents... Fagan, if your Government wish to get rid of me, why do they not give me poison, or have me stabbed?"'

Such tirades were the Queen's only defence. They caused Bentinck some embarrassment, but he hardened his heart. In the meantime he had secret reports of a fresh conspiracy. On January 1, 1812, he found the Queen 'all smiling and *couleur de rose*; she began by saying, let us leave aside all political discourse and have one of friendship'. The King also shunned politics when he visited him at Ficuzza, but he had a negative conversation with Ascoli, the King's

[1] This was untrue.

mentor, who objected to Cassaro directing the new ministry. He also objected to the Queen's behaviour, and remarked that only her death could clarify the situation. Bentinck returned in execrable humour to Palermo, and on January 6 granted a week's delay for the new ministry to be formed; if nothing were done he threatened to declare war. On the 10th he saw the Hereditary Prince: 'I concluded a very long conversation by saying that I should use force if my representations were not attended to... I must confess that I never spoke to a person more dispassionate, honest and apparently well-meaning. He appeared to have deeply at heart the good of his country... I therefore told the Duke of Orléans and the Marquis of Circello of the extreme satisfaction I had derived from my conference with the Hereditary Prince.'

The Queen held frequent Councils of State and bellicose conferences with Castrone, Moliterno and various Neapolitan exiles, harangued the officers of the royal guard, many of whom were French, and tried to show Bentinck that she would resist force with force. These activities created a certain atmosphere of tension in Palermo. But without the British subsidy the Sicilian troops could not be paid; she forgot this hard fact in her frenzy. Fagan told Bentinck: 'The great Lady is more enraged than ever, and a few days past cried out to her guards: "*Ammazzate questi birbanti di Inglesi!*" [Kill those rascally Englishmen!]. Permit me to beg Your Lordship not to have any reliance on their fair promises; every evil... is to be expected from a furious mad woman.' But Bentinck threatened to send the King and Queen and even the Hereditary Prince to Malta, and put the latter's two-year-old son on the throne, under the regency of the Duke of Orléans. On January 11 he embarked his luggage and sent orders to the British troops at Messina, Milazzo and Trapani to march on Palermo. He was about to lower the British arms on his house and declare war, when he received messages from Circello and the Hereditary Prince that the Court had yielded. The King agreed to hand over the government to his son Francis. Bentinck informed Wellesley: 'Her Majesty was highly incensed against the Hereditary Prince whom she reproached in the sharpest terms. She spread about the town the falsest reports... On the 13th both the Prince and the Queen sent for me. I saw the Prince first. He was much affected... with the violent manner in which the Queen had treated him. He was pleased to say that in the execution of my orders I had put *toute la complaisance possible*... I went to the Queen, and I repeated to her what the Prince had just said, that she was the kindest of mothers... She praised him very much... In the latter part of the interview she was so wild that I begged to put an end to it... The Queen not being well, the King came to Palermo on the 14th. The Queen made a last great effort to dissuade the King through the means of his confessor from transferring his authority to the Hereditary Prince.'

Francis had inherited much of his father's weakness, but he had avoided his mother's influence. The Queen had often lamented his mediocrity; she foresaw that he would be docile to Bentinck. But her last great effort failed to dissuade the King. On January 16 he signed a deed of appointment in the form of a letter to the Hereditary Prince: 'Being obliged by ill-health and the advice of my doctors to abstain from all serious application and to breathe the country air... I appoint you my Vicar-General in this kingdom as you have been already twice in my kingdom of Naples,' with all the powers of an *alter ego*.

'I never demanded, directly or indirectly, the King's abdication,' Bentinck wrote to Wellesley. This was merely a regency during the King's 'indisposition', which was to last as long as it suited Bentinck. The King retired to Ficuzza, about twenty-four miles from Palermo; the Queen to Santa Croce, one mile from the capital. Though the King grumbled, he was probably not too sorry to shift his responsibility on to his son in such a crisis. He had no intention of renouncing power for ever. All innovations bothered and upset him, and he was sure these could not last. His son, instead of his wife, would now have to bear the blame, while he would retain his popularity. For he was popular, even with the English. His faults were all attributed to the Queen. The change scarcely affected his daily existence, his round of hunting and fishing and farming, and his cosy liaison with the black-eyed Princess of Partanna. He had no intention of living with his wife. As for Bentinck, what did he know of the Sicilians? Apparently he imagined that they were like the English; he would soon find out his mistake.

The Queen fumed and fretted in retirement at Santa Croce; she was very far from resigned. Bentinck, 'that boorish corporal', had become more odious to her than 'the scoundrelly but too lucky Corsican'.

The Hereditary Prince, who had made a favourable first impression on Bentinck, was left in an unenviable position. He had the domestic virtues of a *bourgeois* paterfamilias, mild, orderly, self-consciously filial and extremely uxorious. He annotated and registered every letter he received, and made a point of answering them himself. A bureaucrat by vocation, pedantically attached to details, he had one ambition: to save all that could be saved and guard the relics of sovereignty until the war was won. Ascoli wrote of him: 'He loses himself in the little and sees nothing in the large'; but he had the strength of his weaknesses. A hero might have upset the apple cart. An ultra-conservative, who had no more enthusiasm for constitutions than his parents, and who was afraid of Bentinck, Francis was forced to play a hypocritical role. *Nescit regnare qui nescit simulare*—'he cannot reign who cannot dissimulate'—was a motto he often repeated. His pathological caution, prevarication and timidity often maddened Bentinck, but helped to preserve his father's throne. He got no credit for it. His mother abused him as 'a rebel against his excellent father'; to Damas she wrote that he had been seduced by a lust for power, sweeping everything aside to achieve his ends, respecting nothing. The King sent him scolding letters, but refused to see him. And Bentinck soon changed his opinion of the hapless Prince: 'The leading feature of his character is distrust... dullness of comprehension, a littleness of mind in all things, a superstitious awe of his parents.' Under the circumstances his distrust was only natural: he had no cause to trust anybody, but he perceived the folly of quarrelling with the English dictator.

Amid the chorus of abuse led by the Duke of Ascoli, an unexpected voice was raised in the Vicar's favour, that of the Prince of Canosa: 'The most virtuous heir to the Crown, ever summoned to cure the dying, saved the sceptre and Sicily, by reconciling not only the Sicilian magnates with the Throne, but by restoring that reciprocal good faith and harmony with our allied protectress Great Britain, whose friendship proved very precious in those critical and stormy circumstances.'

XXXII

Reinstatement of the five barons and exile of their leading opponents—Bentinck's persecution of the Queen—Moliterno's project for Italian unification—Father Caccamo's intervention—The new Sicilian Constitution—A new treaty of alliance—The Prince Vicar's illness—Disputes among the Constitutionalists— The King defiantly returns to Palermo—Bentinck bullies the King—The Duke of Orléans intervenes—The King retires from Palermo—Order for the Queen's departure—The siege of Castelvetrano—The Queen sails from Mazzara—A voyage of eight months to Vienna.

The Regency installed, the five deported barons were reinstated. Their exile had been a stepping-stone to triumph, and the edict revoking the one per cent tax on payments increased their exultation. The Princes of Belmonte and Castelnuovo first went to thank their liberator Bentinck before visiting the Prince Vicar who graciously asked them to forget the past and concentrate on the future; he hoped to see them often and benefit by their advice. Castelnuovo promptly advised the Prince to convoke Parliament at the earliest opportunity. Three of the returning barons were given posts in the new ministry: Belmonte was appointed to Foreign Affairs, Castelnuovo to Finance and Aci became Minister of War. The Princes of Carini and Cassaro were the other members of the Privy Council. Bentinck was usually present at their sessions, and he encouraged them to start reforming the Constitution at once. The drafting of it was entrusted to the Abbé Balsamo, a learned professor of political economy at the University of Palermo.

Bentinck regarded the British Constitution as a panacea for all ills, but he thought the Sicilians should draft one to suit themselves. In the meantime he transferred his army headquarters from Messina to Palermo, and took steps to remove all those he considered obstacles to Sicilian progress. Ascoli, who had advocated the arrest of the barons and urged the King to resist Bentinck to the uttermost, even to escape to Tunis, Tripoli or Constantinople, and embarrass the British by a total abdication, was to be banished. After his debts were paid he sailed to Sardinia. Medici, Belmonte's bitterest adversary, was allowed to go to England, where he was useful as a political observer and unofficial ambassador though resented by Castelcicala. Castrone, who had made a fortune out of the Queen's secret service by pocketing a vast percentage of the sums she so lavishly distributed, was imprisoned in a fortress. Bentinck was convinced that Castrone had been corresponding with the enemy and told the Prince so. 'Did I believe, he said, that the Queen knew of it? I could not say, but under her sanction I was quite certain a treasonable correspondence was kept up.'

One of Castrone's emissaries, Captain Rossarol, had been convicted of conspiring with the enemy and shot, but the Court repudiated the machinations of hotheads, egged on by Murat's agents. Cassetti's confession, which Bentinck received on March 12, 1812, revived his worst suspicions of the Queen, and he now insisted on her removal to some distant part of the island. He wrote to her very bluntly, rebuking her for heaping honours on those who had been dismissed by the new ministry, and for continuing to intrigue against the latter, adding that he knew she had been negotiating with the enemy. The Queen replied verbally asking to see the proofs of this accusation, but Bentinck refused to show his cards. He had an interview with the Hereditary Prince and became annoyed with him for defending his mother: 'He asked me for my proofs. I begged to be excused giving them. I did not accuse the Queen, I did not want to try her. He said, have you any written papers? I said, no. Then, he said, you have only Cassetti's deposition. I said, that, with other circumstances amounting to proofs.'

The Duke of Orléans had recently told Bentinck that the Queen's health was deteriorating—'every evening she was in a state of insensibility for two or three hours'. But Bentinck was pitiless. He gloated sadistically over his persecution of the ailing, elderly Queen. The consul Fagan described with relish how the Queen had been affected by Bentinck's message: 'Her Majesty... shed a flood of tears; and when she was a little recovered she said: "Fagan, take this letter and read it... The French government, Fagan, murdered my sister, and yours will do so to me... Yes, I am convinced your government intend my end to be similar to that of my sister, and this, I suppose, is to take place in England..."'

Castlereagh had succeeded Wellesley as Foreign Minister in Downing Street, and on March 23 Bentinck received letters from him expressing 'H.R.H.'s approbation of the measures you have pursued under the very delicate and arduous circumstances in which you have been placed'. A British Constitution for Sicily seemed to him an admirable antidote to the Napoleonic reforms in Italy, where the liberal afflatus was swelling irresistibly. Amherst had written: 'An independent government and a free constitution would be considered as a boon, the attainment of which would irrevocably bind the Sicilians to the nations which procure it for them.'

Immediately after the Regency was installed, Moliterno came forward with a project for another expedition to the mainland. He proposed nothing less than to unify the whole peninsula under the sceptre of Ferdinand IV as a constitutional monarch. Moliterno himself, of course, was to lead the armada and, as soon as he had occupied Rome, Great Britain and her allies were to recognize the independence and unification of Italy as a single state under His Sicilian Majesty. But apart from Bentinck's conviction that 'hated as Murat is, the old dynasty is more so', he did not consider the moment ripe, and Moliterno was notoriously unreliable. On January 27 he wrote to the Prince Vicar that if it were a question of supporting a total effort of the Italian people, he would feel justified in rendering the utmost assistance: 'The first and sole object must be that of liberating Italy from the French. To wish to impose this or that form of government, to plan in advance the partition of the country into separate states, would have the appearance of conquest rather than of aiding the efforts of a great nation to acquire independence... Here I shall repeat again what I have propounded more than once: that Sicily might be in a position to contribute powerfully towards the conquest of Italy, not with arms but with the example of her felicity. The Italians are an intelligent people; they have long desired a Constitution which would give them a judicious liberty, and will never submit to being transferred from one despotism to another... If by the Prince's desire Sicily be granted a Constitution which will ensure a moderate and reasonable liberty and promote the nation's happiness and prosperity, from that moment I shall regard the conquest of Italy and the restoration of the kingdom of Naples as half accomplished. All eyes on the continent will be turned towards Sicily as a model of happiness and security, and perhaps not only Naples but several adjoining states will seek the good fortune to live under the same chief and the same government.'

Privately Bentinck told the Prince that he was not averse to Moliterno's project because it would distract the Queen's mind from other matters. The Sicilian Constitution came first, and a new Parliament would have to assist its birth. In spite of wretched health the Queen spent all her remaining energy intriguing against the new ministry. The King still had the final word, and he was still swayed by his wife, even at a distance. The Prince Vicar was in an awkward position between Bentinck and his parents: he was less influenced by 'superstitious awe' than by the fact that blood is thicker than water, especially Bourbon blood. The Queen was buoyed up with the hope that Bentinck would never dare go to extremes, and that he would be repudiated by his own government. It was therefore with smug complacency that Bentinck wrote on March 25: 'Fagan told me that when he said to the Queen that I had received letters approving my conduct, she put out her tongue and said, then all my hopes are gone!'

While the new Constitution was being drafted and preparations were being made for the opening of Parliament, Bentinck felt it was essential to eliminate the chief instigator of discord, and Belmonte agreed with him. 'A great deal of our conversation,' he wrote, 'turned upon the mode of getting rid of the Queen... I suggested that the King's authority was the best and perhaps the only way.' But the wily King was inaccessible: he would neither see Bentinck nor his son. Although he would not live with his wife for fear of being compromised by her indiscretions and because he was thoroughly tired of her, he corresponded with her regularly, or rather she, the ever-voluminous letter-writer, corresponded with him; and he could not shake off the habit of deferring to her opinions. The King's passive was thus complementary to the Queen's active resistance: even divided, they were a stubborn team. And Bentinck wished to avoid odious comparison with Napoleon's treatment of the Spanish monarchs. He wrote to Castlereagh on March 31: 'His Majesty, I had reason to suppose, would not see me or receive any letter from me. There appeared... no other channel of communication than through his confessor... Père Caccamo. The Père told me of the King's entire conviction of the necessity of her absence, not only from Palermo but from Sicily also. He informed me that the King during the last two months had been constantly writing to the Queen *andate via, andate via* [go away!], that she had been tormenting him with courier after courier to resume the reins of government... He added that the King observed that he had been married forty-four years and that they had been so many years of *martyre*.'

Father Caccamo, who has been much maligned, seems to have been sincerely anxious to smooth over difficulties, an intermediary by vocation. His task was not easy: although the King respected him, he cut him short when his conversation became irksome. Haunted by Father Strassoldi's sudden death, he never tasted a dish at the King's table of which he had not seen the King partake. After a parley with Bentinck, Father Caccamo approached the Queen. Fagan, a subsidiary go-between, informed Bentinck: 'Father Caccamo has acquainted the great Lady that you insist on her leaving Palermo immediately: she has declared in the most violent manner possible... that she will not leave it alive. It is no longer tears but determined fury.' On April 1 Father Caccamo wrote to the King: 'I spoke to the minister, and he charged me to represent seriously to Your Majesty, that for your happiness and the Queen's, it is necessary for her to leave for any place she may choose, and her present obstinacy is a great embarrassment, since it will injure everybody. May Our Lord enlighten her! Nothing is impossible to the Almighty! As for me, I shall not cease striving for the good of all, and especially of Your Majesty. Yesterday... the English officer sent by the minister came to see me. He told me in confidence that owing to the respect and veneration due to Your Majesty it is expedient that Your Majesty, assuming the tone of a sovereign, should oblige the Queen to leave within a month's time... This effort should be made, and then God will be with us and with her...'

But it was one thing for the King to send his wife away, quite another for a foreign ambassador to dictate her departure. The pressure of Bentinck, who had already antagonized him, struck him as the height of insolence. Weary though he was of the Queen's meddling, he resented the foreigner's more deeply. So he dug himself in at Ficuzza and refused to mention the subject.

The Prince Vicar appealed to Father Caccamo. For the Prince, as for Bentinck, there was no other channel of communication with his parent. The Queen sent him stinging letters, asking him to be kind enough to warn her if he heard of plots against her life; she told everybody that he was an ungrateful, unnatural son. The Prince was distressed by the scandal of her separation from the King, and wished to persuade his father to take her back. He implored the confessor not to forsake him in 'this sea of darkness and woe'. Bentinck had gone to Malta, but might return at any moment. 'You may conceive my awful embarrassment if he should repeat his demand for the Queen's removal.' If Bentinck threatened, to whom could he turn for counsel? He had no friends, and without the confessor's aid he could only take refuge in tears at the foot of the altar. Only God knew what horrors might be published against the unhappy Queen, and how falsely they might be coloured to delude the people. How would the King's refusal to live with her be interpreted in the eyes of the public? Where was the Queen to go if she had to leave the kingdom? What was he to do? 'Advise me for mercy's sake, and tell me what to say to the minister if he makes new demands...'

Still the King kept his door shut. Bentinck wrote again to Father Caccamo on April 17, asking him to use his influence with the King 'in the present imperious circumstances... The King's just esteem for your worthy person is a sure guarantee of the success of an affair of such great import: and I wish to confide it wholly to your zeal and your talents.' This letter was intercepted and taken to the Queen by Father Culotta, a colleague of Father Caccamo, and she told Fagan the same evening: 'If he spits blood, if he stops the subsidy, if he takes down the British arms, I will not go.' To Bentinck she sent word that she intended to move into the royal palace of Palermo on account of her health. When Fagan returned to the theme on the 22nd she told him: 'If he attempts to force me, not an Englishman will remain alive at Palermo... Bentinck's head will ultimately pay for it.' Bentinck wrote to the King repeating his accusations, adding that her intrigues might cause disturbances before the opening of Parliament. He also applied in vain for an audience. On the 25th the Queen wrote: 'Let Bentinck be persuaded that the daughter of Maria Theresa may be persecuted and slandered, but never dishonoured!... The Queen scorns calumny and has sufficient courage to bear with violence and confound her enemies.'

Finally the King replied to Father Caccamo on the 26th, in a letter intended for Bentinck as well as his son. 'I cannot believe there is any truth in what I hear about their insistence on my wife's removal and their threats to use coercion in case she will not go. However, should this be true, let my son realize that I shall allow no joking on the subject, and that for the slightest outrage against her he will be responsible to me, and will have to render me a strict account. God has united us and only God can separate us. She is his Mother and Sovereign; let him venerate, respect and defend her in all circumstances as is his duty... Furthermore you will show my son (although he must have seen them) two pages I have just received, warning him to tell Bentinck to refrain from writing me such impertinences and even more from visiting me. My wife is incapable of being what he believes and dishonestly seeks to represent her. I have not convoked the Parliament, and I know the Sicilian nation as he does not; he will be responsible to God, his government and the whole of Europe for the slightest disturbance or accident that may occur. As Minister of the King of Great Britain our ally, let him therefore respect us as he should, and as General in command of our combined forces, let him only mind his obligation to defend us and our kingdom from the common foe and help us recover that which we have lost because I have always been as loyal as I am now and shall be, in spite of what a few unworthy subjects may insinuate. Let him also know that I shall report all this punctually to England, and when I have received replies and due satisfaction I shall acquaint him with my sentiments.'

In vain the Prince persisted in pleading for an audience: surely his good father would not reject a son who tenderly loved him, whose sole object was to save and preserve his kingdom? What would the public think? He would wait outside his door until he deigned to relent. To Castelcicala he wrote that the Queen's indiscretions were continuous: she herself supplied her enemies with weapons and trusted those who betrayed her. He was cut to the quick by the Queen's taunts while he was struggling, as he said, to temporize and avert the storm. Both his parents behaved as if he were in league with Bentinck against them, which was so far from true that Bentinck, like Belmonte, came to doubt his sincerity and good intentions. Bentinck's persecution of the Queen had the opposite effect to that which he had anticipated. The Queen joined her husband at Ficuzza at the end of the month, and on May 6 they returned to Palermo together. Then the King went to Solanto for the tunny fishing, while the Queen stayed at Bagheria nearby.

Between the opening of Parliament on June 18 and the first meeting to discuss the new Constitution on July 20 there was a strenuous conflict to force the King to accept it. The King kept his son waiting till the last moment before he would approve the allocution which was to be read at the opening ceremony. Again the Prince invoked the aid of Father Caccamo: 'Time flies, our fate is drawing near its end, and the precipice is unknown. . . . Either the

King trusts me and leaves me free to act, or let him act himself. Write to me for mercy's sake, as I shall have to see Bentinck tomorrow and I do not know what to say...' If the King thought of resuming the reins of government, so much the better; far from being displeased, the Prince would be delighted. He would deem himself honoured if the King would allow him to serve as his porter! After several imploring letters the King sent an oracular reply through Father Caccamo on June 12: 'Let the Vicar continue bravely to govern as heretofore, and finish with honour and glory the task he had begun.' Bentinck suspended the subsidy a second time to bring His Majesty to heel. Fagan had informed him that the Queen 'is greatly pushed for money, at least those who attend her tell me that they have not been paid for four months'.

At the first meeting of Parliament, which lasted twenty-four hours in succession, the fundamental articles of the new Constitution were adopted in an atmosphere of tense excitement. Much time was wasted on ancient formalities: such as the coming and going of envoys from chamber to chamber whenever a word was to be added or changed. But the King's sanction was still imperative, and he objected to several articles on the perverse pretext that they did not conform to the British Constitution. Yet again the Prince appealed to Father Caccamo. 'This hesitation', he wrote, 'will be fatal to us all.' Bentinck and Belmonte were blaming him for the delay. The King had in fact won over the Princes of Cassaro and Aci, who subsequently did everything possible to sabotage the Constitution. In the meantime Bentinck wrote to Castlereagh: 'I have done violence to my own judgement and feelings in endeavouring to attain the objects of my instructions by the means of conciliation only. I regret the sacrifices of great advantage to the common cause which have arisen from this undeserved delicacy... it has been all in vain, and I am now in decided conviction that fear, and nothing but fear, can direct a mind which many believe to be as false and cunning as it is certainly weak.' On August 1 he saw the King at Ficuzza. 'He [the King] asked if I would support him? I said I hoped he would not place me in the disagreeable predicament, but certainly if his refusal to comply with the wish, almost unanimous, of the nation should produce disorder, I could not support him. He appeared annoyed at this. He said, "I shall write down your answer and send it to England."' On August 10 the King authorized the Prince Vicar to sanction 'all the articles conforming to the British

Constitution'. On the 12th an 'infernal machine' exploded under the windows of the Sicilian House of Commons, creating a temporary panic but causing no damage. One of the Queen's toadies, the Duke of Craco, was denounced by an accomplice for abetting this. As soon as he was arrested, Craco implicated the Queen in his confession, so that she fled from Santa Croce to take refuge with the King at Ficuzza. Craco was pardoned, but being a Neapolitan he was ordered to leave the island. As the Prince Vicar said, his mother had supplied her enemies with weapons.

The Queen had already written to the Emperor for permission to go to Vienna, and Bentinck had heard this from the Irish-Austrian General Nugent in June. According to Nugent, the Emperor was painfully embarrassed: 'Metternich was very much against her coming, saying she was an intriguing woman and might do mischief. The Emperor thought he could not refuse.' Bentinck was therefore not surprised when, at another stormy interview, the Queen asked him for an armed frigate to convey her abroad. He hastened to take advantage of this request, which had been made in a fit of temper. On September 12 he had signed a new treaty of alliance, guaranteeing Sicily to Ferdinand with a promise to support his restoration to Naples at the general peace. On the 13th he sent Captain Milner with a letter to the King. 'At the last conference which Her Majesty the Queen did me the honour of granting me,' he wrote, 'she communicated to me her intention of leaving Sicily. After this communication, I no longer deemed it necessary to address myself to Your Majesty: but the positive orders I have recently received from my Court oblige me to return to this subject. It is only from Your Majesty that I can expect enlightenment on this point, and I dare hope that Your Majesty will forgive me for begging you to deign to grant it.'

The King was at dinner when Milner arrived, no doubt an additional reason for his irascibility. He told Milner curtly that he would send an answer by his son. The same evening the Queen had convulsions and seemed on the brink of death, but within a week she was back in Palermo, more turbulent than ever. Fagan reported that the King and Queen had never been seen in such a state of affliction, 'that His Majesty declared that he had not heart or courage to oblige his wife to go out of the island'. The Queen remarked to Fagan that 'Bonaparte was a *joli enfant doux* in comparison with Bentinck'. The King informed Cassaro that he did not wish to receive any more impertinent letters from Bentinck, who was to leave the Queen in peace. If Bentinck had any proofs against Her Majesty, let him show them to Cassaro. But Bentinck would only show them to the King. Both the Prince Vicar and Cassaro urged the Queen to yield gracefully, but she remained obdurate. 'Cassaro told her that... it appeared that the British Government was perfectly satisfied with the proofs, and had given me [Bentinck] unlimited powers... The Queen was very angry and told him that he was *un de la généralité*, which piqued Cassaro's pride excessively... She said to him, "And what do these English mean to do with me?" He answered, "To take you away with the troops." She said, "Have they the power to do so?" He said, "What prevents them from sending some regiments?" She said, "The *popolari* will rise in my favour." "Madam, why will you deceive yourself upon this subject. You are surrounded by the worst people. Your antechamber... represents the galleys rather than the room of a Palace..." The Queen was very much enraged with Cassaro for having written so strongly to the King... perhaps her anger arose from the freedom with which he had spoken to her.'

Amid all this pother the Prince Vicar was taken very ill after dinner on September 26, and it was generally rumoured that the Queen had intended to poison him. Apart from the symptoms, she had called her son a traitor and a revolutionary; and as soon as she heard of his condition she sent word to Fagan that the Prince was too unwell to hold the reins of government. It is possible that some of her clique were responsible; these promptly accused the Duke of Orléans. But the weather was hot and the Prince was a heavy eater. Bentinck reported to Castlereagh on October 4: 'The Hereditary Prince has been attacked by a severe illness... it began by spasms in the stomach... The Queen came to the Palace, and the day after the violence of the attacks was so much increased that the greatest apprehensions were entertained as to the result... The symptoms were of a nature so like poison that it was generally believed that arsenic had been administered and... general suspicion was fixed upon the Queen... The result of the illness has destroyed any suspicion of its having been caused by poison, but it is certain that the impression was very strong upon the mind of the Prince himself.' When Bentinck suggested to the Prince's physician that his illness might be due to the great heat, 'he cried out shaking with palsy all over: "*Ce n'est pas la chaleur, c'est sa mère, sa mère!*"' The Prince never entirely recovered from the effect of this mysterious malady; it left him with a mottled grey complexion, a shuffling gait and a senile stoop. The moral shock was even greater than the physical: from now on there was a noticeable change in his attitude towards his mother. If the Queen would only keep quiet, he wrote to Father Caccamo, Bentinck might not insist on her departure. She should go far away from Palermo and stop corresponding with those schemers who had always betrayed her: 'When the tempest raves one must furl one's sails and stay under cover, otherwise he that wishes to brave the wind will be shipwrecked.'

Bentinck returned to the charge again and again, though his letters to the King came back unopened. Besides Cassaro and Father Caccamo, he enlisted the aid of old Circello who had retired; he even delivered a homily to the Queen's faithful Saint-Clair; but it was all so much water off a duck's back. He drafted a letter for the King to sign promising that the Queen should reside at Castelvetrano, and he seriously considered sending a battalion and some cavalry to Ficuzza by way of intimidation. Describing his fruitless efforts to Castlereagh, he wrote: 'I had now no other resource but to solicit a personal interview with the King, and I hoped by appearing unexpectedly at the Ficuzza that the King's mind, being unprepared by the Queen, might not refuse me this request. I in consequence rode down to the Ficuzza on the 15th October... I had not been ten minutes in the ante-chamber before I saw the Queen going into the King's room...' The glimpse was ominous. Though he had had a long ride, the King refused to see him, but he was able to button hole Father Caccamo and threaten to take less friendly steps unless he was granted an audience. After waiting in vain he had much ado to find a lodging for the night, and that of a most squalid description. He had driven his mare so hard in his fury that the animal fell dead. Undaunted, he returned on the morrow. Nor would he leave until Circello and Cassaro had shown him the text of the King's pledge that the Queen would retire to Santa Margherita in the province of Girgenti until the spring, when she would proceed to Vienna.

In the first flush of success Bentinck talked as if he had averted a revolution, and excused his rough behaviour on that score. 'I say what I think and do what I say,' he told Father Caccamo, whom he dubbed 'the minister of peace'. But the King was right in objecting that Bentinck had confused the Sicilians with the English, imagining that they could be governed by the same laws. The new Constitution was excellent propaganda for the Bourbons, although they failed to appreciate it; for the rising sect of Carbonari in Naples began to conspire against Murat in favour of Ferdinand, the constitutional monarch. As Schipa wrote: 'Murat's kingdom seemed the land of bondage and the Bourbon's a haven of liberty.' Most Sicilians, however, failed to understand the nature of this liberty. The transition from absolutism to a more liberal regime was too sudden. Many of the nobles who had voted for the Constitution in a burst of unselfish patriotism were stung by remorse when they realized that it swept their former power away.

The question of *fidecommessi* (entail or settlement on the eldest son) soon split the leaders of the Constitutional party into Belmontisti and Villarmosisti (Castelnuovo was also the Prince of Villarmosa). Belmonte led the 'aristocratic' Constitutionalists, who argued that entails were necessary in order to retain that hereditary influence of great families without which a limited monarchy soon becomes unlimited, and Castelnuovo the 'democratic', in favour of their abolition. The Princes of Cassaro and Aci, both political opportunists, seceded to the royalist party. This split in the ministry helped the formation of a strong opposition which gravitated towards the King. It was further complicated by personal considerations: Belmonte was Castelnuovo's nephew; his uncle had no sons and would therefore gain rather than lose by the abolition of entails; and a scheming Aspasia, the Princess of Paternò, was known to have had a finger in the pie. Libels and slanders pullulated: there was far more licence than liberty. These dissensions would have occurred even if the Queen had left Sicily. They were the inevitable result of too sweeping a change. The foxy Constitutional barons flattered the foreign prig and led him by the nose. That nose could only sniff danger in one direction.

For a while the Queen lay low, but she was determined to make one more bid for power. The cold damp air of Santa Margherita did not agree with her, but her anxiety to persuade the King to resume full authority was the real reason for her joining him surreptitiously at Ficuzza on January 5, 1813. Upon hearing of this Bentinck could not contain himself. He sent fulminating notes to Circello and Cassaro: hitherto the British Government had drawn a distinction between the King and Queen, only considering the Queen as unfriendly. But now the King's conduct had assumed a different aspect: his violation of the engagement—Bentinck called it a treaty —concerning the Queen's sojourn in Santa Margherita denoted a hostile attitude.

The King was justifiably incensed. The Princes of Aci, Cassaro, Cutò and Campofranco, and many other repentant barons, rallied round him urging him to annul the Constitution, 'an unwieldy machine which deprived him of his authority'. 'Everybody is clamouring for me to take back the reins, before everything goes to rack and ruin,' he wrote to Castelcicala. On February 6 he returned to Palermo, where he prayed a long time in the royal chapel before repairing to the Villa Favorita, which became the headquarters of his party. In spite of heavy rain, over a hundred carriages went to meet him three miles outside the city, and a vast crowd acclaimed him on the palace square. Partisan historians deny that this was a popular ovation such as that given to the banished barons; but who is to distinguish between one cheering crowd and another? The King had never lost his popularity. His affability struck all beholders; he had recovered his boyish spirits. But he froze when Belmonte and Castelnuovo came to pay their respects. Cassaro started negotiations with Bentinck for the King's return to power, but Bentinck declared he would never consent until the Queen left the country; he even threatened to arrest her. Anglo-Sicilian troops had occupied the island of Ponza without informing the King, who complained of this secrecy, pointing out that as part of the kingdom of Naples it was outside the Vicar's province. Bentinck swept these protests aside, and again repeated his accusations against the Queen. He had all the proofs of her correspondence with the enemy; even if the King refused to see them, the British Government was convinced that they were authentic. The Queen must go, otherwise he would break the alliance. Cassaro having quarrelled with Bentinck and shown his true colours as a royalist, the King replied evasively through Belmonte.

On March 9 the King returned to the royal palace, summoned the ministers, and told them that since his health had been restored by the blessing of God, he intended to resume government. He would uphold the Constitution so long as it was observed in its integrity, and he would heal party strife. Turning to Castelnuovo, he said: 'The finances should go better.' Castelnuovo replied: 'Your Majesty will correct me.' Next day the King attended a thanksgiving service in the cathedral, which echoed with loud cheers even during the benediction. When he climbed into his coach the crowd wished to unharness and drag it to the palace; and the ovation continued under the palace windows. 'Why don't they go away?' he exclaimed. Cassaro said they were waiting for him to show himself at the balcony. According to the anonymous *Mémoire de la Reine*, Belmonte interposed: 'What, sir? Would you have the King encourage an insurrection?' And Cassaro retorted: 'It is strange to call the applause of his subjects an insurrection. What would you say if they hissed him?' The King bowed from the balcony; hats were flung into the air, after which the crowd dispersed. On the 11th Bentinck had a furious interview with the King, and it is interesting to compare the *Mémoire* account of this with Bentinck's. The former relates that Bentinck came at eleven in the morning. 'The King advanced towards him, imagining that he had only come to salute him. With his usual courtesy the King inquired after his health, but instead of replying as he should have done, Bentinck assumed an arrogant tone hardly tolerable towards an inferior and overwhelmed the King with reproaches for never accepting his advice, adding that he could only predict the direst consequences for such conduct. The King replied to this insolent speech with as much composure as dignity, that having always been the faithful friend of England, he thought he had nothing to fear from her; besides, he had always wished to do what was best for Sicily. Lord William boldly replied: "Thus it was formerly believed, but Your Majesty has given me proofs of the contrary, and I regard you now as no less hostile than the Queen." The King, justly offended, made Bentinck feel that he was doubtless forgetting to whom he was speaking; he added that not only had he never broken his word but he was incapable of doing so. Bentinck then lost all self-control. "Words", he said, "are one thing, facts are another; and Your Majesty will repent of his conduct." The King, at the end of his patience, declared that if he had come to intimidate him he was mistaken, because he only feared God. He begged him to stop his insulting remarks, to which he was not accustomed.'

Bentinck wrote: 'I determined to go personally to the King and see if I could not frighten him. I accordingly went at half-past three and was immediately received... He spoke of the alliance... I said that... it was my duty to warn him of the consequences that might ensue from his persisting in his previous refusal. What consequences, what consequences, he said... I said, *Je suis un homme simple*. He answered, *Je suis plus simple que vous, et plus honnête que vous.* I made a bow, and he recollected himself, *Je suis honnête, vous pouvez l'être aussi...* I said that the object of the King of England was to secure the Constitution . . . the King could never permit that it should be destroyed. The King took fire at the word Permit. Permit, permit, permit, he repeated, England has no right to interfere.'

After this painful scene the King went to lie down with a bad headache. There was to be another *Te Deum* in the popular Church of San Francesco, and Bentinck had warned him that if he chose to attend it he would be escorted by British bayonets. The governor of Palermo, the captain of justice and other officials in breathless succession, broke in upon his rest with sensational news: eight thousand English troops had occupied the strategic points of the capital. The King decided to stay indoors; his headache was followed by fever and convulsions. On the 13th Belmonte brought him an ultimatum threatening to start hostilities unless the Queen left, Cassaro resigned, Parliament were convoked on April 1, a number of foreigners were expelled, and the King promised never to let the Constitution be violated. Belmonte, Castelnuovo and Ruggero Settimo, who had replaced Aci, sent in their resignations when the King replied as before. For the time being Sicily was without a government.

The Duke of Orléans now stepped into the breach as an intermediary. Bentinck considered him disinterested, but he doubtless had one eye on the regency. The Duke visited his father-in-law on the 16th and recorded their conversation most vividly.

'You find me in the greatest embarrassment,' sighed the King.

'Your Majesty may say more than that, you are in imminent danger.' And the Duke recapitulated Bentinck's threats.

'But I do not want these hostilities, you know. I do not want them at all.'

'Your Majesty would have to lose your reason in order to want them... As soon as hostilities begin, farewell to all the treaties by which England is bound to you. The only laws she will observe will be the laws of war. You will be treated as vanquished and Sicily as conquered territory.'

'Alas, that is only too clear. Do you think I do not see it as plainly as you do?'

The King gave vent to his alarm and despair: 'I have been shut up for a week. I can bear it no longer. I am ill, I can neither sleep nor eat. If this continues I shall die. Oh yes indeed, it is a fine story! And you know, it is not a joke. Perhaps Lord William is about to arrive with his troops, to plant guns in the square and fire grapeshot at my windows. Oh Jesus, Mary! I want none of his cannonades, you know. I want none of them at all.'

On March 17, when the term given for Bentinck's ultimatum was about to expire and his secretary, Lamb, was waiting in the palace for an answer, the King, after another attack of convulsions, surrendered in a letter to his son. He retired furtively to the Villa Favorita the night after, so furtively that Bentinck suspected another coup. On the 21st he was required to sign a document renouncing all sovereign authority except his title. This he absolutely declined to do, though the house had been surrounded by British troops and he was a virtual prisoner. Bentinck's purpose was to prevent him from joining the Queen at Castelvetrano, since he heard that she was plotting an insurrection in the centre and south-west of the island. After frantic negotiations the Duke of Sangro and the indefatigable Father Caccamo reached an agreement with Bentinck. The King restored the Vicariate and promised not to return to power without British consent. He even announced that he was ready to leave the island with the Queen; perhaps he would go to Malta. Bentinck then ordered the troops to withdraw and had a more peaceful conference with the King, of which he wrote: 'The King came down and said... "I promise not to interfere with the government of my son. I promise also not to move from here, and if you like it you may place sentries at my gate..." I said I was not that *méchant homme* that I had been represented to him. He took me by the hand, he said he felt sure of me... He hoped I would guarantee his personal security. I gave my word that I would.'

A few days later the King sent Butera to Fagan with a proposal to place him on the throne again, in consideration of which Bentinck was to be made Great Chancellor in perpetuity. Bentinck would not hear of this and again threatened to use force: 'I was fully prepared to have made the King a prisoner if he had not yielded before, so I was resolved to do tomorrow what I had said I would.' This time it was quite true that the King was indisposed. Bentinck described him as looking 'ill and *abattu*'; he would only talk of shooting and fishing, his cows and calves. Later Fagan informed him: 'The King gives signs of approaching insanity. He walks quickly backwards and forwards in his rooms repeating: *Sanctus Deus, sanctus fortis, sanctus et immortalis, miserere mei et fiat voluntas tua.*

Bentinck had cause to congratulate himself. His instructions had been to endeavour to make himself as agreeable as possible to their Sicilian Majesties; perhaps he could make himself even more agreeable. He had induced the baffled King to sign an order for the Queen's departure, 'advising as a friend, begging as a husband and commanding as a King'. The Queen's health had also suffered as a result of the King's defeat, which was in fact her own. But her temper was less submissive than Ferdinand's. Describing the King's 'apparently inconsistent conduct' to Castlereagh on April 4, Bentinck wrote: 'Your Lordship must consider him as the complete puppet of the Queen. Her Majesty solely has access to him. She has constantly impressed his mind with two opinions diametrically opposed to each other... The first that I have had no instructions and that all my measures proceeded from myself... The other that the British government have had no other view than the destruction of the royal family and the possession of Sicily for themselves.' Partly on this account he had not taken command of the Anglo-Sicilian expedition to Catalonia in 1812; owing to his absence, no doubt, it had not achieved much, although the French had the worst of one engagement at Alcoy. He had made preparations for a larger expedition and was eager to sail with it as soon as possible. Only the Queen detained him in Sicily. A doctor had been sent to find out if she was malingering. Fagan reported on April 8: 'The physician Greco has come to Palermo... and has deposed on oath... that he is of opinion that Her Majesty will not survive the voyage.'

Not to be fobbed off with further pretexts, Bentinck sent his second-in-command, General Macfarlane, to Castelvetrano with five thousand men in case the desperate Queen should offer resistance. He had heard that she was ready to defend herself with an armed guard of eight hundred peasants and that she had pawned her jewels to pay them. Macfarlane left his troops a short distance from Castelvetrano and rode with an aide-de-camp and an orderly to the grim castle where the Queen was staying. They noticed some smouldering camp-fires among the dense vegetation of the hill they were climbing. Then some fifty stalwart peasants with muskets rushed out of the undergrowth to bar the way. After explaining with some difficulty that they were friends bringing vouchers for payment, the General's party were allowed to proceed, and the Queen gave orders that they were to be admitted to the castle. They were shocked by the squalor of the sparsely furnished rooms, but the Queen received them with ceremonious dignity. According to his son, the General felt acutely uncomfortable. When he had explained his mission as tactfully as possible, the Queen was overcome with emotion. Her voice rose shrilly through a torrent of words that left her breathless. 'This is a repetition of Bayonne!' she cried. 'Bonaparte did not treat the Spanish royal family worse than Bentinck has treated us! Was it for this that I escaped the axes, conspiracies and betrayals of the Neapolitan Jacobins? Was it for this that I helped Nelson to win the battle of the Nile? For this, that I brought your army to Sicily? General, is this your English honour?'

The General observed that the daughter of Maria Theresa, at all times a majestic woman, was terrible in her rage. As her courtiers had not received any salary for months and had barely enough to eat, he coaxed them with promises of compensation to mollify her. After another tirade she declared verbally and in writing that she would leave as soon as she could embark on an English ship with her son Leopold and her attendants. Her armed guard of Calabrians and Sicilians, who wore red-tasselled caps with the device 'Long live the Holy Faith', wept like children when they heard that she was going to leave them.

Owning herself beaten, the Queen sent Bentinck a proud and eloquent protest, denying the right of the British government to force her to part from her husband and family, for whose sake only she had decided to yield. She made several conditions about the settlement of her debts, which were considerable, and wished to be assured of a respectable income and the payment of her journey expenses. To Ferdinand she wrote with lofty resignation: she pitied and forgave him, but she could not forgive the wretches surrounding him. His throne was tottering; she could only pray for him and for the peace and happiness of the kingdom from which she was driven into exile. To Fagan she expressed her resentment in a tremendous diatribe against her so-called allies, who for seven years in succession had slandered, tormented, dishonoured and made her odious to her subjects and set her own family against her. She maintained that she had always defended the allied cause, with ships at Toulon, with troops in Lombardy, revictualling Nelson's fleet on their way to Egypt, suffering heavy losses in 1798 owing to the assistance she had given the British, and further damage since the rupture of the treaty of Amiens—broken because the British had not withdrawn from Malta, which had been captured by a combined fleet in the name of the Two Sicilies, yet the Neapolitan flag there had been supplanted by the British. In 1805 the British and Russian ministers had obliged her to receive their troops at Naples, who fled before they could face the enemy. The British had then occupied Sicily. She wished to remain friends with England, but had no desire to see Sicily reduced to an English province, and this was the real cause of all the slanders and persecutions against her. After more denunciations of Bentinck, she recommended herself to British generosity, appealing for a loan of a million pounds sterling to pay debts incurred by the maintenance of Neapolitan refugees who had lost everything by following the Court. Needless to say, she did not obtain this loan. The repeated charge that she had offered Sicily to Napoleon in exchange for the recovery of Naples has never been proved.

To Damas she wrote more briefly: 'You will be greatly astonished to learn that I expect to embark at Mazzara between the 8th and 12th of May with my son Leopold, to go to Vienna by way of Constantinople. God alone knows what this cruel departure costs me. To leave the King infirm and old, my children and numerous grandchildren, my property, my position! All this is beyond my power to express. My son Leopold would not leave me, although the august Parliament has thought fit to give him no allowance on account of his filial piety. If I have the good fortune, which I doubt, to arrive safely after this awful voyage by land and sea, I hope to talk to you quietly and show you all the papers and proofs of their iniquity... Leopold is my faithful companion; the Prince of Hesse has also taken a year's leave. I should like to take Cutò as my chamberlain, but I doubt whether they will permit it as I am dealing with contaminated people; it is all incredible but true. I beg you to send me your news in detail to Constantinople. Adieu; my health is so bad that I cannot write at greater length.'

Still she wrote and wrote, until she collapsed with a bilious fever. A British doctor, R. Calvert, Physician to the Forces, was sent to examine her. 'Her Majesty is certainly in an unfit state to embark,' he reported. Bentinck, who was impatient to sail for Spain, lost his temper with the doctor and gave orders that she was to leave as soon as she could do so without danger. But when her health began to improve a piratical Algerian squadron of nine sails came cruising near the coast. Captain Chamberlayne, the commander of H.M.S. *Unity* which had anchored off Mazzara, went to Palermo and insisted on an escort of two ships of the line, the *Edinburgh* of seventy-four guns and the *Leander* of sixty-four. The Queen arrived at Mazzara on June 9, where she attended a *Te Deum* in the cathedral for her safe journey. Although the town councillors had not been prepared for her reception, they were touchingly eager to express their loyalty and stood outside the walls at the gate they had decorated in her honour to offer her the keys of the town. The Queen stayed at the bishop's palace, but as this was too small to accommodate her party, many citizens put their houses, beds and furniture at their disposal. The *Edinburgh* arrived on the 10th, and Captain Duncam, who was to command the convoy, declared they would have to sail on the 14th. He was a rough old sea-dog determined to stand no nonsense from the Queen: he would not even land to pay her his respects. On the night of the 13th she was tortured with violent toothache. A dentist was summoned from Palermo, but as he failed to appear by eleven o'clock on the morrow Captain Duncam had all her goods and chattels taken on board in spite of her plea for a few hours' delay till her pain had been relieved. After a while Duncam approached the shore in his launch and sent for Captain Chamberlayne. Then he took out his watch and told him that unless the Queen embarked in thirty minutes, he would sail without her. She had to forgo the dentist, but wished to attend benediction once more before leaving Sicily. Even then Duncam would hardly wait till the service was over. 'We shall deserve whatever the Queen may say against us,' remarked Chamberlayne indignantly. When she went to pray for the last time in the church by the sea-shore, the whole population followed her in tears. These details are gleaned from the anonymous *Mémoire* edited by R. M. Johnston, which is sufficiently circumstantial without literary pretension, and sufficiently pedestrian to bear the accent of truth.

The Queen's voyage to Vienna by way of the Mediterranean lasted eight weary months. She stopped at Zante from July 19 till August 3, whence she wrote to Damas that she had hoped to wait until her courier returned in order to adapt her plans to the latest reports from Vienna, but the same crooked intrigues which had compelled her to leave Sicily prevented her from staying at Zante. Owing to the plague in Malta, the English threatened to impose a vexatious quarantine. Although she dreaded it, she would leave with her whole caravan for Constantinople, and from there proceed by land to Vienna. 'It is no mean enterprise, and I admit that I very much doubt being able to endure it. If all goes well I expect to reach Vienna by the end of October, and God knows what I shall find there. In a word, I am deeply distressed, but what sustains and encourages me is the knowledge that I have not deserved it.' On August 24 she wrote to him again: 'Since leaving Zante I have been twenty-one days at sea, still hoping for permission to enter the Dardanelles, with the agreeable news that the plague is raging all over Turkey and that it is unlikely that I shall be able to land at Pera; we shall have to apply for permission to go to Varna or Odessa, and at my age, with shattered health, in the beginning of the bad season, after all these horrors and persecutions. Why? Because I wished to prevent the enslavement of Sicily and uphold the rights of my husband, which was my duty. The wickedness of one side and the weakness of the others have made me fly for shelter.'

On September 13 she reached Constantinople, where she stayed with the Neapolitan minister, Count Ludolf. The Sultan sent his Minister for Foreign Affairs to pay his respects with boatloads of succulent fruit, and she was invited to watch the pageantry of the *Bairam* from a palace near the Sultan Achmet's mosque; balls and banquets were given in her honour by the Russian and Austrian ministers. Among her exotic presents from the Sultan were a round silver *tabouret* full of Turkish shawls, dresses of gold brocade, silver bowls of *tzenzut* and *corey* and grey amber, crystal bottles containing balsam of Mecca, attar of roses and rare unguents, besides his cipher in precious stones. A good many of the Queen's suite, more afraid of Polish inns than of political upheavals, left the Queen at Constantinople and continued the journey by way of Hungary. The Queen, who was determined to travel by sea, chartered a merchant ship for Odessa, where she arrived on November 2 after a very stormy passage, saluted by guns from the forts. Here she was exasperated to be detained by quarantine. Supposing royalty exempt from such formalities, she was vexed with the governor, the Duc de Richelieu, for enforcing them, but he had to obey orders. On December 14, when this long ordeal was over, he did his best to counteract it with variety of entertainment, including amateur performances of comedies by Goldoni and operas by Paisiello. In the meantime Gallo, whom King Murat had made a Duke, was fretting at Naples about the Queen's visit to Russia. He was afraid she might go to St Petersburg, where he considered that 'she could be far more dangerous than in Vienna.'

On December 18 the Queen left Odessa, escorted by the Duc de Richelieu, Comte de Saint-Priest, the governor of Podolia, and several Russian officials. Saint-Priest has left a graphic account of the journey. He had been ordered to attend to her comfort, which was not easy in a land where inns were scarce and barely habitable, but the Polish nobility, who lived like medieval barons, were proud of their hospitality and he asked them to co-operate. The first day after crossing the Polish border the party stopped at the castle of Tulczyn, where the widow of Count Felix Potocki lived in opulent state. In her youth the beautiful Countess Sophia had been the guest of Marie Antoinette at Versailles. 'Except for the pride of her glance,' wrote Saint-Priest, 'Maria Carolina had ceased to bear any resemblance to Marie Antoinette. She was little, bent over, and aged by misfortune rather than years. When she alighted before the grand Italian colonnade of the Potocki palace on a cold December night, the Queen of Naples was received by Countess Sophia surrounded by a species of court, by ladies splendidly dressed, gentlemen wearing her colours, a large retinue of servants in respectful attitudes, drawn up at the foot of a vast staircase adorned with a profusion of the rarest flowers blossoming in a tropical temperature in the midst of the snowy season. When her hostess conducted her through a lofty suite of rooms full of precious furniture, lighted by gilt candelabras of colossal dimensions and admirable artistry, the Queen forgot the wilderness and remembered Portici and Caserta, conjured as by the stroke of a magic wand in the endless and almost uninhabited plains she had traversed recently. "Truly I am tempted to cry out in amazement," she remarked to Countess Potocka, "but I should be afraid of being taken for a *parvenue*." From a daughter of the Cæsars dispossessed by Bonaparte the word *parvenue* had singular grace. The Queen liked Tulczyn so well that she stayed there three days instead of a single night. Her ingenious hostess studied to entertain her with every device of imagination and good breeding: there were balls, concerts, plays, all that could be improvised in haste, so that there was some confusion in that noble palace. Perhaps Countess Potocka made more than one *panna stolova* (damsel) pose as a feudal baroness of the district, and the Queen, either intentionally or without her usual perspicacity, like the great Princess she was, did not or would not perceive this. What rendered these substitutes easy was the natural charm and innate elegance of every class of Pole... Here the Duc de Richelieu took leave of the Queen and entrusted her to the care of the Comte de Saint-Priest. Although her retinue had been reduced at Constantinople, it was still considerable and therefore cumbersome, and a great many horses had to be requisitioned. After the coach in which the Queen sat with Prince Leopold, an old lady-in-waiting, and Saint-Priest, there was a long caravan of variegated carriages. The nobility of Podolia had supplied mounted escorts, who were changed from canton to canton. At intervals in the distance huge bonfires of resinous wood lit up the road through the forest and scattered the darkness of the winter nights. At every post there were relays of six-horse teams, caparisoned as for a gala day. A luxury that was soon to vanish still survived in the wealthy mansions of Poland. The Queen of Naples's journey was the swan-song of Polish magnificence. Things were so organized, whether for dinner or for spending the night, that the Queen was always received with sumptuous hospitality. At every station there were tables spread with silver and porcelain, full of all kinds of refreshment. Who could dream that elegance had taken refuge in the land of the Zaporogues and the vicinity of the Cimmerian Bosphorus while civilized Europe was swimming in blood?

'For those who were travelling with Maria Carolina the time flew swiftly. She had seen and suffered so much, and she lent herself so graciously to conversation! The Queen was most amiable and talkative; she expressed herself with simplicity and distinction, sometimes with charm, above all with force and energy, expatiating without reserve on the vicissitudes of her life, and even taking care to explain the chief events in order to justify her own part in them. She spoke much of Napoleon's hatred, which it is no wonder she reciprocated when his rage went so far as to tell the daughter of Maria Theresa that she and her family would be reduced to beggary. When she described how she had crumpled up his letter in indignation after reading it, her expressive eyes flashed, her pale face was suffused with crimson: it was indeed the glance of an outraged Queen. One of her favourite anecdotes was about her solemn audience with Alquier, a former member of the Convention who, as ambassador of the Republic, had heaped every sort of injury on the Court of Naples, when he had to present new credentials from His Majesty the Emperor of the French... Nor did she spare the British government, accusing it of perfidy and Machiavellism not even veneered with civilized forms. In spite of the respect due to her name and sex, the English agents, after keeping her under detention, had driven her from her last refuge. She complained of Lord Bentinck and General Macfarlane more than of the others. Of Macfarlane, her warder at Mazzara, she spoke as her "grandson" was to speak of Hudson Lowe.

'The Queen did not affect any diplomatic reserve... All her memories, even the remotest, those of her infancy and youth, rose from the depths of those deserts as from the tomb, and like delicate phantoms came to besiege her spirit. She remembered her mother, the august Maria Theresa, whose children respected her deeply, she said, but who were very much afraid of her. And her brother Joseph: "He had had love affairs with nearly all the beauties in Vienna!" And Marie Antoinette: "Poor Sister! The world was at your feet... Hail Mary, full of grace... Alas, what became of all that!" And the Princess of Asturias her daughter, who died so young, poisoned!... "And I myself," added Maria Carolina with a fiery glance, "have I not been poisoned with an even more potent venom, that of burning, incessant, persistent calumny... They have represented me as cruel—after I had saved hundreds of ungrateful people! They have portrayed me as ambitious. Yes, so I am, if it is ambitious to defend the crown received from God. It is said that the reaction of 1799 was my doing. I deny this accusation; I disapprove of what happened then; in fact, I was not in Naples, I was in Vienna with my daughters at the time. Apart from which, if we had fallen into their hands, how would they have treated us? Just imagine that one of the ladies of my Court, the Duchess of... (and she named her), imagine that this woman, whom I had covered with kindness, had a crystal scent-bottle made in the shape of a guillotine, and the stopper represented the King's head. Isn't it true, Marchesa?" "Certainly, Your Majesty," replied the old lady-in-waiting with a gesture to symbolize a ceremonial curtsey which the coach rendered impracticable. This question and answer invariably ended the Queen's anecdotes.

'In the midst of one of her most moving narratives, on a road as flat as a garden avenue, we suddenly heard a crash: the axle-wheel of the coach had broken. The heavy vehicle was upset: Prince Leopold, already very fat, fell on top of his mother, the Count of Saint-Priest on top of the lady-in-waiting. The good Marchesa thought she had been crushed and uttered terrifying shrieks. Only the Queen kept her composure and began to laugh. "Take heart," she said, "we are not dead yet! I have escaped worse dangers." A giant suddenly appeared at the door: he was one of the Polish escort, a man of exceptional strength and physique. With one blow of his fist he burst open one side of the coach, and extracting the Queen, he picked her up in his large hairy hands and carried her without a word to another carriage, balancing her fragile form on the palms of his hands. We had to wait awhile, with nothing but the steppes before us, the earth underfoot and the sky overhead. For better for worse all was finally adjusted, the monumental coach was raised and we departed. But the caravan had not come to the end of its trials, because one of those hurricanes of snow sprang up known locally as *metels*, of which people in other climates can have no idea: they blind men and horses and obliterate every track. Saint-Priest did not dare expose the Queen to this danger, and warned her that she would have to stop at the first available shelter until the storm blew over. But this did not suffice. How was that shelter to be found, and as near as possible, since owing to the serenity of the atmosphere such an accident had not been foreseen and no precaution had been taken? There was no sign of a house in the neighbourhood. We were in the centre of a vast domain belonging to Prince Czartorisky, who had no residence there. Scarcely fifty years ago this country had been considered wild, owing to the continual forays of Zaporogues and other savages. Finally, we chose a farm belonging to the Prince called Novaia-Siniawa: it was the least distant dwelling, which we reached almost blindly since the road had become invisible. At the sight of it we breathed again, but what a farm! It was only a hut occupied by a rural agent of the lowest class: a single room which served as hall, kitchen, and even hencoop, filled the whole interior. Its appearance was not reassuring: Saint-Priest's foreboding that it had little to offer was soon justified: except for rancid bacon and stale eggs the farm was bare of provisions... It would be difficult to cater for the Queen and so many attendants with hearty appetites for one day and perhaps even longer, as these storms were apt to last for several days.

'Above all, it was necessary to make the Queen tolerably comfortable in that abode of bliss. She was begged to remain inside her coach a little longer, which was protected from the blast by a shed, until it was possible to usher her into that kind of stable. A hunt for furniture ensued, but none could be found... Finally a rickety armchair of fir-wood was discovered: it was padded with straw, probably for the use of some old invalid. This was placed next to a rough table in the centre of the room, and all being thus prepared for polite conversation, the Queen made her entry. She showed neither surprise nor disgust, which should not cause wonder, for even those with a slight experience of Courts know that princes are easily satisfied, unlike those who surround them, especially their inferior servants. Pretensions soar as the social scale descends.

'The Queen of Naples quietly sat down: her little Court stood round her gloomily; her lady-in-waiting was totally demoralized, unable to do anything but finger the beads of her rosary; Saint-Priest was much worried; the diplomatic officer rolled his eyes, despairing of showing off his profound knowledge of etiquette on that rustic stage. Only the Queen displayed serenity and good humour: she joked about the accident and, from the summit of that throne of recent manufacture, caressed the children of the household, asking their parents a few benevolent questions through an interpreter. She reminded one of Maria Theresa, without any sense of premeditation or rehearsal.

'It became necessary in the meantime to consider means of nourishment, and there was not enough space to observe any distinction in the treatment of persons. An equal penury levelled every class. Woe to the farm hen-coop on that day! All its occupants were sacrificed without exception or mercy. There was no dearth of very black bread, and all were ensured against dying of hunger. But the day threatened to seem inordinately long. How should the time be beguiled? A most unexpected event put an end to the crisis. Suddenly the tinkle of a post-bell was heard, and a moment later two swarthy lancers appeared, charged with valises and wallets full of papers addressed to the Queen. They had come straight from Sicily by way of Hungary. This was the first and only direct news Maria Carolina had received since her departure. Conceive the eagerness with which the fortunate messengers were welcomed! This unthought-of change of scene saved everything and made everybody happy, as curiosity and interest took the place of good fare and appetite. The Queen immediately shut herself up in her cabinet, namely she had her arm-chair moved behind a partition with a warning that she would see nobody till the morrow. She seemed absorbed in feverish expectation.

'Luckily the weather improved on the morrow. The cold was acute, but the air was clear and pure. All were ready and anxious to leave... In a few minutes the Queen reappeared: her expression was grave and majestic, her stature seemed to have increased. She did not utter a word, and with a gesture ordered those present to follow her. When we climbed into the coach and started off, that solemn silence continued one or two minutes longer. The Queen broke it to thank M. de Saint-Priest for the reception given her, repeating several times that she would never forget it. "You have respected my dignity," she said, "and above all my misfortune..." "I have only been able to show my zeal," Saint-Priest replied, "when Your Majesty returns to your states you will immediately find all those things to which you are entitled." The Queen smiled bitterly and said: "Do you think so, sir? Well, now you may judge. Do you know what I found among the despatches I received yesterday?... A prohibition to enter Vienna and an order to stay at least six miles distant from the place where the Court resides." (In Austria this was the usual formula of exile.) "But I shall go nevertheless," she added proudly. "Yes, I shall go; and I shall see if they drive the last daughter of Maria Theresa from Schönbrunn." And she proceeded without paying any attention to the prohibition or even deigning to appear informed of it, and nobody dared order her to leave Vienna. Here M. de Saint-Priest saw the Queen again in 1814 and found her greatly altered. No trace of that vivacity and good humour which she had shown during her troublesome journey. She was the first to realize this. "You do not recognize me," she said, "I am discouraged and oppressed. Here they pay me infinite attentions, but I find myself a burden to all. I am even more of a burden to myself: I have lived too long." Her situation was sadder than when nothing had been settled. She had been sustained by hope. The Allies hesitated a long time between Murat and King Ferdinand. What a humiliation for her! Saint-Priest felt he should offer her some consolation, but the Queen, cut to the heart, only answered with a melancholy smile.'

Maria Carolina reached Vienna on February 2, 1814. Thanks to Metternich, her nephew and former son-in-law was now the ally of King Murat, and though she was treated with respect she was only given the title of Queen of Sicily. But her tenacity was not weakened by misfortune. In her retirement at the Castle of Hetzendorf, almost adjoining Schönbrunn, she was determined to uphold her legitimate rights against the Austrian Chancellor. Only ten days after her arrival Baroness du Montet described seeing her at the Court Theatre: 'The hall was brilliantly lighted, and the loudest acclamations announced the Empress, who saluted with infinite grace. Shortly after, in the same box, appeared the Queen of Naples, and it seemed that she was trying to hide behind the Empress so as not to distract the public from the double homage it rendered, both for the Emperor's anniversary and for the recent victory [of Blücher at Brienne]. But this delicate modesty could not restrain the enthusiastic applause with which everybody expressed sympathy for this last living daughter of Maria Theresa. The Queen of Naples bowed lightly in acknowledgement. The command performance, as usual on such occasions, was very boring, full of allusions to the triumphs of the Allies. I watched Maria Carolina with attention and curiosity... How old she had grown! How bent and curved by the blows of sorrow! All the vicissitudes of fortune had oppressed her: her head, almost white, seemed hardly to bear the weight of her crown... She seemed to be tenderly interested in the young Archduchesses, her grandchildren, and the Archduke Ferdinand, the Emperor's second son: from time to time she urged him to salute the spectators, pushing him towards the balustrade, turning him to the right and the left. But she could not induce the Crown Prince to go forward.'

XXXIII

Bentinck seeks laurels in Catalonia—Murat's indecision—Political factions in Sicily—Bentinck's return and dictatorship—An election campaign—Bentinck's dream—Murat's treaty with Austria, January 11, 1814—Bentinck signs armistice between Sicily and Naples—Murat's double-dealing—Bentinck's proclamation in Leghorn, interview with Murat, and liberation of Genoa—Napoleon's abdication—King Ferdinand's restoration—Sir William A'Court succeeds Bentinck in Sicily—Louis-Philippe's advice—Maria Carolina at Hetzendorf—Her death—Ferdinand's morganatic marriage—Castlereagh's memorandum—Murat declares war on Austria, March 15, 1815—His hasty advance and retreat—The Constitution bequeathed as a parting gift—Treaty of Casalanza—Murat's flight—Miss Davies and Murat's children—Prince Leopold enters Naples—Caroline Murat passes King Ferdinand on his homeward voyage.

Thinking he had made Sicily safe for the splendid Constitution, Bentinck turned his attention to military matters. Catalonia called him with increasing urgency, and he was eager to share the Duke of Wellington's laurels. The Constitutionalists implored him not to go, but he was deaf to their arguments. Having disposed of the Queen, all but deposed the King, and banished the Neapolitans he considered deleterious, he naïvely imagined that the new regime would run smoothly. So impatient was he for martial glory that he sailed before the Queen had reached Mazzara. First he stopped at the island of Ponza, where Colonel Coffin, the commander of the garrison, had been approached by Murat's agents on the pretext of discussing trade under the blockade. Murat had long been wavering between his loyalty to Napoleon and his dynastic ambition. When he sent Prince Cariati as his ambassador to Vienna in April 1813, it seemed that ambition might wean him from loyalty, but he was to waver more and more frantically. Napoleon said he was weaker than a woman or a monk when he was not in sight of the enemy. Bentinck had authorized Coffin to negotiate on the sly, proposing that Murat hand over Gaeta to the Anglo-Sicilians as an earnest of goodwill and join the allies against Napoleon; after the war he might keep Naples until some other kingdom was found for him. As Murat's purpose was to hold

Naples at all costs, these terms were not accepted. Bentinck repeated them on June 2 with a warning that Murat might not have such an offer again, and left a draft convention with Coffin before proceeding to Spain. Though nothing came of these negotiations, they were not without significance as portents.

Bentinck's campaign in Catalonia did little to enhance his military reputation. After a few successful skirmishes he took up positions within sight of Barcelona. On September 12 Marshal Suchet attacked him in force and routed his vanguard at the pass of Ordal. Soon after this defeat he was obliged to relinquish his command at Tarragona and return to Sicily. At the end of August he had written to Lord Castlereagh in pessimistic mood, wishing he could be relieved of his political charge to follow his military career without interruption. 'I am convinced,' he said, 'that such is the weakness of the Hereditary Prince, and such will be the incapacity of any set of men who may be placed at the head of the government; such also the silly, the interested and depraved character of the people, that it will be impossible for the British political authority ever to absent himself.'

Having released so formidable a genie from a bottle on his own responsibility, it had been irresponsible of Bentinck to fancy that he could absent himself in the first place. The Queen had compared the situation in Sicily with that in Ireland, and in one of her arguments with Bentinck she had asked him what England would do to the disaffected Irish if they had recourse to a foreign Power. 'Madam, we would have them hanged,' he had replied succinctly. The author of the *Mémoire* attributed to her comments that this was to pronounce a sentence of death on all those he had championed in Sicily, adding that the claims of the Irish had a better foundation than those of the bunglers protected by Lord William. Others have noted that the Sicilians share many characteristics with the Irish: among these a passion for politics was innate but also ingrown, and it was Bentinck who had awakened it from its long hibernation. He was disagreeably surprised to find what a hornets' nest he had stirred. As Palmieri, the chief literary panegyrist of the Constitution, had to admit, the Queen's absence made no difference to the course of affairs. She had been used by the Constitutionalists, who hated her, as a convenient target. These relied mainly on British support, and did little or nothing to conciliate their opponents. Instead of strengthening their party, they soon broke up into factions. Both Belmonte and Castelnuovo had attracted a number of self-seeking parasites who fomented discord between their leaders. Castelnuovo imagined that whoever had been against the old regime was *ipso facto* for himself, but many of these were steeped in Jacobin ideas and their prevalence in the new Parliament was one of the main causes of its weakness when it was reopened on July 8, 1813. The Prince Vicar pointed out the urgent need for settling the budget, but Emmanuele Rossi, the loudest of the newly elected demagogues, protested that to vote the taxes before publishing the complete text of the Constitution was 'an attempt against the freedom and independence of the chamber'. While the national finances were neglected, the Parliament passed preposterous bills for fixing the price of provisions. The controlled prices were so unpopular that they led to riots on the eve of Santa Rosalia's festival. British troops had to restore order, and a military court condemned two of the ringleaders to be hanged. The Parliament was prorogued, and when it was reopened on July 25 the ministry was accused by Rossi and his gang of violating the Constitution. The consequent hurly-burly showed the necessity for imposing disciplinary rules, but Rossi raised the slogan: 'The Chamber wants no chains.' Far more anti-British than the Queen, Rossi opposed a motion to send a parliamentary commission to England to thank the government for all it had done for Sicily and the Constitution, and also to offer Bentinck a sword of honour and coin a commemorative medal. As the purpose of this motion was to pledge England to maintain the present regime, Rossi was really playing into the hands of the 'reactionary' royalists. Since the plague had broken out in Malta, it was rancorously rumoured that the English wanted to propagate the contagion, and the demagogues in both houses of Parliament fulminated continually against the alleged infraction of the quarantine laws. Egypt was well beyond the infected area, but when a valuable shipload of horses arrived from there for the British cavalry, they were forbidden to land. The House of Commons even voted to send a deputation to England to denounce the British army for attempting to contaminate Sicily. 'Fortunately for the honour of Sicily's reputation,' wrote Palmieri, 'the peers who, whatever their shortcomings, preserved a sense of propriety, rejected that insane and malicious proposal. The British generals with extreme moderation proposed to send the horses back.' The precious convoy returned to Egypt.

The ministers, no longer able to obtain a majority, resigned, and the Prince Vicar appointed a few septuagenarian worthies to step into their shoes. The demagogues merged with the royalists, who spread virulent slanders against Castelnuovo, taxing him with malversation. *La Cronaca di Sicilia*, the Constitutionalist newspaper, published equally vicious attacks against its adversaries. One of these, accusing Rossi's gang of planning to subvert the Constitution 'under the cloak of the Constitution itself', caused another uproar in the House of Commons. But under all the clamour for the punishment of those concerned there was a hidden purpose: to recall the King to power. Lord Montgomery, who was acting as Bentinck's substitute, got wind of this and threatened to arrest whoever introduced such a motion. The House of Commons became so chaotic that the Prince Vicar prorogued it for twenty days, hoping that Bentinck would return in the interval to restore order. He arrived in Palermo on October 3 to find confusion worse confounded, and he promptly resumed the mantle of dictatorship. It was particularly galling that his friend Belmonte had caused the rift in the liberal party by his obstinate breach with Castelnuovo. At bottom Belmonte was an autocrat with a lust for power, intensely vain and susceptible to the grossest flattery. Bentinck had originally described him as possessing 'splendid abilities united to great boldness and conciliation', and as 'the main hope of this country'. But conciliation had not been evident in his dealings with his uncle Castelnuovo. The latter was described by Palmieri as a Plutarchian type, all of a piece, more solid than brilliant and a genuine liberal.

Bentinck told the ministry and opposition that he preferred despotism to anarchy. Great Britain had intervened to improve the conditions of the people and increase the resources of the country; but she would not let the island languish under a misguided Parliament. If necessary he would dictate the laws himself. When nothing further was done, he prorogued Parliament until October 20, and he prorogued it again till the 29th and dismissed the ministry when the motion to discuss the finances was again defeated. His efforts to form a new ministry were hampered by the bickerings of Belmonte and Castelnuovo, and he confessed to the Prince Vicar that he doubted whether these people were adapted to liberty. A new ministry was formed, however, with Belmonte and Castelnuovo as councillors of state, and the Prince Vicar was induced to dissolve Parliament with a paternal reprimand. They had justified the

Queen's remark that they were not ripe for a Constitution. Bentinck was still resolved to snatch victory from the jaws of defeat. He issued a proclamation on his own authority threatening to punish with martial law 'disturbers of the public peace, assassins and other foes of the Constitution'. But Belmonte and Castelnuovo were agreed to disagree, and the guerrilla of factions broke out afresh.

On November 1 Bentinck arranged a two years' truce between Sicily and Algiers through William A'Court, the British envoy there. All the Sicilian slaves were ransomed, and Sicilian subjects were to enjoy the privileges of the most favoured nation in commerce. He hoped that this would influence the next poll. Exhilarated by the victories of Leipzig and Vittoria, he set out on an election campaign in the east of Sicily on November 25, taking all the larger towns in his stride, haranguing local councillors about the benefits of the Constitution and their duty to choose honest and enlightened representatives, warning them not to miss this golden opportunity. Everywhere he was received with festive demonstrations: in such towns as Noto, Modica and Caltagirone he had all the charm of novelty, of an original type of showman. Sicilians revel in sermons and public speeches, and he never minced his words. While thanking the civic council of Catania for the festivities in his honour, he said he would rather they did not elect the same scoundrels as last year—alluding to Rossi, Gagliani and other anti-Constitutional demagogues. The King and the Prince Vicar looked askance at this 'proconsular journey', as they called it, and they were deeply disconcerted when Bentinck sent the Prince a letter describing a strange dream that had haunted him. This dream left no doubt that he had in mind the annexation of Sicily to the British Empire: 'Leave the care of Sicily to England, who alone, I dare affirm, could govern it both for the advantage of Sicily and for that of the kingdom of Naples. Sicily has never been of any advantage to the King of Naples. On the contrary, she has been a liability. Under British government Sicily would be peaceful, and in course of time prosperous...'

Remembering Malta, the Prince Vicar could not conceal his apprehension. Coming from an ordinary traveller, the Prince Vicar replied, he would have attached no special significance to these sentiments, but coming from the representative of Great Britain they had a very different import. Sicily was a 'sacred possession' which could never be renounced; he could not suppose that England would despoil a faithful ally of her last refuge in time of misfortune. At the same time the Prince wrote to Castelcicala in London expressing his alarm. Bentinck continued to reassure the Prince that it was only a philosophic dream of his own; his government had nothing to do with it; but the Prince, who was distrustful by nature, remained unconvinced. Having paved the way for another constitutional victory, Bentinck crossed over to the mainland with other fish to fry.

On his return to Naples after the battle of Leipzig, Murat was still wavering between Napoleon and his kingdom, to which he hoped to add a slice of Central Italy. He, too, had a dream of uniting the whole peninsula, but under his own domination. Such dreams were in the air. According to Villari, Napoleon himself intended to weld the peoples of Italy into a single nation, impressing on them unity of manners and customs. Even if this was true, Napoleon's motives were probably less altruistic than those of Bentinck, who with all his glaring faults had an unselfish passion for the unification of a free Italy. He proved this by disregarding his instructions, and it is a wonder that he was not recalled.

Dissatisfied with Murat's vacillations, Metternich sent General Neipperg to negotiate a treaty with him at once. If he joined the allies now, Austria would guarantee his throne and support his claim to an increase of territory. His wife Caroline, who had been Metternich's mistress, persuaded him to consent; and the treaty was signed by Gallo, his foreign minister, and Mier, the Austrian envoy, on January 11, 1814. In a secret clause Murat renounced all claim to Sicily, and Austria would use her good offices to induce King Ferdinand to renounce his claim to Naples. Metternich thought he could manipulate Castlereagh, but he had counted without Lord William Bentinck, to whom Austrian influence in Italy seemed almost as noxious as Murat's. 'It was lamentable,' wrote Bentinck, 'to see such advantages given to a man whose whole life had been a crime, who had been the active accomplice of Bonaparte for years, and who now deserted his benefactor through his own ambition and under the pressure of necessity.' But Castlereagh ordered him to negotiate an armistice between Sicily and Naples, and after several stormy interviews with Neipperg and Gallo he reluctantly signed one on February 3. It was no more than a truce with certain commercial advantages for England; the rights of the Bourbons were reserved for future discussion. Bentinck had avoided any recognition of Murat as King of Naples. Having made up his mind about 'this extraordinary traitor', as Bonaparte called him, he hampered his activities as much as possible. These were so contradictory that they suggest what modern psychologists call a 'split personality'. Murat protested his devotion to the allies one day and to Napoleon on the next; evidently he intended to occupy the whole of Italy before the Austrians could do so. He continued to exploit nationalist aspirations while his Neapolitan generals scattered leaflets on their northward march, calling on the people to rise for their independence. In Bologna he was greeted with cries of '*Viva il gran Gioacchino! Viva il re d'Italia!*' While he studiously avoided attacking the French or supporting the Austrians in the field, his wife, who became regent in his absence, had no such qualms. Napoleon's sister put an embargo on French shipping and expelled all French officials from Naples; she also grabbed Pontecorvo and Benevento, Talleyrand's principality. But Murat continued to correspond with the Viceroy Eugène Beauharnais until the Austrians began to murmur about his neutrality. Having received the Emperor of Austria's ratification of the Naples treaty, he decided to open hostilities; even then he did more to save the French division at Reggio Emilia from capture than to help his new allies.

A few days later—some say on March 2, others March 9—Bentinck landed at Leghorn with a large Anglo-Sicilian expedition and pronounced his famous address ending: 'Warriors of Italy! you are not invited to join us; but you are invited to vindicate your own rights and to be free. Only call and we will hasten to your relief; and then Italy by our united efforts will become what she was in her most prosperous periods, and what Spain now is.' No mention of Murat. On the contrary, he distributed a declaration that Ferdinand had never renounced the throne of Naples, and this on territory occupied by Murat's troops. On March 15 Bentinck went to see Murat at Reggio Emilia and, waiving diplomatic courtesy, insisted on the withdrawal of his troops from Tuscany; otherwise he threatened to drive them out himself, restore the legitimate Grand Duke and invade Naples on King Ferdinand's behalf. Mier, Gallo and the Austrian generals were appalled; Murat was distracted and mortified. But Bentinck did not care. He wrote to the Austrian Marshal Bellegarde: 'Is there any man in Italy, is there any man or officer in the Austrian army south of the Po, has Your Excellency, or have I myself, any confidence whatever in his sincerity? Do not all believe that his sole object is to gain time?'

Consequently Murat resumed his secret correspondence with the Viceroy Eugène, who pretended to favour a partition of Italy, since he had heard from Napoleon: 'In the present situation nothing should be spared to unite the efforts of the Neapolitans to our own. Later on we shall do as we please, for after such ingratitude, and in such circumstances, nothing is binding.' Eugène's object was also to gain time. Having bedevilled Murat, Bentinck marched his army up the coast to Genoa, which the French garrison surrendered without resistance. Here again he exceeded his instructions; posing as a liberator, he restored the Republic. The unfortunate Genoese 'accepted him as the representative of England, and relied implicitly on English sympathy and protection'.

Murat in the meantime was trying to prevent the Pope from returning to Rome. On March 31 the allies entered Paris; and on April 16 the Viceroy Eugène and Marshal Bellegarde signed a military convention under which the French withdrew from northern Italy. After the most disappointing, and certainly the most muddled campaign in his career, Murat returned to Naples on May 2. With superb aplomb he sported the airs of a victor. At least he had kept his throne, but for how long?

Bentinck sent H.M.S. *Aboukir* from Genoa to Palermo with the news of Napoleon's abdication and the return of the Bourbons to France. On April 23 Marie Amélie wrote in her diary: 'My husband suddenly came into my room shouting: "Bonaparte is finished. Louis XVIII has been restored, and I am leaving on this ship which has come to fetch me." I fell senseless in his arms.' The Duke of Orléans rushed on with the news to Colli, where his father-in-law was staying, and the King was delirious with joy. Sobbing and crying he prostrated himself to thank the Almighty. Already he began to feel that he was back in Naples. Louis Philippe, still considered the black sheep of the family in spite of his domestic virtues, left his wife and children in Palermo while he went to Paris to make sure of his reception.

Dazzled with his vision of a united and independent Italy, Bentinck returned to Palermo on June 8. '*Non era più quel di pria,*' wrote Palmieri; he was no longer the same as before. Beside that vision little Sicily had shrunk in his eyes He had hoped that as a constitutional state it might be 'not only the model but the instrument of Italian independence'. The stark reality would have discouraged a man of less sanguine temperament. He returned to a vortex of irreconcilable factions. His two *protégés*, Belmonte and Castelnuovo, were still at daggers drawn. Bentinck did everything possible to heal the breach: he invited all the ministers to his house to discuss a compromise proposed by Castelnuovo, but they went on bickering. Then Belmonte, out of the blue, proposed that the King should be invited to resume full authority. 'Since things are as they are,' he said, 'I see no reason to come to terms with this or that individual. The best policy is to deal with the head of the faction, who is the King.' The other ministers were too stunned to raise any objection. Only Bentinck could do that with impunity. He merely said that Great Britain had no further interest in preventing the King's return to power. His sympathy for the barons had cooled; the fall of Napoleon had changed the situation. And he knew that his own days on the island were numbered. Why Belmonte should have made this proposal remains a mystery, whether it was due to pique, to a conviction that Bentinck would oppose it or to spite him because they had quarrelled, or because he believed the King had been converted to his views, or that he would reject such an invitation, or even, as many said, that he would become the King's right hand. He boasted that he had saved his fatherland for the third time. Panegyrists of the Constitution say that he dug the grave of Sicilian liberty.

The King, who loved his throne dearly—perhaps it was his only true love—played an exquisitely coy comedy with Bentinck when he knew that it was safely in his grasp. The Prince Vicar and his ministers invited him to return, but as a faithful friend of Great Britain he had promised on March 23, 1813, not to do so without British consent. What did Bentinck think about it? Would he release him from his pledge? The last thing he wanted was to offend his old ally. He seemed so uncertain, so reluctant to leave his quiet country life, that the majority felt sure that he would not accept. Bentinck was almost deceived by his delicate scruples. Since Circello had told him that Ferdinand would respect the Constitution, he assured the King that 'he saw no difficulty in declaring on his own responsibility that His Majesty was entirely absolved from his former pledge'. After repeated prayers the King graciously accepted; he left off tunny fishing at Solanto and returned to the Favorita on July

4, driving through his capital amid frantic acclamations. Next day he announced his restoration 'with the powers and prerogatives which the existing Constitution attributed to the Crown'. He changed the ministry forthwith: all those dismissed by Bentinck were recalled. The Prince of Cassaro returned to his post of chief major-domo and the Prince of Cutò to that of captain of the royal halberdiers. The King was his buoyant self again, surrounded by the henchmen of absolutism paying him homage.

Seeing his Sicilian dream go up in smoke, Bentinck repented of his too hasty agreement. He cantered about the country on horseback to overcome his black depression. For three years he had been the dictator of Sicily, and he fancied he had won the affections of the people. But the wind had changed: it was blowing from Vienna, where Metternich had very different ideas. Bentinck in fact was his pet abomination. With a flash of his former fire Bentinck had an impulse to lead his troops into Palermo, proclaim martial law, and repeat the incidents of March 1813. Prince Castelnuovo dissuaded him from futile reprisals: it was too late. His last gesture was to suspend payment of the subsidy. There was little more he could do, for he had been relieved of his diplomatic post. His indiscreet letter about his dream of annexing Sicily had been complained of by Castelcicala in London and refuted by Castlereagh. The Sicilian minister had demanded his recall. Having served his purpose in time of emergency, he had become a nuisance to his government. '*Ma così fanno sempre gl'Inglesi*,' said the King, '*lascian fare al loro ministro, se riesce l'approvano, se non riesce gli rompano il collo*' ('But this is what the English always do: they leave their minister a free hand; if he succeeds they approve, if he doesn't they break his neck'). Bentinck's neck was not broken, for he still commanded the British forces in the Mediterranean. But his diplomatic successor, Sir William A'Court, had already arrived, a negotiator by vocation, cynical, courteous and ultra-conservative; and on July 11 he presented his credentials to the King, congratulating him on his return to the throne in the name of the Prince Regent of England. On July 16 Bentinck left Sicily for ever, and the Constitution for which he had battled so strenuously soon faded to a memory cherished by a few intransigents. But that memory was effectively revived by Ruggero Settimo in 1848 with the slogan: 'Separation from Naples, or our English Constitution of 1812.'

The opening of Parliament was postponed till July 18 so that the King should open it in person. He had come back like a father to the bosom of his family, he said, in a speech full of honeyed words. The Duke of Orléans, after being benevolently received by his cousin Louis XVIII and recovering much of his Parisian property, had returned to Palermo on July 14 to fetch his wife and three children. As a crony of Bentinck he was viewed with a jaundiced eye. The House of Lords had petitioned the King to dissolve the House of Commons for certain irregularities during the last elections, and the Duke advised his father-in-law to reject this petition. But the King welcomed any excuse to weaken the Constitution and the Parliament was dissolved on July 23. Once more Louis Philippe wrote to Ferdinand urging him to adhere to his British alliance: his kingdom was not strong enough to dispense with foreign aid, and since France and Spain were handicapped, Sicily could only be helped by England. It would be foolish to count on Austrian professions of friendship. Did the King expect to find an ally in Murat? His letter ended: 'Sire, I am leaving, never to return to this country. You may therefore conclude that no selfish interest impels me to offer you this advice.' Belmonte, sickened by the consequences of the King's return to power, accompanied the Duke to France, where he died at the age of forty-eight. After wrecking the Constitutionalist party by his feud with his uncle, he had given it the *coup de grâce* by proposing the King's recall.

On August 6 A' Court informed Castlereagh: 'The King and his ministers continue to make great parade of their constitutional sentiments, but not a day passes without some flagrant violation of the Constitution. In all this they are aided and abetted by Count Mocenigo, the Russian minister, an *intrigant* of the first class.' One of the first acts of the new government was to suppress a pamphlet entitled *A Constitutional Catechism*, which had been published with the approval of the ecclesiastical censors. Monsignor Gravina complained that its tone was irreligious, and the King ordered it to be burnt by the public executioner.

Napoleon's fall had come too late to bring balm to the exiled Queen. Murat still occupied the throne of Naples, and her own son-in-law and nephew, her actual host the Emperor Francis, had given his pledge to maintain him there. He was far more loyal to this engagement, she reflected bitterly, than to his previous engagements to Ferdinand and herself. But she did not despair of seeing the usurper expelled. Not everybody in Vienna agreed with Metternich, who had given Murat's envoys, Prince Cariati and the Duke of Campochiaro, so cordial a reception.

The Emperor Francis had been bored into indifference by the Queen's perpetual complaints and recriminations, so she usually remained at Hetzendorf in comparative retirement with the faithful Saint-Clair and her devoted son Leopold. To her daughter Cristina, the future Queen of Sardinia, she wrote: 'Nothing more on this earth can affect me. My fate was decided on the day I was driven from Sicily like some woman of the theatre... My life in this world is finished... I am only an object of interest for a few old ladies, who never go out except to see the last surviving child of the great Maria Theresa... The Prater is beautifully green, but nothing is beautiful for me any longer.' She was cheered, however, by Ferdinand's declaration of April 26: 'Profoundly indignant at the false news spread by our enemies that we have renounced or are disposed to renounce our rights to the kingdom of Naples, we deem it our duty to publish the falsity of this rumour to the Powers our allies, to all nations, and especially to our subjects and dearly beloved children of the kingdom of Naples, declaring aloud that we have never renounced, and are invariably resolved never to renounce, our legitimate and incontestable rights to the kingdom of Naples, and that our constant and immutable will is to accept no indemnity or compensation whatever for this kingdom.' He could not have expressed himself with more resolution even if she had been at his elbow.

On May 18 her granddaughter Marie Louise, whom she had not seen for ten years, returned to Vienna, a refugee like herself. With her usual candour she did not hesitate to condemn Marie Louise's desertion of her husband although he had been her own arch-enemy. Hatred of the English had made her more sympathetic to the French, and she was particularly amiable to the members of her granddaughter's household. One of these, Baron de Méneval, has described how Marie Louise found comfort in her grandmother's society although she was bewildered by the intensity of her emotions: 'The Queen, who had been the declared enemy of Napoleon in the time of his prosperity, and whose opinion could not be suspected of partiality, professed a high regard for his great qualities. Hearing that I had been attached to him as a secretary, she sent for me to discuss him. She said that formerly she had cause to complain of him, that he had persecuted her and wounded her pride ("for I was then fifteen years younger," she added), but now that he was in adversity she forgot everything. She could not repress her indignation at the manoeuvres to break up a marriage in which her granddaughter should glory, and deprive the Emperor of the sweetest of consolations after the vast sacrifices wrung from his pride. She added that if their reunion was opposed, Marie Louise should tie her bed-sheets to her window and escape in disguise. "That," she repeated, "is what I should do in her place; for when one is married it is for life."'But Marie Louise was miscast for the wife of a man of destiny: she would be quite content to reign placidly in Parma. After six weeks at Schönbrunn she went to take the waters at Aix-en-Savoie, leaving her son by Napoleon, the little 'King of Rome', behind her. The Queen took a morbid interest in her great-grandchild, as if she had a premonition of his melancholy fate. She called him '*mon petit monsieur*', though when he was born she had exclaimed: 'Only this calamity was held in reserve. To become the Devil's grandmother.'

Roger de Damas had left Vienna soon after her arrival to join the Comte d'Artois at Nancy; in April he had been appointed governor of Alsace and Lorraine, but he felt a complete stranger in his native land, having lived abroad so long as a knight-errant of the *ancien régime*. The Queen's last letter to him, dated August 3, 1814, was more optimistic. She looked forward to seeing him before the Congress assembled; she counted on his valuable aid, as his interests could not fail to be the same. 'It would give me such great pleasure to see you,' she wrote, 'that I am always afraid this will never happen. My health is much improved since I have been at Hetzendorf and the pure air combined with a little more quiet has done me a lot of good. Here we are expecting the Congress and the great Powers who will settle it. My life is very uniform; one day resembles another, but I shall not rest until everything has been decided, and well and firmly decided.' Ever mindful of others, she asked him to do what he could for the nephew of Saint-Clair: 'As this worthy man, whose kind heart you know, would like to help him and advance his career, he wished me to recommend him to you and I could not refuse.'

There was a possibility of the Duke and Duchess of Orléans coming to Vienna for the Congress, and the Queen was elated by the last news from Sicily. She would return to Palermo and triumph over her enemies. The frigate *Minerva* was to sail for Trieste to fetch her. On September 7 she received more visitors than usual. The

Comte de Préville had brought her encouraging letters from the King, and had spent part of the day with her discussing the affairs of Sicily and Naples. Talleyrand, having become the oracle of 'the sacred principle of legitimacy', would certainly not tolerate the usurper in Naples. Count Razumovski, the widower of her devoted friend who had been even dearer to Damas, had stayed a long time talking over the tortuous policy of the Tsar Alexander. The Queen was in better spirits but exhausted, and Prince Leopold was relieved when she decided to retire at ten o'clock. She asked her maid not to waken her before seven because she wished to sleep a little longer than usual.

Towards midnight her maid thought she had been called, and found her lying senseless when she entered her room. The Queen's hand was outstretched towards the bell-rope, but she had been struck by apoplexy for the last time. Baroness du Montet, one of the Empress of Austria's ladies-in-waiting, wrote in her *Souvenirs*: 'September 10, 1814.—This morning I went to see the Queen of Naples lying in state. The Court chapel was crowded. Maria Carolina appeared small, extremely small, as if shrunken. She was very simply dressed in a gown of black taffeta with a veil and lace cap, and she wore shoes of silver material. The bier, devoid of any decoration, was placed above a high catafalque: huge candles surrounded her, all bent with the heat. The Queen's corpse was laid on a mantle of silver tissue: at her feet there was a casket containing her entrails, and on a velvet cushion beside her were the insignia of the Order of the Starry Cross [a rare order given to noble dames eminent for their virtues], a pair of gloves and a fan—an old established custom. There was a vast crowd drawn merely by curiosity: of distinguished persons one could only see those who were obliged to be present. In two stalls two Court ladies were praying in low tones; two officers of the Hungarian Guard stood before the catafalque with bare swords raised. In the Queen's last sleep there is the trace of sadness, of infinite weariness. Maria Carolina, who thought she would die in Naples, had had her portrait set up on a tomb in the Capuchin convent in Vienna together with a tender and moving inscription, a gentle testimony of the poor lady's desire to be buried near her august parents. A sensitive but vain precaution, since the Queen's mortal remains have been buried on the spot.'

With the Congress in full swing, there was little mourning for the Queen in Vienna. All except the Court theatres remained open.

Talleyrand wrote to Louis XVIII: 'The Queen of Naples is scarcely regretted. Her death seems to have put M. de Metternich more at ease. The question of Naples is not solved. Austria wishes to place Naples and Saxony on the same level, and Russia wants to make them objects of compensation.' And Cardinal Pacca wrote to Cardinal Consalvi: 'The death of Maria Carolina may serve Ferdinand's interests and smooth his return to the Kingdom of Naples.'

The faithful Saint-Clair's letter to Ferdinand is one of the few that have an accent of genuine grief: 'Your Majesty will surely pity me in this terrible moment if I can only offer him the sentiment of my bitterest anguish.' The King's reply was too rhetorical to conceal his lack of sorrow, and it was written by his secretary Frilli. 'The dreadful blow struck at my soul by the fatal news which came as a thunder-bolt on the morning of the 22nd left me so dispirited that I could do nothing but retire to the country plunged in the most extreme affliction.' There were Masses in all the churches of Palermo for the repose of the Queen's soul; the theatres were closed for a month; and there was to be six months' official mourning. In Naples the Murats stopped a reception at Portici on hearing of the Queen's death, and De Nicola noted in his diary that Caroline Murat expressed her regret because, she said, 'It seems that we were the indirect cause of it.' If, as M. André Malraux has suggested, a man's greatness consists in his defiance of man's fate, Maria Carolina had her share of greatness. At least she strove to attain to something outside herself. Even her failure had a certain lurid magnificence.

In spite of the six months' mourning he had imposed, Ferdinand did not wait two months before marrying his mistress, Lucia Migliaccio, the widowed Princess of Partanna. The morganatic marriage was celebrated privately on November 27, 1814. Ferdinand was aged sixty-three; the bride, aged forty-four, had borne her previous husband seven children, the last of whom was the reputed father of the Comtesse de Castiglione, who embellished the Court of Napoleon III. That gossipy *raconteur* Palmieri di Miccichè was perhaps too loyal to the kindly Princess when he wrote that she had never been nor wished to be the King's mistress, and that it was this stubborn resistance which inflamed his desires and led her to the altar. According to Palmieri she was so impoverished that she had to borrow money from her hair dresser: 'When her financial distress was at its height she threw herself at the King's feet, which moved him so much that he married her.' But Palmieri could not pretend that the Duchess of Floridia, as she became after her second marriage, had been impeccable. She had the faults of her good nature which had blossomed in the Oriental bazaar of Sicily. Palmieri has reported the following conversation between the Duchess of Floridia and the Princess of Santobuono, who often discussed the adventures of their gay past in his presence.

'The Duchess: As for me, my dear, of all the men I have known I have met none to equal Roccaromana.

'The Princess: As for me, dear heart, I prefer Michelino Requisenz without any comparison. His little eyes sparkling with so much wit, his dazzling teeth, the enchanting grace in all he says and does: there is nothing of that in your Roccaromana!

'The Duchess: Listen, dear, you have known both of them, so you are in a better position to make a comparison. I only knew one of them, and can only speak of those who have been my friends...

'And the verb "to have" was invariably used instead of the verb "to know", which I employ here. The Princess of Santobuono, satisfied with having assured the palm to her Michelino, did not push her victory further; and I, being satisfied in turn with this sample, draw the curtain on all that could be said on so delicate a subject.'

It was reported that the Hereditary Prince, who did not approve of his father's second marriage, ventured to remark that the bride had sown too many wild oats to deserve this belated honour, and that Ferdinand had retorted: *'Penza a mammeta, figlio mio, penza a mammeta!'* ('Think of your mamma, my boy!')—a saying which may not be true, although it has become proverbial. There is no doubt that the King was infatuated with the little black-eyed, raven-haired matron, whom he called by the pet name Luzia. As she took no interest in politics, about which she knew nothing, and exerted a wondrously soothing influence over the King's temper, which had gone from bad to worse during Bentinck's dictatorship, she soon endeared herself to all the royal family, including Prince Leopold, his mother's favourite. She was content with the gifts the doting King lavished on her; pretty, placid and practical, she was the antithesis of her overbearing predecessor.

Owing to Maria Carolina's death the opening of the Sicilian Parliament was delayed until October 22, when the House of Commons behaved as obstreperously as the year before, postponing the discussion of finance and splitting up into factious committees.

Thus seven months were frittered away in futile recriminations. The incapacity of the deputies to discharge their ordinary duties brought public business to a standstill. Castelnuovo made a fruitless attempt to remedy the situation. He appealed to Sir William A'Court, who told him to his surprise that the King had the highest opinion of his talents: what prevented him from having a heart-to-heart talk with Ferdinand? Castelnuovo said he was ready to come when called for, but when he saw him he realized that the King hoped to win him over to his own side, and that he was an impenitent absolutist.

Considering the suicidal incompetence of the Parliament, the King can scarcely be blamed for clinging to his prejudices. A'Court soon came round to the King's views. Castlereagh had sent him a long memorandum for official publication, which stated that since the war Great Britain could not continue to exert a direct influence on the affairs of Sicily, but having supported constitutional reforms as the friend and ally of the people, she wished no alterations in the Constitution to be made without the consent of Parliament. Her recent proposal to withdraw her troops from the island was a sufficient proof, if proofs were necessary, that England had not the slightest desire to exert military pressure on the country. The attitude she had been obliged to assume during the war had given rise to many false rumours. She deplored the persistent spirit of faction. The statement wound up with counsels of moderation; the absolute security of those who had promoted Bentinck's measures in the last three years should be regarded as a *sine qua non* of British protection and alliance in future. In other words, the liquidation of Napoleon left Sicily free to find her own way of salvation, and, reading between the lines, Sicily was of no further utility to England, and it had caused her considerable expense. The memorandum was a dignified withdrawal. Only Castlereagh's profound cynicism can explain his toleration of Bentinck. Personally, as Sir Harold Nicolson wrote, 'He had little belief either in Italian unity or in the capacity of the Italians in general, and the Sicilians in particular, to establish parliamentary or constitutional government. While desiring to exclude French influence, whether Bonapartist or Bourbon, from the Italian peninsula, he was inclined to regard Italy as a purely geographical area in which Austria could find compensation for such sacrifices as might be entailed upon her elsewhere. He thus sought to adapt his Italian policy to that of Metternich.'[1]

And Metternich's policy, the restoration of the *status quo*, was incompatible with an independent Italy.

While the Sicilian Parliament was still wrangling, Napoleon escaped from Elba and marched on Paris. Murat sent messages of peace and goodwill to the British government, but as soon as he heard of Napoleon's success he offered to serve him and without awaiting his reply, or declaring war against Austria, he started hostilities on March 15, 1815; Napoleon's example had fired him to march on Milan. Already he visualized himself as King of United Italy. By strenuous recruiting he had expanded his army until it contained 85,000 men at the end of 1814, but only half this impressive number was available for active service. For purposes of propaganda he announced that 80,000 men were advancing to liberate the peninsula. 'The hour has come for the high destiny of Italy to be fulfilled. At last Providence calls upon you to become an independent nation, etc., etc.' But as his columns rushed north, the first by Rome to Florence, and the second by Ancona to Bologna, there was no opposition and no response to his political appeal. A few women waved handkerchiefs at the glittering Gascon on horseback in Bologna. 'Well, you see the ladies are all for us!' he said, smiling to his staff. But he expected all the men who had fought under Napoleon to rally to his standard, while the truth was that Napoleon had worn them out and shattered their faith. They were suffering from an indigestion of nationalistic rhetoric. They wanted rest, not revolution.

The Austrians retired before Murat's advance, as they had few troops south of Bologna. Murat praised the valour of his army and inspirited his officers with talk of future triumphs. General Filangieri distinguished himself on the Panaro by driving the Austrians from the long bridge they should have destroyed; but Murat's other generals were less enterprising and their troops were only half-trained. When the Austrians took up the offensive in earnest at Carpi, on Modenese territory, the Neapolitans retreated towards Bologna, where Murat hoped to make a stand, but the neighbourhood did not seem favourable to defence. At one moment he attempted to negotiate an armistice. Though he fought some successful rearguard actions, an epidemic of desertion broke out with the collapse of the commissariat; provisions were scarce along the line of retreat; hunger increased demoralization. At Tolentino on

[1] *The Congress of Vienna*, London, 1946.

May 3 a pitched battle was forced upon Murat, who behaved with desperate courage, rallying the dispersed and exposing himself to the hottest fire, but he lost all his artillery and 4,000 prisoners, and he had no choice but to retreat towards Naples before he was cut off, while his starving army melted away and the roads were turned into bogs by heavy rains. News had reached him that an Anglo-Sicilian expedition was crossing the straits.

In Naples they were already crying 'Death to Joachim!' and 'Long live Ferdinand!' The Neapolitans were sick of conscription, of exorbitant taxes levied with great rigour, to pay for an army they loathed and for a luxurious foreign Court. They longed for the return of their old King whose manners were like their own. When Murat lost hope of continuing the struggle he imitated the parting gesture of his predecessor and granted the Neapolitans a Constitution. He was actually at Pesaro and he issued the decree on May 12, but he ante-dated it Rimini, March 30, to harmonize with his proclamation to the Italians: 'The hour has come for the high destiny of Italy to be fulfilled...' On the same day Commodore Campbell threatened to bombard Naples unless the armed ships in the bay were surrendered. He also opened negotiations for the surrender of Murat's Queen. As Campbell's force was not large enough to occupy Naples, Caroline decided to stay in the capital to check any outbreak of disorder; excitement was spreading among the *lazzaroni* at the prospect of celebrating their King's return with pillage. She drove through the streets in her state carriage with affected nonchalance, and rode like a Parisian Amazon to review the civic guards.

Weary, haggard and coated with dust, Murat returned to Naples on May 18, escorted by four Polish lancers. He was cheered by a few liberals who had been gratified by his granting of a Constitution, but his wife gave him so frigid a reception that he is said to have exclaimed: 'Do not be surprised to see me still alive. I have done all I could to meet death.' He was to do even more. The Austrian commanders refused to treat with Gallo, whom he had sent to discuss an armistice; they did not recognize Murat as King. He then sent Generals Carascosa and Colletta to make the best conditions they could, and on May 20 they met Generals Bianchi and Neipperg with Lord Burghersh at Casalanza near Capua, and signed the convention that recognized Ferdinand as King and restored peace. Among its provisions, the new nobility were to be maintained with the old; soldiers who transferred their loyalty to Ferdinand were to be confirmed in their rank, honours and pensions; and the King pardoned his former political enemies and consigned the past to oblivion, so that every Neapolitan could aspire to civil or military office in the kingdom. On May 19 Murat rode out of Naples for the last time in civilian garb, accompanied by a few staff officers and his valet Leblanc. After several hairbreadth escapes, he reached Cannes on May 25.

On May 21 Prince Leopold, representing his father the King, joined the Austrian headquarters at Teano; three hundred English sailors landed at Naples the same night, and Caroline Murat embarked on H.M.S. *Tremendous*. According to Miss Catherine Davies, the Murat children's English governess who accompanied them to Trieste—'she was allowed to take whatever she thought proper from the palace with her. The plate, linen, china and many other valuable things she sent on board, with, it may be supposed, an unexpected passenger—a favourite cow with one horn, named Caroline, after herself; that she might have milk for the children during the voyage.' Poor Miss Davies had a harrowing time with the children in the fortress of Gaeta: 'So incessant and tremendous was the firing, that provisions could not be sent us; nor could we venture to leave our dismal place of refuge without danger of being dashed to pieces. This place was extremely damp; in some parts the water was continually trickling down the walls, rendering it both cold and unhealthy. To protect the children as much as possible from the damp, the servants had placed within the cavern the body of a carriage. I filled it with blankets, and did everything in my power to lessen their sufferings. I thought of their kindness and affection for me in their days of prosperity. My heart was overwhelmed with sorrow for the distress they were now enduring, consigned to a dreary cavern without food or bed, after the luxuries of a palace, and the love and tenderness they had ever received. Thus engrossed with cares for their present safety, and fears for their future fate, I neglected to take precautions myself against the overpowering dampness of the place; it occasioned a disease which I have since had the grief of finding incurable: the muscles of my neck became so contracted, as to render me for the future unable to support my head without the assistance of my hands.' Miss Davies and her colleague Mrs Pulsford deserve to be commemorated in the pantheon of gallant English governesses. After seventeen days under fire at Gaeta they were relieved to be picked up by H.M.S. *Tremendous*, although their mistress was now a prisoner. 'The Queen's party consisted of seventy-three persons; yet, hearing nothing but English spoken around, I felt as if I were once more in my own dear country... The Queen thanked us most tenderly for the care we had taken of the children in the sad distress which had overtaken them all, and which had made fidelity of double value...'

Prince Leopold rode into Naples between two Austrian generals on May 22, amid universal jubilation. Everybody flaunted the red cockade; white flags were hoisted; all the trees in the city were stripped of their branches to welcome the deliverers. 'The people are drunk with joy,' wrote De Nicola, 'all run through the streets with branches, shouting "Long live the King!" As soon as they see a soldier coming, a carriage with an officer, whether foreign or Neapolitan, they surround him with the same cry.' Such bantering rhymes were exchanged as: '*Se n'è fuiuto lo mariuolone, e se ne vene lo Nasone*' ("Big swindler has fled; Big Nose comes in his stead"). De Nicola mused sadly on the fickleness of the populace, on whose loyalty the credulous Joachim had relied—'as on his valiant army whose praises have been sung so often in our newspapers, when they never wished to fight'. The Austrian troops camped in the public squares to prevent the *lazzaroni* and disbanded soldiers from looting. Escorted by Hungarian Guards, Prince Leopold went to visit the shrine of San Gennaro, and the simplicity of his equipage formed a striking contrast with the theatrical magnificence to which Murat had accustomed the public eye. The Prince was amazed at the splendid new furniture of the royal palace, including a massive silver bath, which looked as if Murat had not expected to leave so suddenly. Lady Morgan and other writers have made much of Madame Murat's decision not to remove anything that pertained to her royal state, but she would not have been able to do so under the circumstances. She had emptied the Elysée Palace in Paris of all its fine furniture and works of art before coming to Naples, and this proved a minor compensation for Ferdinand's long exile.

It was humiliating for Caroline Murat to witness the festivities for the return of the Bourbons from the quarter deck of H.M.S. *Tremendous* which, like the other British ships in the bay, was dressed with bunting and fired a welcoming salute. But she showed courage in adversity. Within four months, she said, her brother would replace her on the throne of Naples. 'On our way to Trieste,' wrote Miss Davies, 'we met King Ferdinand, whom an English fleet was conveying to take possession of the throne of Naples. Captain Campbell informed the Queen they were passing, and that he was obliged to fire a salute of twenty-one guns, a piece of ceremony we could very well have dispensed with, even had the cause been different, for the noise of the cannon and the shaking of the vessel were by no means a pleasant change to the tranquillity of our voyage.'

XXXIV

Regardless of the Sicilian Constitution the King returns to Naples—His full restoration—Treaty with Austria of June 12, 1815—Bentinck forbidden to land—Murat's fatal expedition—Canosa, the Carbonari and Calderari—The Concordat of 1818—Plague at Noia and destruction of the San Carlo—Stendhal on the San Carlo's resurrection—Rossini—Betrothals of Prince Leopold and Princess Maria Carolina—The crowns of Naples and Sicily united: Ferdinand IV becomes Ferdinand I—Changes in Neapolitan society: Marchese Berio and the Archbishop of Taranto— The Villa Floridiana—The King's visit to Rome—He resolves to part with his queue.

No doubt the technique of constitutional government has to be learned by trial and error. A trial of three years was not sufficient for Sicily, but error had been abundant. For seven months the King had let the Parliament have its way without hindrance, as if to see how far it could sink in the quicksands of its own creation, with an 'I told you so' to his cronies. Even the champions of the Constitution had to acknowledge its scant success so far. Metternich apart, Napoleon's escape from Elba had influenced the new trend of British policy represented by Sir William A'Court, who favoured benevolent autocracy. As soon as the King saw a chance of going to Naples with an Anglo-Sicilian expedition, he asked the Sicilian Parliament to vote 'adequate subsidies'. On April 30, 1815, he admonished the deputies severely: 'The endowment of the state is not a gratuitous gift from yourselves, to be suspended or deferred at your pleasure. It is the first of your duties. For nearly seven months you have failed to fulfil it.' He allowed them six days to vote the sum required. As they did nothing but protest, he dissolved Parliament on May 17 and appointed a special commission for the reform of the Constitution. Marchese Tommasi, Medici's right-hand man, compiled thirty articles for their guidance. The King showed these to Castelnuovo, who protested that they would not modify but annul the Constitution. While this laid down that a prince of the royal family was to remain in Sicily with extensive powers, the new plan envisaged a secretariat for Sicilian affairs at Naples. But the new plan had been sent to London by A' Court and approved by the British government. Castelnuovo retired in disgust from public life, though the King would have appointed him Viceroy had he been accommodating. He preferred, perhaps wisely, to devote his time and wealth to the improvement of agriculture.

In his eagerness to return to Naples the King proceeded to act as if no Constitution existed. The military expedition ceased to be necessary since Murat's defeat at Tolentino. The King appointed the Hereditary Prince Francis Lieutenant-General of Sicily—not Vicar lest it recall Bentinck's dictatorship—and sailed for Messina, where he heard that the treaty of Casalanza had been signed.

'The catastrophe is over,' wrote Medici to the new Lieutenant-General on May 2, 1815, 'Murat has fled like an assassin. Reggio and all Calabria have capitulated, and the capitulations are full of justice and equity. All that is left for me to die content is the amalgamation of the two nations [Sicily and Naples]. Your Royal Highness understands what I mean. His Majesty gave a perfect reception to Murat's officials who came to Messina, and they departed so pleased that they do nothing but shout: "Long live the King!" God bless such good work and preserve for centuries the august House of Bourbon; and all without distinction, Sicilians and Neapolitans, Constitutionalists, Royalists and Muratists, etc., should cry "The House of Bourbon or Death!" My hand trembles with the violence of my emotions...'

On May 17 the King left Sicily in joyful defiance of the Constitution, by which he should have asked for the Parliament's consent. On the first of the month he had announced from Palermo: 'It is now time for me to return to my throne of Naples. Your unanimous sentiment recalls me. The general vote of the other Powers has vindicated my rights; the firm and vigorous support of my allies encourages and sustains me... I return to restore your ancient serenity and to cancel the memory of all past evils... Neapolitans, return to my arms! I was born among you. I know and appreciate your habits, your character and your customs. I only desire to give luminous proofs of my fatherly love, and render the restoration of my government an enterprising period of prosperity and happiness in our common fatherland. One day should extinguish the lamentable series of calamities of many years. The sacred and inviolable pledges of moderation, gentleness, mutual confidence and perfect union should guarantee our tranquillity,' etc. Other proclamations in the same strain preceded the King's arrival. Prince Leopold was so conciliating that the ultra Bourbonists were offended; he received Murat's chief henchmen as amiably as the loyalists they had persecuted during the last decade. The Abbé Taddei, who had been castigating the Court of Palermo for years in the *Monitor*, was allowed to scribble on unperturbed; only the name of his paper was changed to the *Journal of the Two Sicilies*. Many anecdotes were circulated about Prince Leopold's open-eyed wonder and admiration when he saw the decorative improvements made by Caroline Murat at Portici and other royal palaces. He was said to have exclaimed to the King 'Oh, my dear father, if you had only stayed away another ten years!' While on board H.M.S. *The Queen*, the King appointed Circello Minister of Foreign Affairs, Medici Minister of Finance as well as temporary Minister of Police, Tommasi Minister of Justice and Ecclesiastical Affairs as well as temporary Minister of the Interior, while the army and navy were entrusted to Saint-Clair under the nominal aegis of Prince Leopold, possibly as a reward for his admirable discretion as the Queen's favourite. Thus all the old guard were mustered in advance. Medici, who had a stronger personality and a greater reputation for efficiency than his colleagues, became virtual Prime Minister. His ambition satisfied, he grew mellow and complacent. Moderation was his watchword.

The King landed at Portici on June 7. The guns thundering from all the forts seemed the magnified thumpings of his heart, rejuvenated by the sight of his birthplace and capital. He could hardly stop talking for excitement, alternately sobbing and bursting into peals of laughter. De Nicola relates how affably he chatted and joked with the fathers of the Chinese Mission when they went on board *The Queen* to kiss his hand. He told them that it was a miracle of Providence that had brought him back to them, and that he had met Madame Murat on the voyage, after which heaven and earth had broken loose—'and for thirty-one hours we were danced about on this little creature', referring to the ship. He recommended himself fervently to their prayers, saying that he had greater need of them than ever. He was equally expansive with the Gerolomini fathers. But when the Prince of Sirignano, who had served Murat, was announced, his face became solemn. The Prince kissed his hand; he bowed twice very formally in return, and continued to chat with the priests about his vow to build a new church on recovering Naples, dedicated to Saint Francis of Paola, who had spread his cloak on the sea and floated on it from Sicily to Calabria.

This was to be built on the square facing the royal palace, which Murat had widened by demolishing another church. De Nicola, who took his wife to see the King at Portici, describes his tears 'at the memory of the nine years when we longed for him. He repeatedly said to my wife: "Get up, my daughter, get up!" '

Most historians have repeated Colletta's assertion that the King's state entry into the capital appeared drab in comparison with the pageantry of Murat, but at least the uniforms of the British, Sicilian and Austrian troops must have provided the scene with fresh glitter and variety. The King, a dignified eighteenth-century figure, rode between plump Prince Leopold and dashing General Neipperg, the cynosure of the noisiest of crowds waving green branches, banners and handkerchiefs of every hue. 'The King's tears of tenderness and joy rendered the scene more moving,' wrote the diarist. Ferdinand could never play an Olympian role. He was as emotional as these kindly people who idolized him, and as free from affectation. His genuine simplicity stirred their warm hearts; Murat's flamboyance had merely appealed to their eyes. They never dreamt of judging him according to his prowess: they saw him as a genial old paterfamilias whose all-too-human weaknesses were comprehensible and endearing; they accepted him as their true King by divine right. And they were comforted by the survival of a cherished institution. It is more than half a century since the Goncourt brothers wrote: 'Mediocre minds, who judge yesterday by today, are amazed by the grandeur and magic of the word King before 1787. They suppose this love of the King was mere servility. The King was simply the popular religion of that time, as one's own country is the religion of today. When speedier communications will have mingled ideas, frontiers and flags, a day will come when this nineteenth-century religion will seem almost as shallow and limited as the other—to the newspapers all printed in one language.' In Naples the grandeur and magic of the word *Re* still subsisted, in spite of a disgruntled minority of so-called liberals. The public ovations reached a climax when the King returned to his box at the San Carlo theatre on June 19. 'By universal assent such brilliant illuminations had never been witnessed, nor such a spectacle, nor a keener, more perfect and more seemly joy. The King was moved to tears; and when his bust appeared on the stage amid the banners of all the allied Powers, the theatre resounded with applause and continued cheering for half an hour. The King was seen to wipe his eyes, and acknowledge the transports of the public with fervent thanks. The ladies in their boxes cried *Evviva!*' His secret wife, as the Duchess of Floridia was called, did not arrive from Sicily till June 24. Before the end of the month many of the Austrian troops had left for Piedmont. On July 6 *Te Deums* were sung in thanksgiving for the victory of Waterloo; more followed for the entrance of the allies to Paris.

At first the King could not help disliking the survival of so many Napoleonic institutions. Medici's aim was to produce a Neapolitan edition of these and give them a legitimist complexion, but all his tact and patience were required to soothe the King's prejudices. De Nicola noted: 'The King wants the old, but he meets with obstruction.' For instance, Tommasi had shown him a report from the Justice of the Peace at Caserta asking how to deal with a priest who had seduced a young woman, and whose parents demanded his arrest. The Justice maintained that according to the Code no action could be taken because the woman was a major and the Code disregarded the man's clerical profession. The King grew purple with rage. 'What Code, what Code?' he shouted. 'Let the priest be punished with the rigour of our laws!' And when Medici, as Minister of Police, submitted a list of notorious malcontents with a request for the King's decision, he read the list and put it in his pocket. Next day he returned it to Medici, who found Ferdinand's name added to the others. Asked for an explanation, the King replied: 'I have put down my name because I am the first to be dissatisfied with what I am doing.' A satirical sonnet was circulated called 'Joachim Murat's Testament', bequeathing all his achievements to Ferdinand IV and declaring him the executor of his will.

Although Ferdinand could not be said to have moved with the times, he had the sense to realize that these had changed; he wished to restore order with a minimum of confusion. Medici was no statesman, but he seemed adequate. Having long shed his early enthusiasms, which had never been more than the ebullitions of a speculative opportunist, he had come to share the outlook of Metternich, Castlereagh and Nesselrode. His problem was how to govern a state after an interregnum of ten years, when the old regime had been supplanted by new institutions. Medici decided to leave things as much as possible as they had been under Murat without saying so. He thought anybody could be tackled by appealing to his private interest. To him, as Blanch wrote, 'it was an inexplicable phenomenon that soldiers who were paid on the first of the month should mutiny on the second', or that any official should consider upsetting a government which had benefited him. Of the Neapolitans he said: 'Let them steal, and then you can do what you like with them.' The Austrian ambassador described him to Metternich as a man 'who only lives within his own ideas, in his plans for the future, and who seems to shut his eyes to the dangers of the moment'. On June 12, 1815, Cavaliere Ruffo, the King's minister in Vienna, signed a treaty of alliance with Metternich, by which Ferdinand was committed to provide Austria with 25,000 soldiers for the defence of Italy, and to accept an Austrian Commander-in-Chief. In a secret clause he was also bound 'to admit no change in the government of his kingdom that could not harmonize with ancient monarchical institutions or with the principles adopted by His Imperial and Apostolic Majesty for the internal administration of his Italian provinces'. This led inevitably to the amalgamation of Naples and Sicily, which seemed to Medici the ideal solution.

Medici soon discovered that he could manage the King through his wife. The Duchess of Floridia was ignorant of politics but she was susceptible to flattery and fond of dispensing favours. She found Medici infinitely obliging. He would tell her in advance about the topic of the next Council meeting, suggesting whatever he wished the King to decide. In due course the topic would be raised in Council. After enumerating the obstacles which would have to be surmounted he would leave it in suspense, asking the King to ponder it at leisure. When the King visited his wife he would discuss everything that was on his mind, especially any knotty problem which remained to be settled. The Duchess then offered him Medici's solution as her own. The King would mention the subject at the next Council; Medici would recapitulate the difficulties connected with it, and the King would pronounce his opinion like a juggler producing a rabbit. The ministers appeared to be overcome by his sagacity, and a decree was accordingly issued. Medici had learned this ruse from Acton, but the Sicilian duchess was far more pliable than Maria Carolina.

Gradually the King grumbled less. He was more accessible to his subjects than before: in the morning he gave long audiences to those who wished to see him; in the evening he presided over the Council of Ministers. For all that he continued his shooting, *à propos* of which Lady Morgan has recorded: 'The King never goes forth for the chase without arming himself with a heron's foot; which he places in his buttonhole, as the most effective charm against the *Monacello* [the Neapolitan hobgoblin], or against the ill-luck of meeting an old woman or a priest, as he crosses the threshold—both ill-omens for the day! When Lord—— came to an audience to take leave of His Majesty on his return to England, the King told him he had a little *bouquet d'adieu* for him; and when his lordship probably dreamed of a gold snuff-box with the royal face set round with brilliants on the lid, he was presented with the heron's foot, as a spell against all accidents in an English fox-chase, and a remembrance of royal friendship and Neapolitan field sports.' As long as he could the King was determined to enjoy his old age with youthful gusto. According to the same voluble bluestocking, 'many anecdotes were recited to us of His Majesty's joy, at having escaped from the conjugal despotism of *La Mamma* [the late Queen] and in contrasting "*La Moglie del Re*" [the Duchess of Floridia] and his Minister Medici, with Caroline of Austria and her Minister Acton. He frequently exclaims, in his *lazzarone* dialect, "How happy I am! with a wife who lets me do what I will, and a minister who leaves me nothing to do."' The King radiated benignity at the Piedigrotta festival, always the occasion for a splendid military review, combined with piety and popular revels.

Past humiliations had almost been forgotten when Bentinck sent word that he intended to visit Naples. Circello immediately warned A' Court that the King would not allow Bentinck to set foot inside his kingdom. There were plenty of official reasons, such as Lord William's support of the Carbonari, who might make a dangerous use of his name. The Austrian ambassador also wished to prevent his coming, since Metternich had been provoked by his declaration at Genoa, which the Congress had allotted to Piedmont. Characteristically Bentinck swept these objections aside and sailed into the bay on October 4; tact had never been his forte. It was with peculiar relish that the King forbade him to land. He found himself boycotted in consequence. A' Court would do nothing to help him. This time he could not threaten to use force. He could only sail impotently but not mutely—high places in London were to ring with his complaints—out of sight and mind, having swallowed a bitter dose of his own medicine. According to De Nicola, Lady Bentinck had contrived to attend a performance at the San Carlo, and had been escorted from the theatre to the ship like an undesirable by two burly police officers.

This minor satisfaction was followed by a major one. On October 11 the news reached Naples that Murat had landed in Calabria. He, too, had been warned against coming. The Neapolitan police had been informed of his movements: they were only uncertain of his precise destination. Two secret agents, the Corsican Carabelli who had entered Ferdinand's service and the Neapolitan Macirone who had become a British subject, had done everything in their power to dissuade him before he left Corsica. Macirone brought him a passport with a letter from Metternich offering him a residence in Bohemia, Moravia or Upper Austria, and the British frigate *Meander* was waiting at Bastia to convey him to Trieste. Murat declined the ship, but took the passport without any intention of going to Trieste. He had not been able to keep Naples with a big army at his beck and call, yet he expected the whole country to rise against Ferdinand in his favour. He had mustered some two hundred and fifty adherents and equipped seven feluccas. 'I will not give up my kingdom!' he told Carabelli. 'I have only to show myself to succeed!'

He embarked on the night of September 28. The small squadron was scattered by a storm in the vicinity of Naples and Murat's own felucca with another were driven far down the coast. On October 7, when Santa Eufemia was sighted, some of Murat's companions urged him to proceed to Trieste, but Barbara, the captain of his ship, said he would have to land in any case for water and provisions. So he headed for Pizzo, the nearest little port. No doubt Murat was inspired by Napoleon's escape from Elba. 'At the worst I shall die a King,' he had remarked. As a King he would show himself. He donned a magnificent uniform and his feathered hat with diamond clasp and was rowed to the shore at eleven o'clock in the morning. From the beach he marched straight to the market-place with his small band, who raised a cheer for King Joachim. It was Sunday; the square was crowded with a festive throng; but instead of echoing the cheer they scampered away as at the sight of a ghost. These people had no happy memories of Murat's reign; their coasting trade had been ruined by the French occupation; many families were related to the victims of General Manhès; and the magnate of the district was a Spanish grandee, the Duke of Infantado, whose estates had been confiscated under his regime and to whom he was anathema since the *Dos de Mayo* of 1808. A few soldiers were on parade before the coastguard station. Murat coolly ordered them to follow him, and told the sergeant in command that he promoted him captain. But these also ran away from the gorgeous intruder. Having emptied the market-place, Murat decided to go on to Monteleone, the next large town which had always been pro-French. But when he stopped to buy a horse a hostile mob had gathered, and the local police officer, Trentacapilli, summoned him to surrender. Murat tried to bluff—he was on his way to Trieste and his passport was in order—but the mob rushed upon him. There was a scuffle; a pistol shot scattered the crowd, and Murat with a few followers raced to the seashore, but his feluccas had vanished. They were trying to drag a fisherman's boat into the water when their pursuers caught up with them. One of Murat's companions fired and was shot dead. A hideous scramble ensued in which Murat narrowly missed being torn to pieces. Many of his assailants were sharp-clawed women, one of whom struck him in the face, screaming: 'You prate about liberty yet you had four of my sons shot!' Another harridan proudly preserved in a newspaper a handful of hair she had torn from his moustache. Trentacapilli secured his papers and diamond clasp. Famished, exhausted, bleeding and in tatters, the invaders were dragged off to the castle and crammed into a miserable cell. The rest had been rounded up, a total of seventy-nine. General Nunziante, the commandant in lower Calabria, sent the news to Naples by semaphore and a detachment of troops to Pizzo under a humane officer, while the Duke of Infantado's steward supplied Murat with clothes, food, wine and a doctor to dress his wounds. As Murat still had numerous partisans, especially in the army, the King had been nervous about his expedition. It was during an opera at the San Carlo that he was informed of his arrest. A Council was held forthwith, and Medici proposed that Nunziante should assemble a court martial and judge Murat as a public enemy. It is not improbable that A' Court had advised this, while the Austrian ambassador Jablonowsky discreetly retired to the country. Murat was duly court martialled on October 13 by officers whom he had promoted; was found guilty of inciting to civil war and appearing in arms against the legitimate King, and sentenced to be shot. He wrote a touching last letter to his wife, and the vicar of Pizzo, a sincere and saintly man, persuaded him to confess and gave him absolution. 'Aim at the heart, but spare my face,' he said calmly to the firing squad, refusing to be bandaged. The misguided hero fell without a groan. It was an unworthy end to so spectacular a career. But it is difficult to conceive the immediate alternative. Could this inveterate swashbuckler have settled down to quiet domestic life as a pensioner of Austria?

Ferdinand's enemies have taxed him with gloating over his prey; they even invented a myth that he kept Murat's skull as a souvenir. If the King had ever been cruel, it was due to fear and a narrow sense of duty. 'May God be pleased to pardon him,' was his actual comment. He was naturally relieved to be rid of a potential menace. He bestowed upon Pizzo the title of 'most faithful', and awarded a gold medal to the mayor and deputies present and future, to be worn on the chest while in office. The citizens were to be exempted perpetually from the municipal toll on provisions, and each was to be granted an annual supply of free salt. The church was to be rebuilt at the expense of the royal treasury, and a monument was to be raised near the shore to commemorate these privileges and their origin. As the gazette phrased it: 'Heaven has reserved for the inhabitants of Pizzo the glory of saving our fatherland and Italy from fresh revolutionary calamities.'

Medici, who had been harassed by this responsibility, exclaimed: 'At last I can resign from the police!' His successor in that department was the leader of all the reactionaries, the eccentric Prince of Canosa. Medici contested his appointment, but many admired him for his honesty and dogged independence, and the King felt he deserved a place in the government.

So far Circello had been the only minister to disagree with Medici. Circello's ideal, said Blanch, was the monarchy of Louis XIV, but Canosa's was more retrograde: it went back to the Middle Ages. Whereas the average cultured Neapolitan was brought up on the classics and French Encyclopædists, Canosa had been bred on the classics and the Fathers of the Church. He regarded the French Revolution as the fatal result of renouncing mediæval institutions and beliefs, which could still, if revived, produce a generation of Galahads. Since his ill-timed evacuation of Ponza he had been under a cloud, until the King thought of sending him on a confidential mission to his son-in-law, Ferdinand VII of Spain. The choice had been felicitous. Canosa considered Ferdinand VII as the perfect type of restored monarch in contrast with Louis XVIII of France, since he had reinstated the Jesuits and the Inquisition and abolished the Constitution of 1812. The King of Spain appreciated

Canosa's hero worship. It was mainly due to Canosa's efforts that Don Pedro Gomez Labrador, the Spanish representative at the Congress of Vienna, had instructions to insist on Ferdinand IV's restoration to Naples. And Labrador was the most insistent of men. After Tolentino, Canosa returned to Naples with the Grand Cross of the Immaculate Conception, which the King of Spain had bestowed on him for his attachment to the Bourbons. Yet Medici slammed the door to office in his face. While he was kept waiting in the cold, Canosa circulated a sonnet he had written in self praise, exhorting him to flee from treacherous Courts and the envy of his rivals, and to leave his illustrious bones in a soil where the seeds of honour were not dead. Medici was much irritated by this stroke of publicity, but he refused to open the door.

Canosa was about to retire to the country in earnest when he was suddenly ordered to leave for Calabria and make sure that Murat was executed. The semaphore system then known as the telegraph had not been able to function owing to foggy weather, and it was feared that any delay might enable Murat's partisans to rescue him. Canosa set off at once, but along the journey he met the royal courier returning to Naples with the confirmation of Murat's death. He saw this as heavenly retribution for the execution of the Duke of Enghien. His readiness to accept this mission had been another proof of his Bourbonist zeal. Although Medici could keep him out of office no longer, he had to wait another three months before he took over his portfolio on January 24, 1816.

From this moment the Council was divided. Unlike Medici, Canosa regarded the Carbonari as potential instruments of revolution. The origin of this secret sect has been disputed; its character had changed from year to year, but at this time its chief objects were to impose a Constitution and obtain the independence of Italy, or rather these were the objects of its educated leaders, for the majority of its members were frustrated rebels with a passion for conspiracy, always 'agin' the government': Bourbonists under Murat, Muratists under King Ferdinand. Pope Pius VII had denounced them in 1814 as allied to Freemasonry, whose ritual and symbolism they borrowed. Canosa wished to suppress them, but Medici and Tommasi would not hear of anything so drastic. In order to fight them with their own weapons, *faute de mieux*, he supported a rival sect called the Calderari or Braziers, whose aims were to defend religion and the legitimate dynasty against usurpers, and old institutions against the new, especially against those inherited from the French regime. Canosa was reputed to have organized the Calderari, but he denied this in his curious apologia, *I Piffari di Montagna* ('The Mountain Pipes'), and there is no reason to disbelieve him. According to him they had been organized in Palermo in association with Cardinal Ruffo's Sanfedisti; Bentinck had sent many of them under a neutral flag to Naples, where they had joined other secret societies and conspired against the French; at one time they joined the Carbonari. It was a Calderaro who had blown up Saliceti's house.

Canosa was quite frank about his policy. When Medici urged him to crush the Calderari, 'the atrocious remnant of 1799', he replied that the real objects of all these secret societies were the same, to enrich themselves at the expense of their neighbours, and to encroach upon the government in order to usurp its power. Happily all these sects were at variance. Since the Calderari were less powerful than the Carbonari, it was politic to patronize the former, in order to counter balance the latter, and to make use of them as agents for the police against their rivals, since the Calderari took an oath to defend legitimate monarchy, while the Carbonari took an oath to destroy it. 'In reasoning thus,' he wrote, 'the Prince of Canosa frequently used the expression *counterpoise*; and notwithstanding the rule that nothing said in Council is to be revealed, his speech transpired, and gave rise to the reports concerning the organization, or the reform, of the *Calderari del Contrapeso*.'

Medici accused Canosa of fomenting a civil war, and Canosa retorted that Medici had always been a Jacobin at heart. They disagreed on every subject, and their quarrels rose to a climax when Canosa reformed the police department. The treaty of Casalanza was all very well, he said, but how could he trust men who had been appointed by Saliceti, who had thwarted his plans at Ponza and hounded his agents? Medici reminded him of the King's amnesty: so long as these officials did their duty they should be tolerated. To investigate their private opinions, as Canosa had done, would lead to a general upheaval. He complained again of the activities of the Calderari, and called him 'Santa Fede Canosa', a term which had become synonymous with assassin. Canosa retorted that he would challenge him to a duel if he were not so senile, and the King adjourned the Council.

Canosa offered to resign on May 30, and the King hesitated a month before accepting his resignation. His successor soon discovered that he had distributed 16,000 licences to carry arms among the Calderari. All these were now withdrawn; several sectarians were arrested, and Canosa's employees were dismissed. (In his apologia he naively confessed that some of his subordinates had been stupid and corrupt, and excused himself on account of his long absence from Naples.) For a time there was even talk of a trial, but the King, who had supported Medici against his own instincts, pronounced: 'Since we have pardoned the disloyalty of so many, it is only just that we should pardon Canosa, who has rendered us so many distinguished services.' He was given a passport to travel, but he did not go farther than Pisa, where he settled down to write three enormous tomes on 'Why the priesthood of our times and the modern nobility have not shown themselves as generous and zealous as the ancient in the cause of monarchy and of Kings', and made himself ill with overwork. He had always been more of a bookworm than a psychologist. Like most fallen ministers he prophesied woe: he would not admit that he had been defeated; he had only lost the first round. His enemies had exaggerated the danger of the Calderari; the real danger, as he saw, came from the more powerful Carbonari, who were vastly encouraged by his retirement from the scene.

Although secret societies were made illegal Medici winked at them, as he had winked at the republican conspirators in his youth. The storm raised by Canosa was followed by apparent calm. The King seldom interfered with Medici's policy, but in one subject he took an interest as obstinate as it was embarrassing to his ministers, the relations of Church and State. Religion and morality had been undermined during the French occupation. Prompted by his confessor, Monsignor Caccamo, the King wished to remedy this. Though far from spiritual, he was an assiduous, even a bigoted, observer of religious rites. Every day he heard Mass in his private chapel and said his prayers at regular hours; if he met the Viaticum in the street he left his carriage, and knelt before the Blessed Sacrament after accompanying it for a certain distance. Recent events and advancing age had strengthened his religious sentiment. He had already started to build the new basilica of San Francesco di Paola in fulfilment of his vow, a building which owes much to the Pantheon but more to its position in the centre of a handsome colonnade, and to its grey and tomato tints. He now wished to end his jurisdictional differences with the Holy See, and restore as many convents as possible. In this case the reluctant Medici had to yield, and his negotiations with Cardinal Consalvi culminated in the Concordat of 1818, which delighted the King and the masses but annoyed the classes. Gladstone's dictum that the classes are usually wrong and the masses usually right was probably justified on this occasion. The agnostic minority resented that the Catholic Faith should be the sole recognized religion; they resented religious education and ecclesiastical censorship; the lawyers who depended on disputes and the landowners enriched by the sale of Church property had other reasons to dread the Concordat. Confiscated and unalienated property was to be restored to the Church, and suppressed Orders were to be reinstated as far as possible; otherwise there was no great gain for the Roman Curia, except an effective influence over the Neapolitan clergy. Colletta and the Carbonari deplored it as retrograde, but even non-Catholic countries, as Ranke pointed out in his *History of the Popes*, had begun to realize that positive religion, of whatever confession or form, was the best support and guarantee of civil obedience. By the aid of the Pope's spiritual influence Ferdinand hoped the more easily to subdue his domestic enemies. Unfortunately the Concordat deepened the gulf between the monarchy and the ruling classes, who regarded Medici as a time-serving hypocrite.

Towards the end of 1815 an alarming plague broke out at Noia in the province of Bari, but owing to strict precautions it was prevented from spreading. De Nicola relates that a few soldiers of the sanitary cordon arranged for a pack of playing-cards to be smuggled into their barracks from the town. As soon as the Intendant heard of this he ordered them to be confined in the infected area—'a just and indulgent measure because they were guilty of death'. In the meantime the inhabitants of Noia ate, drank and tried fatalistically to be merry: after dancing all night at a party two young men collapsed and died of the plague within twenty-four hours. A calamity that seemed to put all others in the shade was the total destruction of the San Carlo Theatre by fire, which broke out after a ballet had been rehearsed on February 12, 1816. It was caused by sparks from a lamp which had been left burning near the stage, but the people persisted in blaming those they called Jacobins, and the troops were ordered to take up arms. When the King inspected the ruins he said he wished to see the same ballet performed on his next birthday, January 12. Thanks to the enterprising impresario Domenico Barbaja and the architect Niccolini, the whole theatre was rebuilt in less than a year.

Stendhal, who came to Naples in 1817, described the resurrection of the San Carlo as a *coup d'état* which rallied the people to the King far more than any Constitution could have done. All Naples was drunk with joy. And in spite of his cult of the *Code Napoléon* and his passion for dryness, his pen was steeped in something more alcoholic than ink when he wrote about it. His impressions are still warm from his struggle to get into the theatre. 'Here at last is the great day of the opening of the San Carlo: frenzies, torrents of people, a dazzling hall,' he exclaimed, having lost both his coat-tails in the madding crowd. 'At first I thought myself transported to the palace of some Oriental emperor. My eyes are dazzled—[Stendhal did not mind repeating the same word]—my soul is ravished. Nothing is more fresh, yet nothing is more majestic, two qualities which are not easy to mingle. This first evening is entirely devoted to pleasure: I have not the strength to criticize.'

To the San Carlo, Stendhal returned again and again, equally fascinated by the auditorium, the music and the ballets. The auditorium was silver and gold, the boxes were lined with dark blue, their balconies adorned with groups of golden torches intertwined with the Bourbon lilies and separated by silver bas-reliefs. In a *Code Napoléon* moment he counted thirty-six of them... 'Nothing could be more magnificent than the royal box, above the middle entrance: it rests on two golden palm-trees of natural size; the drapery is of pale red metal leaves; the crown, an antiquated ornament, is not too ridiculous.' The ceiling, however, which was painted in the French style on canvas, one of the largest in existence, was altogether too frigid for his taste. Its painter was the then-admired Giuseppe Cammarano (1766-1850), a ponderous exponent of neo-classicism who decorated many palace interiors; and its subject was 'Apollo presenting to Minerva the world's most famous poets, from Homer to Alfieri'. Stendhal proceeded to describe the alarming effect of a dense mist which gradually rose to the boxes, and the 'superb terror' of a beautiful duchess beside him who exclaimed: '*Santissima Madonna!* The hall is on fire! The same people whose attempt failed the first time have started it again.' But after a few sniffs he was able to reassure her: it was due to the heat of the audience in the theatre which was not yet dry. Later on his allegiance to Milan made him compare the San Carlo unfavourably with La Scala, but he divined instinctively the importance of this theatre as the pride and social centre of Naples, apart from which he was drawn to it by the genius of Rossini.

Stendhal was apt to juggle with dates, but even if he did not meet Rossini on February 7, 1817, at Terracina on his way to Naples, his description of this meeting is a curtain-raiser, as it were: 'I distinguished, among seven or eight persons, a very handsome man, fair and rather bald, about twenty-five or twenty-six years old. I asked him for news of Naples and of music in particular; he answered me with ideas that were clear, brilliant and amusing. I asked him if I could still hope to see at Naples Rossini's *Otello*; he answered with a smile. I told him that in my opinion Rossini was the hope of the Italian school; he was the only man of born genius; and he builds his success, not on the richness of the accompaniments, but on the beauty of the songs. I perceived in my man a shade of embarrassment; his travelling companions smiled; it turned out to be Rossini himself... We stayed drinking tea until past midnight; it was the most agreeable of my Italian *soirées*; it was the gaiety of a happy man. At last I took leave of this great composer, with a feeling of melancholy. Canova and himself; that is all that the land of genius possesses today, thanks to its governors...' A few days later he heard *Otello* and was disappointed. The subject did not suit the temperament of Rossini, who was 'too happy, too gay, too greedy'. Besides, he was shocked by the libretto, for which the opulent and cultured Marchese Berio was responsible. Othello had been converted into a Bluebeard, and the famous handkerchief into a love-letter. 'The author of the libretto must have been expert indeed to make the most passionate tragedy of all theatres as insipid as this,' wrote Stendhal. But the Italian critics were bowled over completely. Rossini was all the rage, and Isabella Colbran, whom he eventually married, was the prima donna who held sway at the San Carlo, ruled Barbaja and enjoyed the special favour of the Court. When the Hereditary Prince's eldest daughter Maria Carolina became engaged to the Duc de Berry on April 24, 1816, Rossini composed an official cantata, 'The Nuptials of Thetis and Peleus', in honour of the betrothal. The performance was praised, but the music has not survived. The bass, who had to impersonate the river Sebeto, was reluctant to wear a white wig and beard, since he preferred juvenile roles. 'Never fear,' said Rossini, 'you will be representing the river when it is only between thirty and thirty-five years old!' At the same time Prince Leopold became engaged to his niece, the Archduchess Maria Clementina of Austria.

On December 8 the King, who was Ferdinand III of Sicily and IV of Naples, issued a decree by which he assumed the title of Ferdinand I of the Two Sicilies, to promulgate the union of the two crowns as recognized by the Congress of Vienna. Sicily was thus deprived of the separate institutions of which she was so proud, and her Constitution of 1812 was finally abolished. This meant, as De Nicola wrote, that Sicily would become a province of Naples, and his comment reflects the opinion of the Neapolitan absolutists: 'The Sicilians have deserved this for their treatment of His Majesty, since they practically interned him for the sake of their privileges under the wing of Lord Bentinck, who kept the King a prisoner and made Maria Carolina leave the island, though seriously infirm.' To emphasize the change the King distributed new titles among his offspring. The Hereditary Prince Francis became Duke of Calabria; his first son Duke of Noto, his second Prince of Capua, his third Count of Syracuse, and his fourth Count of Lecce. Leopold became Prince of Salerno.

After Waterloo a swarm of long-delayed travellers rushed to Italy, especially to Naples, where they could combine the maximum of pleasure with instruction, since most of them had been suckled on the classics. The English tourists still continued the eighteenth-century tradition, and poured forth their impressions with the same literary profusion, though they kept the same reserve with fellow travellers. 'We have now nearly three hundred English here,' wrote A' Court, 'I mean presentable people, who expect to be received and entertained at my house. If this continues I shall be ruined.' Here the *douceur de vivre* was to be found even if, like Lady Morgan, they disapproved of the Bourbons. The English have always felt obliged to disapprove of something in the midst of their enjoyment: the dramatic contrasts between splendour and misery, Christianity and Paganism, etc., etc., afforded ample scope for resounding moral platitudes, and the King came in for much liberal abuse. The extravagant voluptuaries who entertained Casanova had vanished without a trace; Neapolitan society had become less ostentatious and more cultured.

Like the Président de Brosses, Stendhal decided that Naples

was the only capital in Italy: all the other large cities were variations of Lyons. Though a Bonapartist he was less censorious than the English, confessing that he enjoyed himself from eight till four in the morning at a royal ball. 'All London was there; the Englishwomen seemed to me to bear away the palm, though there were some very pretty Neapolitans... The host [King Ferdinand] does not deserve the grand phrases in the style of Tacitus which they make against him in Europe: he is the character of Western in *Tom Jones;* this prince knows more about wild boars than proscriptions.' Among his hosts Stendhal mentions the polished Marchese Berio and the republican Princess of Belmonte, who had returned from Paris and made peace with the King by presenting him with one of her allegorical daubs. 'The subject was quite worthy of her brush,' wrote Palmieri di Miccichè. 'A spirit was flying towards Heaven, and at the bottom of the picture you could discern the mortal remains of this spirit, or rather somebody who had fainted, apparently from pleasure, with a smiling face... The spirit was that of the Princess, soaring towards the Creator to announce the happy news of Ferdinand's restoration; the figure at the bottom represented the Princess's body, either dead or fainted or sleeping, I know not which.' But the hospitable dowager had retained little of her pristine charm—'a true skeleton, deserving a place in a natural history museum while still alive: one could have played the guitar on her bosom...' Another vivacious relic of a more riotous day was the widowed Margravine of Anspach, the former beautiful Lady Craven, who had retired to Posillipo—'all eyes, nose, fire and fury, exclaiming against relations who will not allow her to live as she likes, and against beastly Germans who accuse her of leading their gentle Sovereign out of his senses and out of his dominions'. Here at least she could live as she liked, still organizing theatricals as in her frivolous prime, when young Beckford had set one of her pastorals to music.

The two *salons* frequented by the most intellectual residents and visitors were those of the Archbishop of Taranto and Marchese Berio, the ineptness of whose libretti for Rossini's *Otello* and *Ricciardo e Zoraide* was not noticed at Naples; on the contrary, both were applauded, and in the former case Berio was congratulated on his good taste in toning down 'the tremendous catastrophes of the ferocious Shakespeare'. Berio was also a friend of the other genius whom Stendhal brackets with Rossini, and in his Arcadian villa at

Portici three of his daughters had crowned Canova with roses—'the second Pheidias crowned by the second Graces'. In the city he possessed a garden on the second storey of his palace which Kotzebue compared to the hanging garden of Semiramis. 'But it has one considerable advantage over its ancient prototype, in a pavilion containing a charming group of Venus and Adonis, by Canova. It is said to be not among the best productions of this excellent artist. However, the worst performance of Canova's chisel (if the word *bad* is in any of its degrees allowable as applied to them) is always so surprisingly beautiful, that a man of any feeling imagines it impossible in the first quarter of an hour to find defects.' Stendhal remarked that the tone of Berio's salon was approximately that of the best Parisian society, but there was more vivacity and certainly more noise; often the conversation was so shrill that it gave him earache. But to recapture that vanished atmosphere we must turn to a less famous novelist.

'The conversazione of the Palazzo Berio,' wrote Lady Morgan, 'is a congregation of elegant and refined spirits, where everybody converses, and converses well; and best (if not most) the master of the house. The Marchese Berio is a nobleman of wealth, high rank, and of very considerable literary talent and acquirement, which extends itself to the utmost verge of the philosophy and *belles-lettres* of England, France, Germany and his native country. He has read everything, and continues to read everything; and I have seen his sitting-room loaded with a new importation of English novels and poetry, while he was himself employed in writing, *all' improvviso*, a beautiful ode to Lord Byron, in all the first transports of enthusiasm, on reading (for the first time) *that* canto of *Childe Harold,* so read and so admired by all in Italy. Time, and a long and patiently endured malady, have had no influence over the buoyant spirit, the ardent feelings, the elegant pursuits, of this liberal and accomplished nobleman; his mind and manners are beyond the reach of infirmity... Of the conversazione of the Beno Palace, it is enough to say, that its circle comprised, when we were at Naples—Canova, Rossetti (the celebrated poet and improvvisatore), the Duke of Ventignano (the tragic poet of Naples), Delfico (the philosopher, patriot and historian), Lampredi and Selvaggi (two very elegant writers and accomplished gentlemen), Signor Blanc (one of the most brilliant colloquial wits of any country, which the author of this work "ever coped withal"), and the Cavaliere Micheroux, a distinguished member of all the first and best circles of Naples. While *Duchessas* and *Principessas*, with titles as romantic as that which induced Horace Walpole to write his delightful romance of "Otranto", filled up the ranks of literature and talent—Rossini presided at the pianoforte, accompanying alternately, himself, Rossetti in his improvvisi, or the Colbran, the prima donna of the San Carlo, in some of her favourite airs from his own *Mosè*. Rossini at the pianoforte is almost as fine an actor as he is a composer. All this was very delightful, and very rare!—but there was something in these refined circles still more delightful—the most perfect picture of domestic virtue and domestic happiness!—a grandsire and grandame, but just turned the autumn of life; two young unmarried daughters, lovely and well educated, as young ladies of the same high rank in England; and a married daughter, the excellent and amiable Duchess d'Ascoli, always accompanied by her little girls, whose tender age would almost exclude them from society, even in *child-loving* England.' The Duke of Ventignano's tragedies have been forgotten—even his libretto for Rossini's *Maometto II*, the original version of *Le Siège de Corinthe*— but not the rumour that he had the evil eye: Rossini is said to have made the protective 'horn-sign' with his left hand while writing the music. Rossetti is best remembered as the father of our Pre-Raphaelite Dante Gabriel. 'He assured us,' added Lady Morgan in a footnote, 'that having once uttered his inspirations, he could not write them down, nor even remember a word.'

More famous, but more quiet and select, was the *salon* of Monsignor Capecelatro, the absentee Archbishop of Taranto. Nearly all the travel books of the period contain a medallion of this dilettante collector of medallions, coins, cameos, paintings and cats, who had been a Councillor of State under Joseph Bonaparte and Minister of the Interior under Murat, as well as director of the royal museum and the founder of various charitable institutions. He was, as Croce observed in a delightful essay, one of those men who love life and know how to enjoy it in youth, maturity and old age, and die with a smile on their lips. As he did not die until 1836, at the age of ninety-two, this grand old citizen of the world enjoyed a long and glorious sunset. Appropriately he had settled down in the Palazzo Sessa which Sir William Hamilton had occupied. Prince Henry of Prussia saluted him with the words: 'When one comes to Naples, one must see Pompeii, Vesuvius and the Archbishop of Taranto.'

His salon had become a place of pilgrimage. 'But among the *chefs-d'oeuvre* of its pictures,' wrote Lady Morgan, 'among its gems and medals, impressed with the portraits of Grecian heroes and Roman emperors, there is no head in the whole collection so well worth seeing as his own. It is one of the finest illustrations of benignity that Nature, in her happiest mood, ever struck off to reconcile man to his species!... Still attached, with all the enthusiasm of youth, to letters and science, his mornings are given up to his books, his medals and his engraved gems; his early and hospitable dinner-table is seldom without some polished or literary guest; and his afternoons and evenings are devoted to successive circles of friends (whom habits of long and reverential attachment congregate round him) and to some few well-recommended foreigners, who, in the desire of knowing one of the most celebrated characters in Italy, solicit permission to attend his *prima sera*. To this very pleasant Italian season of reception, which begins and ends early in the Palazzo Capecelatro, succeeds the *crocchio ristretto* of his intimate friends of both sexes, including the first persons of rank and talent in Naples; when one or two card-tables, where the stake is next to nothing, vary the resources of the evening.'

A ubiquitous young American, George Ticknor, recorded that a tragedy of Alfieri, the *Stanze* of Poliziano, and a new pamphlet on Pompeii, were among the subjects he heard read and discussed at the Archbishop's: 'In short, it was a literary society. Without pedantry or formality, everyone found himself at ease, and sought to return as often as he could. I have seldom seen a man at the Archbishop's age who has preserved so lively an interest in everything about him; who felt so quickly and simply; who had so much knowledge and made so little pretensions; who had so much to boast on the score of rank, fortune and past power, and yet was so truly humble, so unostentatiously kind. I shall always remember him with the most grateful respect, and think of the Attic evenings I passed in his palace as among the happiest I have known in Europe.'

Apart from his polemical writings on religious subjects, his literary remains are, as Croce said, the versatile effusions of a dilettante. These range from a 'Letter on the sea-shells of Taranto' (1780), addressed to Catherine the Great, for whom he made a rare collection of molluscs, to a dissertation on a painting in the so-called Temple of Isis at Pompeii, where he maintains that Isis is portrayed as a cat, which leads to a disquisition on his favourite animal.

The traveller Simond mentioned that he had cats of all colours, shapes and sizes, and preserved likenesses of them when they died. Simond considered his collection over-rated: 'The ladies who visit him are in the habit of praising his cats, his nicknack tables, and his Murillo too [a picture of Christ bearing the cross, much admired by Mme de Staël], considerably more than they deserve, from a good-natured wish to repay his attentions.'

Kotzebue, who described his collection of coins as 'in many respects unrivalled', has paid humorous tribute to the Archbishop's personal magnetism: 'Sometimes his imagination plays him a trick, as is common with antiquarians. He found, for example, an old copper piece, upon which a man was seated on a horse, covered with a large mantle, and extending his hand forwards: behind him is to be perceived a thing which may certainly be taken for a cap. What does the good Archbishop make of all this? "When the Grecians were before Troy," says he, "their wives at home, not being all Penelopes, found the time long; and by way of shortening it, entertained themselves with their slaves and menservants, and (as it happened) thus produced a number of boys. When the victorious Grecians returned home, not finding much pleasure from this increase of their families, they drove all the boys together out of the city. The youths, united by distress, entered the wide world to seek their living; and, as an emblem for their standard, chose a cap: upon which occasion these coins were struck. The outstretched hand represents a distant journey; the waving of the mantle," which, by the way, does not wave at all, "represents the same; and the emblematical cap renders the whole *perfectly clear*." The good prelate has never put the question to himself: Who struck this coin? The Greeks themselves, to eternize their own disgrace; or the youths, who were hunted away naked and bare, and could hardly take with them the apparatus for such an operation?

'I would just as little vouch that a large square plate of copper with an elephant upon it, is an *ex voto* which the Romans made after the battle lost against Pyrrhus, because that was the first time of their contending in battle, or becoming acquainted, with this animal. However, I must own that all these doubts started in my mind on leaving the amiable Archbishop; for while hearing him speak it was impossible not to believe.'

The King's circle was less cultured, but in his way he had preserved as keen an interest in everything about him as the versatile

Archbishop; his passion for shooting and fishing was undiminished; but he also loved Rossini and Canova: and although he might ogle a *prima donna* or a *ballerina*, his domestic happiness was serene. Dull as they are, his letters to the Duchess of Floridia ooze conjugal affection, and the Villa Floridiana on the Vomero remains a sunny memorial to the old King's tenderness for his morganatic spouse. In his *Royal Delights of a Capital,* Professor de Filippis tells us that when Ferdinand stopped at the Floridiana he was wont to sit with the Duchess near a fountain of white marble, adorned with an allegorical group representing Hymen holding a garland of roses and anemones. A ray of sunshine slanted through this garland on to a sun dial which recorded the date of the King's marriage to the Duchess. The fountain has disappeared like all but one of the statues that used to populate the gardens. The only surviving statue represents a weeping child, 'perhaps the symbol of a happiness flown as soon as glimpsed'.

Antonio Niccolini, who had rebuilt the San Carlo, was the architect engaged to enlarge the house and lay out the grounds, a blend of neo-classical elegance and the romantic picturesque, with all the pretty and fanciful paraphernalia of the period garden, an open-air theatre, a coffee-house, a lake for swans, grottoes, greenhouses, little temples, artificial ruins, an aviary and a menagerie; but the view from the terrace over the whole bay was paramount. When all was nearly completed, the King invited the Duchess to breakfast at the villa on his birthday, and placed the deed of gift in the napkin under her plate.

'A menagerie is, in my opinion, the only drawback to this charming place,' wrote Lady Blessington, 'as the roaring of lions, and screams of the other wild beasts, are little in harmony with so Arcadian a spot. Never were wild beasts more carefully attended or more neatly kept. Their cages are made to resemble natural caverns, and are cut, in fact, in rocks; and the keepers remove every unsightly object, and preserve the dens as free from impurity, as are most children's nurseries in England.' Among the animals were eighteen kangaroos which the King had procured through Sir William A'Court in exchange for an equal number of papyri from Herculaneum, a transaction trounced by Colletta, who called the poor marsupials obscene.

To the luxurious Lady Blessington the bathroom inside the villa seemed the cynosure: 'It is a small chamber, cased with white marble, and the bath occupies nearly the whole of it, leaving only a space sufficiently large to admit of ottomans, formed of the same material, to be ranged round the room. A flight of marble steps, at each end, descends to the bath; whose dimensions would admit not only of bathing, but of swimming. A light balustrade of gilt metal encircles the bath and from the ceiling, which is exquisitely painted with subjects analogous, descend curtains from a circular gilt ring the size of the bath, of snowy texture, which can be secured to the balustrade at pleasure. A lump of snow-white alabaster hangs from the beak of a dove over the bath. Mirrors are inserted in the marble casing of the room, and paintings of nymphs, preparing for the bath, in it and leaving it, are placed so as to correspond with the mirrors. Marble stands for flowers are stationed near the balustrade, so that their odours may be enjoyed by the bather. The dressing-room is equally tasteful and luxurious; and no Eastern queen ever owned two more exquisitely arranged chambers. They look as if designed for some mortal, young and beautiful as the nymphs painted in them, by a youthful lover, whose mind was imbued with the luxuriant and poetical fancies of Eastern climes; instead of the person for whom this fairy palace was created, who is a grand-mother, and the lover who formed it, who is an octogenarian (*sic*).'

Here the Duchess came to spend most of the spring and summer, holding an informal Court of her own; and the King rode over from Capodimonte to join her between his hunting expeditions. Apart from an occasional minor ailment the King was remarkably robust. After a day's shooting at San Leucio he sat on a tree-trunk and remarked to the Prince of Salerno with a happy sigh: 'Leopo', this is the real cure, not like that which the doctors wanted to give me!' During the Carnival he hurled confetti with boyish glee in the Toledo; during Lent he went on foot to visit the sepulchres; and all who saw him agreed that the salutary effects of air and exercise were very visible in his appearance. Colletta was wrong in attributing his anxiety for a Concordat to his failing vigour and morbid fear of death. If he ever thought of death (apart from that of his furred and feathered quarry), he soon put it out of mind. He was slaughtering wild boars at Venafro when Medici signed the Concordat with Cardinal Consalvi on February 16, 1818. By signing it Medici had disarmed his enemies and appeased the King's conscience; above all, he had kept his position, which was his main concern. To salve his own conscience, or its sceptical substitute, he argued that he had merely brought Naples into line with France, Bavaria and Sardinia, which had also negotiated agreements with the Holy See, while Spain had gone so far as to restore the tribunal of the nuncio and recall the Jesuits banished by Charles III. Circello said he would rather have had an arm cut off than have signed that Concordat, and Tommasi considered that the spiritual welfare of the people was not worth such a material sacrifice. 'As progress is made towards the execution of the different provisions of the Concordat lately concluded with the Court of Rome,' wrote the British minister, 'it becomes... every day more apparent that each party has... been the dupe of the other. The palm of Machiavellism must certainly be adjudged to the Chevalier de Medici (in financial matters). In spiritual matters Cardinal Consalvi has over-reached M. de Medici.' But the King was exultant. He called Cardinal Consalvi his dearest of friends, and repeated before his entire Court that the Cardinal was the best friend he had in the world. He decided to go to Rome in October after the pheasant shooting at Caserta. Besides paying his respects to the Pope he wished to see more of his elder brother, the ex-King Charles IV of Spain, and persuade him to return to Naples. Charles had recently revisited his birthplace, for the first time since he had left it at the age of eleven, and had been given the warmest of welcomes by Ferdinand. After being separated for more than half a century the two patriarchs were delighted to find that they had so much in common, and Charles had tactfully come without his wife and Godoy; creature of habit though he was, he had suddenly discovered that he could enjoy life without them.

Ferdinand rattled into Rome on October 24, preceded by four wild boars he had shot at Cardito as a little personal offering to the Pope, and followed by the Duchess of Floridia. Hence the Roman pasquinade

> *Coi peli innanzi e colle corna dietro*
> *Viene Ferdinando a visitar San Pietro.*

('To visit Saint Peter comes Ferdinand
With bristles before and horns behind.')

To provide some light relief from Roman pomp, the King had also sent two Neapolitan comedians ahead of him, Pellegrino and

Casacciello. Colletta says that Ferdinand was the only member of the audience to laugh at their jokes, which were too broad for the supercilious Romans. But they were quick to notice the physical resemblance between Casacciello and the monarch. The Pope gave some splendid entertainments in honour of the Bourbon brothers, and the Duchess was received like a Queen. After a round of banquets and balls and the usual sight-seeing, including several visits to Canova, 'the modern Pheidias', the two Kings travelled back to Naples together. Again Queen Maria Luisa was left behind with Godoy, and it is said that Ferdinand enlightened his simple brother about their illicit relations on the return journey. If so, it was rather too late for so rude an awakening. Charles got very angry, and swore he would never return to them.

For once Ferdinand had been over-strenuous. A few days after his return he was laid up with a tertian fever lasting till the beginning of December, which seemed so serious that the octogenarian Doctor Cotugno was summoned to his bedside at night. The doctor almost died of an apoplectic stroke on the stairs of the royal palace. The patient slowly recovered, but not before the Duchess of Floridia had sent wax candles to the shrine of Saint Rita, 'the advocate of desperate cases', such was the alarm at Court. On December 4 De Nicola recorded that the King had recovered, and that the doctors had persuaded him to part with the queue he had always worn, since he had complained that it had inconvenienced him during his illness. The ex-King of Spain had told him that he was the last sovereign in Europe to wear one. Such was the political importance attached to this appendage that the incident seemed revolutionary. The whole Court gaped, the city buzzed, astounded at the transformation. Had the King's brain been addled by fever? Had he belatedly become a Jacobin? The Carbonari were in a ferment. But the King soon returned to his normal routine, reassuringly static —apart from his physical activity. And the most obstinate of the mandarins ruefully followed his example and bade a symbolical adieu to the eighteenth century.

Another portent almost passed unnoticed: in 1818 the first steamship was launched in the Mediterranean. This was Neapolitan, and the first steamship company to navigate the same sea (in 1823) was also Neapolitan.

XXXV

Death of Maria Luisa of Spain, followed by that of Charles IV—Visiting Russians—The Emperor and Empress of Austria and Prince Metternich—Growth of the Carbonari—The revolt at Nola—General Guglielmo Pepe leads the rebels—Carbonari gate-crashers at the royal palace—Pepe's flamboyant march into the capital—Ferdinand reluctantly swears to a Constitution—Austria's reaction— Repercussions in Sicily—Protocol of Troppau—Ferdinand invited to Laibach: his voyage and arrival on January 8, 1821—The Congress decides to interfere by force—The Constitutional Parliament declares war—Pepe's rout at Rieti on March 7—The Parliament proposes submission to the King—Flight of Carbonari leaders.

After the *Te Deums* for the King's recovery, which was celebrated by Rossini in the form of a special cantata and commemorated by an anthology of prose and verse in Italian, Latin, Greek, Hebrew and Arabic, there were further festivities for the betrothal of the Duke of Calabria's daughter, Princess Luisa Carlotta, to the ugly Infante Francis of Paola of Spain, reputed to be the son of Godoy. These were interrupted by the news of the ex-Queen of Spain's death in Rome on January 2, 1819. 'Let us bring the good news to that poor old man,' said Ferdinand to his gentleman-in-waiting, forgetting that he was not much younger himself. He felt rather abashed when the news failed to cheer his brother.

Charles IV could not help being afflicted. Whatever his wife's infidelities, she had been his companion for fifty years, and her adored Godoy had been almost as dear to him. Perhaps his blindness to her amours had been intentional. Like his father, he had always been ruled by habit, regularity, etiquette. For him the charm of music consisted in the strict beating of time, only it was difficult to find musicians who could keep time with royalty. When his violin teacher ventured to observe that he was playing too fast, he replied with majestic astonishment: 'Well, sir, do you expect me to wait for *you*?' He considered his own tempo unique. Hence his passion for clocks and watches, with which he had a temperamental affinity. He had collected thousands of timepieces which accompanied him everywhere and whose workings he supervised meticulously, and he usually kept half a dozen on his person. Many of his habits were eccentric by ordinary standards. He drank only water, but this had to be served in three decanters, one iced, one hot and one lukewarm: a little was poured from each in turn until he found the right degree of temperature. He ate voraciously but never touched vegetables, which he said were only fit for beasts. De Bausset has related in his *Memoirs* that the King always had his confessor in the next room and would whistle for him whenever he was required, 'as one might whistle for a dog'.

The bereaved King wished to attend his wife's funeral, but his physicians begged him not to risk the fatigue of the journey. Ferdinand was obliged to order Court mourning for four months, which did not interfere with his hunting. Force of habit was too powerful for Charles: he could not long survive such a wrench. He was preparing to leave Naples on January 14 when he had to retire to bed with fever, complicated by gout. Palmieri di Miccichè's account of his dissolution corroborates Colletta's, though it contains more Sicilian than Attic salt: 'Ferdinand was hunting in the woods of Persano when Charles IV fell suddenly and dangerously ill. Feeling that his end was approaching, he asked continually to see his dear brother, to embrace him for the last time, while the ministers, the Court doctors, and especially the Duchess of Floridia, who never left the dying man's bed, sent messenger after messenger to beg the King to hasten his return.

'Upon receiving such distressing news, Ferdinand's first impulse was to get into a rage with Charles IV for choosing such an inconvenient time to die. Then turning to his courtiers, he said in the vernacular: "Bad luck! The King of Spain is very sick!" After pondering a moment he added: "I think there's some exaggeration in these reports. Let us hunt first, and then we shall see." But before he had finished speaking a second and a third messenger, arriving in hot succession, announced that Charles IV was at his last gasp and that he had not a moment to lose for the journey. At this point Ferdinand could bear it no longer: he gave orders not to open any despatches from Naples till the hunt was over, and addressing his courtiers again, he spoke to them almost as follows: "Either my brother will die, or he will recover. In the first case what will it matter to him whether I amused myself hunting or not? In the second, being a crack sportsman himself he will be delighted to see me return with a good bag of game to cheer his convalescence."

...Consequently there was hunting all day with excellent sport and a holocaust of game, and at length the latest despatches were opened, announcing that Charles IV had expired with his brother's name on his lips. Ferdinand stopped another three or four days at Persano, hunting from time to time (some little distraction was needed to mitigate so intense a sorrow), after which he returned to his capital and went into deep mourning.'

Ferdinand wished his brother's remains to receive the honours due to a sovereign, but the Spanish ambassador raised objections, since the Congress of Vienna had recognized Ferdinand VII as the legitimate monarch. However, the Spanish ritual was observed, and the late King was waited upon and sent food for six days as if he were still alive; his name was called out thrice, and each time he was begged to reply, before he was finally confided to his coffin. A dignified elegy was printed and distributed during the obsequies in Santa Chiara, and the ultra-sensitive Spanish ambassador made another fuss because Charles was referred to therein as 'King of Spain and the Indies', insisting on the withdrawal of the elegy and threatening to prosecute its author. Ferdinand had a good laugh when he heard about this and so the affair ended, says De Nicola.

To ward off gloomy thoughts, the King hunted at Caserta and Carditello with unflagging energy. The weather throughout that winter was exceptionally fine. More foreign visitors flocked to Naples for the Carnival. 'The Grand Duke Michael [the Tsar's brother] has been here about a week, and will probably stay till the end of the month,' wrote A' Court on March 7. 'He is accompanied by M. de La Harpe and two or three General Officers. He appears to be heartily tired of his Italian Tour, and disgusted with a country which offers neither parades nor reviews.' A'Court shared Metternich's distrust of Russian motives. La Harpe was Swiss, but as the Tsar's tutor he had exerted an influence over him second only to that of Catherine the Great. Everywhere he proclaimed Russian sympathy with liberal aspirations, and in Bologna he had presided over a meeting of Carbonari. The Tsar's Corfiote minister, Count Capo d'Istria, also paid Naples a fleeting visit. 'I did not mention [the insecurity of the post forbade it],' wrote A'Court on April 18, 'that he had increased the appointments of nearly all the Russian agents employed along the eastern coast of this kingdom, and that he had made some fruitless attempts to procure from the Neapolitan Government an official situation upon the same coast for a certain Duramani, a Greek by birth, who, upon a reference to the books of the police, was found to be one of the most violent incendiaries and revolutionaries who frequent the coffee-houses and other places of public resort in this capital... These circumstances... show the little reliance that is to be placed upon the denial of secret agency so constantly repeated... It is impossible for anyone acquainted with the Russian character to believe that the same system would be invariably persevered in by every successive minister unless there existed a pretty strong persuasion that such a line of conduct was the most certain road to the Emperor's favour.' Society was but little benefited by the Grand Duke Michael's presence, since he declined all invitations on account of his sister's death. 'A number of very indiscreet speeches were attributed to M. de La Harpe during his residence at Naples, but as they were principally expressions of speculative opinion their repetition here would savour too much of *commérage*.'

As a counterblast to the liberals Prince Metternich arrived with the Emperor and Empress of Austria at the end of April. The King, the Prince of Salerno and his wife, a daughter of the Emperor, went to meet these august visitors at Gaeta, while the Duke and Duchess of Calabria awaited them at the royal palace. At first torrential rains marred the public festivities, but these were lavish as soon as the weather cleared. Over a thousand guests attended a party in their honour at Capodimonte, which even the devoutest Muratists had to admit excelled the magnificence of Joachim; there were relays of banquets with the rarest fish and most exquisite viands served in abundance, and any foreign wine asked for was obtainable. The Viennese guests were in ecstasies over Neapolitan *sfogliatella*, a fine-flaked pastry melting in the mouth, 'such stuff as dreams are made of'. Among other spectacles Mademoiselle Cecilia, a fourteen-year-old pupil of the aeronaut Garnerin, went up in a balloon. She was supposed to come down at the exact point of her departure, but she landed some distance away, half suffocated by smoke. At the same time a parachute was dropped with some small unspecified quadruped. A dangerous and useless invention, said De Nicola, since the balloon was at the wind's mercy.

If the *Memoirs* of Guglielmo Pepe, the Carbonaro general, are not wholly the figment of his fertile imagination, he had planned to abduct the King's party and ransom them for a Constitution, but his plan was thwarted by Colletta. He had been ordered to hold a review of five thousand men at Avellino in honour of the Austrian Emperor: 'Before I had read the minister's despatch I became morally and physically feverish. Italy from Trapani to the Alps flashed before my vision, and the enterprise was none too bold to daunt my patriotism. I decided to arrest the King, the Emperor, the Empress, Metternich, Medici and Nugent; to consign them to the custody of a hundred officers and sub-officers of the militia who were all grand masters of the Carbonari, and send them off to Melfi in Basilicata... It is superfluous for me to describe what I hoped to achieve by means of this capture, but I do not think any reader will doubt that it would have led to most important and useful results for the whole of Italy as well as for the Two Sicilies. The King and the Emperor were both so timid that they would have conceded anything. It might be objected that the rulers of Europe would have sent an army against Naples, as Louis XVIII did against Spain in 1823,... but having to deal with a single resolute man is very different from dealing with a congress, in which opinions are many and various.

'I gave due orders for the five thousand militia to assemble, and every man obeyed. Had the sovereigns come, I should have infallibly carried out my plan, leaving the rest to fortune, which mocked me and my intentions. The King, the Emperor and their suite proceeded from Persano to Salerno, and while they were changing post-horses, General Colletta, who was in command of that province, went to pay them his respects. The King wished to know what he thought of the road to Avellino, and the General replied that it was in a very bad state and none too safe for post-travel. Hearing this, the King and the Emperor gave up the idea of attending the review and went on to Naples... Colletta was induced by jealousy to exaggerate the badness of the road, aware that the King was anxious for the Emperor to see my militia, whereas he had not been able to muster a single battalion worth seeing at Salerno.'

Metternich's visit gave rise to many sinister rumours: it was even said that he had urged Medici tacitly to encourage disorders, so that Austria might have a good pretext to intervene and restore the old *status quo*; hence Medici's remarkable forbearance with the Carbonari. Certainly Metternich did not share his confidence in the stability of the government; he was seriously alarmed by the growth of the secret societies.

In Naples this seemed a halcyon period. The King was unquestionably popular; the government, if not 'enlightened', was exceedingly mild and tolerant; and there was reasonable freedom. In the coffee-houses, as in the drawing-rooms of Marchese Berio and the Archbishop of Taranto, everybody could ventilate his personal opinion on any subject without danger of persecution. Medici, the soul of the so-called 'Quinquennium', was powerful but never despotic. Aloof from the excesses both of the Carbonari and the reactionaries, he hoped that his glaring antipathy to the latter—specially since Canosa's removal—would propitiate the new *bourgeoisie*. He fancied he would dissolve the rival factions by creating a state above parties with a moral and material force of its own. His chief fault was complacency: he did not think it possible that anyone should be so foolish as to wish for a better government.

Rossini returned to the San Carlo in May, and his *Donna del Lago*, based on Sir Walter Scott's *Lady of the Lake*, was produced in the following September. Stendhal described the scenery as a masterpiece: a wild and solitary lake in the north of Scotland, on which the heroine was rowing alone in her skiff. La Colbran propelled her boat gracefully while she warbled her first melody, in which nobody could find a flaw. But the first night audience was fractious, and when the tenor, too far from the footlights to hear the orchestra, produced a false note, he was greeted with howls and hisses. 'A menagerie of roaring lions when their cages are unbarred, Æolus unchaining the winds in fury—nothing can give even a vague idea of the rage of a Neapolitan audience offended by a false note,' wrote Stendhal. Though it was a gala night the Court was not present. The young officers entitled to occupy the first five rows of the stalls had evidently drunk the King's health too copiously, for they made such a noise during the military march that they ruined the opera. On the second night, however, it was a great success, though Rossini's nerves had been shattered. In November Stendhal was writing from Milan: 'I saw Rossini yesterday on his arrival: he will be twenty-eight next April, and is anxious to stop working at thirty. This man, who was penniless four years ago, has just invested a hundred thousand francs with Barbaja at seven and a half per cent. They give him a thousand francs a month as director-despot of the Teatro San Carlo... Besides the thousand francs a month, Rossini gets four thousand francs for every opera he writes, and they ask for all he can do. His *Donna del Lago*, on a subject taken from Walter Scott, has had the greatest possible success... Barbaja keeps this great man, and gives him free carriage, table, lodging *ed amica*. The divine Colbran, who is, I think, only forty or fifty years old, is the delight of Prince Jablonowski, of the millionaire Barbaja, and of the maestro.'

The King's life seemed to have fallen into a pattern like the seasons. In October he fell ill again with fever and catarrh on the chest. 'He had become over-heated at the chase and dried his sweat in the sun,' wrote De Nicola. 'His Majesty will not realize that he is sixty-nine years old. May the Almighty prolong his life!' Before Christmas he was hunting again at Persano, as always at this time of the year. The Duchess of Floridia joined him to see that he did not over-exert himself, as his favourite son Leopold had had to take his wife back to Vienna in the hope that her native air might benefit her. Her extraordinary turn of mind, wrote A'Court, had given considerable uneasiness to the whole of the royal family. 'Ever since her marriage she has been subject to lowness of spirits and fits of melancholy, during which she constantly dwells upon the impropriety of her marriage with a person so nearly allied to her as her uncle, and maintains that the Pope has neither authority nor power to render such marriages less offensive to religion and decorum by his dispensation...'

In the meantime the lodges of Good Cousins, as the Carbonari called each other, were increasing all over the kingdom. The army was riddled with them, from the generals who had been promoted by Murat to the lower ranks which had never been amenable to discipline. The generals had retained their honours but resented being placed under the command of the Austrian-Irish Nugent, though they would have resented a Sicilian or a Bourbon loyalist even more, and the junior officers chafed at the slowness of promotion. Under Murat the military career had offered solid advantages which those who had served him compared with their present stagnation. Blanch, himself an officer at the time, said that the army was well treated materially but neglected morally. All the disgruntled were drawn towards the Carbonari, since 'Satan finds some mischief still for idle hands to do'. Provincial landowners, lawyers and prosperous members of the middle class joined the Carbonari for other reasons, the most intelligent because they wanted a decentralized autonomy. Apart from which the mysterious rites and clandestine atmosphere of a Carbonaro meeting were calculated to appeal to the romantic *zeitgeist*, the feverishly exalted spirit of the age. There were similar societies in France, Germany, Switzerland, Poland and even Russia, products of the general unrest after the Napoleonic wars.

In the south of Italy they were more dramatic than elsewhere. Though the meeting-places of the lodges were supposed to resemble barns, with the members sitting on benches along the walls while the Grand Master, the Orator and the Secretary sat at one end before tree-trunks covered with symbols, such crude settings were springboards for rococo flights of rhetoric, of which the literature on the subject gives but a feeble notion. By the dim light of a few candles the huddled initiates shared delicious thrills of secrecy, companionship, devil-may-care patriotism, and, above all, the sweet savour of conspiracy. Initiatory speeches were full of magniloquent abstractions: 'The initiates were addressed more openly as soon as they had shown an aptitude for seizing allegories, or when they belonged to a more enlightened class of society.' The explanation of the symbols varied accordingly: these consisted of a linen cloth, water, salt, a cross, leaves, sticks, fire, earth, a crown of white thorns, a ladder, a ball of thread and three ribbons, one blue for smoke, one red for fire and one black for charcoal. Various illuminated triangles with the arms of the lodge, the initials of the password of the second rank and the sacred words of the first rank, etc., were another important feature.

Ignorance and superstition were easily exploited by all this hocus-pocus, but the Grand Masters knew what they were about. Carbonarism, as Schipa wrote, served to amass rather than fuse different interests and ideas in a single opposition to the government; and this opposition became riveted by a common aim: to force the King to grant a Constitution. The first manifestos had been distributed in Puglia and the neighbourhood of Avellino in 1817: these demanded a Constitution and incited the people to withhold the payment of taxes in case of a refusal. The government commissioner Intonti stopped the agitation by pointing out that it was impossible to yield to their demands while an Austrian army remained inside the kingdom. For a time the Carbonari kept quiet, but after the withdrawal of the Austrian troops in August of the same year their membership multiplied. According to General Pepe they numbered 300,000 in 1819; Colletta doubles this figure. Provincial prelates and magistrates sent Medici frequent reports about the progress of the sect, but he scoffed at them. When they came to the capital he refused to see them. In December Francesco

Patrizi, the prefect of police, became so exasperated by Medici's *laissez-faire* that he decided to open the King's eyes. He told him that there was a conspiracy to make him grant a Constitution, and showed him a list of the conspirators. The King heaped reproaches on Medici and Tommasi. Patrizi had frightened him to death, he said: what were they going to do about it? The ministers soon persuaded him that Patrizi had been talking nonsense and that all was well in the best of possible worlds. The croaking Cassandra was instantly dismissed. Still the Carbonari kept quiet, fearing further revelations. A' Court considered that Naples was 'advancing slowly and silently to a degree of strength and importance never before possessed, notwithstanding the contradictory vapourings of the adherents of the late government'. And Colletta has recorded: 'The rulers were benign, finance prospered, works of charity and public utility were undertaken, and the state was flourishing; the present was happy, the future appeared to be most happy, Naples was among the best governed kingdoms of Europe, which preserved a larger portion of the patrimony of new ideas for which so much blood had been shed.' Evidence from two sources so different in every respect deserves consideration, but the blinkered nineteenth-century liberals are still quoted as supreme authorities, and these could see nothing but decadence and corruption under a rampant despotism.

Pasquale Borrelli, the subsequent chief of police, has stated in print that the activities of the Carbonari would probably have been limited to projects, speeches and sticking up posters in the dead of night had they not been stimulated by the Spanish example. The surprising success of the Spanish mutiny of January 1, 1820, put the Neapolitan conspirators on their mettle. To secure his rights as an Infante of Spain the King perfunctorily swore to the new Spanish Constitution: why then should he not swear to one at home? General Pepe felt he must look to his laurels, but it took him six months to make up his mind to act. Though manifestos and anonymous letters poured in, Medici shielded the King against alarms. An attempt was to have been made during the army manoeuvres at Sessa which the King constantly attended in May, but the King's enthusiasm and affability made him so popular that the ringleaders took fright. However, the Carbonari were able to spread their propaganda among the 12,000 troops collected, and when the camp broke up on May 24 the sect had greatly increased in numbers.

The Duchess of Floridia had been suffering from a liver ailment, but she recovered in time to celebrate the King's saint's day at the San Carlo, little suspecting that another plot had been foiled. Colonel De Concilj (also spelt Conciliis) had countermanded an insurrection at the last moment when General Carascosa warned him that foreign intervention was bound to follow. But as June wore on the movement boiled to a crisis. General Pepe's command had been transferred from Avellino to his native Calabria, but he lingered in Naples to conduct the overture. Finally, two Carbonaro lieutenants, Morelli and Salvati, of the ill-disciplined Bourbon cavalry regiment quartered at Nola, about twelve miles from the capital, persuaded over a hundred men to desert with them. These were joined by the local Grand Master, a priest called Minichini, with some twenty civilian members of the sect; and all took the road to Avellino, thirteen miles distant, on the night of July 1. One loyal officer brought the news to Naples. At the same time De Concilj sent a message to General Pepe to join him as soon as possible.

The King and Prince Leopold were sailing blithely on the corvette *Galatea* to meet the Duke of Calabria and his family returning from Palermo. The Duke had been a conscientious and respected viceroy in Sicily ever since his father's restoration in 1815, and had only been twice to Naples during that period; he was returning on the plea of ill health, though other reasons were assigned for it, which seemed to be supported by coincidence. In fact he was crippled by gout and the Sicilian climate did not suit him; as for his wife, whose brains were as light as her body was heavy, she was pining for the amusements of Naples. But the Court reception that night was not very well attended, although it was Prince Leopold's birthday. Most of the foreign ministers had gone to the country to avoid the summer heat. The King, always happy to be surrounded by his children, appeared in excellent spirits, which contrasted with the gloom of Medici and Tommasi, who were noticeably abstracted in their manner. Neither the ministers nor the generals showed any decision when they met in council. At first they thought of sending General Pepe to quell the revolt, but the King instinctively distrusted him, so General Carascosa was appointed instead. Carascosa did nothing until Nugent ordered him to march on July 3, when the rebels were reinforced by Carbonari from all the surrounding districts and the pass of Monteforte, a long and steep defile on the main road to Avellino, was held by a strong band of deserters. Apparently Carascosa's chief concern was to remain on good terms with both sides. On the 4th he attempted to bribe the Carbonari leaders with 8,000 ducats in gold and safe-conducts from the King. General Nunziante, the commander of Salerno, had evinced more energy, but his troops refused to fight, and those sent in pursuit of the first deserters had joined them. General Guglielmo Pepe remained in Naples, and he was afforded ample time to escape on July 5. His escape was like a triumphal progress; escorted by seventy dragoons and half a company of infantry, he reached Avellino early the next morning and put himself at the head of the rebels. Here he issued a proclamation that his forces would never lay down their arms till the Constitution was not only promised but signed by the King; and to avoid any excuse for delay the Spanish Constitution of 1812 had been chosen as a model. On the night of July 5, while Pepe was riding to Avellino, five Carbonari went to the royal palace and asked to see the King. The Duke of Ascoli received them. Their spokesman said that the whole city was up in arms, waiting for the King to proclaim the Constitution. The Duke replied that the King had decided to grant one, and was actually discussing it with his ministers. The spokesman said it must be ready within two hours: it was now one o'clock in the morning. One of the Carbonari pulled out the Duke's watch to emphasize the time; this happened to be Ascoli's son-in-law, the Duke of Picoletti. A few hours later the royal proclamation was issued: since the general desire of the nation for a Constitutional Government had been expressed, the King consented and promised to publish its details within eight days.

As in Sicily, the unfortunate Duke of Calabria was delegated to deal with the emergency. It seemed as if he had arrived precisely for that purpose. Announcing that his infirmities did not allow him to sustain the fatigues of government, the dear old King, so much heartier than his son and heir, appointed him Vicar-General. Not satisfied with the King's proclamation, the Carbonari collected in front of the royal palace and clamoured for the Spanish Constitution. Their shouts continued while the Prince knelt before his father, imploring him to yield to necessity. The Vicar-General issued a decree accordingly; still the Carbonari were not satisfied until they had obtained the King's own signature. The Spanish Constitution seemed to have become a magical talisman. A'Court wrote that 'of all the grave counsellors who advised the Prince to accept the Spanish Constitution... there was not one who had ever read it'. And Borrelli wrote that Minichini, whom many regarded as the real leader of the revolution, asked him for a copy of the historic document. 'I have done so much for this Constitution,' he remarked, 'and I have not even read it.' Which reminded Borrelli of the chivalrous knight who had fought a duel to prove that Ariosto was a better poet than Tasso. Mortally wounded by his adversary, he murmured: 'My sole regret is that I am dying for an author I have never read.' The masses knew as little about the exotic syllables they were shouting as Grand Master Minichini or the King's grave counsellors. Yet many regarded the triumph of a catchword as the dawn of a new era. 'In the balmy garden of Italy bondage is no more,' sang the ecstatic Gabriele Rossetti, laureate of the Constitutionalists.

A revolution might have been expected in the moon rather than in Naples, exclaimed Prince Jablonowski, the Austrian minister, and his British colleague was equally surprised. A'Court observed: 'A kingdom in the highest degree flourishing and happy under the mildest of governments, and by no means oppressed by the weight of taxation, crumbles before a handful of insurgents that half a battalion of good soldiers would have crushed in an instant.' But a revolution which derived its impetus from the Carbonari, its power from military desertion, and its success from the government's weakness, could hardly inspire confidence. Discipline had ceased to exist in the army. 'It is scarcely a fortnight,' wrote A'Court on July 9, 'since I was assured both by the King and General Nugent that the army might be securely reckoned upon from the General down to the lowest of the soldiers.' Now Nugent had taken refuge with A'Court: 'General Nugent had no hope but in me. I could not quit him an instant, and was obliged to run the risk of conveying him in my carriage [an open one] through the streets to my own house. His wife and family followed.' He had not suspected 'the union of the Carbonari and the army signed and sealed during the camp at Sessa'. According to him private pique had set fire to the mine. 'The nomination of General Church to the command in Sicily determined them to commence operations at once.' The new ministry was composed of the most experienced veterans who had served Murat, including Count Zurlo, Count Ricciardi and the Duke of Campochiaro. 'This choice of ministers is extremely displeasing to the demagogues,' wrote A'Court. 'The present men have some character at stake, and are fully persuaded of the necessity of keeping well with Foreign Powers. They have refused the overtures of the Carbonari of Benevento.' The only real power was vested in the Carbonari, who pervaded all departments military and civil, and began to flaunt their supremacy. 'There is no Government whatever,' wrote A'Court on July 9. 'The Junta named has no power—the Generals very little—the soldiers are abandoning their ranks in all directions. Our sole hope is the *Guardia Civica*.' Another eye witness, Keppel Craven (the Margravine of Anspach's son by her first husband Lord Craven), describes the civic guard as composed of the most respectable classes of inhabitants; it had been much increased, and was assisted by patrols from the few troops who had remained in the capital. At first a strange silence brooded over Naples. 'This suspension of noise and bustle in a city so remarkable for both, seemed to produce an impression nearly akin to terror, and might not unaptly have been compared to that stagnation of the atmosphere which is said invariably to precede an earthquake.'

To crown his bloodless victory, Pepe announced to the Vicar in dictatorial fashion that he would make his public entry into the capital at the head of his legions on July 8. The Prince tried to persuade him to bring only 2,000 men, as the prospect of so large an invasion caused considerable uneasiness, but Pepe was not to be balked of the pageantry of triumph. He allowed an extra day to prepare for his reception, and his entry took place on the 9th. Altogether some 14,000 men marched down the Toledo towards the royal palace. The regular troops, led by General Napoletano, were followed by the motley provincial militia and Carbonari, walking rapidly without any order, headed by General Pepe and the Carbonaro Grand Master Minichini, who attracted more curiosity than his companion, being dressed as a priest, but armed and covered with the symbols of the sect. Keppel Craven, who was well disposed towards the revolution, described Minichini as an intelligent and indefatigable man, and continued: 'The Constitution itself, in a palpable shape, made its appearance in the procession, conveyed in a common hackney one-horse chair, called a *coriccolo*. The spectacle displayed by the bands of provincial militia was singular in the extreme; as, though they were all most formidably armed, their weapons varied as much as their accoutrements: a very small proportion of them were clad in military uniform, the majority being habited according to the different costumes of their respective districts, which at the same time bore a very warlike aspect. It must be acknowledged that the cartridge belt, the sandalled legs, the broad stiletto, short musket, and grey peaked hats, so peculiarly adapted by painters to the representation of banditti, seemed here to realize all the ideas which the inhabitants of the north have formed of such beings; and the sun-burnt complexions, and dark bushy hair and whiskers of the wearer, greatly contributed to render this resemblance more striking.

'A strange contrast was exhibited by the more opulent classes of these same legions, who, though equally well provided with arms of all descriptions, marched among the ranks of their picturesque companions, attired in the full extreme of modern French and English fashions. All bore the Carbonari colours at their breast, while scarfs of the same, or different medals and emblems tied to their waistcoat, denoted the rank they severally held in the sect. Banners with inscriptions in honour of this patriotic association were also carried by them. Nearly the whole of these individuals had been absent from their homes nine days, during which they had never slept in a bed, or even under a roof, but they all seemed in perfect good humour and spirits and appeared amply repaid for all the hardships they might have endured, by the success which had followed them.

'After passing before the palace, they filed off in different divisions, to the respective quarters which had been assigned to them in some of the empty barracks; but more particularly in a long range of buildings on the Portici road, known by the name of the *Granili*. On the first night of their stay at Naples, a considerable proportion of these men slept on trusses of straw, among the oleanders, myrtles and geraniums of the public walk, or Villa Reale...

'The several deputations from the provinces had established themselves in the main street, each forming a place of rendezvous, where their countrymen could apply for any information or assistance they might require: these quarters having the names of their respective districts displayed on draperies of coloured silks, adorned with flowers and illuminated by variegated lamps, added much to the brilliancy and gaiety of the scene.'

This description is pregnant with pathos in the light of subsequent events. The procession was perhaps the most glorious event in the lives of those taking part in it. They saw themselves as heroes.

Of course, the whole city was illuminated for the occasion. The King retired to his bed. The Sicilian Constitution had given him enough trouble, and this seemed far worse. He felt he was surrounded by traitors. Medici had monstrously deceived him. His son Francis had always been flabby despite his good intentions. But were they good? Was he not impatient to succeed, like his Spanish cousin and brother-in-law? The Duke and Duchess of Calabria stood on the balcony over the front entrance to the palace, trying to look cheerful. This was easier for the plump Duchess than for her nervous, gouty husband. General Pepe dismounted and was admitted to an audience with the Vicar, though he was thinking at the time: 'These people are the only real enemies of my country!' Naturally prone to exaggeration, his account of the audience is typical. No doubt he delivered a patriotic harangue, protesting that he would resign his command as soon as the new Parliament assembled. No doubt the Prince, whom he described as a consummate dissembler, uttered a few gracious words in reply, confirming his self-assumed rank as Commander-in-Chief and exhorting him to preserve law and order. It is more probable that Pepe asked to see the King than that the King asked to see Pepe. He was ushered into the royal bedroom. 'I drew near to his bed,' he wrote, 'and perceived that the King was really sick with fever, produced, it must be confessed, by sheer terror.' He extended his hand to be kissed, and Pepe said: 'Now Your Majesty reigns over the hearts of all.' The King merely answered: 'I hope, General, that you will conduct yourself honourably.' Considering Pepe's past record, the King had always treated him magnanimously, as the general admits in his *Memoirs*. It is easy to conceive his disgust when he was subjected to another harangue. He was far from comforted and reassured, as Pepe alleges. He saw Pepe as the criminal leader of a criminal movement, and it was with the strongest mental reservation and under what he considered duress that he consented to swear to a Constitution he abhorred. He read the formula of the oath on July 13 in the royal chapel. According to Colletta, the King then fixed his eyes on the Cross and added gratuitously: 'Omnipotent God, who lookest into the heart of man and can discern the future, if I lie or prove faithless to my oath, do Thou at this moment strike me with the lightning of Thy vengeance!' This is a little too gratuitous to be credible. In public the King was a man of few words, unless he had cause to be elated. And on this occasion, for which he had tottered out of bed, he was profoundly depressed. He kissed the Bible, the oath was taken by his sons, and the new Constitution was proclaimed to the firing of cannon.

Pepe now became the target of the jealousy which had been concentrated against the foreigner Nugent. To placate it he promised to resign as soon as the new Parliament assembled, and to show his disinterested patriotism he refused the sum of 500,000 ducats offered him by the government in remuneration for his services. But he had stolen the thunder of his colleagues and thrust Minichini in the shade. While the Carbonari were still celebrating their victory, he was painfully reminded that military desertion might go too far. Three hundred soldiers of the Farnese regiment, who disliked the prospect of being stationed at Gaeta, forced open the gates of their barracks and deserted with their arms. General Filangieri overtook them in his carriage and persuaded them to return, but on meeting a cavalry regiment which had been ordered to pursue them they thought they were trapped and discharged a volley of musketry at the mounted dragoons, wounding their colonel. The dragoons charged the aggressors, of whom some sixty were shot down. 'General Pepe still sees everything *en beau*,' wrote A'Court, 'but General Pepe, notwithstanding the leading part he has played, cannot be highly rated on the score of discernment or ability.'

The last government had left a large reserve in gold, which the new one immediately proceeded to squander. Keppel Craven naïvely observed: 'Thirteen millions of ducats were found in the treasury, and not only afforded the new Cabinet the means of immediately raising the pay of the army, but relieved it from all those embarrassments which the want of pecuniary resources imposes on most incipient governments. This is not one of the least remarkable circumstances attending the Neapolitan revolution; as a flourishing exchequer is generally the firmest support of a despotic state, and the poverty of the one mostly precedes the downfall of the other.' The complete freedom of the press, decreed on July 26, allowed everybody to 'let off steam'. Zurlo was as ferociously attacked as Medici. The Carbonari wanted an entirely new government, 'neither agents of one tyrant, nor of the other'. Pasquale Borrelli, the chief of police, was tolerated in spite of his service under Murat. He showed exemplary tact and patience in dealing with excitable deputations of Carbonari, and usually succeeded in drowning them in his own superior rhetoric. Some of the extremists were for liquidating the King; it was Borrelli who frustrated their plot. On August 26 A'Court wrote: 'His Majesty sent last night for the French ambassador requesting to see him immediately. The ambassador went to the palace where he found the King in the most dreadful state of agitation. He had come in from Capodimonte, where he considered his life to be in the greatest danger. He said that he had certain intelligence that a plot was formed to put him to death, as well as the whole of his family. He knew that it had been discussed in the *Vendita*. The mildest proposal was to seize him and shut him up as a hostage. He had been advised by his old and confidential servants to devise means for escaping… His Majesty appeared dreadfully ill and agitated… He only wished, he said, to be removed to a place of safety, where he might spend the rest of his days in peace and tranquillity. His conscience reproached him with nothing. He had never had any other wish than the happiness of his people. If he had been mistaken or deceived, it was his misfortune, not his fault.' After a pessimistic analysis of the situation, A'Court concluded: 'I do not see the possibility of aiding him in any way. His departure, could we effect it, would be the signal for the massacre of the rest of the royal family… I am very much embarrassed what line to adopt under the circumstances.'

The British minister walked warily, knowing that Austria was bound to intervene. On July 25 Prince Metternich had informed the German Courts that Austria could not tolerate the revolution of Naples, and would send an army to suppress it if necessary. He had refused to see Prince Cariati, who had been sent as the new envoy to Vienna. Neither Prince Ruffo, the resident minister, nor Prince Castelcicala in Paris, would swear to the Constitution. After Cariati's failure, the Duke of Serracapriola brought a letter from the King to the Emperor of Austria, but no reply was vouchsafed. The Duke of Gallo, who was appointed to succeed Ruffo, was not allowed to cross the frontier. Prince Cimitile was equally rebuffed by the Tsar, but he had a private conversation with Metternich.[1] 'Although the Neapolitan revolution had been provoked by the Carbonari, it should nevertheless be considered as the work of the nation,' said Cimitile. 'While the form under which it had been effected might be blamed, it would be impossible to annul or

---

[1] Reported in a despatch dated August 29, 1820, from the Count of Caraman in Vienna to the Duke of Richelieu.

retract it.' Metternich replied: 'The present revolution at Naples is the work of a subversive sect; it is the product of surprise and violence. The sanction given by other Courts to such a revolution would help to spread its germs in other countries which are still free from them. The first duty and the first interest of foreign Powers is therefore to smother it in its cradle.' 'But my government desires to live in peace with all the world,' Cimitile rejoined, 'it will take great care not to meddle in the internal affairs of other states, and by its wisdom will strive to save the country from the calamities with which it is threatened. Under the circumstances why should the Emperor deprive us of the means of sustenance?' The Austrian chancellor smiled sarcastically. 'Indeed we should be grateful to the new government of Naples for its intention to refrain from a career of conquest!' he observed. 'But don't you see that if we were to proffer our hand, we should shatter the bases of your existence, and at the same time deprive your country of the only means that can save it from anarchy?' 'But what are these means of salvation?' Cimitile inquired. 'Will Your Highness deign to indicate them?' 'They consist in the return to and preservation for the future of the principles on which the tranquillity of states is founded. You may be certain that these principles will triumph, owing to our firm purpose to guard the old institutions against the assaults of innovators and sectarians.'

In pursuit of this policy Metternich summoned a conference of the allies at Troppau in October. Thus when the first constitutional parliament assembled on October 1 with pomp, oaths and speeches full of Carbonaro rhetoric, culminating in a heavy rainfall, omen of celestial displeasure, an assembly of the Allied Powers, from which Castlereagh was notably absent, was considering ways and means to destroy it. Pepe resigned his command of the army, but accepted the post of Inspector-General of the militia and the civic guard, which was almost the same thing. While he was on the worst of terms with General Carascosa, the Minister of War, he was strong in the support of the Carbonari, with whom he had decided to sink or swim. A'Court describes him parading the city 'at the head of an immense mob of people armed with guns, knives, sticks, clubs, swords, etc., carrying a tricolour flag which had previously received benediction from Carbonari priests, filling the streets with tumult and changing the cry of "King and Constitution" to that of "Liberty or Death"... Such disorderly conduct ought to have drawn down on him the indignation of the Vicar-General, and he was in fact summoned to the Council to receive the reprimand he so justly merited. He came; a few firm words were spoken; but the audience terminated rather in compliment than censure.' Since the plot against the King, the Duchess of Floridia had secretly appealed to A'Court for some British ships to safeguard the royal family, 'interspersing her story [of the King's danger] with pointed remarks on the Prince Vicar-General's apathy, who persisted in thinking there was no danger'. Two frigates duly appeared in the bay on October 6, to the King's relief and the Carbonari's rage. Officially Campochiaro, the minister for Foreign Affairs, was forced to ask for the ships to be withdrawn. Unofficially he pleaded with A'Court: 'For Heaven's sake, take no heed of the notes I am obliged to write to you about your squadron. If it leaves the bay we are all lost.' This illustrates the state of mind and nerves of many members of the government, even of those liberals who had served under Murat: they had only accepted their posts to ward off anarchy, and were continually harassed by libellous attacks. As for Pepe and the Carbonari, they were enjoying the fun while it lasted.

The proclamation of the Spanish Constitution in Naples had had immediate and violent repercussions in Sicily. The Sicilians had not been consulted. Possessing by right a Constitution of their own, they were not to be fobbed off with a new-fangled substitute from outside. They wanted a separate government. The news from Naples arrived during the festival of Saint Rosalia, and soon 'Independence' became the national cry. The Irish General Church, who had suppressed the worst brigands infesting Puglia, many of them Carbonari, had recently taken over the military command in Sicily, and he was made the scapegoat of the riots that followed. After being mobbed and almost murdered he escaped to Naples, where he was imprisoned for four months in the Castel dell' Ovo, thanks to the jealousy of Pepe and Carascosa. Civil war broke out, and a large force was sent from Naples to quell it under the command of General Florestano Pepe, Guglielmo's more capable brother. While Palermo was besieged and the inhabitants depended on the leniency of their opponents for their water supply, the spirited octogenarian Prince of Paternò negotiated its capitulation with General F. Pepe on October 5. It was agreed that the forts should be given up to the Neapolitan troops, that the Spanish Constitution should be accepted, and that the deputies of the people should be convoked to decide the question of unity or separation. These terms were obnoxious to the Carbonari of Naples; the government refused to ratify the treaty and sent General Colletta to replace Florestano Pepe, who was accused of acting contrary to his instructions. Colletta enforced submission.

'The proceedings in Parliament are hardly worth relating,' wrote A'Court. 'The members occupy themselves with anything except what really demands attention. They had a long debate last week, which was pushed to a division, whether God was, or was not the Legislator of the Universe. The question was decided in favour of the Deity by a small majority... The names of the provinces are all to be altered... The Asiatic pomp of the theatre of San Carlo, worthy only of a nation of slaves, has also excited the attention of these sturdy reformers. Colonel Pepe has submitted a motion to Parliament upon the subject which will probably lead to the abolition of this splendid establishment, the delight of the capital and the great attraction of strangers.'

While the parliamentarians were reviving the ineptitudes of the 1799 republicans, discussing whether to baptize the kingdom *Regno Italico Meridionale* and substitute Parthenope for Naples and Cortes, appropriately Spanish, for Parliament, etc., the original members of the Holy Alliance were promulgating the Protocol of Troppau, according to which: 'States which have undergone a change of government due to revolution, the result of which threatens other states, *ipso facto* cease to be members of the European Alliance, and remain excluded from it until their situation gives guarantee for legal order and stability... If, owing to such alterations, immediate danger threatens other states, the Powers bind themselves by peaceful means, or, if need be, by arms, to bring back the guilty state into the bosom of the Great Alliance.' The British government repudiated these principles, which would constitute the allies 'the armed guardians of all thrones', but admitted the individual right of Austria to interfere at Naples. The Tsar, however, had renounced his liberal principles. Before resorting to armed intervention Metternich decided to give the King a chance to escape, since he had received a secret letter from him in which he expressed his desire to leave his kingdom and to resume absolute power with the help of the Austrian army. As soon as he was free, the King might act as mediator between his kingdom and Europe. Whatever happened, the principle of legitimacy must be saved. The conference was adjourned, and in the meantime three letters were despatched from the Emperor of Austria, the Tsar, and the King of Prussia, dated November 20, 1820, inviting him to confer with them at Laibach, and 'reconcile the interest and welfare of his people with the duties of the allied monarchs towards their states and the world'.

The King received these letters on December 6, and in his eagerness to accept he sent an elaborate message to Parliament explaining his reasons for doing so. 'I am resolved,' he wrote, 'to sacrifice my every inclination to perform a duty that may avert the curse of war from my subjects. I shall do all to secure for you a wise and liberal Constitution.' But the essentials he defined resembled the French Constitution rather than the Spanish, and the verdict of the special committee appointed to scrutinize the King's message was unfavourable. Unless the King agreed to support the Spanish Constitution the Parliament would not allow him to leave. Knowing that some of the Carbonari were ready to detain him by force, the King pretended that this was just what he meant. After further deliberation the Parliament relented on December 13, when the King hastily embarked on H.M.S. *Le Vengeur* which A'Court had placed at his disposal. The Carbonari had been more turbulent than usual: after presenting the King's message to Parliament the ministry had had to resign under a hail of accusations. The reasonable and moderate Zurlo could not make himself heard in a menagerie of demagogues. Gallo, embittered by the fall of his French idols, still pompous and puffed up with self-importance, took over the portfolio of Foreign Affairs, but the new ministry could do little more than show its medals. Parliamentary deputations went to remind the King of his duty to maintain the Spanish Constitution until the instant he sailed: they pursued him like the Eumenides on board *Le Vengeur*. 'They even come here to tweak my nose!' he grumbled, using a ruder expression in the vernacular. He seemed predestined to meet rough weather at sea, but he felt safer with the elements than with the Carbonari. De Nicola says that on boarding the ship he knelt and kissed the deck. Battered by the blast, *Le Vengeur* was detained at Baia, but early on the 16th she sailed for Leghorn, followed by another vessel containing the Duchess of Floridia. The King landed at Leghorn on December 21 and spent a week in Florence with his nephew, the Grand Duke of Tuscany, to relax before the strenuous journey to Laibach. The Duchess arrived later; she was to stay in Florence until his return. The King wrote to her nearly every day, and these letters have since been published: they describe the minute incidents of his journey in homely language. Instead of a fierce reactionary thirsting for vengeance, they reveal a placid conscience. It is obvious that Ferdinand was convinced that he was doing his best for his people, whom he always regarded as members of his family. His aches and pains vanished: he soon recovered his former zest. In a cheerful letter, on Christmas Eve, he wrote that when he was about to retire for some badly needed sleep some importunate visitors arrived, but two of these were most opportune: 'Two guardian angels sent by the Lord in His infinite mercy, to wit Blacas, who had come expressly from Rome, and Lebzeltern, the soul of Metternich, who had come from Troppau. I conferred with these till half-past ten with the utmost satisfaction, and went to bed at eleven after swallowing some broth. I slept fairly well until five, and the morning passed like a moment as I was intent on the very interesting business I am going to negotiate.' From other sources we learn that the King had been too outspoken. He had told Lord Burghersh, the British minister, that the concessions and pledges he had contracted with the Neapolitan revolutionaries had only been extorted from him by violence, and that therefore he did not consider them at all binding, as in case of refusal he would have been assassinated. It had been through Blacas, Louis XVIII's favourite, that Ferdinand had corresponded with his faithful henchmen Castelcicala and Ruffo, and had protested to other sovereigns against what he had been forced to do at Naples. Hence his reference to the guardian angels.

Already he felt safe and sound. After hunting at Poggio a Caiano he set off for Bologna, but was held up by snow at the old Medicean villa of Cafaggiolo, an ice-box, a Siberia, as he calls it; however, his room was being 'Christianized by a blazing fire'. At Modena he stayed with the Duke and Duchess, 'most amiable and affectionate; the two brothers are in entire agreement about our concerns and full of enthusiasm for the true general good, as they assure me both Emperors are (of Austria and Russia).' He was delighted to renew acquaintance with the Hungarian regiment which had escorted him from Portici to Naples six years ago; and at Vicenza he met General Frimont, the Austrian Commander-in-Chief, whom he liked immensely. The moustaches of his hussars put those of 'our young gentlemen' to shame. Far from complaining of the cold, he found it an excellent remedy for his catarrh, but his hands were covered with chilblains, as when Casanova had kissed them in his childhood. He reached Laibach on January 8, 1821. Metternich wrote: 'This is the third time I am putting King Ferdinand on his feet, and he has the bad habit of tumbling. In 1821 he still imagines that the throne is an easy chair to sprawl and fall asleep in.' But in Laibach the Austrian stoves nearly suffocated him and prevented him from sleeping, besides they were bad for his catarrh, and he suffered from certain cramps which he called 'crabs'. It was a very damp city where you seldom saw the sun, he told Lucia; and his only occupation and amusement was to attend to the present business. In the evenings he played piquet with his old crony the Prince of Ruoti, who never minded losing to his august partner.

The Congress opened on January 11 in an atmosphere of harmony: Ferdinand thanked the assembled monarchs for their anxiety to pacify his kingdom, and asked them for a frank declaration as to how they proposed to achieve this. After a leisurely interval he informed his son the Regent of his prosperous journey and good health, and that his setters had beaten those of the Emperor of Russia. Though his letters contained no allusion to politics, they were communicated to Parliament in order to allay the general impatience. On January 28 he wrote that the sovereigns of the Holy Alliance were determined to employ force to restore the *status quo,* if persuasion was of no avail; and that it had been beyond his power and human possibility to obtain any other result. Should this letter produce the effect he desired—and it was to be given the widest publicity so that everybody should realize the state of emergency— it was the Regent's duty to maintain order until the King changed the administration. The Regent received this on February 9, when the Russian, Austrian and Prussian ministers presented him with letters from their sovereigns simultaneously, repeating that the revolution of Naples had endangered the peace of Italy and Europe, and that an Austrian army, supported by a Russian, was approaching the kingdom, as friends if the people returned to their former obedience, but as foes if they remained intractable. The Regent replied that Parliament would have to be consulted, and the Parliament, swept by a frolic wind of bellicose enthusiasm, fanned frantically by General Guglielmo Pepe and the Carbonari, declared for war. Considering Murat's complete rout by the Austrians in which Pepe himself had been involved, and that the Carbonari had destroyed all discipline in the army, Pepe's pugnacity can only be explained as the desperation of a gambler. Two armies were hastily collected under Generals Carascosa and Pepe, the former to defend the Garigliano, the latter the Abruzzi. The Regent, as honorary Commander-in-Chief, predicted their swift collapse.

General Frimont, the Austrian Commander-in-Chief, told his troops that they were entering a friendly country and should treat the inhabitants well, and the King issued a proclamation that he was returning to his beloved subjects to restore order in a spirit of benevolence; the Austrians were allies. Desertions already began, and soon gathered momentum. On March 7 Pepe risked an engagement with the Austrian advance guard at Rieti, and his troops disbanded before the battle had begun. This defeat caused further desertion on a larger scale. On the 15th Pepe returned a fugitive to Naples. The brave Filangieri wrote bitterly to his commander Carascosa: 'The Neapolitan Generals cannot die otherwise than at the hands of their own soldiers, since we have reached a point at which the unfortunate officers of all ranks will never succeed in seeing the enemy, not even with a field-glass.' On the 13th the Parliament proposed submission to the King, and only twenty-six deputies supported Giuseppe Poerio's protest against the destruction of the Constitution before it closed its doors and a notice 'To Let' was posted over them. On the 18th D'Ambrosio surrendered Capua and signed a convention suspending hostilities; on the 23rd the imperial troops marched into Naples, and the masses cheered for Ferdinand as if the Constitution had been an evil dream.

The Carbonari leaders had fled. The Regent's position had been that of a tight rope walker; though the dynasty came first in his thoughts he was in favour of an amended Constitution, and could not approve of his father's cringing to Austria. Before their collapse some thirty Carbonari, led by the Grand Master Manfredi, had kidnapped the ex-chief of police Giampietro not far from his house and stabbed him to death with forty-two dagger thrusts. A label inscribed 'Number One' was significantly attached to his corpse. Zurlo, Medici, Tommasi and others who had cause to fear the same end escaped. Now it was the turn of the Good Cousins to flee, and the Regent, who loathed excesses, afforded them every assistance. Pepe was given papers as minister to the United States and eventually went to London; Gallo obtained passports for others from A'Court, who was anxious to efface 'the stain of blood upon our character here' which had been left by the events of 1799.

XXXVI

Canosa again Minister of Police— The King's return to Naples—Canosa's conflict with the Austrians and retirement—Medici and Tommasi reinstated—The King attends the Congress of Verona and proceeds to Vienna—Lady Blessington on Neapolitan society—Medici's burdens—Ferdinand's serene old age—A water-fête for the Empress Marie Louise—The King's sudden death.

The dear old King—seventy was then considered old—was in no particular hurry to return to his capital until it had been cleansed of constitutional dross. He had borrowed the money for his journey to Florence from the Emperor Francis, who issued instructions that it was to be repaid out of the Rothschild loan. For the costs of the Austrian expedition and of the maintenance of an Austrian army were to be borne by the Two Sicilies, and Carl Rothschild went to Naples to negotiate a loan which would provide the necessary security. In their martial fervour the Constitutionalists had not dreamt of anything so crassly material, whereas the Austrian Finance Minister Stadion had promptly pointed out that 'the declaration of war by Naples without a shot having been fired is sufficient ground for us to claim our right to indemnity from the date when our troops crossed the Po'. General Frimont sent messages urging the King to return, but he encountered the same obstinacy as Acton and Paget had in the past. The King appointed a provisional government under the stalwart Circello, but its powers were limited. The Hereditary Prince showed A'Court the list of ministers. 'Such a choice was never before heard of!' exclaimed the British envoy. 'Hardly one under seventy years of age, or with talent or capacity enough to govern even a village.' The Duke of Calabria had withdrawn into melancholy seclusion. When Metternich complained that this state of things could not continue, the Prince of Canosa stepped into the breach. Again the King appointed him Minister of Police; the Duke of Blacas and Prince Ruffo, who was Metternich's Neapolitan shadow, both approved of the choice. Here was a man above suspicion of radical sympathies, and he gave promise of vigour. A financial expert was still required. Ruffo proposed Medici, but neither the King nor Canosa would hear of him. 'My poor loyalists!' said the King to Canosa. 'Twice they have made me neglect you, but now that you are going to Naples you must raise a wall to separate the good from the bad. By bad I do not mean merely those who have been active, but also those who seem suspicious to your smell.'

Canosa was greeted in Naples with shouts of 'Long live the King! Long live the Prince of Canosa!' betwixt appeals to lower the price of bread. By coincidence the price was lowered, as the government had purchased a fresh supply of corn, and Canosa got the credit for it. His first task was to punish those who had taken direct or indirect part in the revolution of July 1820, amnesty those who had joined the constitutional movement after the King's capitulation and forget the rest. But Canosa wished to be more thorough, to regenerate the ruling class by eliminating all who had been Jacobins, then Muratists and then Constitutionalists; and reinstate those who had been consistently loyal to the King. In a few hours he had purged his own department; unfortunately the Bourbonists he employed were none too respectable. His pet project was to create an international police to stamp out subversive sects, but such friends as Count Apponyi, the Austrian minister in Rome, pointed out that the time was not ripe for so sublime a scheme.[1] For the present he had to content himself with rough-and-ready chastisements: for Carbonari he prescribed the whip. Contempt and ridicule, he said, were the best medicine for these moral infirmities. Since the majority joined the sects through fanatical vanity, a humiliating punishment was indicated. He applied it on the same day he took office. A doctor who was caught with tell-tale emblems and patents was given a public thrashing. As the culprit seemed a respectable bourgeois the mob went wild with glee: loud cheers for Canosa, the right man for the right job! The Austrians, oddly enough, did not approve of such methods. But Canosa took no notice of General Frimont's protest and proceeded to order the thrashing of another Carbonaro. He was about to inflict the same remedy on a sergeant of the mounted guard who had 'belched indignities against the government', when the Austrian minister, Count Ficquelmont, intervened, and Circello had to humour such

---

[1] The International Criminal Police Commission, known as 'Interpol', was founded in Vienna in 1923.

an ally. Canosa was incensed. So was the King, who wrote to him: 'I understood that the method of the whip and beatings had been adopted for those found with Carbonari emblems, and was sorry to hear that you have suspended both these measures... I believe that the whip is very apt to make the sectarians despised and degraded, and that beating is a useful corrective, and that both should be adopted throughout the whole kingdom.'

On May 9 the Duke of Calabria left Caserta for Rome to assure his father that everything was ready for his return. Countess de Boigne has related in her *Memoirs* that her friend Pozzo di Borgo, who was present at their meeting, gave her a comic account of their conversation. 'In Italy things are called by their names without circumlocution. And it was of their "accursed fright" that the father and son discoursed freely. "What, you were frightened! It was I who was really frightened." "No, dear Majesty, that was nothing. It was since your departure that I became really frightened." And they went on to narrate all the degrees, all the effects, of this terrible *paura* with a candour which left their audience completely cold. Pozzo told me: "After leaving this interview my colleagues and I dared not face each other for twenty-four hours." Prince Metternich has an anecdote on the same subject which depends on a combination of *lazzarone* pantomime with the old King's jargon for its full flavour. Ferdinand spoke to him constantly at Laibach about *questa maladetta paura*—"this accursed terror". As the minister's impassibility persuaded the King that he did not appreciate the full significance of this motive power, he asked him one day if he knew what this *paura* meant. When M. de Metternich replied somewhat disdainfully, the King explained with the utmost bonhomie: "No... no, that's not it... I shall tell you [*ve lo dirò io*]... It is a certain thing [*una certa cosa*] which seizes you there!"—putting his hand on top of his head as if to twist it. "And which clutches the brain and makes it jump until you think it will gush out of your head. Then it goes down to the stomach... you think you are about to faint— you seem to die..." And he placed both his hands on his stomach. "Then it goes lower down." (And both hands followed.) "One feels the devil of a pain and then... then... brebre brebre..." Loosening his hands he ended his physiological description with an expressive gesture.' The Nestor of Monarchs had carried the analysis of fear to a fine art. To paralyse the sects Canosa had to work without fetters, but the Austrians kept invoking the law, a Neapolitan version of the

Code Napoléon which the Minister of Police abominated as an offspring of Satan. As for lawyers, they had a thousand shifts for saving criminals from execution. But the Austrians felt that the eye of Europe was fixed on Naples; as the champions of legitimacy against revolution they were sensitive to criticism. The Minister of Police was giving them a bad name. Ficquelmont asked if the provisional government knew about Canosa's constant arrests, and if the prisoners were put on trial. The government's answer did not satisfy him: he said Austria would never support illegal measures which could not pacify the country. Canosa obligingly sent him a list of those he had arrested, explaining that they had not been tried because the tribunals were composed of Muratists who would have 'canonized notorious culprits as innocent'. The ministers of the Northern Courts (Austria, Russia and Prussia) who were to supervise Ferdinand's restoration on behalf of their sovereigns, decided that Canosa was being drawn by excess of zeal 'towards measures more qualified to ruin than to promote the King's interests'.

In spite of these animadversions, the King was so well pleased with Canosa's cleansing of the Augean Stables that he returned to his capital on May 15 amid suitable rejoicings. Besides the illuminations and triumphal arches, a brilliant 'transparency' opposite the royal palace represented a full-size image of Ferdinand receiving the keys of the city with that of Saint Francis of Paola above him. The people, he reflected, would always be fond of him, whatever happened, and it was a comfort to feel that his affection for them was reciprocated. It was a greater comfort to be protected against 'those others' by the smart well-disciplined Austrians, whose whiskers were so superior to those of the horrid Carbonari. Now he could enjoy the illusions of autocracy in his serene old age. Canosa had been very useful, but he could not last much longer. All the foreign ministers were in league against him except Blacas. To appease them, the King ordered Canosa to draft a decree of amnesty. In doing so he was careful to leave a loop hole for the arrest of Carbonari who had not been compromised between July 2 and 8, 1820. The text was sent to Circello only three hours before publication to elude diplomatic interference. Ficquelmont protested. Canosa replied that not all the Carbonari could be included in the amnesty: many of the most dangerous were still at large. Ficquelmont parried this with the argument that if they were dangerous they would soon give him a fresh opportunity to arrest them.

Canosa modified the decree, but not sufficiently to the taste of the Austrian minister.

The King complained to Ruffo that 'little by little the Austrians wish to meddle in everything'. Poor Canosa was trying to do his best, but he could not do all that was necessary because he was hampered by their perverse insinuations. A secret agent called Barattelli had furnished General Frimont with plausible evidence that Canosa had been helping to revive the Calderari. Frimont denounced this to the Council of Foreign Ministers on June 9, and Ficquelmont observed to Circello that royalists should appear in broad daylight, not at dark conventicles. Though Canosa asserted that an Austrian agent had been distributing patents for the so-called sect, the King's confidence in him had been shaken, and Ficquelmont noted with satisfaction that Canosa, surrounded by traps, was getting panicky. 'My candid and loyal conduct,' wrote Canosa to Circello, 'should place me above all calumny and suspicion. Even in Florence I told His Majesty that earth and hell would be let loose against me. The sectarians have plenty of money, and connexions everywhere. I am serving in this tempest for the glory of God and the King. However, I am very ready to renounce my charge...'

The Duke of Calabria was also at grips with Canosa. The Prussian minister informed his sovereign that 'he neglected no means of saving the revolutionary chiefs from the punishment they deserved and pleaded their cause openly in the King's council, where Canosa durst not open his mouth without being snubbed by the Prince'. The Hereditary Prince had insisted on the release of the four ex-deputies Arcovito, Borrelli, Pedrinelli and Poerio, who had been imprisoned for more than two months. But nothing could satisfy the ministers of the Northern Courts, who considered that it would be wiser to send them out of the country. Canosa told Borrelli that the King, while obliged to him and his colleagues for their good behaviour during the revolution, was constrained by Austria to banish them. Borrelli repeated this to Ficquelmont, who indignantly demanded an explanation. Canosa became more embroiled and had to resign on July 28. The King, who shared his opinions, was grieved to let him go. He did not let him go altogether, for he appointed him a counsellor of state. 'He will do less harm there than in the police,' Ficquelmont told Metternich, 'but he will still do harm.'

Two general commissioners were now substituted for the Minister of Police, one for the capital and one for the provinces: the unscrupulous Austrian agent Barattelli became commissioner for the provinces. Barattelli delved into Canosa's private life and spread libels about his liaison at Pisa with a rag-picker's daughter, by whom he had three children. A battle of scurrilous pamphlets ensued in which Canosa held his own, but he was outflanked and outnumbered by the ministers of the Northern Courts, who wanted Medici to be recalled. Carl Rothschild agreed with Ficquelmont that Medici was the only man who could restore material prosperity. Canosa was the chief obstacle to Medici's return. To avoid such an obnoxious appointment, the King offered Ruffo, his minister in Vienna, the portfolio of Foreign Affairs. Since Canosa had only one foreign supporter, Blacas, Metternich proceeded to flatter the Frenchman's vanity and cajole him into his point of view. Blacas, with his delicate tact, might prevail on the King to change the ministry on his own initiative: a stable government under a *philosophe* like Medici would benefit France as well as Austria. Convinced by these arguments, Blacas began to negotiate with Medici and Tommasi—the pair were still inseparable—on February 15, 1822. They would only accept if Canosa were banished and the King stated in writing that he did not believe Canosa's libels against them in *I Piffari di Montagna* ('The Mountain Pipes'). The King approved of their programme, which was to be a revised version of the Quinquennium which the Carbonari had brought to grief; he agreed to remove Canosa; but he refused to make any statement about 'The Mountain Pipes', which he regarded as a private affair. Medici and Tommasi were so tenacious of this latter stipulation that the King was obliged to yield on June 1. In the meantime he bade Canosa a fond farewell. The fallen minister never forgot the King's heartbroken tone as he clasped his hand tightly and said: 'My son, I suffer so much, try to suffer too without adding to my sorrows!'

The King's sorrows were sincere though they were not very deep. He had the greatest repugnance to taking Medici back, for it was hard to forgive his baneful apathy during the Quinquennium. Tommasi returned as Minister of Justice, General Clary took over the police with Intonti as prefect, and Prince Alvaro Ruffo left Vienna, his spiritual home, to take over Foreign Affairs. If the King groaned now and then over his vassalage, his frequent notes to the Duchess of Floridia are singularly free from shadows of any kind. Like his youthful letters to his father, they are full of the game he had shot. Pheasants at Caserta, wild boars at Carditello, the lists continue. 'A day of Paradise,' he observes, after a successful shoot. And he retires early to bed in order to rise with the birds and for the birds on the morrow. But in October he had to tear himself away from these pleasures, since he had been invited to the Congress of Verona. He had always disliked public business and he was tired of travel, but he wished to be master at home before he died. The cost of the Austrian occupation was a heavy burden: he hoped to reduce it if not get rid of it altogether.

He left Naples on October 22 followed at two days' interval by his wife. Once he had uprooted himself he became impervious to the fatigue of the journey: from Verona he went to Vienna; and he even thought of going to Paris to visit his daughter and granddaughter, the widowed Duchess of Berry. The affairs of his kingdom did not take much time at the Congress: it was decided that the army of occupation should be reduced to 35,000 men, 'who would remain until public tranquillity was fully restored and the Neapolitan army was reorganized'. The Spanish question predominated, and the Congress was again in favour of military intervention. Five months later a French army of 95,000 men under the Duke of Angoulême crossed the Bidassoa, and Ferdinand VII was restored to absolute power, while nearly all the supporters of the Constitution were sentenced to death. Canosa's reaction had been milk and water to this. Of the military deserters who started the Neapolitan revolution only Morelli and Salvati were executed. The King pardoned twenty-eight of the thirty sentenced to death by the supreme court after three months' deliberation. Colletta rings down the curtain of his history on a scene of violence, persecution and cruelty which would have delighted an Elizabethan audience at the Globe. Artistically this is most effective, but Colletta was not there. He had been exiled, but not to the wilds of Africa as the reader might infer. It was in a charming Florentine villa, as the guest of Gino Capponi, that he penned these lurid pages.

From Verona the King proceeded to snow-clad Vienna where he was afraid his dearest Lucia might suffer from the cold, for it was several degrees below zero and even the Viennese said it was exceptional. Baroness du Montet saw him often that winter at brilliant Court balls and concerts. 'He seemed to enjoy himself tremendously here,' she wrote. 'His figure is patriarchal and very dignified without being majestic; his high stature, his fine white hair, his pronounced and venerable features would make him respected in whatever class of society he had been born. In a peasant's cottage or in the garb of a simple fisherman, one could not help honouring him as a grand old man. He speaks very loud and laughs uproariously; at the theatre, and especially at the Italian opera, he applauds with a ringing voice and beats time vigorously on the ledge of his box; at a performance of *The Barber of Seville* he shouted, "*Bravo, lazzarone, bravo!*", in his enthusiasm for Lablache, who used to sing one of the airs in *The Barber* in so astonishing a manner. The actor was delighted by the King's exclamation, which he had heard perfectly.

'The King of Naples is very devout; he fasts with extreme austerity, tells his rosary every day, and often listens to sermons. He has brought his confessor with him. This is a venerable and even very handsome Capuchin who refused the lodging prepared for him at Court to stay in a cell of the Capuchin convent. The King went to the crypt of this church to visit the tomb of the Queen, his wife. He is a stubborn man, and it is very difficult to make him change his mind. He rises very early in the morning, hears Mass, says a great many prayers, dines at midday, takes a nap, then plays cards for fairly high stakes with his favourites, from whom he exacts punctual payment within twenty-four hours, without any remission. The Duchess of Floridia, his wife, keeps somewhat different hours from the King under the pretext of health. She is a little woman, still pretty and very well preserved, plump and dark, who shows infinite tact in her public relations with the King and the imperial family, never above nor beneath the dignity of a king's wife, without the title of Queen. The King gives her magnificent presents; her jewels are fabulous, her diamonds superb; she is generally very well spoken of.

'The King of Naples has a passionate love of the chase, and he is provided with every variety. This reminds me of an old story going back to his first visit to Vienna, almost thirty years ago. He had heard that there were bears in the neighbourhood of Laibach, and he expressed his desire to see them hunted. They did not know how to satisfy him; finally they thought of procuring a performing bear, which used to dance wonderfully, and letting it loose in the woods. They purchased it from its leader, removed its chains, and got ready for the hunt. The poor bear did not go far; accustomed to noise and music, almost tame since youth, it approached at the sound of the horn and, seeing the King's gun pointed at it, imagined that this was the signal for a jig, and began to dance. The King fired and, overcome with joy at having killed a bear, exclaimed: "*O carissima bestia!*"' Baroness du Montet continued to be impressed: it was impossible, she said, for anyone to look more venerable than the King of Naples. 'The extreme affection of this hoary monarch for his children and relations is absolutely touching: his fatherly caresses of the Prince of Salerno, whom he calls his *fanciullo* [little boy] in spite of his colossal size, and the Prince's respectful and tender attentions for his august father, are truly admirable. The King of Naples has not royal majesty, but that of patriarchal old age.'

The King returned to his capital on August 6, 1823, after an absence of over eight months. His domestic circle widened; more and more grandchildren appeared—the Bourbons of Naples were steadfastly prolific—and Ferdinand delighted in them all without ever relaxing his benevolent autocracy. His heir was now aged forty-six, but he was still treated like a somewhat irresponsible juvenile. The vast portrait of the Duke of Calabria's family paying homage to a bust of Ferdinand with Vesuvius in the background, painted by Giuseppe Cammarano, is a delectable illustration of his domestic *pietas*. But he was always slightly afraid of his papa, whose temper had not lost its sharp edge. The Prince of Salerno, who was prone to extravagance, solicited his stepmother's mediation when he was short of money, since the King refused nothing to Lucia. The King always sent the Duchess part of his winnings at cards, which he called his tribute. His anxiety about her health was touching. 'Your letter comforted me,' he wrote, 'and I was glad to hear of the good effect of the castor-oil taken this morning.' The poor lady still suffered from liver, which is not surprising if she did justice to the quantity of game, fruit and dainties, such as hare sausage, fattened quails and sweets of *ricotta*, which he was always sending her. His own health remained florid until the end. His aspect became more venerable. 'The wicked shall flourish like the green bay-tree,' his enemies quoted.

The polyglot society of Naples at this period has best been described by the velvety Lady Blessington in *The Idler in Italy*. The Archbishop of Taranto still presided over a posse of cultured cosmopolitans: 'Russian, German, French, Italian and English might all be heard spoken in the same salon last evening, when the visitants were scattered in groups examining the various objects of virtu that ornament the apartment.' Here she met: '*Son Altesse Royale*, the Prince Gustave of Mecklenburg Schwerin, the Duchesse de Plaisance and her daughter:... General Count Howguitz, who at present commands the Austrian troops here; the Russian Count Benckendorf, brother to the Countess Lieven, Ambassadress from Russia to our Court; Sir William Gell, some Neapolitans; and though last, not least Casimir Delavigne the poet, and his brother.' The English residents asserted themselves with an eccentricity fast becoming extinct. Among those who emerge most vividly from Lady Blessington's circle is Sir William Gell, the topographer of Pompeii, whom she called the laughing philosopher, so gouty at the age of forty-five that he had to be supported by two men when he walked, yet with a taste for gaudy apparel that vied with Count D'Orsay's, and with an appetite unimpaired by his painful disease. He was generally considered the most learned of cicerones, but his learning was spiced with jovial humour, and no wonder, in the company of such epicurean sight-seers as the Blessingtons. Thus, after an archological morning at Pompeii: 'The Forum Vinalia was the spot fixed on for our halting-place; and, on arriving there, we found a *recherché* collation spread on the tables, shaded by weeping willows, the bright foliage of which formed an agreeable protection against the scorching rays of the sun. The table covered with snowy napkins, and piled with every dainty of the united *cuisine à l'anglaise, française* and Neapolitan; from the simple cold roasted meats and poultry, to the delicate *aspics, mayonnaises, galantine de volaille, pains de lièvre aux pistaches, pâtés de Pithiviers, salades de homard et d'anchois*, and *la Poutarga*, down to all the tempting *friandises à la napolitaine*, formed as picturesque an object to the sight, as a tempting one to the palate. Sir William Gell was eloquent in his praises of our superiority over the ancients in the noble science of gastronomy; asserted that Pompeii never before saw so delicious a *déjeuner à la fourchette*, and only wished that a triclinium was added to the luxuries, that he might recline while indulging in them...'

Keppel Craven was Gell's boon companion, a dilettante musician and comic actor, also addicted to fancy waistcoats. Countess Anna Potocka describes him as victimized by his mother, the Margravine of Anspach, with whom he lived at Posillipo. 'Since the Margrave's death she remained in mourning, but she always wore a rose as well as the cross of a decoration which I suspect the Margrave invented for her. Short, wrinkled and very thin, she seemed like a painted mummy under the heavy layer of powder and rouge with which she had coated her face... Mr Fox, whom she treated as a cousin, had become used to her ill-articulated words and had gathered a whole collection of anecdotes which I enjoyed hearing him relate, so comical were they owing to their naïve vanity. She honestly believed that she had offered the world a rare blend of superior wit, vast learning, profound wisdom, all crowned by creative genius. She affirmed very seriously that Rossini owed his reputation to her, that his best operas were copied from those which she had composed at Anspach, where she amused herself directing the Italian company which the Margrave kept in his castle. "That was a very minor service," she said, "compared with those I rendered my husband in inspiring his policy during the wars of the Empire."

'She also said that she alone, in the council, always stood for neutrality, while so many imprudent kings compromised their throne by misplaced presumption. Thanks to her wise advice, the Margrave's flag was always respected, even in the stormiest moments.

'His vast states having been sold to the King of Prussia, she deemed it proper to transport his ashes to England... But when she had his coffin opened to bid a last farewell to her beloved husband, some rats emerged which had feasted on the Margrave. She had this new sort of regicide killed, but as they contained portions of the unfortunate prince, she caused them to be buried in the same tomb. It is impossible to conceive the solemn manner with which she recounted all these details.'

Then there was the dashing General Church, with his weird yarns of the Vardarelli and Ciro Annichiarico, the brigand-priest who founded the Decisi, that gruesome society, whose first condition of membership was that the candidate must have committed two murders with his own hand, and whose decrees and patents were written in blood. The latter were adorned with skulls and crossbones, and their four corners were inscribed: Sorrow, Death, Terror and Mourning. Having captured so many of these outlaws, General Church could curdle your blood very pleasantly over the nuts and wine. He introduced General Florestano Pepe to the Blessingtons, far milder than Church, but 'a flaming apostle of liberty'. The Duke of Roccaromana struck Lady Blessington as 'the very personification of a *preux chevalier*, brave in arms, and gentle and courteous in society... Though advanced in years (report states him to be nearly sixty), his military bearing, and the elasticity of his spirits, give him the appearance of being at least twenty years younger.' 'The devotion of some of the Neapolitan officers to Murat was very touching, and failed not till the last,' she wrote. 'They are now permitted to live free from molestation here; but have not been employed by the present government.'

No doubt Lady Blessington was a somewhat superficial observer, but during the two and a half years she spent in Naples she led a highly civilized existence, associating with many of the most cultured Neapolitans, including Piazzi the astromomer. For all her Byronic sentiment and fashionable poses, she had a sound substratum of common sense. She doted on Count D'Orsay and shared his Bonapartist views, so that she consorted with Muratists rather than Bourbonists. Yet she had to confess: 'We are told that the Italians writhe under the despotism of their rulers; but nowhere have I seen such happy faces. Men, women and children, all appear to feel the influence of the delicious atmosphere in which they live; an atmosphere that seems to exclude care and sorrow.'

The King began to feel the loss of many old ministers and cronies. Circello and the Duke of Ascoli had died, and he had a dismal presentiment of his own sudden death since his return from Vienna. He tried to hurry the building of the Church of Saint Francis of Paola, sighing, 'I shall never see it completed!' In one of his notes to Lucia he mentions his hypochondria; in another that he had been troubled by a series of fantastic dreams; but 'the tonic of the chase in the open air' soon dissipated such distempers.

Medici bore the responsibility of government, and made frantic efforts to reduce the army of occupation. At least he was a stubborn accountant, and succeeded in reducing their maintenance expenses. He peppered Ficquelmont with notes explaining the urgency of relieving the financial situation, for it had leaked out that the Austrian government had saved some six and a half million florins out of the sums extorted from Naples. The deficit was growing to such an extent that Metternich sent Count Apponyi to investigate it. 'Cavaliere de Medici,' he reported, 'regards the presence of our troops as nothing but an intolerable burden, and as Finance Minister he trembles at the idea that the foreign occupation might last until after 1826, and, by compelling him to take refuge in a further loan, still further increase the state's terrifying deficit. This caused him to say to Rothchild a few days ago: "If the Austrain troops remain here after the limit of time fixed by the Convention, I am determined to hand in my resignation."' Fortunately Rothschild agreed with Medici on this qustion; but the Emperor Francis and Metternich did not decide to evacuate Naples till December 1826.

After all, the Austrians would never have come back if Medici had curbed the Carbonari. The King grumbled, but he regarded them as a necessary luxury. The habits of a long lifetime were safeguarded. They were simple habits; and there was as little ceremony and constraint in the King's circle as in that of Lady Blessington. Seeing him at the opera she remarked: 'The King seems to be as partial to dancers as to singers, for he applauded Mademoiselle le Gros last night, quite as rapturously as he had done Madame Fodore, half an hour before. I can sympathize with the love of music in an old man, but a love of dancing in a sexagenarian has something unseemly in it.' Actually he was in his seventy-third year. She saw him again at the Villa Favorita: 'He wore a grey frock coat, high boots, and a broad-leafed hat. He looked the very picture of a respectable farmer: his tall and muscular figure touched, but not bent by age; his clear and ruddy complexion offering a pleasing contrast to the snowy locks and whiskers that edged his cheeks. His Majesty had scarcely entered the garden, when two of the undergardeners ran up to him with the demonstrations of the liveliest joy, and seizing the royal hands kissed them repeatedly with a hearty warmth. The good-natured monarch permitted the familiarity with an air of benevolence very gratifying to witness, and smiled complacently at the vehement benedictions of his humble admirers, as, with light but firm step, he walked from flower-bed to flower-bed, examining all.'

If the King did not grow younger, he grew no sadder: he lived for the passing moment without regrets. 'Let us not talk of the heat,' he wrote to Lucia in August, 'because it is general, and we must endure it with patience.' His granddaughter Marie Louise, Napoleon's widow, came to visit him that summer, and he entertained her with suitable splendour. She, too, had been scarcely touched by the tragic events in which she had been involved. 'A less interesting-looking woman I have seldom beheld,' wrote Lady Blessington. But she described the water-fête given in her honour as one of the most beautiful scenes imaginable. 'A rich stream of music announced the coming of the royal pageant; and proceeded from a gilded barge, to which countless lamps were attached, giving it, when seen at a distance, the appearance of a vast shell of topaz, floating on a sea of sapphire. It was filled with musicians, attired in the most glittering liveries; and every stroke of the oars kept time to the music, and sent forth a silvery light from the water which they rippled. This illuminated and gilded barge was followed by another, adorned by a silken canopy, from which hung curtains of the richest texture, partly drawn back to admit the balmy air. Cleopatra, when she sailed down the Cydnus, boasted not a more beautiful vessel; and as it glided over the sea, it seemed excited into motion by the music that preceded it, so perfectly did it keep time to the delicious sounds, leaving behind it a silvery track like the memory of happiness. The King himself steered the vessel; his tall and slight figure gently curved, and his snowy locks falling over ruddy cheeks, show that age has bent but not broken him. He looked simple, though he appears like one born to command; a hoary Neptune, steering over his native element: all eyes were fixed on him; but his, steadily followed the glittering barge that preceded him. Marie-Louise was the only person in the King's boat; she was richly dresseed, and seemed pleased with the pageant. Innumerable vessels, filled with the lords and ladies of the Court, followed, but intruded not on the privacy of the royal bark, which glided before us like some gay vision or dream.'

Omnia vanitas! It is unlikely that any thought of Maria Carolina or of Bonaparte came to vex either of the protagonists of this starry *fête galante*. Count Neipperg and the Duchess of Floridia were following the royal barge, the morganatic husband and the morganatic wife. The hoary Neptune was proud of his steering. If only Nelson were there to see him! Perhaps Neipperg's black patch evoked that long-forgotten deliverer. The new British minister was called Hamilton, a relative of old Sir William; but Bentinck had prejudiced Ferdinand against his compatriots. He had little to do with them since A'Court had gone to Spain. The malevolent Canning had succeeded good Castlereagh. *Te Deum Laudamus* for Metternich!

The King went to his last shoot on January 2, 1825. Next day he remained indoors with a slight cold, and towards evening he could hardly keep awake over his game of piquet in Lucia's drawing-room; his thoughts wandered; his articulation was blurred. The doctors wanted to bleed him, but he would not hear of it. He asked his attendants not to call him at six o'clock next morning as usual.

They waited with the doctors till eight, when the valet entered the King's room and asked: 'Does Your Majesty command me to open the windows?' Hearing no reply, he drew aside the bed curtains and found the King with his mouth half open and one arm dangling inert outside the bed. Like Maria Carolina, he had died of an apoplectic stroke. The royal household gathered round him weeping, and weeping is contagious. Most of them had followed their master twice into exile; many were as old, if not older. General Danero, who was over a hundred, lamented that he had survived the King he had known as a little boy, playful to the end. For the Prince of Ruoti it was as if the sun had gone out. He was struck down, overwhelmed with grief. Medici tried to prevent the Duke of Calabria from entering the royal chamber, but he was swept aside. After some hesitation the new King decided to announce his father's decease. The guard was doubled outside the palace, and the same evening the royal family retired to Capodimonte, taking the Duchess of Floridia with them, which did honour, said De Nicola, to the hearts of the august sovereigns.

For three days the people flocked to the royal palace to see their beloved King *Nasone* lying in state. Within a week he would have been seventy-five: the elaborate preparations at the San Carlo for his birthday were stopped; all the theatres were closed down. 'He is much regretted,' wrote Lady Blessington, 'for if not a sovereign of superior mental requirements, he was assuredly a good-natured man.' With all his weaknesses he had retained the power of inspiring affection. He had made generous provision for his beloved Lucia in his will. Besides this he made his heir write the following declaration, which was found among the Duchess's papers, dated May 30, 1821:

'I promise after the death of my Father (which God keep ever distant) to His legitimate Wife Lucia Migliaccio Duchess of Floridia, in consideration of the Superlative companionship she has given Him since November 27, 1814, the day of Their Union, to continue exactly during her lifetime the monthly allowance of four thousand five hundred ducats, including her table expenses, stables, etc., etc., and to let her remain in possession of the Apartment She has enjoyed until now in the Palace of Naples.

'Your most obedient and grateful Son
Francis.'

But the poor lady who had done so much to sweeten the King's old age did not long survive him. She died next year on April 26, and it is sad to relate that no member of the royal family attended her funeral. For the descendants of Louis XIV and Maria Theresa of Austria had never really forgiven their father's *mésalliance*.

BIBLIOGRAPHY

Manuscripts
Archivio di Stato, Naples: *Affari Esteri* files.
Società Napoletana di Storia Patria: Lettere di Ferdinando IV.
Borbone a Carlo III dall' Archivio di Simancas.
    Volume I: 1775-1778, pp.719 in folio.
    Volume II: 1780-1785, pp.668 in folio.
(A 19th-century copy, XXXVI a. 6-7.)
Borbone Carlo: Carte relative al suo regno, XXXII a. 2.
Borbone Ferdinando IV: Carte riguardante il suo regno, XXXII a. 2.
Acton Giovanni: Lettere cinque a F. Galiani, XXXI a.
Imperatore Giuseppe a Napoli, XXXI B, 17, p.125, etc.
Public Record Office, London: F.O. 70.

Printed Books and Articles[1]
ACERO, G.: La Sicilia e i suoi rapporti con l'Inghilterra. Palermo, 1848.
AMARI, MICHELE: La Sicile et les Bourbons. Paris, 1849.
AMODEO, F.: Le riforme universitarie di Carlo III e Ferdinando IV
    Borbone. Naples, 1902.
ANGELIS, FRANCESCO DE: Storia del regno di Napoli sotto la dinastia
    Borbonica. Naples, 1817-1836.
ANSPACH, MARGRAVINE OF: Memoirs. London, 1826.
ATTERIDGE, A. HILLIARD: Joachim Murat. London, 1911.
AURIOL, CHARLES: La France, l'Angleterre et Naples de 1803 à 1806.
    Paris, 1904.
AYALA, MARIANO D': Memorie storico-militari dal 1734 al 1815.
    Naples, 1835.
BADHAM, F. P.: Nelson at Naples. London, 1900.
BALSAMO, P.: Memorie Inedite. Palermo, 1845.

[1] Owing to a regrettable deficiency in German, I have been unable to consult Baron von Helfert's 'standard' work on Queen Maria Carolina and Count Corti's recent biography, which to the best of my knowledge have not been translated. The Queen usually corresponded in French, and the Emperor Joseph's account of his visit to Naples was written in that language.

BARTHÉLEMY, ÉDOUARD DE: Mesdames de France, Filles de Louis XV. Paris, 1870.
BAUDRILLART, A.: Philippe V et la cour de France. Paris, 1890.
BAUSSET, L. F. J. DE.: Mémoires.
BECATTINI, F.: Storia del regno di Carlo III di Borbone. Venice, 1760.
BECKFORD, WILLIAM: Italy, with sketches of Spain and Portugal. London, 1834.
BÉDARIDA, HENRI: Parme dans la Politique Française au XVIIIe siècle. Paris, 1930.
(BERTHOLDI, BARON): Memoirs of the secret societies of the South of Italy, particularly the Carbonari. London, 1821.
BEYLE, HENRI (STENDHAL): Rome, Naples et Florence. Paris, 1826.
BIANCHI, NICOMEDE: Storia documentata della Diplomazia Europea in Italia dall' anno 1814 all' anno 1861. Turin, 1865.
BIANCHINI, LODOVICO: Della storia delle finanze del Regno di Napoli. Naples, 1834.
BIANCO, GIUSEPPE: La Sicilia durante l'occupazione inglese (1806–1815). Palermo. 1902.
BLANCH, LUIGI: Scritti Storici, a cura di Benedetto Croce. Bari, 1945.
BLESSINGTON, THE COUNTESS OF: The Idler in Italy. Paris, 1839.
BOIGNE, COMTESSE DE: Mémoires. Paris, 1908.
BONAMICI, CASTRUCCIO: Memorie sulla giornata di Velletri. Naples, 1802.
BONNEFONS, ANDRÉ: Marie-Caroline, Reine des Deux Siciles. Paris, 1905.
(BORELLI, PASQUALE): Casi Memorabili antichi e moderni del regno di Napoli ricavati dal fu Conte Radowski. Coblentz, 1842.
BOTTA, C.: Storia d'Italia. Numerous editions.
BOULGER DEMETRIUS C.: Lord William Bentinck. Oxford, 1892.
BROSSES, PRÉSEDENT CHARLES DE: Lettres familières écrites d'Italie en 1739 et 1740. Paris, 1928.
BUNBURY, LIENT.-GENERAL SIR HENRY: Narrative of some passages in the great war with France from 1799 to 1810. London, 1854.
CACCIATORE, ANDREA: Esame della Storia del Reame di Napoli di Pietro Colletta dal 1794 al 1825. Naples, 1850.
CALVI, F.: Curiosità storiche e diplomatiche del secolo XVIII. Milan, 1878. *Cambridge Modern History.* Vols. VI, VIII, IX, X.
(CANOSA, PRINCIPE DI): I piffari di montagna, etc. Dublin, 1821. CAPOGRASSI, ANTONIO: Gl'Inglesi in Italia durante le campagne napoleoniche (Lord W. Bentinck). Bari, 1949.
CARASCOSA, GÉNÉRAL: Mémoires historiques, politiques et militaires sur la révolution du Royaume de Naples en 1820 et 1821. London, 1823.
CARIGNANI, G.: Il tempo di Carlo III. Naples, 1865.
CARUTTI, D.: Storia della diplomazia... di Savoia. Turin, 1880.
CASANOVA DE SEINGALT, J.: Mémoires. Editions de la Sirène, Paris, 1926.
CASTALDI, G.: Della regale accademia Ercolanese. Naples, 1840.
CASTLEREAGH, LORD: Correspondence, despatches, and other papers. London, 1851–1853.
CELANO, C.: Notizie... di Napoli. Naples, 1858.
CESTARO, F. P.: Studi storici e letterari. Turin, 1894.

BIBLIOGRAPHY

CHASTENET, JACQUES: Godoï, Prince de la Paix. Paris, 1943.
CHIERICI, GINO: La Reggia di Caserta. Rome, 1937.
CHURCH, E.M.: Sir Richard Church in Italy and Greece. London, 1895.
COCHIN, M.: Voyage d'Italie. Paris, 1758.
COLLETTA, PIETRO: Storia del Regno di Napoli dal 1754 al 1825. Florence,1848; numerous editions.
CONFORTI, LUIGI: Napoli nel 1799. Naples, 1886.
—Napoli dal 1789 al 1796. Naples, 1887.
—Napoli dalla Pace di Parigi alla Guerra del 1798. Naples, 1889.
CORTESE, NINO: Il Principe di Metternich a Napoli nel 1819.
—*Napoli Nobilissima, Nuova Serie*, Vol.1, Naples, 1920.
CORTI, EGON CÆSAR COUNT: The Rise of the House of Rothschild. London, 1928.
COURIER, PAUL-LOUIS: Œuvres Complètes. Paris, 1951.
COXE, W.: L'Espagne sous les rois de la maison de Bourbon. Paris, 1827.
CRAVEN, RICHARD KEPPEL: A tour through the southern provinces of the Kingdom of Naples. London, 1821.
CROCE, BENEDETTO: Storia del Regno di Napoli. Bari, 1944.
—La rivoluzione Napoletana del 1799. Bari, 1926.
—Uomini e cose della Vecchia Italia. Bari, 1927.
—Aneddoti di varia letteratura. Naples, 1942.
—La riconquista del regno di Napoli nel 1799. Bari, 1943.
—I Teatri di Napoli. Bari, 1916.
—Aneddoti e Profili Settecenteschi. Naples, 1922.
—Luisa Sanfelice e la Congiura dei Baccher. Bari, 1942.
—Various articles in *La Critica*.
CUOCO, VINCENZO: Saggio storico sulla Rivoluzione Napoletana del 1799. Milan, 1806. Numerous editions.
DAMAS, COMTE ROGER DE: Mémoires publiés et annotés par Jacques Rambaud. Paris, 1912.
DAVIES, CATHERINE: Eleven Years' Residence in the family of Murat, King of Naples. London, 1841.
DE FILIPPIS, F.: La Reggia di Napoli. Naples, 1942.
DE FILIPPIS, F., and MORISANI, O.: Pittori Tedeschi a Napoli nel Settecento. Naples, 1943.
DE NICOLA, CARLO: Diario Napoletano, 1798–1825. Naples, 1906.
DE RUGGERIERO, G.: Il pensiero politico meridionale nei secoli XVIII e XIX. Bari, 1922.
DEGLI ONOFRI, P.: Elogio estemporaneo per la gloriosa memoria di Carlo III. Naples, 1789.
DI GIACOMO, SALVATORE: Ferdinando IV e il suo ultimo amore.
—Lettere di Ferdinando IV alla Duchessa di Floridia. (No date or year.)
DORAN, DR JOHN: 'Mann' and Manners at the Court of Florence, 1740–1786. London, 1876.
DORIA, GINO: Storia di una Capitale. Milan–Naples, 1952.
—Le Strade di Napoli. Naples, 1943.
DOUGLAS, NORMAN: Old Calabria. London, 1915.
—Experiments. Florence, 1925.
DRIAULT, ÉDOUARD: Napoléon I et l'Italie. Paris, 1907.
DUCLOS, CHARLES: Voyage en Italie. Paris, 1791.

DUFOURQ, ALBERT: Le régime jacobin en Italie. Paris, 1900.
DUMAS, ALEXANDRE: I Borboni di Napoli. Naples, 1863.
DUMAS, LIEUT.-GENERAL COMTE MATHIEU: Souvenirs, publiés par son fils. Paris, 1839.
DU TEIL, JOSEPH: Rome, Naples et le Directoire. Paris, 1902.
ESPINCHAL, GUILLAUME THOMAS D': Journal d'Emigration. Paris, 1912.
EUSTACE, REV. J. C.: A classical tour through Italy. London, 1813.
FAURE, MAURICE: Souvenirs du Général Championnet (1792–1800). Paris, 1905.
FERNAN NUNEZ, CONDE DE: Vida de Carlos III. Madrid, 1892.
FOOTE, CAPTAIN E. J.: Vindication of his Conduct, when Captain of His Majesty's Ship *Sea-horse*, and Senior Officer in the Bay of Naples, in the summer of 1799. London, 1810.
FORSYTH, JOSEPH: Remarks on Antiquities, Arts, and Letters, during an excursion in Italy, in the years 1802 and 1803. London, 1835.
FORTUNATO, GIUSTINO: I Napoletani del 1799. Florence, 1884.
GALANTI, GIUSEPPE MARIA: Nuova Descrizione Storica e Geografica delle Sicilie. Naples, 1790–1794.
—Napoli e Contorni. Naples. Ibid. 1829.
GALIANI, L'ABBÉ F.: Correspondance inédite pendant les années 1765 à 1783. Paris, 1818.
GALLO, MARZIO MASTRILLI, DUCA DI: Memorie. *Arch. Stor. Nap.*, XIII pp.205–441.
GALT, JOHN: Voyages and Travels in the years 1809, 1810, and 1811. London, 1812.
GAMBOA, BIAGIO: Storia della Rivoluzione di Napoli. Naples, 1820.
GENOINO, ANDREA: Le Sicilie al tempo di Francesco I (1777–1830). Naples, 1934.
GIGLIOLI, CONSTANCE H.D.: Naples in 1799. London, 1903.
GLEICHEN, BARON DE: Souvenirs. Paris, 1868.
GOETHE, WOLFGANG: Autobiography, translated by John Oxenford. London, 1867.
GORANI, COUNT GIUSEPPE: Mémoires secrets et critiques des cours, des gouvernements, et des moeurs des principaux États de l'Italie. Paris, 1793.
GORDON, MAJOR PRYSE LOCKHART: Personal Memoirs. London, 1830.
GRANT, LIEUT.-COLONEL NISBET HAMILTON: Letters of Mary Nisbet of Dirleton, Countess of Elgin. London, 1926.
GUTTERIDGE, H.: Nelson and the Neapolitan Jacobins. Navy Records Society XXV.
HAMILTON, SIR WILLIAM: Observations on Mount Vesuvius, Mount Etna, and other Volcanos. London, 1773.
HELFERT, BARON VON: Fabrizio Ruffo, Rivoluzione e Controrivoluzione di Napoli. (Italian translation.) Florence, 1885.
HELFERT, BARON VON: Memorie segrete del Gabinetto di Napoli e di Sicilia per servire alla vera storia di quel paese dal 1790 fino al 1816 trovate nel portafoglio d'un Viaggiatore Americano. (Wrongly attributed to Giangiacomo di Cresceri.) Vienna, 1892.
HERVEY, JOHN LORD: Some materials towards Memoirs of the Reign of King George II. Edited by Romney Sedgwick. London, 1931.

IMBERT DE SAINT-AMAND: Marie Amélie et la Cour de Palerme, 1806–1814. Paris, 1891.
JEAFFRESON, JOHN CORDY: Lady Hamilton and Lord Nelson. London, 1888.
JOHNSTON, R. M.: The Napoleonic Empire in Southern Italy. London, 1904.
JOHNSTON, R. M.: (edited by): Mémoire de Marie Caroline reine de Naples, intitulé 'De la Révolution du Royaume de Sicile par un Témoin Oculaire'. Cambridge-Harvard Univ. London, 1912.
KELLY, MICHAEL: Reminiscences. London, 1826.
KNIGHT, CORNELIA: Autobiography. London, 1861.
KOTZEBUE, AUGUSTUS VON: Travels through Italy in the years 1804 and 1805. London, 1806.
LA LANDE, J. J. DE: Voyage d'un français en Italie. Venice, 1769.
LANCELLOTTI, CAV. CARMINE: Memorie Istoriche di Ferdinando I Re del Regno delle Due Sicilie. Naples, 1827.
LEE, VERNON: Studies of the Eighteenth Century in Italy. London, 1881.
LOMONACO, FRANCESCO: Rapporto al Cittadino Carnot, edited by Fausto Nicolini. Bari, 1929.
LORENZETTI, COSTANZA: L'Accademia di Belle Arti di Napoli (1752–1952). Florence, 1952.
MACDONALD, MARÉCHAL: Souvenirs. Paris, 1892.
MAHAN, CAPTAIN A.T.: The Life of Nelson. London, 1897.
MARC-MONNIER: Un Aventurier Italien du Siècle Dernier: Le Comte Joseph Gorani. Paris, 1896.
MARESCA, BENEDETTO: La pace del 1796 tra le Due Sicilie e la Francia. Naples, 1887.
—La marina napoletana nel secolo XVIII. Naples, 1902.
MARINELLI, DIOMEDE: I Giornali, edited by A. Fiordalisi. Naples, 1901.
MARMONTEL, J.-F.: Mémoires. Paris, 1891.
MARULLI, COUNT GENNARO: Ragguagli storici sul regno delle Due Sicilie dall' epoca della francese rivolta fino al 1815. Naples, 1817.
MATURI, WALTER: Il Concordato del 1818 tra la Santa Sede e le Due Sicilie. Florence, 1929.
—Il Principe di Canosa. Florence, 1944.
MÉNEVAL, BARON DE: Napoléon et Marie Louise. Paris, 1843.
METTERNICH, PRINCE: Mémoires. Paris, 1880.
MILES, COMMANDER JEAFFRESON: Vindication of Lord Nelson's Proceedings in the Bay of Naples. London, 1843.
MILLER, LADY ANNE: Letters from Italy in 1770 and 1771. London, 1776.
MINTO, COUNTESS OF: A Memoir of the Right Hon. Hugh Elliot. Edinburgh, 1868.
MIOT DE MÉLITO, COMTE: Mémoires. Paris, 1858.
MONTET, BARONNE DU: Souvenirs, 1785–1866. Paris, 1914.
MOORE, JOHN: A view of Society and Manners in Italy. London, 1790.
MOORE, SIR JOHN: Diary, edited by Major-General Sir J. F. Maurice. London, 1904.
MORGAN, LADY: Italy. London, 1821.
MOSCATI, RUGGERO: Il Regno delle Due Sicilie e l'Austria. Documenti

dal Marzo 1821 al Novembre 1830. Naples, 1937.
MUTINELLI, FABIO: Storia arcana ed aneddotica d'Italia raccontata dai Veneti Ambasciatori. Venice, 1858.
Napoli Nobilissima, Vol. I–XI. Naples, 1892–1902.
NAPOLI-SIGORNELLI, PIETRO: Vicende della coltura nelle Due Sicilie... Naples, 1810–1811.
NARDINI, BENEDETTO: Memoria per servire all'ultima rivoluzione di Napoli, ossia ragguaglio degli avvenimenti che hanno preceduto e seguita l'entrata dei Francesi in Napoli nel 1799. Naples, 1864.
NICOLAS, SIR NICHOLAS HARRIS: The Dispatches and Letters of Vice Admiral Lord Viscount Nelson. London, 1845.
NICOLINI, FAUSTO: Il Pensiero dell' abate Galiani. Bari, 1909.
—Amici e Corrispondenti Francesi dell'abate Galiani. Naples, 1954.
NICOLINI, N.: Luigi de' Medici e il giacobinismo napoletano. Florence, 1935.
—La spedizione punitiva del Latouche-Tréville. Florence, 1939
NICOLSON, SIR HAROLD: The Congress of Vienna. London, 1946.
NUZZO, GIUSEPPE: Giovanni Acton e un tentativo di lega italiana. *Rassegna Storica Napoletana*, Anno IV, 1937.
OMAN, CAROLA: Nelson. London, 1947.
ORLOFF, COMTE GRÉGOIRE: Mémoires Historiques, Politiques et Littéraires sur le Royaume de Naples. Paris, 1821.
PAGANO, MARIO: Saggi Politici. Naples, 1783.
PAGET, SIR AUGUSTUS: The Paget Papers. London, 1896.
PALMIERI, DE MICCICHÉ, MICHEL: Pensées et souvenirs historiques et contemporains... Paris, 1830.
—Moeurs de la Cour et des peuples des Deux Siciles. Paris, 1837.
PALMIERI, NICCOLÒ: Saggio Storico e Politico sulla Costituzione del Regno di Sicilia. Lausanne, 1847.
PALUMBO, RAFFAELE: Maria Carolina Regina delle Due Sicilie, suo carteggio con Lady Hamilton. Naples, 1877.
PANE, ROBERTO: Napoli imprevista. Turin, 1949.
PANNONE, A.: Lo Stato borbonico. Florence, 1924.
PASCAL, C.: Vita ed opere dell'abate Galiani. Naples, 1885.
PECCHIA, CARLO: Storia civile e politica del Regno di Napoli. Ibid, 1869.
PEPE, GENERALE GUGLIELMO: Memorie intorno alla sua vita. Paris, 1847.
PETROMASI, DOMENICO: Storia della Spedizione dell' Eminentissimo Cardinale Don Fabrizio Ruffo. Naples, 1801.
PETTIGREW, T. J.: Memoirs of the Life of Vice-Admiral Lord Viscount Nelson. London, 1849.
PEYRE, ROGER: La cour d'Espagne au commencement du XIXe siècle. Paris, 1909.
PIERI, P.: Il Regno di Napoli dal luglio 1799 al marzo 1806. Vols. XII and XIII of *Arch. Stor. per le Province Napoletane*. Naples, 1926, 1927.
PIGNATELLI-STRONGOLI: Memorie d'un generale. Bari, 1927.
PIOZZI, MRS: Observations and Reflections made in the course of a journey through France, Italy and Germany. London, 1789.
PONTIERI, ERNESTO: Il Marchese Caracciolo Viceré di Sicilia ed il

Ministro Acton. Naples, 1932.
POTOCKA, COMTESSE ANNA: Voyage en Italie, 1826–27. Paris, 1899.
POZZO, L. DEL: Cronaca civile e militare delle Due Sicilie. Naples, 1859.
RACIOPPI, G.: Antonio Genovesi. Naples, 1871.
RAMBAUD, JACQUES: Naples sous Joseph Bonaparte 1806–1808. Paris, 1911.
—Lettres inédites ou éparses de Joseph Bonaparte à Naples. Paris, 1911.
RANKE, LEOPOLD VON: History of the Popes, translated by E. Fowler. New York, 1901.
RAVASCHIERI, TERESA: Il generale Carlo Filangieri. Milano, 1902.
RECOULY, RAYMOND: Louis-Philippe, Roi des Français. Paris, 1930.
RINIERI, P. ILARIO: Della rovina di una Monarchia. Turin, 1901.
RODOLICO, NICCOLÒ: II Popolo agli Inizi del Risorgimento nell' Italia Meridionale 1798–1801. Florence, 1926.
ROSSI, MICHELE: Nuova Luce risultante dai veri fatti avvenuti in Napoli pochi anni prima del 1799. Florence, 1890.
ROUSSEAU, FRANÇOIS: Règne de Charles III d'Espagne. Paris, 1907.
SACCHINELLI, ABATE DOMINICO: Memorie Storiche sulla Vita del Cardinale Fabrizio Ruffo. Naples, 1836.
SAINT-ALBIN, A. R..C. DE: Championnet. Paris, 1861.
SAINTE-BEUVE, C. A..: Causeries du Lundi, Tome II, pp.421–442. Paris, 1853.
SALEMI, L.: I trattati antinapoleonici dell' Inghilterra con le Due Sicilie. Palermo, 1937.
SANSONE, ALFONSO: Gli Avvenimenti del 1799 nelle Due Sicilie. Palermo, 1901.
SARCONE, DR MICHELE: Istoria Ragionata de' Mali osservati in Napoli, 1764. Naples, 1838.
SCHIPA, MICHELANGELO: Il regno di Napoli sotto i Borboni. Naples, 1900.
—Il regno di Napoli al tempo di Carlo di Borbone. Naples, 1923.
—Nel regno di Ferdinando IV Borbone. Florence, 1938.
SCHOLES, PERCY A.: The Great Dr Burney. London, 1948.
SERMONETA, THE DUCHESS OF: The Locks of Norbury. London, 1940.
SHARP, SAMUEL: Letters from Italy in the years 1765 and 1766. London, undated.
SILVAGNI, DAVID: La Corte e la Società Romana nei Secoli XVIII e XIX. Rome, 1884.
SIMIONI, A.: Le origini del risorgimento politico nell' Italia meridionale. Messina, 1925.
SIMOND, L: A Tour in Italy and Sicily. London, 1828.
SMITH, ADMIRAL SIR WILLIAM SIDNEY: Life and Correspondence of. London, 1848.
SMYTH, CAPTAIN W. H.: Nelson's First Visit to Naples; Nelson's Second Visit to Naples. *Royal United Service Journal.* May and June, 1845.
SOUTHEY, R: Life of Nelson. London, 1813.
SPINAZZOLA, VITTORIO: Gli Avvenimenti del 1799 in Napoli. Naples, 1899.
STRYIENSKI, CASMIR: Mesdames de France, filles de Louis XV. Paris, 1911.

SWINBURNE, HENRY: Travels in the Two Sicilies. London, 1783.
—The Courts of Europe at the close of the last century. London, 1841.
TANUCCI, BERNARDO: Lettere a Ferdinando Galiani, con introduzione e note di Fausto Nicolini. Bari, 1914.
TESCIONE, G.: L'Arte della Seta a Napoli e la Colonia di S. Leucio. Naples, 1932.
THIÉBAULT, GÉNÉRAL P.: Mémoires. Paris, 1894.
TICKNOR, GEORGE: Life, Letters and Journals. Boston, 1877.
TISCHBEIN, J. W.: Aus meinem Leben. Reprinted in Berlin, 1922.
TIVARONI, CARLO: L'Italia durante il dominio francese. Turin, 1889–90.
TOYE, FRANCIS: Rossini. London, 1934.
TRITONE, V.: La costituzione del 1812 e l'occupazione inglese della Sicilia. Bologna, 1936.
TURQUAN, JOSEPH: Les sœurs de Napoléon. Paris, 1896.
ULLOA, PIETRO CALÀ: Marie Caroline d'Autriche et la conquête du royaume de Naples en 1806. Paris, 1872.
—Intorno alla Storia del Reame di Napoli di Pietro Colletta. Naples, 1877.
VALENTE, A. Murat e l'Italia meridionale. Turin, 1941.
VANVITELLI, L.: Vita dell' architetto Luigi Vanvitelli. Naples, 1823.
VIGÉE LE BRUN, MME: Souvenirs. Paris, undated.
VINCIGUERRA, M.: La reggenza borbonica nella minorità di Ferdinando IV. Naples, 1918.
VIVIANI, DELLA ROBBIA, E.: Bernardo Tanucci ed il suo piu importante carteggio. Florence, 1942.
WEBSTER, C. K.: The foreign policy of Castlereagh. London, 1931.
—The Congress of Vienna. London, 1937.
WEIL, COMMANDANT M. H.: Correspondence inédite de Marie Caroline Reine de Naples et de Sicile avec le Marquis de Gallo, publiée et annotée par le—et Marquis Di Somma Circello. Paris, 1911
WHITAKER, TINA: Sicily and England. London, 1907.
WINCKELMANN, J. J.: Lettres familières. Amsterdam, 1781.
WINSPEARE, DAVIDE: Storia degli abusi feudali. Naples, 1883.
WRAXALL, SIR N. WILLIAM: Historical Memoirs of my own time. London, 1904.
ZAZO, ALFREDO: Ricerche e Studi Storici. Benevento, 1933.

INDEX

Abrial, commissioner 380, 383, 419
Aci, Prince of 603, 613, 624, 625, 627
A'Court, Sir William
  Algiers, truce 645
  appointment 650
  Bentinck, Lord William 669
  British policy 663-4, 708
  constitution 699-700
  court life 651, 679, 685, 691-2, 695
  Ferdinand 657
  Murat, Joachim 671
  Neapolitan revolution 705, 706-707
Acton, Joseph, Lieut-General 416, 533
Acton, Sir John Edward
  appointment 187-91, 195-6
  character 282, 366, 506
  court life 246
  death 606-607
  foreign policy 207, 233, 239
  France 253-4, 269, 495, 495-6
  grand chancellor 285, 300, 348, 381-2, 422, 441, 445-6, 451, 465-6, 475, 511
  Hamilton, Sir William 263-4
  Jacobins 280-1, 327
  Lock, Charles 439, 440
  Maria Carolina 210-11, 243-4, 253, 255, 296-7, 301, 349, 418, 432, 459, 477
  marine and war, minister 197, 228, 229-31, 247, 257-8
  marriage to niece (aged 13) 447-8
  Naples 396, 401, 463, 471
  Palermo 508, 511, 531
  popularity 203
  resignation 483, 487, 495, 502, 505-6, 505-7, 507-9
  retreat to Sicily 317-18
  return to power 555, 559-60, 562-4, 572-3, 586

Adélaïde, Madame 241, 373
Aix-la-Chapelle, treaty of (1748) 76, 90, 105
Albergo dei Poveri, Reale 85, 86
Alberoni, Cardinal 18-19, 25
Alexander I, Tsar 515, 519-20, 548, 579, 654, 708
Alfieri, Vittorio 266, 381, 394
Allen, Edward 33-4, 61-2
Alquier, Baron
  Acton, Sir John 483-4, 489, 502, 517
  alliance with France 494, 514-15
  ambassador 468, 635-6
  Anglo-Spanish power struggle 476-7
  Bonaparte, Joseph 557
  Bonaparte, Napoleon 519-20, 521-2
  Florence, treaty of 465
  French occupation 501-502
  intelligence sources 487, 489, 532
  King Ferdinand, return 473, 475
  Queen Maria Carolina 484-5, 493, 504, 506-507, 509, 517, 530-31, 559, 599
  treaty with France 536-7
Amherst, William Pitt, Lord 587, 600-601, 602-604, 615
Amiens, treaty of (1802) 470, 483, 489, 631
Angevin dynasty 2-3, 33
Anglo-Neapolitan alliance 264
Anglo-Sicilian treaty (1808) 583
Ansbach, Margravine of (Lady Craven) 168, 225, 242, 680, 701, 724-5
Appolonyi, Count 716, 726
Aragonese period 2-3
Arriola, General Manuel y 285, 326, 608
Artale, Marchese 564, 583
Ascoli, Troiano Marulli, Duca di
  Bentinck, Lord William 613-14

death 726
Ferdinand's equerry 322, 416, 464, 493, 549-50, 699
police superintendent 493, 607
Spanish sympathies 300
Augustus Frederick, Prince 267, 301, 302
Austerlitz, battle of 542, 543, 579
Austro-French peace treaty 546
Austro-Neapolitan convention 460-61
Austro-Russian treaty 515

Baccer, Geraldo 382-3, 397, 449
Baccer, Vincenzo 383, 449
Baia 21, 60, 230, 257, 533, 549, 555, 709
Baiardi, Monsignor Ottavio 91-92
Baillie, Captain 391, 418
Ball, Captain Alexander 408-409, 410
Barbaja, Dominico 677, 678, 694
Bassville, Nicolas Hugou de 251-252, 261
Bausen, Giovanni 196, 590
Beauharnais, Eugène de 528, 647
Beccaria, Cesare, Marchese de 173, 217
Beckford, William 163, 169, 241-242, 680
Bellegard, General de 460, 464, 647-8
Belmonte, Antonio Pignatelli, Prince of 290-294, 295, 296, 297, 423, 456
Belmonte, General Pignatelli di 21
Belmonte, Giuseppe Ventimiglia, Prince of
  baron's protest 601, 603
  death 651
  discontent 624, 626, 643-5
  foreign minister 613, 620, 627
  Sicilian opposition 596
Belmonte, Lucrezia Pignatelli, Princess of 56-57, 191, 241-242, 243, 250, 497, 680
Belpulsi, Antonio 284, 419, 497-8
Benedict XIV, Pope 48, 60, 67, 94, 95, 156
Bentinck, Lord William Cavendish
  Anglo-Sicilian expedition 648-50
  appointment 604-606
  British policy 605-606
  career 604
  Catalan campaign 641-2
  constitution 613, 644-5
  Ferdinand 611, 621-3, 624-5, 626-7, 628-9, 656, 679
  Leopold, Prince 612
  Maria Carolina 606-8, 609, 611, 631, 679
  Murat, Joachim 647
  Sicily/Algiers treaty 645
  threats against Maria Carolina 610, 616-19, 621-2
  unification dream 615-16, 648-50
Berio, Marchese Francesco 678, 680-81, 694

Berry, Maria Carolina, Duchesse de 318, 366, 469, 678, 721
Berthier, Maréchal 309-310, 317
Bianchi confraternity 425, 577
Blacas, Pierre, Duc de 710, 715, 720
Bonaparte, Joseph
  army c-in-c Naples 547-8
  Gallo, Marchese 552
  King of Naples 555, 565-6, 570-72, 579
  King of Spain 584
  Naples 56, 557-8, 587
  negotiations 522
  risings against 571, 582-3
  Rodio, Marches di 566
  Rome 309
Bonaparte, Napoleon
  Anglo-French treaty (Amiens) 470, 489
  Anglo-Sicilian agreement 459
  Austerlitz, battle of 542-3
  Austro-French treaty 536, 546
  Bonaparte, Joseph 309-10, 547-8, 552, 558, 571, 582
  Elba 489, 658, 663
  Emperor of France 509
  First Consul of France 442
  Franco-Neapolitan peace treaty 297-8, 310
  Franco-Spanish alliance 584
  Italy 288-94
  King of Italy 527
  letters from Maria Carolina 490, 521-3
  letters to Maria Carolina 490-91, 519-20, 524, 601
  Madame de Staël 525
  Malta seized 310
  Maria Carolina 304-5, 472-3, 484-5, 528-30
  marriage to Archduchess Marie Louise 505, 598-9, 652-3
  Murat, Joachim 588-9, 597
  Naples occupation 344, 489, 507-508, 535
  Piedmont annexed 489
  Pius VI 297, 299-300
  threats against Britain 514, 590
Bonito, Guiseppe 35, 58-59
Borelli, Pasquale 582, 697, 700, 704, 719
Bourbon, family compact 112, 113, 164, 308
Bourcard, Lieut-General Emmanuel (Burckhardt) 416, 431, 589
Breme, Marchese di 197-8, 197-198, 239-240
Brosses, Président Charles de 9, 10-11, 39, 44, 49, 58, 76, 166, 680
Bunbury, Lieut-General Sir Henry 539-40, 543, 563, 566, 588

Burghersh, Lord 660, 710
Burney, Dr Charles 36, 168, 169
Butera, Prince of 126, 254, 596, 606, 628

Cacault, François 251, 294, 297, 299
Caccamo, Father 616-18, 619-20, 623-4, 628, 675
Cafferello 39, 40-41, 70, 169
Calabria
 Capodemonte kaolin 89
 defence of 553, 559-61, 567
 earthquakes 221-2
 Murat lands 670
 rearming 494, 496, 498
 recovery of 576, 590, 664
 resistance movements 568-70
 retreat from 548
 revolution 351, 355-7, 371-2, 374, 389
Calabritto, Palazzo 99, 470
calderari 673-4, 675, 719
Caleppi, Monsignor 213, 299
Cammarano, Giuseppe 677, 723
Campbell, Commodore George 659, 662
Campo Formio, treaty of (1797) 305-306, 308, 459
Campochiaro, O Mormile, Duke 536, 652, 700, 707
Canevari, Antonio 50, 55, 79
Canlaux, General 298, 302, 307
Canosa, Antonio Capece Minutolo, Prince of
 arrest 383
 carbonari 673-5, 716-17
 military tactics 590, 672
 murder accusation 577
 police minister 715-19
 radicalism 468-9, 571-2, 612
 resignation 719
 Spanish monarchy 672-3
 support of Maria Carolina 564, 565, 571-2, 581
Canosa, Fabrizio Capece Minutolo, Prince of 553, 558
Canova, Antonio 431, 678, 681, 685, 688
Cantillana, Count of 94, 112
Capodimonte
 palace 10, 49-50, 56, 57, 138, 218, 686, 692, 705, 729
 porcelain factory 89-90, 138, 363
Capri 62, 565, 568, 576, 581, 587-9
Capua 21, 25, 333, 335-336, 399, 420-21, 532, 548, 552, 712
Caracciola, Commodore Francesco 196, 287, 315, 328, 348-349, 354
Caracciola, Marchese Dominico 92, 95-97, 106, 173, 205, 207-211, 213-14, 227-228, 230-231
Carafa, Don Lelio 16, 23, 28

Carafa, Marshal Giovanni 20, 21
Caramanico, Prince of 156, 180, 211, 280, 281
Carasale, Angelo 35, 37, 40, 42, 56-57
Carascosa, General 659, 698-9, 706, 707, 712
carbonari 624, 673-4, 676, 693-4, 695-702, 704-708, 711-12, 716-17
Cardel, Father 118, 122
Cardito, Prince of 517, 523, 527-9, 530
Carlo, Prince 212
Carlo Tito, Prince 226
Casalanza, treaty of (1815) 659, 699
Casanova de Seingalt, Giacomo Girolama 160-63, 194, 679
Caserta
 aqueduct 144
 hunting 52, 224, 687, 691, 721
 palace 49, 79-83, 99, 114-15, 149, 185, 209, 225, 300, 481
 treason at 203-204
Cassano, Guilia Carafa, Duchess of 194, 234, 394
Cassaro, F Statella, Prince of 441, 596, 608, 624-6, 650
Cassetti, Captain G (Cassetta) 607, 614
Castelcicala, F Ruffo, Prince of
 character 285, 300, 438
 Foreign Minister 308, 416
 London 258, 263, 531, 614, 646, 650
 Orléans, Duke of 591
 state finances 625
Castelnuovo, Carlo Cottone, Prince of (Prince of Villarmosa) 596, 603, 613, 624-6, 643, 644, 649, 650, 657, 663
Castlereagh, Viscount Robert Stewart 614-15, 646, 650, 657, 706
Castrone, Colonel 564, 571, 581, 607, 610, 614
Catherine II, of Russia 541, 683, 691
Celebrano, Francesco 88, 102
Cestari, Abate Giuseppe 260, 264-5
Championnet, General
 disgrace 378, 379
 Naples 10, 284, 335-6, 338, 340, 343-5, 363
 Parthenopean republic 358-9
 Rome 323, 363
Charles Albert, Prince 226-7, 331
Charles, Archduke 380, 543, 590
Charles Emmanuel III, of Savoy, of Sardinia 19, 60, 63, 64, 76-7, 89, 96-7, 105, 106
Charles III, of the Two Sicilies, of Spain
 Acton, Sir John 199-204
 Austria, defeat by 3
 Caserta 79-83, 185

character 14-16, 72, 74
death 226-7
freemasons 177-80
health 16, 73
King of Spain 106-105, 119-27, 208-209, 211, 212-13
marriage 133-5
Sicily 26-8
succeeds to the Two Sicilies 23-24, 25-8
Tuscany 16-20
Charles IV, of Spain
  abdication 584
  accession 226
  birth 71
  death 691
  Franco-Spanish treaty 288
  Queen's death 689-90
  Rome 687
Charles VI, of Austria 13, 20-21, 27, 60
Charny, Comte de 22, 31, 44
Chastellux, Comte de 373, 502
chinea 32, 213-14
Choiseau, E-F, Duc de 112, 164-5
Choiseul, M de 146, 160
Church, General Sir Richard 700, 707, 725
Cimarosa, Dominico 167, 173
Cimitile, Prince 705, 706
Circello, T di Somma, Marchese di
  Bentinck, Sir William 669
  chief minister 715, 718-19
  constitution 672
  death 726
  foreign minister 529, 531, 573, 649, 665
  Maria Carolina 608, 623
  Moliterno affair 589
  peace moves 295
  Russian treaty 534
Cisalpine republic 460, 503
Clement XII, Pope 20, 33
Cobenzl, Count von 459, 508
Colbran, Isabella 678, 694-5
Colletta, General Pietro 659-60, 666, 685, 692-3, 708
Collingwood, Admiral Lord Cuthbert 559, 564, 585, 586, 590, 596
Colonna, Grand Constable Prince 214, 320
concordats
  1741 60, 113
  1818 676, 686
Consalvi, Cardinal 451, 655, 676
constitution 587, 692, 696-7, 699-700, 703, 707, 709
Corsini, Prince Bartolomeo 15, 23-4, 28
Cotugno, Dr Dominico 302, 304, 688
Courier, Paul-Louis 561, 565, 569-70

Craig, General Sir James 540, 543, 545, 548, 559, 563
cuccagna 45-7, 70, 78, 127-8
Cuoco, Vincenzo 245, 279-80, 345, 360, 362-3, 374, 383, 391, 450
Cutò, Prince of 291, 625, 631, 650

Damas, General Count Roger de
  Acton, Sir John 555, 559, 573
  armistice 464
  army 441, 514-15
  Calabrian resistance 561-2
  Florence, treaty of 465
  French invasions 319-22, 327, 336, 552-3, 558-60
  honours awarded 524
  Maria Carolina 487, 521-3, 558-60
  "revolution" 345
  Russia, alliance 534, 544-5
  wounded 566
Danero, General 353, 357, 729
Dego, battle of 542
Delfico, Melchiorre 497, 681
Deo, Emmanuele de 279, 381
Diderot, Denis 94, 112
D'Orsay, Count Alfred Guillaume Gabriel 724, 726
Drummond, Sir William 472-3, 572, 573, 574, 578, 586-7
Duhesne, General 374, 557
Dumas, Alexander (elder) 53, 382, 391, 450

Elba 296, 489, 670
Elliot, Hugh 493-5, 508, 511, 513, 516, 532-3, 537, 545, 559, 563, 568, 575
Enghien, Duc d' 505, 510, 552, 598, 673
Enrichetta Maria Carmela 212
Épinay, Louise de La Live d' 95, 155, 164, 165, 166, 182, 186, 194
Escurial, treaty of (1733) 19
Espinchal, Comte GT d' 234-6, 241
Esterhazy, Prince 77-8

Fagan, Robert 609, 614, 617, 618, 621, 628, 630
Fanzago, Cosimo 5-6
Farinelli (Carlo Broschi) 41, 97
Farnese, art collection 30, 35, 47
Farnese dynasty 13
Farnese, Élisabeth
  of Spain
    Queen 13-14, 23, 25
    Queen Mother 29, 31, 36, 49, 54-7, 60, 77, 109
    Regent 105
Farnese, Francesco, Duke of Parma 14-15

Index

Fasulo, Nicola 281, 339
Ferdinand, Duke of Parma 122, 133, 289
Ferdinand I, of Aragon (Ferrante, of Naples) 3
Ferdinand III, Grand Duke of Tuscany 237, 288, 295, 455, 459-60
Ferdinand III, of Sicily, IV of Naples, I of the Two Sicilies
  accession 105-8
  Acton, Sir John 197-9, 282, 418, 466, 483, 503, 507
  Anglo-Neapoltan relations 171, 174-6, 282-3
  the arts 166-8, 223-5, 485
  Austria, Emperor Joseph of 138-53
  Bentinck, Lord William 611-12, 626-30, 669
  betrothal to Archduchess Joanna 127
  betrothal to Maria Carolina 130-31
  betrothal to Maria Josepha 127-30
  birth 71
  Calabrian expedition 575-9
  character 124-6, 145, 152-3, 177-8, 204, 215, 236-7, 365-6, 511-12, 541-2, 572-3, 726
  childhood and education 82, 117-19
  children see Carlo, Prince; Carlo Tito, Prince; Charles Albert, Prince; Enrichetta Maria Carmela; Francis, Duke of Calabria; Gennaro, Prince; Leopold, Duke of Salerno; Maria Amalia, Duchess of Orléans; Maria Clotilde; Maria Luisa, Gd Duchess of Tuscany; Maria Theresa, w of Francis I
  children's marriages 238-9, 302-4, 585-6, 591-2
  coming of age 120-21, 124-5
  congress of Vienna 721-2
  death 729
  death of Maria Carolina 655
  descriptions 141-51, 193-9, 215, 365
  escapes from Naples 330-32, 420, 551
  Ferdinandopolis 233
  Franco-Neapolitan armistice 290-95, 310
  freemasons 178-9
  French invasion 289-90, 310, 319
  government 123-4, 210, 281, 422-4, 488-9, 509, 624, 657, 663, 668-9, 674-5, 699, 711-12, 714-17
  hunting 119, 125, 147-8, 171-2, 204, 224, 236, 541-2, 690-91
  Jacobins 277-8, 280, 437-8
  Jesuits expelled 121-2
  legal codes 231-3, 667
  loss of throne 325-8, 520, 557-8, 597
  Maria Carolina dominates 201-2, 210, 231, 347-8, 431-2, 501, 509, 610-11
  marriages 131-8, 148, 655-6
  in Palermo 332-3, 370, 427, 448, 470, 551
  regencies 108, 112-13, 119-20, 123, 711
  regent presumpive of Spain 584
  relinquishes partial power 620-21, 625
  restoration 431, 464
  returns to Naples 418-20, 471, 473-4, 664-7
  Ruffo, Cardinal 353-5
  sexual proclivities 142, 231, 432, 655
  status 208, 326, 329, 431
  unrest against 273-6, 277-82, 697, 700
  Vatican 240-41, 687-8
Ferdinand VI, of Spain 68, 69, 75, 97, 104-105, 107
Ferdinand VII, of Spain 469, 476, 485, 531, 584, 672, 691, 721
Ferrante, of Naples (Ferdinand I of Aragon) 3
Ferri, Fernandino 382-3, 450
Ficquelmont, Count C von 716-17, 718-19, 726
Filangieri, Gaetano 101, 173, 217, 218, 220, 232
Filangieri, General Prince Carlo 658, 704, 712
Fiorentini theatre 161, 164
Florence 2, 16-18, 19-20, 116, 455, 529, 658, 710, 715
Florida Blanca, Count of 199, 203, 212, 239, 252
Floridia, Lucia Migliaccio, Duchess of (Princess of Partanna)
  death of Ferdinand 728-30
  illness 695, 698, 723
  marriage to Ferdinand 655-6, 667, 685, 722
  Medici, Luigi 688
  plot against Ferdinand 707
  status 688
Floridiana villa 685-6
Fogliani, Marchese Giovanni 16, 63, 67, 72, 75, 90, 92
Foote, Captain EJ 405, 408, 412
Forteguerri, Commander 270, 333
Fox, General Hon Edward Henry 568, 572, 577-8, 579
Fox, Hon Charles James 421, 455
Fra Diavolo (Michele Pezza) 372, 392, 428, 431, 567, 568
Francavilla, Prince Michele Imperiali di (younger) 32-3, 125, 161, 162-3, 164
Francis, Duke of Calabria, Hereditary Prince
  Calabria, flees to 554
  character 593, 610, 612

children 678, 679, 689
farming 572-3, 580
France, attitude to 597
French invasion 524
illness 622-3
Lieutenant-General of Sicily 664, 698
marriages 227, 238, 302-304, 469-70, 473, 476, 478-9, 580
mother-in-law 656
portrait 723
regency 553, 615, 711, 712, 715-16, 717, 719
return to Naples 392
succession 703
Vicar General of Sicily 613, 615-17, 620-21, 643, 644-6
Vicar-General of Naples 699, 701, 707
wife's death 469
Francis, Duke of Lorraine 29, 30, 90
Francis II, of Austria 237, 251, 519, 537, 580, 692-3, 715, 727
Austro-French armistice 542, 579
Franco-Spanish alliance 295
Frederick II, of Prussia 91, 103, 117, 484
freemasonry 156, 177-80, 246, 265
French Revolution 11, 228, 233, 237, 245, 246, 252, 272
Frimont, General 710, 716, 719
Fuga, Ferdinando 11, 85

Gabriel, Infante 71, 108, 226
Gaeta 336, 399, 420, 552, 562, 566-7, 641
Gages, General Count de 63-7
Galanti, Guiseppe Maria 173, 231
Galiani, Abate Fernandino
  Ferdinand, King 137
  Hamilton, Sir William 119
  inoculation 186-7
  Naples 164-8, 173, 182
  On money 93
  Paris 94-5, 101, 111-13, 130, 191, 208
  sermons 86
Galiani, Monsignor Celestino 21, 25, 93, 100
Galiani, Vincenzo 274, 279
Gallo, Marchese Marzio Mastrilla (Duca)
  Acton, Sir John 285, 308, 487, 502
  ambassador to Austria 283-4, 287-8, 459
  ambassador to France 472-3, 481, 494-5, 503-504, 505, 509-11, 527
  Austria, alliance 239-40, 253, 287-8, 319
  Bentinck, Lord William 646
  Foreign Minister 552, 558, 659, 709, 712-13
  Maria Carolina, Queen 204-205, 348, 517, 633-4

  Napoleon's influence 527-9
Garat, Joseph 311, 313
Gatti, Dr Angelo 186, 187, 198
Gennaro, Prince 226
Gennaro, San 23, 50, 143, 326, 343, 464, 588-9
  knights of 47, 87, 108
  miracle 103, 156, 339, 386
  shrine 70, 129, 661
  statue 24, 28, 86, 277
Genoa 96, 196, 284
Genovesi, Abate Antonio 100, 101, 104
Geoffrin, Mme 112, 165
George IV (Prince Regent) 608, 650
Giordano, Annibale 247-8, 274, 277-9, 280-82, 283-4, 344, 361, 491
Giordano, Michele 247-8, 277-8
giunta di stato
  1794 274, 279-80, 281
  1799 422, 424, 467, 476, 492
giunta d'inconfidenza 33, 34, 62-3, 77, 97
Godoy, Manuel, (Prince of the Peace) 226, 288, 297, 477, 479, 484-5, 584
Goethe, Johann Wolfgang von 9, 215-22, 223, 314
Goncourt, Edmond de 93, 95, 666
Goncourt, Jules de 93, 95, 666
Goroni, Count Giuseppe 190, 231, 273
Goudar, Sarah 160, 163-4, 193-4
Gouvion Saint-Cyr, Maréchal 489, 490, 493, 496, 498, 502-3, 513, 515, 523-4, 535, 545
granali 230, 398
Gray, Sir James 75, 79, 97-8, 107-108, 119
Grenier, General 600, 601
Grenville, Lord William Wyndham
Grenville 263, 295, 317, 443, 445-6, 457
Guidobaldi, Judge Giuseppe 312, 422

Hackert, Philip 203, 223-5
Hamilton, Lady Emma (Amy Lyon; Emma Hart)
  Caracciola, execution 415
  confidente to Maria Carolina 250, 298, 314, 411-13, 416, 428, 440, 444, 453
  description 216-17, 235, 249, 366-7
  marriage 249-50
  Nelson, Lord 267, 269, 314-16, 367-9, 407-408, 428-9, 437, 456-8
  Paget, Sir William 445-6
  paintings of 222-3
  politics 312, 443-4, 454
  proxy for Maria Carolina 422-3
  return to Naples 407-408
  Sicily 331

Index

Hamilton, Sir William
  Acton, Sir John 188-9, 196, 202-203, 247, 318, 441
  ambassador 119-20, 172
  Caracciola's execution 415-16
  Emma Hart arrives 216-17
  English tourists 174
  events in Naples 130, 146, 438-9
  flight to Sicily 328, 330-32, 366
  journey to Vienna 456-7
  marriage 249-50
  Nelson, Admiral Lord 314-15, 366
  retirement 437, 443-6, 458
  return to Naples 410-11, 413, 420
  royal family 122-4, 134, 135-6, 146, 171
  scientific interests 128-9, 151, 169-71
  social life 222-3
Hardy, Captain Sir Thomas 328, 414
Herculaneum 10, 50-51, 92-3, 295, 363, 481, 485, 685
Hesse-Philippthal, Louis, General Prince of 533, 549, 557, 566, 572, 575, 579
Hetzendorf, castle 640, 652
Hôpital, Marquis de l' 57, 75

Isabella, Princess of Parma 107, 126-7
Ischia 21, 32, 136, 536, 581, 590

Jablonowsky, Prince of 671, 695, 700
Jaci, Prince of (Iaci) 114, 182, 549-50
Jansenists 95, 265
Jerocades, Abate Antonio 260, 264
Jesuits 3, 14, 95, 113, 121-22, 149, 156, 181, 216, 672, 687
Joanna, Archduchess Maria 126-7
Joseph II, of Austria 106, 127, 138-53, 188, 217, 237
Jourdan, Maréchal Comte Jean-Baptiste 380, 587

Karpoff, Baron de 514, 533
Kauffmann, Angelica 223
Kaunitz, Count Ernst 132, 146, 177, 191
Keith, Viscount Admiral 454-5, 465
Kellermann, Maréchal François Étienne Christophe, Duc de Valmy 289, 292, 321, 344
Kelly, Michael 41, 169
Knight, Cornelia 213-14, 313, 315, 328, 332, 369, 455-7
Kotzebue, August Friedrich Ferdinand von 526-7, 681, 684

Lacy, General 530, 533, 539-40, 543-5, 548
Laibach 709, 711, 722
Lalande, Joseph Jérôme Le Français de 35, 39-40, 102-103
Las Casas, Count Somone de 200-202, 211
Latouche-Tréville, Admiral Louis de 257-60, 263, 264, 277, 280
Lauberg, Carlo 260, 265-6, 274, 344, 360-61
Lechi, General Giuseppe 498, 527
Leczinski, Stanislaus, of Poland 29, 30
Leipzig, battle of 645
Leopold II, Emperor (formerly Grand Duke of Tuscany) 132, 135-6, 152-3, 227, 237, 239, 240, 250
Leopold, Prince of Salerno
  birth 227
  Calabian expedition 554, 558
  character 366, 723
  created prince 679
  enters Naples 660-61, 664-5
  envoy to Spain 585
  Royal Corps of Nobles 289-90
  tutor 487
  Vienna 631, 636, 652, 654
L'Hôpital, Marquis de 57, 75
Liveri, Baron de (Marquis) 27, 41-2
Lobkowitz, General Prince of 27, 63, 64-5, 66
Lock, Charles 349-51, 406, 420-21, 429-30, 437-9, 566
Lodi, battle of 289
Lombardy 19, 60, 66, 287-9, 630
Louis XV 16, 27, 40, 76, 105
Louis XVI 234, 248, 251, 262, 307, 308, 311, 468
Louis XVIII 600, 648, 651, 655, 672, 693
Louis-Philippe, Duke of Orléans 584-7, 591-2, 599-600, 610, 614, 627, 648
Louise-Elisabeth, of France, Duchess of Parma 76, 106-107
Lowe, Colonel Hudson 568, 581, 588
Ludolf, Count Gugliemo 254, 633
Lunéville, treaty of 460, 489
Luzzi, Prince of 348, 492, 508, 510, 516, 529

Macdonald, Maréchal Jacques Étienne Joseph Alexandre, Duc de Tarrente 321, 337, 364
Macfarlane, General Robert 629-30, 636
Mack, Field-Marshal Baron Karl 317-21, 322, 323, 326-7, 330, 333, 337-8, 347, 536, 539, 541
Mackau, Baron Armand de 251-2, 253-4, 257-9, 261-2, 264, 267, 296
Maddaloni, Carlo Carafa, Duke of 16, 22, 160, 161, 164
Maida, battle of 567

Malta
  Amiens, treaty of 470, 489, 631
  British garrison 496, 530, 535, 537
  Napoleon seizes 310, 313, 318, 351
  Neapolitan army 494
  plague 632
  recaptured 457
  Russian garrison 528, 537
Manhès, General 606, 670
Mann, Sir Horace 16, 17, 132-3, 149
Manthoné, Gabriele 321, 358-9, 381, 405, 406, 410
Marco, Marchese Carlo de 181, 210
Marengo, battle of 452, 453, 457, 460, 542, 604
Maria Amalia, Duchess of Orléans (Marie Amélie) 366, 452, 528, 580, 584-5, 591, 592, 599, 648
Maria Amalia, of Saxony
  children 55, 64, 69
  death 110
  marriage 30, 43-4, 49
  and Montealegre 67, 72-3
  Naples 108-109
  politics 72
Maria Barbara, of Spain 68, 97
Maria Carolina, Duchesse de Berry 318, 366, 469, 678, 721
Maria Carolina, of the Two Sicilies
  Acton, Sir John Edward 483, 495, 506, 508, 563-4, 573
  Alquier, Baron 505, 514-15, 516-17, 530-31
  ambivalence to Napoleon 495-6, 498-9, 509, 517-25, 528-30, 537
  amusements 157-9, 166, 174, 223-4, 243-4
  Anglo-Neapolitan treaty 583
  Anglo-Russian army 539, 543-4, 549
  attachment to Vienna 133, 237, 370, 448, 527
  attitude to Britain 563, 624, 631
  Austria in Italy 442
  Austro-French peace 597-8
  Bentinck, Lord William 605, 607-8, 621-2, 625, 626, 630-31
  betrothal to Ferdinand 130
  Calabria, defence 560, 562, 567
  character 134-5, 140-41, 144-6, 151, 156-8, 242-3, 273, 300-301, 322, 562, 610-11
  children see Carlo, Prince; Carlo Tito, Prince; Charles Albert, Prince; Enrichetta Maria Carlema; Francis, Duke of Calabria; Gennaro, Prince; Leopold, Duke of Salerno; Maria Amalia, Duchess of Orléans; Maria Clotilde; Maria Luisa, Gd Duchess of Tuscany; Maria Theresa, w of Francis I
  correspondance with Napoleon 482, 490-91, 495, 501-502, 519-21, 524, 547
  council of state 137, 210, 318, 476-7, 509, 537, 579
  death 654-5, 657
  death of children 226, 469
  Drummond, Sir William 578-9
  education 137
  famine 256-7
  favourites 585-6, 623
  financial constraints on 488-9
  flight to Sicily 328-34, 347-8, 351-2, 553-6
  freemasons 156, 177-8, 179
  French revolution 245-7, 248, 252, 260, 262-3, 273, 285-6, 311
  French threat 502-503, 541, 545, 546, 559
  Gallo, Marchese 452-3, 507, 535
  Hamilton, Lady Emma 249-50, 287, 326-7, 348, 416-17, 422-4, 428, 444-5, 453-8
  health 591, 606, 607, 629, 631-2
  journeys to Vienna 454-7, 631-9
  leaves Naples 544
  letter writing 414, 433, 503-504, 545, 558
  Marie Antoinette (sister) 234, 270-71, 313, 327-8, 423
  Marie Louise' marriage to Napoleon 598
  marriage 131-4, 135-8, 347-8
  mourning 226, 264
  Murat, Joachim 589
  Naples recovery plans 575, 578, 589
  Napoleonic war 296, 352
  Napoleon's fall 651
  Nelson 314-17, 427, 443, 453-8, 536
  opportunism 231
  Paget, Sir Arthur 446-7
  Palermo 558-32
  plots against 616-8
  political ambition 177, 210, 305, 435-6, 624
  popularity 582
  power 308, 512-19, 579, 601
  pregnancies 155, 173, 212, 227, 237, 271
  relationship to Ferdinand 140, 144, 431-2, 482-3, 497
  resistance appeal 550-52, 568, 571
  retirement 640, 652-4
  Saint Clair, Marquis de 487
  San Marco, Marchesa di 433-4
  secret services 614
  Smith, Sir Sydney 564-5, 575
  Staël, Mme de 525

INDEX

succession 484-5
tax levy 603
Vatican 240-41
visits to Vienna 128, 238-40, 257, 460-61, 471-4, 621, 640, 651-4, 652-4
Maria Clementina, Archduchess (Clementine; Princess Royal) 227, 302-304, 315, 351, 463-4, 469
Maria Clotilde 212
Maria Cristina, of Sardinia (Mimi) 452, 580, 652
Maria del Carmine, Santa 24
Maria Isabella, Duchess of Calabria, Infanta 469-70, 476, 478-9, 565, 580
Maria Josepha, Archduchess 127, 130
Maria Luisa, Grand Duchess of Tuscany 227, 237, 452, 477
Maria Luisa, of Parma 226, 227, 288, 477, 479-80, 484, 532
Maria Theresa, of Austria 29, 63, 76, 78, 97, 127, 137
Maria Theresa, wife of Francis I 227, 237, 248, 472, 550, 575
Marie Antoinette, of France 131, 167, 234, 254, 262, 270, 636
  execution 267, 271, 272, 298, 423
Marie Antoinette, Princess of Asturias (Toto) 366, 453, 469, 477, 478, 479, 531
Marie Louise, Archduchess (Empress) 248, 471-2, 505, 597, 600, 652-3, 727-8
Marmontel, J-F 112, 167, 207-208
Marra, Ariano Scipione della 392, 414
Martin, Commodore 61-2, 63, 67, 79, 195
Massa, General Orazio 321, 399-400, 405, 410
Masséna, General 284, 549, 557, 565, 567
Maturi, Walter 469, 582
Mazzochi, Alassio S 102, 174
Medici, Cosimo de', Grand Duke 19, 91
Medici dynasty 13-14
Medici, Gian Gastone de', Grand Duke 16, 17, 18
Medici, Luigi, Cavaliere, of Ottaiano
  Acton, Sir John 243-4, 255, 257-8, 280-82, 492
  arrests 393-4, 492
  Austrian army 726-7
  Britain 613-14
  concordat 1818 686-7
  conspiracy investigation 274-5, 277-9
  faction leader 255-6, 266, 278-9, 284, 564, 667
  fall and rise 282, 284, 361, 363-4, 491
  finance, minister of 558, 573, 596, 665, 716
  Floridia, Duchess of 668

Jacobinism 674-6
police chief 246, 255, 266-7, 665, 672, 720
retirement 312
royal counsellor 241
Medrano, GA 35, 49, 50, 79
Méjean, Colonel 400, 405, 413, 418-19, 423
Melas, General 453, 454, 460
Mengs, Raphael 58, 223
Messina
  British at 600-601, 605, 606, 610, 613
  deputy 107
  discontent in 578, 583
  garrison 496, 556, 575, 605, 613
  governor 275, 357
  royal family at 561, 563
  seige 27
Metastasio, Abate 36, 41
Metternich, Prince Clemens Lothar Wenzel
  congress of Vienna 669
  Ferdinand I 711
  Maria Carolina 621, 639, 655
  Naples 692-3, 705-6
  policies 658
  treaty negotiations 646, 652, 668
  Troppau conference 706
Miccichè, Michele Palmiere di 370, 655-6, 680, 690
Michele il Pazzo 338-9, 344
Micheroux, General Antonio 253, 271, 287
Mier, Count Felix 646, 647
Migliano Loffredo, Prince of 322, 433
Milan, State of 19, 25, 63, 658
Milan (city) 380, 527, 529
Miller, Lady Anne 45, 107, 156-7
Minichini, Grand Master 698-700, 701, 704
Miranda, Don José Fernandez, Duke of Losada 15, 74, 105, 110
Modena, Duke of 25, 65, 66
Moliterno, G Pignatelli, Prince of 338, 344, 378-9, 497-8, 564, 589, 610, 615-16
Mondovì, battle of 543
monitore napoletano 359-60, 375, 378, 383, 386, 395, 450
Montealegre, Marquis of (Duke of Salas) 15, 31, 34, 56-7, 61-4, 67, 72
Monteleone, Pignattelli di, Prince 20, 41, 161
Montemar, General Count of (Duke of) 19, 22, 60, 63
Montet, Baroness du 303, 640, 654, 721-3
Monti, Vincenzo 261, 381
Moore, General Sir John 568, 572, 575-6, 577-9, 581, 589

Morgan, Lady 190, 661, 669, 679, 681-2
Mura, Francesco de 35, 58
Murat, Joachim, of the Two Sicilies
  ambition 584, 641, 658
  armistice 464-5
  arrests 536, 659-60, 664, 670-71
  King of Naples 586-9, 600-601, 624, 651-2
  Maria Carolina, Queen 597-8, 639
  Roman republic 309, 648
  trial and execution 671-2

Naselli, General 321, 322, 327, 337, 431, 452, 558
Neipperg, A-A, General Count 644, 666, 728
Nelson, Vice Admiral Viscount Horatio
  Caracciola' trial and execution 414-16
  character 328
  cruise to Malta 453
  duchy of Bronte 428
  Ferdinand 269, 316, 421-2
  Hamilton, Sir William 267-9, 408-9
  Hamilton, Lady Emma 267-9, 367, 408, 429, 437
  hero worship of 316, 318, 410, 428
  journey to Vienna 455-7
  Malta blockade 318
  Maria Carolina 316, 455-7, 536
  Naples 314-17, 376, 388-9, 407-12
  Naples to Palermo 330-31, 333
  Nelson Aria, Haydn 458
  Nile, battle of 313-14, 421-2
Newcastle, Duke of 26, 33-4
Niccolini, Antonio 677, 685
Nicolini, Nicola 25, 228, 361, 491
Nile, battle of the (Aboukir) 313, 421, 428
Nugent, Count General 621, 693, 695, 698, 700, 704
Nunziante, Colonel Marchese 576, 590, 671

Oppermann, General 530, 532-3, 539-40, 543-5, 546, 548
Orléans, Gaston, Duc d' 22, 44
Ossun, Marquis d' 76, 110

Pagano, Mario 394, 424
Paget, Hon Sir Arthur 444-6, 448, 463-5, 470-71, 577
Paisiello, Giovanni 166, 167, 169, 238, 485, 633
Palermo
  court of 579, 605
  deputy of 107
  development of 370
  Ferdinand 334, 427-8

French refugees 332, 351
  Maria Carolina 332-4, 348, 558, 618
  royal family retreat to 329-32
  Turkish incident 430
Palmieri, Niccolo 595-6, 642, 643, 648-9
Paribelli, Cesare 355, 497
Parma
  claims to 20, 29, 30, 60, 297, 460
  Dukes of 14-15, 20, 105, 289
  Papal relations 122
Parthenopean republic 321, 344, 353, 372, 375, 378-84, 425, 499
Partouneaux, General 557, 590
Paul I, of Russia 367, 457, 460, 470
Pepe, General Floristano 707, 725
Pepe, General Guglielmo 692-3, 696, 698-9, 701, 703-704, 707, 711-12
Philip, Infante Don 69, 71, 106, 118-19, 185-6
Philip, Infante Don (Duke of Parma) 63-4, 76, 97, 105
Philip V, of Spain 15, 20, 23, 25, 30, 60, 64, 67-8
Piacenza 14, 19, 25, 29, 76, 105
Piccini, Niccola 167-8
Piedmont 96, 113, 460, 489, 669
Pignatelli, Ferdinando, Prince of Storngoli 265, 284, 321, 588
Pignatelli, General Prince Francesco 177-8, 202, 203, 281, 329, 334-7, 468
Pimental, Eleonora di Fonsica 173, 340, 344, 359-60, 378, 381, 386, 388, 395, 425
Piozzi, Mrs (Hester Lynch Thrale) 88-9, 126
pirates, Barbary 78, 298, 358
Pisa, University 31, 90, 186
Pius VI, Pope 213, 240-41, 260-61, 294, 309, 310, 431
Pius VII, Pope 451-2, 673
Poerio, Giuseppe 712, 719
Poland, war of succession (1733) 19, 29
Pompeii 10, 51, 148, 295, 363, 485, 683, 684
Ponza 565, 571, 588, 590, 625, 641
Popoli, MA Carafa, Duchess of 234
Portici, palace 10, 49, 50-51, 152, 467
Posillipo 2, 116, 163, 193, 256, 427, 724
Pozzo di Borgo, Colonel Count 544, 717
presepe 5, 87-9
Presidi 19, 25, 27, 30, 63, 106, 296, 442, 465
Pressburg, treaty of (1805) 542
Procida 21, 52-3, 54, 56, 136, 376, 581, 590

Ravaschieri di Satriano, Teresa, Princess

INDEX

(Princess --) 218-22
Razoumovski, Countess 559, 562, 654
Reggio, Calabria 494, 563, 575, 664
Reggio, Don Michele 62, 64, 114
Reynier, General 558, 561, 567, 570
Richelieu, Duc de 633-4
Rieti, battle of 712
Roccaromana, L Caracciola, Duke of 335, 338, 339-40, 392, 656
Rocco, Father 85-7, 116
Rodio, Marchese di 513, 565
Rome 320, 431, 442
Rosalia, Saint 208, 427, 643, 707
Rosetti, Gabriele Pasquale Giuseppe 681, 682, 700
Rossini, Gioacchino Antonio 678, 680, 682, 689, 694, 725
Rothschild, Carl Mayer 715, 720, 727
Royal Herculean Academy 92-4, 215
Ruffo, Cardinal Fabrizio
  attempt on life 371-2
  Calabrian expedition 352-7, 371, 372-3
  capitulation of Naples 410-11
  council of state 281
  opposition to Ferdinand 408, 415
  Rome negotiations 544, 548
Ruffo, Commander Prince Alvaro 486, 668, 705, 710, 719, 720
Russia 503, 512, 514, 522-3
Ruvo, Ettore Carafa, Count of 265, 285

Sacchinelli, Abate Dominico 354, 355, 371, 390-91, 421
Saint Francis of Paola, church 665, 675, 726
St Petersburg, court of 519, 520, 522
Saint-Clair, Marquis de 487, 559, 585-6, 652, 655, 665
Saint-Priest, Count Alexis de 634, 635, 636-7, 639
Salandra, Duke of 338, 407, 418
Saliceti, AC 565, 571, 576-7, 581-2, 587, 674
Salis, Baron de 197, 235-6
Sambuca, Marchese della 181, 182, 190, 197-9, 204, 208-10
Sammartino, Guiseppe 88, 102
San Carlo theatre 35-42, 127-8, 173-4, 234-5, 345, 666-7, 676-7, 678-9
San Leucio 231-3, 239, 353, 686
San Marco, Marchesa di 192, 244, 246-7, 282, 284, 286, 433-4, 491
San Martino
  church 5, 146, 383
  hill 397, 400
San Nicandro, Prince of 114, 130, 133, 136
  tutor 71, 108, 117, 119
San Severo, Raimondo di Sangro, Prince of 102-103, 156, 192-3
San Teodoro, Duke of 478, 479, 531, 549, 552, 553
Sanfelice, Luisa 382-3, 449-51, 469
Sanfelice, Marchese Fernando 47, 79
Sant' Elmo castle 3, 61, 374
  seizure 22, 337, 339, 340, 344, 382
  surrender 418-21
Santa Chiara, convent and church 6, 186, 469, 691
Santa Eufemia 567, 568-9, 670
Santa Maria del Carmine 78, 275, 411
Santo Stefano, Count of (Conde de San Esteban) 14, 15, 23-4, 28, 31, 34, 43, 54, 56
Santo Stefano, Countess of 42, 55
Sardinia 297, 613
  King of 97, 254, 289, 334
  state 105, 113
Sarro, Dominico 36, 39
Savoy, House of 76-7, 95
Saxe, Chevalier de 301, 441, 533, 566
Saxe-Teschen, Princess of 7, 180
Schipa, M 28, 340, 624, 696
Schönbrunn 238, 504-505, 639-40, 653
  treaty of (1809) 597
seggi (sedili) 22, 412, 468-9
Sémonville, CL Huguet de 253-4, 258, 263
Seratti, Francesco 439, 489, 492, 551, 564, 573
Seroa, Francesco 59, 101-102
Serracapriola, Antonio Maresca, Duke of 156, 514, 705
Settimo, Ruggero 627, 650
seven years war 96, 195
Sharp, Samuel 37-9, 47-8, 118-19, 136-7
Sicily 221, 284, 370, 444, 457, 493-4, 508
  British concern 590
  conquest 26-8, 447
  Ferdinand flees to 551
  Maria Carolina flees to 553-6
  royal family in 558-73, 575-93
  see also Messina; Palermo; Syracuse
Smith, Admiral Sir Sydney 332, 564-5, 567, 568, 572, 575
Sora, Duke of 43, 56
Speciale, Judge Vincenzo 376-7, 422
Spinelli, Cardinal Archbishop 28, 79
Squillace, Leopoldo di Gregorio, Marchese di 73-4, 90, 96, 108, 114
Staël, Anne Louise Germaine Necker, Baroness de 525-6, 684
Stendhal (Beyle, Henri Marie) 450, 677-8, 694

Stuart, General Sir John 543, 544, 563, 567-8, 581, 583, 589-90, 597
Stuart, Prince Charles Edward 25-6
Studi, Palazzo degli 58, 100, 341, 475

Talleyrand, Baron de 200-201, 251
Talleyrand-Périgord, Charles Maurice de, Prince of Benevento 379, 481, 501-502, 505, 514, 515, 549, 655
Tanucci, Marchese Bernardo
  accession of Ferdinand 107
  anti-clericism 33, 116-17, 121-2
  anti-freemasonry 178, 179
  antiquities 92
  Bourbon compact 111-12, 308
  Britain 113, 120
  character 90-1, 95-6, 125, 150, 175-6
  council of regency 108, 114, 123
  court intrigues 72, 74
  diplomacy 96-7, 149-51
  famine 115
  France 111-12, 124
  Jesuits expelled 121-2
  justice minister 31-3
  legal code attributed to 232
  prime minister/first secretary 122-3, 130, 148-51, 172-3, 175, 180
  resignation 181-3
  royal marriage 132, 135-6
Taranto, Archbishop of (Monisgnor Capecelatro) 680, 682, 694, 723-4
Tatistcheff, Dimitri Pavlovitch 534, 537, 544, 545-6
Termoli, Duchess of 156, 178
Terracina 133, 274, 299, 333
Tesi, Vittoria 36, 70
Thugut, Baron Franz von 210, 300, 357, 406, 448, 451, 455, 457
Thurn, Commodore Count 389, 414
Tilsit, treaty of (1807) 579, 581
Tischbein, Wilhelm 217, 222, 341-2
Toledo, Don Pedro de 3, 78
Tolentino
  battle of 659, 664, 673
  treaty of (1797) 299
Tommasi, Marchese D 663, 665, 667, 673, 687, 697, 698, 712, 720
Torre, Duke della 339, 341
Toulon, siege of 269, 270, 271
Trabia, Prince of 352, 551, 596, 606
Trafalgar, battle of 536
Trebbio, battle of 604
Troppau, conference of (1820) 706, 708-709
Troubridge, Rear-Admiral Sir Thomas 376-7, 388, 408-409, 410, 418, 431
Trouvé, secretary 302, 307-308, 311

Truguet, Admiral 254, 257
Turin, treaty of 19
Turkey 59, 515, 575
Tuscany 14, 16, 20, 25, 30, 289, 460
Tylney, Lord 169-71, 174

Ulm, battle of 536

Valmy, battle of 253
Vanni, Marchese Carlo 281, 312
Vanvitelli, Luigi 11, 79-81, 230
Vasto, Marchese del 226, 281
Velletri, battle of 64-7, 246
Ventignano, Duke of 681, 682
Venuti, Marchese Marcello 50-51, 92, 225
Vergennes, Comte de 204, 211
Verona, congress of (1822) 721
Versailles, second treaty (1757) 97, 300
Vesuvius 86, 101-102, 128-9, 151, 168, 276-7
Vico, Giovanni Battista 101, 218
Victoire, Madame 241, 300
Vienna
  treaty of (1731) 15
  treaty of (1815) 668
  tribute paid to 21
Vienna and Maria Carolina
  attachment to 133, 237, 370, 448, 527
  death 654-5
  journeys to 454-7, 631-9
  marriage in 131
  visits 128, 460-61, 471-4, 652-4
Vigée Le Brun, Mme 234, 244, 250
Viscardi, Pasquale 577, 582
Vitaliani, Andrea 272, 275, 285, 381
Vitaliani, Vincenzo 273-4, 279
Viviani, Senatore Luigi 91, 172
Voltaire, François Marie Arouet de 33, 95, 164, 266, 360

Wagram, battle of 590
Wall, Richard 97, 105
Walpole, Sir Horace 51, 132, 682
Wellesley, Marquis 444, 600
Whitworth, Sir Charles 448, 489
Winckelmann, Johann Joachim 92, 215, 222
Wirtz, General 393, 397
Worms, treaty of (1743) 63

Zurlo, Cardinal Archbishop 275, 329, 339, 344, 345, 378, 386
Zurlo, Count Guiseppe 338, 442, 488-9, 491-2, 700, 704, 709, 712

Printed in Great Britain
by Amazon